The
Startup Company
Bible

The

Startup
Company
Bible

for Entrepreneurs

The Complete Guide

For Building Successful Companies
and Raising Venture Capital

Michael Stathis

AVAPublishing

ISBN 0-9755776-1-1

This book is dedicated first to My Parents and then to the Entrepreneur

Contents

Introduction   xxiiv

Part I: Preparing For Financing

1. Entrepreneurship 101: Establishing Your Company   3

2. Venture Capital and Private Equity Basics   53

3. Fundamentals of Raising Capital   89

4. Investor Profiles: VCs, Angels, and Incubators   125

Part II: Building the Company

5. Intangible Assets & Intellectual Property   157

6. Forming Competitive Strategies   195

7. Alternative Growth Strategies: Licensing Agreements, Joint Ventures & Strategic Alliances   247

8. Managing Growth   279

Part III: Getting the Money

9. Exit Strategies   331

10. Terms of Endearment—Term Sheets & Tactics   367

11. Setting Valuation: Supply and Demand, Risk and Reward, Leverage and Control   395

12. Compensation and Employment   435

Appendices

Appendix A: Legal Agreements   453

Appendix B: Business Plan Guidelines   513

Appendix C: Detailed Explanations   523

Appendix D: Competitive Analysis   545

Appendix E: Investor Groups   553

References

Detailed Contents

Introduction   xxiiv

Part I: Preparing For Financing

Chapter 1: Entrepreneurship 101: Establishing Your Company

A. People   3
  Know Thyself   3
  Forming Your Management Team   5
  Forming Your Boards   9
  Realizing When You Need Help   11
B. Purpose   12
  Vision and Mission Statement   12
  The Business Model   17
  The Business Plan   19
C. Technology   20
D. Money   20
  Equity   21
    Common Stock   21
    Preferred Stock   21
    Stock Dilution   23
    Debt   24
    Mezzanine Financing   24
  Derivatives   25
E. Strategy   26
  Establishing Your Core Competency   26
  Market Profiling and Forecasting   26
  Market Segmentation Analysis   28
  Marketing Strategy   29
  Financial Strategy   29
    Asset Management   31
      Net Cash Flow versus Net Profits   31
      Cash Management   32
      The Working Capital Cycle   33
    Growth Considerations   37
F. Legal Contracts   40
  Founder's Agreements   41
  Nondisclosure Agreements   41
  Noncompete Agreements   41
G. The Boring Details   42
  Selecting a Business Structure   42
  Corporate Charter and Bylaws   43
  Shareholder's Agreement   44

Stock Record Book   44
Business and Liability Insurance   45
Selecting and Starting a Business   46

Chapter 2: Venture Capital & Private Equity Basics

A. The Importance to Venture Capital to Our Future Economy   53
    Historical Background   54
    The Venture Capital Investment Framework   56
    Venture Capital as an Investment   56
B. Understanding Venture Capital   60
    Venture Capital versus Private Equity   60
    Venture Capital Structure   62
    Valuation   64
    Compensation   64
    The VC Process   66
    Venture Financing   68
    Exit   71
C. Modern Portfolio Theory   71
    Portfolio Risk   73
    Risk and Reward   74
    The J-Curve Phenomenon   77
D. Venture Capital Risk Management   79
    Venture Capital Due Diligence   79
    Term Sheets   80
    Syndicates   81
    Staging of Investments: Tranches   82
    Liquidation   82
    What Entrepreneurs Can Expect   82
E. Difficulties Faced By Venture Capitalists   83
    Management Fees and Carried Interest   84
    Transparency and Disclosure Controversies   85

Chapter 3: Fundamentals of Raising Capital

A. Financing Decisions   89
B. Getting the Money   92
    Focus on the Smart Money   93
    Prospecting Rules to Remember   95
C. Prospecting Angels and VCs   104
D. Sources of Capital   106
    Startup (Seed) Capital   106
    Early Stage Capital   111
    Expansion Capital   113

E. Private Placement Memorandum   117
    Overview   117
    Registration Requirements and Exemptions   118
F. Investor Presentations   121

Chapter 4: Investor Profiles: VCs, Angels, and Incubators

A. Introduction   125
B. Deal Flow   128
    Angel Networks   131
    Venture Capital Networks   131
C. Angels   132
    Historical Background   132
    The Angel Profile   133
D. Private Venture Capitalists   136
    Think Like a VC   137
    Profiling Guidelines   140
    New versus Established VCs   142
E. Corporate Venture Groups   144
F. Incubators and Accelerators   146
    Historical Background   146
    Incubators   148
    Accelerators   150
    Due Diligence   151

Part II: Building the Company

Chapter 5: Intangible Assets & Intellectual Property

A. Intangible Assets   157
B. Intellectual Capital   160
    Codified versus Tacit Knowledge   162
C. Intellectual Property   163
    Copyrights   163
    Patents   163
        Historical Background   164
        Types of Patents   165
        Provisional Patents   166
        Conducting a Patent Search and Analysis   167
        Filing For a Patent   169
        The Patenting Process   172
        Patent Portfolios   172
        Patent Valuation   173
        The Startup Company Holy Grail: Serial Innovators   180

Trade Secrets 182
   Keeping a Secret 184
   When to Use Trade Secret Protection 185
   Enforcement of Trade Secrets 186
Trademarks and Service Marks 188
Software: A Unique Intangible Asset 190
D. Conclusion 190

Chapter 6: Forming Competitive Strategies

A. From Business Model to Strategy 195
   Positional Strategy versus Operational Effectiveness 196
   Strategic Approaches for Network Industries 199
     Strategies for Network Effects 200
B. The Competitive Environment 202
   Price Competition 202
     Factors Affecting Price Competition 203
     Competitive Pricing Relationships 204
   The Five Forces Framework 205
   Barriers to Market Entry 209
   Competitive Response to New Entrants 212
   Scaling the Barriers 214
   Porter's Generic Strategies 216
C. Achieving Market Growth 219
   Understanding Product Life Cycles 219
   Methods to Achieve Market Growth 223
   Organizational Integration 224
D. Preemptive Strategies 226
   The Preemptive Planning Process 227
E. Analyzing Competitive Strategies 229
   Market Trend Line Analysis 231
   Other Techniques 233
F. Strategic Planning 233
   SWOT Analysis 235
G. Competitive Intelligence 237
   Resources for Market Profiling 237

Chapter 7: Alternative Growth Strategies: Licensing Agreements, Joint Ventures & Strategic Alliances

A. Strategic Convergence 247
B. Technology Conversion 248
   Core Competencies 248
   Methods of Technology Conversion 249
C. Licensing Agreements 252

Out-Licensing	253
In-Licensing	254
Cross-Licensing	254
When to License	255
How to License	257
D. Valuation of Intangible Assets	258
Prenegotiation Valuation	259
Litigation Valuation	261
Determining Royalty Rates	261
Licensing Valuation Methods	263
License Valuation Using Real Options	265
E. Joint Ventures and Strategic Alliances	270
Joint Ventures	270
Strategic Alliances	272
Alliance and Joint Ventures Management	274
F. Franchising	276

Chapter 8: Managing Growth

A. Introduction	279
B. Capital Budgeting	281
Forming a Project Budget	282
Net Present Value Approach	284
Certainty Equivalent Approach	286
Budget Forecasting	287
C. Financial Planning	288
Percent-of-Sales Method	288
Cash Turnover Method	291
Cash Budget Method	292
Accounting For Project Uncertainties	292
Real Options	292
Decision Trees	294
Scenario Analysis	294
Game Theory	297
D. Financial Statement Analysis	298
Income Statement	298
Balance Sheet	298
Cash Flow Statement	299
Using Financial Ratios to Monitor Performance	300
Liquidity Ratios	300
Cash Flow Ratios	301
Activity Ratios	303
Debt and Interest Ratios	305
Profitability Ratios	306
Equity Ratios	307

Market Ratios	308
E. Corporate Asset Management	309
Balancing Long and Short-term Financing	309
Interest Rates and Inflation	310
Yield Curves	311
Managing Current Assets	314
Managing Accounts Receivable	315
Managing Accounts Payable	316
Inventory Management	317
Cash Management	318
Intellectual Capital Management	320
Emotional Management	322
F. Forecasting Performance	323
Self-Assessment	323
Customer Lists	324
Using the Product Life Cycle to Reshape Strategy	324

Part III: Getting the Money

Chapter 9: Exit Strategies

A. Introduction	331
B. Venture Capitalists	332
C. Investment and Merchant Bankers	335
Investment Bankers	335
Merchant Bankers	336
D. Initial Public Offerings	339
The IPO Process	343
Financial Expense of Going Public	344
Pre-IPO Valuation Process	347
Premature IPOs	351
Venture Capital-backed IPO Timing and Performance	351
Post-IPO Distributions	352
E. Mergers & Acquisitions	353
Reasons to Merge	354
Mergers as a Strategic Alternative	356
Merger Performance	359
The Acquisition Process	360
F. Licensing Agreements	360
G. Corporate Restructurings	362

Chapter 10: Terms of Endearment: Term Sheets & Tactics

A. Introduction	367
B. Term Sheet Basics	368

Term Sheet Valuation 370
Terms during a Down Round 372
Terms during an Up Round 373
C. Assessing the Terms 373
   Opening Statement 373
   Confidentiality Statement 373
   Amount Raised, Securities Offered, Shares Issued, ... 373
     Price Per Share, and Closing Date
   Post-Financing Capitalization 374
   Dividend Provisions 376
   Liquidation Preference 376
   Redemption 377
   Conversion 377
   Antidilution Provisions 378
     Full-Ratchet Antidilution 379
     Weighted Average Antidilution 380
     Narrow-Based Weighted Average Antidilution 381
     Pay-to-Play 381
   Voting Rights 381
   Protective Provisions 382
   Information Rights 382
   Board Composition 384
   Approval Rights 384
   Special Board Approval Rights 384
   Right of First Refusal 384
   Registration Rights 385
   Conditions Precedent 387
   Purchase Agreement 387
   Employee Matters 387
   Legal Counsel 387
   Expenses and Finder's Fees 387
D. Tactics 389
   Dealing with Exclusivity 390
   Closing the Deal 391

Chapter 11: Setting Valuation: Supply and Demand, Risk and Reward, Leverage and Control

A. Understanding Valuation 395
B. Valuation Methods 397
   Discounted Cash Flow Approach 398
   Relative Valuation (Market) Approach 400
   Contingent Claims Approach 401
   Asset-Based Valuation 402
C. Venture Capital Valuation 403

D. Scrutinizing Venture Capital Valuations   407
    Supply & Demand   408
    Risk, Reward, Leverage & Control   409
E. Case Studies   423
F. Conclusions   431

Chapter 12: Compensation and Employment

A. Employment Law & Contracts   435
    Contractors & Consultants   436
    Employee Departure   437
B. Compensation and Benefits   438
    Cash Compensation   438
    Employee Stock Options and Warrants   439
        Vesting and Valuation of Options   441
        Warrants   441
        Antidilution Protection   442
        NSOs and ISOs   442
    Compensating With Stock Options   443
    ESOPs   445
    Golden Parachutes   446
    Silver Parachutes   446
    Split Dollar Life Insurance   446
    Restricted Stock Plans   448
    Worker's Compensation Insurance   448
    Employee Benefits   448
    Key Employee Life Insurance   449

Appendices

Appendix A: Legal Agreements

1. Mutual Confidentiality and Non-Disclosure Agreement   455
2. Consulting Agreement   457
3. Non-Compete Provision   463
4. Confidential Information and Invention Assignment   465
    Agreement
5. Scientific Advisory Board Member Confidentiality,   471
    Non-Disclosure and Proprietary Agreement
6. Investor Questionnaire   475
7. Subscription Agreement   481
8. Incentive Stock Option Agreement   487
9. Stock Option Plan   495
10. Repurchase of Common Stock   507

Appendix B: Business Plan Guidelines

1. Market and Competitive Analysis   516
2. Sales and Marketing Plan   517
3. Guidelines for Writing the Business Plan 517
4. Executive Summary   519
5. Business Plan Outline   521

Appendix C: Detailed Explanations

1. Accredited Investors Defined   525
2. Effects of Portfolio Diversification on Total Risk Reduction 526
3. Venture Capital Due Diligence   535
4. Bond Yields and Yield-to-Maturity   542
5. Calculating the Alternative Minimum Tax   544

Appendix D: Competitive Analysis

1. Market Segmentation Analysis   547
2. Competitive Analysis Chart   548
3. Business Attractiveness Matrix   549
4. The State Department's Contact Numbers   550
5. Comparability of Two Licensing Agreements 551

Appendix E: Investor Groups

1. State Incubation Associations   555
2. Selected Incubators By State   560
3. Angel Clubs & Networks   562
4. Fund Raising & Venture Networks   565

References

List of Figures and Tables

Figure 1-1   The Components of Vision   13
Figure 1-2   Examples of Core Values   14
Figure 1-3   Examples of Core Purpose   15
Figure 1-4   Examples of Envisioned Future   15
Table 1-1   Comparison of Core Values, Core Purpose,
               and Envisioned Future   16
Figure 1-5   The Business Vision is the Heart of the Business Model   18
Figure 1-6   The Six Components of the Business Model   18
Figure 1-7   Components of Financial Strategy   30
Figure 1-8   Common Methods to Increase Cash Flow   32
Figure 1-9   The Working Capital Cycle   34
Table 1-2   General Company Priorities by Stage   40
Table 1-3   Comparison of Different Business Structures   45
Figure 1-10   Guidelines for Selecting a Successful Startup Business   47
Figure 1-11   Administrative Startup Checklist   47
Table 1-4   From Seed Stage to IPO   48-49
Table 2-1   Passive and Active Management Performance
               Spreads   58
Figure 2-1   Institutional Investors Have Balanced
               Investment Portfolios   61
Table 2-2   The Two Broad Categories of Investments   62
Table 2-3   Covenants of a Venture Fund Partnership Agreement   65
Figure 2-3   Overview of the Venture Capital Process   67
Table 2-4   Factors Influencing Investment By Venture Capitalists   70
Figure 2-4   The Two Components of Total Portfolio Risk   74
Figure 2-5   The Relationship between Hypothetical Risk
               and Expected Return   76
Table 2-5   Ownership Required to Support a 30% Return   77
Figure 2-6.   J-Curve Effect on Venture Capital and Private Equity   78
Figure 2-7   Alteration of the J-Curve Effect Due to Portfolio
               Diversification   78
Figure 3-1   The Ten Commandments of Building a Great Company   94
Figure 3-2   Prospecting Rules to Remember   103
Table 3-1   Relative Ease of Financing Sources by Company Stage   116
Figure 3-3   Minimum Risk Disclosures Recommended for Inclusion
               in a PPM   119
Figure 3-4   Minimum Guidelines for the Construction of a PPM   120
Figure 3-5   Topics to Cover During an Investor Presentation   121
Table 4-1   Comparison of Angel and Venture Capital Financing
               Sources   127

Figure 4-1   The Most Common Reasons for Financing Rejections:
              The First Cut   129
Figure 4-2   The Most Common Reasons for Financing Rejections:
              Second & Third Cut   129
Figure 4-3   The Generic Deal Flow Screening Process   130
Table 4-2   Venture Capital Investing by Percentage   133
Figure 4-4   How Angels Find Their Deals   134
Table 4-4   The Required ROI of VCs by Stage of Company   139
Table 4-5   Established versus New Venture Capitalists   143
Table 4-6   Investing Characteristics of Angels and Venture
              Capitalists   146
Figure 4-5   Factors Responsible for the Growth of Incubators   147
Figure 4-6   Characteristics of Successful Incubators   150
Figure 4-7   Initial Questions for Incubator Interviews   153
Figure 4-8   Guidelines for Selecting Incubators   153
Figure 5-1   Classification of Intangible Assets   159
Figure 5-2   Relationships Among Elements of Intellectual Capital   161
Table 5-1   Types of Industry Knowledge   162
Figure 5-3   Common Reasons to Value Patents   174
Figure 5-4   Factors To Consider When Valuing Patents   175
Figure 5-5   Increasing Order of Sophistication of Patent
              Valuation Methods   177
Figure 5-6   Patent Option Valuation Decisions   179
Table 5-2   Technologies with Small Firm Patenting   181
Figure 5-7   Examples of Trade Secrets Owned by a Typical
              Manufacturing Company   183
Table 5-3   Patents versus Trade Secrets   185
Figure 6-1   Sustainable Competitive Advantage Formed by Strategic
              Positioning and Operational Effectiveness   198
Figure 6-2   Example of Direct Spillover Effects   200
Figure 6-3   Factors Affecting Price Competition   204
Figure 6-4   Forces Influencing Arena Attractiveness   207
Figure 6-5   Barriers to Market Entry   212
Figure 6-6   Decision Model for Determining Response
              to a New Entrant   215
Table 6-1   Porter's Generic Strategies   218
Table 6-2   Porter's Generic Strategies versus The Five Forces of
              Industry Competition   219
Figure 6-7   The Product Life Cycle Curve   220
Figure 6-8   The Product Life Cycle Showing Cash Flows   222
Figure 6-9   The Company Value Chain   225
Figure 6-10   Planning for Preemption   229
Figure 6-11   Framework for Analyzing Competitors' Response to
              Actions   230
Table 6-3   Techniques for Analyzing Competitive Strategy   232
Figure 6-12   Steps in Strategic Planning   234

Figure 6-13   Recommendations for Implementing a Strategic Planning
          Process   234
Table 6-4   The SWOT Analysis   235
Figure 6-14   The Strategy Formulation Process   236
Table 6-5   Creative Ways to Gain Competitor Information   244
Table 7-1   Comparison of Acquisitions, Alliances, and Licensing   251
Table 7-2   Factors Affecting Licensing   256
Figure 7-1   Factors to be Considered for Royalty Negotiations   264
Table 7-3   Common Methods of Royalty Rate Determination   267
Table 7-4   Why Alliances are Formed and Why They Fail   273
Figure 8-1   Business Management versus Operational Finance   280
Figure 8-2   Steps for Determining the Incremental Cash Flow   282
Figure 8-3   A Project Analysis Worksheet   283
Figure 8-4   A Generic Comprehensive Budget   289
Figure 8-5   A Sample Cash Budget Chart   293
Figure 8-6   Example of a Decision Tree   295
Figure 8-7   Upward Sloping Yield Curve   312
Figure 8-8   An Inverted Yield Curve   313
Figure 8-9   Recommended Guidelines for Management of
          Current Assets   314
Figure 8-10   Recommended Guidelines for Receivables
          Management   315
Figure 8-11   Recommended Guidelines for Payables Management   316
Figure 8-12   Recommended Guidelines for Inventory Management   317
Figure 8-13   The Cash Flow Cycle   319
Figure 8-14   Managers of Intellectual Capital   321
Figure 8-15   Managing Risk, Equivocality, & Uncertainty
          During the Product Life Cycle   326
Table 9-1   The Fate of Venture backed Companies by Industry   334
Table 9-2   Allocation of U.S. Private Equity Funds (1993-1999)   338
Figure 9-1   Advantages of IPOs   341
Figure 9-2   Disadvantages of IPOs   342
Figure 9-3   IPO Barriers   342
Table 9-3   Roles of Each Participant in an IPO   345
Figure 9-4   Estimated Cost of Going Public   346
Figure 9-5   Product Lifecycle Curve and IPOs   350
Figure 9-6   The Company Value Chain Illustrating Horizontal
          Mergers   358
Table 9-4   Most Common Reasons for Merger Failure   359
Figure 9-7   The Ten Phases of the Acquisition Process   361
Figure 10-1   Summary of the Deal Process   369
Figure 10-2   Sample Term Sheet   375
Figure 10-3   Sample Term Sheet   383
Figure 10-4   Sample Term Sheet   386
Figure 10-5   Sample Term Sheet   388
Figure 10-6   Summary of Important Provisions in a Term Sheet   392

Figure 11-1   The Main Factors Considered By VCs for Valuation   404
Figure 11-2   Relationship Between Risk-Reward and
                    Leverage-Control   411
Figure 11-3   Factors Increasing the Leverage of Venture Investors   414
Figure 11-4   Key Variables When Assessing the Investor's
                    Contributions   416
Figure 11-5   Variables to be Considered By the Company   417
Figure 11-6   Variables Investors Consider Important for
                    Companies   422
Figure 12-1   Questions Used to Determine Employment Status   437
Figure 12-2   Benefits to Companies Issuing Stock Options   440
Figure 12-3   Disadvantages of Stock Options and Warrants   440
Table 12-1   Comparison of ISOs versus NSOs   444
Figure 12-4   Anatomy of an ESOP   447
Figure C-2.1   Price Performance of Securities with Different Betas   527
Figure C-2.2   Price Performance of Securities with Different Betas   528
Figure C-2.3   Two Positively Correlated Securities (companies)   530
Figure C-2.4   The Net Effect of Diversification on Volatility   531
Figure C-2.5   Two Negatively Correlated Securities (companies)   531
Figure C-2.6   The Net Effect of Diversification on Volatility   532
Figure C-2.7   Two Randomly Correlated Securities (companies)   533
Figure C-2.8   The Net Effect of Diversification on Volatility   534

Introduction

The challenges of starting a company and leading it to profitability are extremely demanding due to the wide range of skills required by entrepreneur. And while most would be entrepreneurs have a vision for their business, they lack the sufficient experience and insight needed to successfully raise capital from angels and venture capitalists. Certainly there are several quality books devoted to the subject matter of venture capital and startup companies, but it appears that most contain subject content that is narrowly focused and therefore lacks the comprehensiveness entrepreneurs need in order to maximize their chances of success. Because of this, I sensed the need to write a book from both the venture capital and entrepreneur perspectives so that readers would have a better representation of the demands placed upon early stage companies. Hopefully this text will provide the reader with useful guidelines and critical insights that will be helpful for raising investment capital and positioning their company to achieve success.

The past two decades have witnessed a remarkable growth in venture capital investments paralleled by an unprecedented technological revolution. And although most of the participating entrepreneurs have received at least a fair share of the profits, there have been some unfortunate instances whereby they have received very little return on their innovative ideas and hard work due to uncharacteristic venture finance agreements. Although this represents the exception rather than the rule, the entrepreneur nevertheless must position himself in the driver's seat when approaching venture capitalists and angels for financing.

The best way to achieve this commanding position is by first building a solid business framework, consistent with the demands and expectations sophisticated investors. And this endeavor may only be accomplished by first gaining an understanding of the venture capital industry and using this information to guide the formation of the business. While this book is not centered on valuation or specific negotiation tactics per say, it has nevertheless been written based upon the central theme of negotiation through leveraging a well positioned company and shrewd management team to obtain adequate financing and achieve business success.

The first part of this text is very broad in content and attempts to provide the reader with an overview of initial business considerations for the entrepreneur, aspects of raising money, and an understanding of the venture capital industry. Chapter 1 provides a summary of some of the most important considerations for entrepreneurs as they embark upon their new venture and builds a framework for many of the topics to be presented later in detail.

In order to anticipate the best financing opportunities, it is vital for the entrepreneur to appreciate the motivations, limitations, and strategies of venture capitalists. Chapter 2 lays the framework for this understanding, as the venture capital and private equity markets are discussed at length to provide the reader with sufficient knowledge regarding the objectives and demands of venture capitalists. Chapter 3 shifts the focus back to the entrepreneur and begins with a discussion of basic considerations that should be made prior to structuring a funding proposal. It then discusses several rules for prospecting for capital. In addition, each major source of financing is discussed for the startup, early stage, and late stage company. Next, a rather detailed overview on securities offerings is presented in order to explain the proper procedures for solicitation of privately placed securities. Included in this section are guidelines for the construction of a private placement memorandum and related topics. Finally, this chapter concludes with a brief section on giving investor presentations.

The final chapter in this section is centered on investor profiling and illustrates the significance of this process in achieving optimal effectiveness when raising venture capital. If an entrepreneur is unable to sell his company concept to a prospective investor he will have a difficult time selling his company's services and products to prospective customers. As such, chapter 4 attempts to prepare the entrepreneur for the right psychological mindset when attempting this challenging task. The discussion begins by addressing the needs, advantages, and disadvantages of angel, private venture capital, and corporate venture capital investors. Finally, a brief discussion of incubators and accelerators concludes this chapter and is intended to provide the entrepreneur with an understanding of these organizations so they can decide if this type of assistance will be beneficial.

Part two of this text discusses topics essential for building the business and therefore the subject material is more focused. The key subjects for discussion in this section include management of intangible and tangible assets, valuation of intangible assets, market profiling, competitive strategies, strategic analysis and planning, licensing agreements, royalty rates, strategic alliances, joint ventures, and considerations for managing company growth, such as cash and asset management, budgeting and financial forecasting. Chapter 5 covers the basics of intellectual property and discusses some of the important considerations companies should make when attempting to protect the proprietary content of its intangible assets. Each form of intellectual property is discussed at length with an emphasis on patents and trade secrets. Chapter 6 addresses the critical topic of developing successful competitive strategies. This chapter begins with a discussion of what strategy is and how it can be used to position a company ahead of its competitors. Next, the strategy of pricing is discussed along with considerations for companies that might wish to avoid a price war. Michael Porter's "Five Forces Framework" is then presented as a method of analyzing an industry and the competitive forces within. Next, Porter's "Three Generic Strategies" are discussed as possible ways to overcome barriers within the "Five Forces Framework." In addition, other relevant topics are detailed such as preemptive strategies, strategic planning, and factors affecting price competition. Finally, chapter 6 concludes with a discussion of several resources that may be used to obtain information on competitors.

Developing a revolutionary technology very rarely leads to a successful company in itself. And without a clear and executable technology strategy that exploits the potential customer base, the core technology of the company, and any weaknesses in the market, a company will have a very difficult time competing. Chapter 7 highlights the utilization of intellectual property by presenting methods that can be used to leverage technology for financial and strategic gain. The focus of this chapter is on the use licensing agreements and includes extensive coverage of valuation techniques to assist in the determination of royalty rates, infringement damages, and for other purposes. The final portion of the chapter considers strategic alliances and joint ventures as a means of growth. These can be sensitive issues, as a company might find itself entering into such arrangements with a competitor. And if the necessary issues related to these options have not been adequately addressed, the company could soon find itself essentially shut out from its intended market. Chapter 8 provides an overview of operational finance and attempts to demonstrate its critical importance in determining the bottom line performance of the company. The key topics of this chapter are capital budgeting, budget forecasting, project selection, financial planning methods, asset management using financial ratios, cash management, and debt structuring.

The third and final part of this text is the most detailed and is focuses on topics most directly related to the negotiation process during financing, such as term sheets, valuation methods, exit strategies, and compensation. First, Chapter 9 provides an in-depth discussion of the portion of the financial industry most relevant to the entrepreneur and investor—routes of exit. This chapter attempts to provide the minimum required level of understanding for each of these transactions so the entrepreneur can devise the company's business strategy in parallel with one or more of these routes of exit. By aligning the business strategy with the proper mode of exit, the management team will not only position the company to receive the best financing terms, but they will also maximize the success potential of the company.

Chapter 10 discusses the most generic variations of term sheets along with potential ramifications. Entrepreneurs must understand the full details of all deal terms since the consequences of the agreed upon term sheet may not be apparent until some time into the future. In chapter 11, different viewpoints are made to assist the entrepreneur in determining the amount of control he is willing to exchange for venture capital and angel financing. First, an overview of the different methods of traditional asset valuation is presented to give the reader an appreciation for the factors that are considered when attempting to value company assets. Next, the typical venture capital valuation method is presented. Finally, an innovative valuation assessment model is described. This model provides a basic framework for companies to determine how much control they should give up to a particular venture firm, relative to the specific attributes of a prospective investor. If properly utilized, this valuation approach should empower the early stage company with the needed bargaining elements when negotiating a term sheet. The concluding chapter summarizes employer law and contracts and benefit compensation structures in corporate America. It is very important for the early stage company to understand state and federal employment law, as well as the proper procedures for protection of intellectual property.

The appendices provide examples of many legal documents used by companies, such as non-disclosure and noncompete agreements, stock options agreements, consulting agreements, investor questionnaire, and the subscription agreement. The remainder of the appendices contain more expansive discussions on due diligence, business plan guidelines, forecasting, and information on several funding resources, such as incubators, angel groups, investment meetings, and venture capital conferences.

This book should be kept at the side of the entrepreneur and management team, as they embark on the seemingly endless project of building a successful and profitable company. In addition, this book should serve as an invaluable guide for attorneys, CPAs, and consultants involved in the venture capital industry. A detailed table of contents was created as a substitute for an index and should provide a better guide for identification of specific topics.

Finally, the use of the word "Bible" selected as part of the title of this book was chosen as a generic way to designate this text as a comprehensive source of material for entrepreneurs seeking investment capital and was in no way meant to offend anyone of any religious belief or lack thereof.

The
Startup Company
Bible

Part I

Preparing For Financing

1

Entrepreneurship 101:
Establishing Your Company

"The best way to predict the future is to invent it."
Alan Kay

A. People

Know Thyself

There is often a fine line between entrepreneurs who are able to build a successful company versus those who try but do not succeed. The individual who believes he has an innovative idea that can provide unique value is only able to succeed due to a relentless commitment to transform this vision into reality. And while he does not necessarily need to have the mentality of an entrepreneur, his commitment and fortitude must have a similar motivation, enabling him to execute this vision. Yet these qualities are not sufficient for success, as luck, timing, and perseverance are also key components.

In my opinion, the typical founder of a high-technology startup has holistic intentions, and focuses his innovative skills on creating a positive change for the benefit of all mankind. We can label this type of individual the *holistic entrepreneur*. In contrast, the *pure entrepreneur* is usually motivated by business success, financial reward, and the challenges involved. And while some holistic entrepreneurs are share features of pure entrepreneurs, most are primarily holistic with a vision and perhaps the desire for some sort of public recognition. Entrepreneurs must determine which category they fit because it will determine the best course of action when assembling the company. And the inability to recognize this early on may cost your venture wasted time and potential financing.

Prior to starting a company, it is important to realize your strengths and weaknesses. If you consider yourself the holistic entrepreneur you will need to realize that most of your energy and time should be spent on technology development.   If you are more like the pure entrepreneurial then you will need to focus on the business aspects of the company. If unaware of your motivations and talents, you might otherwise find yourself spending most of your time trying to complete tasks for which you are not prepared.   Too often founders become so involved with all aspects of their companies that they forget they are not strategic business managers.   And this sometimes causes them to overestimate their abilities and underestimate the risks involved with a startup.   *Thus, all entrepreneurs must first learn to separate technology from business strategy and realize that each is equally important for determining the outcome of any high tech company.* If you are the innovator then you will need capable personnel and outside advisors to assist with the business aspects.   If you are the pure entrepreneur then you may need technicians to help implement your technology strategy.

Throughout the course of assembling the company you will probably learn more about yourself than you would have ever imagined.   The venture will be filled with periods of doubt, frustration, anticipation, complications, and hopefully elation.   But in order to succeed, you will need to focus on working smart, devoting time and resources that provide the most efficient results.   While many of the activities should be goal-oriented, others should not.   Examples of goal-oriented activities might include writing the business plan, filing patent applications, and securing adequate financing.   Meanwhile activities, such as attending trade conferences, networking, and developing your sales pitch should not be attached with specific goals or they may be mistakenly de-emphasized.

Even after a founder grows the company to the breakeven point, it may be even more difficult for him to realize when he has reached his limits of effective management skills.   Such individuals may wrongly assume that because they developed the company from the beginning, they also have the skills and experience necessary to further the growth of the company. I suppose it is human nature, similar to parents who raise a child, only to have the child finally leave home without the daily guidance and oversight of the parents.   Many parents struggle with this issue, believing that the "child" at 20 is not yet ready to face the world on his own. Other parents may feel the same of their 28-year-old son.   Is this due to the concern for the child's well being?   Or perhaps there is an element of the "need to nurture" that they are expressing.

Similarly, most founders feel the urge or need to nurture their innovations and this compulsion, when combined with a large ego can be deadly for the fate of a company.   Indeed, it is a very rare event for the original CEO, whether he was the founder or not, to continue as the CEO of the company through maturity.   The reason is that, just as companies and products have different life cycles, so do the abilities of individuals.   And successful startup companies are transformed many times over by the time they reach maturity;

perhaps more so than most individuals can adapt. But certainly securing a partnership with sophisticated investors who make themselves available for mentoring and other business assistance will increase the chances of advancing through all stages of managerial development.

Forming Your Management Team

At some point in the early stages of the startup, the founder should begin the task of assembling a management team. However, this is a process that should not be rushed. Rather, emphasis should be placed on retaining the commitment of initially one or two individuals they know well, are confident of their abilities, integrity, and experience and with whom they can work under stressful conditions. However, the absolute key is to make sure these individuals are equally committed, and this can take a considerable amount of personal interaction to determine.

The underlying component of all successful businesses is that they have the proper personnel in place, which when acting as a team are able to handle all business challenges effectively. And with rare exception, a great service or product is meaningless without an even greater business team. Thus *it is ultimately the quality of the management team that builds successful companies rather than their technology.* A carefully assembled management team will be able to change a failed business strategy and react quickly and effectively to a competitor's charge. Obviously, you cannot start a company with a paper and pen and expect to market the company as a technology innovation. But the technology or concept should be the reason for starting the company and represent its "muscle". The company's "heart and soul" however should be the management team and their ability to lead the company into the battleground against more experienced competitors, yet emerge victorious.

It follows that *most venture capitalists look closely at the strength and characteristics of a company's management team* more so than any other factor, especially in the early stages, when concrete results have not materialized. Venture capitalists and some experienced angel investors have spent an enormous amount of time with the personnel of many companies and have learned to recognize the qualities of capable individuals. They also assess the ability of management to work together effectively and create the synergy needed to operate in a highly demanding, competitive, and stressful environment.

When assembling a management team, the first question you should confirm is whether you are able to work with these individuals for long periods of time under stressful conditions. Next, one should ask *"what skill sets do these individuals add to the company that is complementary to the overall human resources currently in place."* Seldom is the founder of a startup a pure entrepreneur, yet a company will need at least one of these individuals in order to have a chance of achieving success.   This will be the person with the business experience and skills, drive, vision, intensity, leadership, passion for challenge and value creation.   Therefore, when assessing individuals for their potential to succeed in an entrepreneurial situation, three levels of assessment should be considered.

❖ **Character and Personality.** This will give you an idea about the individual's integrity, vision, creativity, fortitude, adaptability, etc.   Is this person a tenacious survivor?   What are his strengths and weaknesses?   These are things that cannot be gauged by looking at a resume.

❖ **Background.** This will give you an idea about the individual's educational and professional background and record of achievements. Does he have the required background in your company's industry? Does he have the aptitude to learn new skills quickly?   Does he have a business background in an entrepreneurial setting?   Has he been involved with a startup before?   Does he have a long history of success in different projects?

❖ **Experiences.** What unique experiences have contributed to this individual's abilities to learn and adapt to change?   How have his experiences contributed to his insights?

Below is a more specific list of questions to ask yourself when considering prospective individuals for a management team.   Keep in mind that the effectiveness of these questions will in large part depend upon your abilities to judge a person's character.   Are you a good judge of character? If not find someone who is and never hesitate to get a second and third opinion about a prospective candidate from a reliable source.

- Does this person have a *unique drive and intensity* that demonstrates his confidence in his abilities to get the job done, whatever the task may be?
- Is this person a *creative problem-solver*?
- Does this person possess a strong *competitive drive*?
- How quickly can this person *react and respond* to unforeseen difficulties?
- To what extent is this person *willing to take risks*?
- Is this person a leader or does he prefer to be led?

- Does this person *inspire you* when he speaks about his interests?

- How *committed and happy* would this person be working to build a successful company with no proven products or guarantees of success?

- What *skills* and other characteristics does this person possess which are *complementary* to yourself and the management team?

- Does this person understand the importance of *teamwork*?

- Does this person have *integrity*?

- Does this person *follow through* with his promises?

- What kinds of *business experience* does this person have?

- To what extent does this person have the *capacity to adapt and learn new skills*, as the company needs change?

- How would this person handle *adversity*?

- Would you feel confident in your chances for *survival* if stranded on a deserted island with this person?

- What is your *gut feeling* about this person's overall abilities?

Of course each person on your management team need not score high marks from each of these questions. You really only need one such individual if you are not already a pure entrepreneur. In fact, *everyone on your management team cannot be a leader and problem-solver; otherwise the ability of the team to work together may be hindered.* The final portion of the selection process should include a *through background check* for issues such as bankruptcy, liens, and history of any criminal record. Individuals with any of these prior difficulties could pose a barrier for obtaining adequate financing from sophisticated investors and these issues should be addressed early on.

If you do not feel confident you have identified committed and qualified individuals who can provide your company with added value, you may consider offering an individual an interim position to assist you in the initial tasks of starting your company in exchange for stock. It is tempting to find individuals who are willing to become associated with your company since you will have hundreds of things to accomplish even before you can begin to approach angel investors. As well it is only natural to seek out employees who share the same level of enthusiasm as you because they provide further validation of your idea, which makes you feel more confident. But assembling a non-committed and/or unqualified management staff prematurely will result in frustration, wasted time, employee turnover, and other adverse effects which could hinder or even prevent your company from succeeding.

The *chief executive officer (CEO)* is the individual most important for the future success of a company and is even more important than the chief technology officer (CTO) of a high-technology company.   After all, the CTO merely controls the development of the company's technology and without a strong CEO, the technology can be likened to a flashlight with two batteries— it will only work so long.   The CEO is needed to execute and constantly monitor the effectiveness of competitive strategies, which will utilize the company's strengths and exploit the weaknesses of competitors.   He reports directly to the board of directors and works with this group on major decisions and strategies the company selects to pursue.   He will also be the one who is responsible for large contract negotiations and other major decisions.   But more important, he serves as the leader who keeps the team focused and unified during difficult periods.

The CEO should have exceptional intellectual, emotional, and social intelligence, and should be a leader, listener, and a problem-solver. Obviously you are not going to attract Jack Welsh, but you would like to recruit an individual who has the potential to become a "Jack Welsh". However, there is certainly no consistently proven formula for a great CEO. And if having a Harvard or Wharton MBA determined a CEO's success, you can bet this would be made evident and everyone would look only for an individual with those pedigrees.   As a matter of fact, I have known many individuals with these exact pedigrees who had a poor sense of business. In short, *look at the person and evaluate his skills based upon what you see in front of you rather than what you see on paper.*

The *chief technology officer (CTO)* is often the founder and obviously without a CTO a high-technology company concept would be difficult to illustrate resulting in low customer and investor interest.   Many founders usually assume a dual role of CTO and CEO initially, and then focus their resources as the CTO once a qualified CEO has been identified.

Similar to the CEO, the chief financial officer (CFO) should also possess exceptional intellectual intelligence and problem solving abilities.   While he should have some knowledge in financial accounting, he should be more skilled in financial analytics, planning and forecasting, fund raising, cash management, and matters concerning terms of financial negotiation.   Ideally, this individual should be a hybrid of an accountant, asset manager, financial analyst, and fundraiser, all of which typically have very different skill sets. However, it is much more important that he possesses the later two skills over the former, as accounting skills can be satisfied through outsourcing or the use of sophisticated software such as Peachtree Accounting.   The CFO will be the financial engineer of the company, serving many roles.

The *chief operating officer (COO)* is responsible for the daily operations of the company, ensuring that every aspect is working in unity and that the business strategies are executed efficiently.   This position is not so important for an early stage company due to the lack of infrastructure but becomes more significant in later stages when the company is generating revenues. This individual should have abilities in production management, inventory, and quality control.

The *business development officer* is needed to form strategic relationships with customers, suppliers, manufacturers and collaborators. Such an individual must have effective communication and interpersonal skills leading to successful negotiation and deal closing. For the early stage company this individual will most likely need to assume the dual role of business development and chief of sales and marketing. Alternatively, the CEO or CFO may assume these responsibilities.

In conclusion, both the CEO and CFO of an early stage company should possess a high level of dynamic intelligence, passion, and vision. Understand that new companies often do not have clear delineations of roles due to the tremendous demands and limited manpower. As such, the responsibilities of the CEO and CFO may show a large degree of overlap until the company matures. And with continued company maturation, the roles of each member of the management team will change to meet these demands. Therefore, *individuals involved in a startup should not only possess basic skill sets, but they should also be able to adapt to differing roles.*

Forming Your Boards

In the early stages of a company, the formation of the *board of directors* serves merely as a legal formality that is mandated by corporate law for companies structured as C corporations.[1] The duties of the board are to make decisions regarding the hiring and firing of top management, establish milestones, review the performance of the CEO, assist in fund raising, and advise the company on matters of large impact. *These individuals have a moral and legal responsibility to decide on matters with the best interest of the shareholders.* Initially, the board usually consists of the founders and management team and therefore results in no change in the company management. As investors are secured, this board is expanded so that the best interests of the shareholders are represented, as required by law.

The investors of preferred stock will expect to have one or more seats on the board of directors since their investment entry occurred at a later development stage, and valuation of the company was represented by a different class of stock. At this time, the company can ask current board members to step down or it can add new positions. Once the preferred board members have been determined, they shall retain their seats on the board assuming there is no unanimous agreement by the preferred board members. In general, *the most current round of financing has at least the same influence in terms of rights, if not more than the previous financing round.*

The *scientific advisory board* should be comprised of individuals with expertise in the company's core technology, as well as others with different but similar areas of expertise. In addition, at least one of these individuals should have relevant industry expertise and corporate contacts that can contribute to the strategic intelligence of the company. Venture firms always look closely at the composition of this board as a partial gauge of technology validation. These individuals should be expected to provide the company with advice on technical issues, help identify market opportunities, and provide industry contacts.

Finally, some companies may need to form a *general advisory board* to fill in gaps of experience and skills of the management team. This is especially true for startup and early stage companies that have not yet received venture financing. *Unlike corporate boards, advisory boards do not carry fiduciary responsibility and their advice is non-binding.* Therefore, it should be relatively easier to secure advisory board members since they will not need to worry about liability for company actions. The composition of the general advisory board should be a balance of industry and financial experts, investors, and management who have differing views and personalities, but who are able to work together cohesively. Proper selection of the general advisory board can contribute a valuable and inexpensive source of human capital to the company. Management should select board members who can provide information on market share, competitive technologies, customer base, marketing strategies, and general business expertise. Below are some general guidelines to follow when assembling boards (see appendix A-5 for a model scientific advisory board agreement).

- Determine the objectives of each board member and make selections based upon the ability of individuals to fulfill those needs

- Clearly define and communicate expectations for each board

- Select board members that think creatively, independently, and who have a diverse skill set

- Every board member should have adequate skill sets to fill a gap in the board but avoid duplication of skill sets

- Require members to sign confidentiality agreements

- Replace board members that are not performing adequately

Realizing When You Need Help

Many companies can have great business plans but the inability to execute these strategic blueprints will jeopardize the viability of the business. Therefore, the company should adhere to its plan, making modifications as needed. In addition, the management team should implement internal and external evaluation guidelines to address the many difficulties and unanticipated hurdles that may be encountered. For example, the company may have met its initial sales and revenue goals but future projections will no be longer sufficient to meet previous estimations. In such a case, the company could be faced with a slow but certain death if the situation is not recognized and corrected in a timely manner. Alternatively, a competitor may develop a superior technology or marketing strategy that threatens the products and/or services, and thus your company's chances of survival. In some cases the speed of detection will be more important than the mode of response. These are just a few scenarios that illustrate the significance of building a strong management team, capable of detection and adaptation.

Nevertheless, despite diligent planning and oversight these critical issues may not be addressed properly until a venture capitalist gets involved. But ideally, the management team needs to be able to work through the difficult challenges encountered during the early stages of the company. This represents the *sweat equity* that venture capitalists and many angels simply do not have the time to assist with. In the later stages, a certain level of control by an angel investor or venture capitalist should provide more synergy, and therefore strengthen the company's competitive positioning.

As the company grows, the inflows of external financing that have fueled this growth will gradually result in a diminished control of the company by the founders proportionate to the amount funded. This can sometimes create internal difficulties because many founders want investment capital but they do not want to give up majority control of their company. Unknowingly, some act as if they should be provided with capital in exchange for minimal ownership because their business concept is a sure success. However, the reality is that *an investment in an early stage company represents amongst the highest risk investments known and in exchange for assuming such risks, investors expect to receive high returns.* This relationship of hypothetical risk and expected returns is an invariable law of finance. I cannot count the number of times I have encountered entrepreneurs who have underestimated the risk portion of this risk-reward concept. And rather than approach financing decisions based upon this relationship, many never get the chance to develop their business because of their unwillingness to relinquish adequate control of their company to investors. In short, most entrepreneurs become greedy because they simply do not understand the risks investors must take.

B. Purpose

Vision & Mission Statement

Discovering your company's vision is the defining moment in the birth of the company concept. Without vision there can be no mission. And *without a clearly defined mission there can be neither the forward direction nor strategic focus needed to create a sustainable competitive advantage.* The mission statement serves to communicate a company's *unchanging philosophy* that is used to assist it not only in the strategic decision-making process, but also as a means of sustaining commercial immortality. The greatest and oldest companies in the world, such as Johnson & Johnson, General Electric, Microsoft, Merck, 3M, Wal-Mart, Hewlett-Packard, Sony, Panasonic, Philip Morris, and Citigroup understand this concept completely. As industries have changed, these companies have been thought at different times to reinvent themselves, but this could not be further from the truth. They never changed their vision. *It was their invariable vision that sought out new markets.*

Prior to composing a mission statement, one must first develop the company vision, which can be divided into *core ideologies* and *visionary goals.* A company's core ideology consists of *core values* and a *core purpose*, both of which are independent to changes in the industry structure and product life cycles (figure1-1). Core ideologies cannot be created but must be discovered by realizing what you feel most passionate about. And it only needs to be meaningful and inspirational for the employees. *Core ideologies do not change* to meet the demands of a changing industry, but remain constant throughout time and can even inspire entry into new industries. When discovering your company's core values, you must ask yourself what issues your company holds deep that will not change over time regardless of the changes in the industry. With rare exception, most companies should have no more than three or four core values, otherwise they may have mislabeled core values with attributes that are subject to change with time or altering conditions, such as corporate strategy (figure 1-2).

Core purpose is the company's reason for existence and also should not change with time or altering conditions. Therefore, it should not be focused on identifying products or customer segments because these things can and will eventually change (figure 1-3). The core purpose is an important component of the core ideology because it provides inspiration and guidance for the company. This not only helps lead the company's product development but it also provides employees with a clear understanding of what the company stands for so that employees are better able to attach value to these projects, making their work more meaningful.

One method that can be used to help identify a company's core purpose is to state what your company does and then begin asking a series of "whys". If your company produces mobile phones, ask yourself why it is doing this. You might answer that the company is doing this in order to provide better hardware for mobile communications. But this is not fundamental to the reason for existence, as this depends upon the mobile communications technology. Asking "why" again might lead you to reason that your purpose for producing mobile phones is to improve the quality of life by providing business consumers with access to the best communication tools. *In keeping the core purpose broader and focused on the consumer, companies are able to change their product offerings as needed over time in order to fulfill the corporate mission.*

Figure 1-1. The Components of Vision

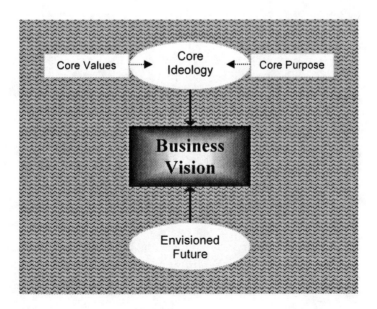

Original illustration by M. Stathis

The second component of vision is *envisioned future or visionary goals.* These are far-reaching goals designed not by logic or projections, but by a dream that may be realized far into the future of the company. They should be clearly stated and promote the excitement and unification of employees. Most visionary goals are thought to target a sales number or product development, overtake a specific competitor, model one's company after an industry leader, or dominate its markets (figure 1-4). And *unlike core ideology, envisioned future must have goals that have ending points so companies will know when these goals have been achieved and when to establish more goals.* Companies should set their visionary goals high and beyond their current capabilities so that management is forced to think more as visionary leaders rather than strategists and tacticians. Meanwhile, strategy should only be used as a tool to achieve the envisioned future of the company.

Figure 1-2. Examples of Core Values

Merck
- Corporate social responsibility
- Unequivocal excellence in all aspects of the company
- Honesty and integrity
- Science-based innovation
- Profit only from work that benefits humanity

Walt Disney
- No cynicism
- Creativity, dreams, and imagination
- Fanatical attention to consistency and detail
- Preservation and control of the Disney magic
- Nurturing and promulgation of "wholesome American values"

Sony
- Elevation of the Japanese culture and national status
- Being a pioneer-not following others; doing the impossible
- Encouraging individual ability and creativity

Figure 1-3. Examples of Core Purpose

Hewlett-Packard: To make technical contributions for the advancement of welfare of humanity

Wal-Mart: To give ordinary folk the same chance to buy the same things as rich people

Merck: To preserve and improve human life

McKinsey & Company: To help leading corporations and governments be more successful

Mary Kay Cosmetics: To give unlimited opportunity to women

3M: To solve unsolved problems innovatively

Figure 1-4. Examples of Envisioned Future

Wal-Mart: become a $125 billion company by the year 2000

Sony: become the company most known for changing the worldwide poor-quality image of Japanese products (early 1950s)

Citbank: become the most powerful, the most serviceable and far-reaching world financial institution that has ever been (predecessor to Citicorp, 1915)

Boeing: become the dominant player in commercial aircraft and bring the world into the jet age (1950)

Reprinted by permission of Harvard Business Review.
From "Building Your Company's Vision" by James Collins and Jerry Porras, Issue 5, Sept/Oct 1996.

Table 1-1. Comparison of Core Values, Core Purpose, and Envisioned Future

	Does it Change	Purpose	Characteristics	How is it Developed
Core Values	Yes	Guide & Inspire	What company stands for	It must be discovered
Core Purpose	Yes	Guide & Inspire	Why company exists	It must be discovered
Envisioned Future	No	Encourage team spirit	Unperceivable Goals	Creative Process

The Business Model

The business model is the key centerpiece of any company's business proposition and is formed from the values of the business vision (figure 1-5). A successful business model serves to connect all the relevant domains of a business infrastructure to form the necessary platform for converting the business vision into economic value and financial profit. *Ultimately it is the business model along with the management team that the venture capitalist chooses to invest.* Chesbrough and Rosenbloom have developed an operational definition for successful business models based upon extensive research. They have proposed that a business model should be able to describe, identify or formulate the following elements (figure 1-6):

- **Value Proposition.** This describes the customer problem, proposes how their product solves the problem and provides a measure of the value created by the product, as thought to be perceived by the customer.

- **Market Segment.** This describes the ideal target customer based upon an understanding of subtle differences within a larger market. Often times, new market segments are created by accurately understanding the needs and of a new technology within the broader market.

- **Value Chain Structure.** This identifies all physical, capital, intellectual, and operational resources required to create and distribute the product. When matched with the company's resources, it can identify deficiencies within the value chain that may be filled by external assets or resources.

- **Cost Structure and Profit Potential.** This identifies the revenue model, cost structure, and profit margins based upon the chosen value chain and value proposition.

- **Position in the Value Network.** This relates to understanding the company's position relative to competitors and complementors as well as suppliers and customers.

- **Competitive Strategy.** This describes the methods that will be used to develop a sustainable competitive advantage over competitors.

While business models are thought to be somewhat constant, this usually proves to be less true for developing companies, as new technologies or unsuccessful business attempts often require new business models in order to effectively leverage their potentials.

Figure 1-5. The Business Vision is the Heart of the Business Model

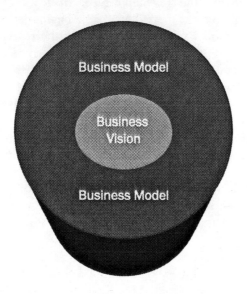

Figure 1-6. The Six Components of the Business Model

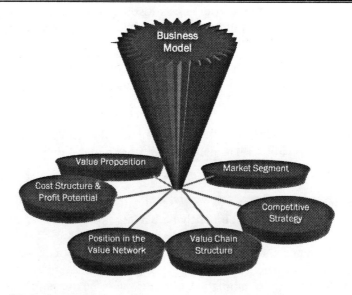

Original illustration by M. Stathis

Business Plan

The task of preparing a business plan is typically viewed with terror and leads to procrastination for the beginning entrepreneur, but it is the first formal step in planning the company. *The best way to think of the business plan is as a detailed blueprint of the overall business model and accompanying strategies,* whose execution will propel the company to overall success and profitability. And when written effectively, it serves as a selling instrument for prospective investors. Prior to writing the plan, certain tasks should be completed, such as developing the business model, conducting market research, (to address the potential market size) a thorough competitive analysis, (to address the competitive landscape) and forming a marketing strategy. Finally, somewhere within the business proposal the company should have identified at least one major competitive advantage, which should serve as the strongest factor in enabling the company to compete successfully within its chosen market.

Keep in mind however, that writing an effective business plan is not something one does just to appease potential investors. The most important reason for writing a comprehensive business plan is to create a hard copy of the company mission, strategy, and goals. This exercise should help the management remain focused on defined goals, as well as provide a means to critique the effectiveness of its strategies, and modify its approach based upon new developments, or the lack thereof.

Rather than attempting to write such a document in full, I suggest dividing the main parts and writing each one on a priority basis. Contrary to what you may have read elsewhere, the two most important parts of the business plan are the *Market Analysis* and *Product Marketing* sections because these two sections allow the company to demonstrate the value add with respect to customers and investors. In many cases, customers will neither care about your strategy nor wish to see a business plan (nor should they have the right to see it). However, in some cases, large customers may become investors at a later time and they will want to be assured that you have structured the course of the company from the onset.

Meanwhile, angels and venture capitalists will want to know the details of how you intend to capture a reasonable portion of the market, precisely how you plan to use the financing proceeds, and over what time period. Finally, it is critical that you understand what type of company you have so that you can position the business strategy accordingly. For instance, are you a distribution company or a platform company? Are you a service company or a product company? What is the best revenue model given the type of company? How are you able to validate this model? Appendix B contains some basic guidelines for constructing effective business plans.

C. Technology

There are several stages of technology development and the entrepreneur should be familiar with some basic terminology. A *concept technology* is the first stage and represents the inventor's idea. Once a company has developed a product and it has been tested by the company and is called the *alpha prototype*. After successful alpha testing has occurred, the product is distributed to select customers for *beta testing*. Typically, the *successful testing of the beta prototype signals the first stage of company development and is one of the optimal points of entry for venture capital financing.*

What is your company's *core technology* or primary technological innovation, and what *sustainable competitive advantage* does it provide? Have you identified all competitors and their products? Does your product address the needs of customers that have not been addressed by the competition?   What are the barriers to entry of this technology?   Have you performed the needed market research that has enabled you to identify your industry market size and your company's expected market share?   How is the industry evolving and what types of regulatory barriers may change the opportunities for this industry?   Is this technology proprietary and defensible by patents and have you conducted the needed patent searches to check for duplication?   These are amongst the first questions sophisticated investors will ask before assessing the viability of your company.   Of course, these issues should be addressed in length in your business plan.

D. Money

Any business that seeks investment capital must provide prospective shareholders and lenders with information related to valuation of the business. The initial responsibility of company valuation will be the founder's, although these numbers typically do not mean much to sophisticated investors. Nonetheless, the founder should develop a rationale for justifying his company's valuation.   More essential however, is for the founder to appreciate the characteristics of each of these financial instruments so that when negotiating financial terms with potential investors, the founder and the management team will be responsive to scenarios that may ultimately affect their compensation, control, and fate of the company.   The easiest way to think of the various instruments available for financing is to divide them into three main categories based upon their distinguishing characteristics.   These three categories are equity, debt, and derivatives.

1. Equity

Common Stock

The issuance of equity to an investor gives that individual ownership of the company proportionate to the amount of stock received. Typically, common stock is the first security issued by the startup company and the shareholders will include the founder, management team, and board members, all of which usually will not have paid cash for the stock but rather, it has been offered in-lue of cash compensation for services in addition to providing financial incentive. Because the founder has invested *sweat equity* into the company in exchange for common stock, it is referred to as *founder's stock*. Investors that usually offer cash for common stock include friends, family, and angel investors. Typically, common stockholders receive one vote on company matters for each share they own but this can be changed by the articles of incorporation if approved by the board of directors.

The main advantage of common stock for the investor is that provides unlimited upside appreciation potential. However, the main disadvantage is that in the event of bankruptcy, common stock holders are the last to receive liquidation assets. In addition, common stock can be very susceptible to a variety of dilutive mechanisms which will decrease the value of each share. Thus, for the company seeking expansion capital, common stock provides a fully transparent mechanism of structuring of company assets in exchange for investment capital.

Preferred Stock

Preferred stock is actually a hybrid of common stock and debt since it has appreciation potential and pays the holder a dividend at regular intervals, when declared by the board of directors. However, *preferred stock is not formally considered debt, since the failure to pay dividends does not constitute bankruptcy*. Nevertheless, holders of preferred stock receive assets before common stock holders when exit occurs, either bankruptcy or IPO. This type of security has many possible variants and can be structured to provide the most ideal investment/financing instrument for the investor/company. As such, the transparency of its structure can be confusing making a careful consideration of all terms essential when determining the particular type of preferred stock to be issued.

It is perhaps due to the flexibility in its design as well as its liquidation priority over common stock that this type of security is invariably favored by venture capitalists. When properly structured, preferred stock can provide investors with a limited downside risk and unlimited appreciation potential.

Thus, the precision and flexibility that can be used to structure a new issuance of preferred stock is a perfect vehicle for venture capitalists to invest institutional money of variable risk tolerance and time horizon. Although dividends are rarely declared prior to an exit, the more common downside protection is provided by clauses that establish *liquidation preferences*, which under certain conditions converts the dividends into additional shares of stock.

Typically, preferred stock issued by private companies is convertible into the analogous common stock at the option of the holder or based upon certain events. A type of convertible preferred known as *redeemable preferred* may be issued to investors as a means of allowing them to redeem their stock if the company is not performing adequately. This stock does not pay fixed dividends, but upon redemption pays the *par value* (the original price of issuance) plus some return on capital. In addition, preferred stock can be constructed to convert on a *"when, and as if"* basis to allow for voting rights and liquidation for IPOs. As will be seen later in this book, the not so obvious advantage of preferred stock is that it provides additional downside protection depending on the specific type of preferred stock issued.

Preferred stock can have a variety of characteristics, depending upon the specific type issued. It pays a fixed dividend at regular intervals and can be cumulative or noncumulative, participating or not participating, dilutive or nondilutive, and can also have special rights attached to it. *Although most preferred stock has voting rights, by definition, it does not have to be issued with voting privileges.* More commonly, voting rights can also be dependent upon certain events occurring. The justification in providing preferred stockholders with such flexibility and downside protection is apparent when one considers that cash is always paid for this type of stock, as opposed to common stock. Therefore, these investors deserve special preferences and rights not available to holders of common stock.

When a preferred stock dividend has not been declared for one or more periods, only the holders of *cumulative preferred* stock will be entitled to receive the dividend from the prior periods as well as the current dividends. However, *noncumulative preferred* stock (which does not allow stockholders to receive such dividends) is much more common in the venture capital industry. Preferred stock can also be issued as *participating preferred*, whereby shareholders are able to participate in excess earnings of the company similar to the holders of common stock. In addition, some participating preferred stock also receives a regular fixed dividend when declared.

Although dividends are rarely declared with startup companies, they accrue with participating preferred (i.e. they are cumulative) so that the holder of these securities is able to not only receive dividends but also participate in the upside of a company sale, similar to common stock. In addition, it also provides a good hedge in the event of a company sale since the holders of preferred stock receive their principal prior to common stockholders.   This is an important distinction during a liquidation sale, when the sales price of the company may fall lower than the original investment.

Stock Dilution

Investors purchase a certain amount of stock with the expectation that they will receive a specific ownership percentage of the company.   However certain transactions can decrease the percentage ownership and when this occurs, the stock is said to be *diluted* from its original ownership representation. *The significance of dilutive transactions is that they can affect the value of previous capital investors committed, in addition to the ownership percentages of the founder and management team.*

Dilution to a shareholder occurs when there is a relative decrease per share as a result of the issuance of additional stock.[2]   Thus, if an investor owns 100% of a company as a result of a $10 million investment and a later round of financing designates the new investor as owning 50% of the company for $2,000,000, this transaction is considered dilutive in terms of shareholder equity. If, on the other hand, the new investor paid $10,000,000 for a 50% ownership position the transaction is not dilutive because the new company valuation is $20,000,000, and the original investor has invested half of this total, which is reflected in his proportionate ownership. Therefore, *dilution only occurs if the proportionate ownership decreases relative to the company valuation.*[3]

No investor wishes to have their equity diluted by a newer investor. However, many times without the additional financing the previous investor may be exposed to a very high level of risk due to the lack of company capital.   Therefore, one must balance the consequences of dilutive provisions in terms of the alleviation of company failure versus the alteration in the investors' *internal rate of return* (IRR). [4]   There are three basic forms of anti-dilution rights that vary in their ability to prevent dilution of previous investors as well as the stock of the founder and management team.   These are full ratchet, broad-based weighted average, and narrow-based weighted average rights.   We will examine these techniques in detail in chapter 10.

Ultimately, performance values such as earnings per share, cash flow per share and gross revenues per share are the most important to venture capitalists when considering the effects of dilution.   Take note that when structuring warrants, stock options, and convertible preferred stock, one must account for possible dilution as a result of the conversion of these derivatives into common stock.   This is also relevant when structuring employee compensation plans.   Finally, dilution must be disclosed clearly in the prospectus of a private placement memorandum in order to maintain the appropriate compliance with state and federal securities laws.

2. Debt

When a company issues debt, it takes out a loan and the holder of these securities becomes the creditor. In return, the company pledges to pay the creditor an interest rate for accepting the repayment risk of this loan by a specified date, known as the *maturity date*. When investment banks underwrite loans for corporations they are called bonds and are usually secured against the assets of the company. When commercial banks underwrite loans for individuals and small companies, they are known as notes and are usually secured against the personal assets of the debtor. Typically, these debt instruments might be used for the purchase of land, bridge financing, specific equipment or machinery and secured against that equipment.

Debt is advantageous to the company because it does not dilute its equity. However, the company must make periodic payments of interest and this can deplete needed cash flows. Meanwhile, debt is attractive for certain investors because it has the first rights of liquidation of assets over both preferred and common stock in the event of bankruptcy. However, it has a limited upside since it cannot participate in appreciation of the company stock value. In addition, *debt holders do not have any voting power to influence company decisions.* Prior to issuance of any debt, the consent of the preferred shareholders is usually required in order to protect their liquidation preference.

For startups and most early stage companies, debt financing is not a viable alternative due to their lack of tangible assets and predictable positive cash flows needed to secure the loan. Nevertheless, some banks will provide loans to companies that have created substantial intellectual property. In addition, banks will provide loans to a company if they can get individuals to sign off on the loan. One way to accomplish this is to offer warrants to such individuals for assuming liability of the loan. If all goes well, the bank will be paid back its principal and interest, and the cosigners will receive rights to purchase company stock at a fixed price anywhere from 3 to 5 years from the date of issuance. This is a common technique used by venture capitalists and angels to enable their portfolio companies to maximize their access to capital without selling more stock. Thus it is a method used to minimize further dilution at a later time when the business risk is much lower than during prior issuance of equity.

Mezzanine Financing

This type of financing can be in the form of equity or debt and is primarily used as a short-term supply of cash when a company is transitioning into another round of financing or just prior to an IPO.   Because of this use, it is often known as *"bridge financing"* since it is used between the major financing stages.   When structured as a debt instrument, mezzanine securities are usually issued with an *equity "kicker"* or a contingent common equity interest in the form of warrants or registration rights which specify a common stock conversion ratio.   These incentives are needed in order to accept the illiquid nature of these investments.   *For the company mezzanine financing can provide a means of short-term borrowing that is not attached to specific milestones.*   For the investor this type of investment, while usually of low risk, also provides low returns.

In the public markets, mezzanine debt may be used to help finance acquisitions, certain capital expenditures, and recapitalizations and it is subordinate to secured senior debt but senior to equity.   In the private markets, mezzanine debt is issued to later stage companies with historical earnings and revenue growth.   When mezzanine equity is issued it is usually structured as preferred equity or convertible equity.   When structured as a convertible debt security, a predetermined conversion rate is fixed at the time of issuance and the interest rate is usually lower than for pure debt since the holder is also receiving the right to convert the security to preferred stock.   Because convertible debt has characteristics common to both debt and equity, it is considered to possess less risk than equity but more risk than debt.   Therefore, this type of security is the preferred means of investment by some venture firms and commercial banks that do not wish to expose themselves to the high risk of equity, but who wish to participate in its upside.

Mezzanine debt is attractive to many later stage companies because it is more flexible than structured bank debt and has no dilutive characteristics.   The flexibility of mezzanine debt occurs on the side of both the issuer and the creditor.   For the issuer, debt covenants are less stringent and typically allow larger leverage.   For the creditors, mezzanine debt structuring provides terms that are highly negotiable with the issuer and offers high interest rates plus upside participation in the form of equity conversion.   The main providers of mezzanine debt have historically been pension funds, endowments, and insurance companies, however private equity funds, LBO funds, commercial and investment banks have increased their demand for these debt vehicles over the past decade.

3. Derivatives

As mentioned previously, stock options, rights, and warrants are known as derivatives because the inherent value of these securities is in part a derivative of the analogous common stock of the company.   Derivatives are attractive investment and compensation tools that when used effectively, provide many benefits to the company. However, one should note that the issuance of options, rights, or warrants is considered to represent the issuance of stock in proportion to the conversion rate. Therefore, earnings dilution will occur when these derivatives are converted into the analogous stock. And this potential dilution must be stated on any future offerings of securities. Finally, warrants are frequently issued in conjunction with preferred stock. Unlike options, which cannot be traded independently, warrants can be separated from the security they have been bundled with and sold separately. In conclusion, the issuance of derivatives should be scrutinized because they will result in earnings dilution, which can have an impact on company valuation.

E. Strategy

Establishing Your Core Competency

Companies should identify their *core competencies* and design a business model that seeks to leverage these competencies in their chosen markets. A company's core technology is often distinct from its core competency. *A core technology represents the company's main technological innovation and can be defined as a composite of skills, technologies, and know-how that when combined, can be used to provide its customers with a valued product or service.* In contrast, *a core competence is a strategic concept that may be defined as all of the know-how, technology, and product development skills behind a company's main technological business idea.* Usually for high-technology companies, core competencies are developed based in part on their core technologies. It is critical that the company properly defines the boundaries of its core competency, making sure that it is not too broad or too narrow. If the core competency is too broad it may cause confusion and misdirection when attempting to design a business strategy that attempts to exploit the competency. If it is too narrow, many potentially significant opportunities may be eliminated.

Market Profiling and Forecasting

After the specific market has been determined, the entrepreneur needs to formulate strategies for effectively competing within this market followed by establishing credible financial forecasts. *Pro forma cash flow and income statements should be estimated for each month for the first year followed by quarterly estimates for the next five years.* Venture capitalists use these projections as a basis for valuation and to determine the amount of equity they will need for a specific financing commitment. Therefore, they will challenge all assumptions behind these estimates to ensure they have been accurately accounted for. *Financial statements that are not credible and without adequate justification will be looked down upon by venture firms and angels. And such oversights will at least cause major changes to the company's valuation. In some cases, it may diminish the company's chances for funding.*

The first step in assessing the growth potential of your company is to measure the size of the market(s) that it will be competing in. This will include identification of competitors and their relative market share. Next, the company should provide reasonable estimates for its potential to capture a certain portion of the market and it should specifically understand how it will achieve this market growth, how much it will cost, and over what time period. From these estimates, financial projections are made over a five year period. Finally, industry multiples are determined, such as price-to-earnings ratio, earnings per share, and price per share.

Using these projections along with the appropriate industry numbers, the company will then have a benchmark that can be used as rough guide to value its business. These preliminary calculations will serve as the basis for the amount of financing that may reasonably be expected. This does not necessarily equate to using the most optimistic data, but rather the best defensible data that will convince prospective investors that the numbers make sense and are achievable. Therefore, intensive efforts should be made to provide the best data for this analysis. Several sources can be used such as industry trade journals, Wall Street research reports, SEC filings, and reports available online. Finally, more extensive sources such as Frost and Sullivan, Forrester, and consulting firms provide industry reports for a fee (usually quite large). We will discuss the valuation process in detail many times throughout this book, but for now let us look at a simple example.

Zip Chips is a semiconductor company specializing in the production of Gallium Arsenide semiconductors. Its competitive advantage is its novel production process that utilizes sophisticated software to minimize the defects of these materials and maximize overall conductivity. The industry average PE ratio for these companies is currently 30 and has averaged 35 over the past 5 years. The company has estimated earnings of $10,000,000 by the sixth year of operation. Therefore, using the PE ratio of 30, Zip Chips is estimated to have a value of $300 million by the sixth year if it meets its earnings forecast estimates. (Note that the 5-year industry average PE is a more accurate measure but the more conservative number has been used to account for error.) If the company expects to need a total financing of $30 million over the next 6 years, this would represent a gross return of investment of 10 times initial investment.   A first round investment of $3 million would represent a 10% stake in the estimated total financing needs of the company. If the company reaches its earnings estimate by year six, the investor would have realized an approximate 70% annualized rate of return.

Companies need to reevaluate their business strategies and modify them at certain times in order to repel an offensive attack or seize market opportunities.   Therefore, management must at all times understand the competition, industry dynamics, and market growth potential.   Therefore, market analyses and financial forecasting will become routine tasks for as long as your company remains in business

Market Segmentation Analysis

The process of market segmentation involves dividing an industry into market segments comprising customers sharing common needs.   These markets may then be further divided based upon more specific criteria. For instance, the computer industry may be divided into customers who use PDAs, PCs, and mainframes.   Within the PDA market, there are several manufacturers, suppliers, and distributors throughout the *value chain* that contribute to the utility of the PDA device.   The electronics components suppliers produce components for the device, the assemblers package the device into a finished product, the software companies provide applications for the device, and the distributors make the product available to end users. A further division exists when comparing those PDAs that use Windows-based versus Palm-based operating systems.   And customers of each device value a specific PDA based upon the merits of the operating system and the utilities provided within.   Similar analogies can be made for the PC and mainframe computer markets, as well as any other industry.

Prior to committing on the specifics of a venture, the entrepreneur should conduct a detailed market segmentation analysis that provides sufficient information to establish potential customers and their needs.   Once the most opportunistic markets have been identified, the entrepreneur can determine whether the business concept or core technology can be leveraged to take advantage of the opportunities within the chosen market.   Next, evaluation criteria should be created that weighs the various aspects of entry, growth, profitability, and exit.   This will assist the entrepreneur when assessing risk and formulation of a competitive strategy.   Also note that a market segmentation analysis should also be used when a company attempts to assess potential areas of market expansion, which may be inevitable as its product life cycle matures.   Appendix D illustrates this procedure in more detail.

Marketing Strategy

Regardless of the industry, marketing strategy may well be second only to competitive strategy in importance. Marketing strategy is even more important than the services and products of a company (assuming a certain minimal level of product/service value). In general there are three factors consumers base their choices on: price, quality, and perception. We see examples of industries focusing their strategies on price selection each day— discount stores, discount brokerage firms, etc. As well, we see examples of companies whose strategy is to deliver the highest quality of goods---brand names versus generic, (although not all brand names represent high quality), excellent versus poor customer service. And finally, perception may be the most difficult to achieve and measure. However, perception often affects price and quality. Many of the most successful companies have a combination of quality and perceived value, such as Nike, Abercrombie & Fitch, General Electric, Intel, Dell, Maytag, and Goodyear, although some of these companies would claim they also have price advantages as well.

Financial Strategy

This is usually one of the least detailed portions of the business plan, in terms of presentation of a specific strategy. Many companies tend to spend enormous amounts of time estimating sales and expenditures that often results in unrealistic projections, lacking the sufficient detail required to solidify the overall business planning process. It is not enough to propose a first round financing of $5,000,000 followed by a second round at $10,000,000, based upon a 5-year revenue projection of $20,000,000 when the company currently has no revenues. This data must be backed up by the proper market research and the details behind each assumption must be included in the footnotes. *In addition, the company also must be specific about how much capital it needs, over what time frame, and for what specific purposes. And it must be able to justify this financing in a manner that yields an excellent risk/return ratio for the prospective investors.*

Thus, the management team must have a clear understanding of the entire financing process, including all potential alternatives, such as joint ventures and strategic alliances. As well, solid revenue models and feasible routes of exit must also be designed by management so that the most effective financial strategy can be implemented. And the overall financial strategy should be directly linked to the company's marketing and distribution strategies to provide overall feasibility of its projections. The company should include a five-year pro forma of financial statements, including the income statement, balance sheet and statement of cash flows with all assumption listed in footnotes.

Typically, overemphasis is placed only on the income statement since the founder feels that the revenue and profit forecasts are the most essential figures and because the company usually has very little if any physical assets and cash flows to assemble a balance sheet and statement of cash flows. However, inclusion of all financial statements demonstrates that the management team is competent and aware of the importance of financial management and forecasting. Finally, management must strike a balance between high revenue growth, minimal expenses, and breakeven time. *Ideally, the financial statements should represent a breakeven point at the 4-5 year mark with an anticipated IPO during years 7 or 8.* Most companies are very optimistic and will therefore forecast an IPO during the fifth year but this is rarely the case.

Figure 1-7. Components of Financial Strategy

Asset Management

It is not enough to make revenue projections in order to satisfy financing requirements. The management team must also plan and demonstrate its understanding of cash and asset management skills because *profits are determined by both revenue generation and expense management.* Efficient cash management may well be the most under appreciated skill a management team can possess, perhaps because there is no systematic method to determine whether one is efficiently managing cash until difficulties develop. Nevertheless, the fact is that *more companies fail due to shortfalls in cash flow than their ability to generate profits, so particular attention should be given to asset management.*

Net Cash Flow versus Net Profits

Let's take a look at the relationships within cash flow and profit generation. *Net cash flow* is the difference between a company's cash inflows and outflows over a given time period. The main sources of cash inflows are sales receipts, bank loans, and proceeds from the sale of underperforming assets. Meanwhile, the main sources of cash outflows are payments to suppliers of raw materials, capital expenditures, salaries and wages, office expenses, interest and principal payments for loans, and taxes. When a company has attained several periods of consecutive or cumulative net positive cash flows it has established the ability to generate the surplus cash needed to maintain its daily operations and therefore has minimal liquidity problems.

In contrast, a *net profit* merely represents the difference between a company's revenues less expenses. And while a company that is showing net profits may be performing well, this says nothing about its ability to pay its bills and continue the needed capital expenditures that will fuel future operations such as product development, marketing, and sales. The reason for this is that sales are recorded when goods and services have been delivered, but customers are usually operating on company credit and thus the cash has not been received. Meanwhile, cash is needed to continue to purchase more raw materials and pay expenses. In essence, one must constantly balance capital expenditures with expenses so that the company is able to pay its bills and still invest in its future operations and growth. If you are not able to invest company funds effectively (judged by the increased revenue growth resulting from this expenditure) why should investors want part ownership of such a company?

Cash Management

The ultimate goal of cash management is to maximize company cash flows so that creditors can be paid and cash can be diverted for other operations, such as growth, wages, and other expenses. Indeed, cash management is an art that can only be accomplished effectively by those who have had substantial experience managing cash or if they have an experienced financial background and understand the demands associated with these tasks. Otherwise, management teams will only develop these skills by making and correcting mistakes.

The general process of cash management can be divided into four basic steps: determine capital needs, speed up collections, delay payments, and make wise use of excess cash flow. There are five general activities that can be altered internally to increase a company's cash flow: affect sales, purchasing, collections, payment, and expense activities (figure 1-8). First, let us consider at *expense management*. Many early stage companies often mistake expense management with minimizing expenses across the board. However, in order to maximize the efficiency of company funds, you should prioritize those expenses that are not durable, while minimizing those that are.

Figure 1-8. Common Methods to Increase Cash Flow

- Increase Sales
- Reduces Expenses
- Increase Prices
- Sell or Return Excess Inventory
- Sell Non-Producing Assets
- Prioritize Discretionary Projects in Terms of Cash Flow Generation
- Decrease the Amount/Time of Credit to the Smallest Customers
- Offer Discounts for Cash Payments
- Enforce Late Payments
- Implement and Execute Efficient Billing and Collection Systems
- Negotiate Increased Credit Time/Amount from Suppliers
- Pay Suppliers Cash When Generous Discounts are Offered
- Raise Equity
- Convert Debt into Equity

In addition, a company needs to assess its discretionary projects in terms of the amount and time until cash flow generation to maximize the most efficient use of capital expenditures. For fixed assets such as land, machinery, and equipment, a lease may provide a more attractive alternative than a purchase due to its ability to increase current cash flow. As well, these items are especially attractive for leasing arrangements due to the relative ease in securing bank loans with liens on the property.

The Working Capital Cycle

The working capital cycle describes the dynamic nature of working capital that is so instrumental in determining the efficiency of business and operational finance. *Working capital* is defined as the difference between current assets (cash or cash equivalents that can be converted into cash in less than 12 months) and current liabilities (short-term debt payable within 12 months). In order to maximize the business efficiency and minimize liquidity risk, management must have an understanding of the company's *working capital needs, or the amount of cash needed to continue operations on a daily basis.* In order to determine working capital needs, management must monitor and balance inventory levels with current assets and liabilities. Therefore, it will need to monitor inventory levels on a daily basis to ensure adequate cash flows to pay company bills.

Keep in mind that receivables (customers that owe you money for goods and services) and inventories are sources of temporarily *"dead cash"* since they are not immediately available in the form of cash for the company to use. In the case of inventories, the costs involved in producing and storing these products cannot be converted into a profitable investment until they are sold. And revenues (expressed as accounts receivables) cannot be converted into cash flows until they are paid in full. In contrast, equity, loans, and payables (your creditors) represent working cash flow. Payables are a form of credit until the company pays its debtors and this money is a form of an interest-free loan (figure 1-9).

Therefore, *the challenge is to minimize the inventory-receivables load and maximize the equity, debt and payables load.* These activities must be balanced carefully however, because companies must have adequate inventory ready for delivery when orders are made. And becoming familiar with customers purchasing behaviors can be a tremendous benefit in the efficient practice of inventory management. In general, the following ratios can be used as a rough guideline to determine the ability to cover short-term debt:

Figure 1-9. The Working Capital Cycle

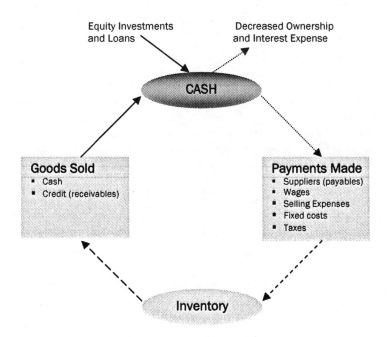

The solid arrows represent cash coming into the company while the dashed arrows represent cash coming out. Each cycle involves payments made, production of product inventory, goods sold, and cash received. There is a certain amount of time involved for each cycle that will depend upon the time it takes to make and sell the product, receipt of credit (receivables), and payment of bills to suppliers (payables). In general, the longer it takes for each cycle to complete, the more working capital a company will need. Any drastic and unexpected changes in this cycle could result in a liquidity crisis.

Original illustration by M. Stathis

Net Working Capital = Current Assets – Current Liabilities

This *net working capital* is important because it determines the amount of cash the company has to fuel short-term needs. Specifically, *it serves as a measure of a company's ability to pay short-term debt and therefore should be monitored closely.* Note that when calculating current assets, one must include receivables and inventory.

Current Ratio = Current Assets / Current Liabilities

The *current ratio* represents the proportion of current assets relative to its liabilities that can be converted into cash/are due within 12 months, and is therefore a measure of liquidity. In general, values under 1.0 represent potential liquidity crisis if not corrected promptly. While a value over 1.0 is theoretically considered liquid, *values over 1.5 are considered healthy. The current ratio may be interpreted to mean that for every $1.50 in assets you generate, you will owe $1.00.* However, these ratios are industry-specific.

Quick Ratio = (Current Assets – Inventories) / Current Liabilities

The *quick ratio* is essentially the same as the current ratio except it accounts for the time delay in converting inventories into sales and thus receivables.

$$\text{Working Capital Ratio} = \frac{\text{(Inventory + Receivables – Payables)}}{\text{Sales}}$$

Since inventory plus receivables are equal to current assets, and current assets minus current liabilities equals working capital, *a high working capital ratio means that the company has demanding working capital needs relative to its sales.* This could be due to various reasons: sales are lagging, customers are not paying, company purchases are low, or a combination of any of these factors. Either way, *a high working capital ratio is an indication that company money is not being efficiently utilized relative to other activities.*

Inventory Conversion period = Inventory / Sales per day

The inventory conversion period tells you how long it takes to convert inventory into revenues. Note however, that *it says nothing about the conversion of inventory into cash*, since upon sales, inventory is converted into receivables, which may take up to 90 days to for cash to be received.

Day Sales Outstanding = Accounts Receivable / Sales per day

This provides a measure of how long it takes for companies to pay their bills. It is important to monitor this ratio regularly in order to predict potential collections issues, which could decrease the company's ability to pay short-term liabilities.

To calculate your company's working capital requirements, you will need to determine how long it takes for each working capital cycle. This may be accomplished by calculating the period of time your cash is tied up or the *cash conversion cycle*. The goal is to minimize the cash conversion cycle so that more cash is available for use by the company.

In order to calculate the cash conversion cycle you need to know the length of your operating cycle, or how many days are required to convert a given lot of raw materials into finished products, sell those products and then receive the cash proceeds. This can be done by adding the inventory conversion period to the day sales outstanding and then subtracting the number of days your company takes to pay its bills. From this formula, it should be apparent that *you can decrease the amount of time your cash is tied up if you delay accounts payable, speed up accounts receivable or sell off inventory faster.*

Inventory Conversion Period

+ Day Sales Outstanding

− Accounts Payable Deferral

= Cash Conversion Cycle

By developing predictable levels of cash flow needs, you will be better equipped to maximize the investment yield of excess company assets.   This is especially important when navigating through periods of seasonality and business cycles, when the cash conversion cycle can be drastically different. And if your company has a sizable cash position relative to its short-term cash flow needs, you will need to invest it properly, through the use of treasury bills, money market mutual funds, and longer-term high-grade bonds. Finally, when preparing cash flow projections, be careful not to overestimate sales forecasts, underestimate costs, and overestimate the ability to obtain financing, as this could create a liquidity crisis.

In conclusion, efficient cash management is just as important as product production, marketing, and sales, as it contributes equally to company performance.   A company needs to think of each dollar as an investment opportunity, whose returns are measured with respect to time: money from products and services, wages, expenses, and excess cash flow.   This topic will be discussed in more detail in chapter 8 when operation finance is considered.

Growth Considerations

As the company evolves, different needs will be required to adequately address new challenges. As such, the skill set of the management team will increase by necessity. Indeed, the responsibilities and demands of the CEO are very different for an early stage versus a late stage company. Therefore, the management team must realize that at some point they may not be permitted to continue in their current position if the company is to succeed. This is especially true for the founder/CEO, who was great at developing the technology, raising $3,000,000, and gaining initial market share, but ineffective in responding to competitive technologies or business strategies that have begun to diminish market share. Indeed, it is a rare event that a CEO takes a company from seed to IPO or acquisition.

Knowing this from the onset will allow one to accept such a resignation or reassignment with responsibility and dignity and still feel proud at the success that has been accomplished, while maintaining enthusiasm for even more success to come.   There have been some individuals who have successfully lead a startup to an IPO, but these cases are rare and were most likely due to a combination of not only determination and external guidance from venture investors, but also a tremendous amount of luck.

When deciding how to ration the expenditure of time and resources throughout each stage of growth one should separate and prioritize tasks depending upon the most immediate needs. Regardless of the stage of growth, there are three basic company activities that should occupy the majority of its time and resources:

- financial issues
- technology and product development
- sales and marketing

Although these priorities may vary depending upon the company and initial resources, a general guideline has been provided in table 1-2.

A *seed stage* company represents an embryonic form of the company. Obviously, the first priority of a seed-stage company is to develop a product/service concept. This would involve sketches of any innovative technologies, plans for implementation, and initial background work on intellectual property issues, such as patent searches and filings. In order to assess potential market demand, one must conduct a market research analysis and attempt to position the company's products and services within the proper market segment. Once this has been accomplished, the founder should begin the task of obtaining seed financing to provide for basic necessities such as office equipment, prototype design and production, and legal work. If friends, family, or friends of family (FOF) money is sought, the business plan can be rudimentary and only consist of a few pages. However, in order to adhere to minimal liability compliance as well as ethical business behavior, this preliminary plan should at least address market demand, total cost, basic strategy, timing of market entry, competitive analysis, and exit.

Although a product may not have materialized at this point, the founder needs to begin the process of establishing relations with potential customers and strategic partners to determine their needs. It is very important for the founder to understand the means of market entry and whether any corporate partners will be needed to augment market penetration. In researching this, the founder should pay particular attention to what potential customers might need so product refinements can be customized to meet the needs of the highest priority customers. Once the needs of the intended customers have been identified, the technology should be tested internally (alpha prototype) to make sure that it works as expected.   Therefore, during the seed stage technology development should be emphasized. And until a technology has been clearly identified and the proper market research performed, financial issues should not even be considered. Once this has been achieved, the company should develop a basic strategy that best utilizes its core technology. And this should provide the entrepreneur with the essential elements required to sell the investment proposal to FOF and perhaps angels.

Thus one may argue that with these three things accomplished (technology validation, compelling story, and resulting money), a company may have progressed to *early stage*. During the initial early stages of a company, the management team should be more focused on developing and refining the company's technologies, including identification of the potential customer base, design and engineering of the product, patent issues, prototype construction and data testing. Although there is much work yet to be completed from the technology and product development side, once you have achieved a certain level of progress enabling you to identify the value add and competitive advantage of your technology, you should focus on raising money so that you can make your ideas and technology a reality.

Notice from table 1-2 that during the seed and early stages of a company, the financial matters are designated as "external", while in the expansion and late stages they are designated "internal". External financial matters refer to fund-raising while internal financial matters are related to budgeting, forecasting, and asset management. The reason external finance matters or fund raising is usually a lower priority during the expansion and late stages is due to the assumption that the previous lead investors will be handling these matters while the management is expected to concentrate on company operations and growth.

Prior to angel or venture capital investment however, a company will obviously need to handle both internal and external financial matters. But internal financing issues during the early stage are usually so insignificant relative to the importance of raising capital that they are not mentioned. Therefore, more time should be spent on developing strategies to execute the attainment of these numbers, rather than spending much of the time making the numbers look good. Remember that in the minds of sophisticated investors, financial projections are mere fiction until they have been attained. But they can be made believable if one has developed a well-devised strategy and execution plan.

After you have succeeded in obtaining a significant amount of capital from either an angel or venture firm and your company has achieved most if not all of its milestones over a two to four-year period (including significant product validation, market share, and consistent revenue growth), it can be considered an *expansion stage company*. From table 1-2, notice that the sales and marketing activities have moved from the third position to become the number one priority and will remain in that position throughout the later stages of the company. During the expansion stage the company is more focused on fulfilling customer demand and allocates more financial and human capital on sales and marketing strategies.

Obviously, each of the tasks is extremely important for every stage of a company's growth. But the key to utilizing the limited financial and human resources of your company most efficiently is to achieve some critical mass in each of these tasks so that more resources can be devoted to the others on a priority basis. And in order for a company to progress to the next stage in a rapid manner, it will need to strike the proper balance of the limited resources available for each task.

Table 1-2. General Company Priorities by Stage

Seed/Startup:
  1. Technology/Products/Services (concept development)
  2. Financial (external)
  3. Sales and Marketing

Early Stage:
  1. Financial (external)
  2. Technology/Products/Services (product development)
  3. Sales and Marketing

Expansion Stage:
  1. Sales and marketing
  2. Technology/Products/Services (refinement)
  3. Financial (internal)

Late Stage:
  1. Sales and Marketing
  2. Technology/Products/Services
  3. Financial (internal)

F. Legal Contracts

Although the wise entrepreneur will use the services of many attorneys throughout the progression of his new venture, he should be familiar with the various contracts that will be needed to protect the privacy of company assets. Most of these contracts are fairly generic and can be modified to suit the needs of the individual or situation. Appendix A contains samples of many of these documents for illustrative purposes only. You should always have an attorney experienced in corporate law review any agreements that were not specifically constructed for your company.

Founder's Agreements

This document is also known as the *Shareholder's Agreement* and is used to structure the proportionate rights and privileges of the founders in matters pertaining to the ownership and transfer of company assets. Issues that are typically included deal with certain restrictions on transferability, intellectual property ownership, and relative commitment of each founder to the venture in terms of time, resources and money.

Nondisclosure Agreements (NDAs)

Nondisclosure agreements are documents that specify what can and cannot be disclosed over a specific time period. The duration of NDAs are highly variable but usually last 2-5 years and include definitions of what is and is not confidential, obligations of the receiving party, and specific time periods of confidentiality. Because NDAs are highly variable in their obligations, exclusions, and other topics, one should always read an NDA carefully and review it with a qualified attorney prior to signing. If there is sufficient proof that a party has violated this nondisclosure, you can sue for damages.

The use of NDAs should be a standard practice when dealing with anyone involved with viewing any proprietary content of the company, including but not limited to employees, founders, directors, advisors, consultants, and partnering firms. NDAs should be used for all employees, parties that received detailed knowledge of patents, trade secrets, know-how and all other proprietary intangible assets. And of course, an NDA should be signed by any investor wishing to conduct due diligence on the company. In practice however, most venture capitalists and sophisticated angel investors will not sign these documents upon initial review of company information. It is simply unreasonable to expect prospective investors to assume liability for initial review of an investment opportunity because beyond a superficial inspection, all that has been presented is a concept. Once serious negotiations begin however, they should be willing to sign an NDA.

Noncompete Agreements

Noncompete agreements (NCAs) are equivalent in importance to NDAs for employees because they provide specific conditions for disclosure of proprietary information and can prohibit an employee from working for a competitor or establishing a business that competes with the parent company. When constructing an NCA, the nature of the company's business must be carefully stated so that there is no ambiguity by the employee. This should be done by describing the business in a manner that is neither too broad nor too narrow.   If the agreement is too broad it may be viewed by courts as being too restrictive to the employee's ability to find further employment. If too narrow, it may lack key elements of protection needed to secure the proprietary content of the company.   Nevertheless, some states, such as California refuse to recognize these agreements altogether. In these cases, the proper construction of NDAs and non-solicitation agreements is critical, as they provide the only method to enforce protection of company intelligence.

The construction of the noncompete agreement should be reasonable for the company and attempt to minimize any unneeded restrictions imposed upon the employee so that if challenged by court, a proper reason for the agreement will be realized and enforced.   The agreement should not be excessive in duration and should last as long as needed by the company to protect its assets.   Finally, because the court system does not like to see noncompete agreements that hinder the ability of the former employee to earn a living, make certain there are valid reasons for each specification which are centered only upon protecting the proprietary assets of the company.

G. The Boring Details

Selecting a Business Structure

In general, venture capitalists prefer to see companies structured as C corporations due to the ease of conversion if the company later becomes a public entity, favorable treatment of the tax structures of venture capital funds, and many other reasons.   However, closely held companies that do not anticipate a need to raise venture capital funds may choose sole proprietorship, S corporation, limited partnership, or limited liability company structures, due to the ease of record keeping, lack of rigorous government regulation, unique tax advantages, and other features.

A *limited partnership* must contain at least two partners, one general partner and at least one limited partner.   In this business structure, all partners are taxed as income and receive profits based upon their percentage of ownership.   While the *general partner* is responsible for all debts and obligations of the partnership, the *limited partners* do not share this liability in exchange for their inability to influence the daily management of the business. However, the limited partners usually have a much larger financial stake in the company. The limited partnership structure is the most common arrangement used by venture capitalists when setting up their investment funds.   We will discuss this type of business structure in chapter 2 when examining the venture capital industry.

Since the formation of the *limited liability corporation* structure in 1988, many companies previously electing a partnership for pass-through taxation advantages have opted for the LCC structure since it receives the pass-through status and has the limited liability of a corporation. Although it is quite flexible in allowing a company to allocate income and loss amongst its partners, LLC has many tax difficulties that creates barriers for tax-exempt institutional investors. Similar to a limited partnership, if an LLC has at least two members, it must file an operating agreement that specifies the relationship between the company and its members.

A C corporation is the most complex form of business organization and is highly regulated by the state and federal government. It is made up of three distinguishing groups with differing roles and responsibilities—shareholders, officers and directors. And while companies can designate any state for incorporation, many choose to incorporate in Delaware due the ease of interpretation of its corporate law, the familiarity of law firms with Delaware corporate laws, and hence their ability to provide opinions on manners regarding corporations registered in that state. In addition, *Delaware corporate law is very amenable for growing companies wishing to go public.* Finally, Delaware has committed extensive resources for the various processes and procedures required for incorporation in that state and has even established a separate court system for hearing issues involving structure and governance of domestic corporations. Table 1-3 shows a summary of the various business structures.

As a rule of thumb, all businesses that anticipate venture capital financing should avoid nontraditional incorporation in favor of a C corporation structure. Many venture firms will not even consider a deal if the company is not structured as a C corporation because they do not want to deal with the legal issues in converting it. In addition, this process can potentially take several months and require several thousands of dollars. Remember, time and money are the most valuable resources of any new venture so startup companies should obtain the right legal professionals that will structure the company in a manner consistent with its objectives so potential difficulties can be minimized.

Corporate Charter and By Laws

The corporate charter is a public record representing a contract between the incorporators and the state of incorporation and serves many administrative and legal functions of a C corporation, including the determination of the company's capital structure. *Specifically, the corporate charter specifies the relationships and responsibilities of company officers and directors, lists the principal place of business and the names and addresses of the officers and directors of the corporation.* It should be noted that many states allow the founder to hold the offices of director, president, treasurer and secretary, making it convenient for startup companies with limited personnel.

The charter will determine any special privileges, such as voting rights, liquidation preferences, and other shareholder issues and is frequently modified based upon investor preferences when closing a round of financing. Finally, the charter specifies the par value of each share of common and preferred stock, the number of shares of stock to be authorized and the rights of each class of stock. The *par value* number is essentially irrelevant but should be assigned a small numerical value, such as one or two cents per share since many states assess annual licensing fees and franchise taxes based upon both the number of outstanding shares and the par value. Otherwise, the state may elect to assign its own value to a no-par value stock.

Bylaws are meant to contain the basic procedural regulations for corporate operation and are specified by the directors in order to describe the rules of governance of board meetings, such as the criteria needed to adopt a motion, the date of the company's fiscal year, duties of the executive officers, location and date of annual meetings, the authorities granted to the board members, and the conditions of amendment of the bylaws. Usually the manner in which any amendments to the bylaws may be passed are contained with the charter. However, they can be amended by the directors without the approval of shareholders and they are not public documents.

Shareholder's Agreement

This document establishes the rights of the shareholders, the duties and responsibilities of the management and board of directors, as well as their composition and compensation. In addition, it specifies conditions for issuance of securities, limitations on secondary distribution of securities, pre-emptive rights, piggyback rights, rights of first refusal, and many other items to be detailed in chapter 10.

Stock Record Book

Because early stage companies have limited resources, they usually assume the responsibilities of the transfer agent. The *transfer agent* is responsible for keeping track of all shareholders and the amount of shares they own, as specified under Article 8 of the Uniform Commercial Code (UCC). A stock record book is used to record all transactions related to the change of ownership of company stock, and since these transactions are small for early stage companies, the management team can easily handle this task.

Table 1-3. Comparison of Different Business Structures

Business Structure	Advantages	Disadvantages
Sole Proprietorship	• Easy to form • Complete control	• Unlimited liability • Limited Inputs (1 owner) • Difficulty raising capital
General Partnership	• Easy to form • Tax Advantages	• Unlimited liability for general partner • Difficulty raising capital
Limited Partnership	• Tax advantages • Not liable for negligence of partners	• Partners are liable for debts & obligations
Subchapter S Corporation	• Avoids double taxation • Losses are offset by owners' income	• Looses stockholder advantages
Chapter C Corporation	• Limited liability • Easier to raise capital • Ownership transferable	• Expensive to set up • Extensive record keeping • Double taxation
Limited Liability Company	• Limited liability • Tax advantages	• Transfer of ownership more difficult than C corp • Dissolution varies by state and can be difficult • Management flexibility

Business and Liability Insurance

There are several types of business insurance that are necessary to provide a margin of safety for a company.   And even a company with a small office and minimal equipment must have insurance.   The replacement cost needed to replace damaged or lost work and equipment can devastate the startup and could set a company back two or more years.

Liability insurance is a must once the company begins shipping products. Even during the period when it may be beta testing, a company needs this type of insurance in order to protect against injury or damage caused by the products. In addition, liability insurance for indemnification of its directors and other executives is needed especially if the company expects to retain high-level board members.[5]

Selecting and Starting a Business

Finally, prior to deciding on a business, some general guidelines should be considered in order to maximize the best chance of success (figure 1-10). The most important rule is that the entrepreneur should start a business that he feels passionate about. The most difficult tasks in life cannot be achieved through monetary incentive alone because there will be numerous barriers involved. The most powerful driving force that we have as human beings is a deeply-rooted passion. Hence, by developing a passion for the intended venture you will be able to scale these barriers. A passionate individual will not accept "no" nor will he let rejection hinder his charge. And with passion soon comes commitment. The next rule to remember is that if you plan to seek venture financing, your company will need to be within an industry that represents a large and/or rapidly growing market. As we shall see later, a large potential market share will create a better investment opportunity for the venture firm.

There are many different strategies companies use to achieve market dominance, but *price leadership and distribution type companies are rarely successful for the startup or early stage company.* Venture firms almost always reject investment in early stage companies with these strategies because they are not viewed as a competitive advantage. Rather, these strategies are usually much more effective for large mature companies. We will discuss these concepts further in chapter 6.

The entrepreneur needs to do the proper amount of market research on both the industry in general and the direct competition. This will not only assist in forming a formable competitive strategy, but will also aid in achieving accurate revenue forecasts, which will become very important when negotiating financing terms with venture firms.

Once the business has been selected, several preliminary administrative activities must be completed (figure 1-11). Table 1-4 summarizes the entire process of forming a company from an idea and growing it to an IPO and serves as a nice summary of some of the considerations and demands entrepreneurs might face.

Figure 1-10. Basic Guidelines for Selecting a Successful Business

- Find a business you are passionate about
- Select a business with a large, rapidly growing market
- Avoid distribution type company concepts
- Avoid price leadership as a strategy
- Establish a sustainable competitive advantage
- Study the industry and competition to develop an understanding of the dynamics involved
- Do Your Homework!

Figure 1-11. Administrative Startup Checklist

- Determine the type of business structure for your venture (LLC, C corp, etc)
- Conduct necessary state and federal trademark and service mark searches
- Register your company with state and federal agencies (certain sole proprietorships and general partnerships may also need to register with local city agencies)
- Obtain all needed permits and licenses needed for your business
- Register for a federal employer identification number (EIN)[6]
- Register with your state for payment of state taxes
- Register with the IRS for payment of federal taxes
- Select adequate business, basic employee, and key employee insurance
- Comply with state and federal regulatory requirements for employee tax and insurance (workers' compensation, tax withholdings)
- Check to make certain business operation is compliant with zoning and building codes
- Check to ensure that your company complies with state and Federal environmental regulations (air, water, and solid waste)

Table 1-4. From Seed Stage to IPO

Key Factors:	Main Focus Activity	Elapsed Time Required	Typical Time Schedule (cum.)	Typical Participants	Help Needed	Major Costs	Main Risks	Results: ROI & Output
Key Stages:								
Stage 1 (Idea)	Secure a Vision	Months to Yrs		Yourself	Creativity	Own time	Lacks commercial realism	Inspiration & Vision
Stage 2 (Kitchen Table)	Solidify a Dream	2-6 months	Month 6	Friends & Founders	Confidentiality Technology Strategy,	Time of several	Secrets Leak out	Crisp view of risk-reward tradeoffs
Stage 3 (Founders' Commitment)	Get firm commitments from key people	1-2 months	Month 7	Founders	Commitment of 1-3 founders	Nerves to commit	Cold feet of founders candidates	Yes or No from founder
Stage 4 (Pullout from Employer)	Leave current employer	1 month	Month 8	Founder Lawyer	Good legal counsel, intellectual property and law	Nerves to start to live on own savings	Counter Offers or threat of legal action	Clean legal separation from former employers
Stage 5 (Business Plan Creation)	Write Fresh Business Plan	2-6 months	Month 14	Founders Consultants CPA, Law	Wise Business Judgment, Sustainable Adv	Time Office Equip	Plan is Not Fundable	Good Strategy Sustainable Advantage
Stage 6 (Filling Management Team)	Attract Vital talent	2-9 months	Month 18	Friends Consultants Media CPAs	Candidates Compensation plan Bright people	Lots of time for interviews	Compromise No money, no hire, leaks of secrets	Recruitment of top notch
Stage 7 (Raising Seed Capital)	Get cash commitment from lead VC	2-12 months	Month 27	VCs Consultants Founders	Whom to contact Coach presentation Valuations	Time, Travel, Patience	No lead VC get shopworn	Firm commitments of seed and VC

Table 1-4. From Seed Stage to IPO (continued)

Key Factors:	Main Focus Activity	Elapsed Time Required	Typical Time Schedule (cum.)	Typical Participants	Help Needed	Major Costs	Main Risks	Results: ROI & Output
Stage 8 (Closing Capital & Incorporation)	Get cash into bank account	1-2 months	Month 28	Lawyers VCs Founders	Good negotiation tactics, financial and legal advice	Legal fees	No cash so must start over	Cash in the bank
Stage 9 (Finding a Home)	Rent working facilities	1 month	Month 29	CEO Real estate broker	Real estate broker facilities construct	Time rental deposits	Bad choice, size, location $ per month	Place to work for a yr
Stage 10 (Startup)	Hire people Start building first product	6-18 months	Month 3	Board of Dir Investors Employees Strategic part	Startup experience	Burn rate: per month	Short of good people, competition starts too soon	Live company
Stage 11 (Secondary Capital Rounds)	Raise more $, leverage equity	2-6 months	Years 2-4 after seed round closes	VCs, CEO, equipment leasers	VC leads equipt leasers	Time of top management out of money	Lack of management focus, run higher than last	Sufficient $ price per round
Stage 12 (Launch First Product)	Get customers from start on work	1-2 years	24-36 mo	Customers Whole comp PR firm	Strong marketing skills, cash resvs	Burn rate: $ per month	Lack of focus Product slips Poor market	Finish first product, begin first sales
Stage 13 (Raise Working Capital)	Leverage Equity	3 months for each banking round	After first quarter of profitability	CEO CFO Banker	Profitability, Savvy banking	Time of CEO and CFO	Have to use precious equity rather then loans	Funding for growth
Stage 14 (Initial Public Offering)	Get shares liquid, cash in some	4 months including road show	Goal: IPO ready at end of year 3	Inv Banker Lawyer Wall St. Anal	Timing, pricing of shares	Underwriting, legal, CPA fees travel costs	Bad price per share, Market window closes	VCs: x5-x10 investment
Overall	Create & grow Successful co.	4-8 y from start to IPO	Aim for 5 y start to finish	Many risk takers	Lots of effort Big breaks	$3-$50 M investors' cap	Co. survives, too small for IPO	Viable co, Great ROI

Notes

[1] However, most states allow a single individual to serve the role of president, treasurer, secretary, and director.

[2] Note that dilution of shareholder value may take several forms depending on the criteria used to assess the value of the company. Here we will define shareholder value as any element that causes the price per share of the stock to decrease.

[3] Keep in mind that the context of dilution is important, such that one needs to realize whether a transaction results in dilution relative to EPS, gross revenue per share, cash flow per share, or net book value per share. For the purposes of state and Federal regulators, however, it is the net book value per share that is assessed for dilution. Perhaps the reason for this is that a dilutive transaction that results in a dilution in EPS, cash flows per share, or gross revenues per share will not be realized until some time after the effects of the financing have taken affect. Hence, it is entirely possible that a transaction that results in a dilution in net book value per share may actually be non-dilutive with respect to EPS at a later date.

[4] Internal Rate of Return (IRR) may be defined as that rate which the present value of a series of investments is equal to the present value of the returns on those investments. The IRR is by far the most common measure of venture fund performance because it expresses a rate of return as a simple percentage, factors in the time value of money, and is able to measure the returns on groups of investments. The IRR is calculated after all the investments have been realized, cash has been paid back to the investors, management fees and carried interest have been deducted. For the academician, derivations of the IRR may be found in several texts.

[5] In order to attract the best qualified directors, an early stage company should be prepared to provide both corporate and personal indemnification in order to limit the potential liability of these directors. Issues surrounding the indemnification of directors should be thoroughly discussed with an experienced attorney.

[6] An Employee Identification Number (EIN) is a federal tax identification number used by the IRS and financial institutions to identify a business entity. All businesses must have both a state and federal EIN if the business is subject to sales tax in the state of domicile. A business owner may only apply for an EIN after it has registered its type of incorporation with the appropriate state and local agencies. Once this has been accomplished, the business owner can either complete and mail or fax (816-926-7988) a Form SS-4 (http://www.irs.gov/pub/irs-fill/fss4.pdf) to the IRS or quickly obtain an EIN by applying over the phone (866-816-2065, Monday-Friday 7:30am-5:30pm EST) and can receive this number in as little as fifteen minutes. If the form is mailed it will take approximately 4-6 weeks to receive the EIN and faxing will take about 24 hours.

Both registration for incorporation and application for an EIN can be handled by attorneys but business owners can save hundreds and possibly thousands of dollars by doing these themselves.   Alternatively, one can also pay a fee of $59 to $100 for companies that specialize in these services.   They usually handle the process very quickly and save the business owner much time.   In contrast, there is no need to pay a third party to obtain an EIN, as this can be obtained easily in one phone call to the IRS.

Finally, the business owner should become familiar with all relevant business tax laws, allowances, and deductions in order to comply with IRS regulations. A good resource is the IRS (www.irs.ustreas.gov).

2

Venture Capital & Private Equity Basics

"When you do the common things in life in an uncommon way,
you will command the attention of the world."

George Washington Carver

A. The Importance of Venture Capital to Our Future Economy

Risk capital provided by venture capitalists and angel investors has been largely responsible for the global technological dominance of the United States. In addition to this robust supply of investment capital, political changes have also helped transform the United States from a manufacturing giant into a technology superpower, responsible for approximately one-third of the world's production of high tech products. And although some industries have declined due to competitive forces from abroad, the United States nevertheless enjoys tremendous royalty revenues from its innovations. Meanwhile, global competition has served to free up the American labor force to provide more brain power rather than manpower. In fact, despite the patenting strengths of Japan and Germany, the number of patents issued to the United States is almost equal to all other nations combined. As well, foreign markets have provided a source of inexpensive labor not only for the production of technology products used by Americans, but also for the benefit of American multinational companies abroad.

Regardless of the source, there should be no argument that risk capital for starting and expanding companies is essential for the economic growth of any society. And fortunately for American entrepreneurs, the financial infrastructure of the United States is well designed to accommodate the needs of business ventures at every stage of their development. The sources of this funding are vast, but a partial list includes the thousands of federal grants and endowments available to researchers for specific projects, and commercial banks providing loans to growing businesses with tangible assets and stable cash flows. *Despite these tremendous sources of funding, it is the venture capital industry that provides the most substantial financing resources for companies that are immature in their development, and therefore associated with the highest risk of failure.* Although many studies have failed to show a direct link between venture capital, employment growth, and overall economic stability, there have been some research reports that have formed these conclusions. Perhaps one only needs to consider the successful track record of the United States as partial evidence of this theory.

Historical Background

The venture capital industry is the newest segment of the financial industry but it has existed in more primitive forms in the United States since the early 20th century, beginning mainly with wealthy families such as the Rockefellers and Vanderbilts. Then shortly after WWII, firms that specialized in this type of investing began to increase in number and became known as venture capital firms. By 1958, the Federal Government had established the Small Business Investment Company (SBICs) program, which permitted these Federally licensed venture capital firms to borrow money at low interest rates from the Federal Government, provided they guaranteed repayment. While the number of these SBICs grew rapidly in the 1960s, they were soon surpassed in number by approximately 900 independently run venture capital firms that used private money. And by 1980, an estimated $3 billion was invested by venture capital firms, soaring to over $23 billion by 1989. Following a short drop off in interest in the early 1990s, venture capital once again took off in record setting fashion reaching over $37 billion by 1995. And as of 1999, this amount soared to over $60 billion. Nevertheless, *investment in venture capital still only represents about 1% of all domestic institutional investment assets* and an even smaller proportion of international assets. Therefore, there is still a large potential for continued growth of this industry.

Prior to the formation of the venture capital industry, Karl Compton, MIT President and Georges Doriot, Professor at the Harvard Business School embarked upon the idea to commercialize innovations resulting from WWII. They named their firm American Research and Development (ARD) and the resulting investment management process they developed later became recognized as the formation of the first modern venture capital firm. However, because this investment concept was still foreign to traditional asset managers and considered highly speculative to institutional investors, they structured their firm into a *closed-end fund* so that ARD could be traded on the U.S. stock exchanges in order to obtain more investment interest.[1]

Although ARD only had a limited number of successful investments during its 26-year life, Compton and Doriot managed to grow a $70,000 investment in Digital Equipment Company in 1957 into $355 million. Meanwhile, as many learned of the success of ARD, several attempts were made to imitate their unique investment approach, even structuring their firms as a closed-end funds. It was not until the mid 1960s that the first venture firm structured as a limited partnership appeared formed by Draper, Gaither, and Anderson. And today the limited partnership structure accounts for the majority of all venture funds in the United States.

Over the past two decades, institutions have become more interested in venture capital funds due to their high returns and the need to diversify excess capital generated from the greatest bull market in the history of America (1992-2000). But the key event that stimulated a more broad institutional interest in venture capital investment was a policy change in 1979 by the Department of Labor, which clarified the meaning of the *"prudent man"* rule. And it was this change in the prudent man rule that opened the door for further pension investment into venture capital.[2]

Prior to this change in legislature, individuals had accounted for the largest share of venture investments (32%), while pension funds accounted for only 15%. However, seven years after its passage, pension funds poured money into these investments and soon represented over 50% of all venture capital and private equity investments. In an attempt to accommodate the fiduciary responsibilities of pension plans, *investment advisors* began to advise and assist institutional investors with their allocation and selection into these funds. When serving in this capacity these investment advisors are often known by the name *"gatekeepers"*. Today these investment advisors or gatekeepers not only provide a significant resource for institutional investors wishing to invest in venture funds but they also account for over 20% of funds raised for venture capital investments.

Corporations have also become much more aggressive in investing their cash and resources in early business ventures. In this case however, the goals are usually more strategic, rather than financial. The large surge in market capitalizations during the 1990s provided corporations with a capital surplus. And rather than invest it all in internal R&D, they realized they could identify more suitable asset acquisitions by investing in early stage companies. However the bear market of 2000-2005(?) has forced corporations to rethink their aggressive nature in venture capital investments. As well, the effects of such a devastating recession have also diminished the amount of investment capital available to private venture firms. And this has of course, influenced their investment approaches due to an emphasis on risk management. Over the next two years, I predict the number of venture firms and total capital raised to contract relative to the record-setting levels seen during the 1998-2000 period.   As well, future dispersements for portfolio companies will continue to dwindle, as venture capitalists continue to focus more on risk management.   But this will only be a temporary correction in what was a prematurely overextended industry fueled by "irrational exuberance".   And when the economic conditions begin to improve, the venture capital industry will rebound with even more vigor than in the past.

The Venture Capital Investment Framework

Venture capitalists create funds by raising money from pension plans, endowments, foundations, corporations, financial institutions, insurance companies, and wealthy individuals.   And these firms are typically attracted to small fast-growing companies in need of capital and management guidance. Venture capitalists typically have no interest in investing in seed stage companies, opting for late-early stage and expansion financing, leveraged buyouts, or turnaround financing.   But ultimately they are sensitive to minimizing risk and securing a healthy annualized return to their limited partners, to which they have a legal fiduciary responsibility.

Venture capitalists prefer to invest in high-technology firms (defined as telecommunications, computers, electronics, biotechnology, medical, and healthcare related companies) and they usually specialize in some type of industry and/or technology (as well as the investment stage of the company). The reasons for this are two-fold.   First, high-technology investments often are associated with large and high growth markets and therefore the potential to participate in large markets with large revenue growth drives high valuations, which results in potentially higher investment returns.   Second, because high-technology industries are characterized by intense competition and rapid change, there is a need for industry contacts, dynamic information exchange, and strategic business guidance, all of which can be provided by venture capitalists due to their industry knowledge and experience.   This preference for high technology investments may help explain why over 95% of all venture capital firms in America are located within the same ten states where technology is the primary focus.   However, investment in high-tech companies comes at a high price, as they typically require more financing rounds and a larger total financing amount than low-technology companies.

Venture Capital as an Investment

We have discussed the impact of changes in the *"prudent man"* rule on the growth of institutional investment in venture capital.   However, the recent surge in venture capital investing by institutions has occurred due to four main events: the growing acceptance by sophisticated investors of venture capital as a legitimate asset class, the superior long-term performance of venture capital funds, the widespread acceptance of the modern portfolio theory, and portfolio rebalancing, which has increased allocations to alternative investments, such as venture capital and hedge funds. And of course, the bull market of 1992-2000 has fueled this need for investment options into alternative investments as a result of rebalancing.

Venture capital has been shown to provide better long-term returns then most other asset classes, with an 18% average annual return. And according to Venture Economics, venture capital funds have yielded average annual returns of 25%, 46%, and 53% over the past 10-, 5-, and 3-year periods as of 2002. But investment in these assets is not without proportionate risk, and *venture funds only have superior long-term returns because they typically experience negative returns over the first 3-5 years.* The unique behavior of venture capital and private equity investments which is responsible for these negative investment cash flows in the early years and positive cash flows in the later years is known as the "*J-curve effect*" and is an almost invariable property of venture investments.

Therefore, due in part to the effects of the J-curve, the dynamics of the venture capital investment process require that these funds be illiquid, and investors are usually locked into partnerships for 8-12 years (*liquidity risk*). In addition, the returns of venture funds have been shown to be highly dependent upon the selection of managers (i.e. the venture firm) such that investors who are not able to conduct a rigorous due diligence screen on prospective venture firms may face poor returns (*manager risk*). Another risk faced by investors of venture capital is *vintage year risk*, which refers to the timing of the fund inception. The financial markets, both public and private go through cycles of good and bad performance, similar to business cycles. Vintage year risk simply refers to the fact that investors are hypothetically at risk for investing in a fund during a time when the venture capital industry or even the industry focus of the fund may be experiencing diminished returns.

Venture capital funds are considered *alternative investments* because they have different risks and financial dynamics relative to the more common *traditional assets* such as stocks and bonds traded on public exchanges. In addition, the performance of alternative investments is much more dependent upon the managers than for traditional investments. From table 2-1, notice that the difference between the performances of the top versus the bottom quartiles for hedge funds, venture capital, and leveraged buyouts (i.e. all categories within alternative investments) for the ten-year period ending in 1997 was much more than for U.S. stocks and bonds, (traditional investments) as indicated by the spreads. The reason for these drastic differences is that *fund managers of alternative investments are in more direct control of their investment assets*, while fund managers of stocks and bonds and other traditional assets are passively managed and therefore have very little say in management of their portfolio companies. Thus, *manager selection is of utmost importance for alternative versus traditional investments.*

In order to fully appreciate the significance of venture capital as a vital component of an institutional investment portfolio, we need to understand general performance characteristics of all asset classes. In general all assets are divided into traditional (stocks and bonds) and alternative assets (venture capital, hedge funds, and distressed debt). Each category of asset classes has general properties which are at times favorable and other times unfavorable depending upon the economic, political, and international conditions. In addition, within each asset category, different assets behave differently based upon the economic environment. Some traditional assets behave more like alternative assets and vice versa. For instance, the stock market generally does very well during periods of economic expansion with low inflation, low unemployment, and low interest rates. In particular, high technology companies needing tremendous amounts of capital for growth and expansion are able to benefit the most from these conditions because the overall cost of capital is relatively inexpensive.

Table 2-1. Passive and Active Management Performance Spreads
(Ten Years Ending in Dec. 1997)

Asset Class	Top Quartile	Bottom Quartile	Spread
U.S bonds	9.6%	8.5%	1.1%
U.S. stocks	19.1%	16.8%	2.3%
Hedge funds	23.6%	13.6%	10.0%
Leveraged buyouts	18.8%	8.1%	10.7%
Venture Capital	21.4%	9.0%	12.4%

Source: Cambridge Associates (from Gompers & Lerner)

In contrast, during high interest rate environments and recessions, basic industries such as food and beverage and larger more diversified companies are generally able to absorb the effects of these adverse economic conditions much better, resulting in superior relative returns. With respect to asset classes, fixed income investments such as Government, municipal, and corporate bonds are favored over stocks during these general economic conditions. And for some investors, the more conservative higher yielding common (utilities companies and REITs) and preferred stock dividends provide a place to "park" assets while waiting for an economic recovery. Because the cost of capital is high in such an environment, fast growing high technology companies find it difficult to obtain a good return on investment, resulting in the collapse of previously high stock valuations.

During the period prior to the recovery of an economic recession and throughout a period of slow corporate growth, cyclical companies usually perform well. In addition, convertible bonds provide good exposure to the analogous stock during recessionary periods, while yielding generous interest rates. By this means, an investor can receive high dividends while waiting for an economic recovery, yet still participate in the equities markets in having the option to convert preferred stock into common. In addition, nontraditional assets tend to show superior returns during adverse economic conditions. Therefore, in general, *when the stock market is under periods of poor performance, the bond markets, and nontraditional investment strategies, such as arbitrage, CMOs, and commodities outperform.*

However, there are periods when economic conditions affect most traditional investments the same way, such as in extreme economic growth or contraction, or during political crises. In such scenarios, both stocks and bonds will show poor returns. Meanwhile, nontraditional investments tend to perform better than traditional assets. In contrast, during periods when the environment is suitable for good stock market returns, (low interest rates, low inflation, and low unemployment) yet the market is down for a variety of other reasons, the opportunity for superior returns is ripe in the risk arbitrage and leveraged-buyout (LBO) markets. In addition, global economic or political volatility can create attractive investment opportunities in the commodities markets.

Furthermore during bear markets, hedge funds with a short strategy tend to yield outstanding returns while performing modestly at best during bull markets. These are general trends which tend to occur given the stated conditions but there are so many other variables to lengthy to mention which can cause contradictions to the results mentioned. Regardless, it should be easy to appreciate that *venture capital investments can add to overall portfolio performance by providing superior returns during periods when other asset classes are under performing.*

In conclusion venture investments have many significant roles that are absolutely vital to ensuring the economic prosperity of our great nation. Surely, this industry assists in the commercialization of new technologies into the world, promoting a better standard of living. But the efforts of venture firms also provide a constant influx of new businesses into our economy that fuels the commerce of existing businesses through their use of goods and services, helping the economy in the United States outpace that of any other comparable nation. And while the United States has great scientific research, there are many other nations with comparably strong research such as Japan and Germany. Therefore, the critical distinction responsible for its economic dominance must be the sociological and political forces in America that have empowered the entrepreneur and assisted the commercialization of revolutionary technologies, of which venture capitalists play a dominant role. Thus, the venture capital industry provides the muscle behind much of the economic and employment growth in the United States.

Finally, this industry supplies an essential asset class for the institutional investment portfolio by helping to reduce overall portfolio volatility during variable economic conditions and increase overall risk-adjusted returns. Due to their illiquid nature, venture capital funds are perhaps best suited for institutional investors that have a continuous source of capital and long investment horizons, such as pension plans, foundations, insurance companies, and endowment funds. And as these investors have grown to account for the majority of venture financing, the venture capital industry has evolved to meet the needs of these investors.

B. Understanding Venture Capital

Venture Capital versus Private Equity

These two terms are often used interchangeably but they are quite distinct. *Venture capital describes the process of private equity asset management while private equity refers the type of financing in both public and non-publicly traded securities.* Both venture capital and private equity are considered *alternative investments*, the definition itself being somewhat ambiguous depending upon whom you ask. Several years ago for instance, international stocks were considered alternative investments, but today are considered to be a component of traditional assets. Other examples of alternative investments typically include hedge funds, high yield bonds, distressed debt, arbitrage strategies, commodities, energy, real estate, leveraged buyouts, and timber. Because alternative investments have different financial characteristics from traditional investments, they serve as excellent diversification instruments and are therefore included in almost all institutional portfolios, as discussed in the previous section (figure 2-1).

Often, *private equity* includes a broad asset class within alternative investments consisting of leveraged buyouts, special situations (distressed debt and mezzanine debt), real estate, or venture capital. *Thus private equity is a more generalized terminology that may or may not include venture capital* (table 2-2). While private equity funds can invest in venture capital funded portfolios, they can also be invested in leveraged buyouts, consolidations, distressed debt financings and many other non-traditional investments. And although venture capital funds sometimes invest in these financial instruments as well, most do not and are mainly equity-linked investments in young high-growth companies. However, the capital supplied by venture capital firms goes well beyond financing, as they also serve interim management positions, board positions, and assist their portfolio companies in a variety of other ways in order to maximize their potential success.

Finally, private equity is also sometimes associated with the term *private placement*, which may or may not be accurate depending upon whom you ask. A private placement is usually structured by an investment bank or financial boutique and can be for either a private or public company. In this type of financing the bank serves as the financier, either directly or indirectly by selling investment units to its clients. And once the transaction is complete, the bank devotes very little if any management expertise, although a banker may hold a seat on the board (also see chapter 9, sections C and F).

Figure 2-1. Institutional Investors Have Balanced Investment Portfolios

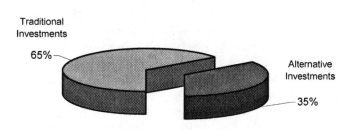

Generic Institutional Investment Portfolio

Traditional
Investments

65%

Alternative
Investments

35%

Table 2-2. The Two Broad Categories of Investments

Traditional Investments	Alternative Investments*
Domestic Common Stocks	**Hedge Funds**
Domestic Preferred Stocks	High Yield Bonds
International Stocks	**Distressed Debt**
Investment Grade Bonds	Arbitrage
US Treasury Bills, Notes, & Bonds	Commodities
Municipal Bonds (Revenue and G.O.s)	**Leveraged Buyouts**
Money Market Mutual Funds	**Mezzanine Debt**
Commercial Paper	**Real Estate**
Asset Backed Securities	Energy
CDs	**Venture Capital**

*Private equity has been designated in bold print

Venture Capital Structure

Venture capital funds are usually structured as private *limited partnerships* and the managers of these funds are known as the *general partners*, while the investors are the *limited partners*. Typically, the limited partners include institutional investors and wealthy individuals that supply almost all of the investment capital (general partners typically contribute about 1% of the capital) but are prohibited from management of the portfolio companies in order to preserve their limited liability status.

In 1996, amendments to *The Investment Company Act of 1940* added incentives to private equity firms that now allow them to accept up to 499 "qualified investors" as limited partners. Otherwise, they can only accept 99 limited partners. And under *Regulation D* of the SEC's rules, private equity firms wishing to qualify for exemption of registration of securities cannot have more than 35 unaccredited investors as limited partners. Subsequently, Reg D states that *an accredited investor must have a net worth of $1 million (or joint net worth with spouse) or have made at least $200,000 in each of the prior two years (or joint income with spouse of at least $300,000) and have a reasonable expectation of making at least that same amount the current year* (refer to Appendix C-1 for a more comprehensive definition).

The *limited partnership agreement* is a legal contract that specifies many expectations and responsibilities of both the limited and general partners. The limited partners have limited liability and contribute the investment capital while the general partners provide the investment management and are fully exposed to the liabilities associated with the invested capital. Typically *venture capital fund limited partnerships are designed with a limited lifetime of 7-10 years, with up to three years extension options.* The agreement also specifies the purpose, investment objectives, risks, duration, investment requirements and restrictions, and the exit and distribution strategies of the fund, as well as the compensation to be received by the general partners.

The *covenants of the partnership agreement* specify the guidelines of fund management, activities of the general partners, and types of investments to be made. There are specific covenants that place limits on the amount of capital that can be invested into one particular portfolio company so that excessive risk is not added to the fund by emphasizing any one particular investment opportunity. The basis behind this restriction is related to the *modern portfolio theory*, which seeks to minimize risk and maximize returns through proper diversification of investment assets.

There are also covenants that restrict the amount of debt venture capital firms may use. In this case, the use of debt may be equated with the direct borrowing to increase the amount of leverage or guaranteeing the debt of the portfolio companies. As well, there are covenants that prohibit continued investment into firms with subsequent fund money in order to increase the valuation of the prior portfolio investment for future fund raising opportunities. Most guidelines require additional investments into such companies with newer funds to occur at previous valuations. Finally, venture capitalists are restricted in the amount and timing of reinvestment of capital gains produced from prior funds. Since they are compensated based upon the value of assets under management or the *adjusted committed capital* (committed capital less distributions), it is in the best interest for venture capitalists to delay distribution of profits to their limited partners and extend the amount of invested capital so that annual management fees will continue to accumulate.

Likewise, the behavior of the general partners is also specified in the covenants of the limited partnership agreement. General partners are limited in their ability to invest their personal assets in their portfolio companies to minimize any excessive attention that may be provided to these firms and thereby result in deviation from the best interests of the total portfolio performance. In contrast, the sale of general partnership interests in a firm is limited to maintain their incentive to maximize total portfolio returns for the limited partners. Additional restrictions are placed upon the timing of efforts of the general partners to raise capital for future funds to ensure that the current fund continues to receive sufficient diligence. The time devoted to outside activities is also specified by these covenants in order to ensure sufficient time and resources are being devoted to the portfolio companies. As well, the addition of new general partners is monitored by the advisory board to ensure that the skills are reasonably in line with the demands of the firm. Finally, the investment covenants set guidelines to control the amount of capital invested in any particular firm and industry, the amount of personal money invested in public securities and the amount if any, allowable for investment into other venture capital funds. Table 2-3 summarizes the main covenants of a venture capital limited partnership agreement.

Valuation

There are many variations on venture valuation methodologies, but the most widely used methods are based on industry-specific multiples, such as earnings, revenues, prices-sales, etc., depending on the industry and stage of development. Typically the *comparables approach* is most frequently used, whereby public or private companies that have recently been acquired and considered similar enough to the company being valued are used as comparisons in determining the appropriate multiples. In addition, other variables are factored into the final assessment such as strength of management, the competitive advantage established by the company, the overall strength of the economy, the strength of the IPO market, and how "hot" the industry is to arrive at a final valuation. Thus a skilled and well-informed management team with an excellent competitive advantage can provide leverage during term negotiations. Valuation topics will be discussed in greater detail in later chapters.

Compensation

The typical compensation structure used by venture capital firms is comprised of two components. First a *management fee* of 1-3% is assessed to the pool of capital committed to the firm. This expense is meant to provide for the entire process of managing the fund, including salaries, wages, and operating expenses. The other component of compensation includes an incentive-based share of the profits of the fund, known as the *carried interest*. The carried interest amounts to about 20% of the profits received by the institutional investors' net profits of the fund and theoretically serves to incentivize the VCs to provide maximum returns. However, venture capitalists do not receive this carried interest fee until the limited partners have received a return of their principal. In addition, some limited partners require a certain return prior to the receipt of the carried interest by the VCs.[3]

Table 2-3. Typical Covenants of a Venture Fund Partnership Agreement

Fund Management Covenants	General Partner Activities Covenants	Investment Covenants
Maximum Investment in a Firm	Restrictions on Sale of G.P. Interests	Diversification
Restrictions on Use of Debt	Timing of Fund Raising Activities	Personal investments
Guidelines for Reinvestment in Firms	Restrictions on Outside Activities	
Guidelines for Reinvestment of Profits	Additions of New General partners	
Compensation Structure	Restrictions of Personal Investments	
	Experience of General Partners	

The VC Process

Gompers and Lerner have discussed what they call the *"venture capital cycle"*, through which fundraising enables the venture capital firm to invest in a portfolio of companies and assist them in building successful businesses. Once the exit occurs, the venture fund is managed in accordance with the investment strategy of the firm, and distributions are made to the limited partners of the fund. Once final dispersements of capital have been made to all limited partners, the process begins again with a new fund. Similar to institutional investors and mutual fund managers, venture capitalists often *"window dress"* their quarterly, yearly, and end-of-period holdings by liquidating their bad investments and investing in the top performers so that they appear to hold the best performing investments when investment statements are printed. This is done with the hope of receiving better returns and as a marketing pitch for future fund raising activities. Finally, because the typical fund can last up to 13 years, each cycle may be influenced by periods of changing business and economic cycles that do not adjust rapidly within this venture fund cycle. Thus it is critical for venture firms to understand and identify these changes and the potential affects they may have upon their current and future funds (figure 2-3).

In general, *as the stage of investment progresses, the duration of investment decreases and the amount of financing increases.* However, this is in contrast to what might be expected, as one might reason that larger financing rounds would be associated with longer financing durations. But the capital-intensive demands required for maturing companies prior to an IPO debut are most likely the primary factors responsible for these observations. In addition, *venture capitalists are more willing to invest more capital in later stage firms because they are viewed as having lower risk.* But with these perceived lower levels of risk is also a lower return, so a larger amount of capital by any one particular venture capital firm is needed to generate returns sufficient to justify its involvement. This is in contrast to the case for early stage investing, where the risk is extremely high, returns are potentially very high, and the investment capital infusion is much smaller.

There have been many studies that have examined the effects of the cyclical nature of the venture capital industry, and Gompers and Lerner have shown that the *health of the venture capital market is strongly correlated with the existence of a strong public market and characterized by intense IPO activity.* Such conditions will enable a higher expectation of liquidity by the venture capitalist. In addition, the relative supply of venture capital available for investment will vary with the economic conditions and is a high predictor of the activity in the private markets. However, determining and predicting these levels can be quite complex due to the number of variables involved.

Figure 2-3. Overview of the Venture Capital Process

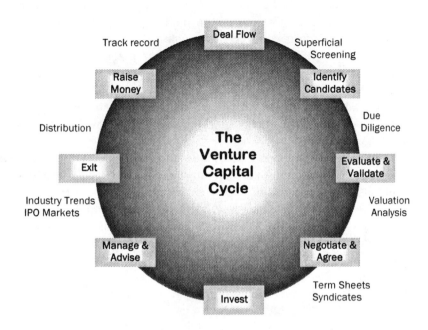

Original illustration by M. Stathis

Finally, Gompers and Lerner (1998) have also found empirical evidence of the effects of capital gains taxes on the venture capital activity. According to these studies, a reduction in capital gains taxes increases the supply of funds committed to venture capital by increasing the after tax returns in assets that are subject to capital gains. This causes the required pre-tax returns to decrease which lowers the risk of this asset class. Therefore, the cost of investment capital is lowered by a decrease in the capital gains tax. While this factor may not be a large element contributing to the supply of investment capital because of the tax-deferred nature of endowments and pension funds, a larger effect is the increase in demand for venture capital funds when capital gains taxes are reduced. Therefore, it is thought that the *number of individuals who initiate startups increases when taxes are lowered because their cost structure is lowered.*

Venture Financing

Once the total capital from a fund has been invested or committed for future rounds in companies that make up the fund (i.e. portfolio companies), the fund is said to have been be "*closed*" for further investments. In addition, because of the investment horizons of the limited partners, the funds will be set up to for a finite number of years, (as stated within the covenants of the limited partnership agreement) after which either extensions can be made (from 1 to 3 years) or investment return is expected to be delivered to the limited partners. Accordingly, when term sheets are constructed by venture capitalists, the necessary modifications are incorporated so that they are able to operate within the investment guidelines specified within the limited partnership agreement.

There are several stages of a company, each with unique characteristics relative to venture financing, and understanding each stage is important for making the most appreciate decisions with regard to a specific financial marketing strategy. The *Seed stage* is formed when an entrepreneur has an idea about how he can form a business and he expresses his vision in a mission statement. This is the beginning of a company so there is no management, no prototype, a rudimentary business plan, and minimal or no market research. The entrepreneur is mainly focused with administrative tasks, such as structuring the necessary legal filings for incorporation, seeking tax and basic legal advice, and preparing a basic office expense budget. This is obviously the riskiest time for a potential investor and with rare exception, no venture capitalist or sophisticated angel would be interested in investing. Usually, the founder will use his own money, as well as friends and family money to finance initial costs for the company.

Once a complete business plan has been written, some of the management team has been selected, and basic resources have been purchased (office equipment), the company may be considered a *startup*. At this point, the company vision and mission have been refined and one or more individuals are working in this company on a part or full-time basis. Development of an alpha prototype begins and market research has been conducted. Market interest is sought and intellectual property (IP) issues are addressed. The company may now be focusing on obtaining funds from angel investors. Venture capitalists however, will rarely be interested in investing at this stage due to the high level of risk and long time for harvesting the investment.[4]

Once the company has a proven prototype with initial customers, the company is said to be in *first stage* financing, although some refer to this as *early stage*. Here, the product is in the β prototype phase or is ready to be manufactured and sold to customers. At this point, the need for a detailed strategic marketing and sales plan is critical. The company is now in a healthier position to receive indications of interest from venture capitalists and will use this investment capital to increase its marketing and sales efforts and for continued production/refinement of the product line. After producing significant revenues and achieving market penetration, the company would then seek *second stage* (expansion) financing to expand the sales and marketing staff to reach a wider customer base. At this stage the management has a better idea of sales growth and effectiveness of its marketing strategy. They also have more accurate estimations of the time when they will break even or become profitable. If a company is able to reach this stage, it has demonstrated its ability to achieve significant market share for its products and the focus gradually shifts from fund raising to revenue growth.

The company would advance to the *third (late) stage* when it has demonstrated several periods of market growth and can provide reasonably reliable predictions for future growth. More effort would be focused on the R&D to secure product competitiveness, or alternatively the primary expenditures may be dedicated to marketing, depending on the products and industry. It is during the third stage that the company might be considering an IPO. If further capital is needed beyond a third round, *mezzanine or "bridge" financing* would be used as a form of temporary funding to finance the positioning of the company for its IPO if needed, rather than issuing more stock and causing further shareholder dilution.

Because the decision to invest in a company is met with great scrutiny, venture capitalists usually seek the further validation of an investment's merit from other venture firms possessing similar expertise. This may or may not result in the use of syndicates (pre-screened investment partners). Nevertheless, in exchange for a commitment of both human and financial capital, venture firms require substantial ownership in the form of preferred stock plus one or more seats on its board of directors. Therefore, *it is important to distinguish between how much a company wants to grow, how much a company is able to grow, and how much a company needs to grow within a specific time period in order to satisfy the investment expectations required by venture capitalists.* At minimum, a new company must either be a part of an already existing large market or it must have such a unique product or service that it is expected to help form a new market. Either way, the products and services must have a strong *competitive advantage*, thereby creating barriers for competitors in order to seize and sustain a substantial market share.

When venture capitalists analyze a prospective investment, one of the first things they do is assess their return on investment (ROI). Many early stage companies do not understand why most venture capitalists refuse to invest money into a business that is expected to require a total investment of $3,000,000 prior to the breakeven point. The reason for this is twofold. First, venture capitalists have more money than manpower and as such, the limiting factor is usually the number of deals they are able manage rather than the amount of capital at their disposal.   And venture capitalists have a legal *fiduciary responsibility* to invest all assets to the best of their ability within the guidelines of their fund.   So if the venture fund consists of $50 million they can only invest in one or two of these companies at best in order to satisfy their investment obligations and not over exhaust their manpower.   Secondly, if the market potential of a technology is $40 million and it expects an optimistic 20% market share, a company seeking $3 million would only expect to generate $8 million dollars in revenues and venture capitalists simply will not engage in such a risky investment for such a small return. Consider that in order to command a 20% market share, it would take several years and even still such a percentage is highly unlikely.   But let us assume that this company does indeed accomplish this feat within six years.   Since VCs look at annual rate of return (ARR), such an investment would only yield an ARR of about 15%, which is unacceptable given the risk assumed.

Finally, throughout periods of venture capital investment, different investment strategies may be implemented due to factors beyond the control of venture capitalists.   It is important to understand some of these factors and recognize when they may be of significant influence in determining a change in venture capital investment preference (table 2-4).

Table 2-4. Factors Influencing Investment by Venture Capitalists

<u>Constant Factors Affecting Venture Capital Investment</u>
- Industry specific risk
- Industry specific liquidity
- Market size
- Total investment capital needed

<u>Variable Factors Affecting Venture Capital Investment</u>
- Health of the economy
- Fund raising results
- Regulatory changes (ERISA, industry-specific)
- Health of the IPO market
- Recent stock and bond market returns
- Future expected stock and bond market returns
- Recent venture capital returns
- Future expected venture capital returns

Exit

The company's route of exit and its underlying strategies are obviously critical considerations prior to investment by a venture capitalist, as a suitable and timely exit provides the limited partners with investment return and venture capitalists with their carried interest. There are many considerations one must account for when selecting a venture capitalist if one has the luxury of choice. One of the main challenges is to develop an understanding of what the management and founder want out of the company versus what the venture capitalists seek to gain. Often these are one in the same but one should never assume this is always the case. Obviously the venture firm wants the best IRR, but to what extent are they committed to the best route and timing of exit for the company? We will address these possibilities in chapters 4 and 9.

C. Modern Portfolio Theory

Venture capitalists invest risk capital entrusted to them by qualified and accredited investors in exchange for preferred equity or convertible debt in private companies. And rather than seeking consistently high rates of returns, such as 25% for each of their portfolio companies, they aim for one or possibly two "*home runs*" in each fund that will provide potential returns in excess of 50-fold, with the acknowledgement that the remainder of the companies will consist of moderate returns, breakevens, and complete losses. The reasoning behind this investment strategy is that it encourages investment in high-risk ventures that could lead to returns of 50 to 100x their original investment. However, in order to exercise prudence, *they diminish investment risk using many techniques, such as asset allocation, tranch funding, use of syndicates, term sheet structuring, and premature liquidation.*

All investors would like inflation-resistant investments providing consistently high returns with low risk and high liquidity. Unfortunately, such investments do not exist due to the proportionate relationship between hypothetical risk and expected return. However, in their attempt to minimize the risk-return profile of an investment, many investors have adapted to the use of the *modern portfolio theory* (MPT). This theory, formulated in 1952 by Dr. Harry Markowitz, takes root in the public investment markets and basically states that *the return on an asset cannot be viewed solely but must be viewed as a contribution to the entire portfolio.*

Within a portfolio of investments, asset risk and performance are thought to have variable degrees of correlation or investment performance with other assets. Thus, while some assets have lower risk and returns, others have higher risk and returns.   And while some asset classes perform poorly during bad economic cycles, others perform much better, as we discussed earlier in the chapter.   Such assets are said to have different correlation coefficients because they perform differently under a given situation.   The MPT basically states that a *diversified portfolio of assets with different correlation coefficients should have a lower risk and provide better risk-adjusted returns than either a non-diversified portfolio or a diversified portfolio with similar correlation coefficients.*

There are two broad asset classes that in general have different correlation coefficients, traditional assets (U.S. stocks, international stocks, and investment grade bonds) and alternative investments.   While both U.S. and international stocks are categorized into the same asset class, they can be divided into different subgroups that have different correlation coefficients relative to each subclass, (such as large, mid, small, and microcap stocks). However, these correlations only have relatively small differences and may not provide adequate portfolio protection under extreme market conditions. Bonds on the other hand, can have very different correlations relative to equities depending upon certain conditions, such as interest rates and inflation.   Meanwhile, a*lternative investments* can be divided into two groups based upon liquidity.   *Liquid alternative investments* would include hedge funds, high yield bonds, distressed debt, arbitrage funds, and commodities. *Illiquid alternative investments* would include energy, real estate, venture capital, leveraged buyouts, and timber.   And while each of these assets have variable correlations coefficients, most are thought to have significantly different correlation coefficients than traditional assets.

The MPT asserts that it is possible to add riskier and thus hypothetically higher performing assets to a portfolio while lowering overall portfolio risk due to the different correlation coefficients in the portfolio.   Hence, *an ideal portfolio would achieve optimal risk-reward characteristics as a result of the proper balance of assets with opposing correlation coefficients.*   The other reason for the use of alternative investments is to minimize inflation risk, which is a sizable problem for endowments.   The proper selection of commodities, real estate, energy, and timber help minimize inflation in a well-balanced portfolio.   Thus for institutional investors, the key to executing an ideal investment strategy is to select alternative investments that have low correlations to traditional investments and maintain a balance of these asset classes (asset allocation) according to economic projections, liquidity needs, risk tolerance, and investment objectives (see Appendix C for a more comprehensive discussion on correlation coefficients).   We will now examine the possible risk characteristics of investment portfolios to further illustrate the utility of the MPT.

Portfolio Risk

The total risk of an investment portfolio may be separated into two distinct components, designated as diversifiable and non-diversifiable risk. *Diversifiable risk* is also known as un-systemic and non-diversifiable risk is known as systemic risk. *Diversifiable risk includes uncontrollable events specific to a company* such as labor strikes, bankruptcies, death of a key employee, unexpected entrant of a competitor, and regulatory actions resulting in legal and financial consequences. This component of portfolio risk derives its name from the fact that it is hypothetically possible to eliminate by diversifying one's portfolio with different securities (i.e. securities with different correlation coefficients).

In contrast, *non-diversifiable risk* includes *equally uncontrollable but more broad reaching events* such as inflation, war, tax changes, changes in oil prices, changes in monetary policies by the Federal Reserve, and political activities, all of which have nonselective effects on securities. As such, *it is theoretically impossible to lower the risk associated with these events through portfolio diversification* because they will theoretically affect all companies. In order to better understand and distinguish the effects of these two components of total portfolio risk, it may be helpful to *think of diversifiable risk as company specific risk and non-diversifiable risk as market risk.*

From figure 2-4, you can see that *the non-diversifiable (systemic) risk of a portfolio is independent of the number of different assets held by an investment portfolio and therefore does not lower the total risk of such a portfolio. However, as the number of different assets within a portfolio of investments increases, the diversifiable (un-systemic) component of the total risk decreases resulting in an overall decreased total portfolio risk.* It follows that *most venture firms seek to minimize risk in their funds by diversification of portfolio companies.* Depending on the investment strategy of the venture fund, firms may achieve portfolio diversification in a variety of ways. For sector-specific venture funds, firms might elect to diversify only by the stage of investment. Alternatively, they may choose to diversify through the use of syndicates. For funds that are broader based in nature, portfolio companies may be selected that have different business characteristics.

In order to apply the basis of the MPT to venture capital portfolios we should account for the fact that these investments are not liquid and are characterized more by default risk rather than price or valuation volatility. Meanwhile, institutional investors typically define risk as volatility of returns (price volatility). Therefore, it is important for institutional investors to consider the *"J-curve effect"* that venture investments exhibit when assessing venture investment volatility, as this could lead to negative interpretations if not assessed within the proper context.

Figure 2-4. The Two Components of Total Portfolio Risk

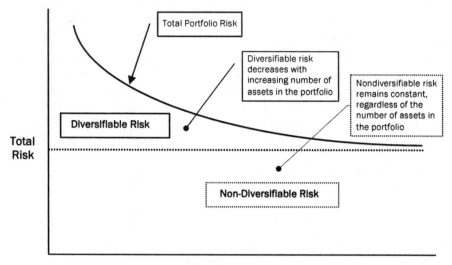

Total Number of Different Assets

The total portfolio risk declines as the number of assets with the portfolio increases. This diminishment in total risk is due to the effects of asset diversification upon the diversifiable portion of the total risk. Meanwhile, increasing the number of assets within the portfolio does not lower the non-diversifiable risk.

Risk and Reward

In theory, the investment process involves estimates of relative probabilities of the occurrence of certain events.   The expected rate of return associated with investments in general is a function of three main factors:

1. The projected economic *benefits* derived from the investment **(how much)**

2. The projected *duration* of these benefits **(how long)**

3. The hypothetical *risk* of not receiving these benefits in their expected amounts and duration **(how certain)**

Venture capitalists estimate an expected rate of return by a variety of techniques that begin with an assessment of the size of the market the prospective investment intends to target followed by the company's expected market share. Then an *expense analysis* is determined to approximate the *total capital infusion* required and time-weighted revenue estimates are approximated to determine the company's breakeven point followed by profit growth. Finally, a *valuation analysis* is performed through a variety of methods, such as the discounted cash flow model or relative (comparables) valuation. For the venture capitalist, it is the average internal annual rate of return (IRR) that is the most important determinant of investment feasibility so that the appropriate investment duration is selected for which the company will have achieved significant revenues timed with favorable market conditions for exit. Meanwhile, *the relative risk of a venture is assessed by quantifying the following factors:*

- **Strength and Execution Ability of Management Team**
- **Financial Management Risk**
- **Competitive Influences risk**
- **Proprietary Content of Firm Assets**
- **Breakeven Point**
- **Overall Health of the IPO Markets**
- **Marketing Strategy and Execution Risk**
- **Development and Manufacturing Risk**
- **Scalability Risk**
- **Business Model Risk**

These risk factors form an overall investment risk profile that estimates both the risk of generating revenues in a timely manner and the risk of default. As with all investments, there is a proportionate relationship between risk and return, as illustrated in the figure 2-5. As you can see, while venture capital investment yields the highest hypothetical returns, it also shares the highest hypothetical risk. And while portfolio diversification used by venture firms serves to minimize many of these risks, we have seen that significant risks (non-diversifiable risks) cannot be lowered by diversification. Fortunately, venture capitalists have multiple layers of protection from much of this risk: intensive due diligence, investment tranches, term sheet structuring, and the use of syndicates.

**Figure 2-5. The Relationship between Hypothetical Risk and Expected Return
(results are over a 20-year period)**

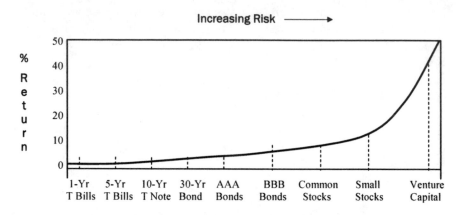

Note that these returns are based upon 20-year historical averages. However, in any given single year, the variance of returns increases to the right of the chart. In addition, due to the initial multiyear period required for capital draw downs in venture capital investments (i.e. the J-curve effect), typically no returns are seen until after a minimum of five years, although the historical returns shown in this chart assume the full harvesting of these investments, which is anywhere from five to 13 years.

Source: Parr & Sullivan

Nevertheless, in order to justify investment in such high risk businesses, *venture capitalists require an average annualized return (ARR) on their investments of 30%-50%.* These risks are in general higher for early stage companies since they have shorter operational histories, little or no revenues, etc., so venture capitalists require either a higher expected return or a cheaper price paid (lower valuation) for their ownership. Typically, *venture firms will take anywhere from 20% to 60% ownership* of a company and will tend not to go below or beyond these limits because they want enough ownership to justify adequate returns, yet they do not want so much ownership that very little is left for management incentive. The investment amount and pre-money valuation can be adjusted so that the desired percentage ownership of the company is obtained. The following formula illustrates these relationships:

$$RCOP = \frac{I}{PV + I}$$

where   RCOP = the Required Current Ownership Percentage

                         I = the Investment amount

                         PV = the Pre-Money Valuation

But this alone is not sufficient, as the venture capitalist must verify a large market capacity and market share for the prospective company. Table 2-5 shows the amount of investor ownership required to yield a 30% return, which is the minimum expected annual return venture capitalists require.

Table 2-5. Ownership Required to Support a 30% Return

Ownership Needed to Yield a 30% Return

	$10	N/A	N/A	80%	60%	48%
	$8	N/A	N/A	80%	60%	48%
Millions of Dollars Invested	$6	N/A	72%	48%	36%	29%
	$4	96%	48%	32%	24%	29%
	$2	48%	24%	16%	12%	10%
		$20	$40	$60	$80	$100

Future Estimated Market Value of Company in 6 Years (in millions of $)

Source: "Three Keys to Obtaining Venture Capital." Pricewaterhouse Coopers, 9th ed.

The J-Curve Phenomenon

When comparing the percentage of positive cash flows versus time there is a tendency for the cash flows within a venture investment to follow a slanted "J" pattern. Hence, a plot of cash flows versus time for private companies yields what is known as a "J curve". Initially, the first few years of an early stage investment are characterized by what are known as "*drawdowns*", which represent the period of investment into the company by investors. At this early stage, the company is financing product development and implementing marketing strategies and therefore has not generated significant revenues. As a result, venture and most private equity funds will show negative cash flows for the first few years. Only after year 5 or 6 does a company usually become cash flow positive and begin to issue cash distributions, which reflect the partial or complete exit of some of the investors (figure 2-6). From the MPT, we can appreciate that venture funds containing portfolio companies that are well diversified in both time and industry can smooth out the effects of the J-curve effect, and thereby provide more stable returns over the life of the fund (figure 2-7).

The occurrence of the J-curve effect can present adverse consequences for institutional investors who are accustomed to traditional asset management and valuation methodologies. For instance, there has been a recent wave of activity in many states, whose pension plans have pressured venture funds to make data publicly available. If this happens, some pension funds may view the J-curve effect as representing too much risk and might decide to discontinue investment in venture capital. Obviously, for institutional investors who hold a sufficiently diversified portfolio of venture funds, the J-curve effect of this entire portfolio will be minimized.

Figure 2-6. The J-Curve Effect on Venture Capital and Private Equity Investments

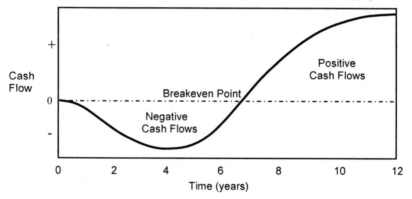

Figure 2-7. Alteration of the J-Curve Effect Due to Portfolio Diversification

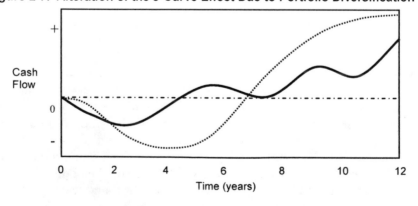

D. Venture Capital Risk Management

We discussed the MPT as one method used by venture firms to lower investment risk, but they have several others. At the first or screening level venture firms use due diligence to minimize risk prior to committing capital. At the investment level, they use term sheets, syndicates, and tranches along with the MPT to minimize risk. And the final level of risk management involves an attempt to salvage an investment. In cases when company failure is certain, they will liquidate company assets with the attempt to recapture principal.

Venture Capital Due Diligence

The *due diligence process* begins once the venture firm tells a company they are interested in looking further into the business proposal and this process serves to help the firm determine if the investment makes sense to them. At this stage the specifics of the company will be assessed such as the competitive strategies, quality and capabilities of the management, the overall risk, and perhaps the most important factor, the internal rate of return. When assessing the company's business strategy, most likely the venture firm will already know the industry space very well so the assessments will mainly be concerned with verification of assumptions, anticipating any IP issues, and determining if the products can achieve the required market penetration. Interviews with each member of the management team and board will be conducted to assess the strengths and weaknesses of both the business and each individual. In addition, they will do background checks on the founders and management team to make sure they can be trusted with money.

There is no standard due diligence process adhered to by all venture firms and the process can proceed at different points throughout the negotiation process. Typically however, some level of due diligence occurs prior to agreement on a term sheet and this can be thought of as *peripheral due diligence.* Many of the primary issues addressed during this phase are largely independent of the company under consideration and involve industry trends, and strategic and competitive assessments. And this data is used to form an overall risk-reward assessment by the venture firm.

While much of the risk associated with company success can be determined by looking at the general structure of the business model and management team, the reward may only be estimated after calculating the IRR. Finally, the risk-reward is largely determined by estimating the expected IRR based on expected market growth versus the risks associated with execution by the management team. In calculating the internal rate of return (IRR), much estimation will be made such as the size of market growth, the expected achievable market share of the company by years 5-7, the possible routes and timing of exit, and the deal terms. If the round of financing is second or later, the venture firm will focus on valuation, since they will have a much smaller ability to control this due to the involvement of other previous investors. Note that the IRR may only be established upon mutual agreement of the term sheet since this critical document contains many of the guidelines that determine company control and valuation.

The second phase of the due diligence process may be referred to as *core due diligence*, and would include examination of corporate records, operating agreements, patents, financial agreements (term sheets, licensing agreements), in-depth interviews, and background checks on the management team. Beyond these issues, the remainder of the due diligence process consists of contracts such as those governing the operation and rights of the company. Of course the due diligence process may result in a lack of further interest by the venture firm at any stage for a variety of reasons. But those entrepreneurs fortunate enough to pass the intense due diligence process of a venture firm should understand exactly what all contracts mean and all ramifications in order to assess any proposals. And they should seek the advice of an experienced attorney who specializes in venture law, as well as a knowledgeable financial professional who has experience with private equity finance (see chapter 4 and Appendix C-3 for more extensive coverage of the due diligence process).

Term Sheets

The term sheet represents an informal description of the investor's terms for financing and may be the most powerful tool venture capitalists have to minimize risk to their limited partners' investment capital. There are many opportunities for venture firms to structure specific guidelines when proposing a term sheet for companies, and each one will depend upon the specifics of the company.

Within the term sheet, various provisions will be proposed within the class of preferred stock to be issued that will account for liquidation, conversion, dividends, antidilution, and voting rights. Therefore, entrepreneurs must absolutely develop a detailed understanding of the various possibilities and consequences of the terms of a financing proposal. Otherwise, what may seem like a favorable term sheet may be favorable to only the venture firm and the company will be powerless to reverse the terms of the financing. We will explore term sheet design and analysis in detail in chapter 10.

Syndicates

A *syndicate* is a group of investors that follow the lead investor's investment into a financial transaction. *The concept of syndication groups is a central theme in the financial industry and serves to provide a diverse collection of information and financial contributions into the investment pool while spreading the investment risk amongst several investors.* Much like Wall Street brokerage firms that sometimes have preferences for outside money managers, venture capitalists have preferences for other venture capitalists they choose to invest with in a particular deal.

There are several possible reasons why an investor may wish to form a syndication group. The first reason is investment by approval. Venture capitalists are no different then anyone else---they seek *investment validation* from their peers in order to strengthen their perceptions of a company's future potential. Syndication also allows investors to share risk among syndicate members and exchange resources. Finally, *syndication helps minimize dilution of shares during future rounds* since syndicates tend to remain committed to funding subsequent rounds, and this helps them maintain control over valuation related issues. Entrepreneurs should also note that *syndication might also represent a method to minimize the risk of securing future rounds of financing since syndicates tend to commit to all future rounds of financings as long as they remain together.*

However, not all venture firms wish to participate in syndicates and some only like them for certain investments. More experienced venture capitalists tend to be more tolerant of syndicate partners with less experience during later stages, while seeking to add equally regarded industry peers to their early stage investments. In addition, some firms like to form syndicates in areas they are not as experienced in so they can benefit from the expertise of more experienced venture firms.[5] In contrast, some venture firms use an investment strategy that relies on a large percentage ownership of the company so the use of syndicate groups would diminish this strategy. And some VCs simply do not click well with others and may not want to join a syndicate. Finally, the size of some rounds of financing is too small to allow sharing by other VCs.

Thus, when venture firms elect to use syndicates, the general characteristics of a syndicate investment structure serves to provide superior investment charactistics by lowering investment risk assumed by any one investor, lowering the risk of default due to the large assembly of human resources, and minimizing individual venture fund portfolio volatility. Therefore, syndication is a very important risk management tool used by many venture capital firms and may also be thought of as a means to conformity to the MPT.

Staging of Investments: Tranches

Tranch funding is a method of fund distribution that allocates separate portions of the total committed financing round into distinct dispersements based upon the attainment of specific milestones.   Venture capitalists are very protective of both the investment capital supplied by their limited partners. Therefore, allocation of investment capital to portfolio companies based upon the achievement of milestones allows specific criteria to be established prior to further funding arrangements.   And if companies have not reached all milestones, management will need to provide adequate justification for this shortfall.   Otherwise, the venture firm may delay or refuse to provide further portions of the committed capital.   Therefore, the use of tranches encourages prudent use of investment capital by both the management team and the venture capitalists.

Liquidation

As part of their ongoing process of financial and human capital management, venture capitalists assess their portfolio companies to identify those with the best time- and investment-weighted return potentials. Unfortunately for the laggards, venture capitalists may begin to spend less time and commit less money to those investments that are underperforming. In fact, they may even exercise their option to force a liquidation event in order to minimize their losses and this could result in dire consequences for a company if not readily prepared.   A venture capitalist most likely will not tell a company that this will happen.   One day a meeting will be called and the announcement made.   That is not to say however that the lead venture capitalist will not provide early indications of this possibility.

It would be a lack of oversight and poor judgment if a company were not aware that their failure to achieve milestones would eventually bring dire consequences.   Despite some common misperceptions, venture capitalists are good people but they have legal obligations to their investors that may cause unfavorable developments to occur with respect to the company.   And *the best way to avoid surprises is to become very familiar with the guidelines and expectations of their investment criteria, as well as understanding the full implications of all the terms of the financing agreement.*

What Entrepreneurs Can Expect

As we have seen, the real value of venture capitalists extends well beyond their wallets.   The best venture firms have tremendous human resources, but this does not mean that they will run the company.   In fact many venture firms typically prefer not to hold a controlling interest in most of their portfolio companies because they will be forced to assume a more hands-on role. And most venture firms simply do not have the time or manpower to run individual companies. Of course there are variable degrees of venture capital investment philosophy and *it is an essential task of the company to understand whether the prospective venture capital is a more hands-on or hands-off.*

Depending on the firm, the industry, and other factors, in general the lead venture capitalist can be expected to visit the company once each month while nonlead venture investors should expect a quarterly visit. While most venture firms do not become involved in the day-to-day management of its portfolio companies, they do receive monthly financial statements and are available for consultation on a daily basis. Many times, conference calls are arranged to handle key timely issues. The venture firm will meet with their board regularly (which includes the major limited partners of the fund) as well to discuss the performance of the fund.

As a company secures additional rounds of financing, the board composition of the company will increase and change. In the early stages, the board consists of the founder and management. Once the company achieves a significant commitment of investment capital, an individual representing these funds will have a seat on the board. When venture capitalists approve financing they will also hold board seats, often times in proportion to their invested capital. As the company increases the number of rounds of investment, some board seats might be forfeited to the newer venture investors. And when the company experiences a needed change in management, such as a new CEO, venture capital representation on the board may increase in order to serve this need for increased guidance.

As difficult as the fund raising process is, the management team cannot rest once they raise their first round, however tempting this may be, as this is just the beginning. The management team will now be held to intense scrutiny, and the investors will expect completion of stated milestones in a timely manner. *Entrepreneurs must keep in mind that the venture capitalist is only concerned with achieving a high IRR in a restricted time period. And if this does not occur he will move on and your company will be difficult to resurrect.*

E. Difficulties Faced By Venture Capitalists

It should be apparent by now of the many challenges encountered by venture capitalists. Needless to say, they have an extremely difficult job. Not only do they have to raise capital for each fund, but also they are responsible for assisting management teams and realizing a certain minimal net profit for their limited partners, all while being held to strict fiduciary guidelines and requirements set forth in the covenants of the limited partnership agreement.   But despite these challenges, the venture capital industry has been highly successful and has transformed our society for the good of all.   However, venture capitalists are now being challenged with administrative and regulatory issues that may pose a threat to the long-term viability of this industry, as we know it today.   And if these changes are not handled in a smooth and cautious manner, it could ultimately damage the entrepreneurial spirit of America.

Management Fees and Carried Interest

As with any maturing industry, venture capitalists are currently experiencing outside pressures that are characteristic of industry regulation. Often, scrutiny is most critical during challenging periods and this holds true for venture capitalists as well as other segments of the financial industry and corporate America.   Specifically, several institutional investors are pressuring venture capital firms to decrease their management fees and carried interest rates, perhaps as an extension of the fee collapse that has occurred for the public financial services industry.   This campaign has been further stimulated by the recent downturn in the economy that has resulted in the decreased performance of the public and private markets.

In large part, much of the recent critism of the industry has been the inability of many firms to fully invest committed funds in a timely manner, yet continuing to assess management fees.   Is this fair?   Well, perhaps not. However, venture firms are merely serving to protect the investment capital committed by these institutions, rather than throwing good money after bad. While a 2% management fee probably should not be assessed when firms fail to invest the capital in a timely manner, *there should be some value attached to exercising good judgment and having reserved a place in the fund.* Remember that this fee is theoretically assessed to pay expenses of the firms' operations towards managing the fund.   And obviously, if a fund remains uninvested, these expenses will not reach maximum levels.

However, *there are certain expenses that must be maintained in order to preserve optimal functional capacity of these firms.*   In order to illustrate this, let us break down venture expenses into three main categories.   First, there are the fees associated with the direct management of each portfolio company, such as travel expenses and office equipment.   Next are the expenses needed to keep the lights on and pay the partners and staff.   Thus if a fund is invested by only 50% by a predetermined time period, how much should the management fee be decreased?   Obviously, each firm must pay the same internal operational costs each month if it is preserve optimal functional capacity.   Should the staff be cut by 50% to reflect the current manpower dedicated to the amount invested? I think not. If this is done, each firm will scramble to restaff when the investment opportunities are better, causing intrafirm instability and decreased investment management efficiency. There is a certain chemistry created at each firm that is built upon each partner and staff member responsible for establishing an optimal level of operating efficiency. Hence, while some decrease in management fees might be justified, it should only be tied to those expenses not being used due to the direct costs of investing. Each firm will have its own formula for determination of modified fees that will depend upon the fund size, the size of the staff, the amount invested, and the estimated direct costs of management of each company.

Meanwhile, other critics that are advocating a decreased carried interest. This would inevitably result in a price war, which we will learn from chapter 6, always benefits the customer, but only in the short-term. If a price war is protracted, it will ultimately drive the value added by venture firms downward to compensate for their decreased budgets. Although they share many activities, venture capitalists do things in a very different manner than asset managers of public securities. And while the same standards of integrity and diligence should apply, venture capitalists should not be held to the same standards of compensation because they actively manage their funds. Likewise, hedge fund managers are also considered active managers because they rely upon skill-based techniques to increase performance. Similar to venture capitalists, the compensation structure of hedge fund managers mirrors that of venture capitalists, having a management fee and a carried interest. Hence, venture capitalists are in a sense, hedge fund managers for private companies and should be compensated in a manner consistent with their responsibilities and performance.

The compensation structure of the venture capital industry is consistent with the entrepreneurial spirit that has fueled the economic and job growth of America over the past 50 years. And if America expects to retain its position as the economic and technology powerhouse of the world, we must serve to protect the incentive based performance that rules the venture capital industry.

Transparency and Disclosure Controversies

As with any type of business, the venture capital industry is currently experiencing some of the adverse effects of increased demand and popularity. As more pension funds and have committed investment capital towards these assets, there has been an increasing pressure to urge the venture capital industry to help comply with the standards that other asset classes are subject to, such as public investments. Although ERISA is the governing body responsible for establishing and enforcing the rules and regulations of pension assets in the United States, it has not been the force responsible for these pressures. Rather, certain state pension plans, such as California, Michigan, and Texas have voiced strong opinions on venture capital disclosure policies. Amongst these reforms are for venture funds to provide increased transparency of valuations similar to the other investments. The problem with this is that it can lead to prematurely discouraging results due to the almost invariable J-Curve effect.

One might argue that investments that are known to carry very high levels of risk and are restricted only to accredited investors such as hedge funds and venture capital should be exempt from such restrictive regulation in order to preserve their unique flexibility. However, when one considers that state pensions invest the retirement money of employees of the state, that changes the entire picture. Perhaps pension funds should allocate more resources towards due diligence of venture funds, rather than demanding increased levels of transparency. Transparency is thought to diminish much of the leverage venture firms have when negotiating exit strategies. *And because valuation information is considered confidential, disclosure of this information could greatly hinder the selling price of their portfolio companies.*

In the opinion of the author, transparency is not the solution and will only serve to assist the pension manager in *window dressing*, which cannot be effectively performed due to the nature of venture investments. In addition, it will greatly diminish much of the proprietary business information venture firms use to position their investments, and therefore diminish the viability and profitability of liquidity events. Nevertheless, it is only a matter of time before the venture capital industry becomes institutionalized much in the same manner that has occurred with the mutual fund industry and which is beginning to occur with the hedge fund industry. But in this process, we should not question the venture-funded company dynamics underlying the J-curve effect. Instead, we should embrace it as one of the peculiarities that lies deeply imbedded within a venture capital industry that has enjoyed tremendous success for decades. Misappropriated accountability standards set forth by institutional investors who have neither the time nor skills to accurately assess them will serve to create more micromanagement by venture capitalists which may hinder the abilities of the entrepreneur to develop the best positioned companies. And we should not alter the entrepreneurial battleground whose victors have built such a great country.

Notes

[1] Closed-end funds (CEFs) are professionally managed investment companies that provide many unique benefits to investors. Similar to the more common open-end funds (mutual funds), CEFs pay out their earnings to investors in two ways: income dividends and capital gains distributions. Unlike open-end funds, CEFs are listed on securities exchanges and are bought on the open market and trade relatively independent of the NAVs. Therefore, investors can buy and sell CEFs like stocks with no sales charges directly assessed (although commissions are charged). In addition, due to the independence of share price with net asset value (NAV), investors can potentially purchase CEFs at a discount to NAV (if the share price is lower then the NAV), unlike the case with mutual funds, which must be purchased at NAV (in addition to any sales charges that may be assessed).

There are several distinctions that should be noted between open and closed-end funds. OEFs offer their shares on a continuous basis and the price of these funds depends upon the NAV. A fund's NAV represents the funds assets minus its liabilities divided by the number of shares outstanding. Unlike OEFs, CEFs have a fixed number of shares outstanding and the share price is only determines by the supply-demand for these funds, similar to stocks. In addition, unlike OEFs, CEFs invest a fixed amount of money that was raised by the IPO of the fund and can only change by authority of the management. There are only a few ways to increase the amount of money in a CEF: rights offerings and dividend and capital gains reinvestments. Likewise, the number of shares can also decrease if the management team decides to repurchase shares from the marketplace or through a tender offer.

While are not as popular as they once were, CEFs still remain excellent investment vehicles and there are still some venture capital funds structured as closed-end funds, such as TINY (ticker symbol). Therefore, because they can be purchased on a securities exchange, they may be bought by anyone, unlike venture funds structured as an LLC.

[2] This change was an amendment to the "prudent man" rule that governs pension fund investments. This rule was enacted by the Employee Retirement Income Security Act (ERISA) to ensure pension funds did not invest in high-risk investments and minimized the amounts that could be invested in venture capital.

[3] When serving as board members on their portfolio companies, venture capitalists usually do not receive stock options or any other form of compensation specifically for this responsibility because the limited partnership agreement governing their funds usually requires any compensation for management of portfolio companies to be subtracted from the fees charged to the limited partners. However, after an IPO venture capitalists are able to receive compensation as board members even if distributions to the limited partners have not yet been made. The reason for this exception is due to the much greater liability assumed by the venture firm for this responsibility. In addition, at this stage, management fees are minimal if even present, so the venture firm is not considered to be "double-dipping".

[4] There are some firms that still prefer to invest in early stage companies, although they represent they minority of all VC firms in the United States. Such firms typically have converged towards an incubator model, offering highly specialized assistance to the entrepreneur with the hope that a large controlling interest early on will yield very large returns within each fund.

[5] Depending upon the relative ownership, the objectives of some syndicate members may not be served when circumstances of the investment change. Some syndicate members are generalists, not focusing on any particular industry or perhaps their focus is not in the industry of their syndicate group. In such situations, these investors will tend to be more risk averse compared to other members who are more experienced in the industry and therefore more willing to assume larger risks. In some situations, when an investment turns into a higher risk than the syndicate member is willing to take on, they may wish to sell their ownership to an existing syndicate member. If the other syndicate members reject this right of first refusal, this investor may be permitted to solicit outside investors. However, this could create problems for the syndicate group, depending upon the personalities and interactional styles of the new group. In contrast, if syndicate members are not permitted to solicit outside investors for previous rounds of financing, the member may be stuck holding a very risky investment with no method of minimizing further potential losses.

3

Fundamentals of Raising Capital

"Whether you think you can, or you can't, you are usually right."
Henry Ford

As the head of a startup company, you will need to convince investors that you will have a reasonable chance of providing them with an excellent return on their investment within a given time period. For investors, the return on investment is only measured in dollars, and there are no moral victories as far as they are concerned. But what constitutes an appropriate financial commitment by an investor? Just what is your company really worth anyway? After all, it's just a startup with little or no revenues and perhaps not even a prototype product. While you may only have a concept and vision, it's your duty to convince investors that you will be able to transform these ideas into profits.

A. Financing Decisions

Entrepreneurs usually do a good job of establishing how much capital their company is expected to need but tend to do a poor job justifying specifically how the proceeds will be spent and over what time period. Likewise, they usually fail to make a proper consideration of the types of financings that will be needed prior to the breakeven point. However, these issues should be resolved prior to prospecting sophisticated investors and should be included in the business plan. Business financing decisions basically involve two choices, debt or equity. However, most successful companies ultimately use both types of financing based upon their specific needs. Thus, the key is not which one you should use, but in what proportions, sequence, and specific terms they can be most effectively utilized.

Debt is defined as a loan collateralized by either company or personal assets. And while debt financing is not dilutive to the ownership of the company, it can hinder its growth because principal and interest payments must be paid back in a timely manner, thereby depleting cash flows. In addition, if the company eventually goes bankrupt, individuals who signed for the loan may be subject to repayment. In contrast, equity financing creates a positive cash flow but has the main disadvantage of being dilutive to the owners' equity in the company and will therefore result in a smaller return on investment (ROI) for the founders and management team. And although traditional finance teaches that the cost of debt capital is less expensive than equity, this really only applies to companies that have a reasonable history of predictable earnings that can be used to service their debt. In contrast, *for early stage companies debt is much more costly from a risk standpoint than equity since the requirements of servicing the debt may deplete cash flows and result in insolvency.*

Management must understand the most efficient use of debt financings because they need to stretch every dollar as far as it will go. In general, companies usually cannot obtain debt financing until they have acquired substantial tangible assets or secured sufficient equity financing from a previous round. However, sometimes companies with minimal assets and a good credit record may qualify for short-term debt financing (payable in one year or less) to be used for *working capital.* Only after the company has more substantial assets will it qualify for long-term debt financings (payable in one to five years).

When considering the types of financial structures for company growth and operations, one should first categorize the types of expenses or assets that are needed for the funding, followed by a determination of the most suitable financing source. In general, money is needed for four types of expenses in a company:

1) **Operating costs**, such as rent and utilities, wages, travel expenses, prospecting, sales and marketing costs

2) **Tangible assets** such or equipment such as office equipment and lab instrumentation

3) **Product supplies** and associated labor expenses, such as reagents, special raw materials, lab animals, machine tooling expenses, etc.

4) **Legal and tax costs**

The first thing a company should do upon securing financing is to apply for a company credit card. In a worst-case scenario of company failure, (resulting in bankruptcy) the company's debt liability from these unsecured loans will not pass on to the management of a properly structured corporation (limited partnerships may not provide this protection). While credit cards tend to have high interest rates, (especially for accounts with limited payment history) this still outweighs paying cash in full. Remember, *preserving cash flow equates into buying more time for the company to mature its products and receive adequate long-term financing.*

Travel expenses and prospecting costs, such as the purchase of lead lists and attendance at conferences should be paid by a company credit card or an unsecured line of credit, once again to preserve cash flow. Depending upon the cost of the equipment and the cash situation of the company, one should always consider issuing debt to pay for expensive lab equipment in order to preserve cash. One of the ways this can be done is by taking a secured loan against the equipment from your local bank that has a technology division specializing in this type of situation. A small business loan is also an option but this could take several months to materialize so companies choosing this route should factor in the delays when constructing the financial plan. Alternatively, you might consider leasing this equipment if such an option is available. In the initial stages, what is needed is the use of the equipment not its ownership and you cannot finance expenses such as rent and travel costs unless you wish to pay a high interest rate on your credit card. So you will want to maximize the company's daily cash flow in order to establish a healthy working capital to provide sufficient liquidity for more critical business operations.

Let us consider a company with $500,000 cash and the need for a $100,000 equipment purchase for prototype data collection and testing. Obviously, this company is far from having sufficient concrete results needed to receive serious venture capital financing. Therefore, preservation of cash flow should be evident. And rather than spending $100,000 on the equipment, the company should obtain a loan secured against this equipment for an extended period. Depending on the situation, the company might be able to receive a loan for prime plus 1-3%. And if the company's funding situation improves, management can then decide if paying the loan off from the lien-holder (in order to save on interest expense) is advisable.

Other costs, such as financial, legal, and accounting expenses can usually be discounted if not completely replaced through company stock. As a matter of fact, for service providers such as attorneys and consultants who tend to charge ridiculous rates, *you should try to find individuals who believe in the success of the company to the extent they will at least allow a partial discount in the form of company stock.* This way, these individuals will be motivated to act in the best interest of the company and not overcharge for services. Below is a partial list of questions an entrepreneur should answer when considering debt financing:

- Will my company qualify for debt financing?
- Over what time period will the loan be needed?
- What are the best sources of debt financing my company will qualify for?
- Am I willing to personally guarantee the debt?
- Can the company accurately predict and deliver the needed cash flow to support the debt?
- Does the company have any assets that can that can be pledged as collateral?
- Will the company be able to comply with all conditions of the debt financing?
- Is venture leasing a viable option?

B. Getting the Money

So how does one get funded? Well the problem certainly has not been due to the lack of money available for venture investments. According to figures compiled by *Venture Economics*, some 364 private equity funds raised $88.4 billion in 1998, up nearly 26% from 1997 and a record estimated $103 billion was raised for 2000.[1] Meanwhile in each of those years, angel investors contributed approximately an additional $20 billion. Thus, investment capital for private equity and venture investments continues to pour in from a variety of sources such as pension plans, endowment funds, foundations, financial institutions, and insurance companies. Nevertheless, *it has been estimated that only 0.2% of companies receive venture backed funding each year.* And if your company is not technology-based, funding options are even more limited, as *only 1 in 4 non-technology based companies are even considered for venture backed financings.*

With this influx of money *many venture capitalists have refocused their strategies on funding fewer companies with more money so they can have more control and higher returns with less risk.* This might explain in part why they focus much more on strength of management as opposed to technology. And since they tend to concentrate their limited human resources on fewer companies, it only makes sense that they would desire to invest in companies with strong management teams who can best utilize their expertise. Meanwhile, as the venture firms have become more selective in their investments, the role of angels has increased, specifically for early stage companies in the biotechnology and healthcare industries.

Now that the economic and stock market bubble of the late 1990s has deflated, the supply of money committed towards these funds has diminished significantly, as the majority of pension plans became under funded as early as 2002. But this merely represents a temporary correction in the long-term trend of increasing institutional investment in venture capital and private equity. As the stock markets have become more widely available to individuals, smaller companies, and banks, this has not only served to increase the competition amongst providers of investment products, but it has also diminished the value of any given investment firm in providing attractive returns for its investors. As such, more institutional investors have sought to separate themselves from the public markets and enter into what could arguably be considered a more controlled environment, free from the influences of Wall Street, yet privy to insider information.

No doubt, venture capital is here to stay and it will continue its growth despite any temporary setbacks. Regardless of the current economic environment, there will always be dark periods separating more robust periods of economic euphoria and entrepreneurs should never let short-term economic trends discourage the realization of their dreams. Progress does not stop when the economy is in a recession, and for some companies it can represent more opportunities than during an economic expansion. Therefore, I have listed what I call the "10 Commandments of Building a Great Company" in figure 3-1 which, when performed with committed dedication, should enable startup companies to persevere despite any adverse economic conditions.

Focus on the Smart Money

During the fund raising process the novice founder will most likely become discouraged in his inability to secure financing after countless months of no success. And this will almost always reoccur, regardless how much money the company has raised in the past. It is simply a reality of the prospecting process. Nevertheless, at some point entrepreneurs may succumb to the desperation to take any amount of money from any number of individuals; do not do it unless you are on the verge of closing shop. *Beyond seed money, accepting investment funds from unsophisticated investors will almost always guarantee failure of the company* for many reasons.

Consider a situation whereby you have raised $500,000 from a total of 100 investors. At first glance that may sound like a great success for seed plus partial early stage money but it will definitely turn out to damage the company and possibly eliminate all chances of success. In reality, this type of financing usually serves to position the company into a slow but certain

Figure 3-1. The Ten Commandments of Building a Great Company

Thou Shalt:

1. Develop a Vision and Create a Mission
2. Do Thy Homework on Competitors
3. Pursue a Large or Rapidly Growing Market
4. Focus on Thy Core Competencies
5. Assemble the Best Management Team Possible
6. Create a Competitive Advantage
7. Go After the Smart Money
8. Construct a Marketable Business Plan
9. Know Thy Prospects
10. Execute Thy Business Model With Determination

death unless it can be reversed through buying out these novice investors. Quite frankly, if they can only afford to invest on average $5000 each, they most likely do not have the experience and knowledge required to be investing in a startup.   And you will most likely be spending 20-40% of your time with these unsophisticated investors going over company progress and addressing educational and administrative issues, thus preventing you from devoting your full attention towards completing the tasks needed to create a successful company, such as prospecting for money, coordinating the efforts of the board members, working on product development, gaining customer traction, dealing with the intellectual property issues, budgeting, refining the business strategy, and several other tasks.   You simply have no time to answer calls from a "large" shareholder who invested $10,000 and wants daily or weekly updates. Nor do you have time to answer weekly questions from the other 99 investors who are wondering, "what has become of their money."

These investors might also hinder the ability of the company to secure financing from venture capitalists since they are aware of the potential problems novice investors can pose for the company. For instance, difficulties could arise if these investors are not in agreement on any changes to the company charter, which is needed for venture firms to invest. Such *inexperienced investors simply do not understand the venture process and could sabotage your efforts if they do not drive you insane first. Therefore, even for seed capital you should focus on finding the smart money.* If your company makes medical devices, you should prospect local physicians who can appreciate your technology. These individuals will not only add validity to your technology but they will also bring in other physicians as angels.

Finally, when companies obtain seed and early stage financing from unsophisticated angel investors, it is recommended that they include a *call option clause* that states something to the effect:

"Upon the successful further financing of __$$, the company will have the option to purchase up to ___ # shares of stock from each investor at a price no less then ___$$."

This will provide a buyout option at a later time and resolve any worries regarding acceptance of the charter when venture capitalists become involved. Be smart from the beginning when you prospect for financing and it will go much smoother in the long run.

Prospecting Rules to Remember

Prospecting for investment capital is difficult for every investment professional so you can bet it is certainly one of the most difficult tasks for a startup company. And unfortunately, the magnitude of its importance in determining company survival parallels the uncertainty of results. In effort to help entrepreneurs structure an effective fund raising campaign, I will now list 15 of the most important rules, in my opinion, when attempting to raise capital for the early stage company.

1. *Maintain Prospecting Intelligence & Etiquette*

Most VCs are very friendly and generous with their limited time because they are smart businessmen and therefore realize that within any given business plan may lay the next great company. However, venture capitalists are always busy. And while you may be able to speak with one in brief upon a cold call, you should not confuse that gesture of attention with serious interest. In short, **Do Not Waste Time Cold Calling***!* It is obviously time efficient to use the phone when prospecting but is it generally not effective and it may serve to destroy many more leads then it generates. VCs do however like email, as it enables them to juggle many tasks simultaneously and prioritize their responses efficiently. My recommendation when using email as a venue of introduction is to introduce yourself and your company in a brief letter similar to the one shown below.

Dear Mr. Big Dollar,

I represent the management team as the founder of MoonStar Technologies, Inc. We are an early stage IT software company headquartered in Omaha, NE formed in 2002. Our core competency technology is based upon proprietary software that drastically lowers cost, improves the speed and accuracy of data storage and retrieval for use in a wide range of applications. We feel this breakthrough technology represents a tremendous investment opportunity for experienced and successful investors such as your firm, who have demonstrated expertise in this field. We have performed the necessary due diligence on your firm and feel that it best meets the needs of our company. Finally, we feel our investment proposition is consistent with your firm's needs and lies within your area of expertise.

Currently, we are in negotiations to license one of our products to local telecom companies for beta testing and we are in need of $3 million to finance this project. I have included an executive summary for your initial review. Please allow me the opportunity to elaborate the details of our company during a 10-minute phone conversation, so that you will be able to determine if our company meets your investment criteria. If you would like to receive any other information about MoonStar Tech prior to this meeting, feel free to contact me by email or phone. I may be reached at 567-786-7273. I thank you for your time and attention in this matter.

This letter accomplishes several things. First, it represents a professional means of communication, since you have introduced your company via their preferred mode of communication. Next, it communicates only the essentials: the technology industry, the relative maturity of the company, the amount of financing needed, and the use of proceeds. And it also informs the VC that you have not randomly selected a name and number out of a book but that you have researched the their firm and are familiar with their investment criteria. Finally, it specifically requests a certain time period, ten minutes, which allows the VC to schedule such a phone conversation when you will have his full attention.

This approach will demonstrate a sense of professionalism and respect, which will definitely provide a favorable first impression to VCs, who is always concerned about the management team's credibility. It will also tend to generate a more favorable response since you have been sensitive to his busy schedule. If after one week you hear no response you should send the same email, as they may have overlooked it. As well, you will want to send this email to the partner at the firm who covers your industry. If the VC shows no interest, you should include him on a list you will maintain to notify for periodic updates.

2. *Generate Leads from Leads: Turn Every Lead Into Two Fresh Leads.*
A good start for generating prospects and referrals should come from friends and colleagues who are familiar with your abilities. You should ask them for potential investor contacts and perhaps a warm introduction. Prospecting is extremely difficult and often unrewarding work and you will undoubtedly encounter no returned phone calls, no responses from executive summary submissions, and perhaps even pessimism that borders on insult. Thus, anytime you receive any form of acknowledgement that you exist by a potential investor, first thank him for his time and consideration then ask for two names of companies or investors that may have an interest in your company. It never hurts to ask, just don't be demanding.

3. *Get Connected: Attend All Local VC-Sponsored Conferences and Other Events.*
These events represent a great opportunity to network in general and get a feel for the current VC environment and latest trends. Even if your company is not presenting, you can learn from the mistakes and successes of companies that present to investors. As well, it presents

a unique opportunity for you to get some face time with VCs and angels so that when your company is ready for consideration, you will most likely receive more attention from those investors you met previously. You can also think of these events as a practice ground for delivering your pitch to individuals you speak with. Obviously, spending $50-$150 for something lacking any direct benefit may at first seem like a waste of company/personal funds, but I can assure you it is one of the best uses of company money if you are able to recognize the potential opportunities of such events.

4.   *Focus Your Prospecting Efforts Towards Local VCs First.*
Many VCs prefer to invest in local companies so they can easily monitor their investments. Such VCs are obviously easier to prospect due to the many opportunities you will have to access them, whether it is from a local investor presentation or simply the opportunity to meet one for a casual lunch. In addition, if you are prospecting VCs outside of your state and they are aware of local VCs who have expertise in your company's space, they will immediately be concerned why you have not secured their interest. Therefore, begin prospecting locally and extend outward as needed.

5.   *Make Friends With The Media.*
Contact the media with a compelling story about your company and how it will change the local area or the way we live. Many large cities have technology publications that are focused on reporting on technology startups in the region. This can be an invaluable source of exposure that may actually cause your phone to ring, and maybe even result in funding. But don't expect reporters to do a story immediately after you meet with them. They have agendas too and the timeliness of their story topics are sensitive to factors other than the developments of your company. Therefore, if they have an interest, they will keep your company information in a file to access at a later date. You should update them on company developments to add to this file.

6.   *Always Have Two Business Plans.*
You should always have a detailed and a condensed business plan. The *condensed business plan* should be submitted upon request by a prospective investor who has reviewed your executive summary. The *extended business plan* should only be distributed to serious investors who have indicated that they have an interest in considering investment in your company. Finally, I cannot count the times I have

lost interest in a company after reviewing their executive summary so make sure it's top notch (see Appendix B for business plan guidelines and format). If you can't even prepare a 3-page summary that compels investors to make further inquiries, how do you expect an investor to have confidence in your ability to run a company? You cannot and they will not. Period.

7. *Know Your Prospects.*
This is easier said than done. The ultimate goal is to develop individual profiles of the most suitable and likely investor prospects and focus most of the prospecting efforts towards them. In the construction of these profiles, you should know the types of investments your prospects prefer, the development stages they prefer to invest in, whether they are hands-on or more passive managers, whether they use syndicates, and if so how often they serve as the lead investors. We will discuss investor profiling in the next chapter.

8. *Learn To Overcome Rejection.*
There is a saying in the sales world that goes something like this, "For every 'No' you get you are one step closer to receiving a 'Yes'." Unfortunately, the "yes" is many steps ahead of all those "no's". But if you realize this from the start, you will be better prepared to rebound from the rejections. So keep charging forward, step by step and think of each "no" as gaining one step closer to a "yes". Regardless of the level of interest by the prospective investor, always thank the individual for allowing you the opportunity to show him or the investment proposal then move on. This will help you preserve your optimism and demonstrate a high level of professionalism. Remember that there are many possible reasons why an investor may not be interested in your company, all of which may be independent of you or the quality of the business. *Therefore, you must learn to never take rejection by a prospective investor personal.*

Never Stop Prospecting. This is true in any type of growth business, whether you prospecting for customers or investors. Even if you have $10 million which you expect to fund the company for six years, do not ever stop prospecting. Prospecting in general, is perhaps the most difficult and time-consuming task for any startup company and it could take one or more years to secure a major investment from a prospect. *Therefore, companies should seek financing that will last them at least 12 months during normal financing environments and 24 months in competitive environments.* It is human nature for people to ask for money only when they need it. However, *it takes some element of fear, greed, and foresight that causes one to prospect for money when it appears they have no need.*

9. ***Have Your Business Plan Reviewed By at Least Two Outside Financial Professionals.***
Many companies often overlook this advice. They have spent several hundreds of hours preparing their business plans and therefore they tend to think that it represents the best possible description of their business. However, keep in mind that financial professionals who work with private and public companies have valuable insight with respect to business strategy, finance, and marketing, and they are better skilled in understanding what investors wish to see in a business plan. In addition, it is very easy for internal management to overlook key aspects of a solid business plan due to their overly optimistic attitudes. There is perhaps no such thing as a perfect business plan, since you will inevitably hear 1000 different opinions from 1000 different people. But with each review from an experienced professional, you might receive feedback that places your plan one step closer to perfection.

10. *Never Give Up!*
This may well be the most important, yet most difficult rule to follow. If you are truly convinced of your abilities and the potentials of your company, and you have an intense drive fueled by a strong passion and desire to achieve success you will eventually succeed in your mission. Period. Regardless of the rejection, the doubt of others, or the lack of early successes that you may face, if you are absolutely committed and determined to achieve success, you will.

However, mistakes are to be expected, especially if you have never led a startup to success, and you must realize they are a large part of the process. However, allowing the rejection and wrong decisions to affect you will ultimately cause you to doubt yourself and the potentials of your company. The key aspect of the entire process is being able to recover from the mistakes you have made and to improve the situation. Remember, starting a company is a growth process involving a steep learning curve and growing pains are part of this process. *Condition yourself to succeed psychologically, like a professional athlete. Winners have winning attitudes at all times; even during signs of possible defeat.* Never give up.

11. ***Assemble The Best Management Team Possible.***
These individuals should be trusted, valued, and passionate about the company's potential. In addition, they should demonstrate an extreme

level of dedication and commitment towards the company's mission. *The personalities of the management team should be different enough to promote a healthy exchange of ideas and opinions, yet not so different that internal conflict could develop.* The backgrounds of the management team should be relevant to the company's technology and each person should have at least one unique and admirable characteristic that adds value to the entire team. As well, at least one member of the team should have significant business experience, preferably from a previous entrepreneurial endeavor.

12. *Conserve Cash: Keep Your Expenses To a Minimum.*

This does not mean not to spend money. It means to use your company's dollar wisely. Until your company has raised substantial funds from venture capitalists, you may wish to consider setting up a home office. I have seen several startups that decide they are a legitimate and successful business once they have raised $500,000 from friends and family, only to close down the business two or three years later due to lack of sufficient funds.

As mentioned earlier, venture capital network events and conferences and other networking events are generally good uses of funds. And make sure to spend adequate amount of money when purchasing leads. But try to minimize the costs of "soft" legal, tax, and consulting business by offering company stock in exchange for cash. Make sure to save the money for the items which are absolutely necessary but non-negotiable in price such as company insurance, equipment and supplies, rent and utilities bills, directories of angel groups and VCs, and subscription costs for conferences. In keeping a check on the best use of funds, you should always ask yourself if the substitution of a product or service for a cheaper one would result in a minimal loss of benefit. Remember, *the number one reason why startups fail is because they run out of money.*

13. *Look Only For Smart Money.*

The importance of looking for the smart money was emphasized earlier in this chapter. Basically, *smart money has two characteristics; it is money that is well spent and it is spent well.* It is well-spent because the investors from which it comes have performed the proper due diligence to understand the companies they have invested, and therefore by investing in such companies they have provided some form of validation to the company. Such investors have tremendous experience in having seen thousands of deals and are very good at identifying the proper elements needed in a successful company. This well-spent money also has the potential to bring in more money from other sophisticated investors familiar with or who respect the commitment of these investors.

This money is also spent well because investors will scrutinize expenditures constantly in attempt to make certain each dollar is spent wisely. In addition, they will protect their investment to the fullest extent and maximize their return on investment through use of the appropriate contacts in their networks. Therefore ideally, *smart money has the elements of good human capital and attracts more money when needed.* Possible sources of such money can be VCs, angels, companies or even very wealthy business leaders.

14. *Do Not Exhaust Your Best Prospects Prematurely.*
In order to succeed in prospecting for the smart money, you need to understand the criteria and psychology of the most suitable prospective angels and venture capitalists, and understand where your company fits relative to their investment preferences. *The worst thing a company can do is approach a venture firm too early during its development.* Inevitably, if approached prematurely, venture capitalists will tend ignore the company at a later date when it may be worthy of investment. In order to fully understand whom to approach at what stage of development is an extremely difficult task, especially given the overly optimistic nature of entrepreneurs.

Finally, *do not "over shop" your deal.* By approaching too many venture firms prematurely, you will not only exhaust your possibilities, but you will also have flooded the deal into the VC community and they will have knowledge of the unsuccessful attempts to gain interest. Venture capitalists are no different than anyone else. They always watch what their colleagues are doing and while they do maintain an independent view of prospective investments, *a deal that has been over shopped will be poorly received due to the unanimous rejections by other VCs.*

15. *Form A Good Business Advisory Board.*
Even the novice learns that a good scientific board is a key element to the company's success from both a technology and fund raising standpoint. However, many startup companies tend to underemphasize or even ignore the importance of having a good business advisory board. There are three main types of boards that every startup company should have; a board of directors, a scientific advisory board, and a general advisory board, which for early stage companies should be called a business advisory board to emphasize

its intent and focus. Business advisory boards are especially critical for early stage companies because they can fill personnel gaps, provide tremendous business advisory assistance, and communicate the investment opportunity to their colleagues, such as other CPAs, attorneys, and financial professionals, who might be well connected with angels and venture firms.

Figure 3-2. Prospecting Rules to Remember

1. Maintain Prospecting Intelligence & Etiquette

2. Generate Leads from Leads

3. Get Connected

4. Focus Your Prospecting Efforts Towards Local VCs First

5. Make Friends With The Media

6. Always Have Two Business Plans

7. Know Your Prospects

8. Learn To Overcome Rejection

9. Have Your Business Plan Reviewed By at Least Two Outside Financial Professionals

10. Never Give Up

11. Assemble the Best Management Team Possible

12. Conserve Cash: Keep Your Expenses To a Minimum

13. Look Only For Smart Money

14. Do Not Exhaust Your Best Prospects Prematurely

15. Form A Good Business Advisory Board

C. Prospecting Angels and VCs

Prior to courting a specific venture capitalist make sure to do your homework. Many VCs do not appreciate inefficient use of their time by companies that do not bother to learn their firm's mission, investment structure, and funding preferences. As a part of the process of *venture capital due diligence*, the company should determine answers to the following questions:

- Do they have an *interest* in investing in your industry space?
- Do they have *experience* investing in your industry space?
- Do they have prior *success* investing in your industry space?
- Do they have relevant *industry contacts*?
- Do they currently have *investments* in your industry space?
  (If so then they are not likely to wish to add another company to their fund. In addition, your company might pose a dilemma for the venture if you are a competitor of their portfolio company).
- Do they have substantial *syndicate arrangements* with other venture firms for additional rounds of financing? If so do they usually serve as the lead investor or as follow-on?

Once you have engaged in discussions with a venture firm and there is a preliminary interest, you should find out the following information for consideration of a match:

- Does the venture firm like a very active management style or do they monitor and advise the management team?

- How compatible are the personalities of your company's management team with the venture firm?

- Does the venture firm have access to potential channels of distribution?

- How many IPOs has the venture firm completed?

It is imperative that you make sure you have completed the minimal tasks before targeting the best venture firms, as they rarely give a company another look if rejected in the past. If you still need further capital to complete essential tasks such as IP work, preliminary data testing, prototype design and construction, you might be better off to focus only on angel investors.

Hopefully prior to seeking financing for your venture, you will have made significant contacts with attorneys, CPAs and other sources of influence. These are the individuals who may be your best chance of introduction to venture capitalists. Some of the most prominent and successful VCs have stated that their best and often only deals they consider come from attorneys and CPAs. It's obvious that these individuals are amongst the first to see deals. Therefore, if they have a relationship with a VC they may have a good understanding of what type of deals the VC would be interested in. The key word here is relationship. This is precisely why you should have an experienced and connected attorney, financial professional, and/or CPA on your general or business advisory board.

There are also venture forums and which might enable you to speak with a VC one on one. If you choose this route you had better have your 30-second pitch down perfectly. Be concise, clear, and after your pitch, provide the VC with an executive summary and arrange for a follow-up call in a week. It would be difficult for the VC to turn you down and say, "No you cannot call me". The worst-case scenario is that they will not take the call. When you do make that call, ask him open-ended questions that allow him to voluntarily provide you with an initial assessment of your summary:

> *"Mr. Voltaire, this is Robert Wood Johnson, from Vibrant Technologies. We met at the Technology 2002 Forum where I gave you a copy of my executive summary. What are your initial impressions of our company?"*

Do not ask if he has read it nor ask if he is interested in your company since these are "Yes" or "No" questions that can easily make the phone call short and unrevealing. After he has commented on your company, thank him for his assessment and ask if he would be interested to see a business plan for further review. If he says "Yes", then ask him if he would like a condensed business plan or a detailed version. Although he will most likely request the condensed version, this lets him know that you have a more detailed business plan if his interest is further heightened. Then ask him what mode of delivery he prefers, hard copy via courier, fax, or email. If he tells you that his firm is not looking to invest in your type of company at this time, thank him nevertheless and let him know that you appreciate the opportunity to present your company proposal to his firm. Ask him if he has any suggestions to improve the attractiveness of your company's efforts. Finally, ask him if he could supply you with names of individuals who might he an interested in reviewing the summary.

D. Sources of Capital

I. Startup (Seed) Capital

As we have discussed, it is important for the startup company to form a comprehensive financial strategy based upon defensible financial projections, backed by solid market research, and tied to financing needs, with the understanding that several rounds of financing will be needed before a breakeven point will be reached. Prospective investors will scrutinize this information, noting the previous use of capital by the company. And companies that demonstrate poor financial judgment will be frowned upon by VCs. Therefore, since the first round of financing is the most dilutive to the current shareholders, one must begin from the onset to manage company expenses diligently because this will ultimately affect the company valuation. In short, *keep the company burn rate under control in order to maximize survival.*

Seed financing is the first of many rounds of financing a private company will need in order to secure the needed capital to assist in the initial stages of forming the company, and typically represents anywhere from $10,000 to $500,000. When conducting a prospecting campaign during the seed stage, top priority should be placed upon obtaining the financial commitment of experienced angels, since often *the individual providing the financing adds to the feasibility of obtaining future rounds of financing.* However, the sources one has for raising seed capital are numerous, ranging from family, friends, friends of family, friends of friends, angel investors, incubators, commercial banks, Federal grants, and occasionally venture firms.

Seed capital is needed to incorporate, file for patents, copyrights, trademarks, web hosting with email, office equipment such as a computer and associated software, printer, and office supplies, funds for prospecting materials, such as directories of angels and venture capitalists, and investor events, plus funds to account for travel expenses and phone bills. During the more mature seed stage, the company will need to demonstrate proof of concept or build and test an alpha prototype. Because this stage is the most risky, it is always the most difficult to secure financing, assuming sophisticated investors are sought. But fortunately for entrepreneurs, not all investors are sophisticated as they should be. However, this situation should never be exploited and each company must take the responsibility for assessing each investor's knowledge of the risks involved in private investments. Adequate education regarding the early stage investment process should be provided to these investors and the proper disclaimers and disclosures should be stated on the private placement memorandum.

Friends of Family (FOF)

This is usually the first source of funding for the entrepreneur. Perhaps the single most important aspect of the financing process in the seed stage is clearly and adequately explaining the entire venture process to these prospective investors. It is also important for them to understand the time involved with the return of their capital so that the lack of liquidity does not impose a financial hardship upon them. Finally, they should be aware that the *seed stage investment represents the riskiest stage of the venture investment process*, which in itself is very risky.

The problem most entrepreneurs have with full and adequate disclosure is that it may scare away less sophisticated investors. However, this is no excuse for withholding adequate information and risk disclosures. Educating these individuals is the best solution for ensuring that they are able to make a well-informed decision. Finally, prospecting to friends and family should be approached with caution, as it could potentially lead to problems with the interfamily relationships.

Personal Credit

Lines of credit established with your local financial institution can provide a source of seed capital or even short-term debt to pay bills in anticipation of receivables. In addition, entrepreneurs should not overlook a unique source of capital—credit cards. There have been many success stories of individuals who have used credit card debt to successfully finance the operations of their company until VC ready. The great thing about credit cards is that they are usually unsecured forms of debt and the financial institutions issuing them do not care how you plan to use them as long as you make your monthly payments on time. An individual with a good credit history can easily establish over $100,000 in credit by applying to several financial institutions.

The obvious drawbacks of credit card debt are that the interest rates are high, and they can increase if you are late on payment. However, during periods such as during the writing of this book, when short-term interest rates are at 40 year lows, one can easily receive 0% APR for one year and low fixed interest credit cards for balance transfer for the life of the loan. As a word of warning, keep in mind that unless you apply for credit cards in the name of the company using the company's tax ID, you will be personally liable for all charges. And even applying for credit in the name of the company will most likely not allow you to escape liability unless your company is the official account holder, which usually only occurs once it has established a positive credit and income history.

Angel Investors

As venture capitalists have sized down their number of investments in favor of taking a larger ownership in fewer companies with smaller risk, they have decreased their investment in seed stage companies. In large part, this abandonment has been replaced by angel investors, who have become more sophisticated and organized.

Angels realize that most VCs do not wish to involve themselves with seed stage companies since they represent the highest risk period of a company's lifetime. However, they also appreciate the tremendous opportunities, since all successful companies must begin at the seed stage. In essence, angels have their own market, seed and very early stage companies, devoid of significant VC involvement, and therefore their only competition is from other angel investors. Locating these individuals can be relatively easy if one learns how they hear about most deals---social events, technology associations and conferences, attorneys, and chance encounters. In addition, most large cities now have angel-sponsored groups that meet regularly and review company presentations. Finally, angel investors can be found by checking with trade journals, law firms, and angel network websites (also see chapter 4 for a more thorough discussion on angels and Appendix E-3 for a list of angel networks).

Business Accelerators/Incubators

Incubators are business assistance organizations that provide companies with enhanced access to resources in the form of low priced office space, assistance with business plan structuring, general mentoring, access to capital, and a network of individuals to further assist their needs. Sometimes, these entities will take an equity position in the company as well. However, many have very little if any direct investment money. Rather, they provide indirect access to capital due to their relationships with venture firms and angel investors. The main advantage of an incubator is that it should have a large and diverse network of external resources with which to supply its companies. And while many incubators can provide tremendous assistance for startup and early stage companies, each company should create a detailed evaluation and selection process to ensure the incubator is able to deliver the specific resources the company requires (also see chapter 4 for a discussion of incubators and Appendix E-1 and E-2 for selected incubators).

Commercial Banks

There are several banks that will loan companies money secured against assets, either personal or company. In fact, many banks have established departments to specifically address this need. And depending upon the current interest rate environment, one can usually secure excellent rates, such as prime plus 1-3%. In addition, approval time can be as fast as a few days. However, most seed stage companies rarely qualify for debt financing under these terms due to failure to meet the collateral requirements of lending institutions. Fortunately, some traditional lenders are becoming more open to consider off-balance sheet assets for debt financing for companies that have substantial intellectual property. One particular bank that has dedicated much of their resources towards early stage financing is Silicon Valley Bank, which has even formed an incubator that provides tremendous access to resources and investment capital.

State Assistance

Most states have programs to help commercialize technology in the form of tax credits, licensing arrangements, low cost facilities, and even incubator type facilities. Many of these are associated with state universities, which also house technology transfer departments for assisting with in-house technology. And while these resources are usually of benefit to entrepreneurs who have formed traditional businesses, they rarely have sufficient resources and expertise required to assist high-tech startups. However, more states are continuing to add premium services and alternative financing terms in order to attract high technology industries. The primary objective of these programs is local job creation. Therefore, as a requirement for funding, companies may need to reside in or relocate to the state providing the investment capital.

Federal Assistance

The Small Business Administration (SBA) is one of the most widely used organizations for virtually every type of small business. This government agency has a variety of loan programs for many situations, but in general they will loan up to 85% on loans of $150,000 and 75% on loans over that amount up to a maximum of $1,000,000. These loans are low interest (usually 1%-3% plus prime) and must be guaranteed by the recipient if they own over 20% of the business. Another drawback is that SBA loans *can take several months to be approved*. So if you have a need for a fast loan you might be consider approaching a professional who specializes in assisting companies with SBA loans sine there are some SBA programs with accelerated application and approval times.

Small Business Investment Companies (SBICs) are private companies regulated and licensed by the SBA. The beauty of this entity as a source of funding is that the government matches the private funding at a 2-1 or 3-1 ratio, so that an SBIC can leverage its assets up to 3 times its amount through the use of government funds. These loans arrange anywhere from $50,000 to

$500,000 and are associated with a broad range of repayment and qualification terms.

The Small Business Innovation Research (SBIR) Program is another Federal program that mandates a specific portion of R&D budgets to be used for small companies for R&D. The agencies included in this program are the NSF, NIH, NASA, and the Departments of Agriculture, Commerce, Defense, Education, and Transportation. The STTP is similar to the SBIR and includes the NIH, NASA, NSF and the Departments of Education and Defense.

Foundations

Foundations are often overlooked but can be quite generous in funding if you are engaged in a project that is specified for financing by the foundation. A web search will provide one with many foundation websites that will detail the purpose of the foundation, the projects funded and other relevant information.[2]

Placement Agents

Placement agents are best utilized for their experience in helping the company prepare its private placement memorandum and as a source of warm prospecting leads. Their main asset is their Rolodex and they usually serve to make formal introductions to prospective investors. Meanwhile, it is ultimately up to the company to close the deal. These individuals may work independently, for boutiques, or larger investment banks, and typically charge 5-9% (cash + stock) of capital raised, almost always on a best-efforts basis.

Placement agents vary in their experience, abilities, and fees. Therefore, if a company elects to employ their services, *I recommend choosing an individual who has a broad knowledge and experience base in the financial industry, such as a former stockbroker or investment banker.* However, be critical of the compensation schedule of these individuals. In general, those firms that charge large retainers and monthly fees should be avoided, as the best interests of your company may be put on the back burner. In addition, *try to find a qualified agent that is willing to accept equity in exchange for any retainer fees and then the standard payment of 6-9% upon successful closing.* As a final note, some agents ask for an *exclusivity clause*, whereby they are the only agent allowed to solicit the company. As well some agents may ask for a *rights of first refusal* clause in the placement contract, which provides them the option of leading subsequent rounds of financing. Careful consideration should be given to such requests prior to agreement due to their restrictive nature.

Venture Capitalists

Although most VCs tend to shy away from seed stage companies, some do invest in selectively screened companies if there is sufficient opportunity to justify the tremendous risk. In addition, other venture capital firms may make exceptions if special situations are exist. These special situations might include investing with an entrepreneur they have had prior success with and companies that have come highly recommended from other individuals they respect, such as finance professionals, consultants and attorneys. However, be prepared to give up 70-80% of the company when seeking venture capital funding during the seed stage.

II. Early Stage Capital

Companies considering themselves candidates for early stage financing should have all the initial administrative activities completed, the technology should be proven (proof of concept), the proper market research should have been performed, and a well focused business plan should include a strategic financial, marketing, and growth strategy, as well as the other essential elements of a successful business venture. Specifically, the company should have completed an α prototype and should be at least in the initial stages of testing the β prototype. Of course these developmental milestones will vary depending upon the type of company. For instance, a pharmaceutical or biotechnology company would need to have sufficient data to prove that its technology and or products are successful at treating an illness. Nevertheless, *the key distinction of an early stage company is that it has received some type of customer demand*, as evidenced by revenues or significant β testing, and therefore has achieved some critical level of market acceptance and needs further capital to build its sales and marketing team. However, the definition of "early stage" is the most variable of all stages and will depend upon both the company type and the investor.

Angels

In general, angels prefer to invest in the more primitive early stage company, due to minimal competition from VCs. However, before approaching these investors, it is best to have all the administrative tasks taken care of and at least be in the process of developing the alpha prototype. Nevertheless, in some cases, angels will recognize that a researcher has not had the time to take care of these details and may be instrumental in serving as an interim CEO.

Corporate Venture Capitalists

While corporate assistance is possible at this stage, it is not likely due to the lack of product development. But if a company seeks the assistance of a corporate sponsor, its products should be seen as having a strategic fit with the corporation's overall strategy. The early stage company should try to identify the needs of a prospective corporate investor and make the necessary product modifications so that the corporation takes notice. *Often, the corporation is first a customer prior to becoming a financial partner in an early stage company.*

Venture Capitalists

For venture firms, early stage usually means mid-late early stage. That is, the company is undergoing or has completed β testing, there is a demand for its products, and financing is needed for sales and marketing. Be wise with your time and prospect elsewhere until you have achieved the venture firm's definition of early stage status.

Commercial Banks

The likelihood of receiving financing from banks at this stage is about the same as in the seed stage since the collateral and income requirements have typically not been met, although as mentioned previously, there are a few exceptions.

State Funding

This stage may be the best time for consideration for state financing. However, as the company progresses, this source will be less effective due to the limited sophistication of state agencies. *As a requirement for funding, the company may have to remain within the geographical boundaries of the state for a certain period of time.* So make certain that you plan for the requirements imposed by these funding sources.

Federal Funding

New companies should always keep these funding sources in mind, especially if the company is high-tech. But the company may have to commit a portion of ownership to a "lame duck" shareholder or may be restricted on certain activities that could adversely affect its future business prospects. Therefore, one should be aware of any restrictions and consequences of the various federal funding agencies prior to committing to this source of financing.

Most of these funding sources will be focused on providing funding for researchers so you will be competing with the professional grant writing skills of university professors and corporate research departments. And if you have no experience writing these grants, look to your scientific advisory board for possible assistance. Finally, because these funding sources typically take a long time to transpire, companies should begin the application process far in advance of funding needs.

Placement Agents

Placement agents may be most effective during the early stage since they often have contacts with ultra-high net worth individuals, angels, and venture capitalists. In addition, small investment banks may be able to assist the company, depending upon the size of the financing proposal. If the capital sought is large enough, they can serve as excellent sources of contacts and even become direct investors, but they usually will not consider companies seeking less than $2 million. There are some groups that will work for a retainer/equity/fee arrangement in order to accommodate smaller clients.

Private Equity Firms

Private equity firms will have a variable degree of utility in providing financing to the early stage company but are generally only moderately useful. In addition, because most private equity firms are associated with large investment banks that rarely lead financings in early stage investments (unless introduced by syndicates or influential institutions), companies should search for boutiques and smaller regional firms for indications of interest.

III. Expansion & Late Stage Capital

Companies that are fortunate enough to have progressed to expansion and late stages will have completed the beta prototype and sufficient market validation and will have significant revenues demonstrating market penetration and at least a reasonable market share. Therefore, expansion/late stage companies will require adequate funds to expand their sales and distribution channels. Companies that have received previous venture financing will continue to get further financial assistance from the previous investors as long as all milestones have been achieved. Therefore, investors involved with previous rounds of financing will usually be more responsible for fund raising during this stage.

Commercial Banks

The best use of commercial banking finance at the expansion or late stage is for debt financings, either secured by the cash flows and assets of the company or by venture firms. Some banks may seek debt with an *equity kicker* (warrants) in order to participate in the upside appreciation potential of the company. Such an arrangement is especially common with mezzanine ("bridge") debt financing.

Private Equity Firms

For some industry types, the availability of private equity financing for expansion and late stage companies rivals that of venture capital, but the difficulty is locating the proper firm since they are not as accessible and do not make their presence as visible in the local community as venture firms. The reason for this low visibility is most likely due to internal sources of deal flow, which typically arise from corporate institutional clients and other financial institutions. And even when these firms have been identified, the entrepreneur needs to understand that many firms have specific preferences for financing, such as convertible debt and mezzanine debt with warrants. Finally, many of these firms are not as "hands-on" as venture firms and will therefore have more stringent investment requirements.

Corporate VCs

Corporate VCs are not likely to become involved in the financing of a company in the expansion stage, unless they have already established substantial relations earlier and have specific interest in the technology. By this stage, most successful companies have already found the necessary financial support from venture capitalists and corporate venture firms are either disinterested in entry due to the control by private VCs, or the private VCs do not allow corporate involvement for strategic reasons. However, there have been many exceptions to this general observation.

Venture Capitalists

Expansion capital represents the most attractive investment opportunity for many venture firms since companies in this stage will have established a solid customer base, making it easier to estimate the potential viability of the business. In contrast, the lead venture firm may not choose to lead the current expansion round, they may wish to sell their interest to other qualified investors, or they may continue to lead the financing and allow no other investors. Companies need to get to know their VCs well so they can anticipate these possibilities during the late stage.

In general, as the company progresses, more investors become involved because more money is needed to cover a shorter time span. Meanwhile, late stage companies often obtain funding from previous venture firms and their syndicates. Occasionally, companies that had been turned down earlier in their history may have blossomed late and could be ready for venture funds in the expansion stage but this is more of an exception than the rule.

State and Federal Funding

In general, the more advanced a company becomes in terms of its revenues, market share, etc., the less it should pursue government funding sources due to their lack of expertise. However, if the company is not growing fast enough for venture financing, government financing may be the best alternative.

Placement Agents

At this stage, unless the agent has direct contacts with investment banks and other institutions that run private equity funds, these professionals will generally not be very useful. If the offering is over $5 million, regional investment banks may be interested to assist the company in the fund-raising process. However, you should expect to pay a retainer fee of $10,000 to $50,000 (depending upon the amount of financing sought) in order to cover their expenses. Make sure that agents charging retainer fees are willing to provide your company with the needed attention.

Direct Public Offerings

A direct public offering involves the direct sale of shares of stock in a company to individual investors. While this strategy is rarely used, it typically seeks financing from existing customers for continued expansion. Therefore, in order for a direct offering to be viable, the company must already have a substantial client base that is overly enthusiastic with the company's products.

Table 3-1. Relative Ease of Financing Sources by Company Stage

	Startup (Seed) Capital	Early Stage Capital	Expansion & Late Stage Capital
FOF[a]	++	+	-
Personal Cash [b]	+++	+++	-
Personal Credit [c]	+++	++	+
Commercial Banks [d]	-	-/+	+++
State	-/+	+	++
Federal	+	+	+
Foundations	-/+	-/+	+
Angels	-/+	++	+
Incubators	-/+	-/+	-
Corporate VCs	-	++	+++
Private VCs	-	+++	+++
Private Equity Firms	-	+	+++

[a] Although it may seem like the ease of raising investment capital from FOF will increase as the stage progresses, this is usually not true for two reasons. First, the investors tend to underestimate hypothetical risk and focus on potential reward. Therefore, they will be most attracted to early stage investments that have seemingly unlimited upside. Second, as the company stage advances more sophisticated investors will not permit less sophisticated investors become involved unless they are syndicate members from previous transactions.

[b] This would depend upon the financial resources of the founder. For some companies that are able to generate large profits early in their life, excess capital can be diverted towards expansion.

[c] Personal credit becomes more difficult to obtain as more is needed during later stages, but this is offset by the increase in tangible assets and cash flows that can be used to obtain debt financings from commercial banks.

[d] Typically, financing from commercial banks in later stages is in the form of straight or convertible debt. The relative ease of capital during the expansion stage assumes positive net cash flows and other significant assets. However, by this stage, usually venture capital has already become involved and will therefore limit the extent of such financing.

E. Private Placement Memorandum

Overview

This document, commonly referred to as the PPM, serves as the offering prospectus for investment into the company and is used by prospective investors as a basis for evaluating the financial merits and risks of the proposed investment. While most companies use a PPM in the process of raising capital, many fail to use a properly structured PPM. In addition, a sizable percentage of companies are not fully aware of the requirements mandated by the SEC regarding the sales of securities, perhaps due to the lack of adequate publicity of these regulations. And even when these issues are discussed in texts geared towards entrepreneurs, this material is frequently presented in an abbreviated and confusing manner.

Regardless of the reason for noncompliance, failure to abide by these regulations could result in potentially disastrous results for the company. Accordingly, if a company does not register its securities with the SEC, structure a Reg D exemption offering appropriately, or comply with all pertinent blue-sky laws, investors may have the *right of rescission*, meaning that they can be entitled to receive their money back if the company fails. In addition, they could also be charged with violation of state and federal securities laws. And with the failure rate of startups so high, companies that do not comply with Reg D laws are essentially playing with a loaded gun.

The PPM should be carefully constructed with the assistance of an experienced attorney and financial professional. The attorney should be utilized to ensure that proper legal guidelines have been adhered to, while the financial professional should be used to maximize the appeal of the investment opportunity. *Statements of pertinent risk factors should always be included as a matter of proper disclosure* and can be an important element of defense against a potential shareholder lawsuit. In addition to a properly structured PPM, the company also needs to issue a *subscription agreement* prior to accepting the investment capital. This document lists the terms and conditions of the investment. For debt financings, a promissory note is also required that details the terms and conditions of the loan between the investor and company. The organization of the PPM should be as follows:

- <u>Cover page</u> specifying the type of financing, (equity or debt) total amount to be raised, amount of shares and price of each share in the offering.

- <u>Summary statement</u> describing the terms of the offering, the business, risk factors, antidilution protection, registration statements, control features, expenses of the transaction, and a summary of financial information.

- Relevant information about the company

- Planned use of proceeds

- Minimum investment amount (optional, see figure 3-3)

- Investment risks

- Financing terms (securities to be offered, preferences, voting rights, conversion privileges, and dividends)

- Discussion of management (curricula vitae of the directors and executive management along with their compensation)

Registrations Requirements and Exemptions

Because the SEC regulates the issuance of securities, all companies must register securities offerings prior to solicitation in accordance with the Securities and Exchange Commission Act of 1933, unless qualifying for an exemption from registration. However, since SEC registration of securities is time consuming and expensive, companies should first determine if they meet one of the exemption requirements, as specified by *Regulation D* of the Act of 1933. *Thus, a company can avoid the burden of securities registration with the SEC by structuring a PPM in accordance with the mandates of Regulation D of the Securities Act of 1933.*

Because the requirements for exemption from registration can be sometimes create ambiguity, the SEC and state securities commissions have clarified specific requirements for exemption, which are listed within Regulation D of this Act and are referred to as *" safe harbor"* exemptions.[3] If the company qualifies for this exemption, it must submit a *Form D SEC Filing* with the Securities and Exchange Commission in Washington, D.C. within 15 days after the first sale of securities so the SEC is aware of the company's intent to use the Reg D structure.[4]

In addition, the company will also need to comply with the *blue-sky laws* of its state. These laws provide the specific conditions by which securities may be offered for sale within the state. And similar to federal securities laws, companies must either register with the state's securities commission or else qualify for exemption. Fortunately, the requirements for state exemptions are often similar to those of the federal agency. Note however, that *the company must satisfy the blue-sky laws of the state of domicile, incorporation, and the blue-sky laws of the states where investors have legal residence.*

In addition, to fully comply with the rules and regulations set forth by the SEC, *companies should also make certain that the PPM provides full and adequate disclose of the nature of risks involved with the company including all detail needed to explain the nature of these risks.* Otherwise, this too could result in legal awards to the investors if the company does not perform as expected. Although many entrepreneurs find statements of risk factors as a deterrent for investment, all sophisticated investors are aware of the universal nature of risk disclosure and its customary inclusion in all well-written PPMs. Therefore, *companies should never worry that adequate disclosure will scare off sophisticated investors. Rather, they should be concerned that failure to identify such disclosures will provide investors with potential legal recourse.* A partial list of typical risk disclosures is presented in figure 3-3, while minimum recommendations for constructing the PPM are shown in figure 3-4.

Unfortunately, adherence to the state and federal securities laws does not absolutely guarantee that the company will avoid all securities violations because there are many other issues the company must safeguard against. Specifically, when investors are required to satisfy the definition of accredited investors (see appendix C-1 for a detailed definition), each prospective investor must provide the company with full documentation and proof of their financial resources and the company should conduct a thorough check on all financial information to ensure its accuracy. Appendix A-6 shows a sample investor questionnaire for prospective investors.

Figure 3-3. Minimum Risk Disclosures Recommended for Inclusion in a PPM

- The company is in the developmental stage and the technology has not been tested/only been tested on a limited level, no products have been made or sold.

- The technology is currently not legally protected by patents (if applicable).

- The success of the company is highly dependent upon the ability of the management team to execute the business plan and none of these individuals have experience/these individuals have limited experience running a company.

- There are competitors that may have resources and experience that exceed this company.

- This offering is only one of several that will be needed for the company to pursue profitable operations.

- These securities are considered illiquid and should only be purchased by those individuals who can tolerate a time horizon of several years.

- Substantial dilution of security valuation may be involved.

In addition, the company should obtain signed releases that verify the investors fully understand the risks of the investment and that they have discussed the proposal, including the risks and any restrictions with a qualified attorney. Finally, because securities sold through a private placement cannot be transferred to other parties, companies should obtain a signed statement verifying that the investor does not plan to resell or redistribute the securities to another party and the stock certificate should be specifically made out to the investor, with a statement that it is non-transferable (known as legend stock). If these securities are resold without this legend notification, the company may be considered to have engaged in a public offering, without compliance of the proper registration requirements.

In conclusion, when companies engage in the solicitation and sales of a private placement of its securities, the management must take these activities extremely serious and understand that they are fully responsible for ensuring these securities have been sold in accordance with the state and federal securities laws. Otherwise, very serious consequences beyond financial damages could result.

Figure 3-4. Minimum Guidelines for the Construction of a PPM

- The PPM should mirror the information in the business plan to ensure consistency and minimize confusion.

- All risk factors should be clearly stated to minimize potential liability from shareholder lawsuits

- Each PPM should be numbered with a handwritten code in order to document the number of copies distributed. A record book should be kept indicating the distribution of each PPM, the date of distribution, and the party delivered to.

- A clear statement of all risk factors thought to be of substantive relevance.

- The date of the PPM should be current and updated as changes occur.

- Disclosures should be clearly stated with reference to the prohibition of reproduction and distribution of the PPM, dissemination of any materials contained within the PPM, each investor should consult their attorney and CPA to help assess the merits of the opportunity, and the offering has not been registered under the '33 Act and the SEC has not approved it.

- All disclosures regarding transactions between the issuer and insiders, such as leasing arrangements, should be disclosed clearly.

- The PPM should not state specific minimum and maximum investment amounts. This may restrict the ability to raise capital and will create inconvenience or even disagreement from previous investors when the company tries to obtain signed authorizations to change these limits.

F. Investor Presentations

As mentioned previously, attendance at investor presentations such as angel and venture conferences may be one of the best ways to get significant face time with prospective investors. Typically, you might pay anywhere from $200-$2000 for the right to present your company to a group of investors, many of which are angels and VCs. *In this type of structured presentation format, it is even more important that your presentation be polished, since there is no relationship-building opportunity in the limited time provided.* Typically, each company will have 10-15 minutes to present information on its business, followed by a Q & A session lasting 5-10 minutes. Figure 3-5 lists the ten key topics that should be addressed during the presentation. You should plan spend roughly one minute on each topic.

Figure 3-5. Topics to Cover during an Investor Presentation

- Company vision and mission
- What the company does
- What needs it addresses
- Define the market size, growth, and market share
- Who the competitors are and why your company is better
- What makes the company unique
- How you plan to acquire and retain customers
- Why your management team is qualified
- Exit strategy
- How much money you need, over what period and for what reasons

Your strategy should be to create a strong level of interest by clearly and briefly stating your company mission, products, markets, customer need, competition, basic financial projections, amount of financing, use of proceeds, and exit strategy. You will also need to demonstrate that your company is unique and well positioned to succeed due to its proprietary technology and strength of management. Remember; *do not loose the attention span of the audience with too many details.* Many companies wrongly assume that the presentation is the most important part of the selling process so they provide the audience with confusing details about how the technology works, which often causes them to loose interest early on.   In contrast, the presenter should try to gain increasing momentum throughout the presentation so that the audience is buzzing with questions.   Understand that the primary goal of an effective presentation is to generate an indication of interest from potential investors, *saving the details for the question and answers session, which is when your real chance to sell your company begins.*

Therefore, *the presenter should prepare sufficiently for the Q & A session, as it is really the most opportune time for potential investors to better understand what your company does and why it is such a compelling investment.*   You will need to work with all members of the management and advisory board to anticipate questions prior to the presentation and make certain to have extra slides prepared to use when addressing anticipated questions.   *Focus on a bottom-line presentation and let the Q&A session dictate the detail of your overall sales pitch.*   A few guidelines are presented below to assist in providing effective presentations.

- **Keep it short.**   You should be able to go through the presentation in 10 minutes even if you are provided with 20.   The main purpose is to generate interest so that questions are raised.   Answering all potential questions during a presentation will tend to bore the audience.

- **Do not give all of the information out.**   This is related to generating questions for the investors. Being able to anticipate possible questions is relatively easy if you have structured your presentation with this consideration.   The ability to handle questions from investors forms a positive impression for you and your company.

- **Keep the overheads basic** and do not clutter with too much print, multiple colors (maximum of two colors), or detailed figures.

- **Practice the presentation** many times in front of many different people, focusing on eye contact and enthusiasm.

- **Videotape yourself** and review to see how you look and sound.   You may be very surprised.

- **Learn from the mistakes of others**. Attend investor presentations and critique them.

- **Be passionate and confident, yet professional and polished.**

Notes

[1] Richards, S. 2002. *Inside Business Incubators and Corporate Ventures.* New York: John Wiley & Sons.

[2] www.foundations.org
www.fndcenter.org/funders/grantmaker/gws_priv/priv1.html

[3] *Company employees who have been convicted of a felony or who have undergone administrative proceedings relevant to the sale of securities must be disclosed in the offering.* In addition, if such individuals are involved with the issuer, the exemption from registration with SEC may not be allowable.

[4] The SEC has attempted to clarify the exemptions from Section 4(2) of the Act of 1933, and these are known as Rule 504, 505, and 506 exemptions of Regulation D. In addition, these "safe harbor" exemptions also include the federal intrastate exemption and the Regulation A exemption. Each of these exemption qualifications specifies securities offerings with different characteristics, such as differing requirements for disclosure, number of investors, and investor sophistication. In assessing whether a company qualifies for the Reg. D exemption, Rule 502 must be met.

In brief, **Rule 504** exemption allows financing sales up to $1 million, with no restrictions on the number of investors or their level of sophistication, and no requirement for issuance of a PPM to prospective investors. **Rule 505** allows up to a $5 million offering, has no limit on the number of accredited investors, but limits the number of non-accredited investors to 35 (see appendix C-1 for the definition of an accredited investor). Finally, **Rule 506** has no limitation on the dollar size of the offering, and also has no limit on the number of accredited investors, but limits the number of non-accredited investors to 35.

Both Rule 505 and 506 require issuance of a PPM to non-accredited investors. However, a PPM should always be provided to all investors since all securities offerings are subject to general anti-fraud provisions of federal securities laws (SEC Rule 10b-5), requiring all "material" information to be provided to investors and that there should be no misstatement of facts or omission of "material" facts necessary for investors to make prudent decisions as to the nature and extent of risk involved. **Note that securities sold through any of these three exemptions are considered restricted and generally cannot be resold. In addition, general solicitation and advertising for prospective investors is prohibited subject to certain conditions.**

The federal **intrastate exemption** is used for companies agreeing to restrict the sales and solicitation of securities within its state of domicile.

Finally, **Regulation A** exemption allows a maximum sale of $5 million of securities and if the total amount of financing sought is $100,000 or more, the company must provide an offering circular containing two years of financial statements to prospective investors. Similar to the case of a public offering circular used for an initial public offering, the Reg. A exemptions requires that the SEC reviews this circular prior to solicitation to prospective investors. The advantages of this type of exemption are that there is no limitation to the number of investors and no there are no special investor qualification requirements. Because a Regulation A exemption is considered a **public offering**, they are not restricted and thus can be resold without restriction (subject to federal security law anti-fraud provisions). This exemption is rarely used due to the expense and time involved in preparing the circular and waiting for the review by the SEC. However, it may provide an alternative means to secure funding if less than $100,00 is needed.

This material is not meant to provide a complete description the restrictions and definitions for each type of exemption and the author highly recommends the reader carefully read and understand the following securities regulations, followed by consultation with an experienced securities law attorney prior to making final decisions on the methods of solicitation and sales of securities.

1933 Act §§4(2) and 5	**SEC Rule 701**
SEC Rule 144	**SEC Reg. D**
1934 Act §10(b)	**1933 Act §3(a)(11)**
SEC Rule 10b-5	**SEC Rule 147**

4

Investor Profiles:
Angels, VCs & Incubators

"Luck is the residue of design."
Branch Rickey

A. Introduction

When constructing a business model, the management team first conducts a market segmentation analysis to identify the best-suited customer base. Likewise, when a company seeks financing it should conduct an *investor segmentation analysis* to identify the current trends in the venture capital industry and understand the different investment preferences and motivations of each firm. If performed with accuracy, the company will be able to screen out those investors that are poor matches and identify the best prospective investors, enabling it to devote more time towards customizing its sales pitch to match the needs of these selected investors. For example, some investors only deal with late stage companies while others only deal with early stage. Some investors have geographical limitations, while others do not. Furthermore, some prefer to be the exclusive investor in a particular round of financing, while others like syndications. In contrast, some investors will only take a minority role as a part of a larger syndicate.

Typically, venture firms search for companies with great management teams that work together well and are easy to get along with. In addition, the company must also have a sustainable competitive advantage, fast growth potential and rapidly growing or large market potential, and a feasible exit strategy. While most venture firms prefer to invest in late-early stage and expansion companies, a small minority prefer to take a large ownership position in startups. Nevertheless, regardless of the stage of involvement, venture firms almost always provide priceless advice and support to the management team by refining and redefining strategies, assisting with staffing needs, and strengthening strategic alliances, thereby promoting overall business and operational efficiency and increasing the chances of future success.

Venture capitalists are rather difficult to categorize on an individual level unless you know them personally or know someone who does. Hence the best thing you can do is familiarize yourself with the philosophy of the firm, their investment preferences, previous successes and failures, management styles, syndicates, alliances, etc. Corporate venture capitalists are very different from private venture firms in a variety of aspects. Rather than focusing on an exit strategy and emphasizing management teams, corporate VCs are more concerned with the value of the technology and its long-term integration and compatibility of the venture with their overall corporate strategy, which as we will see later, can be either a good or bad consequence for the early stage company's long-term success. And while it may be somewhat easier to develop an understanding of their investment preferences, it is often much more difficult to predict their ultimate level of commitment to their portfolio companies since many factors external to the corporate venture group can influence these decisions.

Angel investors are even more difficult to profile and come in all shapes and sizes. However, it is perhaps due to their more focused involvement in the very early stage, as well as their direct source of capital that allows us to better categorize them. *Because they are unique among early stage investors in that they are investing their own money, it is often easier to identify their preferences and motivations.* These individuals account for as much if not more private venture funding than venture capitalists, and should never be discounted as a potential source of significant funding. In general, angels serve an important role early on in the development of the management team by providing a sounding board and source of external advice. Table 4-1 compares the investment involvement of angels versus venture firms.

Regardless of the source of funds, once the company has received the interest from a prospective investor, the management must identify all potential motives of the investor and construct a scenario analysis that will help identify any possible difficulties. Only after such a consideration should serious negotiations commence. For instance, the corporate venture capitalist is primarily interested in forming strategic investments, which can be beneficial to the company since they will not feel the need to produce quick returns, unlike the situation with private venture capitalists. On the other hand, the corporation may alter its strategic direction and decide to abandon all current and future investment in the company. And because it will not want its competitors to access the technology, it will exercise its ownership power to prevent any acquisition attempts by these competitors. Hence, companies funded primarily by corporate venture groups face the possibility of being "run into the ground."

In contrast, private VCs are exclusively motivated by financial reward and will attempt to salvage a lingering company as long as it appears viable. However, they may scrap a struggling venture prematurely in order to minimize financial loss if their overall portfolio has not performed well or if other portfolio companies are more promising. Because most high tech companies will ultimately seek venture funding, this chapter will focus on providing considerations important for understanding the psychology of venture capital firms and builds on the material presented in chapter 2. Finally, it will conclude with a discussion of incubators and hopes to provide methods to examine and select the most appropriate incubation entity if this route is chosen.

Table 4-1. Comparison of Angel and Venture Capital Financing Sources

Angel Investors	Venture Capitalists
• 250,000 Angels invest annually[a]	• 500 Professional venture capital firms
• $20-30 billion	• $35 billion
• 400,000- 500,000 Companies trying to raise capital	• $11.4 billion total investment
• $3.5-4.0 billion: Seed, R&D, and startups	• $1.1 billion: 300 Early-stage investments
• 30,000-40,000 Early-stage transactions	• $7 billion: 1,089 Information tech firms[b]
• 90% of transactions less than $1 million	• $2.6 billion: 426 Healthcare firms
• Mean investment $30,000 to $50,000	• $4 million mean investment ($3M to $7M)
• Mean investment share, 1st round 20%	• $15.2 million median valuation
	• 41% average equity share

[a]Although this number represents the annual number of angels who have invested in any given year, the total pool of angel investors is thought to be approximately 2,000,000.

[b]Software, networking, communications, and electronics.

Source: Benjamin and Margulis, "Angel Financing"

B. Deal Flow

Professional investors must have a continuous supply of prospective financing deals in order to make the best investment decisions, and venture investors refer to their relative abundance and quality of investment proposals as deal flow. *Deal flow* is what drives the private equity and venture capital industries by providing ample channels of lucrative investment opportunity. And achieving sufficient portfolio diversification relies on having access to an adequate supply of quality financing proposals or deals.   However, *each venture firm has preferred routes of establishing quality deal flow.* Similar to all other service industries, *the venture capital industry is relationship driven and relies heavily on establishing key relationships with other venture firms, intermediaries, and the community.*   These are the networks that often account for a large contribution to their deal flow.

Some venture firms prefer to maintain close relationships with local research institutions and cultivate new technologies from developments within.   In contrast, others rely on their syndicate relationships to provide the majority of deal flow. In addition many firms rely heavily on new deals from service providers such as attorneys, financial professionals, and incubators. Finally, some venture capitalists use less direct avenues of accessing deals, such as investor conferences, but this is more the exception than the rule. But regardless of their primary method of deal flow selection, *the invariable characteristic of all venture capital firms is that they actively seek deals based upon their industry knowledge and abilities to leverage their resources.* Therefore in part, the manner by which each firm chooses to establish its method of deal creation will depend upon the individual talents and contacts with each firm.

When deal flow is adequate, a venture firm may receive anywhere from 1000 to 3000 business plans each year depending upon its size and visibility. But almost all of these companies will not qualify for a complete due diligence screen due to one or more of the reasons listed in figures 4-1 and 4-2.   In fact, the great majority of business proposals will be rejected upon initial review of the executive summary (first cut) by the prospective investors for one or more reasons (figure 4-1).   The remaining pool of business plans may be referred to as *prequalified plans* and these will receive a *peripheral due diligence* screen, which may vary from reading the complete business plan, to conducting preliminary market research.   Some of the reasons prequalified plans will not pass the next screen (second cut) are listed in figure 4-2.   However, those plans that make it through the second cut may be considered *qualified plans* and will receive a low level of *core due diligence.* Finally, those proposals that make it through the third cut will move on to be reviewed by an *intense due diligence* process and it is from this group that the final investments decisions will be made. It should be noted that material in figures 4-1 and 4-2 has been provided as general guidelines and the reasons for each "cut" will be highly variable and will depend upon the firm in question.

Figure 4-1. The Most Common Reasons for Financing Rejections: The First Cut

- The investment is outside the scope of the firm's investment expertise
- The firm already has a similar investment
- The market is not large enough or growing fast enough
- The executive summary gained no interest by investors (poorly written)
- Company is too early stage for the firm
- The company does not need enough money
- Value proposition is not convincing
- The ROI is not sufficient
- The industry is currently "dry" for that type of technology

Figure 4-2.   The Most Common Reasons for Financing Rejections: The Second & Third Cut

- Business model is flawed
- The technology does not have a sustainable competitive advantage
- Regulatory approval is imminent
- Company has not achieved the necessary critical mass of milestones
- Growth rate is not sustainable due to lack of sufficient market growth
- The economics do not make sense
- The burn rate is too high
- The management team is inexperienced
- The technology has too many questionable IP issues

Reasons for being cut during this final stage are not as easy to identify but will depend in large part upon the specifics of the venture firm as well as the proposed investment. However, some of the more common reasons may involve final valuation negotiations and the investors' perception of the ability of the management team to adapt and endure throughout difficult periods. Occasionally, negative information about one of the founders may surface, such as a criminal history, and could cause the firm to reject the investment. A schematic illustrating the venture capital screening process is presented in figure 4-3. A more detailed description of venture capital due diligence topics can be found in Appendix C-3.

Figure 4-3. The Generic Deal Flow Screening Process

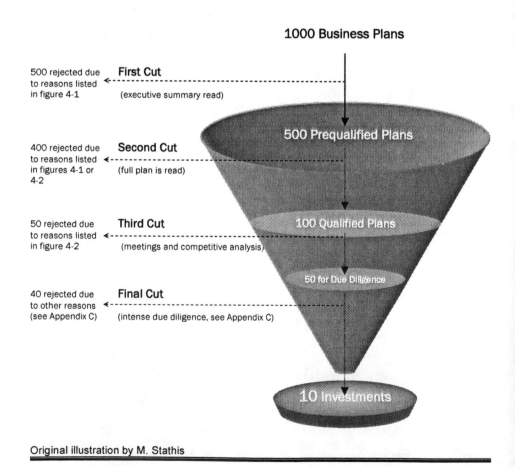

1000 Business Plans

500 rejected due to reasons listed in figure 4-1 — **First Cut** (executive summary read)

500 Prequalified Plans

400 rejected due to reasons listed in figures 4-1 or 4-2 — **Second Cut** (full plan is read)

100 Qualified Plans

50 rejected due to reasons listed in figure 4-2 — **Third Cut** (meetings and competitive analysis)

50 for Due Diligence

40 rejected due to other reasons (see Appendix C) — **Final Cut** (intense due diligence, see Appendix C)

10 Investments

Original illustration by M. Stathis

Angel Networks

These are organized groups of angel investors that meet regularly to collectively review investment proposals. Many are small local groups in larger cities while others are very large and represent very prominent sources of human and financial resources, such as those found in California and Boston. Organized angel groups such as *The Angel's Forum*, *Angel's Network*, *Band of Angels* and others can be a particularly useful source of both financing and guidance. These groups come together to share their industry expertise with companies and have become dominant forces in regions such as Silicon Valley (see Appendix E-3).

A more recent trend has been with the formation of online networks that connect individual angels with specific companies. In this case, the website provider is independent from both parties and serves as an intermediary or broker for company or the investors. An example of a very successful online angel network is NVST (www.nvst.com). Others have noticed the success of this model and are adding these services to their already established resources such a vfinance (www.vfinance.com). Depending on the particular network, compensation may be through subscriber fees from the investors or companies, and a percentage of the closing finance arrangement or a combination of these.

Venture Capital Networks

These organizations hold conferences throughout the world and are organized by geography or industry. The general purpose of these events is to provide a platform for early stage companies to solicit their investment proposal to venture firms and angels, but they also provide education in legal, business, tax, investment, and other areas. One disadvantage to prospective investors is that these networks tend to offer deals that are not fresh, unless they are larger regional or national events that draw a wider geographical audience. The compensation of these organizations is usually in the form of presentation fees by companies, sponsors, and other participants and presenting companies should expect to pay $500-$2000.

Venture capitalists like to participate in these events as one way of keeping open relations with the entrepreneurial community, as some conferences can attract up to 3000 attendees. However, the company should be selective on both the timing and nature of the events. Because companies may be exposed to several hundred attendees, the worst thing would be for a company would be to exhaust its only chance for investment at a time when it is not ready for venture financing. At the very least, *companies should utilize these events to network, make soft introductions to investors and learn from the mistakes of presenting companies.* Very rarely have I seen companies do this, but it is time well spent. Always follow the money, even if you are not in the position to ask for it at that time. Follow it and watch what kinds of companies and management teams its exposed to and interested in. This may be one of the best ways to compile a psychological profile of specific venture firms (see Appendix E-3 for lists of these organizations).

C. Angels

Responsible for approximately $20 billion of private company financing annually in the United States over the past few years, this large group of approximately 250,000 investors does what most venture capitalists will not; they invest in startup companies. In order to formally be classified as an angel investor however, one must satisfy the definition of an accredited investor, set forth by current U.S. securities laws. As such, any individual who has a net worth of at least $1,000,000 or who has an annual income of at least $200,000 ($300,000 combined for couples) over the past two years with the expectation of earning at least that amount over the next year is considered an *accredited investor* by the SEC. An expanded definition may be found in Appendix C-1.

Historical Background

The relative decline in early stage venture investing over the past two decades is a consequence of the venture capital industry shifting from early to later stage investments. However, this has opened the door for more angel financing, as can be seen from the table 4-2. Note that since the mid-1970s, percentage venture capital investing by stage has essentially reversed from a previous emphasis in early to late stage investments. The reasons for this shift are unknown for certain but the less institutionalized nature of venture capital firms three decades ago relative to their current structure has most likely played a significant role in this change in investment behavior.

As discussed in chapter 2, during the 1970s venture capital firms received the majority of their investment capital from high net worth individuals. And only after the modification of the prudent man rule in 1979 did this trend begin to change. As more institutional capital was allocated to venture firms, the industry began to experience a gradual reallocation of capital to late stage companies, perhaps to comply with ERISA guidelines of investment risk and suitability. And although ERISA does not govern the venture capital industry per say, it serves as the regulatory agency of pension funds by establishing guidelines for risk and suitability. As another consequence of increasing levels of institutional investment, venture funds gradually became larger or these firms had more funds resulting in the need for larger deployments of capital. And because manpower became the limiting factor in venture investing, venture capitalists began to invest larger amounts of money in fewer deals, resulting in more late stage deals being funded with larger amounts of capital from any one firm.

Table 4-2. Venture Capital Investing by Percentage (1975-1989)

Year	1975	1976	1977	1978	1979	1980	1981	1982	1983	1984	1985	1986	1987	1988	1989
Early Stage	69.2	92.9	85.7	63.3	70.6	66.7	52.3	59.5	54.9	55.3	47.7	43.1	39.7	40.0	34.5
Late Stage	30.8	7.1	14.3	36.7	29.4	33.3	47.7	40.5	45.1	44.7	52.3	56.9	60.3	60.0	65.5

Source: Gompers and Lerner

The Angel Profile

The vast majority of angels (90%) are male, age 40-60 with advanced degrees, average income range $100,000-250,000, preferred investment horizon of 5-7 years, and invest $25,000-50,000 per deal with a total commitment of $130,000. Typically, they look for startup or early stage companies that can provide a 20% ROI annually. And they usually find out about prospective investments from friends, family, colleagues, or referrals from their CPA or attorney (figure 4-4). While their due diligence is not as sophisticated as that of venture firms, *they tend to invest in industries they understand or companies that are near their residence.* The great thing about these individuals is that they have a high propensity to refer these deals to other angels they know, sometimes forming *angel syndicates.* As early stage investors, they will usually share a portion of common stock similar to the founder and management team and will therefore be subject to certain rights, as provided by the Articles of Incorporation. However, the increasing trend is for angels to receive preferred stock, although it lacks many of the stipulations found in the preferred stock issued to venture capitalists.

Figure 4-4. How Angels Find Their Deals

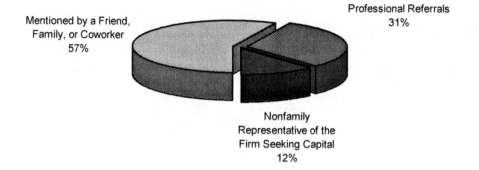

Mentioned by a Friend,
Family, or Coworker
57%

Professional Referrals
31%

Nonfamily
Representative of the
Firm Seeking Capital
12%

Source: Benjamin and Margulis, "Angel Financing"

Angels are usually the first major investors of most deals and are often individuals who were successful entrepreneurs or CEOs with industry knowledge and networks.   These investors seek financial reward but also have the desire to help other entrepreneurs succeed. A distinctive characteristic of angels is *that they usually develop an emotional attachment to the business venture*.   In contrast, VCs only have financial reward as their only incentive and therefore minimize emotional attachment.   This difference stems from their direct source of funds, while as we have discussed, VCs have a fiduciary responsibility to their limited partners.

In addition to having some type of industry knowledge, angel investors are generalists in their business skills and experience. And because they tend to invest in only one or two deals at a time, they are able to provide more nurturing than VCs. Some angels prefer to act as sources of internal due diligence in assessing the decisions and activities of the management, while others may seek to provide a stronger leadership or interim CEO role. This variance usually depends upon the experience level of the angel, as well as his level of investment. Whatever the case, it can be safely stated that the absolute intent of angels' level of involvement is highly correlated with the what they perceive to be the best interests of the company because they are investing their own money. However, good intentions do not always provide good results and one should not assume that VCs have one-sided intentions (or that such intentions, if present will not produce the best results for the company). What may appear to be one-sided from the somewhat limited perspective of an inexperienced management team may very well be in the absolute best interests of the company.

Many of the reasons why angels will reject an investment proposal are similar to VCs: valuation, low growth potential, inexperienced management, and uncertainty about the entrepreneur. However, *they tend to emphasize the technological potentials of the business over the strength of management team.* And once they invest in a company they are usually more patient because they are only held to the scrutiny of their own ROI, unlike venture capitalists. While some angels still accept common stock, most experienced angels will require a convertible preferred issue that will be converted to common stock on a 1:1 basis upon venture financing, sale of the company, or IPO. This stock will have a liquidation preference over the common stock of the founders and the cash dividends will not be paid but will accrue and be converted into an equivalent amount of common stock upon conversion.

In closing, note that there are many accredited investors who claim to be experienced angel investors but most of these individuals are only qualified to be passive investors. Many angels may have profited from the boom of the 1990s and have yet to prove themselves under more realistic times. *Therefore, companies must learn to recognize passive angel investors versus active hands-on angels and make certain that the more active angels know what they are doing.* When prospecting to angels, the best advice is to try and get financing from an angel network that has adequate access to capital and industry expertise. It is a difficult task to look a gift horse in the mouth, but an early investor even with a large investment can potentially hinder future financing rounds.

D. Private Venture Capitalists

Venture capital firms, both private and corporate are very different in terms of their goals, management styles, and levels of financial commitment, resulting in different advantages and disadvantages for a given company. Hence, understanding the mission of each venture firm can assist the company in identifying those firms that offer the most attractive opportunities and the least amount of risk. *Just as venture firms view each company relative to its potential opportunities and associated levels of hypothetical risk, companies must also view venture firms in a similar manner.* This topic is briefly presented here but addressed in more detail in chapter 11.

As discussed in chapter 2, private venture capital firms are usually structured as partnerships, whereby the investors are the limited partners while the venture firms serve as the general partners. These firms mainly invest the capital from public and private pension plans, endowment funds, and financial institutions. And in order to adhere to the objectives of their investors, venture funds are structured with specific investment horizons and levels of risk tolerance based upon the investment objectives of these limited partners. As an added incentive, venture capitalists receive personal ownership in the companies they have chosen to fund (usually 1-2%) so that it really is in their absolute best interest to at least devise a successful exit strategy. *But sometimes, what may be considered a successful exit strategy by the venture firm could prove to yield disastrous results for the company's long-term success.*

There really is no typical makeup of a venture capitalist as they come from variable backgrounds ranging from research scientist, MBA, CEO, attorney, physician, engineer, news writer; you name it. However, the current trend appears to be recruitment of individuals with technology expertise and substantial operational experience at large high tech companies. And although difficult to categorize any particular venture capital firm, one can usually develop a better understanding about their investment philosophy by looking at its list of investors, partners, and results from past investments, while trying to spot behavioral trends. For instance, an *investor segmentation analysis* might begin by looking at whether the majority of a firm's investment capital came from private versus public pension plans versus corporations, whether there is a consistent corporate relationship, whether the firm has other partners it typically works with in syndicate or other capacities, its track record of IPOs and acquisitions, final payout to founders and management after exit, and a host of other factors.

Think like a VC

The best way to position your company with adequate venture financing is to try and think like a venture capitalist, and make any needed changes in order to improve the investment merits of your company. In general, venture capital investment strategies are ultimately dictated by three factors:

- investment objectives of its financial backers **(monetary factors)**

- quality of the company and health of the economy **(performance factors)**

- ability of Wall Street to obtain institutional demand for its underwriting offerings **(exit factors)**.

These three facets are interdependent and will determine the amount and direction of investment capital in private companies. Accordingly, if one understands these elements, an insightful perspective may be formed regarding the psychology of venture capital investment strategy and direction, which can be used as a framework when structuring the company strategy. And this of course can be very useful when prospecting these firms.

Monetary Factors

We have discussed monetary factors at length in chapter two and the reader should understand by now that much of the driving force fueling venture capital investment decisions relates to the investment objectives of their limited partners. Whether the limited partners are corporations or pension plans, and whether the venture firm is private or corporate can determine the timing and mode of exit.

Performance Factors

Private venture capitalists typically look for companies that have a good chance to achieve at least $50-$100 million in revenues within five years. The reason for this requirement is twofold. First, certain minimal sales revenues must be generated by the time the venture firm wishes to exit in order to provide a potentially attractive IRR for the venture firm. Second, yearly revenues can be used as a rough guideline to estimate either a buyout price or a pre-IPO valuation, which along with IPO demand, will determine the post-IPO trading price and therefore the market capitalization of the company. It follows that *without a certain minimal market capitalization, such as $200 to $300 million (depending upon the market conditions), an IPO will be unlikely due to minimum requirements by the underwriting investment* *banking firms* (issues underlying IPOs are discussed at length in chapter 9). Therefore, without this revenue potential, venture firms may turn down the best management team and even the most revolutionary technology in favor of companies that meet these more objective criteria. However, revenue figures are not enough, as they will also look at many other factors such as the size and growth rate of the market, the competitive advantage, previous use of proceeds, the intended use of the current financing, and the burn rate of the company. And the venture firm will view each of these factors with respect to how it will impact their IRR.

Once a company has passed preliminary requirements for market size, revenue growth, and IRR for the venture capitalist, the management team will be scrutinized through an intensive due diligence process that will seek to understand how the company intends to execute its business plan and achieve these revenues. While angel investors serve as guides and devils advocates throughout the pre-venture capital investment period, venture capitalists normally seek a substantial amount of control with respect to ownership and decision-making authority, rather than day-to-day management guidance. And unless the management team has developed a minimal level of competency, VCs would rather replace the entire team with more experienced individuals so that business risk will be minimized.

Table 4-4 shows the typical required return on investment by venture firms for each stage of a company. These results will vary depending upon the industry, economy, and company-specific risk factors. Note that the health of the economy going forward will be a determinant of the amount of risk the venture firm may be willing to take. For example, certain industries will fare better during economic contractions. Meanwhile, emerging markets are more likely to stall during such conditions and may limit the opportunities for investment. Rather than changing the intended makeup of the fund, the venture firm may elect to wait longer and proceed more cautiously prior to closing the fund. In addition, *when investments are associated with more risk, rather than not investing at all, many venture firms will factor in this increased risk by slashing the valuations of companies as a requirement for investment.* Therefore, companies need to have an appreciation for general economic influences on venture capital investment risk and the resulting decreases in valuations. Otherwise, they may never come to an agreement of the financial terms and conditions with VCs.

With rare exception, venture firms view *the quality and adaptability of the management team as the single most important factor in determining the attractiveness of a company for investment purposes.* In order to receive a serious consideration by venture firms, the company needs to demonstrate managerial excellence and maturity. And while they expect company management teams to make mistakes, venture firms will be more forgiving as long as the management becomes better skilled at predicting and implementing new strategies that enable them to better anticipate and react to future challenges.

Much like venture capitalist due diligence, a company must establish mechanisms for self-assessment which go beyond measuring the bottom-line. For instance, it is much easier to give your company an "A" for the quarter because it met its sales goals, but how do you assess the performance of the company if the sales goals have not been met? Is it the fault of the sales force? The marketing plan? Or perhaps the goals were just too optimistic to start with. How does a company learn to micromanage all the day-to-day tasks so that the next two quarters are in line with projections? These are extremely difficult matters to handle but they are just some of the skills venture capitalists will expect from the management team prior to investing in the company.

Table 4-4. The Required ROI of VCs by Stage of Company

Company Stage	Size of Investment	Desired Return	Liquidity (years)	Compounded Annual ROI	Est. Net Annual ROI*
Seed/Startup	$500k-2M	10X	5	58%	40%
		7X	5	47%	32%
First & Second Stage	$2-10 M	7X	3	91%	75%
		5X	5	38%	26%
		4X	4	41%	32%
		3X	5	25%	17%
		3X	4	32%	25%
Third Stage & Mezzanine	$10-20M	5X	3	71%	59%
		3X	3	44%	34%
		2X	2	25%	22%

* The net annual return on investment (ROI) has been calculated by subtracting typical operating costs from the annual ROI.

Exit Factors

In researching potential VC candidates, a review of their previous modes of exit might assist the entrepreneur in determining a matching strategy for the company. However, as we all know, past performance is no indicator of future behavior. Many venture firms have a strong dependency upon Wall Street banks to provide their channels of exit because quite simply, that is where their resources and expertise lie. Accordingly, venture capitalists engage in business negotiations with investment bankers when seeking an IPO. And this is the most preferred choice of exit since the remaining alternatives will in most cases lower their IRR. However, if the current economic conditions are not ripe for IPOs, acquisitions, strategic alliances, and other business transactions will be the prevailing form of exit for VCs. And many times Wall Street banks are also involved in these alternative transactions.

However, bankers merely provide the access to exit while the limited partners (pension funds, endowments, etc.) mandate the exit preference based upon the their acceptance of the covenants of the venture capital limited partnership agreement. Therefore, companies should consider the affects of any financial difficulties pension plans might have upon pension investment criteria. If pension funds decrease the amount of capital invested in the venture capital industry or if they become more risk averse, many venture firms will have to take a more conservative approach when considering additions of portfolio companies to their funds. As well, this same mentality extends to the route of exit. During economic contractions, some pension funds may seek more conservative returns and will therefore settle for alternative exit strategies. And this range of exit possibilities will result in both financial and strategic differences for the company and management. Therefore, companies must consider all conditions that will influence the venture firm's choice in determination of the exit and note the impact each of these exit possibilities will have on the company.

Profiling Guidelines

Regarding the psychology of successful venture capital fund raising, there are three general rules a company should follow in order to maximize its chances for receiving VC money.

Know Your VCs. Throughout this chapter we have highlighted the importance of this point many times. Know if they prefer early stage or late stage investments, funding minimums, maximums, and whether they lead deals or participate in follow on deals? Do they form syndicates? Who are their main limited partners? What is their ability to attract other venture firms? Do they have geographical limitations? Look at their current portfolio companies and determine if they already have a company in your space. If so, they will tend not want another unless that industry is currently a *hot issue* and will therefore be easier to provide an exit at high valuations. As well, if they already have a company in your space, do not overlook the possibility of forming a collaborative arrangement with this company. Also, understanding and preparing for the process of venture capital due diligence will position your company as a better candidate for venture funding. An overview of this process was provided at the beginning of this chapter, however extensive coverage of the due diligence process is presented in Appendix C-3. Finally, make sure to get references from current and previous companies financed by the venture capitalists prior to agreeing to a term sheet. Often, companies can discover how easy a venture firm is to work with and how company-friendly they are when things get rough.

Understand the Current VC Investment Climate and Industry Trends. Is the economy in a contraction or expansion? How will this affect your business? How much will your industry be affected by extremes in inflation? Is your industry currently "hot" or has it "cooled off" in the IPO market? This will affect not only the valuation of your company but also the financial marketing strategies.

Know Where Your Company Fits into the Above. It is human nature for early stage company management teams to be overly optimistic. It is that level of optimism that keeps them energetic and repels thoughts of doubt during those days of endless rejections. However, to be too optimistic can be fatal if not channeled appropriately. Realize from the perspective of a VC where your company stands and use this insight to your advantage. Management teams should exhibit confidence but not arrogance and they should appreciate the viewpoints and perspectives that VCs may offer, despite their disagreements. Finally, always remember that, if you ever reach a point when you think you have accounted for all possibilities and know everything it takes to form a successful company, you need to slap yourself and wake up. Otherwise, you are bound to fail.

In conclusion, the most effective way to get venture capital is by understanding your prospects. Knowing their company preferences, investment goals, and challenges will help management teams position their company in more favorable terms with venture firms. Rarely do venture capitalists have the time or patience to nurture an inexperienced and naïve management team from the onset of a company's formation. Angel investors are not only more willing to do this, but they are usually better suited for this role. In this way, a company is forced to work through the inevitable unplanned difficulties that will be encountered and may benefit from the less pressured assistance by angel investors. Throughout this development process, management can revise and refine its micromanagement strategies and develop a better understanding how they will respond and adapt to meet new challenges. Only after having demonstrated significant results can the human capital offered by venture firms benefit the company. Without this course of progression, the management team will have a smaller chance of achieving the level of autonomy needed to grow along with the company.

New Versus Established VCs

It may seem obvious to conclude that investment by an older and well-recognized venture capitalist would lead to the best chances of success, but this is not necessarily the case. Gompers and Lerner describe the *"grandstanding hypothesis"* to explain the relationship between the amount and ease of investment capital raised by venture firms with the number of IPOs they have completed historically. Specifically, this hypothesis states that the amount of capital a venture firm should be able to raise will be proportional to the number of IPOs it has completed. And the ability of new VC firms to raise money will be sensitive to the number of IPOs it completes relative to established VC funds. A further probe into the grandstanding hypothesis asserts that *the reputation of a venture capital firm can be so strong that it attracts the interest of many other established VCs.* This reputation extends beyond their historical success and can also include significant relationships with prominent investment banks. In contrast, newer VC firms lack an industry-wide reputation, and therefore the benefits that come with this (leading syndications, investment bank support, and loyal investors).

Several studies have shown that the newer VC firms sit on a company's board of directors an average time of 25 months, versus 39 months for more established VCs. Likewise, the average age of an IPO company backed by a new VC is 56 months versus 80 months for established VC firms.[1] *These results imply that newer VCs tend to rush companies to an IPO in order to demonstrate success in the process of building a good reputation.* Accordingly, newer VCs are eager to establish a good reputation within the investment community so they can build more leverage in raising capital for future funds and be viewed as a significant part of the VC network. During the process, it is thought that perhaps these *newer VCs are willing to sacrifice IPO pricing in order to hasten the process*, since the number of IPOs completed is thought to be the most significant determinant of the ability of a newer VC firm to raise capital.

Interestingly, newer VC firms tend to begin raising money for the next fund at a later point than more established funds even though they have induced IPOs earlier. This implies the need for these newer VCs to raise money perhaps selecting the period during its IPOs in order to attract investors. Meanwhile, more *established VCs have many historical accounts of successful IPOs and tend to prefer exercising more caution when taking a company public.* Since they tend to have long-standing committed capital from institutional investors, there are under no pressure to generate fast IPOs so they can "recycle" investor money. Whether or not this is a good or bad for a company is up for debate. Although one should not rely upon these generalizations to guide their choice of venture capitalists, table 4-5 illustrates some considerations of new versus established venture capitalists. It follows that, in an attempt to establish themselves as a part of the more recognized venture capital network, *newer venture firms tend to be more aggressive and have fewer resources. However, companies can use these disadvantages for their benefit when negotiating financial terms.*

Table 4-5. A Comparison of Established versus New Venture Capitalists

	Advantages	Disadvantages
Established VCs	Reputation and credibility	Low bargaining power
	Lower underpricing	
	Good syndicate potential	
	Larger IPO offering size	
	Greater ability to attract high quality underwriters	
New VCs	Desire to build a reputation	Limited funds
	More assistance	Higher bargaining power
	Faster IPOs	Limited syndication ability
		Higher underpricing in IPOs

E. Corporate Venture Groups

The human and structural capital provided by corporate venture arms to their investment companies is usually of tremendous benefit, as the parent company can provide multiple distribution channels, co-marketing agreements, and other benefits difficult to find with other investors. However, intellectual property protection could pose difficulties depending upon the strategic interests of the corporation. Therefore, prior to agreeing to any financing terms, *a company must ensure that it is satisfied with any rights agreements of the assignment of current and future intellectual property.*

In addition, companies should pay close attention to the terms of financing arrangements with these groups because the financial condition of the corporation or its strategic focus should change, resulting in the abandonment of the investment by the venture arm. It is not uncommon for venture arms of very well known corporations to be eliminated under severe economic conditions, only to be revitalized several years later when conditions have improved. As well, if liquidation and redemption clauses are not structured properly, the venture group could claim company assets, further paralyzing its future. It is therefore important to do some research on prospective corporate venture groups to determine how long they have been in operation and the success rate of their ventures. Companies may also attempt to contact current clients of the venture arm and inquire about issues of control and commitment.

Beware of corporate venture groups that obligate you to sign first rights of refusal. This may prevent you from obtaining further outside financing or inhibit a purchasing acquisition by their competitor. And if the corporate strategy changes they may pull out and leave the company hanging. Economic downturns also affect corporate ventures when stock prices are low and justification of funds for these projects is scrutinized by top management of the parent company. *Similar to joint venturing and strategic alliances, corporate venture arms must have the committed support and lines of communication with top management in order to develop a successful venturing business that is able to withstand the effects of diminished corporate earnings and shareholder scrutiny.* And companies should try to negotiate clauses that specify terms for additional capital and buyouts by other companies. Since they will have the controlling interest, such clauses will need to be specified in the voting agreement.

Prior to initiating negotiations with a corporate venture group, the company should determine the type of business model by which the group operates. There are four basic models for corporate VC funds:

- Those that *spin out technologies* (Xerox, Bell Labs)
- Those that *spin in technologies* (Panasonic/ PDCC, Panasonic Digital Concepts Center, Cisco)
- Those that *integrate technologies* (Sony)
- Those that do *all of the above* depending upon the business unit (Microsoft, GE, JNJ)

Within each of these general structures there are hundreds of business models that depend upon the resources, strategy, and culture of the corporation. Developing an understanding of the particular business model of the prospective investor will enable the company to better determine if the goals and capabilities of this firm are compatible with that of the company.

The history of corporate venture capital performance has been well documented by many (see Gompers and Lerner, *The Venture Capital Cycle*). And there have been many explanations for the previous failures of corporate venture capital programs, but the two most significant appear to be related to the inadequacy of corporate strategy and commitment by the corporation's upper management. Quite simply, many corporations have not been clear about their objectives for such a program and often confused emerging technologies with strategic fit. In addition, the inability of upper management to fully understand their significance and commit to these projects resulted in shutting down these ventures prematurely. However, there have been many examples of successful corporate venture capital programs. In fact, *corporate venture programs have been shown to be at least as successful as private venture firms when the investments have a strategic fit with the company's overall strategy.*

Finally, there are some observations that should be mentioned regarding corporate venture backed companies. First, they are much more likely to go public and are less likely to be liquidated. This is especially true if there is a strategic fit between the company and the sponsoring organization. However, *corporate venture funds typical pay more for their investments in comparison to private venture firm when both have invested in the same company.* As a consequence, this can result in a diminished pre-money valuation for further rounds of financing by raising the bar for company performance. Furthermore, if the over funded company fails to achieve its milestones, these results will be even more damaging (valuation issues are discussed in detail in chapter 11). In addition, corporate venture arms tend to make about 3-4 investments every two years while private venture firms make about 43 investments over a seven-year period. However, this should not be interpreted as more contact with the venture arm since they tend to have a much smaller staff. Table 4-6 summarizes some of the characteristics of angels, private and corporate venture firms.

Table 4-6.   Investing Characteristics of Angels and Venture Capitalists

	Angels	Private VCs	Corporate VCs
Lead Startups	Frequently	Rarely	Almost Never
Timing & Buzz	Med Importance	Very Important	Rarely Important
Syndication	Sometimes	Usually	Rarely
Due Diligence	Low-Medium	Very Intense	Very Intense
Main Goal	Success	Financial	Strategic
Industry Knowledge	General-Specific	Mod-Highly Specific	Highly Specific

F. Incubators & Accelerators

Historical Background

An estimated 80% of all new businesses fail within the first five years in the U.S according to the National Business Incubation Association (NBIA). And it is argued by many that incubators are important because they stack the odds of success in favor of new businesses and therefore help stimulate local economic development, creating new jobs and wealth.   They also serve to fill the *venture capital gap* that exists for seed and early stage companies lacking the adequate skills, managerial experience, and resources. Successful incubators also help entrepreneurs bridge the gap between creative technologies and the innovation/commercialization process.   And they are able to accomplish these activities by their broad offering of facilities, internal support, and access to external support and capital.   Thus, it can be said that *the most ideal incubators provide assess to a vast array of physical and human resources that would be very difficult to access otherwise.*

Incubators have been in existence for over two decades, initially beginning as government-sponsored projects headed by the SBA in 1984 to rejuvenate economically depressed areas. Today this same general model is still in existence, however several hundreds of other models have been formed that focus on technology startups. Most of these newer models are aimed at the goals of corporate and private venture capital as opposed to the SBA.

The early success of incubators such as CMGI and idealabs! in the 1990s served to validate the place of technology-centric incubators, which led to the explosive growth of these entities during this period (figure 4-5). As startup companies began to receive funding with sometimes nothing more than an idea and a rough business plan, the promise of an unprecedented high tech revolution created the opportunity for many more incubators to open shop. However, some incubators merely provided executive suite facilities at a discount rate without adequate managerial and capital resources. And most were able to sustain themselves due to the ease of obtaining venture capital financing during the "Internet Boom". However, the realism of what a value-added incubator should be was tested when the Internet bubble deflated and now many of these incubators have either changed their models or have shutdown.

Figure 4-5. Factors Responsible for the Rapid Growth of Incubators

- The early success of incubators such as CMGI, Internet Capital Group, and ideaLab!

- The proliferation of a tremendous number of innovative high-tech startup companies whose founders had very little business experience and an immediate need for mentors, resources, and networks of service providers.

- The need for fast responding Internet companies that could be first to market.

- The economic and financial boom, which poured billions into the private and public markets, thereby increasing the reward for success.

- The excitement generated by the financial industry for entrepreneurs that would be creating a "New Economy".

In 1987, there were an estimated 70 incubators in North America. As of 2003, it has been estimated that there are over 950. However, the peak number of incubators was most likely reached in the year 2000, during the end of the economic boom of the 1990s. And unlike the venture capital industry, a large number of incubators eventually shutdown and the name "incubator" left a bad taste in the mouth of many. And now this industry is fraught with much question as to whether it will serve as a permanent place in the startup process. I think it should be clear that incubators will survive and continue to provide value to startup and early stage companies. The real question is which business models will remain viable (see Appendix E-1 and E-2 for state incubator associations and select incubators).

Incubators

Although many incubators have different goals, *the one common goal (at least in theory) of all incubators is to assist in the successful development of its resident companies so that they graduate and become financially and managerially independent.* According to statistics in a 2002 report from the National Business Incubation Association (NBIA), over 84% of companies graduating from incubators remain in the same geographical area upon graduation and between 80-90% are still in business several years after graduation. However, the percentage of companies that graduate is thought to be very low and the extent of the success of these companies has not been provided.

Incubators and accelerators are structured as for profit or nonprofit companies and many generalizations hold for the majority of these firms, depending upon how they are structured. But before discussing the primary distinctions between for profit and nonprofit incubators, let us first examine what an incubator is and what it is not. Theoretically, an incubator is an entity that provides a host of valuable resources for early stage companies. These resources can be in the form of discounted office or lab space, business services, mentoring, strategic introductions, and access to financing. Some incubators have funds for making small investments in companies, while most require an equity stake and charge fees for services in exchange for sponsoring a company. Others may provide premium rental space and provide services for free. These incubators may also require a 1-3% fee of any financing but several arrangements are encountered depending upon its business model and the source of funding. The compensation structure is highly dependent upon both the source of funding for the incubator as well as its incorporation status.

Prior to signing on with an incubator, companies should make sure they understand the criteria for staying with an incubator, the mission of the incubator, available resources, and knowledge of the main financial backers.

Typically, *most successful incubators have a limitation on the amount of time a company can stay under their roof*, with 2-3 years being the average. By then, it is thought that the company should have obtained adequate financing and/or have outgrown its space so that it requires a separate facility. Otherwise, these companies will be thought of as the *walking dead*. Such companies may pose negative affects on the overall moral of the incubator's other companies and when spotted, they are usually asked to leave.

There is often a link between the incubator's mission and its primary financial contributors, depending upon the type of incubator under question. Within the category of non-profit incubators are business development centers or business incubators that are not necessarily technology based but rather focused on stimulating job growth in the area they serve. In addition, other non-profit incubators may be housed in university centers and other entities funded by government money such as economic development centers. Because these entities typically only generate 25% to 35% of operating costs from their companies, they are primarily supported by state and local governments, universities, corporations, and venture firms. And in exchange for funding, these entities expect the mission of the incubator to reflect their needs.

Similar to any company, the largest investors in the incubator hold seats on the board and vote on major decisions in order to preserve their needs. For instance, a non-profit incubator funded primarily by a local government may have job creation as its primary goal, which could require graduating companies to remain in the immediate area for a certain number of years in exchange for use of facilities at either a deeply discounted rate or for a capital infusion. [2]   Finally, there are some non-profit incubators that are more technology based and are sponsored by corporations and private venture capital firms who also expect their needs to be served by the incubator. *Therefore, it is critical to identify the primary investors of the incubator's source of funds because these entities will dictate the ultimate priorities of the incubator.*

For-profit incubators are almost exclusively focused on high technology incubation and derive their financial support from paying members, private investment, or venture capital funding. And *because they are usually not connected with local funding there is no requirement that its graduate companies remain in the region.* In contrast, incubators funded internally or by venture capital money are more concerned about profits, which may or may not be beneficial for the company. The common consensus has it that the nonprofit incubators will definitely survive while only the most successful for-profit incubators will succeed. But this notion is not based upon the differences in the value add, but rather on the source of funding.

Accelerators

Accelerators are also known as *catalysts* and *venture labs*. The difference between an incubator and an accelerator is easily blurred and oftentimes completely indistinguishable other than by its self-proclaimed designation. In fact, due to the failures of the post-bubble economy, many of these firms would rather avoid the use of the designation "incubator" because of the stigma attached. Thus many of these firms have opted to call themselves accelerators, although many are really incubators in terms of their business models and resources.

If there is any distinction at all, one might generalize that *accelerators tend to house companies for a shorter period of time and take on companies with developed technologies.* The premise of such accelerators is that the guts of the company have been formed and there is a need for technology refocus or management strategy. The most experienced and successful accelerators tend to have more specific skill sets and closer contacts with venture capital firms (which does not necessarily imply they are better at assisting the company in obtaining financing). While some charge fees for services, others prefer to provide minimal financing and business services in exchange for a large equity stake. Some accelerators are independently funded but many are funded by venture capital firms. As with the case with incubators, it really depends upon the accelerator under consideration.

Figure 4-6. Characteristics of Successful Incubators and Accelerators

- They are selective in choosing their companies

- They have a wide range of networks that provide access to capital

- They provide access to facilities and other resources, such as strategic partnerships, suppliers, distributors, consultants, attorneys, and interim personnel to fill gaps in management

- They hold their companies to milestones

- The create synergy within the confines of the environment and diminish the loneliness experienced by the entrepreneur

An improperly sponsored company in an accelerator may benefit more through placement in an incubator if its stage of development is not compatible with the focus and resource capacity of the accelerator. The opposite of course holds true as well. And while most accelerators often host later stage early investments, there are some accelerators with business models that focus on early stage companies, and should be considered incubators. Thus when trying to determine whether a firm is an incubator or an accelerator, one should try to identify whether the mission of the firm is truly acceleration rather than incubation. *Regardless of the designation, the company should be comfortable in the overall value offered by the firm.* After all, in the end you are what you do and how you behave.

Due Diligence

The first step in conducting due diligence on an incubator or accelerator is to *determine the mission of the organization.* This will help identify whether both the company and the incubator/accelerator have the same goals. Like any successful business, incubators and accelerators must have a clearly defined mission that provides direction for the organization and allows candidates to assess whether there is a good mutual fit. And without a clear understanding of its mission, a company will not be able to determine if the incubator or accelerator can meet its needs. *Some incubators are confused about what services they specialize in, and others are disillusioned about what they think they can provide.* Thus the company must filter through the claims versus the reality of the services the incubator provides. The next step is to *determine the capital structure of the incubator* because it will determine the motives and resources of the managers, which may be aligned or misaligned with the company's goals.

Ideally, the best incubator candidates will have adequate access to corporate resources, law firms, business experts, access to venture and angel financing, mentoring programs, and a good track record. Such incubators should have external personnel that are sometimes willing to provide assistance for free, discount or in exchange for equity, and managers of the incubator or their contacts should be ready to assist with advisory board positions and interim management roles if needed. In addition, the advisory board of the incubator should consist of individuals that are experienced in a variety of issues commonly encountered by early stage companies. Finally, *incubators should provide a pleasant atmosphere.* Rather than attractive décor, they should provide a good chemistry for free exchange amongst the other entrepreneurs so that the loneliness factor, common to many entrepreneurs is minimized.

Without proper caution, selection of the wrong incubator could lead to disaster. Non-profit incubators may be staffed with under qualified individuals who are paid by entities, such as local and state governments that do not have the expertise required to monitor the organization. Meanwhile, for-profit incubators that are inadequately funded may feel pressured to generate the majority of their revenues from companies by providing their services for a premium fee, while disguising this business model by providing discounted rent. In addition, *companies should generally be careful when dealing with incubators that they do not shut themselves out to other resources and individuals who are not in the incubator's network* since these networks are usually established through financial contributions to the incubator. Although rarely does this occur, sometimes incubators take the mentality that the companies they sponsor are in fact "their companies" and are overly protective of their interest to the extent that may actually hurt the companies by limiting other sources of assistance. And on occasion, an incubator may wish to keep the needs of the companies it sponsors serviced from within its walls in order to generate more fees. The other word of warning is to *avoid incubators that require a large stake in your company* because it will diminish the bargaining power for financing.

Remember that *just because individuals have established an incubator that does not necessarily mean that these individuals are qualified to run them.* It may be relatively easy to obtain sponsorship funds for an incubator from unsophisticated sources such as local governments or soft dollars from corporations. However, despite the cautions one should take when searching for an incubator/accelerator, there are dozens of high quality facilities that have helped companies obtain financing and guidance. The unfortunate reality is that a company has to be located in the general proximity of the incubator in order to benefit from its resources. And this can present difficulties for those companies located in smaller towns where incubators may be absent or poorly represented. Figures 4-7 and 4-8 contain some questions to ask when interviewing incubators.

Figure 4-7. Initial Questions for Incubator Interviews

- Are you a nonprofit or for profit company?
- What is the source of your funding?
- What is your source of compensation?
- What kind of companies do you look for?
- What value can you add to my company?
- What is your track record and can I see evidence of this?
- What is the graduation rate of your previous companies?
- What is the incubator's graduation policy and how flexible is it?
- Describe your network of outside professionals?
- What is the business experience of the individuals at the incubator?
- What is the vision and mission of the incubator?
- What is the compensation structure of the incubator?
- Are they rewarded based upon the successes they generate?
- Do they have programs in place for introductions to service providers, angels and VCs?
- Can you interview resident companies at your own discretion?

Figure 4-8. Guidelines for Selecting Incubators

- **Selectivity** (How selective are they?
  - How much due diligence do they perform?
  - Are they emphasizing a need to fill occupancy over providing value to the company?
- Extensive **networks** in the community (legal, consulting, and strategic partners)
- Access to **capital** (do they have significant contacts with VCs and angels and do they have platforms of introduction? Verify these relationships)
- **Technology** expertise
- Business **experience**
- Access to structural **resources** (office, lab facilities, T-1 lines)
- Great **chemistry** within the incubator and the host companies
- **Mentoring**

Notes

[1] Data was taken from a study conducted by Barry, Muscarella, Peavy, and Vetsuypens (1990) and consists of 433 venture-backed IPOs taken public between January 1, 1978 and December 31, 1987. New venture capital firms are defined as those less then six years in existence, while established firms are six years or older. The results of these conclusions were borrowed from Gompers and Lerner, The Venture Capital Cycle.

[2] Note that many universities have facilities that may be thought of as incubators, but I would reserve that designation only for universities such as M.I.T., Stanford, Harvard, University of Texas, and a few others. These universities have the sufficient critical mass of resources and experience spinning out successful companies that would qualify for high quality incubation. Many of the other university facilities, while having tremendous technology transfer and licensing departments, lack the adequate business skills, industry contacts, and venture capital ties. The same applies to economic development centers and state assistance organizations, which are more geared to assist the non-high tech entrepreneur in the more basic tasks involved with starting a business.

Part II

Building
The Company

5

Intangible Assets: Intellectual Capital & Intellectual Property*

"Everything that can be invented has been invented."

Charles H. Duell, Commissioner, U.S. Office of Patents, 1899

A. Intangible Assets

For many high-technology companies the largest component of financial value is derived from their intangible assets, defined as those non-physical benefits contributing to future cash flows. These assets include inventions, trade names, customer lists, marketing strategies, production standards, and other proprietary intelligence that is instrumental to the development and delivery of a company's products and services. And despite the challenge management teams face when attempting to represent these assets on the company's balance sheet, (in accordance with the FASB rules and regulations) investors nevertheless appear to recognize and sometimes exaggerate the value of these assets, as judged by the exuberant prices paid for the common stock of many public high-technology companies.[1]

When properly identified, intangible assets are usually protected by different methods afforded by intellectual property law, expressed as patents, copyrights, trademarks, service marks, and trade secrets. It is absolutely critical to companies identify all intangible assets and take the proper measures to secure their legal protection from competitive forces. This is important not only to secure the company's competitive position, but also to assist in the valuation process when negotiating financing with investors.

For some assets, trade secret protection may provide better security than patents, while for others a combination of methods is the best alternative. Therefore, inventors must not only be familiar with each of these methods of legal protection, but they must also develop a detailed business strategy that will guide the ultimate mode of protection and utilization of these assets.

The recent upward trend by investors in acknowledgement of significance of intangible assets may be seen by examining a broad index of publicly traded companies.   According to recent studies, 75% of the assets held by Standard & Poor 500 companies are intangible, where this number was only about 40% a decade earlier.   Most publicly traded companies have identified, protected, and positioned their most valuable sources of intangible assets, such as AOL's subscriber base, Dell's supply chain management system, General Electric's, Microsoft's, Johnson & Johnson's, and Proctor & Gamble's brand names, trade secrets, copyrights, and patents. As well, they have developed the proper infrastructure to allow efficient means of communication of other intangible assets that are more difficult to express and protect by intellectual property laws.   And optimal strategic positioning of these assets have enabled these companies to command higher price-to-earnings ratios (and therefore higher valuations) than their peers, perhaps due to the market's expectation of their full utility.   The same situation applies to private companies as well and perhaps even more so.

Thus, it is essential that companies understand and quantify the approximate value of their intangible assets at all stages of growth so they can divert the necessary human and financial capital towards executing their business strategy and achieve more leverage when negotiating loans, venture financing, and when claiming damages during infringement defense.   While valuation of intangible assets can be somewhat challenging for an early stage company with little or no revenues attributable to these assets, the task becomes relatively easier when such assets begin to generate revenues.

The genesis of all intangible assets within a company arises from its *intellectual capital*, which may be defined as a knowledge-based asset that can be converted into value some measure of value.   Meanwhile, *intellectual property* is the systematic expression of intellectual capital into a form that is protected by legal means.   In effort to better identify and characterize a company's intangible assets, we can divide them into three subclasses (figure 5-1).   *Operating intangibles* are associated with all systems, processes and activities a company has that will enable it to continue normal function and income generation without significant interruption after a change in ownership.   *Production intangibles* are intellectual capital assets resulting from the production design expertise of the company.   Finally, *marketing intangibles* include factors that help a company sell its products and services. While procedures to protect and value some of these intangible assets are more straightforward, (as given by intellectual property guidelines) others are not so clear and therefore should be safeguarded by internal mechanisms to protect the competitive positioning of the company.

This chapter will discuss the hierarchy of intangible asset creation and protection for the purpose of assisting the early stage company in designing effective approaches to harness the maximum value from its intangible assets. And if performed with diligent execution, the strategic positioning of these assets will align companies with a formidable arsenal when approaching investors and market competitors.

Figure 5-1. Classification of Intangible Assets

Categories of Intangible Assets	Examples
A. Operating Intangibles	Trained workforce Administrative systems Corporate culture Distribution channels Corporate practices and procedures
B. Product Intangibles	Patents Technological know-how Production standards Copyrights Software Favorable leases and licenses
C. Marketing Intangibles	Customer lists and relationships Pricing lists and pricing strategies Marketing strategies, studies, concepts Advertising & promotional materials Trademarks and service marks Trade names Noncompetition covenants Franchises

Modified from Source: DePamphilis, D.

B. Intellectual Capital

Intellectual capital is a broad term thought to encompass all knowledge, information, and processes that can be converted into some measure of value, typically expressed as a profitable transaction, financial or strategic. *For many knowledge-based companies, it is their most valuable intangible asset*, as its transformation into intellectual property leads to direct revenue generation and competitive positioning. In addition, the evolution of intellectual capital or intellectual property is often used as leverage for joint ventures, strategic alliances, and provides further opportunities for licensing arrangements. It follows that for publicly traded companies, many people hold the view that a relatively accurately financial measure of its intellectual capital may be estimated by noting the difference between its market and book values.

Intellectual capital can be thought to consist of two main components: human capital and intellectual assets. One of the main challenges of a company is to transform its human capital into intellectual assets so they can be codified and protected by legal means. Once this has been accomplished this intellectual capital is becomes *intellectual property* (IP) and signifies legal protection of ideas, inventions, information, and know-how (figure 5-2). *Consequently, intellectual property is distinguished in that is the only type of asset that provides value and potential investment returns for the company, as well as protection against competition, and therefore should be carefully safeguarded.* However, the selection of the type of IP protection can sometimes be difficult and will depend upon a variety of factors.

Human capital can be defined as the collective experience, skills, and know-how of employees that may be used to solve problems and create solutions, thereby adding value to the company. While critical to the daily operations of a company, *human capital is difficult to express in a written form and therefore cannot be claimed as part of company assets.* In essence, human capital is "what enters and leaves the company facilities each day" and remains within the minds of the employees. *For large companies with many employees, the task of human capital management is critical to maximizing and protecting their intellectual resources.* Employees in these companies need to know what information is important, where to find it, and how it is important to the company's overall internal and competitive strategies. Meanwhile, dissemination of this information must be restricted in order to secure its unauthorized use. Therefore, effective *communication mechanisms must be established in conjunction with specific security protocols in order to prevent intellectual compartmentalization while increasing access to human capital by all employees.*

In contrast, *intellectual assets* are tangible descriptions of knowledge that are codifiable and have been written down in some form allowing protection through intellectual property structuring.   However, even before becoming formal intellectual property, these assets can be protected by provisions of U.S. trade secrets law if the proper measures are taken to secure their secrecy, as required by trade secret law.   Unlike human capital, intellectual assets are owned by the company because these assets can be expressed in a written form and therefore protected by NDAs and trade secret procedures.   Thus, *the ultimate challenge of management teams is to convert all of its human capital into intellectual assets so that the full value of its intellectual capital may be realized and converted into a form that may be legally retained by the company.*

Finally, the transformation of intellectual capital into a legally protected and fully commericalizable product would be difficult without the use of *structural capital*.   These assets are important because they enable human capital to transform its intellectual capacity into intellectual assets.   And while structural capital is not a specific component of intellectual capital, it serves as a provisionary necessity to assist in its formation.   Thus, structural capital is the component owned by the company that provides the needed environment for the transformation of these assets into a form that is protected by law.   The tangible or physical components of structural capital include the

Figure 5-2. Relationships Among Elements of Intellectual Capital

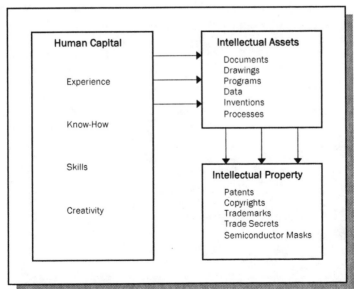

Source: Parr, R.L., Sullivan, P.H.

office surroundings that facilitate a creative and productive flow of intellectual capacity, such as well-designed offices, information libraries and databases, adequate computing power, and ample space for brainstorming meetings. Meanwhile, the intangible components of intellectual capital might include the company's culture, its values, mission, overall objectives, and relationships with customers and suppliers. Together, these tangible and intangible assets can be thought of as a complementary component of human capital, to the extent they assist in its transformation into effective commercialization of intellectual capital.

Codified versus Tacit Knowledge

Intellectual capital comes in two forms. First there is *codified knowledge*, which can be written down, shared, and easily imitated if it is not protected. Subsequently, if codified knowledge is protected legally by patents, copyrights, trade secrets, or semiconductor masks it becomes intellectual property. *Intellectual assets are the codifiable portion of a company's intellectual capital.* In contrast, *tacit knowledge* is difficult to describe and can be thought of as "know-how" represented by the company's human capital. While it is possible to transfer and share tacit knowledge between individuals, this can only occur by on-the-job training and experience. And although it can be demonstrated by those who possess it, tacit knowledge is nevertheless extremely difficult to codify. This characteristic affords tacit knowledge with a degree of inherent protection from duplication, although there are rarely any viable legal means of protection. Examples of tacit knowledge would be that required for manufacturing or process and relationship knowledge used in service firms (table 5-1).

Table 5-1. Types of Industry Knowledge

	Tacit Knowledge (Human Capital)	Codified Knowledge (Intellectual Assets)
Definition	Knowledge that is difficult to articulate and may be embedded in ways of doing things	Knowledge that is written down in in some medium
Ownership	Ownership resides with the holder of know-how; it is difficult to copy and/or transfer	Technology is easier to protect using the mechanism of the law, yet easier to transfer
Examples	Experience Lore Group skills	Blueprints Code Formulae Computer programs

Source: Parr, R.L., Sullivan, P.H.

C. Intellectual Property

1. Copyrights

Copyrights provide for the protection of expressive arts such as literary compositions, fine and graphic arts, musical compositions, phonorecords, photography, video, cinema, chronographic works, and software.   This type of intellectual property lasts for the life of the author plus an additional 50 years or for 150 years if the author is a corporation.   Copyright registration prevents the copying and distribution by any means of written material, works of art and computer programs.   It should be emphasized that expressive works of art may require both copyright and patent protection, as in the case of designs in order to safeguard against unauthorized use.

Although the copyright emblem ©, is no longer required as evidence of copyright protection, the copyright holder should include it to ensure full disclosure so that maximum damages can be awarded in the event of infringement.   However, prior to any attempted litigation for infringement, proper copyright registration with the U.S. Patent and Trademark Office must have occurred.   Consequently, the author may apply for copyright registration within three years after the date of the alleged infringement.   However, damage awards may be diminished due to such delays.

In order to save time and effort, a copyright search should be performed prior to filing for any copyright.   This can be conducted online through the U.S. Library of Congress' copyright homepage.   This website contains helpful information regarding copyright basics, the forms and fees involved in filing for a copyright, and other information, as well as the search database of all records of registrations and ownership documents since 1978.[2]   One can search by author, title, claimant, registration number, or a combination of these.

2. Patents

A patent is the grant of protective rights by the government to the owner from unauthorized selling, producing, or using patented material for a specific time period of anywhere between 14-20 years (depending upon the patent type) from the date of issuance, after which competitors are free to use this information as they choose.   Generally, inventors obtain patents for the following main reasons:

- **Protection** from competition
- **Design** freedom
- **Avoidance** of litigation
- **Basis** for establishing alliances and joint ventures

While some companies use patents individually in the process of commercialization, others prefer to group patents into a strategic *patent portfolio* for use in the company's overall business strategy. The design of these portfolios is not random but very specific and targets predetermined goals within the company's overall technology strategy. There are no restrictions on who may apply for a patent except that the applicant must either be the inventor or the representative of the inventor. *In situations where there may be dispute over who holds patents rights, such issues should be clarified early on to minimize any legal actions by the other party or to prevent the retraction of the patent by the USPTO* (see Appendix A-4, "Invention Assignment Agreement").

Historical Background

As with any form of intellectual property, patents are only as good as their enforcement from infringement. And prior to the mid 1980s, the value of patents had a universally low perceived value relative to their expense. Remarkably, during the 1970s the chances of a patent being deemed valid by U.S. courts, infringed, and enforceable by litigation were about one in three, as the prevailing opinion of the U.S. Department of Justice held that patents damage the economy by establishing anticompetitive monopolies. Therefore, rather than spend the time and expense of paying licensing fees, companies chose to risk infringement knowing that the chances of being found guilty were low.

However, between 1982-1985, several government agencies enacted a variety of laws signaling a paradigm shift in intellectual property law. Specifically in 1982, a federal court of appeals was established for the sole purpose of hearing intellectual property cases. In addition, during that same period the President's Commission on Industrial Competitiveness issued a report stating that the enforcement of intellectual property was one of the keys for the United States to maintain its global competitive dominance. Finally, the Department of Justice reversed its earlier view on patents and stated that they promote competition by providing the needed rewards to incentivize innovators. This significant reversal in political policy signaled a drastic shift in the enforcement and interpretation of patents in the United States. And now the chances of being found guilty of infringement are high so companies now prefer to license patents rather than risk infringement litigation.

Perhaps coincidentally during the same time period of this policy change, America began the gradual dissolution of its manufacturing dominance with a reemphasis on innovation rather than production.   And if one examines global economic business dynamics, they may notice that Southeast Asian nations have replaced much of the U.S. manufacturing and production capacity relative to the period from the 1940s to the early 1980s.   It is the opinion of the author *that this shift was not coincidental but rather intentional and sought to utilize these broad sweeping changes in U.S. intellectual property law.*   Much of the American public has been critical of its loss of manufacturing capacity over the past two decades, but it should be quite clear to the reader at this point exactly what has happened and why.   Intellectual property law is only getting stronger, as the U.S. continues to develop international standards for global intellectual property participation and enforcement.   And NAFTA is a recent example of such policies.   It will be interesting to see the reactions of Southeast Asian nations when they fully realize the momentum and the increasing intensity of international enforcement of intellectual property laws.

Types of Patents

There are three basic types of patent categories specified by the U.S. Patent and Trademark Office (USPTO):

1. **Utility patents** are issued for a process or machine.   They are the *most common patent type* issued and in order to qualify as a utility patent, the invention must be a method or procedure for producing a useful and tangible result, a machine, some composition of matter, a manufactured product, or an improvement of an invention that satisfies one of the above requirements.

2. **Design patents** are defined by the USPTO as "new, original ornamental design for an article of manufacture."   One may distinguish a utility from a design patent by asking the question, "Will removing or smoothing out the novel features substantially impair the function of the device?"   If the answer to this question is yes then a utility patent is not indicated.   Meanwhile, if the answer is no then a design patent is indicated.

3. **Plant patents** are specifically for those who have discovered and reproduced by asexual means a new type of plant.

In order for a patent to be issued, the invention must satisfy all requirements of at least one of the three patent categories, although it is possible that it will satisfy more than one.   In addition, *the invention must be different from all other previous related inventions and be nonobvious to individuals who are very familiar with the area of technological innovation the invention relates to*.   Finally, if the invention has been disclosed to the public or products have been sold, the inventor must file for a patent within one year (even if a provisional patent has been filed) or else all rights of exclusivity will be forfeited (the *one-year rule*).   However, the inventor can still file for a regular patent if this time period lapses, but the process may be complicated if *substantive changes* have occurred.

The basic components of a patent include the names of the inventors, an abstract, drawings of the invention, the name, background, purpose and advantages of the invention, the specifications, and the claims. The abstract is a summary of the invention and the specification is a written description of the invention, how to produce it, and how to make the best use of it. *A patent's claims define the invention's useful purposes and are both the most important and difficult portion of the application process.*

Sometimes   there   is   ambiguity   whether   other   individuals   share inventorship and one should consult a patent attorney to address these issues. *If there is more than one inventor, it is important to determine the extent of contribution and document this in the appropriate legal contract.   Otherwise, an equal share of ownership rights will be assumed by the USPTO.*   Finally note that even the absence of one of the inventor's names on the application can invalidate the patent.   Therefore, it is critical that patent applications be given meticulous attention to detail.

Provisional Patents

Provisional patents are sometimes used to provide a way for the inventor to reserve a spot for his invention to be examined in full at a later time while he finalizes his work.   The advantages of using a provisional patent is that they are less costly, the application is much shorter, and the provisional patent status allows the inventor to use the "patent pending" designation, which is also used during the regular patent application process.   In addition, the patent claims section is not required for provisional patents since the USPTO does not examine the patent at this time.   However, *prior to the one-year expiration, the inventor will need to file an application for a full patent or he will all rights to the innovation.*   During this one year of provisional protection, there is a chance that substantive changes to the invention may have occurred and this could complicate the status.   Therefore, a patent attorney should always be consulted in this situation.

Conducting a Patent Search and Analysis

As discussed, patent protection is an extremely important consideration of any company.   This is especially true for high technology companies offering a unique product or service.   And one of the first tasks one must before registering these innovations is to make certain that they have not already been patented.   *Thus, prior to applying for a patent one must perform a thorough patent search to ensure there are no other existing patents with substantial similarity.*   In addition, the patent filer will need to conduct patent searches in order to include all relevant information for disclosure and use by the USPTO examiner.   As we will see, this is a very important.

The goal of a patent search is to identify all related patented work (as well as any other published description of related work) so that the patent can be shown to be different from all previous works.   Failure to demonstrate such distinctions could invalidate the patent due to "inequitable conduct".   The results of these searches will need to be submitted to the USPTO when the patent application is filed.   In addition, infringement defenses typically attempt to uncover works not mentioned in the patent searches of the patent holder in order to invalidate the patent.   Therefore, *it is extremely important that a diligent patent search is performed and all relevant works noted by the patent filer for the use of the USPTO examiner.*   Finally, when seeking financing from venture capitalists and sophisticated angels, they too will conduct an extensive patent search to assess the distinctiveness of the innovation as a part of their due diligence process.   In general, *the more prior work that is referenced in the search, the better one can distinguish the patent if it is truly unique.*

Patent searches can be a laborious task for those inexperienced with the process but can be conducted free of charge online (**www.uspto.gov**) or in one of the many patent and trademark depository libraries across the United States.   A list of these libraries may be found on the USPTO's website (**www.uspto.gov/go/ptdl**).   Alternatively, the applicant can pay the patent office or an outside consultant to conduct the search.   Delphion (**www.delphion.com**) provides free access to U.S patent searches and charges a small fee for international searches.   Regardless of the method used, the USPTO has professionals ready to assist you throughout the process.

Manual Patent Search

If you live in one of the of cities that contains a patent and trademark depository library, you may wish to conduct a manual search at one of these facilities since they contain earlier patents not accessible online.   If you want to check all patents that may be related to your patent prospect, you should check the subject index (called the *Index of Classification*) of the *Official Gazette of the United States Patent and Trademark Office*.   This publication shows the patent number, the class and subclass, the inventor's name and address, patent rights assigned, number of claims against the patent, and the abstract describing the general design.

The first step in conducting a screening search is to identify the class of patents you wish to examine.   An example of the patent class might be computers.   Then one must identify the subclass, such as computer modems. After identifying the class and subclass of the patent of interest, the *Manual of Classification* should be checked to determine the specific subclass to use. For instance, within the category of computer modems one might wish to examine wireless modems.   A final check should be performed using classification definitions, which detail the information that may be found in each class and subclass.   Once a patent has been identified (the class and subclass has been located), one should check the index (classification of patents), for a listing of each publication and the patent numbers it contains. If the inventor's name, patent rights assignee, or patent number is known, patent searches are much easier.   The patent can be found by referring to the *Index of Patents, Part I: List of Patentees or List of Assignees*.   If the patent number is known, the publication can be checked chronologically, since patent numbers are published in order.

Online Patent Search

Anyone with Internet access can conduct a patent search online using the USPTO *Patent Full Text and Full Page Image Database*.   This search engine contains a database of all patents from 1790 to the most recent issue week. Patents from January 1976 to present provide the full searchable text including inventor's name, patent's title, assignee's name, the abstract, all claims, and images.   Meanwhile, patents issued from 1790 to December 1975 provide the patent number and the current U.S. patent classification in the text display, but not the actual patent.   If the complete patent information prior to December 1975 is needed, you will have to conduct a search at one of the patent and trademark libraries.

The USPTO website provides detailed assistance with conducting a quick and advanced search and can be learned easily.   You can access this search engine by clicking the "site index" icon, then clicking the "Classification Index, Patents".   If you want to enter a search based upon a name, click "classification numbers and titles" at the top left and a list of classes will appear showing a number code.   This code is used to designate the class when searching.   For example, the class "chemistry: physical processes" has been assigned the number 23.   You can click the "go" icon to the left of the number and a list of subclasses will appear.   The subject will be further subdivided once that number is clicked.   This process continues until you have identified the specific area you are looking for.   If you require further assistance with searches you can contact the help line and one or more professionals will be happy to assist you.   I have found them to be very friendly and helpful.

Alternatively, databases may be a time-efficient method for obtaining information on existing and new patent filings.   A simple Internet search for patent databases will provide an extensive list of these sources.   One particularly useful company, CHI Research, Inc. (located in Haddon Heights, NJ) has created large databases of patents filed worldwide and assembled models for assessing competitor strengths, R&D productivity, merger and acquisition target identification, technology valuation, due diligence, cross-licensing negotiation support, and long-term investment strategies.

Filing for a Patent

Depending upon the financial resources and time you have, filing for your patent may be a viable alternative to paying a patent attorney or patent agent. Otherwise, if you use an attorney, a patent may cost you between $5000-$10,000 depending upon the extent of work involved.   Meanwhile, if you choose to file for a patent yourself, it will still cost you around $2000 in filing fees.   *It is not recommended that you file your own patents without the use of experienced professionals unless you have extensive experience filing patents and are confident in your abilities.*

On the other hand, there have been many horror stories of supposedly experienced patent attorneys who have done a poor job filing patents. Therefore, *if you want to file the patent yourself and save needed cash, you should at least pay an attorney a few hundred dollars to review it prior to submission.*   There are a variety of helpful texts that explain how to patent one's innovations, and at the very least, you should familiarize yourself with the process so you can check the attorney's filing because you will be the best source when it comes to the intricate details of the innovation.   A document available in pdf format is available in the help portion of the USPTO website entitled "Manual of Patent Examining Procedure" and details the process of patent examination and patent law.[3]   There is also a publication detailing the patent rules and regulations entitled "Consolidated Patent Rules".[4]

One word of caution; *the strength of patent protection may be the difference between the success and failure of a company.*   Patents are often an extremely important component of a high tech company's competitive advantage and failure to file adequate patents could lead to disaster. Therefore, in selecting a patent attorney, a company should be very cautious and screen the firm based upon several criteria.   The following list is recommended for the initial screening process.

- **Does the firm contain patent agents or attorneys with extensive experience writing patents for your company's technology?** This is such an obvious point that it really does not warrant further explanation. However certain technologies, such a biochips and proteomics for instance, require specific experience in writing these patents that cannot usually be substituted by individuals who have performed work limited to other areas of biotechnology.

- **Are they willing to provide a list of previous clients that can be contacted as references?** This may be difficult to obtain and cherry-picked references may not provide a realistic picture of the quality of work. However, I recommend that unless you can get at least three references who have received patent work in your specific technology, you should continue to shop around, even if it entails working with distant firms.

- **Are they willing to receive partial compensation in company stock as a measure of their confidence in the quality of work?** This may be the most difficult goal to achieve depending upon the policy of the firm, as well as their confidence in the company's future. However, negotiating a fee structure that includes company stock in-lue of cash payment does not always equate to quality workmanship.

- **Does the law firm only write patents or do they also defend them?** This is also an important consideration to keep in mind, as you may end up having to hire a different firm to defend your patent with the liability. Many firms do not write and defend patents and it may be difficult to find one that has the experience and expertise in your technology. But if you can find a firm that does you may be able to negotiate a protective clause that discounts any patent defense services that may arise due to inadequate filings.

Guidelines When Filing for a Patent

- **Understand the Requirements for Patent Eligibility.** As mentioned, an invention must be new or different from any existing device or mechanism and the inventor must be able to demonstrate precisely how it works. In addition, the invention cannot be made for sale or be known about for more than one year prior to applying for a patent.

- **Keep Meticulous Records of Your Invention.** This should be performed as if you were in a laboratory conducting research. Detailed descriptions of the invention as well as all modifications and attempts at prototype production should be documented, dated, and signed by at least one witness if possible. This is very important not only for the future information that will be used for the filing process but as a legal defense in the event that a question of when the invention was made occurs. In such cases, whereby an inventor filed for a patent after another, those with the best-kept records have succeeded in pleading their case in court.

- **Conduct an Extensive Patent Search.** If you have little or no prior experience with patent searches, it is recommended that you hire a professional that specializes in patent searches or at the very least check your results against that of this professional. The fee for this is usually no more than three hundred dollars.

- **Begin Learning How to File for Patents Early.** Even if you follow the recommendation of using an experienced patent attorney, understand that becoming competent in patent filing is a long process that is certain to be accompanied by mistakes. Therefore, entrepreneurs should begin learning the process early on so that the company can become less dependent on patent attorneys when future patents are filed. And while some companies may have the luxury of adequate funding to pay for patent attorneys, the inventor needs to safe guard his innovation by checking the detail of the patents filed by those who are less familiar with the invention.

- **Consider Filing a Provisional Patent Application (PPA).** This is especially recommended for cash strapped companies or inventors that prefer to file for the patent themselves. It allows the inventor to claim a patent pending status, costs only around $150, and only requires an abbreviated version of the patent filing.

- **Require All Parties to Sign a Nondisclosure Agreement.** Prior to discussing the invention with potential customers, an invention that has not been patented needs to remain protected. And the easiest way to ensure this is to require the interested party to sign an NDA. However, an NDA is also recommended even if a patent has been issued.

The Patent Process

When a patent application is submitted to the PTO, an examiner who specializes in the appropriate area of technology is assigned to review the documents to ensure that they meet the basic requirements and that it uses the proper format and language, as specified by the PTO. The general guidelines for patent review are listed in the USPTO's *Written Description Guidelines* which can be obtained from their website. The approval process can last 1-3 years and will inevitably involve many communications between the examiner and the patent applicant.

The goal of the patent examiner is to find specific reasons why individuals who are skilled in the prospective patent technology would not recognize that the written description supports the patent claims. If the patent examiner determines the applicant has fulfilled the written description guidelines of the patent, he is said to satisfy the *"possession test"*. This is meant to imply possession of the patented material by the applicant due to description of the invention that would enable an individual skilled in the given field to create the invention from the description of the patent. Once the patent is filed, the inventor may use the designation *"patent pending"* until the patent has been accepted. A patent number will only be assigned once the application has been approved and accepted.

The USPTO frequently provides instructional materials on their website intended for the training and refinement skills of their agents. Fortunately, these documents are open to anyone with both an interest and knowledge where to find them. You can gain access to much of the countless documents written by the USPTO describing the *Written Description Guidelines* by typing this phrase in the search box of their site. I have provided links for two documents that were written for the training of their agents. These documents should give a patent applicant a better idea of the examination process and therefore prepare him better when filing for patents. I highly recommend the inventor study these documents, regardless of his role in the filing process.[5]

Patent Portfolios

There are two general uses of patent portfolios whose selection will primarily depend upon the company's overall business strategy, resources, industry, and maturity.[6] Companies may use patent portfolios as a *defense mechanism* (called clustering) to block entry of technological access by competitors or they can obtain or design patents around a competitor's innovations in attempt to prevent its further market reach (called bracketing). Companies choosing these strategies typically hold a narrow view of their portfolios and use these assets to protect their technology position rather than to create additional value. In contrast, a patent portfolio may be used as an *offensive* means to add products directly or through alliances and joint ventures.   In reality, *most companies position their patent portfolios for use as both a defensive and offensive tool emphasizing one activity over another in the execution of their business strategy.*

The most effective utilization of patent portfolios is to structure them in a manner that achieves a balance between their strategic and financial utilization, while remaining consistent with a company's overall business strategy.   Hence, portfolios may be structured as an offensive or defensive tool around existing product lines, near-term products, long-term products, or they can have a broad reach structured around the technical competencies of the company.   Each of these IP strategies is selected for specific reasons with the purpose of executing enhanced company performance.   Companies in the consumer electronics industry such as Hewlett-Packard may elect to structure their patent portfolios on near-term products due to the limited profit margins and product life of its offerings.   Meanwhile, Amgen may choose to structure its portfolio around a long-term strategy due to the longer product life and higher profit margins characteristic of therapeutic drug development.   Thus, both companies use their portfolios as a secondary defensive strategy in the course of executing their overall business strategies.

Patent Valuation

The valuation of a company's patents is an art that the entrepreneur should be familiar with so he can understand and scrutinize proposed valuations by prospective investors or infringement awards.   Specifically, patent valuation may be needed for several situations: company acquisition, asset sale, purchase, or swap, infringement damages awards, licensing, and for strategic reasons, such as determination of the relative value of contributions in a strategic alliance, joint venture, or other partnering arrangement. Finally, patent valuation can be used to help determine the R&D and marketing budgets appropriate for expected future revenues associated with the innovation (figure 5-3).

While valuation of patents is difficult for an early stage company, one should note that *some experts equate the number of patents with a higher valuation.*   Thus *early stage companies should always be thinking of ways to increase the number of relevant patents*, as it may be a relatively easy way to build assets in a company that has none.   Although there are no set rules for patent valuation, there are certain guidelines that should be adhered to when performing this assessment.

The first consideration is the *degree or scope of the innovation* under consideration.   For simplicity, innovations can be thought of as either minor, major, or breakthrough relative to their impact on industries.   Second, the *patent's importance within an industry* should be examined for the relative impact it has upon the industry and its ability to derive revenues from its applications. As well, the *size of the markets* and industries served by the patent should be assessed.   The term, or *length of time* the patent has been in force is also a significant factor that should be given proper consideration. Patents that have been in force for a longer duration will have shorter periods of exclusivity but should provide more accurate estimates of revenues due to longer historical track records.   In contrast, newly issued patents will have longer periods of exclusivity but may not provide accurate forecasts of revenue generation.   The next consideration to make is the *number of times the patent has been cited* by other patents.   While this is a lagging indicator, it will only be useful for patents with shorter terms remaining.

Figure 5-3. Common Reasons to Value Patents

- Acquisitions
- Asset Sale, Purchase, or Swap
- Licensing
- Infringement Damages
- Strategic Alliances and Joint Ventures
- R&D Budgeting

There are also additional considerations which delve into the strategic and technological merits of the patent.   Some patents can be expanded to produce other innovations, while others may be used for clustering and bracketing.   In addition, some patents have such broad use that they are able to promote or improve the brand recognition of a company.   Finally, the degree to which the patent is defensible against infringement or designing around the technology is also a critical factor in the valuation formula (figure 5-4).

Once the patent has been analyzed for its term, strength, scope of use, and other variables of impact, these measurements should be factored into any calculations to determine the final valuation. *In general, patents can be valued by applying capital budgeting techniques, such as projecting the future cash flows expected to be generated from its use and discounting back to a present value, then deducting the cost of developing the technology into a commercializable product.*

Figure 5-4. Factors To Consider When Valuing Patents

- Degree or Scope of Innovation
- Market/Industry Applications
- Term
- Third-Party Citations
- Special Considerations
  - Ability to Expand **Scope**
  - Utility in **Bracketing** Strategies
  - Utility in **Clustering** Strategies
  - Patent Equity **Transfer** into a Brand
  - **Defensibility** of the Patent

For more mature companies where the patent is used to produce revenue-generating products, the *avoided cost method* is used to determine its value:

$$PV_{pat} = \sum_{i=1}^{n} \frac{REV_i \times RR(1-t)}{(1 + WACC)^n}$$

where,

PV_{pat} is the present value of the patent

RR is the market-based royalty rate

REV is the future projected stream of revenue

T is the tax rate

WACC is the weight-average cost of capital

If products are the result of many patents, then the patents are grouped together as a portfolio and valued collectively using a single royalty rate multiplied by a declining percentage of the product's future revenue (based upon the determination of its status in the product life cycle, see chapter 7) and discounting this future cash flow to the present value using a discount rate that is indicative of the interest rate environment and risk of failure to execute. The product's future revenue is reduced over time due to the anticipated reduction in marketing that occurs as a percentage of sales as the product establishes a known brand name.

Of course most of the readers of this book are not working in mature companies with revenue-generating products.   Therefore, the valuation process is much more difficult.   If there is no cash flow from the patent at the time of valuation, one may value the patent using the cost of developing a comparable innovation.   However, replacement cost methods such as these do not account for the revenue potential of the patent.   An alternative approach in this case would be to use a *modified comparables method*. Because patents represent unique innovations, finding a true comparable may be virtually impossible.   However, approximate comparables can be used to help estimate royalty potential, market size, and other relevant factors. There are a variety of techniques early stage companies can use to value non-revenue generating patents and summarized in figure 5-5.   These methods are based on cost, market conditions, income, time, uncertainty, flexibility, and changing risk associated with the patent.   In reviewing these methods, keep in mind that they should only serve as a starting point in the more comprehensive task of valuing intangible assets.   And the specific method used will be determined by the purpose of patent valuation.

Cost Based Methods.   This method is considered the least effective since it uses a valuation method that is employed for tangible assets.   As discussed previously, valuation of intangible assets based upon assessing their costs neglects the future potential benefits that may be generated by the asset. This method formerly had utility when companies used cost-based accounting or when tax decisions were used for decision-making but has minimal utility today.

Market Based Methods.   This method uses *comparables* as a gauge for the valuation of intangible assets, whereby recent prices paid for comparable patents are used to guide the price of the given patent.   While relatively easily applied, *the main difficulty with this method is that it can be very difficult to find a close comparable*.   Implicit within this limitation is the possibility that the comparables used may not have been positioned to the optimum strategic advantage of the company, thereby not realizing their full potential value. However, there are two market-based methods worth mentioning.   The first method calculates the value of the intangible asset by subtracting the values of all the remaining intangible assets from the company's market value.   The problem with this is that for private companies, there is no real market value and determination of a company valuation rests upon first assigning a valuation to all assets.   The next method uses price-to-earnings (P/E) ratios from comparable companies and adds a premium to this ratio based upon the expected value of the intangible asset.   A modification of these methods is to determine the actual total return of all remaining intangible and tangible assets and assigning the remaining value to the intangible asset in question.   Once again this is an over simplification that does not take into account the contribution of synergistic returns on tangible and intangible assets.

Income Based Methods. This method is based upon estimating the future income generated by the intangible asset and discounting this value to the present. The main source of inaccuracy with the income method lies with the ability of the individual performing the analysis to accurately forecast the future cash flows attributable to the intangible asset. Even beyond this difficulty is the real possibility that much of the future cash flows will be compromised due to the loss of synergistic assets when the patent is sold. In addition, the need to employ a utilization strategy that is identical with the holder of the patent is important since the assumptions of future cash flow will be based upon this.

Figure 5-5. Increasing Order of Sophistication of Patent Valuation Methods

Least
Sophisticated

Costs
- Cost Based Methods

Market Conditions
- Market based methods

Income
- Methods based on projected cash flows

Time
- DCF Methods allowing for the time value of money

Uncertainty
- DCF Methods allowing for the riskiness of cash flows

Flexibility
- DCF based Decision Tree Analysis (DTA) methods

Changing Risk
Option Pricing Theory (OPT) based methods

1) Discrete time
    a) Binomial Model (B-M) based methods

2) Continuous time
    a) Black-Scholes (B-S) option pricing model based methods

Most
Sophisticated

DCF Based Methods. The discounted cash flow (DCF) method is a widely accepted technique for valuation of both tangible and intangible assets because it accounts for the time value of money and the riskiness in the future expected cash flows. A unique advantage in using the DCF method for patent valuation versus other assets is that *since patents have a limited life, one does not need to estimate perpetual values for cash flows beyond the forecasting period, as is required for other assets.* The main disadvantage of this approach is determination of an appropriate discount rate to account for the possibility of generating the future cash flows. This is especially difficult for patents since, if successfully challenged, an overturned patent can forfeit all future expected income, thereby eliminating all expected revenues. Obviously then, *the discount rate must take into consideration the age of the patent, its prior ability to generate revenue, and its success in patent challenges.* There are more advanced methods to account for this variation in risk with time, but they are beyond the scope of this discussion.

Decision-Tree Based Methods. These methods account for the flexibility of patent utilization by the company. For instance, the company may change its overall operating strategy, rendering the patent essentially worthless. Alternatively, it may create a patent portfolio based around the patent to be valued. Finally, even if the intended use of the patent is realigned within the business strategy, it may still provide value by preventing competitors to access the technology. The basis of the DTA method is to create a decision tree of all possible outcomes of the patent and value each one using the DCF method, applying a different discount rate based upon the consequence of the extent of patent utilization.

In figure 5-6, the main steps for the patent procedure have been listed, along with a cost-benefit decision profile for each step. The patent applicant should use this framework when making decisions regarding the patenting process.

Figure 5-6. Patent Option Valuation Decisions

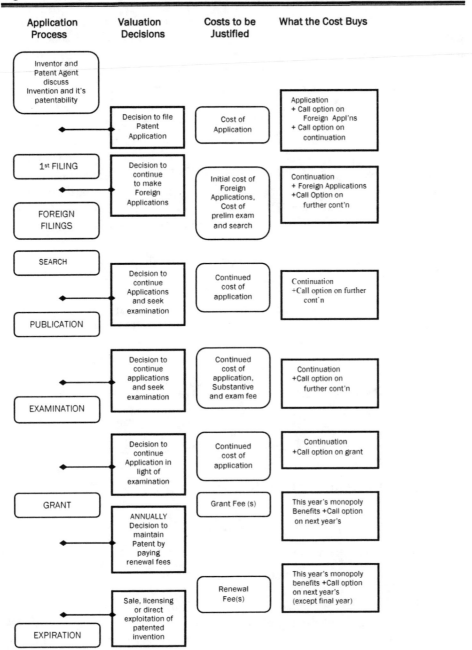

Application Process	Valuation Decisions	Costs to be Justified	What the Cost Buys
Inventor and Patent Agent discuss Invention and it's patentability			
	Decision to file Patent Application	Cost of Application	Application + Call option on Foreign Appl'ns + Call option on continuation
1st FILING	Decision to continue to make Foreign Applications	Initial cost of Foreign Applications, Cost of prelim exam and search	Continuation + Foreign Applications +Call Option on further cont'n
FOREIGN FILINGS			
SEARCH	Decision to continue Applications and seek examination	Continued cost of application	Continuation +Call option on further cont'n
PUBLICATION			
	Decision to continue applications and seek examination	Continued cost of application, Substantive and exam fee	Continuation +Call option on further cont'n
EXAMINATION			
	Decision to continue Application in light of examination	Continued cost of application	Continuation +Call option on grant
GRANT		Grant Fee (s)	This year's monopoly Benefits +Call option on next year's
	ANNUALLY Decision to maintain Patent by paying renewal fees		
	Sale, licensing or direct exploitation of patented invention	Renewal Fee(s)	This year's monopoly benefits +Call option on next year's (except final year)
EXPIRATION			

Source: Pitkethly, R. "The Valuation of Patents: A review of patent valuation methods with consideration pf option based methods and the potential for further research", Judge Institute Working Paper, 1997.

The Startup Company Holy Grail: Serial Innovators

There are some experts who contend that the number and quality of patents is proportional to the success of a company. Leigh Buchanan coined the term *"serial innovators"* to describe those firms that continue to produce new innovations based upon their initial technology or develop new and different innovations that continue to show superiority to competitive technologies. In general, the term serial innovators is meant to describe small firms with ownership rights to many high quality patents enabling them to be long-lived due to their innovative accomplishments and contributions to the value chain. As expected, these firms tend to be concentrated in those industries where technological innovation and patent protection is very important. However, it is not a requirement for a firm to be small in order to qualify as a serial innovator. The characteristically small size is perhaps a consequence of the business dynamics that drive technology strategies of some smaller firms.

CHI research, a consultancy specializing in patent research, has conducted many studies that seek to identify characteristics of serial innovators. In one study, CHI looked at all U.S. firms with 15 or more U.S. patents between 1996 and 2000. One of the primary criterion used was a measurement of a company's *citation index*, or the number of times a patent is referenced in other patents. *The number of citations is thought to be proportional to the technological relevance of the cited patent.*[7]   Each firm was selected due to its longevity and ability to create a high quality patent portfolio and the criteria established by CHI produced 1,071 firms. Upon examination of these firms, the following observations were noted:

- Serial innovators are concentrated in the health and information technology industries

- Serial innovators develop patents that are more highly cited and have a closer link to research

- Firms that patent heavily are mainly manufacturing firms

- Serial innovators are more locally networked than larger firms

- Serial innovators produce patents that are broader based

These observations have many implications for understanding the business dynamics and strategic intent of these firms. First, we should question why these firms seem to be most concentrated in health and information technology areas. In my opinion, technological innovations in the health industry are more highly connected to academic research than any other technology due the interdependence of many scientific disciplines.

On the other hand, information technology is a relatively new discipline characterized by enormous growth and technological innovation and most innovative developments in this industry are also linked to research. Therefore, for different reasons both of these industries are highly dependent upon research.

This is in contrast to the chemical industry, where the level of technology needed is much lower relative to industry demands. While the chemical industry is technology intensive, most of its innovative developments are related to manufacturing processes, consistent with the nature of this industry. Thus, while the chemical industry is dominated by a very high number of patents per company, a small percentage of these patents were developed by small firms. This makes sense since small firms are not operating on economies of scale and therefore will not emphasize the improvement of production and manufacturing standards. Based upon the other results of this study, the quality of these patents, in general is relatively low and characterized by subtle differences from patent to patent.

Table 5-2. Technologies with Small Firm Patenting

Technology Area	% of Patents From Small Firms	Total # of Patents	% of Firms that are Small	Total # of Firms
Biotechnology	25%	3,886	71%	45
Pharmaceuticals	19%	6,453	68%	59
Medial Equipment	11%	8,437	45%	88
Unclassified	11%	2,511	31%	26
Medical Electronics	11%	2,974	64%	14
Chemicals	9%	15,760	29%	91
Agriculture	8%	2,561	28%	18
Semiconductors & Electronics	5%	13,893	44%	13
Office Equipment & Cameras	4%	9,268	43%	37
All Technologies	6%	193,976	33%	1,071

Small firms are defined in this study as those with fewer than 500 employees. To be included in this study, each firm had to be independent, for-profit, not bankrupt, not a joint venture and not foreign owned as of the first half of 2002. This list contains 27 firms of unknown size but whose patenting characteristics suggested they are small firms.
Source: CHI Research

It also makes sense that serial innovators have broad-based patents if one agrees that serial innovators are more closely linked to research. *Broad-based patents are in general thought to be more indicative of innovative technologies since they tend to be founded on core scientific research.* Therefore, they have many potential applications that adds to their quality. Finally, studies of serial innovators have found that these firms do not have a large percentage of software patents relative to other industries. This may in part be due to the various forms of intellectual property available for software protection and the disadvantages of patenting some types of software. Rather, some companies may choose to copyright their programs and hold the proprietary content of the programs as trade secrets so that competitors do not see the algorithms within the program.

There have been numerous studies comparing citations of companies with market values and it has been shown that market prices take into account the number and quality of patents. In fact, CHI research has even performed a hypothetical study of the performance of public companies relative to the strength of patent portfolios. From 1989 to 1998, they made annual hypothetical investments into 25 companies thought to have superior patent portfolio strength, as measured by their algorithms. At the end of each year all stocks were sold and a new set of 25 companies was purchased. At the end of the nine-year period, this hypothetical portfolio had appreciated nine times that of the S&P 500 index. While his study is perhaps crude and may not have accounted for all needed control elements, such as market capitalization, extent of analyst coverage, and other factors. Nevertheless, it provides some support for the importance of patents in determining the valuation of publicly traded companies. And because private companies are in part valued based upon the market values of publicly traded companies, entrepreneurs should extract the full benefit of their intellectual capital.

3. Trade Secrets

"The definition of the term "trade secret" under the Economic Espionage Act of 1996 (EEA) is very broad. But as defined at <u>18 U.S.C. § 1839</u>, it includes generally, *"all types of information, however stored or maintained, which the owner has taken reasonable measures to keep secret and which has independent economic value."* In addition, *trade secrets are not required to be unique or novel unlike patents and the idea need not be complicated, as long as it is not common knowledge.* Examples include anything that can be patented, ideas, production standards, know-how, marketing strategies, customer lists, and any other form of company intelligence (figure 5-7).

Figure 5-7.   Examples of Trade Secrets in a Typical Manufacturing Company*

Technical Information/Research & Development
- Proprietary Technology Information
- Proprietary Information Concerning R & D
- Formulas
- Compounds
- Prototypes
- Processes
- Laboratory Notebooks
- Experiments and Experimental Data
- Analytical Data
- Calculations
- Drawings-All Types
- Diagrams-All Types
- Design Data and Design Manuals
- Vendor/Supplier Information
- R&D Reports-All Types
- R&D know-How and Negative Know-How

Production/Process Information
- Cost/Price Data
- Proprietary Information Concerning Production/Proc
- Special Production Machinery
- Process/Manufacturing Technology
- Specifications for Production Proc. and Machinery
- Production Know-How & Negative Know-How

Quality Control Information
- Information Concerning Quality Control
- Quality Control Procedures
- Quality Control Manuals
- Quality Control Records
- Maintenance Know-How & negative Know-How

Sales & Marketing Information
- Proprietary Information Concerning Sales & Marketing
- Sales Forecasts
- Marketing and Sales Promotion Plans
- Sales Call Reports
- Competitive Intelligence Information
- Proprietary Information Concerning Customers
- Proprietary Customer Lists
- Customer Needs and Buying Habits
- Know-How Concerning Management of Customer Confidence
- Proprietary Sales, Marketing Studies and Reports

Internal Financial Documents
- Budgets
- Forecasts
- Computer Printouts
- Product Margins
- Product Costs
- Operating Costs
- Profit and Loss Statements
- Proprietary Administrative Information

Internal Administrative Information
- Internal Organization
- Key Decision Makers
- Strategic Business Plans
- Internal Computer Software

Vendor/Supplier Information
- Vendor/Supplier Information
- Cost/Price Data

*Note that these may only be classified as trade secrets if they are in compliance with the Uniform Trade Secrets Act of the applicable state.   For instance, these materials and data must be safeguarded.

Source: Mark Halligan, Esq.

In order to safeguard the value of all company intangible assets, trade secrets must be prevented from duplication and use by employees who come across the secrets as a part of their work. Therefore, at the most basic level of protection, everyone who comes into contact with the company's trade secrets should be expected to sign an NDA that was specifically designed to protect the trade secret.   Finally, *even individuals who learn about the trade secret by mistake but had reason to believe it was protected by trade secret law are in violation if they duplicate or use it.*   However, if an individual independently discovers a company's trade secret without the use of any employee of the firm or any other information that is relevant for understanding or duplicating the trade secret, they can legally use it for their own gain. Thus, in contrast to the situation with patents, *there is no legal protection provided for the reverse engineering of trade secrets* (see table 5-3 for a comparison of patents versus trade secrets). An example of this might be an individual who discovers the trade secret formula for Pepsi Cola or Listerine independently.

Keeping a Secret

Unlike other types of intellectual property, *trade secret protection does not involve filing applications with the USPTO or any other agency.* Under the U.S. Uniform Trade Secrets Act (UTSA), companies wishing to qualify for IP protection using trade secret law are expected to keep the items they wish to claim as trade secrets confidential. And they are expected to implement the needed internal controls in order to preserve the unauthorized dissemination of these assets. *In addition, the one-year rule in patent law does not apply to trade secret law. Thus, if you disclose your trade secret to the public there is nothing you can do to claim exclusive rights to it and it becomes public domain. However, there is no set expiration date for trade secret protection, unlike other forms of IP. Therefore, licensing opportunities are potentially limitless,* assuming the demand for the secret survives the test of time and change.

The unique advantage of trade secret protection is that it allows protection against duplication and use without letting the public know what the information is unlike the case with patents. And this may be a preferred method of IP depending on the content of the material. For instance, many proprietary materials such as customer lists, marketing strategies, and production procedures might be difficult to patent but can be protected with trade secrets. In addition, by patenting a unique marketing strategy, you are making it somewhat available to the public since patent filings are listed on the USPTO website.

In order to claim content as a trade secret a company must do more than designate it as a trade secret. It must take specific measures to safeguard the secret from disclosure. Perhaps the best way to accomplish this is to use NDAs in connection with its release to all parties. In addition, the company should implement a system of controls that prevent the content of the secret from being exposed, such as preparing written manuals describing the secret and keeping them locked up in a vault. This not only serves as documented proof of the secret but also shows the intent in trying to keep it concealed from unwanted eyes. [8]

Table 5-3. Patents versus Trade Secrets

	Patent	Trade Secret
Subject Matter	Specific and limited by statute (machines, articles of manufacture, processes, and compositions of matter)	Applies to broad range of intellectual property and business information
Requirements	Must be useful Must be novel Must not be obvious	Must be potentially useful Must not be generally known Need not be novel or obvious
Definition	Defined strictly by language of the "claims"	Often too difficult to define with equal precision, but can be as broad as the "equities" of a particular case require
Disclosure	Required	Any disclosure must be limited and controlled
Protection	Defined by narrow but specific statute Monopoly granted	Varies, depending on circumstances and court; based on many theories Protection only against "infair" users: none against those who independently discover or reverse-engineer
Duration	17 years from issuance	Potentially unlimited
Expense	Procuring	Protection from unauthorized disclosure or use
Risk	Invalidity	Independent discovery or inadvertent disclosure or use
Marketability	Licensing easier	Licensing more difficult, and requires policing of licensee security measures

Source: Fuld, L.M. 1995. *The New Competitor Intelligence.*

When To Use Trade Secret Protection

There are obviously certain advantages and disadvantages for the use of trade secret protection versus the use of more formally recognized forms of intellectual property. The following list provides some examples of when to use trade secrets, followed by some situations when trade secret protection is not applicable.

Trade Secret Protection Should Be Used When:

- The information is not patentable by statute (customer lists, sales forecasts, other lists)

- The information does not satisfy the criteria of patent protection (it is not novel, useful, and non-obvious)

- The information's useful life may extend beyond 20 years so that the potential for perpetual royalties can be preserved

- Patent disclosure may alert competitors of strategic direction and hinder future market gains

Trade Secret Protection Does Not Apply When:

- The invention can be reverse engineered

- Full disclosure of the trade secret has occurred willingly

Enforcement of Trade Secrets

The laws governing the protection of trade secrets vary according to each state, although most of these laws have been derived from the *Uniform Trade Secrets Act (UTSA)*.   In general, if a company suspects that another party has gained access to their trade secret without its permission, it can seek an *injunctive relief* to prevent further use and disclosure.   If the company wishes to claim damages as a result of the theft, use, and/or benefit of the trade secret it must prove that the content was held by the company as confidential information, the defendant obtained the information by illegal means, and the information represents a competitive advantage for parties who have possession of the secret.   Of course this can amount to high legal fees, which could devastate any startup or early stage company.

Even after safeguarding trade secrets using NDAs, there is a possibility of unauthorized use if an employee leaves to work for a competitor or a company in a similar line of business.   And while it may be very difficult to prove that the employee used the trade secret for the benefit of his new company, some states have an *"Inevitable Disclosure"* doctrine which prevents employees from working for competitors if the company can prove that its trade secrets will be disclosed to the competitor due to the nature and intent of the business.   High tech companies that reside in states that recognize an inevitable disclosure doctrine often require prospective employees to sign this document as a mandatory condition of employment.

While the costs of securing innovative ideas by trade secret protection is minimal, trade secret litigation has not reached the status enjoyed by patents in part due to the lack of legal structure supporting trade secrets.   *And unfortunately, trade secrets are not legally recognized until they are litigated.* But even then many times *courts will deny the existence of the trade secret due to improper documentation or failure to safeguard the secret adequately.* The Economic Espionage Act of 1996 specifies six criteria that trade secrets must prove in a court of law in order to validate their protection:

✓**Existence**   ✓**Access**   ✓*Use*

✓**Ownership**   ✓**Notice**   ✓*Damages*

In contrast, copyrights and trademarks only require the last two to be shown.

While some states have made the unauthorized acquisition, disclosure or use of trade secrets a crime, others have not.   However, *the international theft of trade secrets is punishable by the Economic Espionage Act of 1996 and enforces thefts that occur in the U.S as well as those occurring on foreign soil if the thief is a U.S citizen or corporation.*   If convicted under this law, individuals can face fines up to $500,000 and up to ten years prison time and companies can be fined up to $5,000,000.   And these fines and prison sentences are even longer if the theft was performed on behalf of a foreign government.

It has been estimated that the U.S. looses billions of dollars each year to trade secret theft by foreign governments.   However, trade secret protection against foreign governments is a much more sensitive issue that is earmarked with diplomacy issues and potential trade regulations.   In addition, it is much more difficult to prove the direct involvement of foreign governments in trade secret theft.   And even when there is compelling evidence in such cases, pursuit of justice can have longstanding implications on foreign relations. Unlike alleged trade secret theft by corporations or individuals, those implicating foreign government involvement require the approval of the U.S. Attorney General; a fact that might offer one explanation for the lack of historical international enforcement.

Ever since the passage of the act if 1996, U.S. prosecutors have gone after foreign governments only twice out of the forty plus cases that have been discovered.   However, as China continues its tremendous economic expansion and technology infrastructure build out, more trade secret violations will no doubt become the center of attention.   Currently, a landmark case may be heard between a U.S. corporation and two individuals thought to represent the interests of the Chinese government.   U.S. prosecutors have alleged that in November of 2003, two Chinese men, one a U.S. citizen the other a U.S. permanent resident, stole microchip blueprints and other trade secrets from

Transmeta Corp., Sun Microsystems and other companies in order to help China's semiconductor industry. Furthermore, prosecutors have claimed that this plan was funded by the Chinese city of Hangzhou.

The IP community will be watching closely, as this case may determine the future direction of the United States regarding these highly sensitive diplomatic issues. Ever since the policy change by various government agencies in the late 1970s, the U.S. has strengthened its innovative capacity at the expense of production capacity. And it is quite clear that *if trade secret law becomes difficult to enforce between foreign governments, America will experience a very difficult period of diminished technological and economic competitiveness.*

4. Trademarks and Service Marks

Trademarks are privileges granted by the government that ensure the protection of its holders against others using a *symbol of expressive identity associated with a company, product, or concept.* Trademarks are typically used to protect the brand names of products, services, logos, slogans, domain names, and graphic symbols that are used to distinguish the source of products and services from competitors. And because consumers often make purchasing decisions based upon identifiable trademarks, the USPTO protects these identifiers so consumers are not misled or confused about the products and services they are buying. As with the case of copyrights, trademark and patent protection usually do not overlap unless a product design provides brand identity as well as enhanced utility or appeal.

Unlike all other forms of intellectual property, the extent of trademark protection is dependent upon the specific company and its level of brand recognition. While trademark protection requires the mark to be distinctive and not generic, some generic trademarks may become distinctive over time due consumers associating it with a specific product. Thus, while a large well-established company may receive broad protection in terms of geographical boundaries and interpretive decisions, a small newer company may receive a more narrow limitation of protection.

A *service mark* is used to identify services, products or company concepts and is represented by an image. Examples of service marks are Kinko's (photocopying services), Ebay (online auction), and McDonalds (fast food restaurant). A *trade dress* is a distinctive physical feature of a product, such as packaging, odors and colors. Many times the trade dress overlaps with a trademark or service mark, and in such cases can be protected under these laws.

Both trademarks and service marks may be registered in a state for a period of ten years. And similar to the application process for patents, applicants should conduct searches to ensure that there are no preexisting marks registered.   There are four common methods used to estimate the value of trademarks and service marks.

1. **Cost-Avoidance Approach**
    This method is similar to valuating a portfolio of patents responsible for one or more products and assumes that the marketing and advertising campaigns will build brand recognition and contribute added value over the products' life cycle. Because expenditures for marketing tends to be highest initially and declines with product maturity, projected revenues are multiplied by declining percentages to reflect these decreased expenditures.

2. **Recent Transactions**
    Companies that have licensed a trademark or service mark can estimate the future expected cash flows to be generated from the license based upon previous results and the remaining time period the license is in effect. These resulting cash flows are then discounted back to a present value.

3. **Focus Groups & Surveys**
    This method relies on the data from customers in assessing the relative value of brand name recognition and perceived quality versus price as factors for purchase. For instance, if customers are willing to pay 15% more for a company's product, one can reasonable assume that the value of that company's brand name is responsible for 15% of its market value.

4. **Comparable Firm Approach**
    This method involves identifying one or more companies with competing products with similar growth rates and business risk factors but differing cost structures and operating margins as a result of their brand name. Thus, the difference in market valuation between the companies should theoretically be due to the relative differences in the perceived value of each brand name. This information is difficult if not impossible to determine for private companies and is more applicable to public companies, although seldom do two companies exhibit the same growth rates and risk factors.

Software: A Unique Intangible Asset

The Copyright Act of 1980 defined computer programs as "a set of statements or instructions to be used directly or indirectly in a computer in order to bring about a certain result." However, the scope of protection was limited in that it does not protect ideas, but rather only specific expression of those ideas.   To ensure the protection of the idea underlying the software as well as every other expression of that concept, a patent is needed.   Needless to say, the patenting of software is much more difficult than obtaining a copyright because the protection is stronger.

However, the protection of software poses a difficult challenge for companies due to the uniqueness of the products represented by this form of technological expression. Copyright protection provides the holder the exclusivity of reproduction, distribution, and selling of the source and object code of the software but does not provide protection of the concepts of the underlying programs. Some companies do not wish the programming concept to be known and will elect to protect it by use of trade secret protection. Finally, trademark protection can be a very powerful tool in helping to establish the branding behind a software product.   Therefore, in order to provide full protection of its products and technologies, one should determine the best combination of intellectual property tools that allows the company to achieve its goals.

D. Conclusion

The evolution of intellectual property law in the United States has resulted in a drastic shift from its previous status as the world's leading manufacturing nation into an information and technology powerhouse. As such, intellectual capital may be a high-technology company's greatest asset if it can be properly identified and transformed into the most appropriate form of intellectual property.   And the selection of the best structure of intellectual property serves to protect and enforce these assets in a manner that discourages infringement or seeks rapid reconciliation of such violations.

Of the four intellectual property rights, *only patents and trade secrets protect information*.   However, the patent application process is costly, difficult, and requires the patent holder to provide full disclosure of the invention.   In addition, the period of exclusivity of patent use is limited to twenty years, at most.   And by the time a company has fully developed and commercialized the products related to the patented technologies, most likely several years will have been eroded from the patent life.   Nevertheless, companies willing to make these sacrifices have been rewarded by the development of a specific legal infrastructure that serves to protect patent holders from infringement by other parties. For some firms, one or more of these disadvantages may cause them to select trade secret protection as an alternative form of protection since the secret does not need to be disclosed (and cannot be disclosed to the public in order to satisfy its protection as a trade secret), there is no filing time, no specific costs are required, and there is no expiration of exclusivity of rights.

Although trade secret protection can be indefinite, one must be extremely meticulous in following well-devised legal guidelines for establishing and safeguarding intellectual property to be claimed as trade secrets. The one disadvantage of trade secrets is derived from their main advantage; the lack of legal infrastructure. Thus, the ability of companies to predict the strength of legal challenge of its protected status is unknown. However, the best method to enhance the defensibility of trade secrets is to establish systematic controls that at minimum, establish written guidelines for securing the information and distribution of these assets. As with all other forms of intellectual property, all individuals who come into contact with the trade secret should sign an NDA, the secret should be secured in a security vault at all times, and exit interviews and release forms should be provided for all departing personnel. And because of the lack of legal structure dealing with trade secrets, these safeguarding measures are much more important than for other forms of intellectual property. Finally, all intellectual property should be carefully examined to make certain that the founder's previous company has no claims to any work performed while at his previous employer. These issues should be reviewed by attorneys experienced in intellectual property law.

Registering a Patent:

Asst. Comm. for Trademarks, Patent Applications
Arlington, VA 22202
Washington, D.C. 20231
(800) 786-9199

Registering a Trademark:

U.S. Department of Commerce
Trademark Office
2021 Jefferson Davis Highway
(703) 305-8341 or (800) 786- 9199

Applying for Copyright:

U.S. Copyright Office
U.S. Library of Congress
James Madison Memorial Building
Washington, D.C. 20559
(202) 707-3000

Regulatory Information on Importing/Exporting Intellectual Property:

U.S. Customs Office
Intellectual Property Rights Branch
1301 Constitution Avenue, N.W.
Washington, DC 20229
202-566-6956

Notes

[1] It is very difficult to express the full value of intangible assets in the balance sheet, but one alternative is to recapitalize (a method of expensing) R&D, marketing, advertising, and other sources of potentially hidden value and then amortize (i.e. spread the cost on the income statement and balance sheet) them over their future expected lives.

[2] **http://lcweb.loc.gov/copyright/** Note however that this database is not current with the date of filing and there may be a several month lag time between registration and submission into this database.

[3] **http://www.uspto.gov/web/offices/pac/mpep/consolidated_laws.pdf**

[4] http://www.uspto.gov/web/offices/pac/mpep/consolidated_rules.pdf

[5] See http://www.uspto.gov/web/offices/pac/utility/utilityguide.pdf and http://www.uspto.gov/web/offices/pac/writtendesc.pdf

[6] In financial terms, a portfolio is defined as a collection of liquid assets. Patents represent intangible assets of variable liquidity depending upon the patents in the portfolio. Theoretically, unless patents within a portfolio have some degree of liquidity, they cannot qualify as components of such a portfolio. Therefore, the mere collection of patents does not necessarily constitute a patent portfolio.

[7] This assumption is nothing new however, as the number of citations in all areas of science are thought to be somewhat proportional to the quality and impact of the research.

[8] Because the Uniform Trade Secrets Act does not provide specific guidelines for the guaranteed protection of trade secrets, companies should work with an attorney specializing in U.S. trade secret law to develop a systematic and documented procedure for securing the confidentiality of its innovations claimed as trade secrets.

6

Forming Competitive Strategies

*"The concept is interesting and well-informed, but in order
to earn better then a 'C', the idea must be feasible."*

A Yale University management professor in response to student Fred Smith's paper proposing a
reliable overnight delivery service (Smith went on to found Federal Express Corp.)

A. From Business Model to Strategy

Today's marketplace is one of infinite possibilities and limitless boundaries due to recent innovative technologies that have created more efficient and inexpensive means of transportation, telecommunication services, and computing power. Furthermore, the proliferation of the Internet as a business tool has made it possible to extend one's potential customer base to all continents at minimal cost. Thus certain competitive advantages once thought to be effective are now antiquated. However, the fundamental rules of business remain unchanged and no company can expect to succeed without developing a well-devised competitive business strategy. The topic of strategy provides a challenge to introduce in such a limited space because of the complexities associated with the many schools of thought on this discipline. This is in part due to the recent acknowledgement of strategy as a legitimate and universally accepted business discipline. In this chapter we will discuss basic strategies and methods that can be used to help companies create a sustainable competitive advantage and deal with competitive attacks.

Strategy may be defined as the "analyses, activities, and processes associated with linking the internal capabilities of a company with its external environment." And rather than defining strategy as planning, vision, or forecasting, it should be thought of as a set of analytical techniques used to understand one's company, market, and competitors in order to create a positive change in company position.   Finally, the definition of competitive strategy is implicit within the subject content of strategy, since without adequate regard to competitive planning and positioning, a company's strategy would be inadequate.   Strategy development for any company is a very difficult and time-consuming task that should be under continuous cultivation, as the dynamics of one's company, its competitors, and the market are always changing in an interdependent manner.

The most basic elements of a company's business strategy focus on the realization of its goals and mission, which serve as the nucleus for the business model.   From chapter 1, you will recall that there are six issues a business model should address if the company wishes to achieve maximum success.   These six factors are value proposition, market segment, value chain structure, cost structure and profit potential, position in the value network, and competitive strategy.   Rather than an equal component of the business model however, the *competitive strategy may be viewed as the intellectual engine that drives the other five components*.   While the business model is an expression of the methods that will be used to create value, the competitive strategy is the blueprint that serves to capture the full extent of this value by structuring a sustainable competitive advantage over its rivals.

The next tier of strategy formation specifically involves the analysis of and reaction to competitors' activities, enabling the company to navigate through these competitive forces and achieve substantial growth.   For privately held companies seeking outside financing, an exit strategy is a very important issue but is merely the result of superior positioning through the effective execution of its business strategy.   While mention will be made of these strategic elements, the focus of this chapter is on competitive strategy, which should be the most critical focus of the management team.

Positional Strategy versus Operational Effectiveness

One can think of strategy as the careful planning of different activities in order to create a unique and valuable position relative to the competition.   In contrast, the process of *strategic positioning* is best described by Michael Porter as "a system that attempts to achieve a sustainable competitive advantage by preserving what is distinct about a company by performing different activities from rivals or performing similar activities in different ways."   Examples of these activities may be serving specialized needs of many customers, serving the broad needs of a few customers, or serving the broad needs of many customers within a small market.   Effective strategic positioning also demands that a company make *trade-offs* in activity selection. Finally, strategic positioning requires a company to form *cohesiveness* among its activities so that each activity adds reinforcement to the others.

In contrast, *operational effectiveness* focuses on performing the same basic activities of a company's operations with a higher effectiveness and efficiency than its competitors. While operational effectiveness is essential for creating superior performance within a company, alone it will not produce a sustainable difference because it can be easily imitated and thus will not distinguish a company from its competitors. It follows that neither strategic positioning nor operational effectiveness alone is sufficient to create a sustainable competitive advantage for companies. *Rather, companies must be able to execute both operational effectiveness and positional strategy in order to secure a sustainable competitive advantage* (figure 6-1).

As a company perfects its best practices in production, sales, and marketing, costs will decline as the efficiency of production and distribution improve. But competitors will eventually imitate these practices, thereby eliminating the distinctiveness of the company. In addition, as competitors focus on benchmarking in order to match the operational effectiveness of its rivals, they become victims of *competitive convergence*. The result is that overemphasis on operational effectiveness amongst competitors actually has eliminated any distinctions between companies and they begin to resemble each other. Subsequently, the consumer will be the recipient of this industry wide operational effectiveness, as companies slash prices in an attempt to gain an advantage over competitors. Examples of these effects can be readily seen in technology industries, such as telecommunications, computers, and consumer electronics. *Thus the first key step to creating a competitive strategy is to perform different activities than the competition because the essence of strategy is being distinctive in some way.*

However, it is not enough to perform discrete activities as a part of a company's competitive strategy because these activities can easily be imitated, similar to the ease of duplicating the discrete activities associated with operational effectiveness. *In order to produce a sustainable competitive advantage, a company must implement those activities that have the best fit and this involves trade-offs with other activities* so that some activities are emphasized more than others. One might envision emphasizing activities that provide reinforcing value to other activities and de-emphasizing those activities that do not provide much reinforcement.

There are three levels of *strategic fit*, according to Michael Porter. We will only discuss the first two levels for simplicity. *The first level is consistency between activities.* An example of this would be Sam's Club, a discount wholesaler of consumer goods. The consistency of activities in this case is focused on low-cost, and in order to provide discounts of items, customers must buy large portions. In addition, Sam's does not accept credit cards (other than Discover) due to their high service fees. Finally, there are no grocery bags at Sam's, serving to reinforce their "bare bones" cost-cutting

Figure 6-1. Sustainable Competitive Advantage Formed by Strategic Positioning and Operational Effectiveness

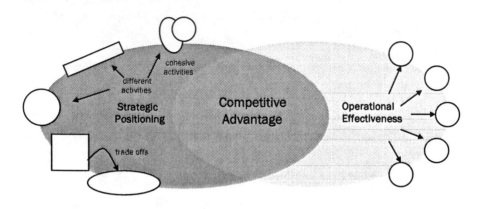

Original illustration by M. Stathis

image.   Thus, the marketing strategy behind Sam's Club is that expenses are minimized and volume purchases are rewarded with wholesale prices. Regardless whether the prices at Sam's are truly the cheapest, the importance of their low-cost marketing strategy is that *customers have the perception* that they are the cheapest because they understand and can identify with the company's business strategy.

The second level of strategic fit involves reinforcing activities, whereby activities influence other activities indirectly.   This may be seen by considering a hypothetical strategy of a computer printer company that sells its printers well below cost.   The strategy would be to gain a large market share, thereby resulting in a large dependency on this company's ink cartridges or laser toners, which will provide recurring revenues.   Perhaps a better example would be Amazon.com building a large customer base by selling books below cost but recovering the loss and making profits on other items it sells.   By building a large loyal customer base, companies can leverage other products and services to its customers and make up any shortfalls in profits from other items.   *Therefore, in assembling a cohesive infrastructure of linked activities, it will be more difficult for competitors to duplicate any single activity such as sales or marketing strategy due to the indirect effects these activities have on other activities in this strategic unit.*

Strategic Approaches for Network Industries

A network spillover (externality) industry is one whose product sales benefit from the product sales of other companies in the same or similar industries.   Such companies have exploded over the past two decades due to the advances and widespread reliance on information technology and telecommunications. A good example of this concept is the network spillover seen in the computer software and hardware industries. For instance, as Microsoft adds updates to its Windows operating system, older computers would eventually begin to experience diminished speed and performance due to limitations in memory and processor speed.   This is great news for Dell, Hewlett-Packard Compaq, IBM and the microprocessor companies Intel and AMD because customers will need to buy new computers or upgrade their current ones in order to run the new version of Windows.

In addition, as new versions of Windows are installed all software applications designed for the previous edition of Windows will be incompatible with the new version and the user will need to purchase updated versions of the software products made for the latest Windows update. Likewise, as Intel or AMD develop a new microprocessor Microsoft will have to develop a new version of Windows so the operating system is compatible with or optimizes the full computing power of the hardware.   It should be easy to see that such network spillover companies have an interdependent synergy and thus indirectly promote need for the products made by companies in different but related industries.   Finally, *despite this apparent mutual dependency between companies within network spillover industries, they are usually dominated by a single company or standard*, as with Microsoft's operating system dominance of the computer software industry.[1]

There are three types of network spillovers. The first is a *direct spillover*. An example of a *direct spillover* was mentioned above and is illustrated in figure 6-2.   The second type is an *indirect spillover*.   An example of this type of spillover would be a software company that focuses its products for use with IBM compatible computers as opposed to Apple, which has a smaller market share.   Companies that wish to benefit from indirect spillover companies will target their products to the largest player so that they will have a piece of the largest market.   The final spillover is *word of mouth*. The larger the network of customers using a product brand, the easier access one has to information about it and the easier it can be serviced.

These three network effects can coexist for the same company or product. And when significant externalities are involved, the best selling product is not necessarily the one providing the best performance and value.   The reason for this is due to the exterior support given to the product by the externalities. Finally, trying *to directly compete with a company that has network effects and that is firmly established within its network should be avoided.* Rather, the best approach is to leverage the network externalities within your company's industry. In other words, when a company wishes to enter a market dominated by network effects, it should learn the rules of the game and play by them in order to maximize its chances of survival.

Figure 6-2. Example of Direct Spillover Effects

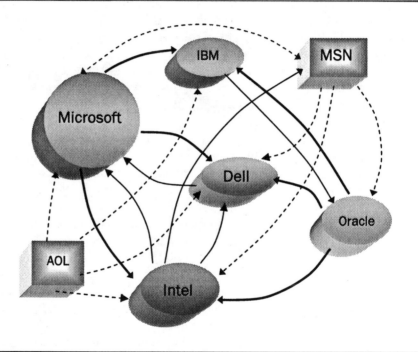

Strategies for Network Effects

<u>Speed</u>. Perhaps the greatest force determining a company's success within an industry with network effects is the *speed at which products and services reach the consumer.* By building an early customer base, a company will be at a strategic advantage to its competitors. Yahoo!, Ebay, Amazon, and AOL began over a decade ago just when the Internet was beginning and therefore, these companies have created a loyal following. They were able to create a customer base when there was none and newer companies will have to compete with the network effects these companies have established. So what does one do? The best approach is to create a company that lies within this

network but complimentary to these providers. New entrants should tailor their products and services with those of the incumbents and these companies provide your customers rather than trying to steal them away.

Buzz. Generating consumer buzz can be an effective method of gaining traction in a network industry and may be the only alternative if your company has not yet completed its product. People always want the latest greatest technology, but sometimes what they want most is what everyone else has. Betamax provided superior video display resolution but VHS became the standard because of their highly successful marketing approaches. At some point prior to the conclusion of the battle between Betamax versus VHS, people began requesting VHS machines because they were led to believe these would become the standard due to the buzz. Apple is now doing this with its iPod, and although there are clearly superior products in the marketplace, Apple's superior marketing strategy has created a tremendous buzz for the iPod.

Creating a product buzz can also be a method of creating competitor sabotage even when a company has not developed a competing product. If people believe your product will be the superior standard, they will hold off buying the competitor's product and this will cause a decreased chance of this competitor to control the market. This tactic can buy time for a company to develop and launch its product without having lost much market share. This strategy is used frequently in the computer software and hardware industries.

Early Adaptors. This strategy is focused on gaining the support of influential customers or a large customer base, much like IBM did many years ago when it convinced computer labs in high schools and universities to use their computers. Apple Computers learned the hard way from the results of this successful strategy and is now doing this globally. Essential to this strategy is having *adequate distribution channels* for product delivery.

Pricing. Industries with network spillovers use the same strategies as those with large economies of scale: penetration by pricing, because competitive pricing helps bring in more users, which creates an economies of scale environment. However, this is difficult for small companies to accomplish because they lack the financial resources required to win a potential price war.

Alliances. The use of alliances may be preferred for newer companies with limited resources in an industry with potential future competitors. In addition, because many industries with network spillovers are high-technology companies, alliances with more experienced companies may be necessary to help establish industry standards.

B. The Competitive Environment

In order to develop an effective business strategy, companies must distinguish themselves from the competition. However, *startup companies will have a difficult time achieving success if they are too different because there is a certain interdependency amongst all high-tech companies within the same industry, even when there are no network effects present.* Therefore, certain aspects of established companies should be imitated while others should be avoided at all cost. We have already seen an example of each of these scenarios in our previous discussions of positional strategy and network effects. This section provides a framework for understanding and identifying the competitive forces so that companies can position themselves in a manner that deflects competitor attacks.

Price Competition

Contrary to popular belief, companies do not make conscious decisions to begin a price war. Rather, price wars occur due the cycle of reciprocating price cuts in response of competing companies. For some incumbents that are loosing market share, initiating a price cut may appear to be the logical solution. But when competitors reciprocate these cuts, this can lead to a long war with the consumers as the only victor. However, a protracted price war may ultimately lead to a diminished quality of products and services over a longer-term period due to the inability or unwillingness of companies to reinvest in further R&D and enhance product development. *Therefore, in the short run the consumer is always the winner of a price war. Meanwhile, in the long run the consumer may or may not benefit from a price war, depending upon several factors.*

The take away lesson is that *when considering a price cut, a company should always perform a scenario analysis on its competitors to assess the complete impact that the initial price cut will ultimately have on its longer-term profitability.* The trick for companies that wish to gain more of the market is to establish price discounts that increase market share and add more profits than the cost of the cuts and to create these price levels in a manner that does not result in a reciprocal reaction by competitors, and hence the beginnings of a price war. Finally, remember that *in order to be classified as a price war, the competitors engaging in the discounting must be viewed by the customers as having products of similar quality.* Otherwise, customers will not react to price cuts. In contrast, increasing product differentiation can lead to leverage, which a company can use to raise prices.

Factors Affecting Price Competition

Number of Companies in an Industry. The more companies within an industry, the less incentive each company will have to lower prices for the chance to gain a small portion of the competitor's market. In addition, such a saturated industry will experience less cooperation among companies with respect to price control due to antitrust laws.[2]   Thus, in industries with a large number of companies competing for a small market, *strong competition is almost always good for the consumer but often bad for the companies.*

Differences Among the Companies Within an Industry.   Due to many differences among companies, the priorities of each may be different. For instance, one company may be structured to benefit more through cost cutting measures while another may receive greater benefit through more advertising. As such, *cooperativity between companies decreases as their underlying differences increase because increasing distinctiveness promotes strength of each brand name, making it easier for customers to make choices and companies to validate price differences.*

Short-run Gain From Cutting Prices.   If product differentiation among competing companies is high, the incentive to cut prices is decreased since consumers will not view the products as comparables and will tend de-emphasize the lower price and focus their emphasis on the difference in products. In contrast, for companies with low product differentiation among competitors, when product capacity is high there is a large incentive to decrease price in order to multiply the effects of price advantage.

Price Transparency.   Low price transparency can cause confusion among management teams when sales have declined as they question whether competitors have cut prices, the quality of its products (as perceived by its former customers) has diminished, or the industry is experiencing a trough in the business cycle.   As such, a company must be very familiar with industry demand and trends at all times in order to localize the effects of price transparency.   *Low price transparency combined with marginal sales will tend to raise the incentive to cut prices.*

Limited Producer Capacity.   This situation results in a low supply relative to consumer demand and is usually seen in two general situations.   The first situation may occur when a company is a provider of an emerging technology or service where the competitors are few.   The capacity of the company to serve the demand of a rapidly growing market can be the limiting factor when the company has limited resources.   It will therefore raise prices to strike a balance between consumer demand and internal capacity. The other situation may arise due to government regulation, as in wireless spectrum licenses. In cases of limited capacity, prices will surpass the inter-company competitive forces and allow all companies to succeed in this market, where customer demand places less priority on pricing and more emphasis on receiving the goods and services. *Limited producer capacity in a market with high demand is obviously one of the sweet spots that allow potentially high company product leveraging.*

Figure 6-3. Factors Affecting Price Competition

- Number of Companies in an Industry

- Differences Among the Companies on an Industry

- Short-run Gain From Cutting Prices

- Price Transparency

- Limited Producer Capacity

Competitive Pricing Relationships

In order to gain a better understanding of their intended market, companies must identify the types of competitive relationships within their industry so they are better able to determine whether to conform to the existing competitive structure or implement an opposing strategy. There are three general types of competitive relationships that give rise to the full spectrum of possibilities. In reality, companies will not exactly mimic any of these relationships but will tend to resemble one over the other. In order to illustrate these relationships we will assume a normal free market economy whereby two competitors seek to maximize profits, which are determined by the overall industry demand, as well as each competitor's share of market demand, as well as the prices charged by each company and the competitors.

1. *Independent (Nash).* Each company determines pricing independent of its competitor's pricing structure so that each company's market share is determined by the prices of both companies.

2. *Leader-follower behavior (Stackelberg).* One company determines its prices for goods and based upon this the competitor decides upon its price for the same set of goods.

3. *Collusive behavior.* Both companies agree on the prices to charge. This is a rare event for truly competing companies. However it can result in high profits by a mutual agreement of price control.

There are three basic statistical methods for determining competitive relationships but the *Granger causality* is the easiest to understand. This method requires only market input data such as pricing and advertising spending and is therefore the easiest to perform. It relates the actions of one company in a previous time period to the actions of a competitor in the current time period. If the actions of the first company result in the actions of the second company but the opposite does not hold, then the first company is the leader and the second company is the follower. However, this method does not detail the nature of this relationship and cannot test for collusive behavior. Furthermore, one must be careful to select time periods that are consistent with actions. Finally, one may be tempted to assess the competitive relationships between companies through mere observation, however this is recommended only as a final check after more accurate determinations have been made.

The Five Forces Framework

In this section, we have discussed some competitive relationships and we highlighted three different models of competitive relationships, whose emphasis was on the prices charged by each company as well as the competitors. Rather than restrict competitive analysis to price factors alone, thereby posing limitations on industries that have factors more important than or in addition to pricing decisions, Michael Porter uses the "Five Forces Framework" to describe the competitive environment, which is subject to a more comprehensive and therefore realistic situation. *This framework is based upon identifying and measuring those elements of a market thought to be most decisive in determining the dynamics of the competitive environment and can be used to determine the overall appeal and potential profitability of entering or remaining in a particular market.*

Figure 6-4 illustrates the five forces framework encapsulated within a triangle. Notice the three broader forces external to the entire five forces framework. Each of these external forces should be examined both in isolation and in combination with each other as well as with each of the five forces because they are potential sources of industry change. **Government and regulatory intervention** can cause major changes to industries in general and can have specific consequences for companies within. Understanding such interventions can help companies recognize potential future opportunities and threats within an industry and therefore allow them to incorporate this information within their overall strategic planning process. For instance, government deregulation in the telecommunications industry created opportunities for certain companies while establishing potential threats to others. Those companies that were able to recognize the full implications of this deregulation were able to adjust their strategies accordingly and exploit these changes for their benefit.

Technological change is an inevitable aspect of any industry and can create opportunities for new entrants while posing threats for existing companies. Understanding the convergence of technologies within neighboring industries can thus provide valuable insight for companies to redirect their operations, production, and technology platforms. The telecommunications industry provides a good example of the importance of recognizing technology change. After deregulation, the door was opened for new entrants to steal market share away from the more traditional telecommunications companies. The entrants included direct competitors as well as competitors attempting to modify the industry by incorporating technological advances in networking, the Internet, and wireless communications. Those companies that were knowledgeable about these emerging technologies were able to create a strategic plan to capture portions of the market unmet by existing technologies.

Market demand influences many dynamics of competitive strategies, as high growth industries experience an increase of new entrants and incumbents are more concerned with meeting customer demand rather than fighting for market share. As the number of new entrants increases, market share becomes more fragmented and increased competition for market share can result in an industry shakeout. In contrast, when an industry is experiencing slowed growth this causes an increased competition for market share and potential new entrants are deterred due to the intense competition.

We now direct our focus to each of the five forces and examine their competitive dynamics. Within the confines of the five forces framework, we see four forces that converge towards the fifth, or the *Direct Rivalry Among Competitors*. *Rivalry among competitors occurs because companies either feel threatened or they perceive opportunity.* And actions taken by one

Figure 6-4.   Forces Influencing Arena Attractiveness

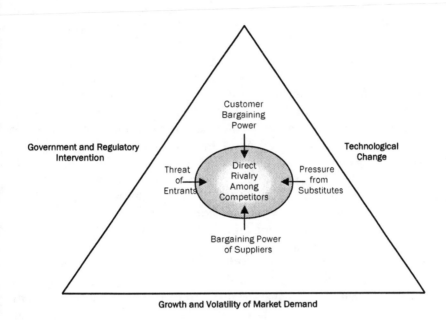

Source: Day & Reibstein

company are likely to result in responsive activities by the other companies within the industry.   Thus, because companies within the same industry share a certain amount of *mutual dependency*, industry conditions can be affected by competitive moves of companies within. *Price competition* is one example of an action that can result in an overall decrease in industry profits of a large number of companies if they decide to react to the company that is determined to be the price leader.

In contrast, *competitive advertising* is used to establish product differentiation within a given industry and can lead to increased profits for all or some of the competing companies.   If the advertising serves to promote the overall industry, the entire market may increase, resulting in benefits for all competitors.   However, this is usually a secondary effect created by the company whose goals are to demonstrate to consumers how their products are different from the competition.   The extent of rivalry will be largely influenced by the specific features within a given industry, such as the total number of competitors, the number of balanced competitors, the growth rate of the industry, the relative amount of fixed costs required for operation with an industry, the extent of product differentiation, the diversity of competitors, the incentives for success of each company, and high exit barriers.

Customer Bargaining Power can create direct rivalry among competitors, threatening to diminish the profitability of the overall industry if the customer group represents strong purchasing power, the industry is highly competitive and comprised of companies with homogenous strategies (see table 6-2), the industry is characterized by a large percentage of fixed costs, the customer group has relatively small switching costs, *backward integration* is a plausible threat of the customers, or the customer group is fully informed about the industry.   If several of these factors are present to variable degrees or one is present to a large degree, customer groups can force prices downward, demand more services, or demand higher quality products and services.   This could result in a battle amongst competitors for the business of these groups. Therefore, the importance of *buyer selection* can provide a formidable preventative strategy for those companies who wish to protect against the potential damaging effects of influential buyer groups.

Bargaining Power of Suppliers can equally promote direct competitive rivalry causing diminished industry profitability if the supplier groups are more concentrated than the industry it sells to, positioned so that they are not required to compete with substitutes, the industry served by the supplier groups is not important to the business of these groups, the suppliers' products and services are important for the business, the suppliers' products and services are heterogeneous, switching costs for the buyers is high, or the threat of forward integration is feasible.

Threat of Substitute Products has perhaps the most direct effect of restricting prices charged for goods and services within an industry.   Certain industries are more susceptible than others to the effects of price implosion, such as commodity-based industries.   Even when an industry is dominated by commodities, it is often possible for competitors to distinguish their products by implementing effective marketing strategies, which will create the perception of higher quality and therefore enhance the company brand.

The *Threat of Entrants* into an industry is dependent upon the barriers to market entry, as well as the reactions of the established competitors within that industry towards new entrants.   Depending upon the nature of the industry, the benefits to each company, and the strategic approach taken, certain strategies can either act to prevent new entrants or the entrants can overcome these deterrents and capture market share.   Because the focus of this book is on early stage companies, we will examine these potential barriers to entry in detail.

Barriers to Market Entry

Product Differentiation. Because new companies lack brand recognition and financial resources, first and foremost *they must establish significant product differentiation that will cause the customer to sacrifice familiarity for promised product attributes.* Product differentiation is thought to be the most important entry barrier in cosmetics, over-the-counter drugs, baby-care products, financial services, and public accounting, perhaps due to the similarity of products and services in these industries and the reliance upon intense marketing strategies that create the perception of product differentiation.

Access to Distribution Channels. Even armed with the best products and services, a new company needs sufficient access to the proper distribution channels to deliver these goods to customers. Without industry knowledge, know-how, and networks, companies will have an uphill battle competing with more established vendors. *Access to the proper distribution networks serves as one of the main reasons some companies elect to form strategic alliances and joint ventures.* Consider a company that has developed an innovative thermostat controlling mechanism that is far superior to any product on the market. In order to gain significant market penetrance, the company will need sufficient industry knowledge and networks in order to secure adequate channels of distribution that will enable it to compete against well-entrenched competitors such as Honeywell and General Electric, whose brand names and distribution channels are firmly entrenched.

Legal barriers. These represent a relatively static and virtually impenetrable portion of defense for new companies and specifically includes intellectual property and government regulatory policies. While little can be done to overcome these negative forces, the well-prepared company can scale many of the other barriers, which are far more prevalent in emerging markets. In addition, *regulatory change or industry consolidation often provides opportunities to gain market share* if companies can recognize these trends and are able to modify their business strategy to exploit these changes.

Economies of Scale. This is the advantage afforded to large companies that have achieved a large market share and results in decreases in production and operation expenses, as higher volumes of product are made. In some industries, economies of scale are absolutely necessary, such as those requiring substantial fixed costs, while in others, economies of scale can assist the companies in competitive pricing strategies. Since newer companies lack the needed financial resources and customer base needed for economies of scale, *price advantages are rarely successful with early stage companies.*

High Minimum Efficient Scale Relative to Market Size.   This means that a certain market share must be controlled in order for the company to recover its cost of capital (i.e. its total business expenses).   This relates to market capacity, which is determined by the overall industry dynamics influencing factors such as business expense (production, research, sales and marketing costs), market growth potential, and competitive landscape (number of incumbents relative to market size and growth potential).

Cost Disadvantages Independent of Scale.   This refers to cost advantages of well-established companies that are not matched by new entrants, regardless of economies of scale.   In particular, established companies' proprietary product technology, tying up resources, favorable location, government subsidies, and experience curve factors can all contribute to cost advantages of the experienced companies.   Of particular note, *experience curves can cause manufacturing and production expenses to decline as the labor force becomes more skilled and product design changes are made.* These effects are usually strongest in industries with high labor content or requiring complex manufacturing assemblies.   *The most important aspect of the cost declines associated with the experience curve is to transform and protect this know-how into intellectual property so competition cannot duplicate it.*

Government Policy.   This can be a major source of barriers for new entrants depending on the industry.   Typically, highly regulated industries such as trucking, railroad, liquor retailing, airlines, and telecommunications can be subject to variable periods of tight regulation which can either create a barrier for entry or a window of opportunity, depending upon the company.   Such policy changes can result in limitations on access to raw materials, product standards, environmental standards, and other limitations that can increase the cost of doing business in these industries due to the costs of compliance and thereby favor those companies that have achieved economies of scale. In contrast, policy changes can also ease restrictions within an industry in order to promote the entry of more competitors.

Large Sunken Expenditures.   This refers to industries whose companies have assets that are not liquid and have a low resell value.   Companies will consider the purchase of such assets as a high risk, as will financial institutions, which will make it difficult for them to receive external financing due to poor collateral.

Network Externalities.   This was discussed earlier in this chapter, but essentially occurs when the value of a product is greater when it has more end-users. It is very difficult to compete with companies that have network externalities and in order to have a chance, the entrant must become a participant within the existing network and play by the rules established by the incumbents or else it will have very little success competing.

Capital Requirements. Industries such as the airlines, utilities, semiconductors, and oil exploration are very capital intensive and often require rapid increases in capacity to accommodate new trends in customer demand. Without adequate capital to finance such operations, companies can miss out on market share independent of competitive forces.

Switching Costs. These are one-time costs associated with some change occurring within the company, such as employee training costs for expansion, costs associated with switching suppliers, new equipment or facilities. Once again, the new entrants will be limited to the extent by which they are able to absorb these costs.

Incumbent First Mover Advantages. Incumbents are better-positioned than new entrants if they have established distribution networks, customer loyalty, and a reputable brand name. The effects of *first mover advantages will depend somewhat on the nature of the products and services, and to a larger extent on the growth and capacity of the market.* Emerging markets with unmet capacity make it easier for new entrants to gain entry since the incumbents might be experiencing difficulties meeting consumer demand and will therefore tend not to devote significant resources towards attacking these entrants. This might provide sufficient time for these entrants to establish their own branding and customer loyalty, thereby positioning them when competition becomes intense.

It should easy to appreciate that the early stage company has very little influence over many of these barriers, however the alert management team that is able to recognize their presence will have a better chance in navigating around them. Finally, note that *entry barriers can change with changing economic and industry dynamics* and although such changes will usually be independent of the company, specific strategies can influence the ease or difficulty in scaling these barriers. Just as firms with adequate financial and technological resources may be able to scale certain entry barriers, *those companies with well-planned strategies and a sustainable competitive advantage will also increase their chances of surpassing these barriers.*

Figure 6-5. Barriers to Market Entry

- Access to Distribution Channels
- Economies of Scale
- High Minimum Efficient Scale Relative to Market Size
- Cost Disadvantages Independent of Scale
- Government Policy
- Large Sunken Expenditures
- Network Externalities
- Capital Requirements
- Switching Costs
- Incumbent First Mover Advantages
- Legal Barriers
- Product Differentiation

Competitive Response to New Entrants

When the presence of a new entrant is detected, competitors within the industry must decide their responses in a timely manner.   Likewise, *when early stage companies plan to enter a new market, they need to anticipate the most likely responses of their competitors so they are prepared for any possible retaliatory actions from incumbents.*   Therefore, we examine here the possible actions of incumbents upon new entrants in order to prepare for methods of counterattack.   When an incumbent detects the presence of a new entrant, it should address five key issues relative to the entrant: competitive stance, magnitude, speed, domain, and weapon (figure 6-6).

Competitive Stance.   The company must first decide if it will respond at all. It may choose to do nothing, taking the more conservative "wait-and-see" approach, which will give management more time to fully assess the situation. In contrast, the company may decide to respond by accommodation, abandonment, or retaliation.   *Accommodation* would be the preferred method to avoid possible confrontation with the new entrant but would only be feasible if the market is large enough for all competitors. On the other hand, such a passive gesture could be interpreted as a sign of weakness by the remaining incumbents, who may recognize this as an opportunity to attack the accommodating incumbent. Therefore, if accommodation is chosen, the company should attempt to communicate its reasons to the competitors, such as relying messages that "the size and growth of the market necessitates more entrants in order to fulfill customer demand."

If the entrant has a tremendous competitive advantage and the current market is already saturated with intense competition, an incumbent may elect to *abandon the market* in order to prevent potential losses in fighting a loosing battle for small rewards. Meanwhile, *retaliation* by increasing sales and marketing expenditures could send a signal to the entrant that the company is committed to the market. And while such a move could result in temporary decreases in profit margins, it might prevent future companies from entering the market and therefore represent a good long-term investment.

Magnitude. When attempting to determine the relative magnitude of the retaliation, the incumbent can either match the move of the entrant or try to outdo it. If the incumbent seeks to match the moves of the entrant, it is attempting to send a message that it will counter every move made by the entrant in order to protect its highly valued market share. In contrast, if the incumbent chooses to aggressively retaliate, it will mirror the entrant's moves with more intensity hoping to cause direct damage and deter any further advancement.

For instance, if an entrant provides a price advantage, an incumbent's matching strategy might involve a similar decrease in price. If this tug of war continues, it could quickly result in a price war. For early stage companies, price competition is almost always accompanied by failure because such companies do not have the financial power to withstand a potential price war. Of course, incumbents realize this and may react with such a move if the entrant's products have minimal differentiation. A more likely scenario might be that the entrant has introduced a higher quality product than the incumbent, in which case a matching approach might involve an increase in R&D expenditures or an asset acquisition. Meanwhile, if the incumbent decides to outdo the entrant, it might enact a combination of price cuts, increased sales force and marketing efforts.

Speed. If the incumbent decides to match the entrant's move, it will need to determine how quickly to react. It can react immediately, take a "wait-and-see" response, or anticipate the move before it happens. Each of these responses has unique advantages and disadvantages and the final choice will depend on the industry and competitiveness of the market. An immediate response might be suited for a new market that has yet to become saturated with established leaders. On the other hand, such markets usually provide adequate room for additional competitors so the incumbents may choose to spend their resources gaining market share rather than battling with a new entrant with minimal market presence. When the market is more competitive, an immediate response might be indicated for preventing the entrant from becoming entrenched. Finally, the best approach might be a preemptive strategy, whereby the entrant is deterred even before it begins to access the market. We will detail this approach later in this chapter.

Domain. The incumbent can respond in the same market of the entrant or in a different market. The typical response is to defend the market of the entrant's attack as a way to protect its market position and demonstrate its market commitment. However, if the entrant has differentiated itself sufficiently, the incumbent may find that it makes more sense to fight back by moving to a different market segment. This decision will depend upon the competitive position of the incumbent and the entrant, the potential market losses, and the estimated expenditures involved in the response.

Weapon. The final consideration for the response to the entrant is to choose the type of retaliation. Although incumbents usually react with the same threat used by the entrant, this may not necessarily provide the best result and would depend upon the magnitude of the entrant's threat, as well as the resources of the incumbent. Examples of responses can be demonstrated through pricing, advertising, increasing sales force, distribution, promotions, and introducing new products. Finally, the decisions involved in the response to the entrant will depend on how important the market is to the incumbent, the ability of the incumbent to respond, and the relative size of the threat created by the entrant.

Scaling the Barriers

Regardless of the sophistication of the technology, there will always be formidable barriers that prevent market entry for those companies that have not analyzed, planned, and structured a sound business strategy that identifies and incorporates its internal strengths and weaknesses and any perceived industry threats and opportunities. *Simply having the best technology will not guarantee a company's success, as the preeminent technology of today can soon become the obsolete technology of tomorrow.* All too often, early stage management teams with fantastic technologies think they have a guaranteed success and therefore downplay the importance of competitive strategy and execution. However, *management teams must recognize the importance of strategic planning and positioning in securing the growth of their company.*

Figure 6-6. Decision Model for Determining Response to a New Entrant

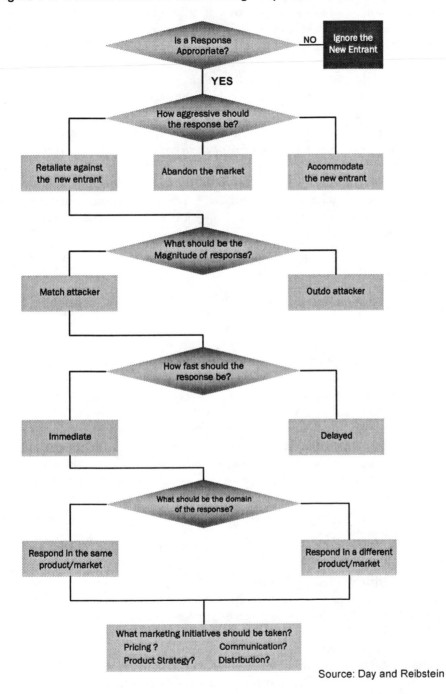

Source: Day and Reibstein

A startup or early stage company should think of their technology as a "generic resume," which merely provides a potential opportunity for entry into the marketplace.   However, the ability to achieve and sustain rapid growth is dependent upon how well the technology is positioned with respect to the target market and the competitors within.   Therefore, management teams must fully assess the dynamics of their market, looking beyond the competitors' technologies and focus on how they have achieved their success. For instance, *understanding the competitor's channels of distribution, its supplier relationships, marketing strategies, sales force structure, supply chain management techniques, and revenue models will assist the company in gaining an overall understanding of how the competitor has translated its business strategy into market leadership.*   If you build it they will not come unless they know you have it and they are convinced it adds value above the competition's products.   We will look more closely at methods to scale entry barriers during our next discussion of Porter's generic strategies.

Porter's Generic Strategies

In dealing with the five competitive forces, Porter identified three generic strategies for outperforming industry competitors.   These strategies are generic because they are not dependent upon industry type.   They include overall cost leadership, differentiation, and focus, and are based upon applying a cost advantage and differentiation in either a broad or narrow perspective (table 6-1).

The *cost leadership strategy* targets a broad market and aims to sell products at average industry prices while offering a higher quality product or the same product quality at a lower price.   As noted previously, price advantages are rarely effective for early stage companies due to the lack of adequate resources and market share required to produce efficient economies of scale.   In contrast, for more mature companies, price advantages may be achieved by lowering operation costs, purchasing raw materials in large quantities, improving production efficiency, efficient use of outsourcing, and vertical integration.

Companies that are successful in creating cost leadership will often have better access to external capital, improved operational efficiency, and efficient channels of distribution.   However, many companies will not be able to develop an effective cost leadership strategy due to the nature of their products, industry, or the markets served.   In general, *the best products for a cost leadership strategy are those that are closer to the maturity phase in the product life cycle* (discussed in the next section) or require very little cost for reproduction and modification, combined with readily accessible distribution channels.   Thus, most small companies will not be able to execute this type of strategy effectively.

The risks of a cost leadership strategy are that competitors may mimic the efficient processes and operations of the company and render the advantage useless. Thus, there must be necessary changes that are protected in the form of patents and trade secrets and these implementations must work synergistically with the overall strategy. However, companies choosing a cost leadership strategy can be overtaken by early stage companies with innovative products of high quality and utility, as there will always be a healthy market for products that are differentiated based upon high quality. Dell Computers Inc. serves as a prime example of a company that has evolved into a broad based cost leader and possesses all of the above attributes. But perhaps the greatest risk for these companies is that *cost leadership tends to cause the participant companies to focus more on cost and less on product and market change, which can lead to loss of market share.* Finally, severe economic conditions, such as inflation can diminish the price differential held by the cost leadership company, making product differentiation a stronger force in determining market share.

A *differentiation strategy* is the more common path for successful early stage companies and offers a unique product or service than the current market provides. As opposed to the cost leadership strategy, the differentiation strategy highlights a product or service's unique value and enables it to charge higher prices. *The main advantage of this strategy is that it is somewhat immune to supplier price increases, since the higher costs may be passed on to consumers who will continue to pay a premium for a unique and highly valued product.* Companies pursuing a differentiation strategy must place a high emphasis on research and development, creative product development, and a strong sales and marketing team. However, one of the main challenges of this strategy is how to communicate this perception of higher quality to a market that may have great loyalty to larger, firmly entrenched competitors. *Accordingly, the sales team may be the biggest factor in the success of the differentiation strategy because they are responsible for the product perception.*

A *focus strategy* attempts to create either a cost advantage or product differentiation within a specific market segment. By focusing on one particular group, the company hopes to become more familiar with the specific needs of these customers and promote greater loyalty and customer service. Rather than a general cost advantage, these companies must rely more upon differentiation of products and services since the ability for high volume purchases and thus an economy of scale advantage tends to be lower. In addition, if the only advantage is cost leadership, larger competitors serving broader markets may be able to overcome these barriers.

For some industries, notably commodities based businesses, there are few opportunities for either focus or differentiation so cost factors are the primary

drivers of success.   In other industries such as high technology, cost
leadership is insufficient to overcome product differentiation and focus.
When properly implemented for the appropriate market and industry, each of
these generic strategies provides strong barriers against competitive forces.

Table 6-1. Porter's Generic Strategies

Target Scope	Competitive Advantage	
	Low Cost	Product Uniqueness
Broad (Industry Wide)	Cost Leadership Strategy	Differentiation Strategy
Narrow (Market Segment)	Focus Strategy (low cost)	Focus Strategy (differentiation)

Table 6-2 examines the effects of Porter's generic strategies on the five forces
influencing industries. The reader should study this table in detail.

Table 6-2.Porter's Generic Strategies vs The Five Forces of Industry Competition

	Generic Strategies		
Industry Force	Cost Leadership	Differentiation	Focus
Entry Barriers	Ability to reduce price discourages entrants	Core competencies can discourage entrants	Customer loyalty can discourage entrants
Rivalry	Better able to compete on price	Difficult for rivals to match unique values and sway customer loyalty	Difficult for rivals to match unique values and sway customer loyalty
Supplier Power	Substantial market share and economies of scale provide purchasing power	Can pass on price increases to customers due to loyalty	Can pass on price increases to customers due to loyalty
Buyer Power	Can offer lower price to powerful buyers	Diminished ability to negotiate price due to few substitutes	Diminished ability to negotiate price due to few substitutes
Threat of Substitutes	Can use low price to defend against substitutes	Customers become attached to differentiating attributes, reducing threat of substitutes	Specialized products and core competency protect against substitutes

C. Achieving Market Growth

Understanding Product Life Cycles

The product life cycle attempts to explain the typical course of a company from infancy to decline, and when the number of units sold is plotted versus time, an S-shaped curve is produced. However, this model can also be used to explain industry evolution and individual product life cycles as well as the company life cycle (figure 6-7). During the early stages of a company sales are low, as it has no established brand name, limited distribution networks, and very little resources for sales and marketing. Most of its resources are spent for R&D as it struggles to compete with the incumbents. However, after a gradual period of increasing market penetrance, the company will emerge from its *incubation stage* and begin to experience *rapid sales growth*. During this phase, the company is transitioning to mass production as it struggles to meet customer demand for its products. The company now begins to spend less on R&D and more on manufacturing, marketing, and sales.

However, at some point, this rapid sales growth begins to slow down and the company reaches a *maturation stage* due to a saturation of the market and entry of competing products. The products are less differentiated than before due to competitive products but it has reached a sufficient sales volume that enables it to derive the benefits from *economies of scale*, so its expenses are much lower. Finally, the company reaches a point whereby the sales growth begins to *decline* as competitive technologies have made the product obsolete. As sales continue to fall, profit margins begin to diminish, as the decreased sales volume destroys its ability to maintain economies of scale. At this stage the company will either stabilize to a lower sales growth, continue to decline until it reaches insolvency, or it will rebound if it takes the appropriate actions prior to entering the decline stage. The ultimate fate will depend on many factors internal and external to the company.

Figure 6-7. The Product Life Cycle Curve

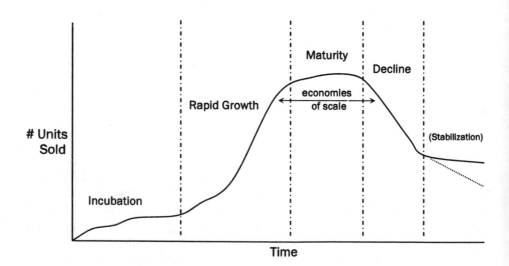

The importance of accepting the product life cycle cannot be overstated, although there are many critics of this model. Some of these criticisms are that each stage will vary in length depending upon many variables and it is often difficult for companies to know with certainty which stage in the cycle they reside. In addition, not all companies progress through the cycle in the order shown and some companies skip certain stages completely. Nevertheless, the life cycle model is only meant to provide a general framework for each company to customize based upon more detailed information.

One can point to some specific examples to illustrate the adverse effects of the failure to recognize the product life cycle model, or at the very least to respond to it in a timely manner, such as the failure of Polaroid to update its product portfolio or Eastman Kodak and Xerox's failure to deliver digital products to the marketplace in a timely manner. Fortunately for the latter two, their business diversification and strong brand name has thus far allowed them to survive. *Although easier said than done, the most successful companies understand where their products lie on the life cycle curve and are able to react appropriately, prior to experiencing significant declines in market share. Alternatively, they can introduce new products and leverage their loyal customer base.*

Keep in mind that regardless of the specific strategies selected to achieve market growth, *the company must have an excellent understanding of not only its own product life cycle, but also where along the cycle the industry lies* so that it can identify opportunities and implement effective mechanisms of exploiting them. For instance, the telecommunications industry is currently experiencing a decline in sales growth. While it may be premature to categorize this industry as in the decline stage, we should feel comfortable understanding that there have been many recent regulatory and technological changes that will provide opportunities for this industry to either rebound or for other industries to assume the higher end of its services and products, while the telecom industry declines and serves only the most basic customer needs. We should be able to appreciate that the larger companies have been slow to integrate wireless and broadband products and services into their business models as a way to replenish lost revenues due to the price collapse of telecommunication services. Meanwhile, Internet Services Providers (ISPs), such as AOL and MSN have seized these markets as a way to enhance the volume of customers accessing their digital content. Fortunately, the distribution channels and of these local and long distance carriers is so strong that they will most likely recover substantial market share for these newer products and services.

The next chart (figure 6-8) illustrates the dynamics of product investment capital versus cash flow at specific periods of the product lifecycle. Notice the decline in investment capital at the onset of product maturity and the continued decline as the lifecycle approaches its end.   Also note that towards the end of the rapid growth phase the product generates positive cash flows for the first time, as price erosion has not yet hit the product and the investment capital required for the product has begun to decline.   This investment capital continues to decline further, as the effect of economies of scale increases during the maturity stage.   The effect this has is to lower the product cost but the profit margins also decline due to the lowered price of the product, which is needed to remain competitive with at this phase.   *Thus the sustained increase in cash flows is a result of the effects of economies of scale for the early portion of increased cash flows, followed by the result of lower capital investment needed, once the economies of scale effect has disappeared during the decline stage.*

Figure 6-8. The Product Life Cycle Showing Cash Flows

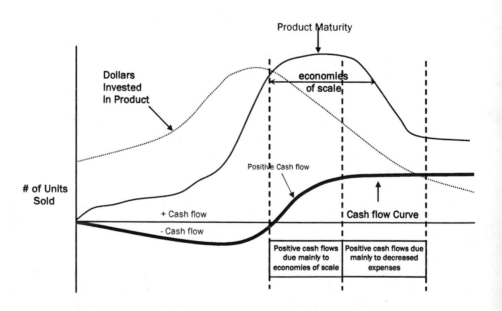

Original illustration by M. Stathis

This illustration serves to highlight several important concepts. First, a company's products are like any other investment; the longer you are able to sell them the higher your cumulative returns. Second, as the product matures and assuming no major alterations are made, the capital expenditures required for the continued (although diminished) sales of the product should continue to decline until a critical point is reached, whereby any further decline in expenditures will compromise sales independent of product acceptance. This critical point will be company and industry dependent and will reflect the fixed costs associated with the product. Thus, *companies that are able to interpret their products with respect to the life cycle curve will not only be able to redirect specific strategies, but they will also be able to use the positioning on this curve as a tool for financial planning and budgeting.*

Methods to Achieve Market Growth

Conglomerates. From the modern portfolio theory (MPT), we know that companies can reduce risk by diversifying their business assets. Accordingly, most companies have historically sought acquisition candidates to achieve diversification. However, many mergers and acquisitions have demonstrated poor results, perhaps due to the inadequacy of identifying complementary fits between companies. Nevertheless, there are a few examples of companies that have perfected their abilities to diversify and add to shareholder value, such a General Electric and Johnson & Johnson, but these are exceptions. Therefore, *growth and diversification strategies should focus on building the core competencies of the company, followed by leveraging these competencies to diversify their product offerings.* And when acquisitions are made based upon the goal of expanding the core competencies of a company, these transactions will have a greater chance of success.

Vertical Integration. While a common trend two decades ago, vertical integration has recently been on the decline, as outsourcing now represents a more efficient and cost effective method for earnings growth through cost reductions. However this method of growth may become more favorable at some point when global economies change.

Synergy. This represents the leveraging of a company's core competencies, and can be a very powerful growth strategy. Synergy may be formed by a variety of methods, such as acquisition, licensing, strategic alliances, and joint ventures. Regardless of the method used, a company must identify appropriate lines of business that represent effective overlap between its core competencies followed by careful execution of its business strategy.

Globalization. Due to macroeconomic trends, many companies seek growth through globalization rather than diversification.   Globalization provides tremendous access to less costly labor products, more supplier options, and may create new distribution channels.   However, regulatory barriers present in certain countries may diminish the overall appeal for expansion by this method.

Market Penetration.   This should seem as an obvious way to grow market share, but the most effective strategies in achieving market penetration are often very difficult. A fragmented industry might benefit from a consolidation approach, as was achieved by Waste Management.   In contrast, a new market might be dominated by more contemporary approaches such as outsourcing or innovative pricing models.

Establish Alliances.   Forming strategic alliances with companies can represent an excellent way to gain access to distribution channels and provide resources otherwise unavailable to the early stage company.   We will discuss this strategy in further detail in the next chapter.

Organizational Integration:
Horizontal and Vertical Integration

Organizational integration involves the coordination of activities between multiple interdependent groups within a business process.   This is often difficult to accomplish because specialization within each group promotes differentiation amongst groups, making it difficult to achieve coordination between groups.   Therefore, *the goal of effective organizational integration is to achieve the maximal coordination between groups, yet preserve the specialization activities of each group.*

Organizational integration can occur through horizontal or vertical integration.   *Horizontal integration* occurs through either *forward or backward integration*, whereby different operations of a company are integrated into the main infrastructure in order to establish a lower cost product.   All of the processes and operations essential for a company to produce its products comprise its value chain (figure 6-9).   The designation of the *direction of integration* relates to the position of the newly integrated operation on its *value chain* relative to the company's primary operations. If a company adds operations upstream (to the right) from its primary strength, the integration is referred to as forward.   If it adds operations downstream (to the left) relative to its core strengths, the integration is known as backward.

In contrast, vertical integration involves coordination of groups not directly related to the production, sales, and distribution of a product.

An example of this would be a direct order computer manufacturer such as Dell purchasing an ISP (Internet Service Provider). As previously mentioned, the current trend has shifted away from this in favor of outsourcing. However, one should not overlook some of the potential advantages of this approach, as the merits of vertical integration will be case dependent.

In conclusion when deciding whether to outsource or vertically integrate, the manager must identify any synergies, cost savings, coordination, and loss of specialization problems and then weigh these against the benefits and cost of outsourcing. Because the process of vertical integration is complicated and difficult to complete successfully, early stage companies should not seek this option, but instead should use outsourcing and strategic alliances if viable, so they can focus their efforts on achieving market share. Finally, note that outsourcing does not always have to mean a company looses potentially synergistic opportunities. If structured properly, outsourcing arrangements can lead to mutually beneficial results that may not be achievable through vertical integration.

Figure 6-9. The Company Value Chain

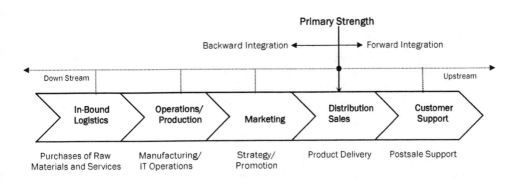

If we assume a company's main strength is in distribution and sales and it wishes to integrate a productions business unit rather than continue to outsource, this would be a *backward integration* since productions is behind distribution and sales along the value chain. If the same company wishes to integrate customer support directly within its business, it would be called a *forward integration*.

Source: DePamphilis, D. (modified)

D. Preemptive Strategies

Basic competitive strategy focuses on analysis, planning, and offensive or defensive reactions to a competitor's activities.   Initiating a price cut would be an example of an offensive competitive strategy, while reaction to the price cut would be an example of a defensive maneuver, potentially creating a price war.   In contrast, a *preemptive strategy is a maneuver used by a company that attempts to prevent a planned action by the competitor*.   While the intent is defensive in nature, preemptive strategies take an offensive approach in shutting down avenues of potential opportunity or activity so that the competitor either cannot or chooses not to proceed.   When executed effectively, a preemptive strategy can delay or permanently halt the competitive activities before they have been implemented.   The following descriptions illustrate examples of common preemptive strategies:

Locking up capacity.   A company that is able to accurately forecast industry changes before its competitors can boost production and gain a competitive edge.   In 1984, Sony did this when it correctly forecast the future growth for 3.5-inch floppy disks and announced a five-fold increase in production capacity.   Shortly thereafter, IBM announced that it would become a producer of next generation computers.   This preemptive action by Sony discouraged potential rivals due to the first-to-market effect.

Locking in markets.   Companies that introduce a new product into many different markets simultaneously or within a short period will prevent or make it more difficult for competitors to react by introducing a comparable product. This can be a highly effective strategy but is also accompanied by high risk, since the product is being distributed to different markets without having been proven in the primary one.   Gillette executed this preemptive strategy effectively with Sensor by releasing it into 19 countries almost simultaneously.   As well, Proctor & Gamble released Pampers Phases into 90 countries within a year.   However, these companies have worldwide brand recognition and the products launched were improvements to their predecessors so they had reasonable cause for their actions.

Locking up minds.   A well-known company may announce that an innovative product will be released within the year, causing consumers to wait for this product rather than buying the existing one made by the competitor. Even if the product is never made or is made several years later, this strategy has decreased the sales of the competitor's product that has been on the shelves all along.

Blocking a competitor's intended action. In 1990, Kellogg announced that it would be launching a new fortified shredded wheat cereal that stated on each box that it was the "most nutritious shredded wheat you can buy." Kellogg had already produced several thousand cases of this cereal and was in the initial process of shipping it to grocery stores. Just before the shipping, the attorneys for Nabisco sent a letter to Kellogg stating that they would also be launching their own fortified shredded wheat cereal, which would therefore invalidate Kellogg's claims. Nabisco threatened to sue Kellogg for "false and misleading" claims if they did not remove these this statement from the boxes. Thus, Kellogg's new position in the market for a shredded wheat cereal was preempted by Nabisco's intended product launch.

The Preemptive Planning Process

The preemptive planning process begins by analyzing the current market and using this information to predict the moves of competitors. Market dynamics such as capacity, pricing, and technology trends are good indicators of future market shifts. Each of the competing companies will have different levels of financial and human resources and will try to utilize their best resources to benefit from expected changes in the market. Therefore, preemptive strategies are formulated and tested for the possible effects on each competitor. Next the company assesses the consistency of these preemptive strategies with its own core strategies and constructs potential outcomes of these strategies for each competitor. Finally, the company analyzes the dynamic responses of these competitors to the preemptive actions in order to understand possible reactions and prepare for retaliation. This process is shown in figure 6-10.

Market Direction. A preemptive strategy is only as good as the accuracy achieved in forecasting market and competitor direction. One must first have an understanding of the dynamic forces within the market that have caused it to be shaped the way that it is. This process is similar to what an analyst does in determining the investment opportunities of publicly traded companies. Historical data is examined in order to identify the most dominant factors causing the markets and companies to react in specific ways. Some industries are influenced more by regulatory actions than others. Meanwhile, other industries are affected more by direct factors such as consumer trends and the direct effects of competitor activities.

Determining Intended Moves of Competitors. Instrumental in the process of preemptive strategy planning is the ability of a company to anticipate the future moves of its targeted competitors. There are a variety of ways a company can identify such intentions prior to their implementation, and the list below is by no means exhaustive.

- *Competitive signals.* Companies provide hints of this by their acquisition choices, test marking, strategic alliances, and joint ventures.

- *Competitive analysis.* Understanding a competitor's complete history combined with a market analysis will assist the identification of intended activities.

- *Distribution channels.* Companies can either be limited or assisted in expansion activities. Understand the competitor's channels of distribution and analyze its limitations and advantages for product expansion.

- *Environmental analysis.* This includes, legal, political, economic, cultural, and technological factors that may create new opportunities for some and result in adverse consequences for others. As an example, consider the effects of deregulation of the airlines and energy industries. Examine the market leaders prior to and after deregulation.

Evaluating Opportunities for Preemption. Prior to the final determination and execution of a specific preemptive strategy, a company should evaluate each of the candidate strategies, along with its feasibility and consistency with the corporate strategy and determine an estimated magnitude and duration of the candidate strategies on the competitor. In addition, a company should understand how implementation of the preemptive strategy would affect its ability to continue its core strategy. Each category should be designated by a numerical or grade scoring system then the final decision made.

Analyzing the Dynamic Response of Rivals. In forming the final preemptive strategy, a company is assuming its competitors will or will not make certain moves. After execution of the preemptive strategy, the competitors' predicted moves might be different due the response of the strategy. Therefore, an effective preemptive strategy should account for all possible reactions to the initial preemptive strike.

Figure 6-10. Planning for Preemption

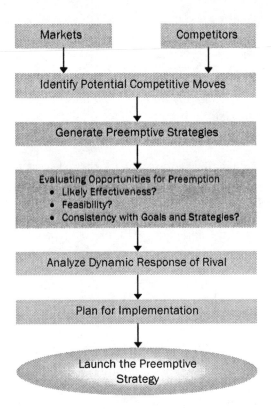

Source: Day and Reibstein

E. Analyzing Competitive Strategies

Frequently, issues arise that are material to both the company and its competitors. The following are examples of such dilemmas:

- *How should a new product be positioned to minimize a competitive threat yet maximize market penetration?*

- *Is a decline in sales an indicator the company's failure to execute effectively, a reflection of the competition's lack of success, or just a reflection of the economy?*

- *What should be done if a competitor increases its advertising? Should the company follow this activity or ignore it?*

- *Should a company cut prices or wait until the competition does? How much should they cut prices by or how much of a price cut by competitors is allowable?*

- *What will the company do if competitors cut prices? Will they follow suit or do nothing?*

To address these concerns, companies need to assess the cause and effect relationships that might result from such actions both within their own company as well as potential reactions and resulting consequences from competitors. This may be accomplished by one of several ways depending upon the resources of the company. Figure 6-11 provides a basic framework that can be used to create a decision tree analysis in order to predict potential responses of rivals to actions made by the company. Meanwhile, the remainder of this section discusses specific methods that can be used to analyze competitive strategies.

Figure 6-11. Framework for Analyzing Competitors' Response to Actions

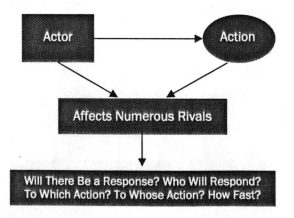

Source: Day and Reibstein

Market Trend Line Analysis

This technique provides a relatively simple yet effective way to analyze industry, competitor trends, and other information required for the strategic planning process. Note that the various market trend line methods listed below are also very effective when planning for preemptive strategies (table 6-3).

Natural line extensions. Broad consumer trends, such the growth and popularity of fat-free foods, low-calorie sweets, online shopping, etc. can be used to predict the expansion of new products and services within these established trends. In addition, demographic and socioeconomic data show strong correlations with preferences for colors, shapes, styles, etc. One way to capture a currently underserved market would be to extend the cultural appeal preferences of a successful product into these underserved ethnicities. For instance, the Hispanic population in the United States is expected to continue its rapid rate of growth over the next three decades. Meanwhile, this ethnic group is already underserved relative to its size and purchasing power. Thus, by analyzing socioeconomic, demographic and cultural data, a company such as Gap Stores might use this data to design a marketing strategy to capture this new market. This example obviously extends to virtually every aspect of consumer goods and services. Large corporations, especially those with large marketing operations have been conducting such analyses for several years. In this current age, activities such as this might be viewed as a form of racial profiling, but the facts speak for themselves and there is no law prohibiting the capitalization of group trends; not yet anyway.

Next-generation products. This can be understood by reexamining the product-life cycle. Thus when a product has reached maturity, one might expect the need for technological improvement or complete replacement in order to maintain its current level of revenues.

Innovative products. New products not only create additional markets, but also can also significantly alter preexisting markets through changes in consumer behavior. For example, the DVD has been integrated into the U.S. consumer marketplace faster than any other electronics device in the history of America. Within a few years of its introduction in the mid 1990s, the price dropped from over $400 to as low as $40 currently. This has already begun to reshape other markets such as the VHS, video camera, personal computer, and movie industries.

Table 6-3. Techniques for Analyzing Competitive Strategy

Technology	Example	Advantages	Disadvantages
Trend Lines	Historical Analysis	Fast, easy, inexpensive, Requires little future data Reflects real events	Assumes future will mimic the past, does not allow for creative thinking. Limited in number of factors measured
Brainstorming	Idea-Generation Teams	Fast, easy and creative	Is qualitative and judgmental
Forecasting	Economic Models	Quantitative and rigorous Uses many factors that assess the activity measured	Ignores competitive reaction of multiple scenarios for the future. Assumes future will mimic the past
Qualitative Scenario Planning	Scenario Planning	Creative, can be quantified evaluates many possible scenarios; more rigorous form of brainstorming	Hard to evaluate which scenarios are best, does not assess competitive dynamics
Simulation	Strategy Simulations	Can incorporate results of all the above methods, Can test specific strategies and counterstrategies, can assess competitive dynamics	Costly and rigorous, scarcity of adequate software, difficulty in developing the software

Source: Day and Reibstein

Customer analysis.   This should be self-evident, as consumers ultimately determine the success of a company through their willingness to purchase its products.   However, determining the most influential factors affecting consumer choice (price, brand recognition, style, etc) can be very challenging.

Emerging new business paradigm.   It is important, although usually difficult to spot trends in new business models prior to widespread acknowledgment.   Understanding the feasibility of new paradigms by examining market and consumer trends can assist in forming preemptive strategies and can even help in shaping a new business paradigm. This is perhaps the easiest way to gain control of a new market that is still open to change.

Other Techniques

Brainstorming is a relatively simple, yet highly effective method for identifying competitor trends and can be equally instrumental in the development of effective counteractive strategies. While simulation techniques may provide the greatest benefits for competitive analysis, the financial cost involved is quite high and thus inappropriate for many large companies, not to mention early stage companies. In addition, the development of an in-house simulation program is a long process that requires ongoing revisions as industry and environmental changes occur. Therefore, perhaps the best approach for a small company would be to use the combined efforts of a trend line analysis and brainstorming sessions. Forecasting is limited in creativity and too intensive to justify the effort for a small company. But if the company has adequate resources, it can provide valuable information when combined with other methods.

F. Strategic Planning

In this chapter we have provided a brief overview of strategy, focusing many discussions on competitive strategy. And we have examined many of the tools that can be used to analyze competitors and establish a competitive position. Because market conditions are constantly changing, strategy formulation is a dynamic and complex process that must be formally structured, and constantly reassessed. *The strategic planning process is used to help achieve or maintain a company's visionary goals by providing focus and reestablishing priorities.* When performed successfully, this process helps companies respond to change more effectively and vigorously (figure 6-12). An overview of many tasks required for an effective strategic planning process is presented in figure 6-14.

Central to the development of a strategic plan is the identification of a company's mission and objectives that serve as the framework for exploring future opportunities. Subsequently, the strategies devised should be centered on the company's vision, expressed in the mission statement. The next step is to perform an analysis of the internal environment (a self-assessment) in order to identify strengths and weaknesses of the company. First, one must gain an understanding of past performance, which may be accomplished through the use of historical financial statements, milestones, growth rates, and other data. Next, the company must examine its external environment to uncover opportunities and risk within its industry. The best method used to conduct these analyses is by use of the SWOT analysis.

Figure 6-12. Steps in Strategic Planning

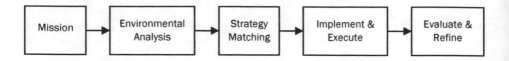

We previously learned that Porter's five forces could be used to analyze the competitive forces within an industry. Using this analysis in combination with a SWOT analysis, a feasible strategy should be devised that links the firm's strengths with the opportunities available within the industry, while staying clear of its weaknesses and minimizing external risks. Further refinement of this analysis may be conducted by using one or more of the various analytical tools briefly mentioned in the previous section, such as trend lines or scenario analysis. After the most effective strategy has been identified and selected, it is implemented. Finally, in order to achieve maximum effectiveness, the strategy execution must be continuously monitored and revised until the desired results are achieved. Figure 6-13 lists recommendations for implementing a strategic plan.

Figure 6-13. Recommendations for Implementing a Strategic Planning Process

- Make certain that all employees understand the mission statement

- Objectives must be measurable and time sensitive

- External analysis is performed periodically and seeks to identify threats and opportunities

- The operating environment is regularly assessed

- The company should analyze its internal operations seeking to identify strengths and weaknesses

- Decision analysis should be based on all information and consistent with preserving the vision of the company

- Results of the strategic plan should be written down, and adhered to

- The results of the strategic execution should be constantly evaluated and refined as needed

SWOT Analysis

Once the mission has been clearly defined, an assessment of the environment must be made from the both an internal and external perspective. This is traditionally known as a SWOT analysis and seeks to identify the *Strengths and Weaknesses* as well as the potential *Opportunities and Threats* external to the company. The importance of a SWOT analysis is that when performed accurately, it provides the critical information that may be used to match the company's resources with the demands created by its competitive environment. Examples of company strengths can be strength of intellectual property, good reputation with customers, good suppliers, good access to distribution networks, and any other attribute that gives it a competitive advantage. In contrast, a company's weaknesses may be shortcomings in any of the previous categories.

When assessing the external environment, the company should consider all potential possibilities for future growth, such as favorable regulatory changes that could extend market share, unmet customer demand, and strategic alliances. Threats could be the result of deficiencies in the above factors. Once all strengths/weaknesses and opportunities/threats have been identified, strategies should be designed to meet the demands of each combination of strengths/weaknesses and opportunities/threats. For instance, S-O strategies would be designed to utilize company internal strengths best suited to exploit industry opportunities, while S-T strategies would involve the use of strengths to minimize competitive threats. Likewise, W-O strategies would seek to minimize weaknesses in order to pursue opportunities, while W-T strategies would use the knowledge of the company's weaknesses in effecting a defense against possible competitive threats (table 6-4). [3]

Table 6-4. The SWOT Analysis

External Environment	Internal Environment	
	Strengths	Weaknesses
Opportunities	S-O Strategies	W-O Strategies
Threats	S-T Strategies	W-T Strategies

Figure 6-14.   The Strategy Formulation Process

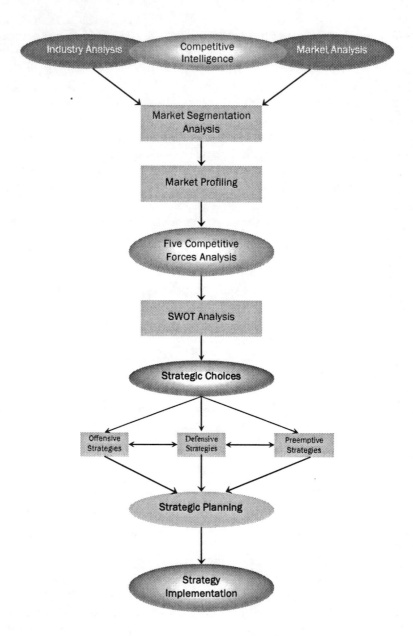

Original illustration by M. Stathis

G. Competitive Intelligence

In order to design and execute the most effective competitive strategies, management must acquire strategic and tactical information on its competitors. *Competitive intelligence* may be defined as specific information that has been collected and analyzed about competitors and can be used in the decision making process of a company's strategy. The key issue here is how to most efficiently obtain the needed information with which to conduct these analyses. This can be a difficult task, especially if the companies are not public and therefore critical information is not readily disclosed. However, according to Admiral Ellis Zacharias, (*The Story of an Intelligence Officer*) 95% of all necessary intelligence, corporate or military, may be found in the public arena. That claim may be even more accurate today, as the Internet has greatly enhanced accessibility of information. In general, the extent of information availability on competitors depends primarily on five factors:

1. *Rationality.* The more local a competitor's operations are, the easier it will be to find information on it.

2. *Dynamism.* The more dynamic and the industry, the easier it will be to find information on it.

3. *Regulation.* The more regulated an industry is, the easier it will be to find information on companies in that industry space since they are required to comply with government policies.

4. *Concentration.* The more concentrated an industry (there are fewer players) the easier it will be to find information on competitors.

5. *Integration.* The more a company has integrated its value chain, or all components of its business from sales and marketing to supply and distribution, the more difficult it will be to obtain information on these companies since the exchange of information is limited to company insiders and therefore does not leak out as readily.

Resources for Market Profiling

Prior to beginning the process of forming a competitive strategy, one must first develop a detailed understanding of the market, customers, and competitors. Thus the first step is to conduct a market analysis so that the competition can be analyzed. After this task has been completed, the company can then apply this information to the Five Forces Framework and SWOT analysis to uncover opportunities and detect competitive threats.

There are many excellent research reports available from market research firms specializing in every major industry, although such reports can cost in excess of $5000 each. Initially, one should gain a basic understanding of the competitors in the industry from information made publicly available and free. There are a variety of free sources online that provide information on demographics (U.S Census Bureau) and industry research reports (U.S. Government). In addition, one should examine the 10K, 10Q, 8-K and other SEC filings of publicly traded companies in the industry of interest in order to compile an assessment of the relevant industry. These are available through www.freedgar.com and other sources.

Market reports should examine industry averages such as sales, growth rates, etc. and compare them with those in the given industry, noting distinctive patterns of success and detriment. Industry averages may be found by many sources online such as Yahoo! Finance. Of particular interest should be industry-wide and individual figures for earnings per share, industry growth rate, debt, debt to assets, profit margins, inventory turnover, price to sales, price to book value. As well, one needs to specifically dissect each company's product and services portfolio and the relative impact on revenue and earnings. Finally, note that in many cases these resources can be used for much more valuable and specific information since companies will publish licensing agreements and other strategically relevant information as required by the SEC if such arrangements are material to corporate operations. The following provides a partial list of available resources.

- **SEC Filings**

  10-K: A public company's annual statement. Detailed information on a company's annual operations, financial statements, accounting changes, business conditions, competitors, market conditions, legal proceedings, risk factors, names and compensation of directors and executive officers, listings of shareholders of more then 5% of company stock and other information.

  10-Q: Quarterly updates on company financial statements, operations, discussions of any legal proceedings, and payment defaults.

  20-F: An annual filing by foreign issuers of securities, similar to the 10-K.

1933 Act Registration Statements: (S-, S-2, S-3, S-4, S-6, S-8, S-11, S-18, S-20, F-1, F-2, F-3, F-4, F-6, SE, N-1A, N-2, N-5, N-14): Filed when a company plans to register new stock and includes proposed use of proceeds, risk factors, offering price, dilution, related financial statements, individuals and entities planning to sell the stock, and expenses involved with the new issue.

8-K: Filed when a company faces a "material event", such as an acquisition, divestiture, bankruptcy, resignation of directors, change in fiscal year or change in accountants.

10-C: Same as 8-K except used for over-the-counter securities.

13-D: Filed when a company plans to acquire more then 5% of a class of stock.

14D-1 and 14D-9: Filed for a tender offer.

13E-3: Filed when a company wishes to go private and is filed after the transaction has occurred.

13E-4: Similar to 13-E.

13-G: Annual filing by individuals or institutions owning more than 5% of a stock.

6-K: Filed by foreign companies whose stock is publicly traded in the U.S., this filing contains financial information.

Schedule 14A: A proxy statement. Gives information about annual meetings, information about executive management, officers and directors, and their compensation.

Proxy Statement: Filed annually and for special meetings, it is used to give shareholders adequate information for voting on corporate matters.

- **Credit Reporting Agencies.** These services are inexpensive means to obtain potentially useful data about a company. They can be obtained either by contacting affiliated trade groups or independent services such as Dun & Bradstreet. While they have limited utility for small privately held companies, the following is a list of information that may be obtained from these reports: name, address and industry classification, age of company, and parent-subsidiary relationship, sales or net worth figures, general purpose of business, payment record, and court cases outstanding.

- **Uniform Commercial Codes (UCC).** These are filings initially completed by banks when commercial loans are used to make purchases. These forms are then filed to the secretary of state's office. This information may be accessed easily be ordering a *business information report* from Dun & Bradstreet.

- **Trade Organizations, Directories, and Magazines.** These are excellent sources of industry-specific information and trends such as market data, sales volume, and major players. Most of these associations are headquartered in Washington D.C. and make it their job to keep industry statistics. Many of these directories and studies can be found in business libraries or you can request their annual reports directly. There are hundreds of industry-specific directories and journals too lengthy to mention here but an Internet search should be performed to locate the industry of relevance. In addition, do not overlook the utility of searching databases of articles from the *Wall Street Journal, Barron's*, and the *New York Times*, as these publications have great information. Many of the past articles from these publications can be located from an Internet search. Finally, I have found the site www.findarticles.com to be extremely useful, containing articles on virtually every subject imaginable from hundreds of magazines, newspapers, and journals. Write that address down and keep it posted on your computer!

  - Directory of Associations in Canada (Micromedia Ltd.)

  - Directory of European Industrial and Trade Associations (Gale Research, Inc.)

  - Encyclopedia of Associations (Gale Research, Inc.)

  - National Trade and Professional Associations of the United States and Canada and Labor Unions (Columbia Books, Inc.)

  - World Guide to Trade Associations (K.G. Saur)

  - Corporate Directory of U.S. Public Companies (Gale Research, Inc.)

- Directory of Corporate Affiliations (National Register Publishing Company). A great resource listing subsidiaries and their parent companies along with the address, product line and sales. There is also an international edition.

- Million Dollar Directory (Dun's Marketing Services). Conatins, sales, numbers of employees and other data.

- Thomas Register of American Manufacturers (Thomas Publishing Co.). Very helpful resource consisting of 26 volumes.

- Value Line Investment Survey (Value Line, Inc)

- **Consumer Groups and Market Research Companies**
  - FINDEX (Campbridge Information Group) is a very comprehensive reference listing of the latest market research studies.

- **Consultants**
  - Bradford's Directory of Marketing Research Agencies and Management Consulting in the United States and the World (Denlinger's Publishers Ltd.)

  - Consultants and Consulting Organizations Directory (Gale Research, Inc.)

  - Dun's Consultants Directory (Dun's Marketing Services)

  - European Consultants Directory (Gale Research, Inc)

- **Government Agencies**

  - **U.S. Department of Commerce** tracks industry shipments and trends, and this information can be found in the *U.S. Industrial Outlook Handbook* and *Current Industry Reports,* which are published annually. In addition, this guide can tell you how to contact government industry analysts which you can interview.

  - **The State Department** collects information on companies worldwide. Appendix D contains the numbers of Asian, Pacific and European desks.

- **International Trade Administration** (ITA) is a subagency of the U.S. Department of Commerce established to study the effects of imports on U.S. commerce. It conducts competitive investigations on industries called "322 cases" and the Unfair Import Investigations Division hears investigates and hears cases involving patent infringement and unfair trade practices. The ITA's country desks will assist exporters with trade exhibitions and even provide free legal counseling to locate an international banker and freight forwarder. The ITA desk phone numbers are listed in Appendix D.

- **Federal Communications Commission** (FCC) requires that manufacturers identify source suppliers and present the schematics of products sold. They also identify the U.S. assembler or marketer of the equipment as well as the original manufacturers. They can be very useful for competitive analysis due to their comprehensiveness.

- **Environmental Agencies.** All companies that are planning to build plants or change production facilities that may affect the environment must file with local and sometimes federal environmental agencies. The general form is called the environmental notification form (ENF) and provides information on the project's name and address, size of the plant, processes used, number of employees, production cost of the facility, and the number of production sites that will be created. These forms are especially useful for companies in the chemical and pharmaceutical industries.

- **Business Libraries.** These can provide a tremendous amount of information, depending upon the facility. Specific use should be made of the reference librarian, who is intimately familiar with publications and journals you may be unaware of. In addition, for a small fee, these libraries will conduct database searches for journals and articles pertinent for your analysis. Finally, most business libraries will contain publications such as those listed in this discussion, as well as many others.

- **Trade Shows.** These are potentially tremendous platforms for obtaining competitor information. Company staff at these shows typically are more than enthusiastic about discussing virtually any aspect about their company, including revenues, profits, market share, new technologies, distribution and marketing strategies. These individuals are there to gain new customers and therefore have their guard down. Attendance at the appropriate trade show may provide the best-spent time and money for obtaining competitive intelligence in your industry. The attendee should prepare a list of information sought for each relevant exhibitor. Among the information that may be obtained from these shows are product literature, demonstrations, discussions about market share, general financials, customers, distributors, suppliers, strategic alliances, and virtually any other piece of information depending upon the representative of the company. From this information, one can conduct interviews of distributors and suppliers to refine data. One can easily identify industry relevant trade shows by browsing trade magazines in libraries. For regional or local trade shows, the best resource is the local chamber of commerce. Below are some of the most comprehensive publications on trade show information.

- *Exposition Trade Shows & Fairs Directory* (American Business Directories, Inc.)

- *International Exhibitors Association*-Membership Directory & Product Service Guide (International Exhibitors Association)

- *Trade Shows & Exhibits Schedule* (Bill Communications)

- *Trade Shows Worldwide* (Gale Research Co.)

- **People.** Interviewing distributors and manufacturers can be a helpful method to obtain information on the competition.

- **Creative Resources.** These methods are inexpensive (although sometimes time consuming) means of estimating data on competitors (table 6-5).

Table 6-5. Creative Ways to Gain Competitor Information

Variable	Resources
Number of employees	Count Parking Spaces of Facility
Sales	Identify Distributors Count Truck Shipments
Market share	Identify Product Suppliers Identify Distributors Identify Box Suppliers (check the box for company; many companies use more than one box maker) Trade Shows
Financials	Trade Shows UCCs

Notes

[1] The case of Microsoft with this network industry is quite unique however, due to its overwhelming influence (some might even call it monopolistic control) over the computer industry. For instance, if Microsoft chose to they could refuse or perhaps delay updating the new version of Windows to support AMD's new microprocessor. And while this would obviously be advantageous for Intel, because Microsoft controls the operating systems market, AMD would have very few alternatives. Normally, there are no monopolies permitted and cooperation between network companies is exercised for the mutual benefit of all companies within the network, rather than as a means to avoid charges of anti-competitive behavior, as in the case of Microsoft.

[2] The pharmaceutical and biotechnology industries are unique in that the intellectual property protection afforded to its products can create a temporary virtual monopoly in cases where there are no substitutes. Consider the case of Amgen, which introduced two highly effective drugs to the marketplace, Neutropin and Epogen. These drugs neutralized many of the devastating side-effects of chemotherapy by causing the body to increase its production of white and red blood cell counts in these patients, thereby restoring their immune function and oxygen delivery capacity. The success of these billion dollar drugs helped make Amgen the most successful biotechnology company in the world. Yet without patent protection, these drugs could have been imitated. Other technology companies can sometimes design around innovative solutions and add similar products. But the pharmaceutical industry, by nature of the tremendous expense of R&D and risk involved in drug approval, has the unique luxury of monopolistic behavior and can therefore control the prices charged for its products.

[3] Another way to look at the possible external threats faced by the company is to conduct a PEST analysis, which seeks to identify all possible macroenvironmental events such as Political (fiscal changes, employment laws, industry regulatory laws), Economic (monetary policy, economic conditions such as inflation and employment rates), Social (public attitudes, demographic), and Technological (product life cycle lengths, innovations).

7

Alternative Growth Strategies:
Licensing Agreements, Strategic Alliances & Joint Ventures

"I think there is a world market for maybe five computers."
Thomas Watson, Chairman of IBM, 1943

A. Strategic Convergence

In the previous chapter we reviewed some of the basic principles of strategy and highlighted various ways by which to analyze and understand a company's competitive position. We learned that some of the most important elements of any strategy is that it must be dynamic, reactionary, and adaptive. As well we discussed some of the methods to assist the strategic planning process. This is not the end of the story however, as *a formidable business strategy includes a strong technology strategy integrated within the framework of the company's overall strategic blueprint.*

Many of the sales and operational-based strategies that companies use serve to enhance corporate value by increasing their market share and reduction of overall expenses, which may enhance their price competitiveness. But many of these strategies only provide a temporary competitive advantage, such as Just-In-time inventory management, customer loyalty programs, and many others. Once competitors implement these same programs the advantages dissipate from those companies without adequate competitive barriers. *It follows that for the successful knowledge-based company, the most formidable competitive barrier is the optimal positioning of its intangible assets and intellectual property.* And while intellectual property is an assumed trait of all high technology and innovative companies, *a technology strategy that is misaligned with the business strategy can create internal disruptive forces and serve as a self-defeating entry barrier.*

B. Technology Conversion

The need for companies to assemble a carefully designed technology strategy within their business model cannot be overstated. Such strategies might include in-licensing, out-licensing, cross-licensing and perhaps joint ventures, alliances, and acquisitions, depending upon the size, specific needs, and resources of the company. One or more of these strategies are often required at specific growth stages in order to fully utilize the intellectual capacity of the company, due to the technological interdependencies within the high tech industry. Thus, these methods of technology conversion when appropriately utilized, can provide viable means for companies to transform their intellectual capital into a stream of revenues.

In chapter 5 we discussed the different types of intellectual property, as well as some of the difficulties involved in converting human capital into intellectual capital. This chapter builds upon this previous discussion and focuses on commercialization strategies available for converting intellectual property into revenues and leveraging these assets to improve competitive position. Most companies recognize and place tremendous value on securing the right personnel that can provide intellectual capital. However, without adequate intellectual property protection and viable commercialization strategies, a company cannot reasonably expect to capture the full financial value from its intellectual capital.

Core Competencies

Companies that wish to succeed must identify their core competencies and position these skill sets in a manner that promotes a stronger competitive position. Not to be confused with core ideology (discussed in chapter 1), *core competency is a strategic concept* that may be defined as all of the know-how, technology, and product development skills behind a company's main technological business idea. In contrast, core ideology is a defining concept of what the company represents and its reasons for existence. While a company's core competency is a reflection or a means to achieve the core ideology, the two concepts are obviously distinct. *Core competencies can and often do change over time but ideally a company's core ideology should never change.*

Ideally, core competencies should be difficult to imitate, add to the end product supply, and broaden the markets served. And they are used to develop core products, which are leveraged to build a larger collection of end-users. This concept is similar to forming a *platform technology*, whereby the primary technologies are assembled in such a way that many different markets can be accessed and the competitive position is protected by many layers.

By positioning their core competencies appropriately in developing core products, a company can augment its competitive advantage and insulate itself from competitive attacks. For instance, a company specializing in the production of biochips should position its technologies so that many different uses can be applied from the proprietary technologies.

Establishing core competencies for startup and early stage companies is rather difficult if the technology is cutting-edge because it's so new that clearly defined applications may be lacking. As well, *technologies that are too innovative are rarely funded by traditional venture firms because they like to jump on the bandwagon in order to minimize risk.* Often, the "me-too" company that does it better and faster is preferred over the "lone ranger" because the venture capitalists can more easily envision market acceptance, demand, and exit.

Methods of Technology Conversion

Due to the technological advances that have been made over the past two decades, self-sufficiency among companies is a trend of the past and interdependence between competitors is the reality of the present and foreseeable future. Brandenburger and Nalebuff have made this premise popular in their book "Co-opetition". *Because we have experienced a large shift in the base of corporate assets from tangible to intangible, the absolute need to gain access to competitors' technologies requires vigilant cooperation with other companies.* And this trend is especially important for newer companies, who lack adequate patent portfolios and sufficient access to capital.

We have already seen evidence of this technological interdependence with the rapid growth of licensing agreements, strategic alliances, and joint ventures over the past two decades. Dell Computers is a prime example of the success of these interdependent relationships. Rather than produce the various components of a computer, Dell has established agreements with suppliers and has, in essence outsourced much of this business unit. Dell has rewritten the rules of supply chain management and all its competitors seem to be lost in its tracks. Even automotive companies have shifted from complete in-house production facilities to outsourcing auto supplies. The need for such strategies has risen mainly from the expense and rapid progression of technologies, and companies can often benefit from sharing the risks as well as the benefits of resource pooling.

Licensing agreements allow the originating company to retain the ownership rights of its intellectual capital while receiving royalty payments in exchange for allowing another party to use these assets. Joint ventures are agreements between one or more companies with a common goal, each company possessing the complete pool of business assets required to commercialize the innovation, but seeking to spread the risks of projects over other companies. In contrast, strategic alliances occur when a company with an innovation and the necessary business assets required to commercialization does not have adequate access to the target market. An example of this might be a biotechnology company that produces a drug but has no sales force. This company might choose to form a strategic alliance with a pharmaceutical company in order to gain access to its sales force. Meanwhile, the pharmaceutical company can leverage its sales force and increase its product offerings at a fraction of the equivalent cost for R&D. Finally, some companies prefer to engage in a sale of rights, which involves an exchange in ownership of intellectual property for cash or other assets.

Historically, acquisitions were the transaction of choice for companies seeking to expand their market presence into countries with restrictive barriers, such as cultural and political dissonance. In chapter 9 we will discuss acquisitions as an exit strategy from the perspective of an investor. From the management's perspective however, an acquisition also represents a means to provide growth into new markets and geographies, and can provide synergy and economies of scale. Finally, some countries limit the extent of direct foreign investment, making collaborative arrangements and licensing agreements a necessary alternative to acquisitions. In such instances, the use of horizontal alliances can provide a good alternative when antitrust concerns arise.

When analyzing the feasibility of an acquisition, companies may also consider strategic alliances, joint ventures, and licensing agreements as potential alternatives or even as a noncommittal way to test the business model. While it is thought that *acquisitions enhance value through commitment, alliances and joint ventures do so by flexibility*. Once an acquisition has been completed, the partnership cannot be easily dissolved and corporate cultural mismatches may only become evident well after the transaction has finalized. In contrast, *alliances and joint ventures commit resources in a stepwise manner*, usually attached to achievement of specific milestones. And this should theoretically allow both companies to minimize downside risk while participating in returns (table 7-1).

In the process of interaction with the partnering company, each participant develops a better idea of the value of its partner's assets and can respond by allocating investment and human capital towards those assets that show the most value and have the best strategic fit with its operations. Therefore, information asymmetry is minimized and investment expenditures become efficiently aligned. Regardless of the type of transaction chosen however, each participating company must realign its incentives so that employees focus on contributing to the new company mission.

Table 7-1. Comparison of Acquisitions, Alliances, and Licensing

	Advantages	Disadvantages
Acquisitions	-Company gains complete control of all assets -Synergy possible -May result in economies of scale	-Post-acquisitions integration costs can be high -Most acquisitions fail -High cost -Integration is slow -Potential earnings dilution
Strategic Alliances and Joint Ventures	-Asset utilization can be targeted towards strategies consistent with company's overall strategy -Works well when information asymmetry is present -Shared costs -Flexibility -Partially retractable commitments -Quick access to complex resources	-Internal conflict -Proprietary loss -Shared rewards -Partner may become competitor -Objectives may diverge
Licensing	-Licensor maintains IP ownership -Provides a predicted stream of revenue -Allows Licensor to capture revs from nonstrategic assets -Expands business networks	-Licensor may miss out on direct market expansion

Source: Parr and Sullivan

Another method for achieving market growth and enhancing the utilization of a company's intellectual capital is through entering into licensing agreements with other companies. This may be achieved through in-licensing, or exchanging some form of asset for the rights to use outside technology. Alternatively, out-licensing may contribute to market growth indirectly by converting non-core assets into royalty payments, which can be used as a financial engine for market expansion of its core technologies. Furthermore, larger more diverse corporations often achieve market growth through cross-licensing agreements, or the mutual exchange of technologies between two companies.

Licensing arrangements also provide methods for expanding a company's technology portfolio and capturing value from nonstrategic assets, and are less intrusive than an acquisition, alliance or joint venture. In addition, in-licensing provides a company a with much higher level of control than with alliances and joint ventures and at a smaller cost and effort than an acquisition (table 7-1). While out-licensing may seem to deplete a firm's intellectual assets, its utility is that it provides a means for companies to convert non-strategic assets into revenues that can be used to finance technologies and operations that are more compatible with their business strategy.

The best method of technology conversion will depend upon the specifics of the company, its business strategy, the intellectual capital, and the external resources from which the company has at its disposal. Those companies that are able to leverage their intellectual property towards achieving the best use of these conversion mechanisms will have contributed towards their efforts in establishing a sustainable competitive advantage.

C. Licensing Agreements

A license grants the rights to the use of intellectual property to another party in exchange for some type of asset. Although the assets used for compensation are typically in the form of royalty payments, sometimes licenses are exchanged for patent portfolios or other licenses, access to customers, equipment, production facilities, and other assets. Thus, licensing provides companies with greater options and flexibility in the course of capturing the full value of their intellectual property and can become a critical component of a company's business strategy. Licensing can be viewed from the perspective of the licensee (in-licensing), the licensor (out-licensing), or a combination (cross-licensing). An understanding of the goals of the in-licensing or out-licensing firm is an essential task for identifying the most effective licensing relationship. Table 7-2 lists some of the key issues, goals, and considerations for licensing arrangements.

Central to the success of a company's licensing strategy is devising a method to gain access to *complementary assets* from the licensee. Recall from chapter 5 that we divided intangible assets into operating, marketing, and product intangibles (figure 5-1). We can also categorize intangible assets by noting whether they are complementary or non-complementary to a company's business strategy and technology portfolio. Those *assets that are complementary can be considered strategic assets* because they represent vital links to the execution of a company's technology strategy. In contrast, those assets that are nonstrategic can be considered noncomplementary or essentially "junk" because harvesting these assets would deviate from the company's strategy and waste both financial and human resources.

Furthermore, *complementary intangible assets* may be divided into critical and generic. *Critical complementary intangible assets* are those that are difficult to duplicate or develop and include specialized production facilities, brand name recognition, and established channels of distribution. These critical assets are used for the commercialization process during the licensor-licensee business relationship. Critical complementary intangible assets can also include complementary technologies, customer lists, etc. *In contrast, generic complementary assets* are easily duplicated or developed and include general production facilities, generic branding, and channels of distribution that are open to many companies. These assets are used for other activities so that critical assets may be saved for the commercialization of the innovation. It is very important for the management team to place the proper level of attention and resources to each of these asset types.

Out-Licensing

Although most early stage companies are in no position to establish out-licensing activities, it is important to understand the motivations of companies with dedicated licensing offices so that the early stage company can position itself with both in-licensing and out-licensing opportunities if and when they become more feasible. Some companies prefer not to license out their core technologies for defensive reasons. Meanwhile, others recognize the when lack of resources, such as market reach limit the potential revenue of in-house technologies and set up these offices in attempt to extract maximum value from these untapped technologies. Still other companies have intellectual property that is outside of their core competency and wish to convert these dormant assets into revenues by licensing them to other companies.

The anatomy of a corporate out-licensing office is highly varied and depends upon the goals and missions of the office, the strength and breadth of its intellectual property, and the financial commitment to this office from the executive management and corporate budget. Although there are no proven guidelines for structuring an effective licensing office, typically an out-licensing office consists of a variable mix of IP attorneys and businessmen with experience in technology, mergers and acquisitions, divestitures and joint ventures. The relative size and mix of these professionals is highly dependent upon the purpose of the office. Thus, an out-licensing office created with the purpose of expanding the market reach of the company's core technologies will tend to have a large office consisting of a balanced mix of attorneys and businessmen. Meanwhile, an office designed to convert unutilized non-core technology IP will tend to be rather small and staffed primarily with businessmen.

Licensing offices may be highly connected to different business divisions within the company or there may be other teams that serve to link these groups. In contrast, some corporations choose not to establish a formal licensing office but rather handle licensing matters through their corporate legal department. But the ultimate decisions that are involved in structuring these offices are reflected in the company's overall business strategy and performance expectations. Early stage companies should form a good repor with potential licensing candidates and interview each so that they understand the organization and goals of each licensing office.

In-licensing

When developing an in-licensing program, the company must first establish a conceptual commercialization strategy initiating from the research, product development, manufacturing, distribution, and sale to the customer. Then a conversion mechanism must be designed in order to transform the intellectual capital into sales. The conversion strategy should be a core portion of the overall vision and business strategy of a company and should represent more than revenue generation. Ideally, the imported innovations should serve to enhance the hosting company's core technologies, with the ultimate goal of building stronger brand recognition in the respective market.

In-licensing strategies are not usually viable alternatives for the pure startup or early stage company due to their lack of adequate financial resources and undeveloped technology strategies, but as the company develops market maturity and a more definitive picture of its specific technology strategy, in-licensing opportunities should be carefully reviewed as an alternative source of revenue and asset growth. In this process, understanding the structure and requirements of a corporation's in-licensing technology office can assist the early stage company in designing and refining their technologies to meet the needs of large potential partners.

Cross-licensing

In a cross-licensing agreement, rights to certain technologies are exchanged for an entire portfolio of patents and a one-time payment to compensate for differences between the value of rights exchanged. Therefore, *no royalty fees are involved with cross-licensing arrangements.* Cross-licensing strategies are very popular with larger industries where large patent portfolios are involved in overlapping industries. The majority of these industries require cross-licensing in order to commercialize many of the products due to the overlapping nature of the technologies and difficulty with patent protection. Without such arrangements, many companies would not have sufficient design freedom necessary to produce the most competitive products and would need to spend large amounts of money to navigate around protected technologies. It is not uncommon to have products using technologies with very broad ownership in industries such as semiconductors, computers, and electronic components. IBM has made tremendous use of cross-licensing strategies for the benefit of its overall corporate strategy. In particular, as the number one patent awardee in the world nine years running, IBM has leveraged its intellectual property to enable it to achieve the remarkable turnaround from over a decade ago.

In contrast to cross-licensing strategies focused on the enhancement of design freedom, *cross-licensing strategies may also be implemented for technology acquisition.* This strategy focuses more on the exchange of intellectual property from more narrowly defined technologies and does not involve the exchange of know-how and ongoing support, unlike cross-licensing strategies for design freedom. Finally, the use of cross-licensing agreements has also found utility during the remediation process of litigation resolution. Thus, cross-licensing may be a mandate awarded by the court for an infringement violation or may even be a result of pretrial negotiations to prevent the high costs of litigation.

When To License

As we have seen, licensing represents one of many alternatives for transforming intellectual capital into revenues. Other choices include vertical integration, outsourcing, strategic alliances, and joint ventures. Vertical integration may be the best strategy for commercialization when a company possesses some complementary assets but needs critical complementary assets for commercialization, the intellectual property protection is good, the company can financially support the entire integration process, and competitors are not better positioned. However, if any of these conditions are violated, companies should seek alternative strategies for commercialization, such as joint ventures, licensing, or buyer-supplier agreements.

Buyer-supplier agreements are best implemented when the supplier either possesses intellectual property or generic assets for its commercialization, while the buyer possesses distribution channels or generic assets for the production of the commercialized assets. When engaging in buyer-supplier co-development agreements, both parties must secure protective measures to safeguard their investments. The supplier should ensure that the buyer is committed to preserving an agreed upon profit margin and does not use the commercialized innovation as leverage for its other products, which could result in lowered prices and a bad investment for the supplier. Even more important, the supplier must ensure that the buyer does not gain access to its branding or production know-how. As a healthy compromise between these

Table 7-2. Factors Affecting Licensing

Source: Parr and Sullivan

Factor	Licensors		Licensees	
	Aggressive	Passive	Seekers	Infringers
Protection	Have protection, are willing to exchange for financial consideration		Want guaranteed protection, particularly if protection is a competitive issue	Want protection for as long as possible in order to reduce any future payments
Exclusivity	Prefer not to offer exclusive license as this precludes other income from the patent.		Wants exclusive	
Utility/Advantage			Saw cost advantage of not having to recreate technology	See cost advantage of minimizing costs by obtaining license
Commercial Success	Unable to guarantee commercialization success unless other licensees or patent holders have already commercialized		Want some guarantee of commercialization success	Already know about commercialization success, wants to minimize cost outlay
Refinement	Probably see little refinement required		See more need for refinement, which lowers potential profits	Further refinements unnecessary, by definition
Competition Where Licensor & Licensee Are Competitors	Seek cross-licensing terms			
License Duration	Minimize duration in order to be able to renegotiate	Offer license for life of patent	Seek license for life of patent	Seek maximum terms e.g. license for like of patent
Royalty Amount	Seek maximum	Seek standard	For new technology seek running rate, for known technology seek one-time payment	Seek one-time payment
Support/Train	Offer after-sale training and support		Seek after-sale training and support	No training sought to minimize cost
License Commitment	De facto commitment to license because it is a source of strategic revenue	Commitment to license must be requested of passive licensors	Very interested in commitment to license	Commitment to license not an issue
Enforcement Burden	Already interested in enforcement	Enforcement interest unsure; licensee may need press for guarantees	Does not want to have enforcement, will seek guarantees of enforce-ment	Enforcement already demonstrated
Foreign vs. Domestic	No preference		No preference	
Crossover Sales	Cross-over sales may be possible		Allow crossover sales if terms are advantageous	Minimize crossover sales to reduce costs
Advice of Expert				

two strategies, licensing offers many attractive alternatives for building a commercialization strategy that is unachievable with vertical integration or buyer-supplier agreements.

- Licensing agreements provide access and to the other company's complimentary assets, which can minimize duplication of assets and lead to economies of scale.

- Licensing agreements typically use pricing schedules that include a fixed fee and a royalty rate, which is effective in aligning the incentives of the commercialization risks shared between both companies.

- Licensing agreements can also include legal provisions against misuse and misappropriation of the given technology and can provide for grantbacks when complementary innovations are developed by the licensee.

However, there is a fine balance between the decision to license technologies in order to compliment the overall business strategy and the risk of depleting intellectual property to current or future competitors. *A licensing strategy should be viewed as a way to access complimentary assets, decrease the total cost of commercialization, access expensive and protected technologies, avoid infringement litigation, and provide a source of revenue from its competitors.* But these goals do not come easily. And a company that wishes to implement a licensing strategy into its business model must engage in an ongoing industry competitive analysis in order to understand the benefits and risks of such strategies relative to specific companies.

How to License

Once a company has located a potential licensor or licensee, the proper background research should be performed in order to aid in the negotiation process. The first step should be to research various licensing agreements within the industry and conduct an analysis of licensing terms so that one can get an idea of compensation standards. Next, if the prospective licensing partner is a public company, the terms of all previous relevant licensing agreements should be investigated. Companies that have engaged in prior licensing agreements tend to use generic agreements, modifying them as needed. The SEC requires for all public companies that "any franchise or license or other agreement to use a patent, formula, trade secret, process or trade name upon which [the] registrant's business depends to a material extent" must be included in the company's SEC's filings.[1] If the company is not public, obtaining this information may be impossible, but that should not stop one from requesting to see previous agreements (with the name of the other party removed of course). Whether they will provide this information will depend upon the specific case, but it certainly will not hurt to ask. Regardless, licensing terms for each industry can be standardized by checking SEC filings of public companies. This information can be used as an initial starting point when negotiating terms with private companies.

There are three basic methods for determining standard industry and company specific licensing terms but all three use the SEC filings. One can conduct the searches manually, using on-line and CD-Rom databases, or by hiring consultants who specialize in this field. *When checking SEC filings, one should look at company 10-Ks and registration statements, which often disclose the terms of licensing agreements.* While there are no financial costs for manual searches, the time required can be very demanding and unless one has access to the small number of SEC reference rooms available in the U.S., an online search (www.freedgar.com) will be required. Other online and CD databases can be expensive and will most likely only include the most recent filing statements of companies, which may not yield adequate information. If one has the financial resources, the best approach would be to pay for professional assistance while the company can focus on preparing for the negotiation process.

Once the appropriate licensing agreements have been located, the company must then analyze and compare each relevant agreement so that some estimation of normality can be determined. Appendix D-5 compares two licensing agreements and provides an example of some of the most significant issues to consider when assessing these agreements.

D. Valuation of Intangible Assets

Valuation of intangible assets is a very difficult task to perform with accuracy, even for certified valuation professionals. And most entrepreneurs have neither the time nor expertise required to conduct these analyses. However, there are certain guidelines that when followed, can yield relatively quick and accurate estimates, which can serve as a starting point for refinement by other parties involved. The first step in calculating the value of a firm's intangible assets is to determine the proper valuation methodology to be used, as well as implementation of the appropriate assumptions. And this may only be accomplished by determining the primary objectives of the valuation.

In general there are three situations for which valuation of intangibles is needed; these are precommercialization, prenegotiation, and litigation. The precommericalization valuation is marked with perhaps the most inaccuracy due to the level of uncertainty of the ultimate success of commercialization. It is usually performed when seeking financing and involves determining the feasibility and commercial viability of the assets. Precommercialization valuation begins by conducting a market analysis and expense estimate of commercialization of the assets. From this information, one should have a reasonable estimate of the market size, growth rate, market share, revenue streams, and costs involved. Consider that the possibilities of commercialization can be licensing, franchising or complete autonomy, and therefore, calculations for each of these possibilities will obviously result in large differences in revenue and cost estimations.

Prenegotiation Valuation

A prenegotiation valuation is usually performed during licensing, acquisition, an asset sale or swap, or liquidation negotiations. Thus, it is very important that a company has a financial estimate of its intangible assets in order to arrive at a fair and mutually agreeable value with the opposing party. Without adequate knowledge of these asset values, the company will have diminished leverage in final negotiations and may not receive adequate compensation. Listed below are some factors to be addressed for each of the four situations that might prompt a prenegotiation valuation:

1. **Licensing Valuation.** This is important in order to determine the royalty rate for the intellectual property. One should consider each of the following factors when making a determination of the final value of the royalty rate.

   - *License Terms*. The most important factors to be addressed in the terms are the length of time the license will be in effect, the extent of exclusivity of the assets, such as the all rights granted, and geographical coverage.

   - *Competitive Advantage*. Emerging or completely innovative technologies are potentially more valuable to the licensee than improvements to existing technology and will therefore command a higher royalty rate.

   - *Cost Savings*. If the technology poses a potential threat to the licensee's technology or overall strategy, then it may be more cost and time effective to license the technology. Therefore, the licensor should be familiar with the costs of developing a patent around the prospective licensee and the potential loss in market share that may be at risk to the licensee.

- *Legal Protection*. No license is valuable without adequate infringement detection and legal protection. Therefore, the extent of these commitments must be determined.

- *Technology Maturity*. If the licensee has to spend enormous time and money to refine the technology into a commercial product, the license will not receive the best royalty rate.

- *Commercial Success*. Obviously, those technologies that have proven success in the marketplace will command a higher royalty rate and their valuations will be more accurately determined.

2. **Acquisition Valuation.** The valuation of intangible assets for acquisition negotiations is usually the primary component of the overall valuation of a high-technology firm. In general, the same factors considered for licensing agreements can be applied to asset acquisition as well: term, competitive advantage, cost savings, legal protection, technology maturity, and commercial success. However, the methods used to value these assets will vary depending upon whether these assets have generated revenues. If they have a historical and predictable stream of revenues, the Black-Scholes equation can be used (refer to the section on "Licensing Valuation Using Real Options"). If they have not generated sufficient revenues, one of the approaches in table 7-3 can be used.

3. **Asset Sale or Swap.** This strategy is typically used by companies wishing to augment their asset portfolios in conjunction with their business and technology strategies. When a company has recognized the existence of "dead" or nonstrategic assets in its portfolio that are inconsistent with the business strategy, they will often look to sell or exchange these assets to companies whose strategies would benefit from their addition to their portfolio. Once again, the same factors used for licensing agreements can be used for assets sales.

4. **Liquidation Valuation.** Some of the factors mentioned for valuation of licensing agreements may or may not be critical in a liquidation valuation, depending upon the characterization of assets and the prospective buyers. If a late stage company fails, they may have acquired substantial tangible assets, but its intangible assets may be viewed by the market as essentially worthless since the company was given adequate time and financing yet was not able to convert these assets into significant positive cash flows.

Thus, the intangible assets underlying the core technology may be viewed by outsiders as ineffective. Finally, the bargaining power in a liquidation may be close to zero depending upon the nature of the event. If the company is in bankruptcy proceedings, then the leverage to negotiate may be exclusively in the hands of the creditors. Otherwise, the equity shareholders will determine the conditions and price of the sale. If the majority shareholders (assumed to be VCs) are not able to locate an interested firm that views the assets as complementary, then deep discounts may be needed to increase the appeal of these assets.

Litigation Valuation

Valuation of intangible assets for litigation determination may either be practiced as a reactive or proactive exercise. Infringement cases are heard in a federal court of appeals specifically created for intellectual property cases. In order to prove that infringement exists, a company must satisfy what are know as *Punduit tests* (after a U.S patent case, *Panduit Corp. v. Stahlin Bros. Fiber Works Inc.,* 575 F.2d 1152, 1978). These tests require the patent holder to demonstrate that "demand existed for the product, there were no noninfringing substitutes, the patent holder has the manufacturing capacity to exploit the demand, and the amount of lost profits can be quantified." Even if the patent holder is not able to show that there were no noninfringing substitutes, the court will usually award a royalty rate to the patent holder if all the other tests have been met.

Usually companies will only perform this valuation after detecting competitors who have infringed on their protected intellectual property. However, an alternative approach employed by some companies is to conduct this valuation analysis and approach companies that are suspected of infringement, or the infringement is questionable. Because litigation costs can be tremendous and the intellectual property holder wins the majority of contested cases, many companies will opt to settle with the challenging company for a licensing agreement of some other form of compensation. While perhaps considered unethical, some firms use this intimidation tactic so companies should be aware of this possibility.

Determining Royalty Rates

When determining and negotiating royalty rates for innovations, several factors must be assessed due to their impact on the final royalty structure. Although we discussed six factors in the previous section, we will highlight the two most important factors to determine the terms of the agreement; competitive strategy and duration. The licensor must determine the potential impact of the license on the recipient and whether they are or might become a competitor. Finally, the licensor should understand all business relationships of the potential licensee to ensure they are not connected with competitors.

Since the ultimate goal of a conversion method such as a licensing agreement is to enhance the strategic position of the company, caution should be exercised when allowing the innovation to be placed in the hands of an outside company. *Candidates who are potential competitors should only be considered for licensing of non-strategic intellectual assets, while strategic assets can be licensed to noncompetitors with caution.* Alternatively, licensing can serve as a defensive activity by preventing competitors from developing their own technology. This might prevent the competitor from building a *clustering patent portfolio* around the company's core technology. Finally, cross-licensing agreements can be created that may decrease the likelihood of infringement.

The duration of the agreement is also a significant factor in determining the royalty structure of a licensing agreement. It is important for a company wishing to license its innovations to understand its potentials in the market as well as assessing the amount of leverage a prospective suitor may gain from such an agreement so that the maximum price is secured over the given period. *If the innovation is expected to result in large revenues for a company, the licensor will want to lock in a large fee over a shorter period so that renegotiation can lead to higher fees once the innovation has produced large revenues. Likewise, the licensee should seek the opposite.*

Assessing Risk

Much of the focus in royalty determination is with the assessment of the financial benefits and duration of these expected benefits with the cost of alternatives. Nonetheless, *the identification and measurement of the various possible forms of risk involved with the license is perhaps the most important leveraging device a company can use in negotiations.* Thus, when assessing the viability of licensing agreements, the company should perform a quantitative analysis in order to identify and measure all potential risks and rewards. Licensing transactions considered high risk are those technologies characterized by numerous factors that decrease the probability of receiving the expected benefits or increase the probability of receiving undesirable consequences. For instance, a high-risk transaction would have no record of commercial viability and involve further development and testing. Figure 7-1 shows factors affecting the structure and compensation of royalties.

Licensing Valuation Methods

In the previous two sections we discussed considerations thought to be most relevant for determining the value of licensing agreements and we learned that the specific valuation method used should be reflective of the reason for the valuation analysis. Here, we outline the most commonly used valuation techniques for licensing agreements based upon the reason for valuation. However, the calculations and assumptions selected for the valuation of patents and licensing agreements demonstrate wide variability and there is currently no universally preferred method.

Once an assessment of the costs, benefits, and risks has been made the company needs to determine a valuation for the project that reflects this information. Although there are more sophisticated techniques, the utility of the methods presented here should be sufficient to assist management in successfully negotiating the final terms of a royalty agreement. However, the reader is encouraged to refine each method based upon the details of the six factors discussed previously for determining valuations. Table 7-3 provides a detailed comparison of these methods.

The 25% Rule. This method states that the licensor should receive at least 25% of the pre-tax gross profit resulting from the use of the intellectual property. In general, *this results in a royalty rate of about 5% of the licensee's selling price.* However, this method should be refined for use with each particular asset. Patents are all different and the efforts of commercialization will be different. Some technologies will need refinement, while others will need a large sales force to capture revenues. Thus, the cost structure of the commercialization process should be factored into the final calculation in order to determine an equitable rate. Primarily used for precommercialization.

Market of Industry Norm Approach. This method consists of obtaining a market-based consensus of royalty rates. However, absent from this approach is a consideration of growth rates, market size, net profits, and risks. Finally, a discount factor can be used to account for any risks of revenue shortfall. Such information may be difficult to obtain but a good source might be through patent attorney interviews. In addition, for public companies this information can be obtained by checking SEC filings. Primarily used for precommercialization.

Figure 7-1. Factors to be considered for Royalty Negotiations

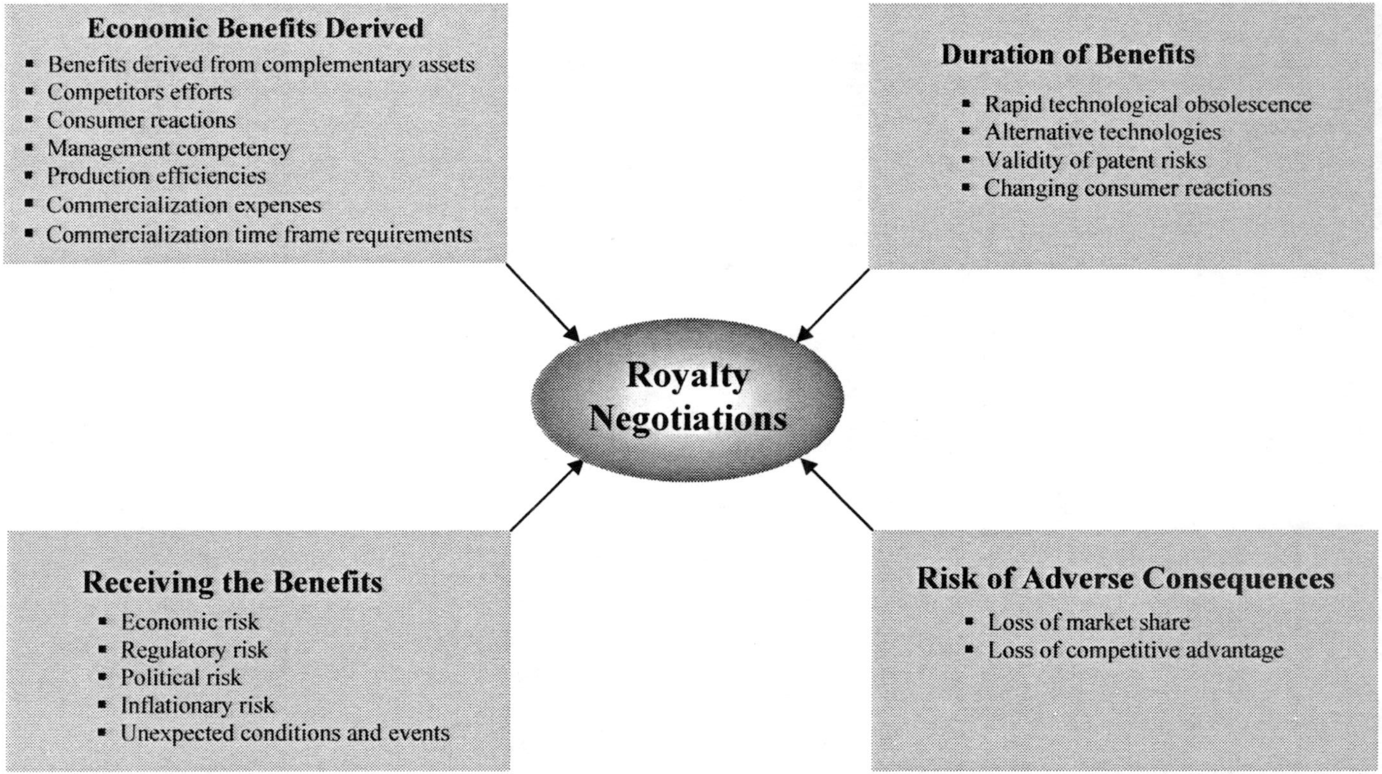

Economic Benefits Derived

- Benefits derived from complementary assets
- Competitors efforts
- Consumer reactions
- Management competency
- Production efficiencies
- Commercialization expenses
- Commercialization time frame requirements

Duration of Benefits

- Rapid technological obsolescence
- Alternative technologies
- Validity of patent risks
- Changing consumer reactions

Receiving the Benefits

- Economic risk
- Regulatory risk
- Political risk
- Inflationary risk
- Unexpected conditions and events

Risk of Adverse Consequences

- Loss of market share
- Loss of competitive advantage

Royalty Negotiations

Return on Sales. This method calculates a royalty rate based upon net profits as a percentage of revenues. However, the return on sales method does not consider risk involved or other assets used for the product, but a discount factor may be added. Primarily used for precommercialization.

Return on R&D Costs. This method places a value on the intellectual property based upon the costs of its development and adds a fair return on investment. This is considered *the most misleading of all methods* because a "fair return" is calculated only by a determination of the cost of development and not on the benefit that it has provided. Hence, this method is similar to the replacement cost calculation used by insurance companies, minus the fair return component. Primarily used for precommercialization.

Income Approach. This method is based on the income generated by the property and projects this income through the expected life of the asset. It is essentially the discounted cash flow method mentioned in chapter 5 (see chapter 11 for more detail). The problem with the income approach is that it can be very complicated and relies on multiple data and assumptions which may difficult to obtain. However, *it does factor in risk, market data, and the value of any complementary assets used in the project.* Primarily used for prenegotiation and litigation.

Lost Profits or Reasonable Royalty. This method is based upon infringement and so the company must satisfy the Panduit tests. In addition, many experts are needed to demonstrate the nature and extent of lost profits and this can be a very costly process for both parties. Used for litigation.

License Valuation Using Real Options

In chapter 5, we discussed various ways to value intangible assets such as patents, trademarks, and service marks. While the following method can be applied to determine the value of other intangible assets such as those described in chapter 5, it is more applicable to the process of licensing valuation. This method utilizes the Black and Scholes Option Pricing Model that is typically used to determine the value of financial options. Those familiar with options may have bought and sold puts and calls listed on the Chicago Board of Options Exchange (CBOE).

In financial terms, an option represents the right of the holder to buy, sell, or utilize an asset for a specific period of time in exchange for a mutually agreed price. A *call option* provides the holder the right to purchase a given security within a certain time frame at a predetermined price in exchange for an upfront payment for this right.   In contrast, the holder of a *put option* pays an upfront fee in exchange for the right to sell a given security at a predetermined price within a given time frame.

In contrast to options of publicly traded securities, licenses, patents, copyrights, trademarks, property and equipment purchase rights, and other intangible assets that are not traded publicly are called real options. Specifically, one can think of the ownership rights of these assets as call options, whereby the owner or holder of the asset has the right to derive benefit from the asset until the options contract expires.   The contract can be thought of as the term of a licensing agreement or a patent expiration date.

$$C = SN(d_1) - Ee_f^{-R,xt}N(d_2)$$

where C = the theoretical call option value

$$d_1 = \frac{\ln(S/E) + [R_f + (1/2)\sigma^2]t}{\sigma(t)^{-2}}$$

$$d_2 = d_1 - \sigma(t)^{-2}$$

S = stock price or underlying asset price
E = exercise price
R_f = the risk-free rate of interest
σ^2 = variance of the stock's or underlying asset's returns
t = time to expiration of the option
$N(d_1)$ and $N(d_2)$ = cumulative normal probability values of d_1 and d_2

The most difficult variables to estimate in this equation are $N(d_1)$ and $N(d_2)$, which represent the risk associated with generating the projected cash flows. However, numerous factors may be applied in order to construct a scenario analysis to determine the relative probabilities of the license yielding these projected cash flows. These variables are Z-scores from the normal probability function and may be found in cumulative distribution function tables for standard normal random variable.

Table 7-3. Common Methods of Royalty Rate Determination

Method	Strengths	Weaknesses	Context
25% Rule	-Easy -Inexpensive -Ballpark estimate	*Does not consider:* -true profitability -risk/return of investment	**-Precommercialization** -Provides initial ballpark of value
Market Approach	-If data are available, provides credible way to determine industry range of average royalty rate	-Assumes current industry norms are correct -High cost of obtaining data -Requires active market of similar transactions	-If data is easily obtainable then this is ideal for **precommercialization** -If data not readily available but possible to find, then prenegotiation
Return on Sales	-Quick -Easy -Inexpensive	-Low level of precision -Difficult to determine proper allocation of profits between two parties *Does not consider:* -Value of complimentary assets -Risk/return of investment	**-Precommercialization** -Provides initial ballpark estimate of value
Return on R&D Costs	-Easy -Inexpensive -R&D costs easy to determine	-R&D costs rarely equal IP value *Does not consider:* -Low level of precision -Value of complementary assets -Risk/return of investment	-Use only as last resort during **Precommercialization**
Income Approach	-Highly credible method *Does not consider:* -Value of complimentary assets -Risk/return of investment -Market size -Competitive assessment -Requires cross functional input	-Accuracy of valuation highly dependent on precision of assumptions -Getting consensus on appropriate assumptions may take some time -Time consuming to get accurate data -Need detailed knowledge of marketplace & environ.	-Because is more resource-intensive, good for **Prenegotiation** and ideal for **Litigation**
Lost Profits	-Highly credible methodology -Very precise valuation Does consider: -Value of compl. assets -Risk/return of investment -Market size -Competitive assessment	-Requires very precise assumptions -Time consuming and costly to get accurate data -Need detailed knowledge of marketplace & environment -Requires independent expert -Takes a long time -Often must rely on infringer's cost of production	**-Litigation**

Source: Parr and Sullivan

Note from the equation that increasing time to option (license) expiration and increasing variance of cash flows are more valuable than when decreasing. However, it is the opinion of the author that while increased variation yields more value of the option due to the increased probability of expected returns when valuing financial options, the same does not hold for real options.   The reason for this discrepancy is that unlike financial options, in which the holder can buy out his contract prematurely by selling these calls on the options exchange, licensees and patent owners are typically restricted to the expiration time periods given by non-negotiable contracts and government regulation, for licenses and patents respectively.   Simply stated, real options are typically not liquid assets. Therefore, such increased variance may result in a lowered cash flow over an extended period leaving the owner of real options with limited or no ability to sell the rights to a third party.   As such, real options with high variance values should be viewed with caution.

Example of Real Options Calculation for Licensing

Assume that a company has a 10-year license to produce and market a product in a designated geographic area to a specific set of customers. The cost of retooling the firm's manufacturing operations, training, sales force, promotional literature, advertising, and license fees requires an initial investment of $100 million. The present value of projected cash flows from utilizing the license is $80 million. Although the product is currently expensive to produce in small quantities, the cost of production is expected to fall as larger volumes are sold. Furthermore, improvements in production technology are expected to lower production costs, which will enable a reduction in the price of the product. It is uncertain by how much sales of the product will increase due to the declining price. An analysis of similar projects in the past suggests that the variance of projected cash flows is 3%. The current 10-year Treasury bond rate is 6%. Even though the project has a negative net present value of $20 million, estimate the value of the license as a call option, which could be sold to another party.

Solution:

Value of the asset (PV of projected cash flows from utilizing the license) = $80 million

Exercise price (PV of the cost of developing and marketing the product) = $100 million

Variance of the cash flows = 0.03

Time to expiration = 10 years

Risk-free interest rate = 0.06

$$d_1 = \frac{\ln(\$80/\$100) + [0.06 + (1/2)0.03]10}{(0.03)^{.2}(10)^{.2}}$$

$$= \frac{-0.2231 + 0.7500}{0.1732 \times 3.1623}$$

$$= 0.9620$$

$$d_2 = 0.9620 - 0.5477$$

$$= 0.4143$$

$$C = \$80(0.8531) - \$100(2.7183)^{-0.06 \times 10}(0.6736)$$

$$= \$68.25 - \$36.97$$

$$= \$31.28$$

If this company were being valued for possible acquisition, the acquirer may choose to add $31.28 million to the total valuation for this firm due to the value of this license.

Notes:
1. Z scores: The probability of drawing a value from the distribution of possible outcomes associated with this investment opportunity that is less then or equal to $d_1 = 1.1501$ is 0.8944 and of $d_2 = 0.6024$ is 0.7422.
2. The Z scores were calculated at the 5% significance level

E. Joint Ventures & Strategic Alliances

Generally speaking, any formal arrangement between two or more organizations for the purposes of creating mutual gain can be represented by joint ventures, strategic alliances, licensing agreements, minority equity investments, and consortia.   Obviously, joint ventures and strategic alliances are a broader expression of these cooperative arrangements and can be structured to include co-marketing agreements, co-developing agreements and other activities.   When assessing the merits of partnering arrangements versus an acquisition, companies must weigh the benefits of direct asset acquisition, determine the ease of asset assimilation into the overall strategy, estimate the amount of expected synergy and quantify the increased access to capital/debt liability as well as cost/value of operational flexibility.

Joint ventures and strategic alliances are prevalent in certain industries where acquisitions do not provide equivalent risk-reward alternatives.   For instance, *in industries where there is significant uncertainty, alliances provide the needed flexibility for companies to alter their course if the regulatory atmosphere changes or product launches fail or are delayed.*   In addition, alliances provide an opportunity to enter a foreign market with minimal investment while a company assesses the potential benefits of a full commitment.   Thus, *alliances provide cost-effective and low risk methods to test intended strategic direction.*

Joint Ventures

There has been much inaccurate use of this terminology over the past few years, perhaps due to the absence of a clear and consistent definition of what a joint venture is within the financial literature.   In part, this may be a consequence of the absence of legal definitions for these arrangements.   However, for the purposes of this discussion, *we will define a joint venturing arrangement as a unique entity formed when two companies unite to form a third company.*   This would be defined as a corporate joint venture and would be governed by particular state laws of incorporation, with separate by-laws and a board of directors governing the decisions of the CEO of the venture, similar to a separate company.   In addition, *separate supply, managerial, license, and technical assistance agreements are needed to ensure that the venture is conducted as a separate legal entity with bias proportionate to the ownership of each partner.*

The first task in assessing the feasibility of a joint venturing arrangement is for each party to reveal the value it expects to add to the overall mission. Typically, both companies possess adequate assets to accomplish the goals of the venture individually, but each wishes to spread the risk with one or more participants. Similar to licensing programs, the relative effectiveness of any joint venture program rests upon the ability of the venture unit to receive the needed resources and control from both companies. In addition, frequent reporting and milestone achievements are critical for preserving each company's interest and commitment toward the venture. Several examples of joint ventures are presented below.

Risk-Sharing Joint Venture. This is perhaps the most common joint venture arrangement and usually takes the form of an *equity joint venture*. This is basically a partnership in which both partners contribute both tangible and intangible assets towards the common goals of the agreement. These ventures are formed more for the purpose of sharing the risk rather than due to a lack of sufficient resources by each partner. However, the total asset contribution by each partnering firm may result in a stronger competitive position towards the completion of the goals of the venture.

Disguised Sale. One company may wish to transfer a low-basis, high-value asset to another party to minimize taxes. Instead of selling the asset outright and incurring a capital gains tax, the selling company may organize a joint venture with another company interested in obtaining this asset. The strategy is for both companies to utilize the asset for a limited time then dissolve the venture in a way that allows the company to transfer the asset to its partner in return for cash proceeds generated by the asset during the time of the unification. Such an arrangement should be crafted carefully in order to avoid tax assessments by the IRS. While this arrangement is usually structured as a limited partnership, it is nevertheless a common arrangement considered as a joint venture.

Pro-competitive Joint Venture. This strategy would be used when a dominant competitor plans to force others out of the market. One of the smaller competitors may wish to form a joint venture with the dominant competitor to protect itself from the effects of this attack on the industry.

Critical Issues

Dissolution of joint ventures can be messy and may present adverse consequences for those companies that have not secured the appropriate safeguards in advance. Proper scenario planning should account for resolution of the pre-joint venture conditions within each firm in order to ensure a smooth transition once the venture has dissolved. In addition, the *joint venture agreement should define and protect the value of the relationship established by the joining of the firms and should specify any and all conditions related to asset disposal and any other benefits created by the venture.*

Control issues are perhaps the biggest hurdles for structuring and executing effective joint ventures since each party may have unequal ownership rights. Therefore, specific financial and managerial control issues should be clarified prior to the formation of a joint venture. For instance, one company may wish to sell assets to an outside party which may hinder the success of the venture. Such an action could be prevented by establishing rights of first refusal in the venture agreement, thereby allowing the partner to have first choice of purchasing these assets. Alternatively, a company may wish to exit the venture prematurely, which might impede the success of the other company's interest in the venture. This can be protected by drafting clauses within the agreement that specify the conditions under which exit or liquidation may occur. *The venture agreement should also address the manner by which intellectual property established as a result of the venture should be allocated upon termination of the joint entity.* Finally, the agreement should attempt to clearly define the responsibility of each party in disclosing all resources that might potentially provide gainful assistance to the joint venture. In some cases, one company may want to protect resources from its partner for fear of expansion of its core businesses into their markets.

Some companies have argued that joint ventures should have call options in order to enhance their potential leverage. Such a call option would specify a price at which one of the companies could increase its equity stake at some future time if it chooses. This would help minimize investment risk while allowing for enhanced participation in returns.

Strategic Alliances

Strategic alliances are formed when two companies agree to share resources and information in pursuing the outcome of a single project. They are usually formed in order to increase a company's global presence, to provide synergy, economies of scale, or to respond to industry consolidation, convergence, and product life cycle compression. Typically, when companies are attempting to develop multiple sources of competitive advantage simultaneously, strategic alliances can assist in the extension of external collaborative networks with customers, suppliers, government agencies, and even competitors. While the focus of strategic alliances has changed over the years, the current motivation for their formation is to assist in the creation and development of new products and technologies. However, some are still formed to enhance one's channels of distribution. *One overlying common feature of strategic alliances is that they are created during periods of industry transition when new strategies are required in order to maintain and build competitive advantages.*

Many companies initially opt for alliances over acquisitions because they want to create synergy without the financial risk and commitment required by a merger or acquisition. Despite the initial preference for alliances by some firms, *acquisitions are often the end result when these strategies provide mutually successful* and financially rewarding results. While the success of alliances can be small and the risks large, they have experienced a tremendous growth rate by U.S., European, and Japanese firms over the past two decades.[2] However, the formation of alliances does not come without significant risk. One of the most feared outcomes by a company is that one partner will exploit the alliance to gain a competitive advantage over the other partner. This outcome could result despite the lack of specific intentions by the firm gaining the advantage, but rather as a consequence of the structure and management of the alliance.

Unlike joint ventures, *strategic alliances are less formal in their structure and do not form a third entity*, but are nevertheless amongst the most complex business arrangements that can exist due to the lack of legal structure which can create ambiguity of control and ownership of assets. When both companies attempt a temporary unification, the corporate cultures of each partner can cause many difficulties. As a consequence, the results of these alliances have not been particularly successful in the past. The following recommendations for achieving a successful alliance come from Dr. Gussin of Johnson & Johnson:

Table 7-4. Why Alliances are Formed and Why They Fail

Why Alliances are Formed	Why Do Alliances Fail
-Overcome barriers to entry	-Lack of cooperation
-Gain access to a restricted market	-Lack of trust
-Acquiring technologies, products, or new skills	-Inadequate advance planning
-Pooling of resources	-Too much detailed negotiation, too little management of the alliance
-Reducing uncertainty	-Lack of organizational capabilities and resources to manage cooperative relationships
-Sharing risky projects	
-Speeding entry into new markets	-Size, Strategic, or Cultural mismatch
-Deriving new sources of revenue from combining complementary assets	-Change in strategy of one partner
	-Wrong choice of partner
	-Wrong initial strategy

- Develop a clear understanding of the goals of the alliance

- Form a clear strategy for reaching these goals

- Identify milestones for assessing the progress of the alliance

- Engage in extensive up-front planning

- Clearly define roles of responsibility

- Engage in frequent communication between partners at the operating management level

- Gain enthusiastic and continuing support from upper management

In addition, *the alliance must be successful in forming the appropriate internal networks that provide access to the needed resources of the parent companies involved.* This task can be extremely difficult to accomplish unless the alliance involves the core competencies of both partners. Only when the core competencies of each company are involved will the alliance maintain the mutual commitment needed to achieve the goals of the alliance. Without this requirement the alliance with fail.

Alliance and Joint Venture Management

Companies can maximize their success in these partnering arrangements by planning for and executing three essential tasks:

Pre-Alliance/JV Planning. Prior to entering these arrangements, the first step that should be taken is to define the structure of the alliance/JV. This would consist of determining what each participant wants from the partnership, determining the feasibility of the arrangement by performing several risk/benefit analyses, and identifying the best candidates. Next, after prospective partners have been identified and the decision to consider the partnership has been made, each partner should list its expected level of tangible and intangible asset contributions. This is followed by each partner notifying the other of its objectives, and modifying these as needed during a negotiative process. Finally and most importantly, control issues must be agreed upon. The following questions serve to help this process.

Feasibility:

- What goals does the company have that are not achievable without outside assistance?

- What company could best help you achieve these goals?

- Can your company help the potential partner achieve its goals?

- What are some possible long-term benefits of partnering with the candidate?

- What resources is your company willing and able to contribute towards the goals of the alliance/JV?

- What information and/or processes do you want to keep the candidate from learning?

- How should you organize to attain short-term and long-term goals?

- What are the estimated costs?

- What are the estimated benefits to my company?

- What are the estimated benefits to the partner?

- What are the possible risks to my company?

Control:

- Which partner has the best ability to manage the partnership?

- What will be the ownership representation of each partner (joint ventures)?

Dissolution:

- Under what conditions can the partnership be dissolved?

- How will assets resulting from the partnership be distributed?

Post-Alliance/JV Education. This activity involves learning from the partnering company and teaching the employees to understand the merits and restrictions of the alliance. The need to remain autonomous may seem like an obvious recommendation but *alliances can sometimes cause a dependency on the other company, which is only noticed after the alliance has ended.* In addition, the each company must protect its most valued assets, human and intellectual capital, as the partner of today could become the competitor of tomorrow. *Knowledge flows must be managed by each partner so that the* *alliance maintains the equity originally set forth and no competitive advantages develop.* Below are some questions that may be used to help satisfy this activity.

- How can principal employees of each company be educated regarding the benefits of the common goals of the venture?

- How will the company institute the proper programs to handle any corporate culture conflicts?

- What processes need to be developed to ensure efficient cooperation, yet minimize the possibility of becoming dependent on the patenting firm?

- How will your company contribute assets to the project yet ensure the partner develops no competitive advantages?

Corporate Alliance/JV-Management Capabilities. Each company should form a corporate alliance-management unit that treats the alliance as a business unit representing a portion of the company's overall business strategy. This is in contrast to treating the alliance as a subsidiary that has an autonomous strategic focus.

F. Franchising

A franchise is a contractual agreement between two legally independent companies whereby the franchiser provides the right to the franchisee to sell the franchiser's products or to conduct business under its trademarks over a specific time period. The compensation paid to the franchiser is usually an origination fee, royalties, and advertising fees, both calculated as a percentage of annual revenues. Franchising is an attractive alternative for the entrepreneur since it combines the attributes of a large corporation, such as economies of scale, and the incentive based performance of an owner run business. Obviously, certain businesses are better suited for franchising, namely retail trades such as fast food, car dealerships, real estate and tax agencies, fitness clubs, hair saloons, and gas station/mini-marts. By far the U.S. leads the world in both the number of franchisers (over 3000) and franchises (over 250,000).

While usually not a good method of business expansion for high tech companies, franchising can be a good method to expand a technology services business, such as IT consulting or computer technician businesses. The unique advantages of franchising are that it allows a company the ability to rapidly expand its business rapidly with minimal capital since the franchisee is responsible for the costs of the facilities. This can provide a tremendous advantage for businesses that require several offices in order extend its geographical reach. Finally, franchising provides a cost effective method for building the brand name of the franchise.

Notes

[1] 1991 SEC GUIDELINES; Rules and Regulation, Warren, Gorham & Lamont, Boston, MA (1995), Section 229.601(b)(10)(ii)(B), p. Reg S-K.69.

[2] The estimated failure rate for strategic alliances is 40-60%.

8

Managing Growth

A. Introduction

Throughout Part II of this book we have discussed intellectual property positioning and market profiling techniques needed for offensive, defensive, and preemptive strategies central to the establishment of a sustainable competitive advantage. And we have emphasized the importance of maintaining an ongoing assessment of your industry and competitors, essential for completing this task. However, positioning the company competitively only contributes to its *top-line*, or revenue. And because companies are ultimately judged by their ability to generate profits, we must also address other activities that influence the *bottom-line* or overall profitability. Thus it is ultimately the financial management of company operations that is responsible for converting revenues into earnings.

To further illustrate the significance of financial management, it may be helpful to think in terms of two broad aspects in the process of driving company profits; business management and operational finance. *Business management* includes those activities directly responsible for revenue generation, such as the *strategic planning and execution* of R&D, sales and marketing, production and distribution, growth and market penetration. Meanwhile, *operational finance* is concerned with the most efficient *utilization of company assets* and involves budget formation, cash management, management of accounts payable and receivables, inventory management, collections, administrative and product related purchasing decisions. As such, operational finance is also involved with the financial decisions related to R&D, sales and marketing, production, distribution and expansion. Therefore, when attempting to prioritize human resources to be committed towards business management and operational finance, one should keep in mind that *profits are derived from both revenue generation (business management) and expense management (operational finance)*, as illustrated by figure 8-1. This chapter discusses the main activities of operational finance thought to be most essential for optimal company performance. Also included towards the end of this chapter are topics more concerned with business management, but can also be utilized to assist in the financial operations of the management team.

Figure 8-1. Business Management versus Operational Finance

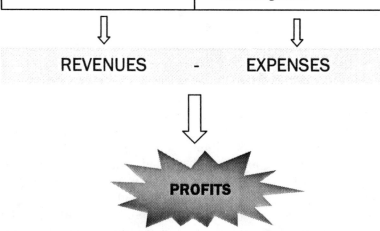

Business Management	Operational Finance
Technology Strategy	Capital Budgeting
Sales & Marketing Strategy	R&D Expenditures
Production & Distribution	Sales & Marketing Expenditures
Growth & Expansion Strategy	Production Expenditures
Intellectual Property Strategy	Direct Materials Expenditures
Profit Margins	Labor Expenditures
	Administrative Expenditures
	Asset Management
	Accounts Payable
	Accounts Receivable
	Collections
	Inventory Management
	Cash Management
	Debt Management
	Tax Management

REVENUES   -   EXPENSES

PROFITS

B. Capital Budgeting

Capital budgeting is the process of determining how a company plans to allocate its financial resources based upon revenue and expense forecasts. More specifically, capital budgeting is concerned with expense forecasting and income utilization associated with longer-term projects and operations. Within a capital budget one finds financial projections for business operations and expansion, purchase and replacement of equipment and land, and repair of equipment and facilities. Despite generating tremendous revenues, without an accurately prepared budget a company may not use its cash efficiently and can quickly become insolvent. *Indeed prospective investors can form discriminating conclusions about the management team that has historically either met its budget or fallen short. And this will no doubt affect earnings and/or cash flows resulting in an alteration of company valuation.*

Well-designed budgets inform the management of the breakeven point and allow them to implement specific milestones for sales and revenue, cost control, and the efficient management of cash flows. And for high growth companies, budgets are critical for controlling the demanding expenditures required to fuel such growth. In general the budget should contain not only the company's future projections, but also its past performance, all of which may be obtained from the financial statements (which will reveal the cash flows, expenses, sales and revenue, earnings, and debt of the company). *Thus a well-designed budget helps form the basic outline for the annual financial management plan of the company and therefore may be thought of as its financial business plan.*

For convenience, we can divide company expenditures into two categories. *Current expenditures* include items such as salaries, wages, sales and marketing expenses, and cost of raw materials, and these items are entirely written off in the same year that these expenses are incurred. *In contrast, capital expenditures* are longer-term investments in projects such as R&D, purchase of machines and equipment, replacement of existing equipment, office expansion, and land purchases. In this case, each type of expense is amortized (a gradual reduction in value) according to guidelines mandated by the IRS. However, both the IRS and Generally Accepted Accounting Principals (GAAP) allow considerable flexibility in the choice of methods used, which can result in large differences in the financial statements of the company. In addition, even more flexibility is allowed with pro forma financial statements. While current expenditures are accounted for by cash and asset management activities, the management of capital expenditures is more complex and may involve a combination of cash, debt management, forecasting, and selective choice of accounting methods.

Forming a Project Budget

Within the process of creating a capital budget, several other budgets must first be constructed. For instance, many companies wish to know the estimated expenses required for a project in order to determine its feasibility. As well, companies must determine the best use of capital for investment in projects that are expected to return the highest payout with respect to time. Therefore, when forming a *project budget*, the company first needs to determine the expected initial cost of each project to ensure that the investment is reasonable. The initial cost is calculated by subtracting the initial revenue from the initial expense (see figure 8-3). Next, the *incremental cash flow*, or that portion of a company's cash flow due to the hypothetical project must be calculated (figure 8-2).

Incremental Cash Flow = Incremental EBIT + Incremental Tax Benefit of Depreciation

Figure 8-2. Steps for Determining the Incremental Cash Flow

---

1. Calculate Additional Net Earnings.

Additional Net Earnings = Estimated Total Net Earnings – Estimated Net Earnings
(with the project)   (without the project)

2. Calculate the Tax Benefits of Depreciation.

Additional Tax Benefit of Depreciation = Tax Rate x Additional Depreciation

3. Add Additional Net Earnings and Tax Benefits of Depreciation

---

This method can provide an initial screening tool for capital budgeting decisions. However, in order to arrive at a final decision, more sophisticated methods should be used that account for the time value of money, risk of generating cash flows, interest rate risk, and inflation. For companies with earnings predictability, analysis of conservative projects can be approximated using the average rate of return and payback period, since both methods use earnings as a basis for their calculations. The ease of these two methods is reflected in their neglect of the use of cash flows and calculations for the time value of money. However, because the time value of money includes factors for estimating interest rate changes and inflation, as well as the increased risk associated with periods of increasing cash flows, these two methods do not yield the most accurate results. *In contrast, net present value, internal rates of return, and profitability indexes rely upon cash flows, account for the time value of money, and the first two include the discount rate.*

Figure 8-3. A Project Analysis Worksheet

Initial Expense	Amount	Initial Revenue	Amount
Price of New Items		Revenue from Sale of Existing Machinery	
Additional Expenses, Packing and Delivery		Tax Credit on Sale of Existing Machinery at Loss**	
Installation			
Inspection			
Other			
Taxes on Sale of Existing Machinery*			
Change in Net Working Capital		Total Initial Revenue	
Total Initial Expense		Initial Cost of Project	

*Note that if the machinery is sold above its book value, there will be a recaptured depreciation amount equal to the difference between the amount sold for and the current book value. The amount of recaptured depreciation will be taxed at the capital gains rate of the company. The book value is calculated by observing the IRS schedule for depreciation. Equipment and machinery is typically depreciated over 3 or 5 years depending on the category.

**Note that if the machinery is sold below its book value, there will be a loss recognized that will result in a tax credit, which will be equal to the difference in the book value of the equipment minus the sales price, then multiplied by the capital gains tax rate of the company.

Source: Barron's Finance

Net Present Value Approach

Calculating the investment strength of a project using cash flows is preferred to earnings since depreciation can be accounted for in the former. *The net present value approach simply discounts the future cash flows of a project to yield a present value and compares this to the initial cost of the project.* Therefore, if the present value of the future expected cash flows of the project is greater than the initial costs of the project, it is considered financially feasible. The formula for the net present value is

$$NPV = PV - I$$

where   NPV is the net present value

PV is the present value of the future cash flows

I is the initial investment outlay

We can calculate the present value, PV by the following equation:

$$PV = \frac{M}{(1 + i)^t}$$

where M = the amount expected to be received at a specified time

t = the time period under consideration

i = the interest rate or for the purposes of this discussion, the annual rate of return of the project

The selection of the interest rate should reflect the alternative project or other methods the company has to invest this cash.

Example calculating the present value of future cash flows for a project

A company has been profitable for several years due in part to efficient reinvestment of excess cash flows back into operations. This year it is trying to decide whether to invest in a new project. Historically, the company has yielded an annual return of 10% by investing its cash flows into the company. Based upon a detailed market analysis, the company estimates that it should be able to earn the following revenues from this expansion over the next four years: $500,000, $850,000, $1,300,000, and $2,600,000. The initial expenses for this project are estimated to be $2,200,000 and $150,000 for each of the three remaining years. Determine if this new project makes sense purely from a financial perspective.

Year	Cash Flows	Expenses
1	$500,000	$2,200,000
2	$850,000	$150,000
3	$1,300,000	$150,000
4	$2,600,000	$150,000

The present value of future estimated cash flows are:

$$PV = \frac{\$500,000}{(1 + 0.10)^1} + \frac{\$850,000}{(1 + 0.10)^2} + \frac{\$1,300,000}{(1 + 0.10)^3} + \frac{\$2,000,000}{(1 + 0.10)^4}$$

PV = $454,545 + $702,479 + $977,444 + $1,369,863

PV = $3,504,331

The total expense for this project during the four-year period is $2,800,000. But we must calculate the present value of the future expenses.

$$PV = \frac{\$2,200,000}{(1 + 0.10)^1} + \frac{\$150,000}{(1 + 0.10)^2} + \frac{\$150,000}{(1 + 0.10)^3} + \frac{\$150,000}{(1 + 0.10)^4}$$

PV = $1,818,182 + $123,967 + $112,782 + $102,740

PV = $2,157,671

Therefore, if all estimates are accurate the company is expected to benefit by a present value of $1,346,660 by engaging in this project. Note the assumptions used for this example. First, the company chose to use a discount rate of 10% based upon the historical returns earned by previous reinvestment of capital into the company. Finally, the company assumed that the historical 10% earned by reinvesting excess cash flows into the company was not necessary to sustain its profitability. That is, this reinvestment was independent of the company's ability to continue to make profits at levels consistent with historical accounts.

The determination of the *discount rate* is a very important variable and *will increase as the length of time of the project increases, the risk of execution of the project increases, interest rate or inflation increases.* Remember that the discount rate is a premium attached to the present value calculation that reflects the investment risk relative to the risk-free rate, which is usually denoted by the U.S. Treasury bill. Finally, note that in order to maximize accurate results, one must also account for the effects of inflation. A simple way to account for this is to subtract the annual rate of inflation from the discount rate to yield the *real discount rate*, and then calculate the present value as before.

Certainty Equivalent Approach

While the net present value method may be useful in comparing the relative financial strength of two or more projects, it ignores risk factors associated with generating the expected cash flows. Often, projects do not go as planned. Therefore, when there is uncertainty of future cash generation, it is more accurate to use other methods, such as the certainty equivalent approach, the capital asset pricing model, sensitivity analysis, and simulation techniques. These methods can be found in most corporate finance textbooks but we will briefly describe the certainty equivalent method here due to its relative simplicity.

The strength of the certainty equivalent approach is that it accounts for both the risk in generation of future cash flows and the duration risk of expected future cash flows in calculating the net present value of a project. A key portion of this calculation requires one to determine the percentage of future cash flows that are certain or can be relied upon with minimal risk. These percentages are called the *certainty equivalent factors.* The steps needed to calculate the financial strength of a project using the certainty equivalent approach are outlined below:

1. Estimate the expected cash flows of the project under consideration.

2. Determine the certainty equivalent factors. For instance, there might be a 50% chance of generating $1,000,000 and an 80% chance of generating $500,000. The accuracy of these estimations will depend upon the assumptions underlying the project and can be refined using a scenario analysis.

3. Calculate the *certain cash flows* by multiplying the values from the previous step with the analogous future expected cash flows.

4. Calculate the present value of the project by discounting these certain cash flows by a risk-free discount rate. Mostly commonly, U.S treasury bills are used for this rate.

5. Calculate the net present value of the project by subtracting the initial investment required from the present value of certain cash flows.

6. The project is deemed acceptable if the net present value is zero or positive and unacceptable if it is negative.

Budget Forecasting

Prior to making capital budgeting decisions, a company must undergo the difficult task of budget forecasting. There are many types of budgets the company must create, but generally speaking the operating and financial budgets are the most important. The *operating budget* consists of a sales budget, production budget, direct materials budget, direct labor budget, selling and administrative expense budget, capital budget, and pro forma income statement. Meanwhile, the *financial budget* consists of the cash budget and the pro forma balance sheet. Each one of these budgets has a distinctive role in helping the company plan for and manage operations and they are all combined into what may be called the *master budget*, which is used to create the financial statements for the end of the quarter and the fiscal year. *The sales budget is by far the most important portion of a company's budget plan because it establishes numbers by which all the other budget types depend.* Next in importance is the *expense budget,* otherwise known as the cost of goods or inventory budget. Figure 8-4 illustrates the components of the master budget.

Of course revenue, expenses, and cash flows will not always go according to the proposed budget and when this happens it is known as the variance, or the difference between the forecasted and actual numbers. *Variance analysis* by management can often uncover problems within business units of the company due to underperformance. For instance, the discrepancy between operating expenses and the sales budget could be due to direct factors such as the inefficient use of company resources or indirect factors related to cash and inventory management. Nevertheless, if these variances are not interpreted with caution, any misinterpretation could result in misappropriated adjustments to corporate strategy.

Finally, it should be emphasized that accurate forecasting of economic data is a critical element of constructing an accurate master budget. And any unanticipated change in economic conditions (inflation, interest rates, currency exchange rates, changes in oil prices, political changes) or any other factors influencing the overall business environment could result in drastic variances in the master budget or any of its components. As well, failure to account for any possible seasonal or business cycle changes will also result in variances. Therefore, companies should understand how such changes would affect their customers, suppliers, distributors, and the industry in general and account for these possibilities in advance.

C. Financial Planning

As we learned from the previous section, the methods used for capital budgeting analysis can be used to determine the financial merits of individual projects. *However, the primary objective of capital budgeting is not to determine financial feasibility of projects but rather to estimate the future financing needs of a company so that it does not face a liquidity crisis.* Such a disastrous situation could occur with even a highly successful company that is generating substantial revenues if proper planning and budgetary decisions are not made in advance.

Controlling expenses or the *burn rate* should be one of the keys concerns of an early stage company, as investors will scrutinize the use of cash flows prior to and after they have invested capital with the company. And management teams without an adequate understanding of the basic skills for cash management and budgeting may be shunned by investors. Therefore, in this section we will discuss three methods that can be used to estimate capital needs when forming a budget: percent-of-sales, cash turnover, and cash budget methods. When project delay or alteration of investment amount occurs, additional methods may be required, so we will also discuss methods that allow one to incorporate the flexibility of such events.

Percent-of-Sales Method

This method calculates the financing needs of working capital (the amount of cash needed to pay short-term debt) by assuming that changes in sales alter the amount of assets needed by a company. At first glance, this seems reasonable, since changing levels of sales will affect the need for inventory changes and alter the amount of accounts receivable. The correlations are as follows:

- As sales increase, inventory is depleted and needs to be replenished. Likewise, accounts receivable will increase.

- As sales increase, liabilities will increase due to the need to purchase raw materials for inventory replenishment.

Figure 8-4. A Generic Comprehensive Budget

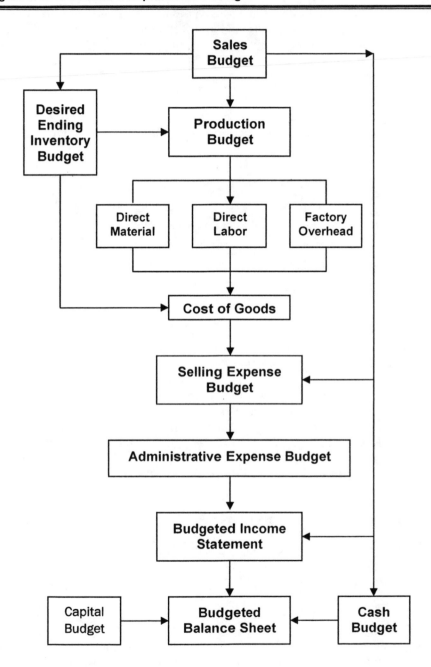

Source: The Vest-Pocket CPA, Dauber, Siegel, and Shim

In order to use this method, a company must examine its historical financial statements to calculate ratios of differing types of assets and liabilities to sales so that the dependence of assets and liabilities upon sales volume will be known.   Once these ratios have been determined, they are used to predict the amount of external financing needed to provide for future sales forecasts. The formula for determining this financing is as follows:

Required External Financing = A/S (ΔS) – L/S (ΔS) - rS

where, A/S = assets that change with sales
ΔS = expected change in sales forecast for the year
L/S = liabilities that change with sales
r = ratio of net profits after dividends to sales
S = total expected sales forecasted

Example of the percent-of-sales method

The CFO of company X has examined previous financial statements and determined that the ratio of assets that change with sales is 50%, while the ratio of liabilities that change with sales is 10%.   A budget analysis has shown that sales are expected to increase by $500,000 in the next fiscal year, making the total expected sales $1,000,000. The company has historically maintained 5% of its sales revenue as net earnings after dividends.   Estimate the amount of external financing needed to support this expected sales.

Required External Financing = A/S (ΔS) – L/S (ΔS) - rS

= 50%($500,000) – 10%($500,000) – 5%($1,000,000)
= $250,000 - $50,000 - $50,000
= $150,000

Thus, company X will need to arrange for $150,000 of external financing in order to support the expected sales increase for next year. Without this financing, it will not be able to make the needed purchases for inventory or fulfill its short-term debt obligations.

Cash Turnover Method

This method calculates the minimum amount of cash needed to continue operations by relating its annual operating expenditures (cost of goods, raw materials, salaries, wages, interest and dividends) to its cash turnover. Therefore the *cash turnover method is a measure of liquidity needs* of a company. Note however, this method assumes that there are no major changes in operating expenditures within the period examined, which may be in contrast to the situation with an early stage company. *Cash turnover* is defined as the number cash cycles that occur in a year. A *cash cycle* (also known as the operating cycle) is defined as the number of days that pass between the purchase of raw materials and the collection of sales proceeds from these raw materials. When we discuss asset management later in this chapter, we will see that there are many ways to alter the cash cycle. An example of the cash turnover method is provided below.

$$\text{Cash Turnover} = \frac{360 \text{ days}}{\text{Cash Cycle}}$$

$$\text{Minimum Cash Required for Operations} = \frac{\text{Annual Operating Expenditures}}{\text{Cash Turnover}}$$

Example of the cash turnover method

Company Y has annual expenditures of $1,000,000 and its cash cycle is 100 days. Determine the minimum required cash company Y needs to maintain throughout the year in order to satisfy these expenditures.

$$\text{Cash Turnover} = \frac{360 \text{ Days}}{120 \text{ Days}} = 3$$

$$\text{Minimum Cash required} = \frac{\$1,000,000}{3} = \$333,333$$

Cash Budget Method

This method is also useful for maintaining adequate liquidity by estimating any shortfalls in cash flows. While it is relatively simple to use, it is somewhat time consuming because the company must examine old and current receipts and payments. Figure 8-5 shows a sample cash budget chart used for estimating monthly cash flows. Receipts and payments are recorded, and then payments are subtracted from receipts to yield the monthly cash flow, as shown in columns 1-3. Next, the amount of cash at the beginning of the month is added to this cash flow to obtain the ending cash, as shown in columns 4 and 5. Finally, any cash reserves the company maintains are added to the ending cash. If this final number is positive then the company has sufficient cash to continue operations without external financing. Otherwise the company could face a liquidity squeeze. It is important to note that these estimations assume timely collections of receivables and any departure from these assumptions could create liquidity problems. Therefore, know your customers, as your company's fate may rest on their goodwill.

Accounting for Project Uncertainties

Much like anything else in life, projects don't always go as planned. A project may be delayed due to shortfalls in cash or unexpected actions by competitors. Therefore, to help account for unforeseen circumstances, companies may wish to use the methods previously discussed in combination with one or more of the following three methods.

Real Options

This method uses the Black-Scholes option-pricing model that was discussed in the valuation of licenses in chapter 7. The Black-Scholes equation determines the price of an American call option for a non-dividend paying equity whose returns are assumed to lie within a specific range of returns. The advantage of the real options method over others is that *it does not rely on the selection of a discount rate* (which can lead to many inaccuracies) and provides a quick financial assessment of a project. Instead, it uses data from comparable publicly traded companies so that *the discount rate is cancelled out of the calculation.* The drawback is that it cannot be used when suitable publicly traded companies cannot be identified. Therefore, the accuracy of this method will be highly dependent upon the ability to identify a true comparable.

Figure 8-5. A Sample Cash Budget Chart

Source: Barron's Finance

Month	Column 1 Receipts	Column 2 Payments	Column 3 Net Monthly Cash Flow (C1 – C2)	Column 4 Beginning Cash	Column 5 Ending Cash (C3 + C4)	Column 6 Cash Reserve	Column 7 Cash Surplus or Deficit (C5 + C6)
January							
February							
March							
April							
May							
June							
July							
August							
September							
October							
November							
December							

Decision Trees

Decision trees are schematic representations illustrating the complete range of cause-effect scenario possibilities within a given project. Representation of these scenarios allows the decision-maker to account for the possible effects of uncertainty that may occur for a given project and therefore provides a host of remedies for the final decision analysis. *This method is best used when projects have a moderate level of uncertainty with respect to the course and extent of adverse events affecting the outcome.* For instance, in assessing the merits of an expansion project, financial methods may be able to provide accurate estimations on the cost structure of this expansion but they will not provide a solution that addresses the strategic components of the expansion, such as the number of units to be made and when the production should occur (figure 8-6).

If the company can identify a publicly traded comparable, one may wish to calculate a rough estimate of the financial merits of a project using the real options method and then make the final decision by constructing a decision tree that incorporates other areas of uncertainty. Otherwise, the use of decision trees in conjunction with one of the three financial methods reviewed in the previous section should suffice.

Scenario Analysis

Scenario analysis is a technique designed to minimize the individual biases that tend to surface when confronted with uncertainty in the course of decision-making. The analysis involves generating and analyzing a variety of related and unrelated scenarios that may be possible for a given project or strategy and consists of *scenario creation, scenario elaboration, and scenario integration* into the decision-making process. Although related to decision tree analysis, a complete scenario analysis is much more detailed. However, the use of decision trees can provide an initial framework for the scenario analysis.

There are two approaches that can be used to construct a scenario analysis. In the *"bottom-up"* approach, the decision-maker assembles scenarios from a detailed description and assessment of all possible uncertainties. In contrast, the decision-makers electing to conduct a *"top-down"* analysis construct creative scenarios then distinguish each one based upon the number and extent of possible uncertainties within each scenario. The following example illustrates the use of both a bottom-up and top –own scenario analysis.

Figure 8-6. Example of a Decision Tree

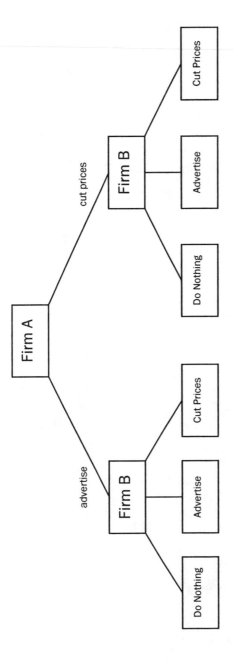

Firm A wishes to implement a new strategy to increase market share but it wants to analyze the possible reactions of Firm B before determining which strategy to use. For each strategy, Firm B will do nothing, advertise, or cut prices. If Firm A decides to advertise, Firm B might decide to advertise as well and this could result in increased overall product awareness and benefit the entire industry. In contrast, an advertising battle could also result in a smearing campaign, which could hurt the image of Firm A. If Firm B instead decides to respond to Firm A's advertising campaign by cutting prices, Firm A could focus its ads to promote the distinctive quality of its products. This analysis can be extended to include the possible advertising approaches, estimated price cuts, and any other possibilities. By detailing this exercise, Firm A will have a better understanding of the possible consequences of its actions and can make a final decision based upon the possibilities of these responses by Firm B.

Example of a "bottom-up" ands "top-down" scenario analysis to form a genomics business unit

Bottom-up analysis

A biotechnology company wants to assess the financial and strategic merits and risks of forming a separate genomics business unit that is expected to enhance its drug discovery resources and reduce overall R&D costs in the long run, leading to improved profitability. The management first details the uncertainties involved with the project:

Step 1: Scenario Creation

- Time involved in creating the facility and executing synergist operations

- Difficulty integrating the genomics facility into the long-term capital budget and overall company operations

- Threat of legal restrictions regarding patenting of genes will render much of the intangible asset value of the investment worthless, wasting developmental and patent costs.

- Response of competitors

- Cost of legal protection of patents

Next each of these uncertainties is analyzed to identify dependencies on other uncertainties. For instance, the ability to provide the necessary capital expenditures for the project will depend upon the time required to achieve full execution and integration. The response of competitors may depend upon the government's policy regarding the extent of intellectual property recognition and protection. Then further extensions of each scenario are continued to express these interrelationships (steps 2 and 3 are continued below).

Top-down Analysis

Since the ultimate goal of the proposed project is to increase profits, through the enhancement and availability of genetic resources and the lowering of R&D expense, the "top-down" decision-makers will first approach the feasibility of this project by determining other methods to increase its experimental resources and reduce its R&D cost structure.

Step 1: Scenario Creation
- Outsourcing to labs and companies may provide similar access of genetic materials

- The cost structure of outsourcing the genetic materials will decline if the commoditization of this industry occurs.

- Strategic alliances may allow complementary asset sharing, lower overall execution risk, and create synergies.

Next, separate scenarios are created for each of the above examples in order to formulate approximate end result scenarios.

- Those companies used to provide genetic materials may control prices due to limited competition

- The intellectual property protection policies for genomic content may not be challenged by the government and the commoditization of these materials may not ensue, causing prices to remain relatively high.

- Strategic alliances may assist in the formation of competitors from partners.

<u>Step 2: Scenario Elaboration</u> (bottom-up and top-down)
The decision-makers will then quantify and/or qualify these scenarios to gain a better understanding of the risks involved. The financial models will reflect the non-strategic aspects of these scenarios, while qualifying models will provide strategic perspectives and may be created by extending the previous scenarios.

<u>Step 3: Scenario Integration.</u> (bottom-up and top-down)
The final step is directed towards integrating each scenario into the broad strategic decision-making process. If the emphasis is quantitative, the financial results of each scenario are merely multiplied by their individual relative probabilities of likelihood. If the emphasis is qualitative, the assessment is more difficult. Each scenario must be viewed as a strategic option and weighed against its overall strength and compatibility to the overall company strategy and its inherent flexibility, which will provide for redirection if needed.

Game Theory

This method is an extension of scenario analysis but has the added feature of accounting for *strategic uncertainty*. It may be thought of as a systematic decision analysis modeling technique that *allows companies to predict possible outcomes when strategic uncertainty exists.* Strategic uncertainty may be thought of as the inability of a company to predict the actions of its current and future competitors, buyers and suppliers.

In the discussion on scenario analysis we saw that strategic uncertainty was largely unaccounted for. In contrast, game theory is able to account for these uncertainties by considering the decision analysis that results from your company actions. However, game theory should not be misused as a sole tool for absolute decision-making but rather as a learning tool that allows a company to understand the full array of potential reactions from a competitor. The depth of coverage required to give justice to the topic of game theory is beyond the scope of this discussion and perhaps beyond the level needed by early stage companies, but even early stage companies should be aware of it.

D. Financial Statement Analysis

In addition to its utility in forecasting based on historical numbers, financial statement analysis may also be used to identify any potential problems that may go unnoticed until a point in the future when resolution of such problems may be extremely difficult or even irreversible. Therefore, a company needs to be able to dissect its income statement, balance sheet, and cash flows in order to make certain that the business is at maximum operational efficiency, has adequate liquidity, and is maximizing shareholder value.

When used correctly, financial ratios provide a means of interpreting the financial statements and can often uncover potential problems that might otherwise go unnoticed. When looking within an individual financial statement to assess the relative proportions of two or more variables, this is considered a *vertical analysis*. When comparing previous statements to determine changes in variable (revenues, assets, liabilities, etc.) this is referred to as a *horizontal analysis*. The analysis of financial statements is well-beyond the focus of this book and the reader should refer to some of the recommended texts at the end of the chapter for more extensive coverage.

Income Statement

The profit performance of a company is represented by the income statement, sometimes referred to as the "P & L" (profit and loss) statement or statement of earnings. When one hears the words revenues, profits, income, and EPS, they should envision the income statement since these are some of the values contained within this document. Some other terms frequently used when referring to the income statement are *"top line"* and *"bottom line"*, which refer to the physical locations of the sales revenue and net income data within the statement respectively. Hence, "top-line growth" refers to revenue growth, while "bottom-line growth" means increased profits. *An income statement provides a measure of how well a company has performed over a specific period and is therefore best interpreted by a horizontal analysis or comparing previous statements.* It is designed to be read sequentially from top to bottom, with deductions being made as one progresses down the top line of each major category.

Balance Sheet

The financial condition of a company at any point in time is given by the balance sheet and consists of the company's assets, liabilities, and owner's equity. This is why you may have heard it referred to as the *"statement of financial condition"*. It is referred to as the balance sheet because it is typically presented with assets on the left and liabilities and shareholder's equity on the right side of the sheet and both sides are in essence, in balance. *The balance sheet does not tell us anything about revenues or cash flows.* Rather, it tells us where a company's assets came from and how the liabilities arose. The classic equation to remember is:

Assets = Liabilities + Shareholder's Equity

You can think of the balance sheet as a description of a company's net worth since all that you own minus all that you owe is equal to your net worth. When we rearrange the above equation, this relationship becomes more evident.

Assets - Liabilities = Shareholder's Equity

Cash Flow Statement

Unfortunately, there is no unanimous definition of cash flow and the term is often used rather loosely even by Wall Street analysts. However, the improper usage of this term could lead to inaccurate assumptions about a business' financial status. *Cash flow can either be negative or positive and is determined by the summation of all money that has been received and disbursed.* The main sources of positive cash flow of a company come from product or service sales, stock sales, and debt. In contrast, operating expenses, capital expenditures, and debt service payments result in negative cash flow. The summation of these items determines if a company is cash flow positive (has a cash surplus) or cash flow negative (has a deficit in cash).

A statement of cash flows is of critical importance to investors and creditors of a company because this is from which liquidity and company valuation are derived.[1] However, one needs to realize the utility of a cash flow statement so that misinterpretations do not occur. Unlike the balance sheet and income statements, which are recorded using the accrual principal in accounting, the cash flow statement reports all cash received and dispersed in during the reporting period, similar to the process of balancing ones checkbook.[2] A statement of cash flows shows the cash flow from profit-making operations a company has generated as well as how this cash was spent, but not necessarily its profit.   Unlike the balance sheet, the *statement of cash flows does not indicate the financial condition of the company at the end of that reporting period.*   Rather, it reflects the company's ongoing abilities to satisfy short-term debt obligations.

Note also that cash flows from profits and the actual profits are not the same.   The profit, indicated by the net income portion needs to be examined carefully in order to understand the true meaning of its value.   And this may only be done by examining the income statement and balance sheet in conjunction with the cash flow statement.   As such, when analyzing a statement of cash flows, one must examine *the change in cash from one period to another (horizontal analysis), rather than the actual dollar amount.*

Using Financial Ratios to Monitor Performance

One of the best ways to analyze the operating performance of a company is to examine key financial ratios obtained from its financial statements. *The use of financial ratios serves to assess the relative degree of a company's liquidity, debt position, asset utilization, and profitability and can therefore be used to help management monitor performance and plan for future operations and growth.*   Invariably, financial ratios are also used by banks and other creditors to assess the earnings, debt load, and liquidity of a company in the process of determination of its creditworthiness.

More notably, when interpreted and applied correctly, ratio analysis can help the management team identify areas of operational inefficiency.   Rather than an absolute gauge of company efficiency however, these ratios should be used to identify possible areas of weakness upon which further inquiry should be directed.   However, in order to use these ratios effectively one must be able to interpret them correctly.   Therefore, companies must be familiar with the appropriate industry averages for each ratio used, which can be obtained from trade journals and online financial sites.   Finally, *perhaps the best way to utilize these ratios is as a screening mechanism by looking for large ratio changes over a period of time, which should prompt an in depth investigation into the areas each ratio addresses.*

Liquidity Ratios

These ratios measure the extent of asset conversion into cash and are therefore determinants of a company's solvency. *Liquidity ratios are important to consider in the day-to-day cash management activities of a company as it seeks to pay its short-term liabilities.*   In general, ratios below 1.0 are considered evidence of insolvency, while ratios above 1.5 are thought to represent liquidity.   However, these numbers will vary with each industry. It is very important for companies to monitor these ratios regularly to ensure they have adequate funds to pay short-term liabilities.

Often the use of the current ratio is insufficient to accurately assess a company's liquidity. Therefore, *the current ratio should be used in conjunction with the quick ratio*, since the later accounts for the time delay in converting inventories into sales (receivables).   For example, consider the case whereby a company has both a large number of current assets and a large inventory buildup.   In this scenario a company will most likely have low liquidity due to its inability to convert inventory into sales or because it is overstocking.   An inventory buildup represents a waste of working capital since this money could be spent on investment transactions elsewhere. Therefore, when this is detected, it should prompt reason for reevaluation of inventory management operations.   By comparing both the current and quick ratios of a company over a period of time, *one should be concerned about increasing inventory levels if the current ratio increases while the quick ratio remains relatively constant.*

$$\text{Current Ratio} = \frac{\text{Current Assets}}{\text{Current Liabilities}} \qquad \text{Quick ratio} = \frac{\text{Current Assets - Inventories}}{\text{Current Liabilities}}$$

Cash Flow Ratios

For newer companies without predictable cash flows or extensive credit facilities, cash flow ratios are a better predictor of liquidity than current and quick ratios. This view has been taken by credit rating agencies, which place a large emphasis on cash flow ratios in their rating decisions.   Whereas current and quick ratios are obtained from the balance sheet, cash flow ratios are obtained from the statement of cash flows, which as we know describes the current cash position of the company.   Meanwhile, data from the balance sheet is relatively static, is based on the accrual method (which recognizes revenues and expenses when these transactions occur and not when cash has been received or paid) and only measures a single point in time.   Thus, it makes sense that cash flow ratios provide a more accurate measure of liquidity.

During periods of economic stress, even older companies with historically predictable cash flows may begin to resemble newer companies with respect to their financial condition.   Therefore, cash flow ratios are closely monitored to determine the ability of such companies to repay current liabilities (short-term debt obligations). Finally, when using these ratios, it is important to compare values specific for the chosen industry as well understanding the significance of these values to your company.

$$\text{Operating Cash Flow} = \frac{\text{Cash flow from operations}}{\text{Current liabilities}}$$

> The numerator is calculated by determining the net cash flow from operating activities. This is the net value from the cash flow statement, adjusting for noncash items and changes in working capital. Note also that the net cash flow number also includes cash paid out for interest and taxes.

$$\text{Funds Flow Coverage} = \frac{\text{EBITDA}}{\text{Interest} + \text{Tax-adj* debt repayment} + \text{Tax-adj* preferred dividends}}$$

> EBITDA (earnings before interest, taxes, depreciation, and amortization), thus this calculation does not consider the effects of the taxes and interest. In the denominator, debt repayment and preferred dividends are adjusted for taxes by dividing each value by the compliment of the corresponding tax rate. This calculation provides an estimate of the company's abilities to repay its interest, short-term debt, and dividends if any. If this ratio falls below 1.0, the company will need to raise additional funds for these debt and interest obligations.

* divide by the compliment of the tax rate to adjust for taxes.

$$\text{Cash Interest Coverage} = \frac{\text{Cash flow from operations} + \text{Interest paid} + \text{Taxes paid}}{\text{Interest Paid}}$$

> The cash interest coverage provides a measure of the company's ability to make interest payments on its total debt load. Obviously, companies with high values have good abilities to pay this debt. If the ratio falls below 1.0, the company could have difficulties paying its debt. This ratio is similar to the times-interest-earned ratio (below) except that the CIC ratio uses the operating cash flows rather than earnings.

$$\text{Cash Debt Coverage} = \frac{\text{Operating Cash Flow} - \text{Cash Dividends}}{\text{Current Debt}}$$

> The cash debt coverage measures a company's ability to repay its current debt. For early stage companies, the cash dividends value can be ignored.

$$\text{Capital expenditure Ratio} = \frac{\text{Cash flow from operations}}{\text{Capital expenditures}}$$

> This ratio measures a company's ability to pay debt after maintenance or investment on plant and equipment.

$$\text{Total Debt ratio} = \frac{\text{Cash flow from operations}}{\text{Total debt}}$$

> This ratio measures the ability of a company to service its short and long-term debt.

Activity Ratios

Activity ratios are used to estimate the rate which companies are able to generate cash if needed. The *average collection period* indicates the time a company must wait before receivables are converted into cash. It provides a means to determine whether a company is meeting credit obligations in a timely manner over the course of a year, weighted against the size of its purchases. The *average payment period* is a measure of a company's ability to pay for goods and services from its suppliers. Inventory ratios indicate the time taken to convert inventories into cash.

$$\text{Average Collection Period} = \frac{\text{Accounts Receivable}}{\text{Annual Credit Sales} / 360 \text{ days}}$$

In managing receivables, it is important to know the time it takes to convert receivables into cash. These numbers should be compared with the company credit policy to determine whether customers are paying on time. And any problems may prompt a revision of credit policy. Note that because this calculation groups all sales together, it may not give an accurate picture of the collection activities of individual companies. Finally, note this calculation does not account for cash sales.

$$\text{Average Payment Period} = \frac{\text{Accounts Payable}}{\text{Annual Credit Sales} / 360 \text{ days}}$$

Since annual credit purchases are not distinguished on financial statements, the company must keep separate records of these transactions in order to obtain accurate calculations.

$$\text{Inventory Turnover Ratio} = \frac{\text{Cost of Goods Sold}}{\text{Average Inventory}}$$

Inventory represents dead assets that can neither earn interest nor generate revenues. In contrast, the company may actually be paying interest on the capital used to stock these inventories. Thus, it is in the company's best interest to establish a delicate balance between high inventory turnover and having sufficient inventory to meet the demands of anticipated orders.

$$\text{Inventory Conversion Ratio} = \frac{\text{Inventories}}{\text{Cost of goods sold} / 360}$$

A better feel for inventory and production management can be obtained by calculating the number of days to convert inventories into cash. The inventory conversion ratio accomplishes this.

Debt and Interest Ratios

Important for measuring a company's relative financial leverage, these ratios are typically used by banks and other financial institutions to determine the company's suitability for obtaining loans and monitor its ability to service existing debt. Companies strive to achieve the optimal capital structure, consisting of the right balance of debt and equity so that financial leverage is in balance with the cost of capital. Normally, equity is more costly than debt for companies that have consistently positive cash flows. However, *for early stage companies without predictable and positive cash flows, debt is more expensive from a risk management perspective since these companies lack sufficient cash flows to service their debt. Therefore, in the early stages of a company, these ratios are not expected to be relevant unless the company has substantial debt obligations.*

As a company takes on increasing levels of debt, the cost of equity capital increases for the company since the new equity investors will demand proportionate compensation for bearing the risk of a company with a higher debt load. In general, high debt loads tend to be associated with higher rates of bankruptcy, and in such a case, the creditors (debt holders) receive top priority of repayment. Rarely, do equity investors receive any return of their principal in such situations.

Consequently, as a company increases its debt, its financial leverage also increases and results in a higher earnings value during healthy business conditions. This is in part due to the tax-free interest paid by the company, which translates into more operational cash flow. However, during a recession or difficult environment within the industry, a highly leveraged company may encounter difficulties servicing its debt. Therefore, management must periodically assess the amount of leverage and make sure the equity-debt mix is amenable with the companies liquidity needs.

$$\text{Debt Ratio} = \frac{\text{Total Liabilities}}{\text{Total Assets}}$$

$$\text{Debt-to-Equity Ratio} = \frac{\text{Long-term debt} + \text{Value of Leases}}{\text{Stockholders' Equity}}$$

$$\text{Long-Term Debt Ratio} = \frac{\text{Long-term debt}}{\text{Total Assets}}$$

$$\text{Times-interest-earned ratio} = \frac{\text{EBIT}}{\text{Annual Interest Expense}}$$

As mentioned, the TIE ratio is similar to the CIC, except it uses earnings. Therefore, this ratio can only be used for companies that have earnings. In addition, even for later stage companies that have earnings, the CIC ratio may provide more accuracy since the earnings may not be consistent or reliable.

Profitability ratios

It is obviously an ideal situation for a company to maximize its net profit margin and to demonstrate incremental increases in this number over several years. Hence, profitability ratios are important for valuation and assessment of management leadership, as they can provide a measure of how well the company is utilizing its assets to affect sales, generate income, and control expenses. Companies should know the typical profit margins for their industry, although these industry averages may show large deviations for early stage companies.

While sometimes difficult to achieve for older, more established companies, increasing profit margins are expected for newer companies with products in the rapid growth phase of the product life cycle, through improvements in operational efficiency and achieving economies of scale. In contrast, older companies are usually very limited in affecting these margins because they have achieved an operational efficiency that is difficult to alter. More readily, older companies can improve profit margins through development of new business lines that are complimentary to existing lines of business, restructuring activities, and/or or additions of new businesses and products by acquisition. Also included in profitability ratios are the equity and market ratios.

$$\text{Gross Profit Margin} = \frac{\text{Sales} - \text{Cost of Goods Sold}}{\text{Sales}}$$

Operating ratios indicate how well a company is managing indirect expenses, such as overhead. Operating margins should be compared with gross profit margins to ensure that both are changing at the same rate and in the same direction. Otherwise, this could indicate problems with controlling indirect costs or cost of goods.

$$\text{Operating Profit Margin} = \frac{\text{EBIT}}{\text{Sales}}$$

$$\text{Net Profit Margin} = \frac{\text{Net Profits after Taxes}}{\text{Sales}}$$

Equity Ratios

While these ratios are also used in part for valuation purposes, they can also be helpful for the management to evaluate their overall performance.

$$\text{Return on Equity} = \frac{\text{Net Profits after Taxes}}{\text{Stockholder's Equity or Net Tangible Worth}}$$

$$\text{Return on Investment} = \frac{\text{Net income}}{\text{Sales}} \times \frac{\text{Sales}}{\text{Total Assets}} = \frac{\text{Net income}}{\text{Total Assets}}$$

ROI is a bottom-line measure of how well a company uses assets to generate sales and how well it generates profits. The above equation illustrates the Du Pont Method, which allows companies to determine the individual effects the ROI value.

Market Ratios

A company's price/earnings (P/E) ratio is a very common metric used to value both public and private companies as it represents the amount multiple investors are willing to pay for each dollar of earnings per share (EPS). A simple way to calculate this number is to divide the price paid per share for a company stock by its earnings per share. However, a more accurate method of calculating the P/E ratio that considers risk, earnings growth, and payout ratio may be determined by the following:

$$P/E = \frac{\text{Payout Ratio}}{K - G} \qquad \text{where} \qquad \text{Payout ratio} = \frac{\text{Dividend}}{\text{Earnings}}$$

K = the discount rate assigned to the company
G = the expected earnings growth

Of course, for private companies that typically do not pay dividends, this formula cannot be used. Even when they may declare dividends for preferred stock, this ratio is not valid since these dividends are rarely paid in the form of cash. Therefore, dividends in such case do not represent a typical cash paying investment.

The more practical utilization of P/E ratios for private companies is to be used in relative valuation calculations, such as the comparables approach. In such a case, the P/E would be calculated using the price paid divided by earnings per share. Even still, many early stage companies do not have earnings with which to calculate a P/E ratio. Therefore, an alternative method to determine value in this case would be to calculate the price-to-sales ratio.

Due to the lack of tangible assets that typically characterize private high-technology companies, use of the price-to-book value ratio in determining valuation would be inappropriate. However, when companies have a large proportion of tangible assets, other metrics must be considered to ensure accurate interpretation of price-to-book ratios, such as the debt-to-asset and debt-to-equity ratios. Each industry will have accepted standards for metrics used in valuation analysis and it is critical that companies are aware of these metrics prior to attempting such an analysis.

E. Corporate Asset Management

Certainly, by now you are convinced of the importance of proper strategic positioning and management of intellectual capital. However, as we have demonstrated, efficient management of a company's financial assets can be equally important for profit generation. This is a critical point that many inexperienced business managers fail to recognize in a timely manner. Rather than maintaining a balance between efficient business management, sales and marketing, and technology issues, early stage companies tend to de-emphasize the importance of what really is the bottom line; earnings. The reason for this may be that inexperienced management teams feel that the bottom line is really sales and revenue, but this is far from the truth. In this section, we will delve into examples that illustrate the importance of asset management towards affecting the bottom line. The first concept relevant to this discussion is to understand the definition of *net working capital*. This is simply the money remaining after subtracting current liabilities from current assets.

Net Working Capital = Current Assets – Current Liabilities

Net working capital is an excellent measure of a company's liquidity since the amount of net working capital determines its ability to pay its short-term debt. At this point, the reader may wish to review the working cash cycle material presented in chapter 1 (figure 1-9).

Balancing Short-term and Long-term Financing

Every business has an optimal balance between the use of short and long-term debt instruments that minimizes the cost of capital, maintains adequate liquidity, and improves its operational efficiency by minimizing financial and business risks. The goal of short-term financing is to secure adequate levels of cash to substitute for temporary cash shortfalls (payables), in anticipation of cash inflows (receivables) to repay the debt and other expenses. For instance, credit lines or over drafts may be accessed in order to satisfy accounts payable or to increase inventories prior to an anticipated increase in business orders. Of course long-term financing would achieve this goal with much less effort but there would be excess cash available when the company would not need it. Thus the cost of financing would increase, thereby decreasing the bottom line or earnings.   Therefore, a company must make a best efforts attempt to identify all fixed assets and finance these with long-term debt, while financing current assets with short-term debt.   Accordingly, all land, machinery and equipment (fixed assets) should be financed with long-term debt.   Finally, *some companies may choose to lease equipment since this will decrease its liabilities as reported on the balance sheet. However, management should understand the tax and financial reporting differences between operating versus capital leases prior to making this selection.*

When considering long-term debt financing options, companies should be aware of all variables affecting the premiums charged for these debt instruments so they will be able to utilize these factors for their benefit.   In brief, the company's credit history, its current financial health, and the interest rate environment are the most significant factors determining the expense and ability to obtain long-term financing.   Early stage companies rarely have adequate credit histories required for obtaining the highest quality financing (i.e. the lowest interest rate) but they can sometimes obtain low interest rate loans (usually 1-3% + prime) if they have positive cash flows or substantial tangible assets such as machinery, land, and equipment to use for collateral.

Interest Rates and Inflation

Throughout this book we have identified several reasons why companies must understand the economic environment of their industry when making strategic business decisions.   As we shall see in later chapters, economic conditions also influence exit strategies and company valuations.   However, in order to improve the efficiency of business and financial operations, companies should also be aware of general economic conditions such as business cycle dynamics, interest rate, and inflation forecasts prior to long-term debt structuring.   If inflation is expected to rise over the term of the financing arrangement, purchasing power will diminish.   If interest rates rise, the cost of borrowing increases, as it costs more to borrow funds.

There is a direct relationship between short-term interest rates and the money supply, or the relative amount of money made available by the U.S. Treasury for businesses and consumers.   And although other factors influence interest rates, in general as the money supply is increased interest rates will decline.   Thus, the U.S. Treasury helps control interest rates by changing the money supply available for business activity.   All other factors being constant, when interest rates are high, the U.S. Treasury increases the money supply by repurchasing U.S Treasury bills, notes, and bonds, thereby releasing cash into the banking systems, in effort to lower these rates. Similarly, when the U.S. Treasury issues bonds, it decreases the money supply available for businesses and consumers, which raises short-term rates.

Meanwhile, the Federal Reserve Bank is responsible for keeping inflation low, and one of the ways it does this is by directly altering the Fed funds rate (or short-term interest rates). The Fed determines short-term interest rates based upon their assessments of the current and future economic environment of the U.S. If the money supply is large and interest rates are low over a sustained period this could result in large increases in inflation, which would reduce the purchasing power of the dollar. Therefore, to diminish the appeal of borrowing, the Fed will increase short-term interest rates, which should decrease the money supply.

Note that short and long-term interest rates are usually not correlated, as long-term interest rates are influenced more by more complex factors. In general, long-term rates are determined by the 30-year T-bond market price, which is somewhat influenced by the demand for these securities by the public. Because a significant amount of these investors are foreign institutions, you can begin to appreciate the complexities involved since currency exchange rates, foreign trade policies, and political dissonance can be contributing factors. However, one can develop estimations of the direction of short-term rates by examining the yield curve.

Yield Curves

A *yield curve* illustrates the relationship between a bond's yield-to-maturity (YTM) and time-to-maturity and can be used to give investors an idea about the direction of future interest rate changes. In brief, the *YTM is a value that expresses the total return rate of the bond relative to its price and will change as current interest rates change* (see appendix C-4).[3] When considering bonds of equivalent credit quality, the YTM depends on the bond price, changes in interest rates (the Fed funds rate), its maturity date, and its coupon rate. However, *because the coupon and maturity date of the bond are constant, the price will vary based upon changes in interest rates.*

Figure 8-7 shows a plot of bond yields (expressed as the YTM) versus time of T-bills (3-, 6-, and 12-month maturities), T-notes (2-, 3-, 5-, and 10-year maturities) and 30-year Treasury bonds.[4] Note also in figure 8-7 that securities with smaller maturities (T-bills) have less time until expiration and therefore a lower yield, and will exhibit price changes similar to newly issued short-term debt (i.e. they will be strongly affected by changes in the Fed funds rate). Meanwhile, bonds with longer maturities dates (10-year notes and 30-year bonds) have higher yields. And investors expect a higher dividend (coupon) payment for assuming this longer time of repayment of principal. Therefore, bonds with longer maturities will be affected the least by changes in the Fed funds rate since these changes would not be expected to last throughout the duration of the maturities.

Figure 8-7. Upward Sloping Yield Curve (bonds with longer maturities have higher YTM)

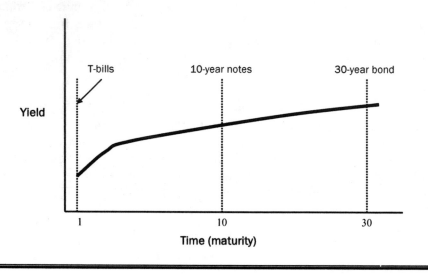

Under normal conditions and assuming all other factors are held constant, as bond maturities increase the bond yields also increase since investors demand a higher compensation for buying bonds with higher default risk (there is a higher risk of default for long–term debt).   Therefore, under normal circumstances, a yield curve plot assumes an *upward slope* as in figure 8-7, reflecting this relationship between bond yields and time to maturity. In addition, *when interest rates are low, the yield curve also tends to slope upward*, reflecting the relative expectations of forthcoming interest rate increases towards their historical mean of about 5%.

However, the shape of the yield curve can also become *inverted*, and now bonds with intermediate and longer maturities will have lower yields than those with shorter maturities (figure 8-8). *This relationship indicates that the market predicts an eminent decrease in short-term interest rates*, making bonds that will mature in only a few years more valuable because they will be paying a higher rate than the expected issuance of bonds with lower rates.[5]

Prior to forming this inverted slope, the yield curve goes through a period when the slope is *flat*, during which bonds with short maturities have similar yields as those with intermediate and long maturities.   Flat yield curves tend to exist only for short periods of time and indicate the bond market's relative uncertainty of the future direction of short-term interest rates.   However, once the direction of interest rates becomes more certain, the yield curve will adjust to factor in the expectations of future interest rate changes. *Therefore, the normal shape of the yield curve is thought to have an upward slope, reflecting low interest rates with expectations that these rates will increase.*

Since interest rates are typically high at the peak of a business cycle and low during troughs, companies can use yield curve data to plan financings prior to the period when rates are expected to increase. Finally, the importance of understanding yield curves and making accurate interest rate change predictions extends beyond the debt financing decision process. *Because interest rates are so significant in determining the overall economics underlying business dynamics, they can alter industries, individual companies, consumers, and competitors.* Therefore, companies should follow news regarding these yield curves and consider how possible interest rate changes will effect its operations and competitive strategies. Fortunately, one does not need to analyze these curves, as yield curve information and analyses are provided daily in financial newspapers and online financial websites.

Figure 8-8. An Inverted Yield Curve (bonds with shorter maturities have a higher YTM)

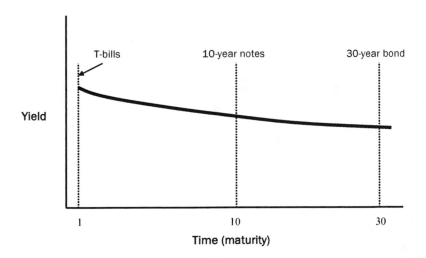

Over different periods, both long and short-term interest rates may show large deviations from their historical means. However, economic and market forces are always in action to pressure these rates towards these historical means. Therefore, if one studies yield curves over several decades they will notice oscillation of upward and downward (inverted) movements, serving to keep the average overall short-term rates at about 5% and long-term rates at about 8%.

Managing Current Assets

Current assets may be defined as cash, cash-equivalents, and receivables that can be converted into cash within 12 months. Throughout the fiscal year, a company will have variable amounts of currents assets due to sales fluctuations and the timing of accounts payable and receivable. *During the process of budget formation, management should predict minimum and maximum current asset levels for each year in order to manage company assets efficiently.* A company with an established operational history should be able to accomplish this activity with relative ease. However, it may be a more difficult task for new companies and companies experiencing rapid growth. Nevertheless, this exercise is a very important step in the overall management of assets.

The *minimum level of current assets* may be defined as that period in which the current asset levels reach a minimum over the year and the likelihood of current assets descending below this amount for an extended period is minimal. Likewise, the *maximum current asset level* would be the period in which the current assets reach a peak over the same year and are not expected to ascend above this level. The difference between these two levels represents the company's *seasonal financial requirements,* or the amount of assets needed by the company throughout the year to finance current liabilities. Therefore, when structuring company finances, *the minimum current asset level for the year can be financed with long-term debt* since it can be considered a fixed asset and will therefore remain on the books for an extended period. Meanwhile, *the seasonal financing portion should be financed with short-term debt,* such as a line of credit. To reiterate, the most appropriate choice of financing assets will affect the bottom line or company profits, since the cost of financing increases as the term of the loan increases.

Figure 8-9. Recommended Guidelines for Management of Current Assets

- Use the cash flow ratios or current ratio and quick ratio to determine any inventory buildups

- Calculate the average collection period to help determine the timeliness of receivables

- Estimate the minimum and maximum current assets levels at the beginning of each fiscal year to determine the seasonal requirements

- Use short-term debt to finance seasonal requirements

- Use long-term debt to finance minimal current assets

Managing Accounts Receivable

We have discussed the drag on net positive cash flows that delayed receivables can have on a company. Not only can mismanagement of these assets result in the inability to maintain proper inventory levels, but also it can ultimately lead to decreased liquidity, and under extreme situations possible bankruptcy. Given their nature, newer and smaller businesses are more easily affected by mismanagement of receivables and should therefore devote a large amount of attention to prevent and correct these situations when they arise.

Companies should establish and follow clear guidelines that address the management of receivables such as performing adequate credit checks, obtaining credit references, and strict enforcement of late fees. Each customer should understand the guidelines for payment and the company should be strict in its enforcement of these policies. Finally, companies should offer small discounts for immediate cash payments, provide allowances for only their best customers, and consider outsourcing collections when collection of receivables begins to consume an inordinate amount of time (figure 8-10).

Figure 8-10. Recommended Guidelines for Receivables Management

- Perform Credit Checks on each New Customer Prior to Issuing Credit

- Obtain Credit References

- Establish Written Credit Limits for each Customer

- Indicate Customer's Credit Balance on Each Invoice

- Periodically Review Customer History and Revise Credit as Needed

- Invoice Customers Immediately After Receiving Products

- Offer Discounts for Cash Payments

- Establish Late Fees and Enforce them

- Provide the Best Credit Terms to Your Best Customers

- Outsource Collections when Results are Productive

Managing Accounts Payable

Management of payables is equally important as receivables and theoretically should be an easier activity to control since company management is involved in making most of the decisions. However, management must be proactive in understanding and negotiating the various credit policies of each creditor. In addition, a company can best manage its payables by developing a complete understanding of the business behavior of its products and the needs of each customer. For instance, as previously discussed, each industry has specific business cycles that relate to differing seasonal demands. Therefore, the ability to predict future inventory levels will influence purchase decisions so that quantities purchased should reflect demand forecasts. And by understanding the needs of the customer, companies can structure their inventory levels to match their buying patterns.

Alternatively, companies that are able to establish multiple duplicate supplier arrangements can minimize their inventory with comfort knowing that the timeliness of delivery is not dependent upon one supplier. Companies should not hesitate to ask for a returns policy and a charge back provision if there is a delay in shipping, especially with suppliers for which they have established good business relations. For larger companies that order in bulk, suppliers that can deliver supplies on a just-in-time basis, enabling these companies to save tremendous amounts of money over the year by minimizing inventory and thereby maximizing cash flow, as well as minimizing the cost of inventory storage (figure 8-11).

Figure 8-11.   Recommended Guidelines for Payables Management

- Calculate the average payment period to monitor the timeliness of payables

- Calculate net working capital frequently to monitor cash flow

- Calculate cash flow ratios frequently to assess ability to provide for payables

- Negotiate with creditors for time extensions (without additional fees) when needed and ask for discounts when paying with cash

- Understand the industry and specific business cycle and anticipate variations in business; arrange for bulk order discounts during peak season

- Establish multiple supplier arrangements to increase bargaining power

Inventory Management

Having a certain level of inventory is necessary to avoid delays in customer orders and therefore establish a high level of reliability. However, holding *excess inventory* represents an opportunity cost because money invested in the inventory is tied up, thereby preventing it from earning revenues from other investible activities. In general, the nature of the product will dictate consumer demand, and therefore determine the extent and timing of inventory levels. And companies can often predict periods of high and low inventory levels required for each operating cycle based upon the historical buying patterns of repeat customers. However, for companies without a sufficient operational history this task may be much more difficult to achieve. In some cases, approximations may be obtained through analysis of industry competitors and customer interviews to at least determine seasonal demands.

Successful early and expansion stage companies typically experience periods of inconsistent and rapid growth that can lead to a misinterpretation of inventory levels. Thus, it is vital that these companies monitor inventory levels frequently so that efficient use of capital will be directed towards the continued growth efforts of the company while still maintaining adequate liquidity. Finally, the supply-demand-pricing dynamics of a product will influence the company's ability to pass cost increases rapidly to customers and an understanding of these dynamics will also affect the levels of inventories. *Therefore, in determining how much inventory to hold, one should consider three factors: the nature of the product, the seasonality of the product, and the opportunity cost of deploying assets to other investible activities* (figure 8-12).

Figure 8-12. Recommended Guidelines for Inventory Management

- Use the inventory turnover ratio and inventory conversion ratio to monitor inventory surpluses and correct as needed

- Understand customer purchasing patterns and business cycle to anticipate inventory needs and minimize excessive inventory

- Establish multiple supplier arrangements to increase just-in-time delivery capacity and therefore minimize inventory

Cash Management

When considering a company for financing, one of the first questions a venture capitalist will ask is when the company will be cash flow positive or what the breakeven time is. The reason this information serves as an initial screening question is because it will strongly influence their hypothetical IRR. Thus, in addition to influencing internal operations management and productivity, cash management decisions can impact the valuation of a company, the ability to receive financing, and can therefore ultimately determine its success or failure. It follows that the *financial statements of a company are directly connected with its previous and future annual budgets, and the activity that links these items is the process of cash management.*

Cash flow is simply the summation of all money that has been received and disbursed. The main sources of positive cash flow of a company come from product or service sales, stock sales, and debt. In contrast, operating expenses, capital expenditures, and debt service payments (payment of interest and principal) result in a negative cash flow. The summation of these activities determines if a company is cash flow positive (has a cash surplus) or cash flow negative (has a deficit in cash). When operating on a tight budget and dealing with supplier expenses and other product-related costs, management must have a strong grasp of their company's cash flow needs and restrictions in order to maintain good business relations with companies that supply needed raw materials, products, or services.

Cash flow management is vital to the survival of early and late stage companies. And improper cash management decisions could result in a financial crisis, diverting the management's time and energy towards solving this problem instead of running the business. Even for companies that are experiencing tremendous growth, cash flow problems can potentially hamper their future success if effective cash management techniques are not implemented. Rapid growth means rapid sales, but not necessarily rapid payment by customers. And while the company is waiting for receivables, it will have payables to suppliers and distributors that are due. And until they are paid, the company will not be able to continue to purchase the raw materials needed for its products. Such delays could lower barriers for competitors and result in decreased market share.

Thus, effective management of the cash flow cycle involves the interdependent management of all company assets and liabilities. Management of accounts receivable and payable, and inventory management involves estimation of the timing of cash payments, payment to suppliers, and product orders. In addition, companies must account for other current assets and liabilities and ensure their cash balances are sufficient to make payment to suppliers, service debt, pay wages and expenses, and otherwise continue current operations.   In part, financial ratios can be used to assist companies in the management of their cash flow cycles.

Figure 8-13. The Cash Flow Cycle

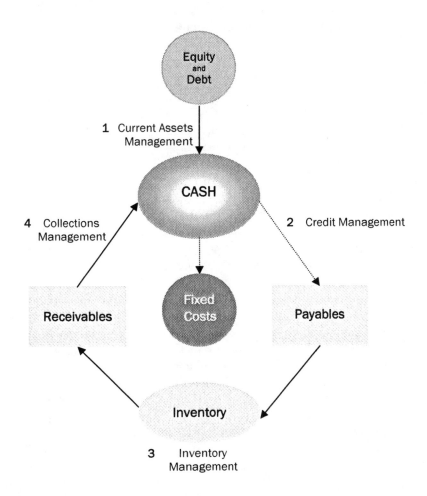

Each financial operation can be assisted by the use of previously discussed financial ratios, provided below:

[1] Use Current & Quick Ratios, Cash flow ratios, Average collection Period, and Debt Ratios
[2] Activity Ratios and Cash Flow Ratios
[3] Activity Ratios
[4] Activity Ratios

Intellectual Capital Management

In chapter 5 we discussed the importance of intellectual capital to the knowledge-based company. We defined intellectual capital as knowledge that can be converted into profit and is comprised of human capital and intellectual assets, whose transformation into intellectual capital occurs with the use of adequate structural capital. Meanwhile, legal protection of the rights to exclusive use of intellectual capital is secured by its transformation into intellectual property in the form of patents, copyrights, trademarks, and trade secrets. Therefore, *intellectual capital management* seeks to maximize the value expression of a company's intangible assets by positioning them in ways that strengthen the company's value chain, thereby improving the efficiency of business operations.

For larger companies, the most difficult task in orchestrating efficient use of human capital involves designing managerial systems that provide rapid transfer of relevant information between employees, yet maintaining safeguarding mechanisms of information flow to unwanted parties. Employees must be able to utilize the tacit knowledge of the entire company. Therefore they must know this information exists, how it is relevant, where it can be found, and how to access it. In order for a company to have a freely flowing distribution of human capital, all employees must be able to accomplish these tasks. For early stage companies, this is quite easy to achieve, but as companies grow larger and add more key employees, additional human capital is spread among more individuals, making it more difficult to monitor and share this information. Subsequently, human capital becomes compartmentalized and less accessible as companies increase in complexity and size. Therefore, in order to preserve the accessibility of human capital yet maintain its security within the company, employees must develop a *collective intelligence*, whereby they understand the roles of all other employees, which helps them know who has what knowledge.

Parr and Sullivan provide a model for human capital management that offers several explanations for the variable degree of intellectual capital creation within companies. Figure 8-14 illustrates four management philosophies that may provide possible operating solutions for management of intellectual capital. The y-axis shows management styles resulting in increasing employee autonomy, while the x-axis shows the increasing response of employees. Meanwhile, the slope of these axes measures the ease of intellectual capital output and increases outward.

Paternalistic managers underestimate the abilities of their employees and therefore exercise strong control over their actions. The employees under a paternalistic manager feel as if they are being treated as children and therefore react to this style of management with reluctance. Thus, the paternalistic management style is thought to inhibit the human capital component instrumental for the creation of intellectual capital.

Theory Y managers maintain a subordinate relationship with employees but feel that they possess the sufficient skills to accomplish all activities if provided with adequate resources. The employees respond by reaching success only in the activities directed by the management. While more productive for the development of intellectual capital, the employees' creative skills are not being maximized.

Figure 8-14. Managers of Intellectual Capital

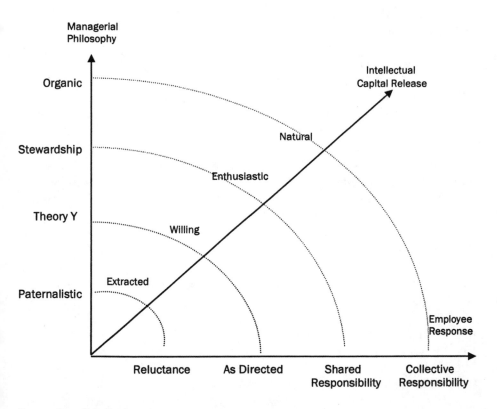

Source: Parr & Sullivan

Stewardship managers hold the view that employees are managerial partners while the manager serves only to oversee the overall coordination of the business.   Employees view this style of management as shared responsibility.   This is usually the realistic limit of management styles within large companies with tremendous intellectual capital.

Organic managers represent the most idealistic management style, where there are no traditional managers, no leadership or supervision.   Rather, each employee understands his role and responsibilities, as well as those of all other employees, and each is able to complete group tasks when needed. This management style is obviously extremely difficult to emulate in large companies, but it is sometimes present within early stage companies by coincidence.   Nevertheless, it promotes the most effective leveraging of human capital towards the creation of intellectual capital.

Emotional Management

And now, brief mention will be made of a less obvious realm of management that may well be the key to leading a company to success. Today's future successful business leaders require skills beyond those found in the traditional management disciplines of finance, marketing, and strategy. More important are qualities that are difficult to gain and to measure—the ability to fully appreciate risks and the propensity to take them, understanding and interacting with multiple cultures, creativity, tenacity, and dynamic leadership skills.   While some of these are skills that can be learned, others are a cumulative product of one's unique life experiences.

Emotional intelligence may be defined as that portion of social intelligence that is able to simultaneously analyze one's own emotions, as well as those of others and react in a manner that influences the behaviors, emotions, and activities of individuals. We know from studies of neurologists and psychologists that specific areas of the brain are responsible for emotional expression and decision skills.   And these regions are thought to be responsible for the decision-making processes involved in *social adaptation*. While we have fairly reliable methods to measure intellectual capacity, we have not developed reliable gauges of social and emotional capacity, although arguably, this type of intelligence is more important (once a minimal IQ threshold has been reached) than one's IQ.

The topic of *emotional intelligence* has recently gained widespread acceptance as an essential element for business leadership and success. Tichy and Sherman popularized the importance of emotional intelligence in their 1994 book *Control Your Destiny or Someone Else Will*, but there have been many other equally significant pioneers.   Clearly, this area of study is open to many different theories and approaches, but *the one common element shared by emotionally intelligent individuals is their ability to monitor and interpret their own and others' emotions in a variety of situations, and to use these emotional signals to influence outcomes for their benefit.*

We all know at least one individual who has the ability to attract the respect and admiration of those who they come into contact with. Some of these individuals display emotional characteristics that almost demand respect through their decisiveness, fortitude, and diligence. Meanwhile, other individuals may reflect a more solemn display of emotional expression that produces respect and admiration through their overall appeal and sense of empathy. What this all boils down to however, is *relationship management.* The ability of a CEO to lead with relentless courage and confidence or to become an active listener of employees in times of employee doubt requires not only a highly sophisticated social awareness, but also the ability to understand how to leverage one's own emotions and the emotions of others.

Perhaps the best examples of the effectiveness of emotional intelligence may be demonstrated by analyzing former presidents, military leaders, and successful CEOs, such as Presidents Clinton and Reagan, Winston Churchill, Martin Luther King, Generals Macarthur and Patton, Jack Welsh, Bill Gates, and Larry Ellison. No doubt these are just a few examples of individuals who were able to leverage emotional intelligence to attract widespread support and achieve tremendous business success.

F. Forecasting Performance

Self-Assessment

Critiquing one's own performance may be one of the most difficult managerial tasks to perform with accuracy due to the high level of optimism and confidence deeply embedded within the management of an early stage company. However without this skill, companies will continue to miscalculate their strengths and weaknesses. A more indirect method of self-assessment may be achieved by analyzing the relative strength of the company. The *business attractiveness matrix* accomplishes this and captures a dynamic image of the company and it attempts to identify factors thought to be essential for market success. Similar to the market attractiveness matrix to be used when conducting a market segmentation analysis (chapter 1, Appendix D-1), the business attractiveness matrix uses a set of evaluation criteria scored based upon the relative weight each factor has on the company's competitive strength. A total score is calculated that should provide a rough measure of the company relative to its competitors (see Appendix D-3).

Customer Lists

Customer lists can be considered trade secrets if they are treated as such but they will have variable degrees of significance depending upon the company and the industry served.   In cases of high correlation, it is sometimes acceptable to determine projected revenues from historical rates of revenue and customer growth.   The contract length and customer history is a very relevant determinant of such a projection, and longer contracts should be receive more weight then agreements of short duration.

Many types of Internet companies are valued in part by the number of registered users, number of monthly "hits", or length of time and number of times the users access the site per given period.   This data is used to correlate revenue projections based in part on advertising revenue forecasts, and thus as a method to value the company by correlating revenue projections with projected customer growth rates.   However, in order to make these correlations reasonable, one must determine the effects of customer attrition upon these growth rates when projecting revenues.

Using the Product Life Curve to Reshape Strategy

Corporate finance techniques used to determine project feasibility, such as those presented in section B of this chapter only assess the financial merits of a project.   However, the strategic merits of such projects are equally, if not more important in the overall determination of project feasibility. Incorporation of decision trees and scenario analyses to these financial methods helps account for strategic fit, project delay, and other possibilities. Likewise, when constructing R&D, production and distribution, and advertising budgets, we can also use the product life cycle in conjunction with financial techniques to maximize the accuracy of results.

Throughout this book we have made mention of the product life cycle several times to illustrate various aspects of a company's positioning.   We shall now examine this curve further and correlate it with a company's core technology and R&D strategies in order to assist the company in determining the needed changes management must make to remain competitive. Assuming one accepts the validity of the product life cycle model, every product is thought to have a limited lifespan.   As we examined in chapter 6, the amount of investment and the cash flows from the products change as the product progresses through the cycle.   Hence, management teams must strive to understand where their products are located on the life cycle curve and allocate the proper amounts of human and financial capital in future core technologies prior to the maturation stage.

According to Sapienza, the process involved in developing and distributing technology by a company can be described by considering three properties: uncertainty, equivocality, and risk. *Uncertainty* refers to the fact that there are gaps in knowledge and experience or know-how needed to complete its transformation, as product commercialization and production are embryonic. *Equivocality* refers to the presence of multiple interpretations regarding the use and extent of the technology. Both uncertainty and equivocality are high during the emerging and growth stages of a technology life cycle, as the processes involved in transforming the raw materials into commercial products, the supplier and distributor relations, operational aspects, and the full range of use and ease of integration of the products into the overall consumer marketplace are uncertain.

Risk may be defined in this case as the time required to transform the technology into a usable product and distributed to the consumer. Therefore, high levels of uncertainty and equivocality lead to a higher inherent risk. It follows that each stage of the life cycle may be described by variable levels of uncertainty, equivocality, and risk. From figure 8-14, we can see that the levels of *uncertainty, equivocality, and risk are all high during the incubation stage* of the life cycle. At this stage, a reduction of either uncertainty or equivocality alone is not sufficient to reduce the risk. However, *when equivocality declines, the product is thought to be in the rapid growth stage* of the cycle since there is now a common agreement amongst the management regarding the use and role of the technology due to market penetrance and consumer demand.

When uncertainty declines but risk and equivocality remain high, the product is thought to be in the *late growth stage*, as sales growth declines due to better innovations by competitors. At this point, the company begins to question the future demand of its products. Finally, sales growth ceases causing the uncertainty, equivocality, and risk to be low, signifying its maturation stage and the product can no longer be considered a core technology, as competitors have successfully seized a good portion of the market.

In chapter 6 we examined a generic representation of internal investment capital and resulting cash flows generated from a typical product as it progressed through the cycle (see figure 6-8). Accordingly, if we superimpose these curves with the one shown in figure 8-15, we now have a more comprehensive illustration that relates risk, product demand, and investment capital, with return on investment (as approximated by cash flows). Thus, by developing a dynamic understanding of where the company and products lay on this curve, the most effective deployment of financial and human capital resources can be allocated for R&D, marketing, and budgeting strategies. If this can be achieved, the company will maximize its chances of completing its objectives thereby maximizing corporate value and competitiveness.

Figure 8-15. Managing Risk, Equivocality, & Uncertainty during the Product Life Cycle

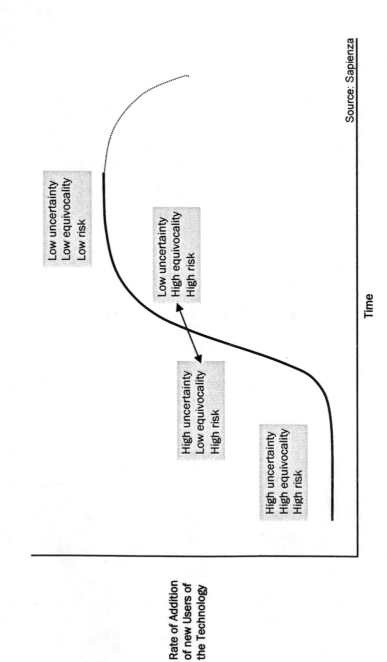

Notes

[1] When the discounted cash flow (DCF) valuation method is used, cash flow statement projections are used as the source of cash flows. However, for many early stage companies, the comparables method or a combination of the DCF and comparables methods are used for valuation purposes. The balance sheet is also used to assess default risk.

[2] The accrual principal treats payments and expenditures similar to a credit card because there is a delay between the time accounts receivable and payables are converted into cash.

[3] A bond's price will also be affected by changes in the default risk of the company, as reflected by credit rating agencies.

[4] U.S. Treasuries are chosen since they have essentially zero default risk, thereby minimizing any outside forces in the shape of the curve. However, any bond can be chosen as long as the all of its characteristics are equivalent, except the variable to be assessed. Quite often, the yield curve of U.S. Treasuries is compared to that of corporate bonds to measure the relative yield spreads between the two curves. It is thought that such an analysis provides information about the default risk of corporate debt.

[5] It is actually the demand for these short-term bonds in the market place that drives the prices higher, resulting in a higher yield.

Recommended Texts for Financial Statement Analysis:

(1) John Tracy. How to Read a Financial Report. 1999. 5th edition. New York: John Wiley & Sons.

(2) Thomas Ittelson. Financial Statements. 1998. Franklin Lakes, NJ: Career Press.

(3) Ciaran Walsh. Key Management Ratios. 2003. 3rd edition. London: Prentice Hall.

Part III

Getting
The Money

9

Exit Strategies

"Opportunities multiply as they are seized."

Sun Tzu

A. Introduction

Perhaps the most significant event that occurs with any venture-backed company is the exit. No matter how great the investment opportunity may seem, without a viable route and timing of exit, no venture capitalist will receive your company's proposal with much interest because the exit event represents their only measure of success. For each party involved however, the attractiveness of the various exit possibilities will depend upon a multitude of factors, many of which will be discussed in this chapter. As the founding entrepreneur leading a startup company, it will be important to understand the details of the various types of exit strategies available, their possible impacts on the company, and the psychology of all potential parties involved so that the company can be prepared to minimize any execution failures and identify potential hidden agendas.

A frequent oversight made by individuals involved with startup companies is their failure to recognize the *interdependent nature of the financial industry.* Many entrepreneurs seem to think that angels and venture capital firms (and to a smaller extent banks and SBIA loans) serve as the only prospects for early stage financing. Only several years later after the company is financially stable does the idea of investment bankers surface as a viable resource. However, the fact is that *at any stage of a company's maturity, both investment and merchant bankers can be a tremendous, if not primary source of investment capital.* In fact, depending on the particular professional and company, an investment banker can be almost as valuable for the early stage company as is the venture capitalist.

Investment and merchant bankers may have a direct interest in the company for inclusion into one of their firm's private equity funds, or may serve to raise capital directly for the company. In addition, they can provide business advise, analyst research, and information regarding M&A and IPO trends, which can assist the company when determining industry and competitive analysis, valuation metrics, and exit strategies. Of course establishing relationships with these individuals early on can also be helpful down the road when the company is considering an exit. However, this is easier said than done, as even some less established venture capitalists have difficulty getting their attention unless a financial transaction is ripe.

The management team must at all times have accurate and adequate knowledge of the current trends in the public and private markets because these dynamics will affect the business and financial marketing strategies of all private companies. For instance, between 1998-2000, the IPO market was very hot and many venture firms *"table dressed"* early stage companies to take advantage of this mode of exit. Unfortunately, many of these companies are either no longer around or are struggling to avoid bankruptcy, but the banking firms that took them public and the venture firms who liquidated their holdings profited well.

Since 2001, the public markets have been in a period of greatly reduced IPO demand, as Wall Street feels repercussions of an overextended bull market. Accordingly, many venture firms have changed their exit strategies and therefore the way they view companies is drastically different, as are their standards for valuations, exit strategies, and risk tolerance. For the next several years, mergers and acquisitions will be a very important form of exit for many private companies and this will have a direct impact on company growth and exit strategies. As well, collaborative agreements and licensing fees will serve to provide the core revenue for many companies until they become buyout or IPO candidates.

B. Venture Capitalists

Throughout this book we have described the structure, strategies, and activities of venture capitalists. In chapter two, we learned that venture capital firms are typically structured as limited partnerships, acting as the general partners in providing investment capital to early and late stage companies on behalf of their limited partners. And each fund constructed by these firms has characteristics specified by its covenants, such as lifetime of the fund, investment return objectives, risk parameters, liquidity clauses, management fees, transparency issues, and many other features. Like all sophisticated investors, venture capitalists ultimately seek the best risk-adjusted and time-weighted investment opportunities for inclusion into their funds so they are able to generate a healthy carried interest, while serving the best interest of the limited partners. And it can sometimes be a difficult balance to preserve the best interests of these limited partners and still maintain the best direction and advice for their portfolio companies. However, when push comes to shove it will always be the interest of the limited partners that prevails.

In serving the needs of their limited partners, venture capitalists attempt to provide the best and most efficient expenditure of financial and human capital in order to obtain the best exit relative to the company's products and services, as well as the economic and market conditions. Typical exit strategies for venture capital-backed companies in order of highest preference include IPO, acquisition, sale to a private equity fund, and licensing arrangements. Meanwhile, liquidation is the preferred method of exit when companies have not done well and are expected to continue their underperformance.

IPOs are always the preferred route of exit for venture firms due to the high returns achieved and the high level of corporate finance structure that secures these returns. In addition, as we have seen, an IPO looks good on the venture firm's resume as they begin the process of raising capital for new funds. However, on average only about three in ten venture-backed companies achieve an IPO over the lifetime of each venture fund. Table 9-1 shows the outcomes (expressed as a percentage) of 794 venture capital-backed firms categorized by industry from the Venture Economics database.

Contrary to what many entrepreneurs may believe, the best innovations and business opportunities are not always funded, or venture firms fund them in a less timely manner if those industries are not in favor with the financial community. *Rather, venture capitalists balance the supply-demand dynamics of business opportunities, investment risk, investment capital, and human capital in locating, growing, and then exiting from their investments, much like a hedge fund manager.* Similar to this type of asset manager, venture capitalists must be able to access an adequate supply of investment capital to fund their chosen companies and survive through business and economic cycles. In addition, both must not only have established a plethora of value-added asset management skills, but there must be a high level of demand for those skills by investors so the venture capitalist can successfully close on deals and the hedge fund manager can add to his investable assets. As well, both types of investment managers must be able to recognize and participate in the most lucrative exit strategies or else risk diminished future demand for their skills by investors. Finally for both, exit means providing a sufficient annualized IRR, which is best achieved through IPOs for venture capitalists and through execution of successful trading strategies for hedge fund managers.

Table 9-1. The Fate of Venture backed Companies by Industry
(from a sample of 794 companies, as of July 31, 1992)*

Industry	IPOs	Mergers/ Acquisitions	Liquidations Bankruptcies	Private**
Communications	24.6	24.6	13.0	37.7
Computers	20.0	28.0	36.0	16.6
Computer related	29.0	27.5	21.7	21.7
Electronic components	11.8	35.3	0.0	52.9
Other electronics	20.0	30.0	20.0	30.0
Biotechnology	50.0	27.8	11.1	11.1
Medical/Health	30.4	30.4	21.4	17.9
Consumer products	27.9	14.7	8.8	48.5
Industrial products	7.0	35.1	10.5	47.4
Transportation	41.7	16.7	8.3	33.3
Other	11.1	13.9	12.5	62.5
Total	**22.5**	**23.8**	**15.6**	**38.1**

* While this data is informative for more general purposes, caution is advised when making conclusions regarding industry results for venture capital-backed outcomes, as these results may be indicative of certain time-specific trends. And the relative feasibility of each exit will depend upon the industry and the economic conditions, as well as the performance characteristics of each company. For instance, note that although 22.5% of the companies in this study went public, the biotechnology and transportation industries were twice as likely to exit via IPO. Whether or not this was due to short-term trends cannot be determined from this study.

** Note the fourth column represents firms that have not received financing since January 1, 1988

Source: Gompers and Lerner

C. Investment and Merchant Bankers

Investment Bankers

In its most restricted definition, *investment banking* is the process of raising money in the form of equity and debt for corporate clients or public institutions. As a complement to these financial activities, *investment bankers* also provide strategic and tactical advise, screening and due diligence, valuation analysis, deal structuring, negotiation, and execution of transactions such as issuance of equity, debt, and convertible securities in the form of an IPOs (primary offerings), secondary offerings, shelf offerings, or tender offerings; mergers, acquisitions, corporate restructurings, divestitures, leveraged buyouts, private equity transactions (including private placements), and many other financial transactions.

A public issuance of a security (either as an IPO, secondary, shelf, or tender offering) involves the investment bank acting as an underwriter of the securities, purchasing the securities from the issuer, and reselling them on the public market. In order to provide its clients with a full suite of corporate finance support, large banking firms also provide supplementary services such as sales and trading, research, and a syndicate function (sharing the underwriting responsibility with other investment banks). Prior to raising capital for their IPO-bound companies, investment bankers must first determine the funding needs of the client then identify investors who will be willing to supply these funds. Usually they call upon their large list of institutional investors to supply these funds in exchange for ownership of a portion of the security offering.

In contrast to public offerings, a private placement provides a means for financing public and private companies and calls for the investment bank to act solely as an *agent*, as opposed to the issuer. *In this case the company seeking financing is the issuer* and the bank will match the issuer of the security with potential investors in an offering, which is not made available to the public (hence the designation "private placement" since it occurs outside of the securities markets). In this transaction, investment bankers concentrate their efforts on identifying alternative sources of capital and developing innovative techniques to match the interest of users and providers of capital. *For public companies, private placements can occur when the offering is not made available to the general public and is therefore is not offered on the stock market exchanges. This type of private placement transaction is often called a P.I.P.E. (private investment in public equity).*

In the case whereby an investment bank sells ownership of a private company to its clients in exchange for company stock, this transaction is also called a *private placement* and it can be thought of as a *venture capital financing arrangement without the control element* taken by venture capitalists. Regardless whether they occur with a public or private company, private placements offer the unique advantage that the issuer is not required to register the securities with the SEC if specific exemptions have been met (refer to chapter 3, footnote 4), and therefore is not required to provide a prospectus to interested investors. In addition, the issuer is not required to publicly disclose its financial statements, competitive position, and new product developments. *Therefore, private placements offer the company a way to receive long-term financing without the rigorous scrutiny of the SEC, disclosures of financial statements, costly fees associated with registration, and generation of a prospectus.* Hence, capital can be raised in a short period of time and with minimal company transparency.

The typical compensation for private placement transactions is usually 6-9%, depending on the financing amount and terms of the deal. And in general, once the placement has been sold the investment bank has no further ties to the company, other then a portion of company stock that they may have structured into the deal as partial compensation. The investment bank's primary incentive is the 6-9% fee charged for raising the money and unless they are serving on the board of directors, all formal ties with the company will cease upon closing of the deal. Larger banks will not even consider any private placement deal below $25-50 million but there are always exceptions, especially during a recession, when the markets are down and banking business is lagging. The smaller regional banks and boutiques may engage in private placements of $2-$5 million and up even during good economic times. There are obviously several advantages and disadvantages to using large versus small banks, the discussion of which is beyond the focus of this book.

Merchant Bankers

It is perhaps not through neglect that most people do not understand the role of a merchant banking department, as their activities are extremely broad and their roles often ill defined. Likewise, a specific definition of merchant banking has not been provided by U.S. banking and securities laws and therefore its meaning is often misunderstood even by most financial professionals. However, the Federal Reserve has issued laws that govern their involvement with investment activities. *With respect to the private equity industry, merchant bankers are financial professionals working for investment banks (and some large commercial banks) and are involved with the transactional and managerial aspects of virtually any non-financial private or public company for the purpose of establishing the portfolio companies for their firm's private equity fund.*

In general, merchant bankers are lenders, advisors, and investors that participate in negotiated private equity investments by financial institutions in the unregistered securities of privately or publicly held companies. Some of the activities performed by merchant banking departments include equity investment, (common stock of private and public companies, convertible preferred stock, and subordinated debt with conversion privileges or warrants) non-strategic asset sell-offs in corporate divestitures, taking a public company private, leverage recapitalizations, and management buyouts. And while both investment and commercial banks are permitted to conduct merchant banking business, the range and expertise of offerings by investment banking firms are clearly superior to those of commercial banks due to their rich supply of financial and intellectual resources.

When considering private equity transactions, and specifically private placements, it can often be confusing to distinguish between the duties and limitations of investment bankers and merchant bankers. Although both can handle private equity transactions, it can be generally stated that *investment bankers tend to focus on the corporate finance activities of public companies while merchant bankers usually concentrate in corporate finance issues with private companies.* Hence, most investment bankers handle private placements of public companies in addition to much other public corporate finance business, such as corporate restructurings and IPOs.

Typically investment bankers' involvement with private equity transactions is mainly focused on the non-venture capital side, such as private placements involving public companies, leverage buyouts, and other activities involving at least one public company. However, there are instances whereby investment bankers work with private placements for private companies, but they typically serve as the middle man, either providing the initial due diligence screen prior to referral to private equity fund managers of the bank, or by serving as placement agent for the private company in the fund raising process.

In contrast, merchant bankers tend to handle corporate finance of private companies (excluding IPOs), such as venture capital-based private equity and other transactions occurring outside the public markets. When attempting to distinguish between the roles of each of these two bankers within the private placement financings, the main point of distinction between is that *merchant bankers typically have dedicated investment funds with which to construct a private equity portfolio.* Therefore they serve as the direct investor, unlike the case with investment bankers. Note however, that these are very generalized rules of thumb, and the distinguishing characteristics of these two professionals seems to be even more blurred with smaller investment and commercial banking firms since they tend to have less manpower but often attempt to maintain full private and public corporate finance capabilities.

Private equity financing (private placement) is often an attractive alternative for private companies that need capital but have a poor financial history, as other financing options for such companies may otherwise be unattainable or too costly.   Furthermore, a private company may wish to pursue this type of financing to change the ownership while remaining private and to avoid the cost of debt financing.   However, *the majority of private equity financing transactions for private firms is focused on financing startup and early stage companies, similar to venture capital.*   Likewise, as previously discussed, public companies may also pursue private equity transactions when they want to obtain financing with minimal regulatory approval and expense and wish to avoid public disclosure.   Often, when public companies seek this type of financing alternative, the proceeds are used for conversion into a private company through a leveraged buyout.   The diversity of financial transactions available to private equity funds and merchant bankers accounts for a tremendous amount investment capital allocated to these firms each year (table 9-2).

Table 9-2. Allocation of U.S. Private Equity Funds (1993-1999)

Year	Total Private Equity	Venture Capital	Buyout/Mezzanine Financing[a]	Other
1999	$108.1	$46.6	$44.6	$16.9
1998	$105.4	$28.0	$61.2	$16.3
1997	$73.8	$15.7	$48.7	$9.4
1996	$45.2	$10.6	$29.8	$4.9
1995	$41.1	$8.2	$27.3	$5.6
1994	$30.9	$7.2	$20.5	$3.2
1993	$22.0	$3.9	$16.9	$1.2

[a]Mezzanine financing generally consists of subordinated debt with equity conversion privileges or warrants issued in tandem with the equity issue in a buyout.

Source: Craig, V.V. 2000. *Merchant Banking Past and Present.*   Division of Research and Statistics, FDIC.

Similar to venture capital, private equity firms are usually structured into limited partnerships, whereby merchant bankers and other equity managers serve as the general partners, investing the capital of its limited partners. Also identical to venture funds, the limited partners of private equity funds are usually institutional investors, such as pension plans, endowments, and insurance companies. Another similarity with venture capital funds is that the general partners of private equity funds are required to invest 1% into the funds they sponsor, which by law have a limited life of between 10-15 years. Therefore, private equity funds, like venture capital funds are very illiquid, and thus best suited for only a small portion of pension fund investment. The most common exit mechanism of these funds is by IPO, although private sale to another private equity or venture capital fund is not uncommon.

However, unlike venture capitalists, merchant bankers do not provide ongoing management of their portfolio companies and are prevented from doing so by law, although they can intervene when situations arise that could jeopardize the investment. Finally, the methods of distribution of investment capital back to the limited partners of private equity funds are more variable than in venture funds. In addition to the common methods of profit distribution to the limited partners of a venture fund, private equity funds also market ownership units of the fund and resell them to retail markets.

D. Initial Public Offerings

There are a variety of reasons a company may elect to sell its shares in an initial public offering. *For the venture capitalist, an IPO offers a convenient method for return on investment and the added advantage of providing flexibility in the liquidity event,* since the company stock will have a daily market for buyers and sellers. However, some venture capitalists choose to hold their stock with the hopes of further appreciation over a longer-term horizon. Likewise, for the founders of the company, an IPO may provide a means of capitalization of their hard work and assumption of risk. While the management team may also have this motivation, from a purely corporate finance standpoint *an IPO may be the most economical means to secure expansion capital and provide better access to long-term debt financings, when the cost of further debt financings might be otherwise very expensive or difficult to obtain.* Finally, for companies that have achieved significant market share and many periods of revenue growth, both the cost and risk of equity financing is less than debt financing.

Prior to its IPO debut, a company will undergo numerous scrutinies by both the sponsoring investment bank and the Securities and Exchange

Commission (SEC).   The investment bank will tend to value the shares at a price that will be attractive to investors, which may or may not result in undervaluation.   And much of this will depend upon the market conditions and the relative demand for the issue.   Meanwhile, the founders will want to maximize the price per share in order to obtain the highest liquidation proceeds.   *Likewise, the management team will also seek the maximum price per share to increase their compensation, but should ideally be focused on a public offering that fairly values the company so earning expectations will not be unattainable.*   The final pricing decisions are determined based upon the negotiations between the venture investors and the lead underwriting bank. But ultimately, pricing is based upon the demand for the company.   Thus, the company management is sometimes left in the dark, not having any idea what the company may be truly worth and must rely on the valuations provided by the venture and investment banking firms.   However, it is human nature to overlook such issues when anticipating the excitement, prestige, and financial benefits of an IPO.

Companies must address many issues when considering an IPO as a means of obtaining long-term financing.   When the original shareholders of a private company offer their shares to the public they are relinquishing exclusive control of the company's future.   With that said, why would an IPO be the preferred route of exit for a company?   In general, *public companies have tremendous access to capital and the company stock is usually liquid.*   In addition, companies may issue additional shares at a later time *(secondary or shelf offerings)* and will have greater access to credit lines and debt financing transactions.   Further reasons companies wish to go public are listed below and in figure 9-1.

- **Complements Product Marketing.**   National publications and the general media cover the events and business offerings of public companies to a much greater extent than private companies because the entire nation potentially has a vested interest.

- **Improves Employee Recruitment and Retention.**   Because public companies are relatively liquid, their stock options and repurchase programs tend to be more vibrant and active than those of private companies, resulting in more extensive participation by employees.

- **Facilitates Mergers, Acquisitions, Joint Ventures, Strategic Alliances and other Business Activities.**   Due to the rigorous disclosure guidelines of the SEC, potential strategic partners are more assured of company transparency and better informed of potential partnering opportunities of public companies.   In addition, the access to capital provided by treasury stock and stock-repurchasing activities can add tremendous financial leverage towards a company's acquisition activities.

Keep in mind that no matter how great a company is, there must be a marketplace established for an IPO. This marketplace is created first by the venture capitalists, who sell the idea to the investment bank, and second by the investment banking firm and analysts, who promote the company through road shows and issue optimistic research reports to their institutional clients.

Figure 9-1. Advantages of IPOs

1. Potentially Higher Price (valuations tend to be overstated)

2. The Most Desired Exit by Management (status symbol)

3. Management Can Participate in Future Growth (stock options)

4. Provides Capitalization of Company for Growth and Increases its Financing Alternatives

5. Proceeds are Unrestricted

6. Provides for Stock Incentive Compensation Plans (used to attract and retain top talent)

7. More Liquidity for the Company Stock is provided

8. Enhanced Ability to Expand

9. Lower Cost of Capital versus Debt

On the other hand, IPOs are very expensive for companies and these high costs are even surpassed by the ongoing annual costs once it becomes a public corporation. In addition, public companies must publicly disclose their financial statements and other information thought to be material for investors to make reasonable decisions regarding the investment merits of the company stock. Finally, shareholder and Wall Street analyst scrutiny can result in a refocus in growth strategies, due to emphasis on shorter-term earnings, all of which may lead to diminished job security for the executive management team. Figure 9-2 lists some of the main disadvantages of an IPO, while figure 9-3 lists IPO barriers.

Figure 9-2. Disadvantages of IPOs

1. Higher Cost

2. High Recurring Costs associated with filings, audits, legal fees, shareholder meetings, investor relations, public relations, annual reports and so on. These fees can add up quickly and can be a drag on earnings if not managed properly. In addition, if not handled with diligence, oversights such as material within disclosing statements in annual reports could initiate shareholders litigation.

3. Must Have Sufficient Valuation

4. Lock-up Agreements Prevent Initial Liquidity

5. Loss of Control

6. Company Must Answer to Wider Range of Shareholders (this could jeopardize long-term growth strategies for short-term performance due to shareholder pressures)

7. Many corporate strategic decisions will be based upon the relative health of the stock price which could hinder future growth.

8. Public Disclosure of key information becomes available. Financial statements, licensing agreements and other important items can be accessed and exploited by competitors.

9. IPO Valuations tend to be Artificially High, which may cause a period of market retreat; as the stock is sold off, access to capital may become extremely difficult.

Figure 9-3. IPO Barriers

Internal Barriers
- Must Have Valuation of at Least $200-$500 Million (depending upon market conditions)
- Key Investors and Management Must be in Agreement on the Decision to Go Public (otherwise problem could develop from individuals with a significant ownership position).

External Barriers
- Company Proceeds Dependent on Economy and Market Conditions
- Company is Vulnerable to Analysts Agendas and Corporate Finance Support

While most large corporations in the U.S. are public, there are some notable exceptions. For instance, Enterprise Rent-A-Car and Fidelity Investments are two of the leading companies in their industry, yet they remain private companies. Upon closer examination, one may realize that these two companies are in industries that are capital intensive. Yet, both have grown tremendously and are the largest among their peers. Hence, these two examples seemed to have trivialized the main reason for going public—the need for extensive access to credit and equity capital in order to fuel continued growth. However, one should note that these companies are not high tech and therefore have different financial dynamics, timing of capital requirements, and cash flow patterns. Specifically, both are income-generating businesses, unlike high tech companies, which usually require a long return on investment.

Perhaps those companies wishing to remain private place the highest priority on retaining absolute control of their company. However, going public does not always mean losing majority control. For instance, consider the case of Dell Computers, Microsoft, and Fossil. Although there are many more examples, in each of these cases the founders have retained a very large percentage of ownership of company stock making them by far the single largest shareholder. And while they may not hold the majority of their company stock, the founders of these companies have sufficient ownership to influence corporate decisions through shareholder voting rights even if they were not the CEO. In addition, their large ownership percentage enables them to repel any potentially hostile takeover bids through utilization of sophisticated asset leveraging techniques. Nevertheless, it is interesting to consider the reality that companies can and have grown to become market leaders without going public.

The IPO Process

The IPO process begins with the selection of a primary investment banking firm as the *lead manager*. The lead banking firm will be responsible for pricing the issue, advising the company of market conditions relevant for the pricing, providing the legal paperwork, and distributing the issue. The first step is gaining the approval of the SEC by submission of a *red herring* by the investment banking firm. This document contains a description of the security, the total amount to be raised, the number of shares issued, the curriculum vitalae of the management team and their compensation, outside shareholders, board of directors, the competitive position of the company, relevant products and markets served, inherent risks, and pro forma financial statements from the past 4-5 years structured according to the rules and regulations of the SEC.

After the SEC has approved the red herring, it becomes the *prospectus* and is distributed to all interested potential investors. In the mean time, the lead banking firm has formed an *underwriting syndicate* composed of other investment banking firms, whose responsibility is to assist in the distribution of the shares. *Tombstone* ads are then circulated in various financial publications indicating the intent of the issue to be sold in the public markets, the amount to be raised, number of shares, the tentative offering price, and the list of syndicate members. Table 9-3 shows a timeline listing the main tasks and individuals involved with an IPO.

In the process of selection of the investment bankers, companies should identify those financial institutions that will be committed to them several years prior to and after the IPO if possible, as they can be instrumental in advising the company on early preparation for the IPO process. In addition, securing the committed support of this firm after the IPO can provide better access to financing transactions and analyst coverage, needed to maintain a sufficient level of visibility for investors. One way to help strengthen such a commitment might be by granting one of the bankers a seat on the Board of Directors. At the very least, the company needs to develop a good relationship with the lead bank so that it can interpret its subtle actions, in effort to maintain continued support for the stock after the IPO. Fortunately, venture capitalists usually take care of soliciting companies for IPOs and acquisitions.

Financial Expense of Going Public

An IPO is a very demanding and stressful period for all parties involved and the preparation can take up to one year to comply with the rules and regulations of the SEC and the listing exchanges. It is also the time during which the founders, management, angel and venture investors are rewarded for their investment of human and financial capital. But for the management team, it also represents a period of difficult transition that will consume much time and capital in order to comply with these stringent regulations. Figure 9-4 lists the typical fees associated with bringing a private company public on the NASDAQ market exchange. *In addition to annual listing fees required for all exchanges, there are certain listing requirements that a company must meet on an annual basis or it may be delisted from each exchange for which it fails to meet the criteria.* Some of the listing requirements for these exchanges include minimal numbers for:

- Stockholder's Equity
- Public Float (shares)
- Market Capitalization
- Total Revenue
- Minimum Bid Price

- Pre-tax Income
- Total Assets
- Operating History (time)
- Market Value of Public Float
- Shareholders (round lot)

Table 9-3. Roles of Each Participant in an IPO

	1-2 Years Before	1-6 Months Before	1-3 Months Before	1-4 Weeks Before	1-10 Days Before	1 Day Before	Day of IPO	3 Days After	0-30 Days After
Company	Act like a public company	Select the team; Execute letter of intent	Select Printer & transfer agent	Executives present road show	Issue press release	Price the offering; execute under-writing agreement	Security Trades	Provide certificates; Collect proceeds	Provide additional certificates; collect additional proceeds
Company Law Firm		Perform housekeeping of company records; Draft S-1; file with SEC; File listing applications	Prepare & file preliminary registration	Clear SEC comments		File final registration		Deliver documents	Update closing documents
Company Accounting Firm		Clean up and restate balance sheet; prepare and review audited Financial statements	Prepare draft comfort letter	Prepare updated financial stmts	Deliver draft comfort letter			Deliver bring-down comfort letter	Second bring-down comfort letter
Investment Bankers		Assess market and make presentation to board	Continue due diligence	Orchestrate road show; solicit indications of interest	Form syndicate; place tombstone ad	Execute under-writing agreement		Provide net proceeds	Exercise over-allotment option determine issuance of research report
Investment Banker's Counsel		Begin due diligence	Prepare NASDR filing; undertake blue-sky filings	Clear NASDR comments	Continue due diligence			Assist in closing	Assist in second closing
Financial Printer		Print preliminary registration stmt/ prospectus	Produce SEC & NASDR filings			Print final registration statement/prospectus			
SEC		Confer regarding Problems if needed	Review preliminary registration statement Issue comment letter			Declare offering effective			
NASDR		Request prefiling Advice, if necessary	Review preliminary registration statement	Resolve comments		Declare no objections			

Figure 9-4. Estimated Cost of Going Public

Offering Value:	$25 Million	$50 Million
Total Shares Outstanding:	5,880,000	5,880,000
Item	Estimated Fee	Estimated Fee
Underwriting Discounts And Commissions	$1,750,000[1]	$3,500,000[1]
Item 13 From Registration Stmt		
SEC Fees	$9,914[2]	$19,828[2]
NASD Fees	$3,375[3]	$6,250[3]
Printing and Engraving	$100,000[1]	$100,000[1]
Accounting Fees & Expenses	$160,000[1]	$160,000[1]
Legal Fees & Expenses	$200,000[1]	$200,000[1]
Blue-Sky Fees*	$25,000[1]	$25,000[1]
Miscellaneous	$34,200[1]	$34,200[1]
Nasdaq Entry Fees	$63,725[4]	$63,725[4]
Nasdaq Annual Fees	$11,960[5]	$11,960[5]
Transfer Agent & Registrar Fees	$5000[1]	$5000[1]
Total	**$2,363,174**	**$4,125,963**

1 Mean value; issuers should be aware that all aspects of the relationship, including underwriting, can be   negotiated.

2 1/29 of 1 percent of the offering value, inclusive of over-allotment shares.

3 $500 + 0.01 percent of the offering value, inclusive of over-allotment shares, not to exceed $30,500.

4 Includeds a $5000 one-time company initial fee and a fee based on $5,880,000 total shares outstanding.

5 Fee shown is a full year's fee. On Nasdaq, first year annual fee will be prorated based on month listed.

Source: Nasdaq. *Going Public and Listing on the U.S. Securities Markets*

By far the American Stock Exchange has the lowest fees (not counting the Nasdaq small cap market) for both entry (ranging from $10,000 for up to 1 million shares, to $50,000 for over 125 million shares) and annual continuation fees of $6,500 to $14,500 for the same share numbers. The New York Stock Exchange charges the highest fees for entry, at $150,000 for up to 20 million shares and up to $250,000 beyond 75 million shares. Likewise, its annual continuation fees also remain constant for up to 25 million shares but can reach as high as $500,000 for share amounts beyond 125 million.

The Nasdaq market lies in the middle with entry fees of $34,525 for up to 1 million shares and $95,000 beyond 16 million shares. Nasdaq continuation fees of $10,710 for up to 1 million shares and $50,000 for beyond 100 million shares (all data is as of 06/01; source: Nasdaq, NYSE, Amex). In addition, the fees associated with attorneys, accountants, printing costs, filing fees, blue sky fees and transfer agent fees can range from $250,000 to $750,000.

As you can see, the financial cost of going public is high. Meanwhile, the financial and human resource costs of remaining public are perhaps even higher, as public companies must abide by SEC and exchange mandates that require SEC filings, audits, legal fees, shareholder meetings, investor relations, public relations, annual reports and so on. Thus, it is easy to see that going public requires tremendous expense and commitment to meeting the continued compliance required by the regulatory bodies overseeing public companies.

Pre-IPO Valuation Process

We have discussed some of the difficulties in determining the final IPO price of a company. But the starting point used for this determination begins by establishing a pre-IPO valuation. Once this value has been determined, the final offering price will be based upon the relative expected versus actual demand for the issue by investors, and this is usually set a few weeks in advance and revised if needed two or three days prior to the IPO. And while the final price of the offering may be under the control of the market, the entrepreneur should nevertheless understand the methods used by venture firms and investment banks to arrive at this initial figure.

The *comparables approach* is a relatively simple method that can be used to estimate the pre-IPO valuation and involves identification of similar companies that are publicly traded. Price-to-earnings multiples can then be associated with key financial data such as revenues, revenue growth, earnings, earnings growth, etc. Finally, the price-to-earnings ratio for these comparables can easily be converted into a sales price for the company by multiplying by the forward earnings projections. The time period of these projections is variable. This method is presented in more detail in chapter 11.

An interesting phenomenon frequently occurs with companies prior to their IPO debut. During the underwriting process, a valuation is determined for the candidate company. Depending upon the industry type, one of several possible valuation methods is used to determine this figure, such as the comparables approach mentioned previously. However, keep in mind that *many companies are taken to the public marketplace prematurely, often during economic expansions and bull market conditions.* Consequently, many company valuations can have large margins of error because in part, the estimations are based upon inflated valuations of comparable public companies that always accompany bull markets.

Support for these observations has been confirmed through several studies that have examined the results of timing venture-backed versus nonventure-backed IPOs. Specifically, these studies by Gompers and Lerner have concluded that venture firms tend to take companies public during stock market peaks, when they can receive higher valuations, hoping to improve their reputations and thereby increase their ability to raise additional capital for their next fund. In addition, because they are very familiar with the business cycle of the company, venture firms can time the public offering during a period when the company earnings are spiking, which will also tend to maximize the offering price and secondary market demand. From the venture capitalists' perspective, taking a company public during market peaks will serve to minimize dilution since the stock will tend to be offered at a higher price. In addition, the stock price will tend to appreciate in advance of company fundamentals due to high demand in the marketplace. This is a very important part of the venture firm's investment strategy because their IRR is determined based upon the time immediately prior to making share distributions or liquidation of shares to their limited partners.

In addition, there are other factors that can contribute to pre-IPO overvaluation. Companies with limited operating histories may have insufficient data periods for prediction of future revenues and earnings. In the case of the discounted cash flow (DCF) valuation method, future cash flows are estimated based upon assumptions formulated from a financial model. In accord with this method, a *perpetual (terminal) cash flow forecast* is determined for use in these calculations based upon an amount the company is expected to generate indefinitely. These future cash flows are then discounted back to a present value based upon the risk of achieving them. However, *these cash flow estimates are often determined during a period when the company is experiencing rapid acceleration of revenue and earnings growth and therefore its cash flows are not representative of the longer-term growth assumed by the DCF method.*

To further illustrate this problem, we need to examine a typical life cycle product curve (figure 9-5). As you can see, *companies typically make their IPO debut during the rapid growth stage, when revenue and earnings growth rates are peaking.* Thus, when valuation for the companies is performed, the revenue, earnings, and cash flow figures are not necessarily representative of the longer-term cash flow and revenue growth expected based upon its position in the product life cycle curve. Therefore, when estimating future cash flows and determining a perpetual (terminal) value, the numbers used are usually significantly inflated, resulting in a high valuation. And when bullish market conditions are present, these estimates are exaggerated even further through the use of the comparables approach. Finally, when the company begins to report lower than expected earnings, the stock price suffers.

When these events do occur, that is not to say that the company never again reaches these inflated levels, as inferred by the chart. As companies reinvent or improve their products they can be considered essentially new, so that they may eventually reach these valuations. The main questions are, how many years does this take and how much have these exaggerations in shareholder value affected investors? The possibility of this scenario and its consequences are important considerations for the company management and founder, as they may be able to catch that window of opportunity and liquidate a large portion of their stock after the lockup period, prior to significant declines in the stock price. Unfortunately, however, founders and management usually have lock-up periods of one year or more, in contrast to the venture firms.

Perhaps the most significant consequence of excessive IPO overvaluation is that a subsequent series of earnings misses or downward revisions by the company could result in a devastating decline in the stock price that could hinder corporate credit facilities. Consider that credit rating agencies use ratios involving shareholder's equity when assessing a company's credit risk. And a large sustained decline in the price of a stock may not only result in diminished credit, but could also cause *debt covenants* to be violated, which might trigger the immediate recall of all debt principal.

In addition, we have seen that each exchange has certain listing requirements such as market capitalization and minimum trading requirements, and Wall Street analysts also observe these requirements for research coverage. Accordingly, any company that falls below $5 and remains there for an extended period will be considered a "penny stock". Because of its penny stock status, most analysts will discontinue research coverage, which would inhibit the ability of pension funds from purchasing the stock due to ERISA guidelines. Thus, the stock would essentially be abandoned and ignored and the laws of supply and demand would most likely cause the stock's public valuation to dwindle once lockup periods for IPOs began to expire. Even more detrimental, the main advantages public companies have may no longer be available such as increased access to credit facilities.

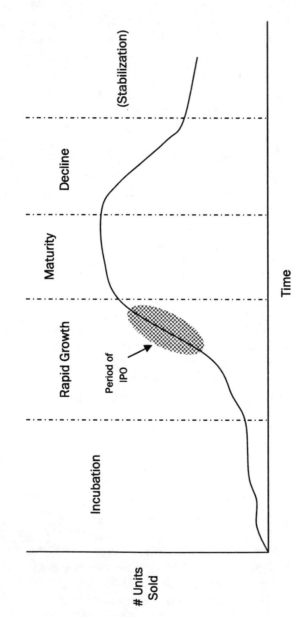

Figure 9-5. Product Lifecycle Curve and IPOs

Premature IPOs

In an attempt to establish a successful track record, some newer venture firms may rush the IPO of a company that may not be fully prepared to endure the intense scrutiny of public shareholders and Wall Street analysts. This behavior is known as *"grandstanding"* (discussed in chapter 2) and was a common practice especially during the ending stages of the bull market of the 1990s. As discussed previously, companies without revenues, erratic revenues, or with small revenues relative to their valuation, when placed under the scrutiny of public shareholders, can quickly begin to experience devastating pressures that could lead to their demise. In addition, such actions could not only result in the ultimate failure of the business but also the inability of the management and founders to cash out, due to the disintegration of the stock price prior to lockup periods. It should be obvious that these effects can be even more devastating when premature IPOs are issued during bull markets, which will further exaggerate their value.

An example of this situation can be found by examining a formerly well-known high-tech company. This was a company that appeared virtually from nowhere and formed by an individual who had no background or experience in technology. Yet he was opportunistic and created the needed network of individuals and companies to help support a growing business during a period when such companies were very well received by the public and private markets. But after the Internet bubble burst in 2000, the company began experiencing many difficulties after Wall Street analysts became more critical of their revenue recognition methods.

Eventually, Wall Street analysts dropped support for the stock when it was discovered that the company was involved in questionable revenue sharing practices between its business partners. The stock price gradually declined to pennies, and was later delisted. The once lavish lifestyle of the founder/CEO rapidly dissipated, as the majority of his net worth was tied into the stock. This example illustrates the failure of the proper level of due diligence by Wall Street investment firms, analysts, and perhaps questionable guidance and oversight by the venture firms that sponsored it. And unfortunately, this company was only one of hundreds that experienced the first hand effects of being taken public prematurely during the peak of a tremendous bull market.

VC-backed IPO Timing and Performance

Historically, *venture capital-backed companies have about a 30% chance of going public through an IPO (Gompers and Lerner).* Nevertheless, because this route of exit represents by far the highest rate of return for venture firms, only a couple of companies in each venture fund need to go public in order to provide good overall returns for the entire fund. Therefore, when the IPO period approaches, venture firms will be more focused on maximizing their return and will conduct activities towards this end.   As such, it is possible that some VCs may advise companies in ways that may hinder their longer-term productivity, perhaps unknowingly. Of course this is not the norm, as most venture firms will have a vested interest in the company for a significant period post-IPO and will thus be protective of its fate.

Despite the common occurrence of IPO overvaluations, it has been shown that *companies that go public via venture capital sponsorship tend to perform better than those without venture capital assistance.* Studies for venture-backed IPOs versus nonventure backed IPOs from the period of 1972-1992 have shown that venture backed IPOs have 5-year returns that average 44.6% while nonventure backed IPOs average 22.5%.

There are many possible explanations for these results. First, many venture capitalists retain board seats well after the IPO and provide sources of strategic insight as well as additional avenues of financing. In addition, many of the established venture firms have good relations with top investment banks and may be able to gain favorable analyst coverage for their companies. Finally and perhaps most significantly, because most of the limited partners are institutions, common stock distributions to these partners tends to be held over a longer time period rather than being liquidated immediately. Therefore, the stock price is supported over a longer period of time, perhaps helping to minimize the affects of early earnings disappointments.

Post-IPO Distributions

In the hopeful situation whereby the liquidation event is an IPO, the compensation of the venture capitalists in large part may be influenced by the restrictions of the *lockup agreement* that is negotiated by the lead underwriter of the IPO. *Typically, the lockup agreement restricts the sales and distribution of shares of the recent IPO for typically 40-180 trading days.*[1] This period is thought to provide adequate time for the volume of shares traded to stabilize so that the stock price is not affected much by liquidation of large blocks within a short time frame.   Upon reaching the end of this lockup agreement, venture capitalists usually distribute the shares to their limited partners, although they sometimes sell the shares and distribute the cash proceeds.   In the latter case, this would trigger a capital gains tax for the venture capitalist and is therefore rarely done.[2]

In addition, most venture partnership agreements allow the venture firm to use its discretion when making distributions of committed capital versus profit enabling them with the flexibility to potentially increase their relative compensation through diligent execution of market timing techniques.   The actual return the limited partners receive however, may not be indicative of that calculated by the venture firm, due to the timing of liquidation of the limited partners' shares. Nevertheless, once the shares have been distributed, the venture capitalist uses the current market price for these shares in calculating the return on investment. However, the stock may be overvalued and could experience sharp declines over the ensuing period prior to liquidation by the limited partners, making the reported returns much higher than the actual returns.

E. Mergers and Acquisitions

Merger activity hit record levels even prior to the bear market of 2000-2005(?). And the mega mergers of the 1990s set the stage for the biggest mergers in the world; AOL-Time-Warner and Pfizer-Warner Lambert-Pharmacia. Fueled with soaring stock prices, many companies would have been considered financially irresponsible to have not used their inflated stock price to acquire companies with significant intellectual capital and strategic assets. The best example of this was America Online's acquisition of Time-Warner. With an increasing churn rate and intense competition from MSN, AOL was nevertheless able to hold off doubts about its earnings projections until after the acquisition of Time Warner. And unfortunately, the accounting fraud of AOL did not show up until after the two companies united.

Aside from high stock prices, this recent intensity in merger activity may also be attributed to the expansion of global competition, industry consolidation, deregulation, and strong consumer demand for the latest technological innovations. Finally, the antitrust regulatory agencies have shown ease, seen by the rapid consolidation in the telecommunications industry during the 1990s. Perhaps the recent telecommunications implosion along with the bear market will signal these regulatory bodies to alter their antitrust policies going forward, but this should have very little impact for acquisition opportunities of private companies.

While most venture capitalists view an IPO as the best exit route, it may not provide a viable alternative if it is not consistent with their investment strategy or time horizon. In such cases, acquisitions may provide the best exit. The topic of mergers and acquisitions is extremely complicated, detailed, and very difficult to present as a survey in a single text. And because this book has only dedicated a small portion of this chapter to this topic, our discussion will be quite limited. However, I will attempt to describe the most common reasons for mergers, the most common reasons for their failure, and provide on overview of the process so that early stage companies can gain some familiarity with these business strategies.

Reasons to Merge

In general, mergers occur when two companies combine but only one company's identity remains. A *statutory merger* occurs when the acquiring company assumes the assets and liabilities of its acquisition target according to the statues of its state of incorporation. We have discussed vertical and horizontal mergers in chapter 6 but there are many other subcategories such as subsidiary, conglomerate and many more. In general, the most common reasons motivating companies to pursue mergers are the following:

1. **Synergy (financial or operational).** This relates to *economies of scale* (the spreading of fixed costs over larger production levels) and *economies of scope* (the enhanced utilization of specific skills and assets to develop a wider range of products). Financial synergy should occur when the combined companies produce a lower cost of capital than the acquiring company if the cash flows of the two companies are uncorrelated or the merger allows the formation of financial economies of scale.[3] *Operational economies of scale should result in lower costs for items such as depreciation of equipment, maintenance spending, interest expense, lease payments, and taxes. Economies of scale are best applied to manufacturing industries that are associated with high fixed costs such as utilities, chemicals, pharmaceuticals, steel and aircraft manufacturing.*

2. **Diversification.** Companies may wish to diversify products or enter new markets in order to reduce shareholder risk by stabilizing revenue streams through periods of normal and abnormal business and economic cycles. An example of such a technique would be Goodyear Tire acquiring a defensive company such as a food and beverage or drug company (similar to the financial synergy described above). When Goodyear's earnings decline due to the cyclical nature of its industry, the earnings of the food and beverage company may provide stabilization to the overall stream of combined earnings since this industry is relatively resistant to business cycles.[4]

3. **Increase Market Power**. Increasing market share to better control prices is an obvious advantage and may be accompanied by the added benefits of economies of scale.[5]

4. **Tax Advantages**. Depending upon the specific situation, a merger may permit the acquiring company to obtain unused losses, credits, and substitute capital gains for ordinary loses from the

acquired company as well as the tax-free nature of the acquisition.

5. **Buying Undervalued Assets.** This strategy seeks to acquire assets at a discount when the stock of the target company is less than the cost of buying the assets elsewhere. This rationale was dominant during the 1970s when high inflation and high interest rates made the cost of capital high and depressed the prices of stocks often below their book values.

6. **Managerialism**. Managers who equate the size of a company with their relative compensation may engage in poorly researched and executed mergers.

7. **Strategic Realignment Due to Regulatory Changes and Technological Innovation.** The thought is that mergers are able to achieve a rapid shift in corporate strategy to utilize any regulatory changes that have occurred in a given industry. This rational has resulted in thousands of mergers over the past two decades due to deregulation in the health care, financial services, utilities, media, telecommunications and defense industries. There is some evidence that this provides a good reason for merger activity if one examines specific companies, such as AT & T, Citigroup, and Pfizer. Technological changes have created the need for corporations to quickly integrate new means of product and services delivery, and the continuing trend of decreasing product life cycles has pressured producers to rapidly and increase their portfolio of products at a low cost in order to continue earnings growth. Therefore, *many companies elect to engage in acquisitions to add technologies at prices lower than would be required to build them from scratch.* This has been especially common with biotechnology and computer networking companies.

8. **Hubris (managerial pride).** The competitive nature of many managers is often overcome by an ego-driven decision making process, that frequently results in overpaying for acquisitions during highly competitive bidding wars, leading to the "winner's curse", whereby the winning bid is stuck with paying too much.

9. **Agency Problems with Mismanagement.** To replace inadequate managers or managers whose goals are inconsistent with those of shareholders.

Regardless of the reason for the acquisition, in most cases acquisitions pay off at least initially for the company that has been acquired, since there is a general tendency for overpayment for these transactions. However, there is more uncertainty in determining whether merger activities payoff for the acquirer, and more importantly for the shareholders. This is an issue of great debate and unfortunately, the answer is case-by-case dependent. However, it is the opinion of the author that, while mergers tend to produce unfavorable results when large public corporations acquire other large corporations (especially when the transaction is an all stock deal), they may have much better chances for mutual success if the acquired company is significantly smaller or both companies are relatively new. The rational for this hypothesis is that *much of the problem with creating a successful merger stems from the difficulties associated with the post-merger integration process*, which includes conflicts in corporate cultures, management problems, strategic misdirection, and poor post merger communication.[6] And it appears that the combination of small companies with much larger ones produces an smoother transition, due to the lack of fully developed corporate culture and strategic flexibility by the smaller firm. However, even prior to post-merger integration issues, many mergers are destined for failure from the beginning due to poor due diligence, overpaying, and inexperienced acquirers. In fact, the prevalence of *inexperienced acquirers has been shown to be the major factor contributing to the success or failure of mergers.*

Therefore, all of these factors must be considered when assessing the probable success of a proposed merger-acquisition. In addition, companies must determine at an early stage what impact a variety of acquisition types could have on its future. While some acquisitions are made for the purpose of *strategic lockout*, or to eliminate the competition, the vast majority are for *strategic synergy*. Regardless of the reason, once the buyout has been completed, the management team of the acquired company may be dismissed. Therefore, companies should address these possibilities with the VC prior to the closing of the deal, as they may be able negotiate a temporary management position with the acquiring company. This is an important issue to bargain for with the VCs and the acquiring company, as it will provide these individuals paper experience with a larger corporation and add to their employment appeal after separation from their venture.

Mergers as a Strategic Alternative

Many share the opinion that an acquisition is a second place finish to an IPO for the acquired company, but this is not necessarily true. For venture capitalists, however, this is almost always the case since IPO have historically provided the best IRRs, not to mention the added benefit of a more controlled exit environment.   In contrast, for the company executives this may or may not be true since wise management teams should be focusing on the best exit strategy that will secure the *long-term survival* of the company. Nevertheless, when a company seeks complete control over another company's assets, acquisitions are often the preferred alternative to joint ventures, licensing agreements, franchising deals, and strategic alliances. Let us consider the advantages of a typical acquisition.

1. **Acquisitions can materialize with a shorter operational history of a startup versus an IPO.** This is especially true for a high tech company that has developed software or other technology that is clearly superior, but whose revenues are limited by the operational and marketing inability of the founders. It might take these entrepreneurs an additional ten years to generate the required market penetration that captures the full revenue potential of this product. By that time, the technology would most likely become obsolete. In contrast, a large company in the same industry with various channels of distribution and customer reach might be able to capture the true value of this technology almost immediately.

2. **Acquisitions can be structured with great flexibility of payout option, allowing the founders to select their level of return risk.** For instance, acquisitions can be done with all stock, cash, or a combination. In an all-stock transaction, the recipient will have a holding period (lock-up period) attached to the liquidation, adding a return risk especially if the acquiring company is publicly traded. For private companies the return risk may be less, as the holding period, if any will be less and the liquidation price will only be a factor of the business valuation.

3. **The acquiring company can immediately add to its valuation.** Public companies are valued in part, by a multiple of their revenues, earnings, earnings growth, profit margins, or other financial metrics. If a public company is being valued by earnings growth for instance, and the market has attached its earnings at a rate of 10% per year, it can acquire a company that is growing its earnings at 30% per year and therefore claim that its future expected earnings growth will be proportionate to the size of earnings contributed by the acquisition.[7] And therefore, the market will place a premium on this acquisition assuming it sees no problems with integration. However, these assumptions are most likely not accurate due to the complexities and difficulties involved with post-merger integration. Nevertheless, market demand ultimately dictates public company valuation in

setting the price of its shares on the public exchanges and reality often lags behind perception.

We discussed horizontal mergers in chapter 6 as an alternative to licensing, strategic alliances, and joint venturing activities when the acquiring company to wants to *permanently* fill one or more deficiencies in its production or *value chain*.   Figure 9-6 is a generic representation of the corporate value chain for an information technology company and will be used to illustrate the concept of horizontal mergers.   For instance, if a company's primary strength is marketing and it wishes to add distribution channels by acquisition, the horizontal merger is referred to as *forward integration* since the company to be acquired is ahead of the acquirer in the value chain.   Likewise, if this same company wishes to add more production facilities, it is known as *backward integration*.   This form of asset addition is viewed by the company as a less expensive and more rapid alternative to assembling these business segments from scratch.

Figure 9-6. The Company Value Chain Illustrating Horizontal Mergers

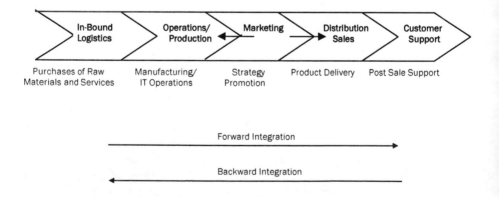

Source: DePamphilis, D.

Merger Performance

There have been numerous studies investigating the effects of mergers on shareholder value, and while these results have been mixed overall, merger activity in general tends to add no shareholder value and in some cases destroys it. [8] However, there are certain attributes of an acquiring company that typically result in increased post-merger shareholder value, such as prior experience with mergers and cash payment versus stock. In addition, *during certain periods of merger history, there have been specific merger strategies that have demonstrated more post-merger success than others due to uncharacteristic economic environments or regulatory changes that have created new opportunities in specific industries.*

Finally, it has been shown that *most mergers fail due to three main reasons: inadequate due diligence, poor merger integration, or valuation issues.* Obviously for the acquired company, valuation issues are not important (unless the management plans to hold the exchanges stock for an indefinite period), therefore when private companies assess acquisition proposals, they should focus on those factors that will result in an enhancement of company value. Table 9-3 represents a list of the most common reasons for merger failure for each of these categories.

Table 9-4. Most Common Reasons for Merger Failure

Inadequate Due Diligence	Poor Merger Integration	Valuation Related
Overestimating Synergy	Poor Post-Merger Communication	Overpaying
Poor Assessment of Technology	Slow Pace of Integration	Payment in Stock
Large Size of Target Company	Conflicting Corporate Cultures	
Poor Strategy	Poor Post-Merger Cultures	
Weak Core business		

Note the findings of these studies are valid only when the acquiring company is a publicly traded corporation while the company acquired may or may not be public. The methods of assessing post-merger performance include comparison of industry financial performance versus S&P peer companies and recovery cost of capital within the first few years.

The Acquisition Process

The process of searching, screening, and planning a company's acquisition candidates for inclusion into its corporate strategy is very similar to the process a startup company engages when determining its intended market, goals for market share, competitive factors, and overall production and distribution strategies. The general acquisition process can be divided into ten broad phases, as shown in figure 9-7. The first step for a company is to develop a strategic business plan that incorporates the need for acquisition of additional assets. Next, a plan of acquisition is created. With these two plans, the acquiring company will have a clear idea of the attributes candidates should have and a search is initiated using these general guidelines, followed by a screening process, which seeks to identify the best candidate that fit into the acquirer's overall strategy.

Once the best candidate has been chosen, contact is initiated and an informal proposal is made. If the candidate is open to the acquisition possibility, negotiations commence. During this phase, company information is exchanged so that each party can perform valuation analyses and due diligence. If each has passed the due diligence screen, a financing proposal is created that specifies the deal terms. However, many revisions are usually needed before both companies to reach a compromising agreement. Assuming each company has approved the acquisition, an integration plan is developed for assisting with the integration of all retained personal, operations, and assets of the acquired firm. Then final approval is sought by other controlling parties, such as the shareholders and the S.E.C., and if approved the closing process begins. Upon closing, the integration process commences and is reviewed periodically to ensure maximum transition.

F. Licensing Agreements

We have discussed the financial and strategic benefits of licensing in chapter 7. And although licensing is typically thought of as a growth strategy, it can also it provide a means of return on investment for angels and venture capitalists. If extreme adverse circumstances develop, licensing might represent the only method of revenue generation and therefore the only viable exit strategy available to the investors. In contrast, many research institutions, such as universities choose to license their innovations rather than spend the money and take on the risk of establishing a company. For these institutions, licensing represents a major exit strategy, devoid of substantial business risk and capital infusion.

Regardless of a company's financial and market strength, consideration of licensing agreements is of vital importance when seeking methods to improve a company's long-term financial stability and technology strategy. And venture capitalists can provide tremendous assistance to companies considering licensing due to their previous experience with these arrangements, as well as industry knowledge of royalty rates and other compensation terms.

Figure 9-7. The Ten Phases of the Acquisition Process

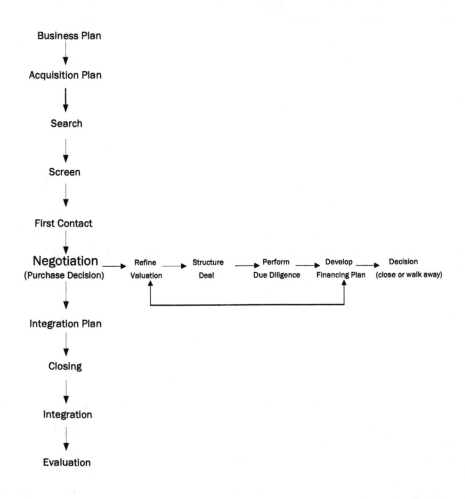

Source: DePamphilis, D.

G. Corporate Restructurings

Restructuring activities can range from mergers, acquisitions, strategic alliances, divestitures, and many other transactions. In our brief discussion of mergers and acquisitions we summarized the motivations for these transactions, reasons for failure, and presented an outline of the basic process. However, we did not discuss the critical topic of restructuring activities that often occurs prior to or after the merger has closed. *Large companies may restructure in order to focus their asset pool prior to a planned acquisition of a smaller company.* For instance, in a *consolidation* merger both companies restructure some of their assets in order to improve the operational and financial efficiency of the newly formed entity.[9] As well, a restructuring might occur only after the acquisition has been made. Finally, *some companies elect to restructure one or more business units in order to improve the overall company efficiency or to decreases operating expenses.*

A *divestiture* is the sale of certain company assets that have either become strategic misfits or low profit generators for the purpose of increasing shareholder value and are the most common activities used to restructure companies. The most common divestiture transactions include sell-offs, spin-offs, split-ups, and satellite launches. A *sell-off* is the most common type of divestiture and occurs when a company sells one or more of its business units to another company. A *spin-off* occurs when a company sells off one or more business units needed to enable it to survive as an independent company. It typically occurs when a division of the parent company is receiving a lower valuation than the division is actually worth. Alternatively, some companies wish to detach divisions that are costly or debt-ridden hoping that the parent company will increase in valuation, (as measured by an increase in EPS) as a result of removal of these liabilities. Thus, *spin-offs are done in order to maximize shareholder value.* Shareholders of the parent company usually receive a pro-rata distribution of stock or dividends from the newly formed spin-off company based upon a conversion ratio that is determined by valuing the spin-off and the parent company separately. Simultaneously, the remaining shares of the new company are distributed through an IPO.

In the case whereby shareholders of the parent company do not receive shares of the spin-off and the newly formed company distributes its shares exclusively through an IPO, it is labeled an *IPO carveout*. The parent company may or may not choose to retain a significant interest in the spin-off. When the parent company does retain an interest it is called a *divestiture IPO*. A *split-up* involves the disassembly of an entire company into two or more smaller companies. Unlike a spin-off, which involves the selling off of one or more business units of the parent company, a split-up involves the complete break up of the company.

Typically, when a venture capital firm selects a *restructuring* transaction for one of its portfolio companies, it is more of a salvaging effort rather than an exit route for return on investment. When a venture capital firm decides to cut its losses in a particular portfolio company, it may decide to engage in an operational restructuring arrangement with a larger company. Essentially, this amounts to selling off assets in attempt to recapture investment principal. For later stage companies, the venture capitalist may choose to engage in a financial restructuring transaction in order to gain more control of the company or to lower the cost of capital by issuing debt in exchange for stock. Alternatively, restructuring activities might be used as a method of increasing the financial appeal of the company prior to solicitation of an acquisition to prospective buyers.

Notes

[1] Unfortunately for the founders and management teams, this lock-up agreement is considerably longer, and while this period can be negotiated in the term sheet financing document, the SEC also has rules pertaining to the sell of these restricted securities, known as SEC Rule 144.

[2] A study in 1995 by Lin and Smith reports that during the period from 1977 to 1990, the shares sold by venture capitalists totaled less then $400 million, which was only about 1% of the total amount of money raised by venture capital funds during that period. This data sample was collected from 77% of the total number of venture-backed IPOs in that period.

[3] Uncorrelated cash flows refer to cash flows due to products or services in different industries or business sectors. The addition of uncorrelated cash flows is thought to decrease the volatility of expected cash flows, thereby creating a more stable source of cash and enables more accurate earnings forecasts, which improves the overall financial health of the company.

[4] Because this example provides no synergy whatsoever, the company would need to weigh the risks of being able to integrate this business into their overall operational strategy versus the potential benefits expected. This difficulty demonstrates the relatively poor success this strategy has had in providing an increase shareholder value, as the expertise required by the management team of the acquiring company is usually insufficient to capture the intended value of the new company. In contrast, it has been shown that *companies that focus in their industry (measured by spin-offs of diverging entities) tend to perform better than their peers.*

[5] However, if a company begins to focus on becoming a price leader, it may miss significant changes in consumer trends and lead to a decrease in market share over a long-term period.

[6] In addition, it is the opinion of the author that most mergers financed by cash or a 50:50 combination of cash/stock seem to fare better than those financed with only stock. This may be due to the failure of proper due diligence, the market's inaccurate valuation of the stock price, or a combination.

[7] For the acquisition target with no earnings, a similar estimation can be made by transforming its revenues into earnings at some point in the future.

[8] When discussing the relative success or failure of these transactions, shareholder value is only measured by the post-merger improvement in earnings-per-share (EPS) versus the premium paid for the acquired assets. Other measures of merger success such as strategic synergy or market expansion are considered only to the extent they contribute to the EPS of the post-merger activity.

[9] A consolidation is usually a more favorable event for the acquired company since the new entity is recognized as a new company, implying that the assets of the acquired company are expected to add tremendous benefit to the new entity. Otherwise, the acquired assets from this company may only be viewed as a primary strategy to provide a moderate level of additional assets or revenue to the company.

10

Terms of Endearment:
Term Sheets & Tactics

"The mistakes are all waiting to be made."
chessmaster Savielly Grogorievitch Tartakower

A. Introduction

Financing a startup with external capital comes with difficult concessions for both the founder and management team. When venture capitalists become involved they will want a substantial ownership stake in the company. And each subsequent round of financing will be dilutive to the original shareholders' ownership, potentially diminishing their rights to manage the company. Because venture capitalists are active investment managers, they will usually require a controlling interest in the company so they can exert strong influence over company actions. Otherwise, they will not agree to invest. Accordingly, an early stage venture capitalist might demand up to a 70% ownership of the company.

Venture capitalists seek to minimize investment risk by negotiating for a certain amount of ownership and control that will enable them to impact major company decisions, such as strategic direction and the hiring and firing of personnel. However, they also have indirect techniques that focus on minimizing investment risk, such as extensive due diligence, portfolio diversification, use investment tranches, and syndicates. Yet none of these methods provides them with the level of company control needed to influence the ultimate fate of the company and protect their investment. *The only tool venture firms have to gain an adequate amount of control over their investment is by the way their preferred stock has been structured. As such, the term sheet serves to establish the blueprint for specifying the rights, restrictions, and conditions of the preferred stock shareholders.*

Hopefully, at some point during the lifetime of your venture, your company will be presented with one or more term sheets by venture capitalists and angel investors. The term sheet is an extremely important document because it is responsible for establishing the desired changes to relevant legal corporate documents governing the company. Therefore, the term sheet serves to create a post-financing risk management tool for venture firms because it specifies the assignment of rights, privileges, and preferences to the class of preferred stock they will receive in exchange for a given round of financing. The goal of this chapter is to familiarize the reader with the basics of term sheets, as well as some important considerations prior to acceptance of such an agreement.

B. Term Sheet Basics

The term sheet outlines the financial and legal terms for investment in a prospective company and serves as an informal letter of intent to purchase shares of company stock.[1] Because most startups begin with complete ownership by the founder, only one class of stock is issued initially, which is typically common stock or (sometimes known as *founder's stock).* And while common stock is also issued to most angel investors, some insist on a convertible preferred. However, when venture capitalists become involved, additional classes of stock must be issued to provide cohesiveness with their limited partnership agreement, specifying guidelines for the amount of capital to be invested in any one round, the time horizon of investment return, and other mandates. Therefore, in the process of constructing a term sheet, a venture firm will include those clauses necessary to maintain consistency within their fund's limited partnership agreement, such as antidilution, liquidity, redemption options, and so forth. In addition, they will also construct specific time-sensitive milestones for the company to achieve in order for installments of committed capital (tranches) to be continued, such as achieving further advances in product development and sales revenue by a specified time period.

Upon mutual agreement by both parties, the term sheet is further used as a template for the final drafting of the required legal documents involved with the issuance of the types of securities and assigned rights to be distributed upon financing. *Consequently, in order for new stock to be issued, alterations must be made to the company's Articles of Incorporation or Company Charter, as well as the Purchase and Sale Agreement.* The relevance of this from the founder's and management's perspective is that certain powers, (which may have been granted prior to venture capital involvement) may now be modified in order to make the investment attractive for the most current investors. *However, all shareholders and directors must approve any changes to the Articles of Incorporation, as well as the Purchase and Sale Agreement, and this can cause difficulties if the original shareholders are not in agreement.*

Figure 10-1. Summary of the Deal Process

---

1. Term sheet created by the venture capital firm

2. Acceptance of the conditions within the term sheet by the company

3. Construction of a modified Articles of Incorporation to reflect the desired preferences by the venture capital firm (subject to approval by the shareholders and directors)

4. Formation of the Purchase and Sale Agreement from the term sheet to reflect the terms of the investment, as well as the changes proposed within the Articles of Incorporation

5. Acceptance of these documents by both parties

6. Company receives the investment capital

Term sheets are used every time financing is sought by a company and such periods are known as *financing rounds.* Typically there are three rounds of financing known as A, B, and C rounds, and sometimes a "bridge" or mezzanine round. And when more than one venture firm is involved in supplying capital in a particular round, the *lead investor* is responsible for creating this document. *It is the lead investor who will be the majority financier during the current round and will therefore set the valuation of the offering.* And because all components of valuation are contained within the term sheet, the lead investor directs its composition. Once the valuation has been set, it will serve as validation for other prospective investors for that round. Meanwhile, rounds of financing subsequent to the current one are usually supported by at least the lead investor who was involved in the subsequent round so that his portion of ownership will not be diluted (right of first refusal). And this will almost always occur unless the company is not performing up to expectations and the prior lead investor feels that either the company will not succeed, too much money will be needed to turn the company into a success, or the investor's money could be put to better use.

If a company is having difficulty raising funds for a round of financing, investors involved with prior rounds may offer the deal at more attractive terms relative to the previous round. This would be considered a *"down round"* of financing since the *price per share offered would be less than that of the previous round.* Therefore the valuation of the company would be lowered on a per-share basis relative to the previous round of financing. Likewise, if the opposite occurs and the demand for investment into the current round is high, the investors will provide financing terms which are not as favorable to investors as the previous round and this is called an *"up round"* of financing, characterized by a price per share and valuation higher than the previous round of financing. Finally, if a term sheet offers the company stock at the same price per share as in the prior round, the deal is designated a *"flat round"*.

There are many different reasons why a round of financing may result in an up, down, or flat round. The most obvious reason would relate directly to the success or lack thereof in the company's ability to achieve its milestones. However, there are indirect effects of company performance that may also result in alterations of future financing rounds. For instance, changes in market and/or economic conditions might alter the relative valuation of the company similar to what occurs with the stock price of publicly traded companies. Furthermore, *if economic conditions are extreme, companies could face a down round although they had achieved all milestones. Finally, a down round could result from the previous round of financing being overvalued, despite the attainment of all milestones.*

Term Sheet Valuation

Valuation of a company may be thought of an estimation of the total value of the company's outstanding stock, and this value is used by the company to determine the percentage of ownership it must sell in order to raise a specific amount of money. Likewise, the company's valuation estimate is also used by the prospective investors to determine what percentage ownership they need to achieve a specific IRR.

When discussing an offering, the investor will be interested in distinguishing between the company's pre-money versus post-money valuation. The *pre-money valuation* is the assessed value of the company prior to the current round of financing and may be calculated by many ways.[2] If the previous round(s) of financing did not involve a venture capitalist then the venture firms who are considering the current financing will determine the current pre-money valuation. For instance, an investor may agree to invest $100,000 for a 10% ownership position in the company. If agreed upon by the founder, this would set the pre-money valuation at $900,000 and the post money valuation will therefore be $1,000,000. *The pre-money valuation is an issue that is very important for the venture capitalist to negotiate because it will strongly influence future valuations of the company.* This is especially true for early rounds of financing, when the ability of venture firms to dictate valuations is much easier.

Company management seeks to maximize the pre-money valuation because higher values will mean they do not have to give up as much ownership of the company for a given amount of capital. In contrast, the venture capitalist seeks to minimize this the pre-money valuation because they will be able to obtain more of the company for a smaller amount of investment capital. Somewhere in between this virtual tug of war lies a reasonable valuation that is negotiated by each party. *Being prepared to justify your valuation goal by the use of meticulous assumptions and detailed analysis is the best way to convince the investor that your valuation is fair.*

The *post-money valuation* is the pre-money valuation plus the current round of financing. Note that *the post-money valuation of the previous financing round is always the starting point for the pre-money valuation of the next round.* And this number will be adjusted based upon the performance of the company during the previous round, as well as current and future economic factors.

Post-money valuation = Pre-money valuation + Investment Amount

Therefore, the pre-money valuation is:

Pre-money valuation = Post-money valuation - Investment Amount

Let us consider a scenario whereby an early stage company is seeking its first institutional round of financing.

Example showing pre- and post-money valuations. SoftSpace Inc. is an early stage business-to-business software provider that is seeking to raise $5 million in a Series A Preferred round. Previously, $400,000 was raised from the founders and angel investors as seed capital. The tangible assets have been valued at $100,000 after depreciation, and the intangible assets have been valued at $10 million by the management based upon the company's financial projections.[a] Therefore, the company feels that its pre-money valuation is $10 million, but neglects to factor in a discount rate that accounts for the risk of generating the future expected cash flows.

Venture firm Z shows interest in the SoftSpace and submits a term sheet, which assesses a $2 million pre-money valuation. SoftSpace Inc. agrees to the terms of the financing and is provided with $5 million of staged installments of $1 million each. Therefore, since the pre-money valuation was set at $2 million and $5 million was invested, the post-money valuation becomes $7 million, and the venture firm receives 71% ($5 million / $7 million) of Softspace Inc.

Two years later, SoftSpace Inc. begins to raise a $10 million round of financing. Because the company reached all of its milestones and the market for the software industry experienced an increase in demand, the pre-money valuation was set (by firm Z) at a 30% premium or a $9 million pre-money valuation, constituting an "up-round". However, SoftSpace was only able to find one potential investor, Venture firm Q. Firm Q asserts that they will only finance this round if the pre-money valuation is set at $6 million. However, this would mean that the company had lost value since the prior financing round. The current round would therefore be termed a down round.[b]

Whether or not SoftSpace would accept this pre-money valuation would depend upon venture firm Z's acceptance since they own the controlling interest in SoftSpace. If firm Z disagrees with firm Q they may wish to finance the current round themselves or find other investors. Thus, *the pre-money negotiation is highly subject to negotiation but becomes less negotiable as the number of financing rounds increases and the number of venture firm involvement increases.*

Notes:

a Because the company currently has no revenues, a certain degree of inaccuracy should be factored into the valuation of the intangibles.

b Although the company achieved all milestones, it was faced with a down round due to the limited supply of investors willing to provide capital.

Terms during a Down Round

No company or prior investor wants to be faced with a *down round*, as it means that the current valuation of the company has declined since the post-money valuation of the previous financing. As mentioned, this could result from the failure of the management to execute effectively or it may be due to changing market conditions. Regardless whether it is a down, flat, or up round, *the most recent preferred stock investor that is leading the deal typically receives liquidation and redemption priority over previous investors.*[3] And in order to secure investment in down rounds, the company and previous investors will need to allow provisions that are very favorable for the new investor, such a higher dividends, board member restructuring, and perhaps even a full-ratchet dilution in extreme cases. Finally, the new investors may call for a new CEO as a condition for investment.

Terms during an Up Round

Achieving an *up round* is the goal of both the company and the prior investors (both common and preferred shareholders), as it reflects the success of the company and represents an increased valuation relative to the previous round of financing. However, if the company receives an increased valuation in an earlier round of financing and subsequently fails to meet its milestones, future rounds of financing can be difficult to obtain. Thus, *companies must make certain that overvaluation does not occur at an early stage of the company*, as it will be that much harder to reach inflated expectations of the new investors.

C. Assessing the Terms

When examining a term sheet, keep in mind that the legal language used can result in situations that favor the investor, company or is neutral. In addition, terms will be indicative of the strength of the economy as well as whether the current round of financing represents a down, flat, or up round. A fictitious example of a "boilerplate" or typical term sheet has been included (figures 10-2 to 10-5) to demonstrate the most common features encountered for early stage companies. Critical phrases throughout the term sheet have been highlighted and should be analyzed for their full impact.

Opening Statement

This portion is generic and often absent, as it meaning is implicit. It serves to summarize the nature of the transaction, that it is non-binding, and includes the name of the company, the amount offered, the number of shares and the investor leading the round (figure 10-2).

Confidentiality Statement

This is also an optional portion and frequently not included, but rather assumed. It has been included in this sample term sheet (figure 10-2).

Amount Raised, Securities Offered, Shares Issued, Purchase Price per Share, and Closing Date

These sections are self-explanatory and describe the class of securities offered, the amount raised, the number of shares, information on the company stock option plan, and the total enterprise value of the company (figure 10-2).

Post-Financing Capitalization

The purpose of this section is to inform the investor what the capitalization structure was before and what it will look like after the current proposed financing. It will list the total number of shares outstanding, the types of stock issued up through the current round, and the number of shares issued for each type of stock. Finally, it will also list all options and warrants, both granted and ungranted. Venture firms are interested in the relative distribution of company stock and options prior to the financing because they want to make sure that too much stock was not given to previous investors since this will affect the valuation. Thus, they are interested in seeing the post-financing distributions because it will allow them to clearly analyze the relative ownership percentages to confirm they are within normally accepted ranges. This section will be included unless a current securities section is provided, because one can easy determine the post-financing capitalization from the current securities and new securities offered sections. From this information, the investor should be able to determine the pre- and post-money valuations.

Capitalization tables are also checked to make certain that the stock ownership percentages (i.e. founder's stock and employee stock options) make sense relative to the round of financing. The company must make certain that it accounts for standard dilution transactions that will occur during each round of financing raised. *In general, companies should expect about a 15 to 20% dilution for each round of financing due to allocation of about 15% for stock options for the executive management team, 1-2% for each board member, and 1% for each advisory board member. This stock may be the only mechanism of providing at least partial dilution protection for the founder and management.*

Figure 10-2. Sample Term Sheet (page 1)

MEMORANDUM OF TERMS FOR

THE PRIVATE PLACEMENT

OF

SERIES A PREFERRED STOCK OF

COMPANY A, INC.

The intent of this document is to describe, for negotiation purposes only, certain principal terms of the proposed Series A Preferred Stock financing of Company A.   This document is not intended to be a binding agreement between the Investors and the Company with respect to the subject matter hereof, except for the paragraph immediately below regarding confidentiality. A binding agreement will not occur unless and until all necessary approvals have been obtained and the parties have negotiated, approved, executed and delivered definitive agreements. Until execution and delivery of such definitive agreements, the company and the Investors shall each have the absolute right to terminate all negotiations for any reason without liability or obligation.

Confidentiality

The terms and conditions of this Term Sheet, including its existence, shall be confidential information and shall not be disclosed to any third party without the consent of the Company and each Investor, except that the Company and the Investors may disclose the terms and conditions described in this Term Sheet including its existence to their respective officers, directors, employees, attorneys and other advisors, provided that such persons agree to the confidentiality restrictions contained herein.

Amount to be Raised: $5,000,000

Type of Security: Series A Preferred Stock

Number of Shares: 5,000,000 shares

Purchase Price: $1.00 per share based on a pre-money valuation of $2,000,000

Closing Date: The initial closing of the sale of the Series A Preferred Stock (the Initial Closing) will be on or before December 7, 2004, subject to a minimum sale of $2,000,000 in Series A shares. Subsequent sales of Series A Preferred Stock may occur within 120 days of the Initial Closing until the maximum of 5,000,000 shares have been sold.

Post-Financing Capitalization:

Class of Securities	Number of Shares	Percent
Founder's Common Stock	10,000,000	50.0%
Additional Common Stock o/s	1,000,000	5.0%
Common Stock Committed	500,000	2.5%
Series A Preferred Stock	5,000,000	25.0%
Option Pool:		
Outstanding	500,000	2.5%
Future Grants	3,000,000	15.0%
Total	20,000,000	100.0%

Dividend Provisions

The dividend section specifies the *rate and priority of dividend payout and serves to provide venture capitalists with a method to protect their investment in the event of a premature liquidation* due to poor performance. Dividends can either be *accrued,* known as *cumulative preferred* or *non-accruing,* referred to as *noncumulative preferred* stock.   If the shareholder has *cumulative dividends,* the company would be required to pay the investor declared dividends from the previous years in which they were not issued, prior to paying out dividends to investors for the current year in which dividends are declared and issued.   In contrast, *noncumulative dividends* mean that while a company votes to declare dividends for a given year, it may not decide to issue dividends in that year.   But following the issuance of dividends in the subsequent year, the company is not responsible for paying dividends from the previous year for which dividends were declared.

Dividend payments can either be mandatory or "when, as and if" declared. Mandatory dividend payments are rarely seen in venture capital financings because they would deplete the company of cash flows, which could create insolvency.   However, *venture investors often use cumulative dividends as a means to minimize downside risk in the case of liquidation* of the company. Typically, if the company is liquidated, the holder of cumulative preferred stock will convert the cash value of accrued dividends into the equivalent value of preferred stock and therefore increase his liquidation ownership percentage.   *In contrast, another alternative is for cumulative dividend provisions on a "when, and as if" basis to be waived only if the company reaches the requirements for a Qualified IPO.*   This is an IPO that has been defined by certain minimum requirements given by the venture firm.   Since the accrual of dividends serves to protect the downside in the event of liquidation, venture capitalists can justify waiving the cumulative dividends upon a Qualified IPO.   From figure 10-3, we can see that the term sheet calls for noncumulative dividends, issued on a "when, as and if" manner, which is favorable to the company.

Liquidation Preference

This clause details the *priority of liquidation* of company assets if the company was to be liquidated due to bankruptcy or poor performance.   It is one of the most important sections to understand and should be carefully examined because it can result in an inequitable share of proceeds for the company in favor of the investors.   *It is customary for the liquidation section to require complete return of the preferred investors' investment prior to returning any capital to the common shareholders.*   It also usually provides for a return on investment by a minimum multiple of usually 1.5 to 2 times the original investment in addition to any declared but unpaid dividends relative to the initial value of the securities offered (figure 10-3).

The following scenario illustrates a possible outcome regarding this clause. In the case of a liquidation event whereby the common stock shareholders have a 50% company ownership and the preferred investors own the other 50%. In addition, note that the preferred stock is a $5 million cumulative preferred offering paying 10% dividends which had been declared but not paid in the past 6 years. Therefore, a $10 million sale of the company could result in the preferred stockholders receiving their principle plus the accrued 10% for each of the 6 years, amounting to {$5 million + [6 x (10% x $5,000,000)]} or $8,000,000. The remaining $2 million would be then paid out to the common and preferred stock shareholders at a 50% distribution. Therefore, the preferred holders would receive $9 million ($8,000,000 + $1,000,000) and the common holders would receive $1million. As you can see, the original 50:50 ownership share resulted in a 90:10 ratio in favor of the preferred shareholders. Although the above example is not uncommon, there are many variations of this clause that can be structured to protect the venture capitalists' investment.

Redemption

This clause is included in order to provide the venture capitalist with alternatives to liquidation by a specific time frame if sufficient liquidity and ROI have not been generated. The redemption clause is very important to the venture capitalist since their funds are set up with limited lifetimes in accord with the investment needs of their limited partners. VCs will stipulate that *if sufficient returns have not been generated by a specific time period, they can redeem some or all of their preferred shares for some multiple of the price paid in addition to any declared but unpaid dividends.*

The time of liquidation will in large part depend upon past the success of the company. However, it will also depend upon the overall performance of the venture fund (in the case of venture capitalists). Understanding this reality can serve to provide more incentive to the management team to achieve better results. When analyzing a term sheet, *the company should specifically study the liquidation, dividend, and redemption sections together* to assess the full impact of the provisions and weigh all potential consequences (figure 10-3).

Conversion

This section states the conditions by which conversion from preferred into common stock is to occur, including the conversion ratio, as well as any conversion restrictions. The *conversion ratio* is a numerical value that is used to convert different classes of preferred stock into common stock and is calculated by dividing the original per-share purchase price by the conversion price. *This clause is included so that venture capitalists are able to participate in an IPO that will provide a higher return than the multiple set forth in the liquidation preference.* Since underwriters usually require all company stock to be of one type, it is a rare instance that IPOs are successful if holders of preferred stock do not convert their shares into common so this clause is included to maximize the success of the IPO. However, the venture capitalist will want to maximize the conversion multiple and the amount of money that will be deemed as a qualified IPO so that when the IPO does occur, it is assured a certain value and the conversion is assured a certain ratio.[4]

Most venture capitalists insist upon both an automatic and voluntary conversion of stock. *Automatic conversion* would occur upon certain events (specified by the venture firms) in order to secure some minimum return. In contrast, *voluntary conversion* allows such the stock conversion to occur at any time the investor chooses, such as during a liquidation. Typically, the *automatic conversion clause is provided to trigger this conversion when an IPO is scheduled.* From figure 10-3, you may notice that the automatic conversion clause states a conversion ratio of 1:1.5 given that the original price of the Series A in this example was $1.00. *Typically, venture capitalist will seek a conversion ratio of three or four times the original purchase price.* Finally, *the conversion price will be adjusted if additional shares are issued and if either up or down rounds occur to adjust for the effects of dilution.*

Antidilution Provisions

These provisions are constructed to address dilution of share price during future rounds of funding. Venture firms want to minimize the possibility of dilution so that future financing rounds do not result in share prices that are cheaper than earlier rounds since this would dilute their ownership percentage. Because some of the most critical issues for VCs are valuation related, dilution provisions are of utmost importance since they can drastically alter the value of their investments, and therefore not only their IRR, but also their abilities to control company decisions through diminished ownership percentage. Therefore, *venture firms always require dilution protection as a requirement for investing in a company.* In small part, this may be served by the Right of First Refusal clause (to be discussed shortly). However, during subsequent down rounds, this clause will not counter the effects of a decreased valuation, so specific antidilution protection mechanisms are needed.

There are two broad categories of antidilution protection. *Mechanical or simple antidilution provides protection against structural changes in common stock such as dividend payments, stock splits and the issuance of additional stock by adjusting the conversion ratio* so that the same proportion of preferred stock can be exchanged for common. Therefore, in the instance whereby a company offers a 2-for-1 stock split, the holder of 1,000,000 shares of common stock will now have 2,000,000 shares. *However, because holders of preferred stock cannot participate in stock splits, the holder of 1,000,000 shares of preferred will not benefit from such a change. Therefore, in order to preserve his proportionate amount, the conversion ratio would have to be changed by a factor of two.*

The other category of anitdilution protection is based on **price** *and provides the investor with protection against dilution resulting from an alteration in valuation or a down round.* If investors do not have protection against lowered valuations, they can be *"smashed" or "crammed down"* (the ownership percentage is diluted so much that it becomes essentially worthless) by investors during new rounds of financing. The basic mechanism underlying a price dilution occurs when *the conversion price is changed, which changes the conversion ratio.* It is rare that the management team receives such antidilution protection since they are directly responsible for achieving these milestones, and therefore ultimately influence whether the next round will be up or down.

There are three general forms of price-based antidilution protection, each with drastically different potential consequences. *The most severe antidilution provision for the company is known as a "full ratchet" clause.* The effects of a "full-ratchet dilution" can be devastating and the management should be very careful to consider its full consequences. **Potentially, the venture capitalist could provide a very generous pre-money valuation only to include a full-ratchet clause.** The company, not knowing the full implications of this a full ratchet could mistakenly think they are receiving a great valuation, when in fact, by the time liquidation occurs they could end up with very little.

Full-Ratchet Antidilution. *A full-ratchet provision lowers the conversion price of a previously agreed upon conversion ratio if a subsequent financing is issued at a lower conversion price,* **regardless of how many of these new lower priced shares have been issued.** For example, assume the founder initially owned all 2,000,000 shares of the common stock and a venture firm decides to invest $1,000,000 into the company in exchange for 1,000,000 shares of convertible preferred stock. The conversion price is set at $1 per share of common for each share of preferred. Therefore, the post money valuation is now $2,000,000 and each party has a 50% ownership. At a later time when the company needs more money, *it is faced with a down round, so the price per share is decreased in order to attract new investors.* Upon agreement by the board to issue an additional round of 50,000 shares of preferred stock at say $0.50 per share, at a conversion of $0.50, *the original venture firm now adapts to this new conversion price for its previous investment* resulting in a doubling of their 1,000,000 shares into 2,000,000 shares of preferred and the founder's ownership position drops from 50% (1,000,000 shares out of 2,000,000 total shares) to 33% (1,000,000 shares out of 3,000,000 total shares).

Thus, it does not matter how many shares of this new round are issued, and even one share issued at the new conversion price of $0.50 will serve to fully dilute all the common shares because the venture firm holding the preferred stock containing the full-ratchet clause receives the new conversion price. Fortunately, the use of "full-ratchet" antidilution is not as common as in the past but when used, it can result in devastating ownership changes for the founders and management. In addition, use of a full-ratchet antidilution can also create a barrier for entry of new investors who may be unwilling to provide such benefit to the previous investor. This type of protection was more common during the Internet Boom, when the average time to IPO was only about two to three years.

Weighted Average Antidilution. *In a weighted average antidilution, **the number of shares issued at the lower conversion price does matter** and the common shares issued prior to this financing are diluted to this new conversion price in proportion to the number of shares issued relative to the original number the founder holds.* Because this mechanism of antidilution provides protection proportionate to the level of investment made by venture capitalist, it is viewed as a more reasonable approach against antidilution. The conversion in a weighted average dilution arrangement can be calculated by the following formula:

$$NCP = OCP \times \frac{SOB + \frac{\{NS \times NSP\}}{OCP}}{SOA}$$

where   NCP = the new conversion price

OCP = the old conversion price

SOB = the number of shares outstanding before the new issuance, on a fully diluted basis (i.e., including all shares of common stock that are issuable on conversion of convertible securities and exercise options)

NS = the number of newly issued shares

NSP = the new share price

SOA = the number of shares outstanding immediately after the new issuance, on a fully diluted basis

Narrow-Based Weighted Average.   Finally, the variation most favorable to companies is *narrow-based weighted average* antidilution protection. This type of protection is *limited to some finite amount of shares*, such as the original number of outstanding shares prior to the new financing. Thus, if new shares were issued at a lower conversion price, holders of common stock from previous financings would only be diluted up to a specific number of shares. Meanwhile, investors with this antidilution protection would receive the new lower conversion price up to the number of shares specified by this finite amount. The effects of a narrow-based antidilution may also be determined by the same formula used above.

Pay-to-Play.   Regardless of the antidilution mechanism used, *pay-to-play provisions require that holders of preferred stock must participate in their pro-rata share during down rounds in order to activate these price-based antidilution mechanisms. However, these provisions are usually advantageous to both the initial venture firm as well as the company.*   For the company, pay-for-play provisions help to commit the venture firm into future rounds of financings. Meanwhile for venture firms, it helps hold the syndicate together by requiring them to commit their pro-rate share towards future financings in order to receive the benefits of these antidilution mechanisms.

   Remember that the **valuation and terms of financing will be influenced to a large extent by both internal factors** (strength of the management, competitive advantage, expected IRR for the investor, overall business proposition, and whether the current financing represents an up or down round) **and external factors** (the economy, the health of the public markets, and the popularity of the company's industry as viewed by institutional demand in the public markets). As such, during down rounds or economic recessions, many venture capitalists will seek to account for the risks associated with these conditions. Finally, it should be noted that *antidilution clauses are sometimes negotiable if the company management team is able to deliver superior performance.   For instance, the management team can set additional milestones, which if fulfilled could be rewarded by additional stock options* (figure 10-3).

Voting Rights
   Since preferred stock is typically not granted with voting rights, this section grants investors voting rights as if they had converted into an equivalent number of Common Shares. This provision is an obvious mandatory requirement for venture investment (figure 10-3).

Protective Provisions

Protective provisions are included to secure certain rights by the investors relative to future rounds of financing, such as the issuance of additional stock, declaration of dividends, alteration of the rights, privileges or preferences of the Series A Preferred, redemption of any shares of Common Stock, any merger, reorganization or any other transaction in which all or substantially all of the assets of the Company are sold or licensed, amendments to the company's bylaws, amendments to the Articles of Incorporation, changes in the size of the board, redemption of employee stock, and other events cannot occur without a some type of shareholder approval. This is also a standard clause not subject to negotiation. *The company should therefore understand the ability and willingness of the venture firm to add additional investors in future financing rounds because only they will decide if additional classes of preferred stock will be issued.*

In addition, protective provisions are *used to require management to seek the approval of the preferred shareholders for certain major decisions and disallow changes in the nature of the company's line of business.* The extent of these provisions will determine the relative favoritism of the investor versus the company. Obviously, it would be in the company's favor to not include provisions allowing the Series A Preferred to vote on changes in the number of the board members, redemption of Common Stock, and amendments to the Articles of Incorporation. These provisions are usually weighted towards favoring the most recent investors so that the most current money invested has controlling protective clauses (figure 10-3).

Information Rights

This clause defines the extent of investor review of company documents on file, audited or non-audited. The management style of the venture firm will dictate how often they request access of company financials and other relevant documents (figure 10-3).

Figure 10-3. Sample Term Sheet (page 2)

Dividends: The holders of Series A Preferred shall be entitled to receive **noncumulative dividends** in preference to the holders of Common Stock at the rate of **8% per annum** from funds legally available of the purchase price per share **when, as and if** declared by the Board of Directors.

Liquidation Preference: In the event of dissolution, liquidation or winding up of the company, all holders of Series A Preferred Stock shall be entitled to receive the amount of **$1.00 per share plus any and all declared and unpaid dividends, if any, in preference to the holders of Common Stock.** Thereafter, the remaining assets of the company shall be distributed ratably to the holders of Common Stock. A sale, conveyance or other disposition of all or substantially all of the assets or business of the company, a merger, consolidation, or any other transaction or series of transactions with or into any other corporation in which shareholders of the company immediately thereafter, other than a consolidation with a wholly-owned subsidiary of the company, a merger effected exclusively to change the domicile of the company, or an equity financing in which the company is the surviving corporation, will be deemed to be a liquidation for purposes of the liquidation preference.

Redemption: At the election of the shareholders of a majority of the Series A Preferred Stock shareholders, the company shall redeem the outstanding Series A Preferred in **two equal annual installments commencing on the fifth anniversary** of the closing. These redemptions shall be at a **purchase price equal to the original purchase price plus any declared but previously unpaid dividends.**

Conversion Privileges:
Voluntary Conversion: Each shareholder of Series A Preferred shall have the right, at the option of the holder at any time, to convert any and all shares of Series A Preferred Stock into shares of Common Stock at an initial **conversion ratio of 1:1, subject to possible adjustments as given below.**

Automatic Conversion: The Series A Preferred shall be automatically converted into Common Stock **at the conversion ratio set forth at the time of conversion,** in the event of the election of the shareholders of a **majority** of the outstanding Preferred Stock at the time of conversion, voting together as a class, or during the closing of an underwritten initial public offering of the company's Common Stock pursuant to a Registration Statement under the Securities Act of 1933, as amended with aggregate proceeds of at least **$40 million at a public offering price of at least $1.50 per share.**

Antidilution Provisions: The conversion price of the Series A Preferred stock will be subject to a proportional adjustment for stock splits, stock dividends, recapitalizations and the like and to adjustments on a **weighted average adjustment** (based on the total number of outstanding shares of both the common and preferred stock) to reduce dilution

Voting Rights: The holder of Series A Preferred will be entitled to that number of votes equal to the number of shares of Common Stock issuable upon the conversion of the Series A Preferred on all matters presented to stockholders.

Protective Provisions: Consent of the holders of a **majority of Preferred Stock** will be required for increases or decreases in the number of authorized shares of Series A Preferred, creation of any new class or series of shares having preference over or being on parity with the Series A Preferred, redemption of shares, declaration or payment of any cash dividend, alteration or changing the rights and preferences of the Series A Preferred, any change in the authorized number of directors, amendments to the Articles of Incorporation or Bylaws of the Company which materially adversely affects the holders of the Series A Preferred, or any transaction in which the control of the company is transferred or the Company is acquired.

Information Rights: So long as an Investor continues to hold shares of Series A Preferred Stock or Common Stock issued upon the conversion of Series A Preferred, the Company shall deliver to the Investor audited annual and **semi-annual** financial statements and will provide a copy of the Company's annual budget within **30 days** prior to the beginning of the fiscal year.   So long as the Investor continues to hold no less then _____ shares of Series A Preferred or Common Stock issued upon conversion of Series A Preferred, the Company shall deliver to the Investor **unaudited monthly** financial statements.   Each Investor shall be entitled to standard inspection and visitation rights of the Company. These provisions shall terminate upon a public offering of the Company's Common Stock or upon acquisition of the Company.

Board Composition

This section would determine the control of the company based upon the number of shares held.   It can be slanted in either way in favor of the founders and management team or the investors depending upon how many board members are permitted for each type of stock (figure 10-4).

Approval Rights

These are special rights which are *granted to the board members* and *enable them the authority to vote* in matters such as new stock issuance, stock options programs, compensation of employees, annual budgets and financial plans, hiring of all company officers, and purchase decisions.   These rights obviously can determine the fate of the company as well as impact the IRR of future investors.   *Although VCs negotiate for approval rights themselves, they will request waivers of these rights by previous investors who may have been given these rights.*   This can result in a power struggle that will be won by the VC who has demonstrated its ability to provide a large amount of value to the company it looks to represent (figure 10-4).

Special Board Approval Items

These are included to provide board members with control over additional matters of the company and should be carefully considered (figure 10-4).

Right of First Refusal

The right of first refusal defines the extent investors have to control the sale of securities and *provides them with an option to purchase additional shares when the company seeks further rounds of financing so that their proportionate control is not diminished.*   Earlier we discussed several antidilution mechanisms that serve to protect venture firms from declining valuations due to down rounds.   But dilution can also occur when the round is flat or sometimes even when it is up unless the previous investors are given the chance to buy a sufficient number of shares from the new financing round that will preserve their original ownership proportion.   Thus, First Rights of Refusal is a standard non-negotiable clause that only provides a minimal level of antidilution protection for the investor.   Many times, angel investors will also require this clause and when venture firms become in involved, and any reluctance by angels to forfeit their right of first refusal could hinder the willingness of venture firms to provide financing.   Therefore, the company should make certain that a prospective angel investor understands that any right of first refusal granted to him will only apply to future financings of other angel investors and the company may want to add this stipulation in the angel's term sheet (figure 10-4).

Registration Rights

These rights are important for investors when they hold a minority position and will therefore have insufficient say in forcing the company to go public. For whatever reasons, the majority shareholders may not wish to go public, at least in a timely manner. Therefore, *these rights force the company to register their shares with the SEC for a public offering when exercised.* There are two basic registration rights that are frequently encountered; demand rights and piggy back rights. *Demand rights* are important for the venture firm to ensure liquidity through an IPO and require the company to file a public offering (register shares with the SEC) when exercised, usually after a certain time has elapsed to provide it the chance to mature.

Companies should attempt to limit the number, dollar amount, and extent the timing of demand rights. *Piggyback rights* allow investors to offer their shares along with those of the company in subsequent public offerings. These rights also specify the transferability, termination of rights, and provisions for lock-up agreements. Typically, investors will include a transfer clause but this is optional. The *termination of rights* clause is favorable for the company. Finally, the period of stock *lockup* is designated in order to restrict the liquidation or transfer of shares of the securities relative to the date of registration. Companies should not underestimate the high expenses involved with registration rights and should negotiate these costs with the investors (figure 10-4).

Figure 10-4. Sample Term Sheet (page 3)

Board Composition: The size of the Company's Board of Directors shall be set at **five**. The board shall initially be composed of (name 1), (name 2), (name 3), (name 4) and (name 5). Board of Directors will be elected annually and Board of Directors meetings shall be held no less then four times per year. The holders of the **Series A Preferred voting as a separate class, shall be entitled to elect two members** of the Company's Board of Directors, **the holders of the Common Stock shall be entitled to elect two members**, and the **fifth member shall be mutually agreed upon** by the holders of the Series A Preferred and the Common Stock.

Special Board Approval Items: The consent of the majority of Board of Directors will be required for the following items:

(1) Hiring of all officers of the Company
(2) All employment agreements
(3) All Compensation programs including base salaries and bonus programs for all officers, key employees, and contract workers such as consultants and attorneys.
(4) All stock options programs as well as the issuance of stock and stock options
(5) All annual budgets, financial and business plans
(6) All real estate leases or purchases
(7) Other purchases or leases such as equipment, having a total value that is greater then ($____) and that are not within the most recent budget, business or financial plan approved by the Board of Directors

Right of First Refusal: The right of first refusal will be assigned to shareholders of at **least _____ percent of the shares of Series A Preferred Stock originally issued**, in the event the Company proposes to offer equity securities to any person (other than securities issued in accordance to employee benefit plans or pursuant to an acquisition). **These shareholders shall be entitled to purchase their pro rata portion of such shares before the Company makes any equity securities available to any other person.** This right of first refusal shall terminate upon a Qualified IPO.

Registration Rights:

Demand Registration: Beginning on January 5, 2004 or 180 days after the Company's Initial Public Offering, which ever occurs first, **investors holding no less than 30%** of the Series A Preferred Stock may demand that the Company file a Registration Statement for at least $8,000,000, upon initiation of holders of a majority of the outstanding Registrable Securities. The Company will not be required to effect more than **two registrations** under these demand registrations and will not be required to effect a registration during the **180 day period** beginning on the date of the Company's initial public offering or if it delivers notice to the shareholders of the Registrable Securities within 30 days of any registration request of its intent to file a registration statement for a Qualified IPO **within 90 days**.

Piggyback Registration: Holders of Series A Preferred Stock will have **unlimited piggyback registration rights**, subject to a pro rata reduction in the number of such shares proposed for the registration of **no less than 20%** of the total number of shares to be offered in any offering subsequent to the Company's initial public offering at the discretion of the underwriters.

Form S-3 Rights: Holders of **no less than 25% of the Series A Preferred Stock** shall have the right to require the Company to register on Form S-3, if the Company is able to utilize such form (i) shares of Registrable Securities for an aggregate offering price of no less than $1,000,000 (ii) the Company shall **not be obligated to effect more than one S-3 registration in any six-month period.**

Registration Expenses: Registration expenses (exclusive of underwriting discounts and commissions, stock transfer taxes and legal fees to counsel to the selling shareholders) will be borne by the Company for all demand, piggyback and S-3 registrations.

Transfer of Rights: Registration rights may be transferred to any family member or trust for the benefit of any individual holder or any transferee who acquires **at least one-third of the shares** of Registrable Securities originally issued, provided the Company has been given prior written notice.

Termination of Rights: The registration obligations of the Company will expire (i) beginning in the fourth year after the initial public offering (ii) upon Acquisition of the Company, which ever occurs first.

Lock-up Provision: In connection with the IPO, each shareholder of registration rights will be denied the right to sell or otherwise dispose of any securities of the Company for a period of **180 days following the effective date of the registration statement.**

Conditions Precedent

This discusses the final conditions necessary for the financing transaction to be completed, such as the due diligence by the investors, mutual agreement of the purchase and sale agreement by both parties, and other formalities.

Purchase Agreement

The purchase agreement must be signed by the investors before they can purchase company stock, and this item outlines the topics that will be included in its construction (figure 10-5).

Employee Matters

The most important portions of this section are the *Reserve Shares* and the *Vesting*. *Reserve shares* are used for further compensation of management when performing at or above expectations. Thus the use of reserve shares serves to maintain a high incentive for future performance and acts as their only means to minimize dilution that will occur in later rounds. Investors will also require all employee shares to be vested in order to keep them tied into the company for a certain period of time. This is a standard requirement (although vesting schedules can vary) and ensures that key employees will have an incentive to remain with the company. In addition, founders will also be required to subject their stock to vesting (figure 10-5).

Legal Counsel

This section specifies under what conditions the company will be responsible for legal fees involved in the financing (figure 10-5).

Expenses and Finder's Fees

This section discusses the treatment of any finder's fees in conjunction with the financing arrangement (figure 10-5).

Figure 10-5. Sample Term Sheet (page 4)

Conditions Precedent: This proposal is non-binding and is subject to:

(1) Completed due diligence reviews satisfactory to the Investor and Investor's counsel.

(2) Customary stock purchase, stock options plan, and related agreements satisfactory to the Investor and the Investor's counsel.

(3) Intellectual property, confidentiality, and non-compete agreements with all key employees of the Company satisfactory to the Investor's counsel.

(4) Satisfactory review of all compensation programs, stock allocation, and vesting schedules for all officers, key employees and others, as well as any existing employment or similar agreements.

(5) Both the Company and the Investor shall negotiate exclusively and in good faith toward an investment as outlined herein and agree to **"no-shop" provisions for a period of** _____.

Purchase Agreement: The purchase of the Series A Preferred will be made pursuant to a Stock Purchase Agreement and Shareholders Agreement drafted by the counsel of the Company reasonably acceptable to the Company and the Investors. The Stock Purchase Agreement shall contain, among other things, appropriate representations and warranties of the Company, covenants of the Company reflecting the provisions set forth herein and appropriate conditions to closing which will include, among other things, qualification by the counsel of the Company of the shares to be sold under applicable Blue Sky laws, and the filing of Amended and Restated Certificate of Incorporation. The Purchase Agreement shall provide that it may only be amended and any waivers thereunder shall only be made by the approval of the majority of the holders of the Series A Preferred. Registration rights provisions may be amended or waived solely with the consent of the holders of the majority of Registerable Securities.

Employee Matters:

Reserved Employee Shares: The Company has **reserved** _____ **shares of Common Stock** for issuance to key employees. These shares will be issued under such arrangements, contracts, or plans as are recommended by management and subject to approval by the Board of Directors. **All such shares will be subject to vesting restrictions.**

Stock Vesting Schedule: All stock and stock equivalents issued after the Closing to employees, directors, consultants and other service providers shall be subject to the following vesting schedule: **20 percent will vest at the end of the first year following issuance, with the remaining 80 percent to vest monthly in equal installments over the subsequent four years.** Upon termination of employment of the shareholder, with or without cause, the Company retains the option to repurchase at cost any unvested shares held by the shareholder.

Restrictions on Sales: The Company shall have **a right of first refusal** on all transfers of Common Stock, subject to normal exceptions.

Confidential Information and Invention Agreement: Each officer, director, and key employee of the Company and each person serving in any such capacity in the future shall enter into the Company's standard Employee Confidential Information and Inventions Agreements.

Co-Sale Agreement: The shares of the Company's securities held by the Founders of the Company _____ shall be made subject to a co-sale agreement with the shareholders of Series A Preferred such that each shareholder of Series A Preferred has the opportunity to participate in the sale, transfer or exchange of their stock on a pro rata basis prior to any offering to other parties. This right shall terminate immediately prior to a Qualified IPO or Acquisition of the Company.

Key-Man Insurance: Within a reasonable period after the Closing of financing, the Company shall submit all required qualifications for securing a key-man life insurance policy for _____ in the amount of $1,000,000 naming the Company as beneficiary.

Management: The Company will, on a best efforts basis and subject to **majority** approval by the Board of Directors, hire a chief _____ officer within 180 days following the closing of the financing.

Legal Counsel, Expenses, and Finders:

Legal Counsel: The Company shall select legal counsel subject to the approval of the Investor. The Investor's counsel shall draft all financing documents for review by Company counsel unless agreed otherwise.

Expenses: The Company and the Investors shall each be responsible for their own legal fees and expenses pursuant to the transaction.

Finders: The Company and the Investors shall each indemnify the other for any finder's fees for which either is subject to.

D. Tactics

Through examination of this model term sheet, we have seen that a carefully structured preferred stock series can be a powerful investment tool for the venture firm, which when designed with full severity, can result in a loss of both significant ownership and control of the company for the management. Obviously, some of the provisions in a term sheet demand special attention and should be analyzed in conjunction due to their potential consequences, such as dividend, liquidation, redemption, conversion, and antidilution. In contrast, many of the remaining provisions, such as voting, protective, and approval items by themselves do not seem to be attached with potentially adverse consequences. However, when combined with other clauses and performance scenarios, they could become much more significant. Therefore, in order to understand the full impact of all potential consequences, the company should construct an extensive scenario analysis detailing the possible effects of adverse events prior to signing the terms of financing.

When attempting to negotiate the terms of a financing deal with venture firms, *you must understand what clauses are open to negotiation and which ones are not.* There will be some variance depending on the venture firm, the stage of financing, the company's position, and other factors but in general, *venture firms will not negotiate liquidation or redemption clauses,* due to the fiduciary responsibility to their limited partners.

Finally, throughout the entire negotiation process, founders must be on their best behavior and keep their egos in check when dealing with venture firms. The last thing you want to do is give venture associates an indication that you will be demanding and difficult to work with, as they would rather pass on a promising company with a difficult team, than subject themselves to potential headaches and frictional relationships. And if you think your company is the greatest in the world that is perfectly fine. But do not expect venture capitalists to share this idea because as far as they may be concerned you don't really have a company yet. All you may have is some promising technology and a few customers. What they see in your company is potential, as reflected by your business concept and strength of management. And you can bet that they have been involved with better companies and management teams in the past. So maintain your level of confidence and optimism, but don't let this turn into belligerence, antagonism, or disillusion when trying to negotiate with VCs. You need to convince yourself that you absolutely need venture capital assistance beyond their financial capital. Like all inexperienced entrepreneurs, you will need their human capital most of all. And if you are not able to convince yourself of this reality then you're probably not going to be successful raising capital from VCs.

Dealing With Exclusivity

If the term sheet presented to your company has no *exclusivity clause* (see "no-shop" provisions under the conditions precedent, figure 10-5), you have no legal responsibility to cease soliciting other prospective investors. However, there is a certain code of ethics and respect implied within a term sheet negotiation and companies should assume exclusivity exists even if there is no specific mention of such a requirement.   Remember, venture capitalists invest a great deal of time and effort towards the construction of a term sheet.   And this process has consumed several hours in the form of personal meetings and interviews, and other tasks involved in their due diligence process.   So you need to develop an appreciation and respect for their efforts in this regard.   In addition, by "*shopping your deal*" during the negotiation process, you will raise questions about your integrity and cast doubts upon your company's management team.   Nevertheless, even if you plan to shop your deal to other investors inform the venture firm you are working with, but never go behind their back and try to get more stew in the pot.   That would represent you as dishonest and if they cannot trust you they will not invest their money in your company.

Therefore, when dealing with a term sheet that has no such restrictions, the recommended approach is to inform the prospective investors that while you have had interest by other VCs, you respect their commitment and promptness in their actions and will therefore voluntarily end all other negotiations with investors until having adequately assessed the term sheet. In addition, you may want to inform the other prospective investors of your success in receiving a term sheet, taking care not to disclose the terms or the prospective investor, and that your company has voluntarily suspended all other negotiations, unless such firms are willing to provide term sheets as well. Inform these other investors that your company has specific requirements it seeks from a potential investment partner, and if these guidelines are deficient or absent from the current term sheet, you would be appreciative if they accepted your offer to continue negotiations.

This approach demonstrates your integrity, while preserving the ethical and professional business relationship established with the current VC. First, it signals to all firms involved your acknowledgement and responsibility with respect to the venture firm that has offered the term sheet.   It also indicates to all firms that your company operates in a professional business manner and understands the ethics involved with such an arrangement.   Finally, it lets all investors know that your company has currently established a serious investment interest, yet is focused on securing the best overall investment proposal from the most qualified VC, rather than accepting the first money it is offered.

Closing the Deal

Once you have been offered a term sheet and carefully reviewed it with your attorney and any financial professionals on the advisory board, the last step is agreement of the terms set forth by the prospective financing entity. The first major issue that may be a source of disagreement is the valuation. In general, venture capitalists tend to be somewhat flexible in negotiating major financing terms such as valuation, but this depends in large part on market conditions. In addition, if other investors have approached your company you may have some leverage in determining the final value.

Prior to final acceptance of the term sheet, companies should also determine the ultimate level of commitment of the venture firm by asking what preferences they have for future rounds of financing. Some VCs may not want a company to open another round of financing or increase the current round because they may wish to retain the same level of ownership and control. Likewise, some VCs may feel that further financing at the current time is inappropriate and would only serve to decrease their IRR.

Understand as well that *valuation can be altered in ways that could be unapparent to the company through the use of many clauses in the term sheet*, as we have seen in this chapter. However, keep in mind that the initial pre-venture capital funding valuation is not nearly as important as the ultimate valuation of the company, which will be strongly influenced by the guidance and advice the venture firm provides. *Therefore, when addressing valuation concerns, the most important consideration should be the quality and resources the venture firm has that can help add value to the company down the road, and thus help maximize the final exit valuation.*

Finally, note that getting funded is not automatic once the terms have been agreed upon because venture capitalists will continue the due diligence process to ensure their complete satisfaction. As a matter of fact, *some VCs will not conduct the most intensive portion of the due diligence process until after both parties have accepted the terms.* This is especially true during economic periods where valuation is the key determinant and major barrier for obtaining venture financing. In such cases, venture firms prefer to resolve the more difficult issue of valuation prior to committing the intense time and effort involved in an extensive due diligence process.

Figure 10-6. Summary of Important Provisions in a Term Sheet

1) **Dividend Provisions:** specifies rate and priority of dividend payout

   a) **Cumulative Preferred** shareholders are issued dividends from previous years when they were declared by not issued in those years prior to payment of current dividends to noncumulative shareholders.

      i) **Mandatory** payment of dividends means that cumulative dividends will be paid without conversion to stock

      ii) **When, as and if** dividend payment means that accrued dividends or conversion to stock will be waived if the company reaches a Qualified IPO.

   b) **Noncumulative Preferred** shareholders are not eligible to receive declared but unissued dividends from previous years.

2) **Liquidation Preference:** specifies the conditions and priority of liquidation of company assets. Usually, investors will require that the complete principal is returned in addition to some multiple of the original investment prior to any proceeds to common shareholders.

3) **Redemption Provisions:** specifies under what conditions, how much, and over what time frame shareholders of preferred stock can redeem their shares. Redemptions usually occur with some multiple of the original investment in addition to any unpaid dividends

4) **Conversion Rights:** allows for conversion of preferred into common stock and specifies a conversion ration by which this will take place

   a) **Automatic Conversion:** triggered by the occurrence of specific events, such as an IPO

   b) **Voluntary Conversion:** allows the preferred shareholder to convert his shares into common stock at any time he chooses. Needed during a liquidation event, especially when the shareholder has cumulative preferred stock that will have dividends to be converted into common stock

4) **Anidilution Provisions:** provides dilution protection for the investor as long as he participates in his pro-rata share during down rounds (Pay-to-play)

   a) **Full Ratchet:** lowers the conversion price of a previously agreed upon conversion ratio if a subsequent financing is issued at a lower conversion price regardless of how many shares of the new shares are issued.

   b) **Weighted Average:** lowers the conversion price of a previously agreed upon conversion ratio if a subsequent financing is issued at a lower conversion price in proportion to how many shares of the new shares are issued.

   c) **Narrow-Based Weighted Average:** lowers the conversion price of a previously agreed upon conversion ratio if a subsequent financing is issued at a lower conversion limited to a finite amount of previously issued shares.

5) **Registration Rights:** specifies the conditions and requirements for registration of securities, including lockup periods, transfer and termination of these rights.

6) **Employee Matters:** specifies the amount and conditions by which employees will be granted reserves shares, as well as the vesting schedule of these shares

Notes

[1] Although the term sheet can be considered a letter of intent, it is typically not legally binding, unless it contains a statement which makes this statement, which is rarely encountered.

[2] The initial pre-money valuation is associated with the most subjectivity since the company has minimal assets and revenues, and a minimal operational history.

[3] The exception is when the previous investors have been issued secured debt, which always receives a higher liquidation priority than stock.

[4] The minimum IPO proceeds will typically be at least $40-$60 million in order to be considered a Qualified IPO. This numerical range is chosen to ensure that the venture capitalist receives a minimum return.

11

Setting Valuation:
Supply and Demand, Risk and Reward, Leverage and Control

"Argue for your limitations, and sure enough they're yours."
Richard Bach

A. Understanding Valuation

Sophisticated investors are concerned with the valuation process because it serves as a measure of the future earnings potential of the assets under consideration, and will therefore influence the expected return on investment. Unfortunately there are numerous valuation methods, whose ultimate selection will depend upon the reason for the valuation, the revenue potential of the assets, the type of assets under consideration, and the investor's opinion as to the most appropriate method.

We will now consider a simple example to illustrate some of these concepts. As we learned in chapter 5, assets can be classified as tangible or intangible. Obviously, a tangible asset such as a 2005 Honda Accord is somewhat easy to value since prices may be found in either the Blue or Black Book, depending on whether you are a dealer or consumer. Nevertheless, this valuation exercise is relatively simple in this case because there is an active and stable market for these cars due to the balanced supply-demand ratio. That is, the manufacturer only produces a few more cars than the demand preventing an inventory buildup and subsequent decline in price in order to move the inventory. Therefore, a predictable price range for this automobile exists, as the manufacturer is able to neutralize the effects of changing demand by altering the supply. It follows that because the market for these automobiles is active and the prices are relatively stable, this asset can be considered a somewhat liquid *commodity*.[1]

Let's now consider a 1959 Corvette. In this case, although it is still a tangible asset, it is also considered a *collectible* so it will have an intangible element associated with its valuation and pricing.[2] And since this vehicle is out of production, the manufacturer cannot alter the supply within the marketplace. In addition, there are no dealers with large inventories that could help control the supply of these vehicles within the marketplace, unlike the situation for newer Corvettes or the Accord. Thus, the market demand will be the only variable controlling the price, as the prospective buyer will not only consider the current value of the car, but may also estimate its future appreciation potential due to the intangible value of collectors' appeal. Because of this potential market price volatility, the 1959 Corvette is therefore more difficult to value and is considered less liquid than the new Accord due to the supply-demand discrepancy. *Therefore, the dominant factor involved in assessing a value for this car is the disparity between the supply and demand within the collector's market, which will potentially result in large price fluctuations* over a five-year or longer period.

Likewise, for early stage companies that anticipate high growth, valuation methods attempt to determine the future earnings potential of their assets rather than the current value because the majority of these assets are intangible and therefore have not realized their full potential value. In addition, *supply-demand forces will also affect the valuation of the company.* If it is innovative and has few competitors, the demand for investment in this company will typically be high, (assuming the risk is reasonable) resulting in a high valuation. However, as competitors enter the market, investors will have more alternatives and the price for the company will decrease accordingly. Therefore, this company will also potentially experience price volatility over a longer period of time and such an investment would therefore be considered illiquid. *Valuation measurements that take into account the supply-demand forces of the marketplace,* such as in the examples above are called *market valuation approaches* and can be applied to any asset type because the valuation is closely tied to the price investors are willing to pay for the assets.

However, there are other valuation methods that do not rely primarily on market approaches, such as *asset-based methods.* An asset may be defined as any resource that can potentially either generate future positive cash inflows or reduce future cash outflows. As we have seen, all companies have some combination of both tangible and intangible assets responsible for the nature of their financial capabilities. Tangible assets of a company could be plant facilities and lab equipment, any vehicles or real estate it owns, and any other physical property owned by the company. Meanwhile, its intangible assets might include trade secrets, patents, licenses, goodwill, and even key employees, such as the individuals directly responsible for the technology development, marketing, customer service, and operations.

The first step towards determining the valuation of a company using an asset-based approach is to categorize the types of assets and liabilities on the balance sheet, followed by individual valuation of these assets. While tangible assets can be valued with some degree of accuracy, *the traditional method for valuing intangible assets with the asset-based approach uses replacement cost, which does not account for the revenue generating potential of these assets,* and is thus very inaccurate. Hence, this is where the utility of this approach ends and the value of intangible assets must be determined using other methods. For some intangible assets, such as intellectual property, we have seen there are a variety of valuation methods that may be used (eg. DCF and real options methods). However, if the full capacity of revenues has not been realized, valuation of these assets will rely more heavily on market approaches. *Therefore, because of this limitation on intangible asset valuations, asset-based methods are best used for businesses with minimal intangible assets.*

B. Valuation Methods

There are many methods that can be used to value companies, but they will all be influenced to variable degrees on supply and demand or market factors. Hence, all components contributing to company valuation are based upon the willingness of investors to acquire a portion of ownership (demand) relative to the availability of other investment alternatives (supply). *Even approaches that do not use market factors, such as the discounted cash flow method will still be influenced by supply and demand based upon the assumptions underlying these calculations.* It follows that when the demand is large relative to the supply, the assumptions used for the discounted cash flow model may produce a higher valuation numbers and vice-versa.

Regardless of the method, valuation of companies may be considered either an art or a science, with most companies fitting somewhere in between. And in general, *the earlier stage a company is, the more subjective the valuation determination.* Likewise, more established companies are typically associated with more objective valuation approaches since they have more fully realized the value of their assets. In an effort to provide the reader with a more comprehensive understanding of valuation, I will provide an overview of the four traditional methods used to value individual assets and companies so that they can be better prepared to adapt to any future changes in venture capital valuation methods.

Discounted Cash Flow Approach

Throughout this book, we have seen that the DCF method in one form or another has been used for many different valuation determinations, and with good reason.   *Because valuation is theoretically a predictor of future earnings, and cash flows are roughly correlated with earnings, many hold the view that the best method to determine the value of an asset is by using its cash flows.* (You may also recall from chapter 8 that cash flow ratios are the best predictor of liquidity for early stage companies).   In the DCF method, assets of a company are valued based upon the present value of expected future cash flows of those assets.   The calculations are determined by developing cash flow projections over a multiyear period then applying a *risk-adjusted rate*, called the *discount rate* to these cash flow projections. Implicit in the best use of this model is a thorough understanding of the company's business, its market, and past operations.   Take note that the assets of a company and price-earnings ratios are ignored in this method.

The critical step in this valuation method is an accurate estimation of the risk-adjusted discount rate, which is determined by assessing the amount of risk in generating the future cash flows. The discount rate is really the *default risk*, or the risk that the security will default on its return of these expected future cash flows.   For example, the discount rate, or amount of risk when applying the DCF approach to a U.S. Government (default-free) zero-coupon bond would be 0, because the future cash flow would be guaranteed.   On the other hand, corporate bonds have a default risk based upon the financial strength of the company.[3]   And since the cash flows in corporate bonds take the form of a coupon rate (or payable dividends), one would estimate the value of this bond by discounting the cash flows (or coupon rate) at an interest rate that reflects the default risk.   When estimations of future cash flows are accurate and the appropriate discount rate has been applied to these assets, the DCF approach should yield an asset's *intrinsic value*.   The six basic steps to determine the value of a business using the discounted cash flow method are:

1.   Estimate debt-free projections of the company's future operations.

2.   Determine the net positive or negative cash flow in each year of company financial projections.   In the case where a company has debt, interest charges are not factored into the projections prior to determining the cash flows.

3.   Approximate a cash flow value for the last year of projections.   This is called the *terminal value* and is a very important estimate that will greatly influence the final valuation.

4. Determine the discount rate to be applied to the cash flows. This rate should be indicative of the amount of business and investment risk involved. *A large discount rate will result in a lower valuation indicating that there is a large risk associated with generating the expected cash flows.* Often, discount rates are determined using two extremes, the cost of borrowing and the cost of equity investment. For instance, if the cost of borrowing is 4 points plus the prime and the equity investors want 40% return for their investment, the discount rate is chosen to reflect the risk of business failure. [4]

5. Apply the discount rate to the cash flows (surplus and deficit) each year and to the terminal value. These values will estimate the present value of the future cash flows. Then add these values.

6. Subtract all debt (long-term and short-term) from the present value of future cash flows to get a value of the company.

While the DCF method works well with companies having positive cash flows, it becomes less accurate as cash flows become less predictable, cyclically negative, when companies are distressed, for assets that are underutilized, companies involved in restructuring, undergoing acquisition, or for private companies. *When cash flows become less predictable, the discount rate is larger to reflect this uncertainty and larger discount rates are associated with lower degrees of accuracy with this method.* Meanwhile, cyclical companies may have periods of negative earnings and cash flows that may not truly reflect their true value. For these companies, the business dynamics of the industry are more the problem than the internal fundamentals of the company. Therefore, in determining the discounted cash flow for cyclical companies, the most important estimates are when the business cycle will reach its peaks and troughs. In contrast, distressed companies have more internal issues that can result in negative cash flows and because these companies face a good possibility of bankruptcy, it is extremely difficult to determine whether they will ever have any positive cash flows.

Calculating a present value for companies with negative cash flows, by necessity, results in a negative equity valuation for the company. Therefore, the DCF method must be modified when used to value such companies. Nevertheless, many subjective assumptions and estimations must be made. In addition, companies with underutilized assets such as intellectual property may not be receiving a fair valuation since these assets either produce an underutilized cash flow or none at all. Obviously, for companies in the midst of an acquisition, discounted future cash flows are difficult to assess due to the inability to determine the level of synergy that would result from the integration with the partnering company.

Finally, when attempting to use the DCF approach for early stage companies, the measurement of the discount rate is theoretically not feasible due to the various uncertainties involved with these estimations. Nevertheless, many *venture firms estimate discount rates based upon the stage and industry of the company and make adjustments for more specific factors.* There are however, some early stage companies that can be valued using the discounted cash flow approach legitimately if they have a history of predictable cash flows. And while this approach has many limitations when applied to newer companies, it nevertheless remains significant in the overall process of determining valuation based on other methods.

Relative Valuation (Market) Approach

Unlike the DCF approach, which seeks to value assets by determining their intrinsic value, the relative valuation approach is completely influenced by market demand. When comparing these two methods, it may be easier to think of the DCF approach as a way to estimate the present value of future expected rental payments over a specified period. In contrast, the relative valuation method would look at the real estate market and compare similar property values in order to determine the sales price of the house.

In the relative valuation method, *the value of an asset is estimated based upon comparisons of variables with those of similar assets.* Most often, these variables are earnings, revenues, cash flows, book values, P/E and price-to-earnings growth (PEG) ratios, price to book, price to sales, and price to cash flows. There are typically two methods to determine the appropriate multiples; however the most commonly used is the *comparative method,* whereby the multiples of comparable companies are used to estimate the most realistic situation of the company being valued. *The key to this approach is the accurate determination of what constitutes a comparable company.* Unlike the DCF model, *the comparative method is especially useful for companies that have negative cash flows and cannot be accurately valued using the DCF method.* In this case, metrics such as revenues would be selected to determine the value based upon a comparable company.

Although a comparable company can be thought of as one with similar cash flows, growth rates, and risk characteristics similar to the company under consideration, one must be careful to include companies in the same types of business, since they will share similar business dynamics and therefore more accurately reflect any interdependencies of risk, growth characteristics, and cash flow patterns. In addition, one should be aware of the relative size and maturity of the comparable companies being used and the appropriate changes made for those companies that have inherently lower risk and/or growth rates due to their maturity and/or size. Estimations of these disparities may be obtained by a relative comparison of the product life cycle curves for each company. Finally, in order to ensure that companies are comparable, they should use the same accounting methods. There are three basic rules to adhere to when using the relative comparison approach:

1. Define the multiple consistently and measure it uniformly for all companies being considered.

2. Understand how these multiples vary so that you can identify under- or overvaluation within the industry you are considering relative to the overall market.

3. Identify the most closely comparable companies and modify the numbers using a discount or premium rate to account for differences between comparing companies.

While this method is relatively easy to apply, it should be apparent to the reader that several potential inaccuracies may develop. If the sector for which the company being valued has been under or overvalued, a similar level of under or overvaluation will be determined for the target company. And because each company has unique characteristics, the reliance on the comparative method could be severely flawed if the closest company is not identified for comparison. Finally, *valuation results based upon this method can change dramatically with changes in the market, which may not reflect an accurate valuation.* Nevertheless, when diligently performed, *the relative valuation method is perhaps the best valuation technique used to value assets expected to be sold in the near future since it relies on supply and demand, which ultimately determines pricing.*

Contingent Claims Approach

This method uses the *options pricing model* to measure the value of assets that share characteristics with their underlying options. The basis for this valuation approach is derived from the *Black-Scholes Option-Pricing Model* that was discussed in chapter 7. Recall from that discussion that a call option is a contract that gives the owner the right to buy company stock at a specific price by a specific expiration date. The formula for valuing a call option is:

$$C = SN(d_1) - Ee_f^{-R,xt}N(d_2),$$

where $\qquad$ C = theoretical call option value

$$d_1 = \ln(S/E) + [R_f + (1/2)\sigma^2]t \,/\, \sigma\,(t)^{-2}$$

$$d_2 = d_1 - \sigma\,(t)^{-2}$$

S = stock price or underlying asset price

E = exercise price

R_f = risk-free rate of interest

σ^2 = variance of the stock's or underlying asset's returns

T = time to expiration of the option

$N(d_1)$ and $N(d_2)$ = cumulative normal probability values of d_1 and d_2

This method does not work well with assets that are not publicly traded on an exchange, due to the uncertainties in estimating projected cash flows. However, for revenue generating assets, it can be an excellent method for valuation.

Asset-Based Valuation Approach

As discussed earlier, this approach values individual assets owned by a company and combines them to obtain a complete valuation. There are several variants of this approach such as liquidation value (the present value of assets based upon their sale) and replacement cost (the present cost necessary to replace the assets). Liquidation value becomes important when companies are distressed and face the possibility of bankruptcy. These methods estimate the current market value of the company equity by determining the cost/sale of replacing/from liquidation the company's assets at current market prices minus the present value of its liabilities. *The drawback of this approach is that in valuing assets separately, it does not account for the value of use of these assets in combination.* In addition, as discussed earlier, the asset-based method does not provide a way to value intangible assets appropriately. Thus, it is an especially poor technique to use when valuing startup companies with many intangible assets.

C. Venture Capital Valuation

There really is no objective standard consistently used to value a startup company lacking historical revenues, earnings, cash flows, etc. In essence, one can assume such a company to represent a collection of intangible assets, (like concepts, know-how, and technology) for which there is no established demand, but with the potential to create a demand and therefore to ultimately form a market of willing buyers. Therefore, when estimating the value of an early stage company, *venture capitalists try to determine the full value of these unrealized intangible assets, estimate the risk involved in achieving these values, and then determine if they can achieve an IRR that justifies the investment relative to the relative risk.* The three main factors that they consider are their required IRR, the risk involved, and the projected revenues generated by the time of expected liquidation. Meanwhile, variables such as the quality of management and competitive advantage are used to estimate the probability of achieving the financial projections. *With this information, they try to strike a balance between the amount to be invested and the percentage of ownership, hoping to obtain an adequate level of control while minimizing the amount of capital infusion.* Figure 11-1 lists the key elements that determine the extent of these three valuation factors.

Let us now look at the typical approach used by venture capitalists to value a company. First, the venture firm estimates the number of years required before the company will be ready for an exit, which is usually based on the estimated time to breakeven. Next, for later stage companies with more predictable cash flows, estimates of these cash flows are made up to the time of exit and then discounted to a present value based upon the risk of achieving these cash flows. This is essentially the discounted cash flow approach. Meanwhile, *for early stage companies venture capitalists may use comparable companies to attach a value to expected cash flows, revenues, or other measures.* Thus future cash flows or revenues are assigned a multiple based upon the IPO or acquisition price paid for a public or private company that is generating certain cash flows or revenues.

If public companies are used as comparables, sometimes a discount factor is also used since private and public companies are only moderately comparable due to differences in size and other factors. For instance, if a comparable company similar to the one being valued was generating $100 million in revenues and was sold for $400 million, it received a valuation of 4 times its revenues. But because this company was public, a private market discount of 25% might be applied to reflect differences in business risk due to the difference in size, for instance. In this case, a multiple of three times revenues would be used to value the company.

Figure 11-1. The Main Factors Considered By VCs for Valuation

- Intangible elements within a company, including IP, experience and quality of management team, competitive advantage, proprietary nature of technology, know-how, and customer lists.

- Revenue forecasts and expectations of revenue growth

- Breakeven time

- Current and expected future valuations of similar companies.

- Developmental stage of company

- Market conditions (including IPO and merger/acquisition markets)

- Concept "buzz" (the market appeal for the company's products)

- Anticipated exit route and timing

- Total amount of financing needed prior to exit

- Risk of execution failure (dependent on quality of management, technology, and the nature of the competitive forces within the industry)

- Future stock options allotments for management team

Finally, the venture capitalist determines a discount rate based upon the risk associated with achieving the forecasted cash flows to arrive at a present value of the company. The selection of the discount rate is very important, as are the assumptions behind and will be influenced by the interest rate environment, quality of the management team, and time involved until exit. An example of the most basic form of this method has been provided.

Example of the Valuation Process. Logic Tech is a semiconductor company seeking a Series A Preferred financing round of $4 million. The company locates a venture capitalist that agrees to invest $4 million in the Series A with 10% cumulative dividends, and they both agree that the pre-money valuation will be assigned at $16 million. Therefore, the post-money valuation is $20 million and the venture firm now has a 25%

ownership. The venture firm has determined that the Logic Tech will require an additional of $20 million beyond this recent financing in order to take it to a liquidity event. Assuming the venture firm exercises its right of first refusal throughout each additional round, it will have retained a 20% ownership and invested a total of $8 million.

The venture firm has determined that similar private companies have recently sold for four times revenues and they have estimated that Logic Tech will have revenues of $50 million within five years. Therefore, the current value of Logic Tech using this approach is $200 million and the venture firm expects to gross $40 million ($200 million x 20%). However, a discount rate of 25% is attached to these revenue projections to account for the relative risk estimated by the venture firm. Therefore, the VCs will gross $30 million or 3X their investment which comes to an IRR of 30% annually. Assuming a 25% overhead for each year the money is invested to cover travel costs and other expenses of the venture firm, the net proceeds to the firm will be $23 million or a net IRR of 25%, which is nothing to get excited about considering the risk taken. However, for simplicity the cumulative dividends of 10% would increase the IRR. Finally, in this example there was no discount for the use of the public company as a comparable, although this could have been a reasonable assumption.

The *three main assumptions in this method are that the company meets its revenue forecast, the market is still paying four times revenues for similar companies, and a true comparable was used.* Other significant factors considered are growth rates and financial leverage used (amount of debt). The company should note that *of all variables used by venture capitalists, the discount rate is the most subjective and should be the variable targeted for negotiation by the company.* Therefore it is critical for the management to understand all assumptions used by the venture firm when determining this rate. *Most venture capitalists use a rough guide when determining the discount rate, with early stage companies having the highest and later stage the lowest, due to the relative risk involved.* The industry and economy also have an influence on this rate as well, but VCs will typically assume a large error with the pro forma financial projections and will factor this into the determination of the final discount rate. Therefore, *more important than having great numbers, the company should be able to discuss all assumptions behind the projections in detail* and should have spent sufficient time developing the business strategy to further increase the chances of achieving these estimates.

Regardless of any projections for a company, the venture capitalist will always make certain that his preferred ownership percentage and investment amounts are in balance with the hypothetical risk and expected IRR. In this process, they will estimate the total expected future capital needed so they are able to determine their final percentage of ownership. The following formula can be used to determine this value.

$$\text{Post-money valuation} = \frac{I}{RCOP}$$

where I = the Investment amount

               $RCOP$ = the Required Current Ownership Percentage

$$RCOP = \frac{RFOP}{RR}$$

where $RCOP$ = the Required Current Ownership Percentage

               $RFOP$ = the Required Final Ownership Percentage

               RR = the Retention Ratio

The *retention ratio* is the percentage of the original amount of the company owns after dilutive activities such as further financing rounds. This number is very important for the VC to determine because it will impact their IRR estimations. As a simple example, if a venture firm owns 60% of a company and it is expected to need an additional round of financing that will consume 50% of the stock, the retention ratio for the venture firm would be 30%. Note that in order to accurately estimate the retention ratio, one must have a good idea what the total amount of financing will be, as well as no major alterations in valuation (i.e. no down rounds).

D. Scrutinizing Venture Capital Valuations

As we learned in the previous chapter, there are certain items in a term sheet that are not open to negotiation, such as voting rights, right of first refusal, liquidation preferences, and redemption clauses. Meanwhile, equally significant provisions such as *antidilution and reserve shares are negotiable and may have a tremendous impact on the exit valuation.* And while the pre-money valuation is usually somewhat negotiable, one of the biggest mistakes made by early stage companies is overemphasizing the valuation of their company and overlooking all factors relevant for achieving a high exit valuation, such as term sheet provisions and selecting the best venture firm. *Thus, while pre-money valuation issues are important, companies must understand that there are many other issues directly related to valuation and they should focus on these rather than pre-money valuations.*

Even when a company receives a pre-money valuation it is pleased with, it may not have received financing from the venture firm that has the best ability to help them achieve the *maximal exit valuation.* Therefore, *the absolute most important factor in trying to achieve the best valuation is securing the highest quality investor.* And we can define such an investor as the one who can help the company achieve the best exit valuation. A high valuation early on, while seemingly attractive, is irrelevant if the company doesn't survive to benefit from the rewards of a timely exit strategy. In contrast, a good venture firm is the company's best partner in helping to extract the maximum value from a company, thereby securing the highest possible exit valuation.

Although certainly not the norm, there are some venture firms that might offer your company substantially less than you feel is needed to get through the next growth phase and subsequent round of financing at a reasonable valuation. Thus, severe undervaluation can pose a threat to the long-term viability of the company. This *undervaluation strategy* would increase the firm's chance of securing a higher valuation in the next round of financing. Therefore, some venture firms use undervaluation as a means of lowering risk. Likewise, *overvaluation can be equally detrimental.* Companies that receive a large amount of money and subsequently fail to reach milestones will have a very difficult time obtaining another round of financing without agreeing to a substantially lower valuation (down round). *Furthermore, when the valuation is extremely high, the next round can be down even if the company has achieved its milestones.*[5] While the management team should guard against such extremes, they should focus on the resources and long-term benefits of the venture firm that will assist the company in achieving a maximum exit valuation.

Supply & Demand

Earlier, we discussed the influence of the supply-demand relationship on company valuation.   We can further illustrate more extreme effects of supply and demand on valuation by looking at the investment environment of the late 1990s.   During that period, the U.S. economy was doing extremely well, and along with tremendous returns in the stock market, low unemployment, low inflation, a very bullish Wall Street, and widespread access to the markets, billions of dollars were being poured into the stock market daily.   And while the supply for IPOs was robust, the public demand for ownership in public high technology companies was so overwhelming that the relative supply paled in comparison, and the stock prices soared reflecting this large disparity.

This demand was first created by those venture firms that cultivated the big name Internet companies like AOL, Yahoo!, Ebay, Amazon.com, and countless others.   And while many investors purchasing shares of these companies realized VC-type returns, the sponsoring VCs received returns that were much larger.   Consequently, these tremendous returns fueled a vicious institutional demand for IPOs, especially for those groups that had not been participants of earlier private financing investments.   Of course Wall Street further assisted in elevating the demand within the investment community with praises such as "The New Economy".   Then we all know what happened a couple of years later.   Reality check.

Another example may be illustrated by considering what happened in the biotechnology industry during that same period.   In 1999, the biotechnology genomics market was in high demand, sparked by exciting developments in the human genome project.   In addition, the same favorable economic and market forces remained in place to fuel the launch of several very rewarding genomics IPOs.   This demand funneled back down the investment chain to the VCs, who recognized the spectacular investment and exit opportunities within this sector.   As such, private genomics companies were receiving extremely high valuations because venture capitalists knew there was intense institutional demand for public ownership in these seemingly lucrative companies.   Therefore, during this period, many VCs were not as concerned with valuation as they were with identifying genomics companies having the potential to provide a fast exit in the form of an IPO.   Thus, *the demand for such companies was much higher than the supply and this caused the valuations to skyrocket,* as VCs battled to invest in these companies. However, in an attempt to ride this wave of demand for genomics companies, some VCs got caught in 2001, when the trends changed and somehow the "words of wisdom" proclaimed that the proteomics companies would be the true beneficiaries of the human genome project.   As a consequence, many VCs who had not exited or provided an exit for their genomics companies by the end of 2001 suffered large losses due to the diminished institutional demand for genomics IPOs. Of course, after 2001 the demand for proteomics companies faded as well.

In both of these cases, market demand for investment in these companies drove valuations to ridiculously high levels. This demand was orchestrated by the concerted efforts of venture capitalists, Wall Street firms, and the media and was further enhanced by a tremendous bull market and a booming economy. Of course that period was an extreme representation of market valuation affects. But it serves to emphasize the point that *management teams must be able to recognize supply-demand dynamics because they can assist their companies in achieving the best valuations if exits are timed appropriately.* That said, when using the valuation framework discussed in this chapter, understand where your company's representative industry lies within this investment spectrum. Is it in the midst of a huge surge in demand, or trailing off? Perhaps it has not yet occurred, which might be the best situation because you know it will happen at some point and you will be more opportunistic when positioning your company to capitalize on its effects.

Risk & Reward, Leverage & Control

The main lesson one should have taken from the discussion of valuation methods is that they are always subjective, especially for early stage companies. Thus, management should be satisfied that the venture firm has adequately justified its *subjective valuation* of the company. Yet for the entrepreneur, it remains a difficult task how to challenge this valuation convincingly. Therefore, I will attempt to provide some guidelines that should be considered by the management throughout the valuation process. After all, it's not only the venture capitalist's IRR that is important but also that of the original founders and management of the company. But once again, keep in mind that it is the exit valuation and thus the quality of the venture firm that is most important.

When a VC exerts some control over the company, the management team should have a certain expectation of the amount of leverage added by this firm. [6] Or, stated in a different way, a company might be willing to accept increased control (majority voting and percentage ownership) if it is confident in the VC's ability to provide a proportionate level of added benefits (leverage). Leverage may be defined in many ways depending upon its usage. In general, there is financial leverage, mechanical leverage, and human leverage. Regardless of its form, leverage can be a powerful force, positive or negative.

When considering financial leverage it should be apparent that there is a certain level of proportionate risk that is introduced. For instance, when a company takes on debt, it has increased its leverage in order to secure financing for expenditures. If the company is able to improve its business position through the use of this debt (and is able to repay the interest and principal) then the leverage was positive. In contrast, if the company is not able to service the debt, (due to the inefficient use of the debt proceeds or the inability to repay the loan) the leverage manifests its power in a negative way and results in a situation that is worse for the company than if it had not incurred the debt.

While venture firms certainly provide added financial leverage through investment in their portfolio companies, this discussion more specifically refers to the *"human leverage"* attributable to the firm, which would include their experience in dealing with startup companies, contacts, strategic planning, management skills, and insight. *It is this human leverage that serves as the distinguishing characteristic between different venture firms.* We can define human leverage as the accentuation of an individual's abilities, influence, or actions upon another person, object, or event, so that the magnitude and intensity associated with a leveraged individual upon these people, objects, or activities is much greater than without their involvement.

When the human leverage contributed by the venture firm is high, it follows that there should be a proportionate reduction in business risk for its portfolio company. *Hence, there is an inverse relationship between "human leverage" and business risk, which accounts for a major reason why the venture capital model works.* Any investor can provide financial leverage, but good venture capitalists provide excellent "human leverage" which ultimately lowers the risk of company failure. Meanwhile, less talented venture firms may only provide financial leverage, which by definition has an inherent amount of risk built in (see the notes below when defining leverage). And if the human leverage provided by the firm is insufficient, this may ultimately result in a negative financial leverage for the company.

What is the proper balance between control and risk? The ideal amount of control by a VC should be determined by the optimal level of added leverage by the VC that results in the maximum decrease in risk. Recall that we learned of the invariable risk-reward concept in chapter 2. In discussion of this concept we mentioned that the Modern Portfolio Theory, while unable to change this relationship, could alter the ratio so that hypothetical risk is lowered relative to the expected return through proper diversification of investment assets. A similar situation applies for those venture firms that have added human leverage. Such venture firms will possess a broad array of resources which, when applied to the company, can mitigate business risk. And because these firms are able to lower business risk by leveraging their human capital, they should be rewarded with a proportionate amount of control in order to execute this reduction in risk (figure 11-2).

Earlier in this chapter we discussed some of the ways by which supply and demand can affect valuation. It follows that there should be some method to express the complexities between business risk, control, return, and leverage. I will now present a method for the purpose of providing a basic framework for critiquing the venture firm's valuation assessment of a company. *Rather than a tool to be used for negotiating the pre-money valuation, companies should utilize this methodology when assessing the human capital capacities of each venture firm in question.* If this approach is emphasized, the company will be more focused on retaining the venture firm that is more likely to maximize the exit valuation, which is really the only valuation that matters.

For simplicity, we shall assume that reward is defined as the return on investment (ROI). In the ensuing discussion many of the variables to be presented have been assigned numerical ranges to reflect their relative weight and relationship when combined in the equations that follow. The reader should focus on the interrelationships between each variable rather than being concerned with specific equations. Also note that for simplicity, some variables have intentionally been assigned value ranges less than 0 rather than

Figure 11-2. The Relationship between Risk-Reward and Leverage-Control

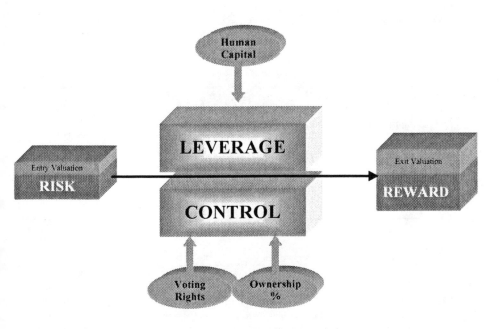

Original illustration by M. Stathis

expressing them as fractions.   Therefore, when this occurs, note that the interrelationship between variables will be reversed. First, we will define the variables to be used.

t_i = time; measured in fiscal years from the point in time outside investors become involved

C = control; measured by ownership percentage and control over company decisions (voting rights and special board approval items)

> Assume a range of $1.0 - 9.0$ with 1.0 representing no added control by the investor(s). Note also below that the risk ratio (R_r) and total leverage (L_A) would also equal 1.0, the hypothetical starting point before investors become involved.

R_c = risk of company failure

R_{vc} = risk of company failure when the venture capital firm is an investor

> This would depend on the quality and abilities of the venture firm (total financial commitment beyond the current round, syndicate ability, industry experience and contacts, and potential human capital commitment). As well, it will depend upon the ability of the venture firm to improve the characteristics of the company (management, potential market, market barriers, and positioning of proprietary technology) in decreasing the risk of business failure. Therefore, this value is related to the leverage.

R_r = risk ratio, whereby $R_r = R_{vc} / R_c$

> The risk ratio should always be less than 1.0. Otherwise, the VC firm has not lowered the risk of company failure and we can assume that any company is better off with rather than without the assistance of a venture firm.

L_A = actual leverage; $| L_{ob} - L_{exp} | = L_A$

> This represents the actual leverage relative to the leverage observed and expected of the venture capitalist. [7]

L_{ob} = observed leverage

> This is the amount of overall value and increased performance added to the company attributed to the VC's involvement. This may be assessed by say, increased sales/revenue growth, for instance. It would also include the ability of the VC to increase the demand for the services/products of the company through their guidance. This value cannot be determined until after the VC has invested and results compared prior to their involvement.[8]

L_{exp} = expected leverage factor

> The amount of leverage expected to be added by the VC, which would affect the future performance of the company as well as the success of any exit strategies. It would be more dependent on the longer-term abilities of the VC, such as strategic adaptation skills, overall vision, exit strategy success rates and other factors expressed with R_{vc}. One way to assess this number is to study the results of each investment a particular VC has made and speak with past and current portfolio companies.[9]

HR = hypothetical return; where 1.0 represents a 100% return on investment

> It is important to calculate this as an annual rate of return (ARR). In general, a good annual rate of return for a venture capitalist is 50%, while anything above 60% might be considered excellent; 25-30% would be considered mediocre.

P_q = performance quotient

> This number may be different in each time period of assessment, such as the company's fiscal year. A reasonable period must be chosen and used throughout to assess performance of the company by reviewing the ability to reach stated milestones.

The boxed equation below is a very important underlying relationship in this exercise and simply states that control is proportional to the product of leverage and risk and can be rearranged to demonstrate that leverage and risk are inversely proportional. Therefore, increasing leverage should result in decreasing risk, assuming control is constant. From the parameters defined thus far, it should be apparent that the control exerted by the venture firm should be dependent upon both the leverage added and the risk lowered by the VC's involvement, R_{vc}. Specifically, the expected leverage, L_{exp} is the variable related most to R_{VC}. And although these two variables are interdependent, adding leverage does not always result in decreased business risk.

$$\textbf{Control = Leverage x Risk}$$

$$\textbf{Leverage} = \frac{\textbf{Control}}{\textbf{Risk}} \qquad \textbf{Risk} = \frac{\textbf{Control}}{\textbf{Leverage}}$$

Equation 1.0 $C = L_A \times R_r$ where $L_A > R_r$

OR

Equation 2.0 $C = (\, |L_{ob} - L_{exp}|\,) \times (R_{vc} / R_c)$ where $L_A > R_r$

In theory, if a venture firm is expected to provide a tremendous amount of leverage, L_{exp}, for a fixed amount of business risk, it can justify more company control. In addition, this also holds true for future financing rounds and may be assessed by measuring the relative L_{ob}. Therefore, when attempting to assess L_{exp} versus L_{ob}, the company should review features of their investment strategies and historical results of the VC's portfolio companies versus the amount of leverage delivered by the VC for subsequent rounds of financing respectively. Thus, it will be virtually impossible to determine the L_{ob} and therefore the L_A, until there has been formal VC involvement. Therefore, the only estimate of leverage for a first time investor must be given by L_{exp}.

Meanwhile, if the VC is a follow on investor from a previous round, then L_{ob} can be measured and weighed against the L_A to assess the cost to the company of any prior shortfalls in the expected versus observed amount of leverage. Therefore, each equation in the remainder of this discussion will be separated to show values for each the L_{exp} and L_{ob}, denoting the case for a new investor versus a subsequent investment by the same VC. Finally, note that the VC will only be able to exert this human capital leverage to a certain extent if not provided with the proper amount of control. Figure 11-3 lists some of the positive factors that might be associated with high leverage and hence diminished business risk. If the investor is an angel with limited private investment experience, he should be able to demonstrate some evidence of being able to produce beneficial results to the company, such as significant managerial experience or the ability to bring in other angels.

Figure 11-3. Factors Increasing the Leverage of Venture Investors

- Historical success of portfolio company performance
- Industry experience
- Extensive industry networks
- Ability to form syndicates
- Ability to secure good investment banks
- Distribution channels

The control/risk ratio should not only be greater than 1.0, but it should ideally increase by some multiple greater than 2, since with each increase in control, leverage is automatically increased without a lowering of risk due to the mathematical relationship. Rearranging equation 1.0, we obtain:

$$L_A = C / R_r \qquad\qquad R_r = C / L_A \qquad\qquad \text{where } L_A > R_r$$

Rearranging equation 2.0, we can solve for both the company's risk (equation 2.1) and the venture capitalist's risk (equation 2.2).

Equation 2.1 $R_c = R_{vc} (L_{exp}) / C$

$R_c = R_{vc} (|L_{ob} - L_{exp}|) / C$ where $L_A > R_r$ (for subsequent rounds)

Equation 2.2 $R_{vc} = (C \times R_c) / (L_{exp})$

$R_{vc} = (C \times R_c) / (|L_{ob} - L_{exp}|)$ where $L_A > R_r$ (for subsequent rounds)

Equation 2.1 shows that company risk is directly proportional to the risk assumed by the venture capitalist and the actual leverage to be added by the VC firm, and indirectly proportional to the control given up to the venture capitalist. This means that the business risk is a product of the investment capital contributed by the VC and their human capital (leverage). The relevance of this is that if the amount of investment capital is increased by any one venture firm, the level of control will automatically increase due to a proportionate share of voting and ownership rights. And because human capital within each venture firm is relatively constant, the only way to lower business risk is by giving up more control via board seats, special approval items, and perhaps even generous antidilution privileges for the venture firm. Therefore, if L_{obs} is significantly different that L_{exp}, too much control may have been provided to the VCs.

Meanwhile equation 2.2 shows that VC risk is proportional to the product of their amount of control and company risk, and inversely proportional to the absolute value of the actual leverage. This also makes sense if we consider the fact that the risk of loss of their investment capital will decrease as their leverage increases. Keeping either the company risk or the control constant and noting the expected effects is not an accurate representation due to the fact that an increase in control will be accompanied by a dimishment of company risk according to the amount of leverage provided by the VC. Therefore, if the VC offers only minimal leverage but receives a large amount of control, not only will the company risk increase, but the VCs will cause an increase in the risk of their investment capital through mismanagement.

Solving equation 2.0 for L_{exp}, we get:

Equation 2.3 $$L_{exp} = (CR_c / R_{vc}) - L_{ob}$$

Equation 2.4 $$L_{ob} = (CR_c / R_{vc}) - L_{exp}$$

These equations show that the leverage added by the VC is proportional to the product of the amount of control the VC has and the risk of company failure, and inversely proportional to the risk of company failure when the VC is an investor. Figure 11-4 summarizes factors the company should consider when assessing the benefits of a prospective venture firm. However, this is only a partial list and there will be other factors that ultimately affect the valuation of a company, such as the current and expected market conditions, the buzz, and current accepted IPO and acquisition multiples (figure 11-5).

Figure 11-4. Key Variables When Assessing the Investor's Contributions

• Risk taken by company	What is the business risk without the investor? How much can the investors lower business risk? Will there be sufficient management incentive left?
• Control Investors	How much can be justified? What are the possible effects of each control element on the company?
• Risk taken by the investor	How much human versus financial capital?
• Hypothetical Return	How does it change with investor assistance?
• Leverage (expected)	How much might the investor lower business risk? How much can investors add to the overall success based upon their resources?
• Leverage (observed)	How much does the investor improve company performance?
• Return	How can the investor improve the exit valuation How much can they improve it by?

Figure 11-5. Variables to be Considered By the Company
               (Independent of the Investor)

- Demand of Company (Buzz)
- Overall Economics of the Venture
- Acquisition or IPO Valuation Multiples
- Market Conditions
- Strength of the Economy
- Systemic Business Risks

The formula for estimating the hypothetical return of an investment may be given by the following relationship:

$$\boxed{\textbf{Return = Time x (Performance + Leverage)}}$$

Equation 3.0a $\mathbf{HR_c = t_i \; x \; (P_q + L_{exp})}$

    where $P_q + L_{exp}$ = expected leveraged based performance

Equation 3.0b $\mathbf{HR_c = t_i \; x \; (P_q + L_{ob})}$

    where $P_q + L_{ob}$ = observed leveraged based performance

Algebraically, we can solve for the performance quotient, P_q:

Equation 3.1 $P_q = HR_c \, / \, (t_i - L_{exp})$

Thus, after a certain period of VC involvement we can measure the P_q to determine if the VC is continuing to add the same amount of leverage by assessing any significant changes in performance. Therefore, this equation will only be useful for estimating the effect of VC involvement after financing has been agreed upon. However, it can also be used to assess performance for future rounds of financing for which the VC will be involved. And depending upon the results, the management team may be able to negotiate more reserve shares or other benefits if they can demonstrate that the VCs did not increase the performance relative to their ownership percentage and expectations of the management team. And although the ultimate responsibility of achieving stated milestones is with the management, the extent of assistance expected from the VCs may influence the ability to achieve certain milestones. Solving equation 3.1 for L_{exp}, we obtain:

Equation 3.2 $$L_{exp} = HR_c / (t_i - P_q)$$

Substituting equation 2.3 and 2.4 into equation 3.0a and 3.0b, we have two equations showing the effects of time, performance, control, risk and leverage on the hypothetical return. This would represent the hypothetical return with respect to the company's opinion:

Equation 4.0 $$\mathbf{HR_c = t_i \,[P_q + (CR_c / R_{vc}) - L_{exp}]}$$

$$\mathbf{HR_c = t_i \,[P_q + (CR_c / R_{vc}) - L_{ob}]}$$

It is important to recognize that not only is the management team responsible for estimating company risk without VC involvement, but they must also determine several of the variables attributable to involvement by the venture investor. And since each VC will prioritize different factors in assessing the company's strengths and weaknesses, the management team should interview them thoroughly to determine the relative weights of these numbers when assessing an appropriate level of control, leverage expectations, and risk. If this is done, the management team will at least understand areas of disagreement in opinion and can factor this into their overall rebuttal of the valuation proposed by the VC.

Keep in mind that most VCs will be valuing your company based on similar, although slightly different and much more simplistic measures. For example, while your main concern is a healthy control/leverage exchange resulting in a lowering of risk, VCs will be mainly concerned with the strength of your management team, the competitive advantage of the company, and the potential market share. Thus, the company should be concerned with how the VC will lower business risk. Meanwhile, the VCs will be concerned with how the company can lower business risk and therefore the risk of their investment capital. But both considerations are really assessing the relative risk involved in the business. As such, we could devise a formula representing these variables to illustrate how a venture firm might attempt to place valuation on these subjective factors, (although they certainly would not use an equation). Typically, they will base these assessments on their experience with the industry and results from previous portfolio companies. Obviously, the hypothetical return would be directly proportional to the time of investment, the performance quotient, quality of its proprietary technology, and the strength of management. The **hypothetical return from the perspective of the venture capital firm would therefore be:**

Equation 5.0 $$HR_{vc} = t_i T_p \; x \; (P_q + M_c)$$

T_p = degree of proprietary technology

This not only includes IP but also staying power in the market; this range might be 0.5-3.0, whereby 0.5 would represent a technology that would have poor IP protection and one that would be relatively easy to replace by competitors. At the other extreme, a value of 3.0 would represent a technology that would be difficult to replace and would be properly protected with the proper IP.

M_c = strength of company management team

This is a fraction in the range of -0.3 to +0.3; the degree to which the management team is expected to affect the future performance of the company (independent of the VCs) as well as the success of any exit strategies.

Keep in mind that equation 5.0 is very crude and says nothing about the attractiveness of the market with respect to its size, growth rate, and competitive environment. In addition, it also neglects to factor in all significant company strengths or weaknesses such as distribution channels, quality of customers, and many other factors. However, we are assuming that the market size and growth rate are adequate, otherwise the VC would not wish to invest. In addition, other factors such as customers and distribution networks may be unfair to assess for early stage companies lacking sufficient capital. *This equation only addresses the most common issues VCs will be able to provide an opinion on with confidence.*

Before we illustrate examples that demonstrate the use of these relationships, let us review the general guidelines that venture capitalists use to value companies so management teams will understand how venture valuation is determined prior to actually doing any math. Each of these categories has different treatments depending on whether the company is early, middle or late stage, as well as the health of the economy and the markets. Only a few qualities for each category will be listed although there are several others (figure 11-6).

Management: For early stage companies, VCs will determine if management is experienced, passionate, entrepreneurial, committed, easy to work with, can adapt to change, and respond to adversity. Throughout the period of investment, there will most likely be periods of extreme stress experienced by the management team due to perhaps competitive forces, low-yielding marketing efforts, and even a need to refocus company strategies. As such, VCs will need to feel comfortable the management team is levelheaded and would be willing to accept their guidance. For later stage companies they will be more concerned with management's ability to execute their business strategies, deal with competitors, reach revenue targets, and ease to work with.

Technology and Competitive Advantage: For early stage companies venture firms will determine how proprietary the technology is, the quality of IP protection, and how well it can be defended for possible infringement violations. For later stage companies they will assess the strength of the technology once immersed within the market, and the success of any revisions. In addition, they will determine if the competitive advantage is valid and sustainable.

Market Potential: They will assess the growth potential of the company based on the value added to the consumer, competition, current market size, and industry growth rate. They will also estimate the potential market share the company can feasibly command. For later stage companies, VCs will have a better idea about these issues and will now focus on the extent of market penetration and technology validation, as well as growth rates.

Exit strategy: VCs will consider what the best routes of exit are for a company given its industry, strategic buyers, and investment horizon or timing of exit and how this will impact their IRR. They will have a good idea what form of exit they anticipate and will groom the company in alignment with this strategy.

Financial Commitment: Venture firms will consider the total committed capital required or how much capital the company will ultimately require before an exit strategy becomes feasible. This determination will be based upon the company's financial projections and a discount rate will usually be added to account for uncertainty based upon the industry, stage of the company, and strength of management. For later stage companies with positive cash flows, VCs will have a better idea regarding the ability of the company to meet its financial projections and may use the DCF method in combination with the comparables method to arrive at a final valuation.

Return on Investment (ROI): This is obviously one of the most important factors for VCs, however it has been placed towards the end because other factors such as management and technology are more difficult to assess. VCs reject many more companies due to weakness in management and technology platform than their ability to provide an attractive return on investment. Most VCs look for an annualized return of at least 30%, with 50% considered good. However, even with a 50% IRR, after accounting for expenses and fees, the return to the limited partners of the VC fund may only be about 35%. In addition, the time horizon for exit is also a factor because the longer the horizon, the greater the chance of failure. It is obviously an easier task to determine the ROI for later stage companies that have achieved a notable market penetration and revenue.

Company Maturity: Different venture firms have variable expectations of the management, depending upon the stage of the company, the industry and competitive landscape, and the relative strength of the competitive advantage. In addition, they also have variable levels of expertise, resulting in different abilities to add leverage. Therefore, depending upon the VC, very early stage companies with unproven results and limited market penetration may be favored in exchange for a large percentage ownership. The strategy of these VCs might be to bring in further rounds of financing and exit in the middle stages of a company. Alternatively, corporate VCs might be able to recognize the potential technology benefits to their company and may add significant value such as distribution channels and complementary patent portfolios, and might want a large percentage of ownership for a smaller price.   However, keep in mind that as a group, corporate VCs tend to overpay relative to private venture firms.

Still there are other VCs who might invest in a company regardless of its maturity due to an emphasis in forming strategic partnering arrangements with one of their portfolio companies, or in the case of corporate VCs, their own company.   Within this subgroup are companies themselves who seek to benefit from acquiring the rights to the proprietary technology and / or sales and distribution channels of the company.   In this case, the company seeking the strategic relationship usually prefers to invest in later stage companies that have already secured a lead investor.

Deal Terms: VCs will need to consider how much if any dilution has already occurred, as well as any current and/or future commitments in place such as stock options, warrants, and liquidation preferences, all of which may effect the ultimate valuation and/or control of the company and perhaps even the incentive of the management team.   In addition, they will consider the current investors.   What can be a detriment for investment by a VC here is a company that has previously raised $500,000 from 100 or more investors. Such investors could make it difficult for the VC to exert the needed control over company decisions.

Figure 11-6.   Variables Investors Consider Important for Companies

Company Dependent	Market Dependent
• Strength of Management • Competitive Advantage • Proprietary Technology • Stage of Company • Market Potential • Total financing needed • Time of Investment • Exit Strategy • IRR • Ownership Percentage • Concept Buzz	• Industry Valuations • Market Conditions • Economic Factors

E. Case Studies

Case Study 1

The Company: Light Vision is an early stage fiber optics company seeking a Series A Preferred equity financing of $2.5 million. The company has been operating for six years and the management team has matured slowly but nicely. The technology and business strategy represent a strong competitive advantage and the IP is solid. They have no customers but have established good relationships with corporations which have indicated interest in their products once they have completed beta testing, assuming the product works as claimed. The company expects an IPO within seven years based upon the attainment of its financial projects and milestones. While the market for fiber optics is huge, the current economy and market conditions make barriers to entry very difficult, resulting in an extremely competitive market.

Light Vision's previous capital consisted of $800,000 in F&F money and $200,000 in long-term debt with a coupon of 16% secured against the assets of the company. Based upon their 5-year pro forma projections, the management has estimated the current valuation of their company to be $10,000,000 using the comparables approach. Despite many previous attempts, the company has been unsuccessful in obtaining either angel or venture financing. The company is cash poor, although they have minimized their burn rate. For lack of adequate compensation, the management previously decided on a generous stock options plan, which has helped morale somewhat.

The Investor: The VC firm is a well respected and has helped many of its previous portfolio companies achieve great success and financial rewards. However, it has had limited success with fiber optics companies and its only two fiber optics investments have previously been with competing technologies. They present a term sheet to the management team of Light Vision calling for substantial control over the company through a variety of mechanisms (i.e. dilution, possible replacement of a portion of management team, etc.), based upon a pre-money valuation of $1,000,000. Without showing any specific numbers for potential market, etc. you should be able to provide a reasonable assessment of the terms of this offer.

Analysis: We are concerned with the value the VC can bring to the company (i.e. leverage) versus the amount of control they should receive. Within this assessment, we will need to estimate the relative risk and the potential reward, or HR from the perspective of the company (HR_c) and the venture capitalist (HR_{vc}). Let's review the information:

- The company is a struggling early-stage investment
- The management team has proven its endurance and managed to stay afloat up to this point
- The technology has good IP
- The competitive advantage is strong
- The company is cash poor
- Management has gained significant corporate attention but has no customers
- The total market potential is huge but competition is intense
- Company is seeking $2.5 million in first round financing based upon an expected $10,000,000 pre-money valuation.
- Management controls a large portion of stock through warrants and options

This is one of the most unfortunate situations that can occur with an early-stage company. Essentially, they are victims of a down economy. Loans will need to be paid and since they currently have no customers or cash so they are vulnerable to the current pattern of diminished corporate spending. And if they fail to meet the interest payments on their debt, they could face foreclosure. Let's review what the VCs add to the deal:

- They are successful and well-known
- They have some expertise in fiber optics and therefore may have some relevant industry contacts
- They are your only offer and you have liens on company assets

On the other hand, the disadvantages are:
- They have no expertise in your specific technology
- They have expertise (and possibly portfolio companies) with competing technologies
- They want too much ownership

Based upon the Light Vision's pre-money valuation, ($10,000,000) they are expecting to give up only about 20% ownership interest to a first round investor. However, based upon the pre-money valuation assigned by the VC firm, ($1,000,000) the company would have to give up about 70% ownership to the VC. Now we examine the relative values of each variable in the following equation:

$$HR_c = t_i \left[P_q + (CR_c / R_{vc}) - L_{exp} \right]$$

We have an idea of all the above variables, except the HR_c. Therefore, we look at this value only after consideration of the others.

t_i: exit is expected to occur with 7 years via IPO

P_q: decent at best but poor on a time-weighted scale

C: the VCs want a huge ownership stake

R_c: at this point the company has substantial risk since it has a $200,000 loan due with minimal cash so the risk of failure without VC funding would be considered high

R_{vc}: the VC has a decent ability to lower the risk of the business from its human capital, based upon its experience. However, in this case, the greatest amount of leverage added would be financial, since the company is in immediate need of cash. Therefore, the business risk would be greatly diminished by VC involvement, but it is unclear whether the VC would be able to contribute significant human capital.

L_{exp}: the VC is well-established and successful but has limited expertise in the specific technology, although they may have significant industry contacts.

HR_c:

So the real question here is does the high level of control sought by the VCs justify the risk ratio? From the above results, it appears as if it does. In this case however, it is the financial leverage rather than human leverage that is most attractive for the company since all funds will be exhausted soon. Before making final conclusions we need to assess the variables in the equation below so that we can estimate the attractiveness from the perspective of the VC.

$$HR_{vc} = t_i T_p \text{ x } (P_q + M_c)$$

t_i: the time for expected exit is within acceptable ranges

T_p: the strength of proprietary technology is high

P_q: the performance of the company thus far has been submarginal. However, this could be due more to the economy and market rather than the ability of the management team

M_c: the strength of management is questionable, as they have not produced any solid results (management teams will always give themselves high ratings). However, they are up against a difficult economy so the results are inconclusive.

Therefore, we can conclude that the HR_{vc} is not good, as the performance thus far has been inadequate and the management team's ability is questionable. The strongest factor in this case is the strength of proprietary technology. Note that the management team will tend to overestimate these values since they are assessing themselves.

The first question the company must now determine the answer to is why the VCs want to invest in this technology if they have no experience and if they represent companies with competing technologies. The answer to this question is vital but finding this information out safely could be tricky. The last thing the company would want to do is to imply a lack of trust in their future possible investor. However, they would need to tactfully determine why the firm would be interested in investing in a competing technology, since this is uncharacteristic behavior for VCs.

Essentially, investment in a competing technology could be viewed one of three ways. Either the VC has decided to no longer fund the competing technology going forward, they are considering a synergistic partnering strategy for this company, or they could possibly be want to utilize the strength of the company for the benefit of their existing portfolio companies. The latter situation is rare, but nevertheless should always be considered as a possibility when such a situation arises. Even in a partnering or strategic alliance situation, the management team must find all details involved, since it may have major implications for the company's future growth, management team tenure and ultimate success of the company.

The next assessment to make is how much leverage these investors can bring to the company. The most difficult part here is making sure the management team performs an accurate self-assessment of its abilities. How can they demonstrate their competence when they have no customers or revenues? The investors will determine the abilities of the team through the due diligence process, which will consist of numerous interviews and review of company strategy and execution. Therefore, the management must be ready to illustrate the specific details of their skills and abilities. The investors will not care so much about what accomplishments prior to this venture the management team has achieved, since they have failed to produce significant results after six years. Therefore, what they will be looking for is the ability of the team to understand and execute business and marketing strategy.

This company has a great technology, questionable management, and no revenues. The reason for the large discrepancy between the management's valuation of $10,000,000 versus the VC's ($1,000,000) is due to a number of factors, such as different comparables used. However, most likely, the main reason is due to the discrepancy between the discount rates used. Under a better economic environment perhaps the company would have more traction.

But a slow economy means a longer exit for the VC and since he is sensitive to annualized ROI (or the IRR) and the company has no revenues, a 70% stake is not unreasonable in this situation.

And finally, the management must determine if they are willing to risk the failure of their cash-poor company if they decide not accept the terms. This is a complicated situation due to the competing portfolio companies of the venture firm, as well as their limited experience in Light Vision's technology. On the other hand, in reality the company does not pose an immediate threat to any competition since it has no customers. Therefore, the management team should sacrifice the control and focus on a modified arrangement that ensures the integrity of the VC, as one can never be too sure what could happen.

As an example, the company might propose that a scaled ownership be structured whereby the initial ownership is 40% in increments of 20% based on certain milestones. This would provide the original owners with a majority stake in the company until certain hurdles have been reached. To give up majority ownership of the company under the proposed valuation assumptions to a VC with competing technologies and limited expertise in this technology would be foolish. Therefore, this suspicion should be managed appropriately, rather than cast aside their only suitor.

Alternatively, they could more aggressively pursue their corporate contacts and attempt to raise some money. If structured appropriately, this might provide the company with more leverage down the road, depending on the management philosophy of the VC. Ultimately, if the management truly believes in the potential success of Light Vision and is willing to assume the potential default risk, they may decide to pursue other investors if they are not able to secure a graded ownership structure from the VCs. However, they should discuss renegotiation of the debt financing terms with the lender prior to abandonment of the offer from the VCs, as it is their only offer.

Case Study 2

The Company: Computer Health is an early stage healthcare IT solutions company for patient data mining, primarily for hospitals. While it has only been in formal existence for 8 months, research and product development have been going on for nearly ten years at a world-renowned hospital by the founder, who is a recognized world leader in the field of bioinformatics. They are neither willing nor capable of assuming a direct leading role in the financing and growth of this company. Rather, they prefer to leverage their relationships and reputation to help the management team build a large client base.

After a few failed attempts to receive a buyout, the venture arm of the hospital located an experienced individual to help lead this company to success. This individual paid $1,000,000 in cash for a 51% ownership of the company and assumed the role of CEO. He has former experience as project leader at an unrelated technology corporation, as well as questionable experience leading a company to an IPO, but no startup experience. As such, he really is not quite sure what to expect in terms of fund raising or working with VCs, but he was able to establish interest with a well-respected VC after attending a conference. He has assembled a preliminary management and sales team, which is ready to commit to this venture on a full time basis once the round of funding has been raised. Currently, all staff is either at the hospital or working from their home for no cash compensation.

Approximately $10 million has been spent towards the development of these emerging technologies and the market is expected to reach several billion dollars over the next 10 years. The company is seeking $5 million for equipment and expenses for sales and marketing and production costs. The β prototype is complete and the company expects to generate revenues of $1-2 million over the next 12 months and is already in serious negotiations with two leading medical research hospitals for these products. The CEO is optimistic and confident in the future success of the company and is not willing to give up exclusive control. Based upon the 5-year pro forma revenue projections, he assesses the company's current valuation at $20,000,000.

The **Investor**:   The venture firm considering the deal has had previous success with a life sciences venture capital fund and has recently started a telemedicine incubator. This firm has a strong syndicate membership including two established venture firms and the venture arm from a well-known medical device company. They offer the Computer Health a term sheet with a pre-money valuation of $2,500,000.

Analysis: Once again we must compare the HR_c with the HR_{vc} in order to determine if the control proposed by the VC can be justified based upon the expected benefits. Let us review the facts.

This company is somewhat of a mixed bag due to several factors. The CEO has former experience with a corporation but he has no startup experience. While the lack of startup experience is not necessarily an issue, what matters more is that he has been in a corporate environment his whole life and therefore may not understand the entrepreneurial world. This is where the VCs would interview him to determine his abilities to lead a startup. Based on the company's pre-money valuation of $20,000,000, Computer Health expects to exchange a 20% ownership position for the $5 million. However, based upon the VC's pre-money valuation of $2,500,000, it will have to exchange a 66% ownership stake for the $5 million financing round. In order to attempt to bridge this gap we need to list the strengths and weaknesses of the company, management team, and the VC. Let's first summarize the potential leverage the VCs can contribute:

- They have started a telemedicine incubator and this would add synergy to the company.
- They are well respected, have previous success in a life sciences fund, and they understand the sector well
- They have expertise in the technology
- They have a strong syndicate including a venture arm of a large medical devices company
- They have industry contacts from at least their syndicate partners

The only drawback of the VC is the terms of financing, thus valuation. The Company was expecting to sell 20% of the company for $5 million, but the VCs want 66%.

The Company has a low level of risk due to many factors:
- The previous financial backing of a well-renowned hospital.
- The founder is renowned for his work in bioinformatics.
- The company is a startup only from a managerial perspective, but could be considered late early to early middle stage from a product development perspective.
- The company has indications of interest from several hospitals which could provide it with the needed critical mass needed to tap into its target market.
- The burn rate for the company is modest.

Overall, Computer Health appears to have good bargaining power, as they have established an excellent competitive advantage based upon their technology and the influence of the founder. In addition, the cash requirements for current operations are low and they are under no pressure from creditors. However, they do need capital to begin a rollout of the product, as the technology is very time sensitive. Let us look at the hypothetical return equation from the company's perspective.

$$HR_c = t_i \, [P_q + (CR_c \, / \, R_{vc}) - L_{exp}]$$

t_i: exit is expected to occur with 7 years via IPO, which is acceptable to VCs

P_q: good, since although no revenues, the company is less than a year old and is in negotiations for 2 contracts

C: the VC wants a large ownership stake

R_c: the main risk to the company is the potential for the technology to become obsolete or more competitors entry into the market

R_{vc}: although it does not appear that the VC would be assuming an enormous amount of risk due to the situation, they nevertheless appear to have the proper resources to added significant leverage beyond the financing and therefore significantly lower business risk.

L_{exp}: Strong syndicate and telemedicine incubator

HR_c: very good but time sensitive

Therefore, it would be difficult to agree to the valuation given by the VC in this case.   Given the $1,000,000 by the CEO and the $10,000,000 soft money invested by the founding hospital, it is fair to conclude that a minimum valuation could be set at $6,000,000.

$$HR_{vc} = t_i T_p \; x \; (P_q \; + M_c)$$

t_i: the time for expected exit is within acceptable ranges

T_p: the strength of proprietary technology is very high but market penetrance is critical before standards of the new technology have been accepted.

P_q: the performance of the company thus far has been submarginal. However, this could be due more to the economy and market rather than the ability of the management team

M_c: the strength of management is good but lack of knowledge of the early stage environment will cause delays developing the business if the company is not funded in a timely manner

The result of this analysis also shows that both the HR_c and HR_{vc} are expected to provide very good results and the VC appear to have the potential to add tremendous leverage by providing significant distribution channels, in exchange for tremendous control. The CEO is very resistant to the terms but the fact is that without further financing the company potentially faces a slow death, since the technology is time-sensitive. Without the proper funds, this company will either make it on its own and with minimal future investment from the hospital or the technology will become obsolete by the time the part-time staff and hospital gains enough market exposure. Therefore, if the company could negotiate with the VC for ownership below 50% this would be the most ideal situation. However, most VCs will want a controlling interest so it should be expected that 51% is more likely.

F. Conclusions

This chapter was written with the intent to assist the entrepreneur's efforts in obtaining a fair valuation. We began by discussing an overview of the most common asset valuation methods and then extended this discussion to include variations used by venture firms. In general, venture capitalists are not likely to accept drastic alterations of their terms unless your company is a "hot issue" (sought out by many venture capitalists). Therefore, the method presented in this chapter is only recommended as a tool to assist the entrepreneur in avoiding extremes in valuation, as this could ultimately destroy the incentive of the management team. Nevertheless, it may be of particular use when negotiating with angel investors, since they rarely use term sheets, and therefore are prone to more flexibility when agreeing upon a fair valuation.

Fortunately, in most cases venture capitalists are alert to extreme deviations in valuation and tend to view these situations as detrimental to the company's future success. Therefore, in most cases, management teams will not be faced with financing terms that could jeopardize the fate of the company. Rather, other issues are more important, such as assuring fair liquidation, redemption, conversion, and antidilution provisions in the term sheet. Nevertheless, if used appropriately, the exercise presented in this chapter should help the company's financing efforts when attempting to negotiate term sheets. Perhaps of more importance, *this methodology should be used as a means to assist the company in identifying the best venture firm that will maximize the exit valuation, which is all that really matters.* However, like most things in life, this information, if misused could be a detriment to obtaining venture financing.

Finally, companies must take special care to present their differences in opinion to prospective investors in a manner that will avoid tensions with the venture firm since many VCs stress the importance of investing in companies that have management teams that are easy to work with. And it would be a tragic event to lose the interest of a VC due to the stubbornness of the management in over looking the big picture. Remember that VCs and angels represent your best chances for success, so you need to work with and not against them in trying to negotiate a fair valuation for your company.

Notes

[1] A commodity can be considered a product or service that is relatively inexpensive and easily obtained due to its supply or adequate channels of distribution. While a car may not be considered a commodity in a formal sense, relative to the automobile industry it may be approximated as one and serves to illustrate an important point in this example.

[2] In contrast to a commodity, a collectible is relatively expensive and difficult to obtain due to a relatively high demand and low supply. And it is this disparity between supply and demand that in itself causes the market price for these items to rise above their inherent value.

[3] Zero coupon bonds are unique in that their dividend payment is incorporated into the price at maturity. Therefore, the holder of these bonds receives a value at upon the maturity date that includes the principal and interest, as opposed to semi-annual interest payments. A rough measure of the corporate bond default rate can be determined by looking at its rating, as provided by Moody's and Standard and Poor's.

[4] Most VCs have specific discount rates based upon the stage of the company. These rates are then modified based upon the inherent risks within the industry combined with the amount of confidence in the management team, the competitive advantage and other factors. Typical discount rates are early stage (60-80%), middle stage (30-60%), and late stage (15-30%).

[5] Of course, market and economic conditions affecting the supply and demand for venture capital, which can also affect valuations independent of company performance as well.

[6] Control would include voting power over important company decisions as well as ownership percentage.

[7] Note that because the actual leverage, L_A is a positive number, (notice the absolute value sign) negative leverage is not a possibility in this hypothetical analysis. You may recall from real estate and equity investments that leverage has an inherent element of risk built within it, such that positive leverage can turn into negative leverage and therefore a lower return. The leverage we are considering here is "human leverage", rather then equity leverage so we can assume that for the purposes of this illustration, leverage and risk are two completely independent variables. And unlike financial leverage, human leverage is not necessarily associated with an increase in hypothetical risk.

[8] Note that we are assuming that the leverage created by the venture capitalist is positive. In reality, however, the VC could generate negative leverage and therefore have a value < 1.0.

Note that we are assuming that the leverage created by the VC is positive. In reality, however, the VC could generate either no leverage or negative leverage and therefore have a value of 0 and < 0 respectfully. This unfortunate, but realistic scenario could occur with VCs who are not able to either raise additional funds for future financing rounds, secure other rounds of fund raising from other sources, decide to discontinue further rounds of financing, or mess up earlier valuation, thereby causing other potential investors to pass on future rounds.

12

Compensation & Employment

"All paid jobs absorb and degrade the mind"

Aristotle

One of the last issues a startup company will want to consider are human resource activities since management has so many other tasks that are seemingly of higher priority. However, if adequate planning for human resource matters is observed, even the most difficult issues can usually be handled with ease, preventing potential misunderstandings and legal problems down the road. The first section of this chapter briefly discusses employment law and basic employee benefits, emphasizing the necessity of handling the hiring and release of employees with extreme care. The second section provides a survey of the various types of employee compensation and benefits packages available in corporate America. Because most entrepreneurs delay the investigation of this complex and time consuming process, I have included it due to its importance in promoting employee satisfaction and incentive. An understanding of these benefits is important in the founder's overall strategy of recruitment and retention of the most talented employees. And hopefully, when working with a human resources consultant, the reader will be better prepared to make these decisions.

A. Employment Law and Contracts

The employment contract is important for defining the responsibilities of the employee, publication rights, and issues of confidentiality. In addition, it outlines the criteria for promotions, bonuses, benefits, and stock options. Although specific non-disclosure agreements (NDAs) should also be used, the employment contract should address the protection of issues related to trade secrets and know-how. Therefore, it is important to make certain that the employment agreement is consistent with the separate NDAs to be used (see appendix A-1 for a sample NDA).

Most states recognize the concept of at-will employment, whereby the employer or the employee may terminate the employment contract at any time, with or without cause and with or without notice. However, termination of employment cannot be for reasons deemed to be illegal, such as discrimination[1] or whistle blowing.[2]   Employers should make all formal offers for employment in writing in an employment contract and should state the possible reasons for cause of termination consistent with state law. The management should also become familiar with state and federal employment laws since the threat of litigation, even if invalid could sideline the priorities of an early stage company and hinder its future success.[3]

Upon hiring any employee or contractor who will be exposed to intellectual property or any other proprietary assets, the company should require each to sign non-disclosure and non-competition agreements (appendix A-3).   Furthermore, each prospective employee should be interviewed and investigated to determine whether they are subject to non-compete agreements from their former employers. Failure to identify these contingencies could create legal problems for both the company and employee.   In addition, each company should determine whether their state employment laws recognize non-compete agreements, as their use may show absence of good faith by the employer if such agreements are not recognized by the state.   Finally, exit interviews between the employer and departing employee should be performed in order to make certain that the employee fully understands the agreements signed.

Contractors & Consultants

When considering whether to hire independent contractors, consultants, and other part-time employees, the company should be careful to abide by all state laws regarding the treatment and classification of these individuals. Obviously, hiring personnel for a fee can save the company expenses usually associated with employee benefits but there are specific legal criteria for classification of these individuals.   Two frequent tests used to determine whether a worker should be classified as an employee or independent contractor are the "rights of control" and "termination at will" test.   The *"rights of control"* test considers whether the worker is granted the right to control the manner in which the work is performed versus only having control over the results of the work. If the later is the case then the worker can be considered an independent contractor. The *"termination at will"* test examines whether the worker-employer relationship is binding upon specific results of work expected or can terminate the relationship at any time (figure 12-1).

If your company intends to treat workers as independent contractors you should make sure they sign a consultant/contractor agreement (shown in appendix A-2) that specifically states the compensation, the objectives for the worker, and other information that may help to clarify the status of the relationship. However, this will not automatically guarantee the judgment of the court of an independent contractor relationship. Misclassification of workers can potentially create many problems that could jeopardize the future of the company so management should seek the guidance of experienced human resources professionals and employment attorneys to determine the proper classification of workers.[4]

Figure 12-1. Questions Used to Determine Employment Status

- Is the worker paid by the project or hourly?

- Does the worker have the right to conduct the work in any way he or she deems fit?

- Does the worker relationship cease upon completion of specific projects or objectives?

- Does the worker hold himself/herself out as an independent contractor?

- Is the worker currently performing work for other companies as well?

- Does the worker hire his or her own employees to assist in the completion of the projects?

- Does the worker hold a specific license related to the projects he or she is engaged in?

Employee Departure

There are many issues to consider when key employees are scheduled to depart from the company. Amongst the most important is the protection of intellectual property rights such as trade secrets. As you will recall from our discussion of intellectual property in chapter 5, because trade secrets do not have the formal protection controls seen with patents and other types of intellectual property, it the responsibility of the company to safeguard these assets. Therefore, each new employee or anyone else exposed to company assets should not only be required to sign NDAs related to all proprietary information, but they should also sign a Noncompete Agreement if such agreements are recognized by the state. Finally, each employee should undergo an exit interview to ensure that he understands the full meaning of these signed agreements.

It should also be noted that upon termination of an employee who has been participating in an incentive-based stock options plan, the law sets a maximum of three months by which he may exercise his vested portion of options. However, the company may reduce this time period by specifying it in the stock options agreement. Regardless, in order to qualify for the ISO tax advantages, the employee must hold the options for one year prior to selling them. More detail on this topic will be presented in the next section.

B. Compensation & Benefits

In general, there are three basic psychological motivations for emphasizing compensation. First there is the individual who is focused on and overemphasizes compensation from the very beginning due to a "greed element" if you will. Usually, such an individual is destined for failure due to the adverse effects of misguided motivations. These employees are usually the dreamers who are only motivated by easy money and do not possess the commitment, passion, ability, perseverance, and selflessness necessary for creating a successful and profitable venture. Next, there is the individual who only emphasizes compensation once either the success or failure of the company is a reality or because certain complexities arise which only then necessitates their evaluation of the compensation schedule. This employee's motivation for a later reconsideration of compensation is driven by a "fear factor." This could represent a fear in being liable for potentially severe tax consequences from stock options, or not receiving an appropriate amount of compensation in proportion to his efforts and achievements, which may cause a moral problem within the company. The third type of employee considers the compensation schedule during the initial structuring of the company through the advice of an outside advisor, not due to greed or fear, but simply as a matter of good business sense, to protect his own interests, as well as the best interests of the company. Hopefully, your company will have employees with this final type of mentality.

Cash Compensation

The most obvious element of compensation is cash, as most employees recognize need for immediate payment for their efforts. The problem is that cash is absolutely the most important resource of any new venture and perhaps even more important than the business concept itself. Of course, it is always best if the management team is able to sustain themselves through other means without the use of company funds but unfortunately for many this is not always a viable alternative. If members of the management team do have this luxury, it is recommended that these individuals receive promissory notes for back pay once the company has been adequately financed for at least two years. If this funding does not materialize within a year then modifications in salary should be made to reflect this uncertainty.

The more difficult situation is with the individuals who are working in a startup or early stage company with no other source of income. Many entrepreneurs begin their company working on a part-time basis, but make the mistake of quitting their salaried job once they receive what they deem to be a significant source of money from FOF, such as $500,000. To the salaried employee making $80,000 per year, this amount seems to justify the decision to quit their full time job and commit to the company full time. Of course, what it really represents is poor judgment, lack of understanding the startup process, and poor financial planning. Even though this person is now working full time towards the development of a successful company, he has yet to experience the challenges and harsh realities of growing a startup. Therefore, he might exercise poor judgment due to the success in raising this early money. And even though he may think that this money was hard to raise, it will be much more difficult to convince experienced angels and venture capitalists to part with their money.

Finally, another method that could be used to conserve cash is similar to venture capital investment tranch financing, whereby the company founder needing a certain amount of cash compensation attaches payments to certain milestone developments within specific timeframes. This would provide an additional incentive to produce results and would allow the founder to assess the longer-term feasibility of company survival prior to making a full commitment.

Employee Stock Options and Warrants

The implementation of a broad-based stock options plan in companies is now an integral part of the overall equity compensation strategy. This trend is especially true for high-technology companies due to the high risks involved. Stock options are financial derivative securities that can be thought of as call options. In the financial markets, a *call option* gives the holder the right to purchase a specified security at a predetermined price prior to a set expiration date. Similarly, stock options are issued by the company to employees at specific periods during their tenure granting them the right to buy a specified number of shares of company stock at a specified price up to an expiration date, which may be as long as 10 years. The price at which these stock options are awarded to the employee is called the *grant price* and usually coincides with the current market price of the company stock, although the *exercise price* (strike price) can be higher or lower. When the employee decides to buy the stock he has "exercised" the option and he can elect this options exercise anytime prior to the expiration period.

The purpose of stock options is primarily to incentivize optimal employee performance and retention, improve employee moral, attract talented employees, and preserve company cash. In structuring a stock options plan the company must make certain that its future growth is sustainable, future employee growth is known, and most of all the company must identify the main purpose of the plan as a way to provide a one-time non-cash compensation benefit or to promote long-term employee ownership. Once these determinations have been made, the most suitable plan can be structured that makes the most effective use of the variable degrees of eligibility, allocation, vesting schedules, valuations, holding periods and grant price. Figures 12-2 and 12-3 list some of the most common advantages and disadvantages of using a stock options plan. A sample stock option plan agreement has been provided in appendix A-9.

Figure 12-2. Benefits to Companies Issuing Stock Options to Employees

- Provides a portion of employee compensation that serves to conserve cash until a later date.

- Provides a financial incentive to help maximize employee performance.

- Provides reward proportionate to company success and thereby serves to create employee/company unity.

Figure 12-3. Disadvantages of Stock Options and Warrants

- Affects the company's balance sheet.

- Triggers a taxable event that may potentially result in disastrous consequences.

- Causes dilution of shareholder equity

Vesting and Valuation of Options

The idea is for the employees to exercise their eligible stock options at a time when the stock is valued or being sold on the market for a price higher than the exercise price, so that a profit is realized. However, options are usually not awarded immediately and there are certain periods that an employee must have served for the company prior to the award of these options. This is known as the *vesting period* and it is the necessary time the employee must be a member of the company prior to receiving all rights to the options. *Only when vesting has occurred can the employee exercise his stock options.*

There are two general types of vesting periods, known as graded and cliff. In a *graded vesting* structure, a percentage of the stock options are allocated to the employee on a yearly basis, such as 20% after year one, 40% after the second year, (60% after the third, 80% after the fourth and 100% after the fifth year) so that each year of stock options award requires five years of further employment before the employ can receive 100% of the option award. In contrast, a *cliff vesting* stock option structure awards the entire stock option to the employee after 3-6 years, but none prior to that. Therefore, under a three-year cliff vesting stock option plan, if an employee works for a company for less then three years, he will not receive any stock options and will have forfeited them due to his departure.

To avoid any possible legal actions from terminated employees, companies should be very careful about termination just prior to their vesting period. There have been many former employees that have claimed they were terminated just prior to the vesting of their stock options in order to prevent them from receiving these assets. The potential legal and financial distractions that may result from such allegations could ruin a company's chances for survival, and should therefore be avoided.

For a private company, valuing stock options is difficult, but there are several ways one can get an idea of these values. First, you will have an idea once you have raised money, as the valuation of the latest financing (the post-money valuation) can be used to estimate the value of the company and thus the company stock. Second, you can do a market comparison analysis to project what the company is worth by comparing it to similar public companies. Finally, you can hire a business valuation specialist to assess the value of the company stock.

Warrants

Although typically issued in combination with debt or convertible securities financing, warrants are also used for employee compensation.[5] Warrants usually have expiration periods of three to five years and are detachable from the main security with which they are issued. What this means is that they *can be separately sold to other investors, unlike stock options.* Because they provide the holder with the right to purchase stock at a predetermined fixed price up until expiration, *the exercise price (the purchase price) of warrants is usually set at 10% to 20% above the current value of the stock when issued*, with the expectation that the stock price will have appreciated above the exercise price prior to expiration.

Antidilution Protection

As a growing company progresses through multiple rounds of financing, dilution will inevitably affect the founder and management team. For the founder, this can mean decreasing from 100% to 5 or 10% ownership, which can result in demoralization and diminish the incentive to perform. This is especially true when an early round investor, who most likely has antidilution protection is able to maintain a constant ownership throughout several rounds of additional financing. And as discussed in chapter 10, dilution can be even more significant if the company experiences down rounds. Thus, the issuance of stock options serves more then a means of non-cash compensation, but as a method to minimize the effects of ownership dilution.

Obviously, venture capitalists do not want to dilute the management team's ownership to the point where their incentive disappears. Rather, they want to maximize their IRR, which can only be accomplished by striking a delicate balance between minimizing pre-money valuations prior to financing a round and making sure the founder and management team have enough ownership to maintain a high incentive. Therefore, the terms of each round of financing can set aside additional options to be granted by the board of directors known as *reserve shares*, whose purpose is to counter the effects of dilution and preserve the high level of incentive of the founder and management team. If structured properly, these reserve options can even intensify the drive and performance of the management team by attaching them to the achievement of specific milestones.

NSOs and ISOs

There are two general types of stock options that must be distinguished. *Nonqualified Stock Options (NSOs) are more commonly distributed since they may also be used as payment for non-employees* (i.e. taxes are not withheld from their paychecks and they do not receive a W-2 from the company) such as attorneys, consultants, non-employee directors and freelance workers. In contrast, *Incentive Stock Options (ISOs) are reserved for executives and are also known as qualified stock options because they are qualified to receive special tax treatment* by the IRS under IRS code 422. However, the annual *limitation for ISOs is $100,000 per employee.*

The key distinction between these two types of options is that **upon exercise of NSOs, the recipient incurs a tax liability if the stock has appreciated above the grant price, regardless whether the holder sells the stock or holds onto it.** In contrast, *with ISOs, the holder only incurs a tax liability if the stock is sold at a price above the grant price, provided the holder has held the shares for two years after the grant of options has been awarded and one year after he has exercised the options.* This tax liability is the option holder's current capital gains tax rate multiplied by the difference between the sales price and the exercise price. **If however, the holder of the ISOs sells the stock either prior to the two-year plus one-day award date or the one-year plus one-day exercise date, these options are taxed like NSOs and thus taxable once exercised.** Table 12-1 compares ISOs with NSOs.

While *ISOs provide a major tax advantage over NSOs, they have the disadvantage of being subject to the alternative minimum tax* (AMT). Specifically, the difference between the purchase price of the stock and the grant price is the portion subject to the AMT (see Appendix C-5 on the calculation of the AMT). The AMT was created to make sure that high-income earners pay a minimum tax amount on money they receive that is not considered income, since they are benefiting from potential tax exclusions and deductions produced from the difference between the grant and exercise prices.[6] Although no formal guidelines have been established to indicate when individuals may be candidates for AMT tax rules, *employees earning over $75,000 in one year are generally AMT candidates.*

The incentive stock options plan will specify the maximum number of shares that may be issued to participants of the plan and this figure usually amounts to about 10-20% of the total stock outstanding. In addition, *the plan also informs the shareholders the maximum amount of dilution they will incur if all options are granted and exercised.* A committee must be formed to administer the plan, and because these individuals are responsible for granting the options and establishing the criteria for compensation, they cannot be eligible participants of the plan. Appendix A-8 shows a sample ISO agreement.

Compensating With Stock Options

How much should a founder compensate its management team? Well as we have seen, the percentage ownership of the company that the founders and management begin with is usually nowhere near that after a liquidity event. Therefore, *prior to beginning a fund raising campaign directed towards venture capital firms, the company should structure an "ideal" ownership percentage to be implemented within all term sheets if possible.* These ranges can vary greatly, but Alex Wilmerding has reported that this range is 3 to 13 percent for CEOs, 1 to 2.5 percent for CFOs, and 0.5 to 1.5% for key executives. In order to maintain this percentage ownership, the management team will need to demonstrate consistent superior performance throughout each series of financing so that the investors will be encouraged by their results and wish to maintain an optimal level of incentive for these individuals. In structuring the stock options compensation for board members and advisory members, the company should set a fixed percentage aside so that as the size of these groups is altered, the total percentage does not change. The amount can range from 0.5 to 1.0% and should be closely tied to the value each of these boards contributes.

Table 12-1. Comparison of ISOs versus NSOs

	ISOs	**NSOs**
Indications	Executives	Employees and non-employees
Limitations	$100,000 value per year per employee (calculated on the date of the grant)	None
Holding Period	2 years + 1 day after grant 1 year + 1 day after exercise	None
Strike Price	Must be equal to greater then current fair market value of stock	Can be less then, equal to, or greater current fair market value of stock
Basis	Fair market value of the stock at the time of exercise	Fair market value of the stock at the at the time of exercise
Taxes	Long-term capital gains on spread between exercise and sales price.	Regular income tax on spreads between exercise price and current market value at the time of grant and capital gains tax on the sales.
AMT	AMT is assessed if greater than regular income tax.	None as long as holding periods are observed*
Recommended Execution Strategy	Gradual exercise each year to minimize the AMT liability	Gradual exercise each year to minimize chances of increasing your tax bracket
Special		Be careful when exercising because this immediately triggers a tax liability and stock could decline causing a large tax burden.

* Note that a person may also have an AMT liability if they have substantial long-term gains from NSO or even traditional stock sales.

Finally, while ideally attractive for the company, striving to restrict ownership to a specific percentage by the management team is a very difficult task. Therefore, the company may wish to focus on negotiating for a set amount of reserve shares that would be dilutive to the preferred stock. In order to create this the company would need to have board approval.

ESOPs

In the early stages your company probably will not be concerned about ESOPs, nor will it have many resources to provide for them. However, assuming that the company progresses to become a successful business entity, you will need to consider these types of benefits in detail. An Employee Stock Ownership Plan (ESOP) is a qualified contribution plan similar to profit sharing plans, except instead of cash contributions an employer can make *tax-deductible contributions of cash, stock, or a combination into a trust for the benefit of its employees.* Thus, ESOP plans provide a mechanism for employees to obtain company stock at a low cost to the employer due to tax savings.[7] And because employees are not taxed until these assets are withdrawn, ESOPs are a convenient instrument for *tax-deferred compensation.* While the engagement of an ESOP can clearly cause existing shareholder dilution of nonparticipants and thus a decrease in voting power, this can be used as a defensive strategy against a hostile takeover of a public company. In addition, ESOPs can also be used for a management buyout by employees. Figure 12-4 illustrates the operational dynamics of an ESOP plan.

For the company that sponsors the ESOP, the *principal and interest on ESOP loans are tax deductible, as are the dividend payments on stock contributed by the ESOP if they are used to repay the ESOP debt. Furthermore, tax credits up to 0.5% of employee payroll can be earned if ESOP contributions in that amount were received.* In a long-term study of publicly traded companies, it has been shown that companies with ESOPs experience an increase in sales, employee retention, and sales per employee by approximately 2.3% per year relative to periods prior to implementation of the ESOP. In addition, these same studies found that companies with ESOPs also tended to remain in business longer and overwhelmingly provided more retirement benefits programs to their employees versus non-ESOP companies. However, there has been no similar study with private companies, due to the lack of available data.[8]

It is important to note that ERISA legislation requires that *if shares of the corporation are closely held (private) and more then 10% of the plan's assets are invested in the employer's stock, ESOP participants must be given voting rights on certain corporate issues such as mergers or acquisitions, recapitalizations, reclassification, liquidation or dissolution, or sales of a substantial portion of company assets.* While this may not represent a dilemma for most early stage companies whose staff mainly comprises management, it could pose difficulties for later stage companies that have several non-executive employees. Finally, private companies must repurchase the shares of departing employees, which will require an outside valuation of the company to be generated. And while the minimum initial cost to establish an ESOP is $15,000 to $20,000, it can provide substantial longer–term tax savings for the company and create an incentive-based staff similar to larger companies.

Golden Parachutes

These are employee severance plans that cover top management and are usually triggered whenever a change of control occurs. They are added to increase the job security of these individuals who at some point might be forced out of their position. These benefits are similar to the compensation plans you may have heard of when the CEOs of Compaq and WorldCom resigned. Typically, golden parachutes provide for employee benefits and salaries of one to three times the current salary of qualified executives for one to ten years after termination of employment, depending upon the size of the company.

For private companies, a typical golden parachute might include an annual payment of the employees' salary for up to three years. The tax considerations for such plans are unique and specified by the 1986 Tax Act and *penalties are imposed on companies issuing such plans if payments exceed three times the employee's salary over the past five years. In addition, these payments are not tax deductible to the sponsoring corporation and the recipient of this plan must pay an additional 20% surcharge in addition to his normal state and federal income taxes.*

Silver Parachutes

These are similar to golden parachutes but they cover more employees at the mid management level. Rather than providing up to three times the employee's salary for up to ten years, these employees might receive six months to one year of payments totaling 50% to 100% of their salary.

Split Dollar Life Insurance

This is an insurance policy that shares both the costs and benefits between the employer and the employee. It is used as a low cost insurance benefit for the executive.

Figure 12-4. Anatomy of an ESOP

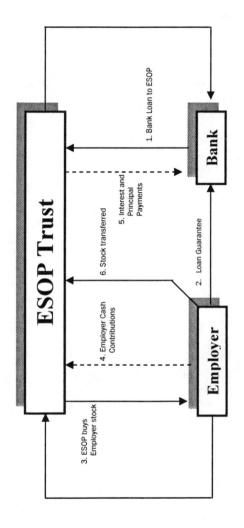

The ESOP trust borrows from funds from a bank (1), and the employer guarantees this loan (2). The ESOP trust uses these funds to purchase company stock from the employer, which is used as collateral to secure the loan (3). The employer then makes periodic cash contributions to the ESOP trust for repayment of principal and interest on the bank loan (4) and the ESOP trust sends these payments to the bank (5). Portions of the stock are transferred to the ESOP trust as the loan principal is repaid to the bank (6).

Source: Leimberg, S.R., McFadden, J.J.

Restricted Stock Plans

Venture investors certainly do not want members of the management team to jump ship when things get tough, knowing that they can retain full rights to ownership of their stock. This is especially true during the early stages of the company, when investors are investing more in the management team then anything else. Therefore, they will usually require founders and key management to submit a portion of their stock under a *restricted stock agreement* so that it is only vested after a number of years with the company. In addition, *reserve shares are also tied into a restricted stock agreement* for the same purpose. The timing and extent of restriction of this stock can and should be negotiated within the term sheet.

Benefits

Workers' Compensation Insurance

One of the first activities that a new company wishing to hire personnel must accomplish is establishing workers' compensation insurance for its employees. *Failure to do so is not only a professional and moral oversight, but also a violation of federal law and may be punishable by imprisonment and/or fines.* According to U.S. law, if an employee suffers any work-related injury or illness, the employer is required to provide benefits to the employee immediately. These benefits include all medical care required to heal the employee, temporary disability indemnity (partial wage replacement during the recovery period), permanent disability indemnity (monetary compensation if the injury is permanent and the employee does not fully recover), vocational rehabilitation (retraining resources if the employee cannot carry out his or her prior duties), death benefits, and burial expenses to the dependents of a deceased employee.

Employee Benefits

Unfortunately employee benefits plans can be costly but must be prioritized as an essential business expense. As a company grows and begins to generate revenues (either through sales and/or financing), the need to provide competitive medical benefits, IRC Section 125, and retirement plans becomes more important in the process of attracting experienced corporate professionals into the startup organization. These individuals will expect to receive benefits comparable to their previous corporate employer. However, typically 40-60 employees must be covered in order to begin to offer the most competitive packages.

The number, types, and extent of employee benefits have changed dramatically over the past decade and the choices, fees, and exclusions found within the benefits universe are so highly varied that it can be a full time job structuring and maintaining this aspect of the business. Perhaps this explains the recent growth in the human resources industry. Therefore, the most efficient use of time and money devoted towards this segment of the company may be achieved by the management's understanding of the basic fundamentals of employee benefits and employing the services of a qualified benefits specialist. At minimum, a benefits specialist should be knowledgeable in stock options plans, 401k and alternative plans, life and term disability insurance, business insurance, and medical insurance.

Key Employee Life Insurance

This type of insurance is an individual life and/or disability policy *that insures a company against the loss or disability of a key employee. Therefore, the owner and beneficiary of the policy is the company rather than the employee.* A key person certainly includes the owners or founders but can also be any person of the company whose unexpected death or disability could result in serious economic loss to company operations. While this type of insurance is usually needed for any startup company due to the limited numbers of individuals involved, (and therefore the higher dependency upon each individual) it is an absolute must for the technology startup due to the nature of these knowledge-based businesses.

For small companies, the life insurance portion usually goes up to $10,000,000 with a coverage period of to 30 years, while the disability product is difficult to insure in excess of $2,000,000. In order to provide the most coverage for the lowest price, a company should purchase term insurance. However, no fees are recoverable in the event that the policy never issues a claim unlike with life insurance. If the company so chooses, this term insurance can be converted over to life insurance at a later date if requested.

Usually, the minimum requirements for acceptance by these plans are a basic medical examination of key employees, financial information on the company and any information on large investors in the company. And depending upon the policy amount, person's age and the issuing company, the insured may have to submit to more specific medical procedures, such ECGs and treadmill tests.

Notes

[1] Title VII of the Civil Rights Act of 1964. http://www.eeoc.gov/laws/vii.html

[2] National Whistleblower Protection Act.
http://www.whistleblowers.org/html/model_whistleblower_law.html

[3] Key Employment Laws
http://www.li.suu.edu/Library/Circulation/Lewis/acct3360tlEmploymentLaws.pdf

[4] One helpful resource for these issues is the website of the Society for Human Resources Management www.shrm.org.

[5] More often however, they are used as "*sweetners*" to encourage investors to accept a lower interest rate that is typically offered by convertibles or to provide a justifiable means for a company to offer a low interest rate debt instrument.

[6] Note that a person may also have an AMT liability if they have substantial long-term gains from NSOs or even traditional stock sales.

[7] One should note that because partnerships cannot issue stock, ESOPs are unavailable to these entities. In addition, while S corporations are permitted to establish ESOPs, they are not permitted to receive all of the tax benefits of this plan, making ESOPs a unique advantage for C corporations.

[8] Consequently, there is no positive evidence correlating CEO stock options compensation at public companies with increasing financial performance.

APPENDICES

APPENDIX A

Legal Agreements

Appendix A courtesy of

Peter B. Finn, ESQ,
Senior Partner, Rubin and Rudman LLP
(www.rubinrudman.com)
for educational purposes only

APPENDIX A-1

MUTUAL CONFIDENTIALITY AND NON-DISCLOSURE AGREEMENT
(THE "AGREEMENT")

XYZ Corporation [the "Corporation"] a _____ corporation duly organized under law and having an usual place of business at _____ _____and _____, a _____corporation duly organized under law and having a usual place of business at _____ _____(the "Company") are willing to disclose to each other certain confidential, non-public information concerning their respective proprietary products, technology, business plans, financials, capitalization, facilities, business records and any other proprietary information prepared by or for each of them (the "Confidential Information"). All material that is written, in hard media, digital or other format shall automatically be considered as Confidential Information. If the information is disclosed orally, then it shall be deemed to be Confidential Information if the disclosure is reduced to writing, marked "CONFIDENTIAL" and delivered to the other party within thirty (30) days of the date of disclosure. The "Corporation" or the "Company" shall include the respective entities and their successors, assigns, legal representatives, affiliates, employees, agents, servants, advisors, attorneys, accountants and consultants (hereinafter sometimes referred to as the "Representatives"), all of whom agree to be bound by the terms and conditions of this Agreement.

In consideration of the willingness of the Corporation and the Company to disclose to each other their respective Confidential Information and, in recognition of the confidential nature thereof, the Corporation and the Company hereby each agree that the Confidential Information received from the other, will be kept strictly confidential and will be used solely for the purposes stated in this Agreement; and will not be disclosed to any person, firm or entity other than a Representative without the prior written consent of the other. The Corporation and the Company agree that their Representatives shall keep such Confidential Information confidential. The Corporation and the Company further agree to take such steps to protect and maintain the security and confidentiality of the Confidential Information as the Corporation and the Company would take in the case of their own confidential business information.

The restraint on confidentiality provided herein shall not apply to any Confidential Information which:

a) Is or subsequently becomes part of the public domain through no fault of either the Corporation or the Company; or

b)   Was known by the Corporation or the Company at the time of disclosure and such prior knowledge can be demonstrated by the Corporation or the Company; or

c)   Is required by law to be disclosed, after notice to the Corporation or the Company and an opportunity for the Corporation or the Company to seek injunctive relief and/or an appropriate Protective Order.

It is agreed that all documents and other materials which embody the Confidential Information will be returned to the Corporation or the Company as the case may be, immediately upon the request of the other, and no copies, extracts or other reproductions shall be retained by the Corporation, the Company or the Representatives.

The Corporation and the Company agree that money damages will not be a sufficient remedy for any breach of this Agreement by the other or their Representatives, and the Corporation or the Company as the case may be, shall be entitled, in addition to money damages, to specific performance and injunctive relief and any other appropriate equitable remedies for any such breach. Such remedies shall not be deemed to be the exclusive remedies for a breach of this Agreement but shall be in addition to all other remedies available at law or in equity.

This Agreement shall be governed by, and construed in accordance with, the laws of

_____.

The purpose of this Agreement is for _____.
This Agreement is being executed in multiple copies each of which shall be deemed to be an original, under seal, this ____ day of _____, _____.

XYZ Corporation

By: _____
                    [Name]   [Title]
Hereunto Duly Authorized

This Agreement and its terms
and conditions are hereby
acknowledged, accepted and
agreed to:

By: _____
[Name]   [Title]
Hereunto Duly Authorized

APPENDIX A-2

CONSULTING AGREEMENT

THIS CONSULTING AGREEMENT (the "Agreement") is made and entered into this_ day of _____, 200_ (the "Effective Date") by and between XYZ Corporation, a _____ corporation duly organized under law and having an usual place of business at _____(hereinafter referred to as the "Company") and _____ of _____ _____(hereinafter referred to as the "Consultant").

WHEREAS, the Company wishes to engage the Consultant to provide the services described herein and Consultant agrees to provide the services for the compensation and otherwise in accordance with the terms and conditions contained in this Agreement,

NOW THEREFORE, in consideration of the foregoing, and for other good and valuable consideration, the receipt and sufficiency of which are hereby acknowledged, accepted and agreed to, the Company and the Consultant, intending to be legally bound, agree to the terms set forth below.

1.   **TERM.** Commencing as of the Effective Date, and continuing for a period of ____ (__) years (the "Term"), unless earlier terminated pursuant to Article 4 hereof, the Consultant agrees that he/she will serve as a consultant to the Company. This Agreement may be renewed or extended for any period as may be agreed by the parties.

2.   **DUTIES AND SERVICES.**

(a)   Consultant's duties and responsibilities shall be _____

_____

_____

_____

(collectively, the "Duties" or "Services").

(b)   Consultant agrees that during the Term he/she will devote up to ____ (__) days per month to his/her Duties. The Company will periodically provide the Consultant with a schedule of the requested hours, responsibilities and deliverables for the applicable period of time. The Duties will be scheduled on an as-needed basis.

(c)   The Consultant represents and warrants to the Company that he/she is under no contractual or other restrictions or obligations which are inconsistent with the execution of this Agreement, or which will interfere with the performance of his/her Duties.   Consultant represents and warrants that the execution and performance of this Agreement will not violate any policies or procedures of any other person or entity for which he/she performs Services concurrently with those performed herein.

(d)   In performing the Services, Consultant shall comply, to the best of his/her knowledge, with all business conduct, regulatory and health and safety guidelines established by the Company for any governmental authority with respect to the Company's business.

3.   **CONSULTING FEE.**

(a)   Subject to the provisions hereof, the Company shall pay Consultant a consulting fee of _____($_____) Dollars for each hour of Services provided to the Company (the "Consulting Fee"). The Consultant shall submit monthly, on the Company's standard reporting form, a listing of his/her hours, the Duties performed and a summary of his/her activities. The Consulting Fee shall be paid within fifteen (15) days of the Company's receipt of the report and invoice.

(b)   Consultant shall be entitled to prompt reimbursement for all pre-approved expenses incurred in the performance of his/her Duties, upon submission and approval of written statements and receipts in accordance with the then regular procedures of the Company.

(c)   The Consultant agrees that all Services will be rendered by him/her as an independent contractor and that this Agreement does not create an employer-employee relationship between the Consultant and the Company. The Consultant shall have no right to receive any employee benefits including, but not limited to, health and accident insurance, life insurance, sick leave and/or vacation. Consultant agrees to pay all taxes including, self-employment taxes due in respect of the Consulting Fee and to indemnify the Company in the event the Company is required to pay any such taxes on behalf of the Consultant.

4.   **EARLY TERMINATION OF THE TERM.**

(a)   If the Consultant voluntarily ceases performing his/her Duties, becomes physically or mentally unable to perform his/her Duties, or is terminated for cause, then, in each instance, the Consulting Fee shall cease and terminate as of such date. Any termination "For Cause" shall be made in good faith by the Company's Board of Directors.

(b)   This Agreement may be terminated without cause by either party upon not less than thirty (30) days prior written notice by either party to the other.

(c)   Upon termination under Sections 4(a) or 4(b), neither party shall have any further obligations under this Agreement, except for the obligations which by their terms survive this termination as noted in Section 16 hereof. Upon termination and, in any case, upon the Company's request, the Consultant shall return immediately to the Company all Confidential Information, as hereinafter defined, and copies thereof.

5.   **RESTRICTED ACTIVITIES.** During the Term and for a period of one (1) year thereafter, Consultant will not, directly or indirectly:

> (i)   solicit or request any employee of or consultant to the Company to leave the employ of or cease consulting for the Company;

> (ii)   solicit or request any employee of or consultant to the Company to join the employ of, or begin consulting for, any individual or entity that researches, develops, markets or sells products that compete with those of the Company;

> (iii)   solicit or request any individual or entity that researches, develops, markets or sells products that compete with those of the Company, to employ or retain as a consultant any employee or consultant of the Company; or

> (iv)   induce or attempt to induce any supplier or vendor of the Company to terminate or breach any written or oral agreement or understanding with the Company.

6.   **PROPRIETARY RIGHTS.**

> (a)   <u>Definitions</u>. For the purposes of this Article 6, the terms set forth below shall have the following meanings:

>> (i)   <u>Concept and Ideas</u>. Those concepts and ideas disclosed by the Company to Consultant or which are first developed by Consultant during the course of the performance of Services hereunder and which relate to the Company' present, past or prospective business activities, services, and products, all of which shall remain the sole and exclusive property of the Company. The Consultant shall have no publication rights and all of the same shall belong exclusively to the Company.

>> (ii)   <u>Confidential Information</u>. For the purposes of this Agreement, Confidential Information shall mean and collectively include: all information relating to the business, plans and/or technology of the Company including, but not limited to technical information including inventions, methods, plans, processes, specifications, characteristics, assays, raw data, scientific preclinical or clinical data, records, databases, formulations, clinical protocols, equipment design, know-how, experience, and trade secrets; developmental, marketing, sales, customer, supplier, consulting relationship information, operating, performance, and cost

information; computer programming techniques whether in tangible or intangible form, and all record bearing media containing or disclosing the foregoing information and techniques including, written business plans, patents and patent applications, grant applications, notes, and memoranda, whether in writing or presented, stored or maintained in or by electronic, magnetic, or other means.

Notwithstanding the foregoing, the term "Confidential Information" shall not include any information which: (a) can be demonstrated to have been in the public domain or was publicly known or available prior to the date of the disclosure to Consultant; (b) can be demonstrated in writing to have been rightfully in the possession of Consultant prior to the disclosure of such information to Consultant by the Company; (c) becomes part of the public domain or publicly known or available by publication or otherwise, not due to any unauthorized act or omission on the part of Consultant; or (d) is supplied to Consultant by a third party without binder of secrecy, so long as that such third party has no obligation to the Company or any of its affiliated companies to maintain such information in confidence.

(b)   <u>Non-Disclosure to Third Parties</u>.   Except as required by Consultant's Duties, Consultant shall not, at any time now or in the future, directly or indirectly, use, publish, disseminate or otherwise disclose any Confidential Information, Concepts, or Ideas to any third party without the prior written consent of the Company which consent may be denied in each instance and all of the same, together with publication rights, shall belong exclusively to the Company.

(c)   <u>Documents, etc.</u>   All documents, diskettes, tapes, procedural manuals, guides, specifications, plans, drawings, designs and similar materials, lists of present, past or prospective customers, customer proposals, invitations to submit proposals, price lists and data relating to the pricing of the Company' products and services, records, notebooks and all other materials containing Confidential Information or information about Concepts or Ideas (including all copies and reproductions thereof), that come into Consultant's possession or control by reason of Consultant's performance of the relationship, whether prepared by Consultant or others: (a) are the property of the Company, (b) will not be used by Consultant in any way other than in connection with the performance of his/her Duties, (c) will not be provided or shown to any third party by Consultant, (d) will not be removed from the Company's or Consultant's premises (except as Consultant's Duties require), and (e) at the termination (for whatever reason), of Consultant's relationship with the Company, will be left with, or forthwith returned by Consultant to the Company.

(d)   <u>Patents, etc.</u> The Consultant agrees that the Company is and shall remain the exclusive owner of the Confidential Information and Concepts and Ideas. Any interest in patents, patent applications, inventions, technological innovations, trade names, trademarks, service marks, copyrights, copyrightable works, developments, discoveries, designs, processes, formulas, know-how, data and analysis, whether registrable or not ("Developments"), which Consultant, as a result of rendering Services to the Company under this Agreement, may conceive or develop, shall: (i) forthwith be brought to the attention of the Company by Consultant and (ii) belong exclusively to the Company. No license or conveyance of any such rights to the Consultant is granted or implied under this Agreement.

      (e)   <u>Assignment</u>. The Consultant hereby assigns and, to the extent any such assignment cannot be made at present, hereby agrees to assign to the Company, without further compensation, all of his/her right, title and interest in and to all Concepts, Ideas, and Developments. The Consultant will execute all documents and perform all lawful acts which the Company considers necessary or advisable to secure its rights hereunder and to carry out the intent of this Agreement.

7.   **EQUITABLE RELIEF.** Consultant agrees that any breach of Articles 5 and 6 above by him/her would cause irreparable damage to the Company and that, in the event of such breach, the Company shall have, in addition to any and all remedies of law, the right to an injunction, specific performance or other equitable relief to prevent the violation or threatened violation of Consultant's obligations hereunder.

8.   **WAIVER.** Any waiver by the Company of a breach of any provision of this Agreement shall not operate or be construed as a waiver of any subsequent breach of the same or any other provision hereof. All waivers by the Company shall be in writing.

9.   **SEVERABILITY; REFORMATION.** In case any one or more of the provisions or parts of a provision contained in this Agreement shall, for any reason, be held to be invalid, illegal or unenforceable in any respect, such invalidity, illegality or unenforceability shall not affect any other provision or part of a provision of this Agreement; and this Agreement shall, to the fullest extent lawful, be reformed and construed as if such invalid or illegal or unenforceable provision, or part of a provision, had never been contained herein, and such provision or part reformed so that it would be valid, legal and enforceable to the maximum extent possible. Without limiting the foregoing, if any provision (or part of provision) contained in this Agreement shall for any reason be held to be excessively broad as to duration, activity or subject, it shall be construed by limiting and reducing it, so as to be enforceable to the fullest extent compatible with then existing applicable law.

10.   **ASSIGNMENT.** The Company shall have the right to assign its rights and obligations under this Agreement to a party which assumes the Company' obligations hereunder. Consultant shall not have the right to assign his/her rights or obligations under this Agreement without the prior written consent of the Company. This Agreement shall be binding upon and inure to the benefit of the Consultant's heirs and legal representatives in the event of his/her death or disability.

11.   **HEADINGS.** Headings and subheadings are for convenience only and shall not be deemed to be a part of this Agreement.

12.   AMENDMENTS. This Agreement may be amended or modified, in whole or in part, only by an instrument in writing signed by all parties hereto. Any amendment, consent, decision, waiver or other action to be made, taken or given by the Company with respect to the Agreement shall be made, taken or given on behalf of the Company only by authority of the Company's Board of Directors.

13.   NOTICES. Any notices or other communications required hereunder shall be in writing and shall be deemed given when delivered in person or when mailed, by certified or registered first class mail, postage prepaid, return receipt requested, addressed to the parties at their addresses specified in the preamble to this Agreement or to such other addresses of which a party shall have notified the others in accordance with the provisions of this Section 13.

14.   COUNTERPARTS. This Agreement may be executed in two or more counterparts, each of which shall constitute an original and all of which shall be deemed a single agreement.

15.   GOVERNING LAW. This Agreement shall be construed in accordance with and governed for all purposes by the laws of _____ _____applicable to contracts executed and wholly performed within such jurisdiction. Any dispute arising hereunder shall be referred to and heard in only a court located in _____ .

16.   SURVIVAL. The provisions of Sections 5 to 9 and 15 to 16 of this Agreement shall survive the expiration of the Term or the termination of this Agreement. This Agreement supersedes all prior agreements, written or oral, between the Company and the Consultant relating to the subject matter of this Agreement.

        EXECUTED, under seal, effective as of the Effective Date.

XYZ CORPORATION   CONSULTANT

By:_____   _____
[Name]   [Title]
Hereunto Duly Authorized

APPENDIX A-3

FORM OF A NON-COMPETE PROVISION

NON-COMPETITION.

(A)   <u>Non-Competition Period</u>. The Employee shall not, directly or indirectly (including, without limitation, either alone or as a partner, officer, director, employee, joint venturer or stockholder of, or as a consultant or other independent contractor to or agent or representative for, any company, business, individual or other entity), engage in any business activity which is directly or indirectly in competition with the Company's Business, as hereinafter defined, at any time during the Employment Period and for a period of _____(__) years after the termination, for any reason, of the Employment Period (the "Post-Employment Period") (collectively, the Employment Period and the Post-Employment Period are herein referred to as the "Non-Competition Period"); provided, however, that nothing in this Agreement shall prevent or restrict the Employee from owning, directly or indirectly, not more than three percent (3%) of the securities of any publicly traded company for the sole purpose of a passive investment. For purposes of this Agreement, the Company's Business shall be defined as: _____

(B)   <u>Restricted Business Activities:</u> During the Non-Competition Period, the Employee will not, directly or indirectly:

(a)   solicit or request any other employee of or consultant to the Company to join the employ of, or begin consulting for, any individual or entity that researches, develops, markets or sells products that compete with those of the Company;

(b)   solicit or request any individual or entity that researches, develops, markets or sells products that compete with those of the Company, to employ or retain as a consultant any employee or consultant of the Company;

(c)   divert, directly or indirectly, to any competitor of the Company, any customer of the Company; or

(d)   induce or attempt to induce any supplier or vendor of the Company to terminate or breach any written or oral agreement or understanding with the Company.

EXECUTED, under seal, effective as of the Effective Date.

XYZ CORPORATION   EMPLOYEE

By:_____   _____
[Name]   [Title]
Hereunto Duly Authorized

APPENDIX A-4

XYZ CORPORATION
CONFIDENTIAL INFORMATION AND
INVENTION ASSIGNMENT AGREEMENT
(THE "AGREEMENT")

As a condition of, and in consideration of, my employment by XYZ Corporation ("XYZ"), and my receipt of the compensation now and hereafter paid to me by XYZ, I agree to the following:

1. **Confidential Information**.

(a) **XYZ and Third Party Information.** I agree at all times during the term of my employment and thereafter, to hold in strict confidence, and not to use, except for the benefit of XYZ, or to disclose to any person, firm or corporation without written authorization of an officer of XYZ, any Confidential Information. I understand that "Confidential Information" means any research conducted by me either alone or with others during my employment by XYZ, and all results and data generated in connection therewith, and any confidential or proprietary information, technical data, trade secrets or know-how of XYZ, including, but not limited to, research and product plans, products, services, customer lists and customers, markets, developments, inventions, processes, formulas, technology, marketing, finances or other business information disclosed to me by XYZ, either directly or indirectly, in writing, orally or otherwise. I recognize that XYZ has received and in the future will receive from third parties confidential or proprietary information of such third parties subject to a duty on XYZ's part to maintain the confidentiality of such information and to use such information only for certain limited purposes, and I understand that such information is also Confidential Information. I further understand that Confidential Information does not include any of the foregoing information or items that has become publicly known and made generally available through no wrongful act of mine or of others who were under confidentiality obligations to XYZ as to the information or items involved.

(b) **Former Employer Information.** I agree that I will not, during my employment with XYZ, improperly use or disclose any proprietary information or trade secrets of any former or concurrent employer or other person or entity and that I will not bring onto the premises of XYZ, any unpublished document or proprietary information belonging to any such employer, person or entity unless consented to in writing by such employer, person or entity.

2. **Inventions and Publication Reports**.

(a) **Inventions Retained and Licensed.** I have attached hereto as Attachment "A" a list describing all inventions, original works of authorship, developments, improvements, and trade secrets that were made by me prior to my employment with XYZ (collectively referred to as "Prior Inventions"), that belong to me, that relate to XYZ's business, products or research and development, and that are not assigned to XYZ hereunder; or, if no such list is attached, I represent that there are no such Prior Intentions. If, in the course of my employment with XYZ, I incorporate into a XYZ product, process or machine a Prior Invention owned by me or in which I have an interest, XYZ is hereby granted and will have a non-exclusive, royalty free, irrevocable, perpetual, worldwide license, with the right to grant sublicenses, to make, have made, modify, use and sell such Prior Invention as part of or in connection with such product, process or machine.

I further agree that with respect to all Inventions or other matters that may arise during my employment that may result in publishable material, with or without consideration, all such publications rights shall belong exclusively to XYZ. When and if such materials and items are published by the Company, the Company agrees to note my involvement and development of such materials and items.

(b)   **Assignment of Inventions.** I agree that I will promptly make full written disclosure to XYZ, and will hold in trust for the sole right and benefit of XYZ, and hereby assign to XYZ, or XYZ's designee, all my right, title, and interest in and to any and all inventions, original works of authorship, developments, concepts, improvements or trade secrets, whether or not patentable or registrable under patent, copyright or similar laws, that I may solely or jointly make, develop, conceive or reduce to practice, or cause to be made, developed, conceived or reduced to practice, during the period of time I am in the employ of XYZ (collectively referred to as "Inventions"). I further acknowledge that all original works of authorship that are made by me (solely or jointly with others) within the scope of and during the period of my employment with XYZ and that are protectable by copyright are "works made for hire," as that term is defined in the United States Copyright Act.

(c)   **Maintenance of Records.** I agree to keep and maintain adequate and current written records of all Inventions made, developed, conceived or reduced to practice by me (solely or jointly with others) during the term of my employment with XYZ. The records will be in the form of notes, sketches, drawings, and any other format that may be specified by XYZ. The records will be available to and remain the sole property of XYZ at all times.

(d)   **Patent and Copyright Registrations.** I agree to assist XYZ, or XYZ's designee, at XYZ's expense, in every way to secure XYZ's rights in the Inventions and any copyrights, patents, mask work rights or other intellectual property rights relating thereto in any and all countries, including disclosing to XYZ all pertinent information and data with respect thereto, and executing all applications, specifications, oaths, assignments and all other instruments that XYZ shall deem necessary in order to apply for and obtain such rights and in order to assign and convey to XYZ, XYZ's successors, assigns, and nominees the sole and exclusive rights, title and interest in and to such Inventions, and any copyrights, patents, mask work rights or other intellectual property rights relating thereto. I further agree that my obligation to execute or cause to be executed, when it is in my power to do so, any such instrument or papers will continue after the termination of this Agreement. If XYZ is unable because of my mental or physical incapacity or for any other reason to secure my signature to apply for or to pursue any application for any United States of America or foreign patents or copyright registrations covering Inventions or original works of authorship assigned to XYZ as above, then I hereby irrevocably designate and appoint XYZ and XYZ's duly authorized officers and agents as my agent and attorney in fact, to act for and in my behalf and stead to execute and file any such applications and to do all other lawfully permitted acts to further the prosecution and issuance of letters patent or copyright registrations thereon with the same legal force and effect as if executed by me.

3.   I agree that, during the term of my employment with XYZ, I will not engage in any other employment, occupation, consulting or other business activity directly related to the business in which XYZ is now involved or becomes involved during the term of my employment, nor will I engage in any other activities that conflict with my obligation to XYZ. I agree that, at the time of leaving the employ of XYZ, I will deliver to XYZ, any and all documents or property, or reproductions of any such documents or property, developed by me pursuant to my employment with XYZ or otherwise belonging to XYZ, its successors or assigns.

4.   **Representations**. I agree to execute any proper oath or verify any proper document requested by XYZ to carry out the terms of this Agreement. I represent that my performance of all the terms of this Agreement will not breach any agreement to keep in confidence proprietary information acquired by me in confidence or in trust prior to my employment with XYZ. I have not entered into, and I agree I will not enter into, any oral or written agreement in conflict with the terms of this Agreement.

5.   **Arbitration and Equitable Relief**.

(a)   **Arbitration.** Except as provided in Section 5(b) below, I agree that any dispute or controversy arising out of or relating to any interpretation, construction, performance or breach of this Agreement, will be settled by arbitration to be held in _____, _____ in accordance with the rules then in effect of the American Arbitration Association. The arbitrator may grant injunctions or other relief in such dispute or controversy. The decision of the arbitrator will be final, conclusive and binding on the parties to the arbitration. XYZ and I will each pay one-half of the costs and expenses of such arbitration, and each of us will separately pay our counsel and witness fees and expenses.

(b)   **Equitable Remedies.** I agree that it would be impossible or inadequate to measure and calculate XYZ's damages from any breach of the covenants set forth in Sections 1, 2 & 3 herein. Accordingly, I agree that if I breach my obligations under any of such sections, XYZ will have, in addition to any other right or remedy available, the right to seek an injunction from a court of competent jurisdiction restraining such breach or threatened breach and to specific performance of any such provision of this Agreement. I further agree that no bond or other security will be required in obtaining such equitable relief.

    6.   <u>General Provisions</u>.

    (a)   **Governing Law.** This Agreement will be governed by the laws of _____ without reference to conflicts of laws principles.

    (b)   **Entire Agreement.** This Agreement and the attached Letter Employment Agreement set forth the entire agreement and understanding between XYZ and me relating to the subject matter hereof and merges all prior discussions between us. No modification of or amendment to this Agreement or the Letter Employment Agreement, or any waiver of any rights under these Agreements, will be effective unless in writing signed by the party to be charged. Any subsequent change or changes in my duties, salary or compensation will not affect the validity or scope of this Agreement.

    (c)   **Severability.** If one or more of the provisions in this Agreement are deemed void by law, then the remaining provisions will continue in full force and effect.

    (d)   **Successors and Assigns.** This Agreement will be binding upon my heirs, executors, administrators and other legal representatives and will be for the benefit of XYZ, its successors and its assigns.

Dated: _____   _____

                                                       [Signature]

Name of Employee: _____

Address:_____

               _____

Social Security Number: _____

XYZ CORPORATION

By:_____
[Name]   [Title]
Hereunto Duly Authorized

ATTACHMENT A

LIST OF PRIOR INVENTIONS

AND ORIGINAL WORKS OF AUTHORSHIP

Identifying Number   **Title or Brief Description**
           Date

_____   No inventions or improvements

_____   Additional Sheets Attached

Signature of Employee: _____

Print Name of Employee: _____

Date: _____

Accepted by:
XYZ CORPORATION

By:_____
[Name]   [Title]
Hereunto Duly Authorized

APPENDIX A-5

XYZ CORPORATION
SCIENTIFIC ADVISORY BOARD MEMBER
CONFIDENTIALITY, NON-DISCLOSURE AND PROPRIETARY
AGREEMENT
(THE "AGREEMENT")

With respect to my engagement as a member of the Scientific Advisory Board ("SAB") of XYZ Corporation, (the "Company"), and for the remuneration and other valuable consideration to be paid to me as set forth below, I hereby warrant and agree with the Company as follows:

1.   I acknowledge that, as a member of the SAB and advisor to the Company, I will have access to Confidential Information, as hereinafter defined, belonging to the Company and that improper use and/or disclosure of such Confidential Information would cause the Company substantial loss and damage. I agree that all Confidential Information shall be and remain the sole property of the Company.

2.   For purposes of this Agreement, "Confidential Information" is defined to include: all information that has been created, discovered or developed, or has otherwise become known to the Company including, without limitation, information created, discovered, developed or made known by me during the time spent interacting with or performing a service for the Company as a member of the SAB, and/or in which property rights have been assigned or otherwise conveyed to the Company which information is essential to the Company. By way of illustration but not limitation, Confidential Information includes: (a) any trade secret, idea, improvement, invention, technique, innovation, process, procedure, protocol, test, treatment, development, technical data, know-how, design, formula, device, pattern, concept, computer program, training or service manual, plan for new or revised services or products, item compilation of information, or work in process, or any Invention (as hereinafter defined) or parts thereof, and any and all revisions and improvements relating to any of the foregoing (in each case whether or not reduced to tangible form); and (b) the name of any client, employee, prospective client or employee, sales agent, supplier or consultant, any sales plan, sales forecast, marketing material, plan or survey, business plan or strategy, or opportunity, product or service development plan or specification, business proposal or information relating to the present or proposed business of the Company.

3.   My obligations with respect to the Confidential Information will cease after the Confidential Information or any portion thereof: (i) becomes part of the public domain through no wrongful act of my own or my representatives, agents or employees, (ii) is lawfully received by me from a third party without contravention of this Agreement or any similar nondisclosure agreement (whether or not with the

Company) by which such third party is bound, or (iii) is approved for release by written authorization of the Company.

4.   All documents, data, records, apparatus, equipment and other physical property, whether or not pertaining to the Confidential Information, furnished to me by the Company or produced by myself or others in connection with my engagement as a member of the SAB, shall be owned by the Company and promptly returned to the Company as and when requested.

5.   In consideration of the services to be rendered hereunder, I will, upon execution of this Agreement, be granted a Non-Qualified Stock Option Grant to purchase _____(_____) shares of the Company's Common Stock (the "Option"), vesting annually over a four (4) year period and otherwise in accordance with the terms and conditions of the Company's 200_ Stock Option Plan (the "Plan") and Stock Option Agreement (the "Grant). In addition to the Grant, I will be reimbursed for all of the out-of-pocket expenses incurred by me as an member of the SAB.

6.   I understand that my engagement as a member of the SAB is at-will; meaning that the relationship may be terminated by either party at any time with or without cause. While a member of the SAB, I agree to attend quarterly SAB meetings; to be reasonably available for advice and consultation including, telephone discussions and conference calls, and assume such other responsibilities as mutually agreed upon.

7.   I acknowledge that, as a member of the SAB, I will be, individually and collectively, advising and assisting the Company in its business and scientific development and will therefore be involved in improvements, inventions, patents, patent rights, general intangibles, formulae, processes, techniques, know-how and data, whether or not patentable (hereinafter individually and collectively referred to as the "Inventions"), and I hereby agree that all such Inventions shall be owned by and belong solely to the Company, and hereby assign all of my right, title and interest in and to such Inventions to the Company.

8.   I further agree that with regard to the Company's Inventions, to assist the Company in all ways (but at the Company's sole expense) to obtain and, from time to time, enforce rights with regard to the patents on the Inventions in any and all countries, and to that end, my obligations hereunder will be limited to executing and delivering all documents for use in applying for and obtaining such patents thereon and enforcing the same, as the Company may desire, together with any assignments thereof to the Company or persons designated by it; and it is understood and agreed that I will not be involved in the construction of the patents. My obligation to assist the Company in obtaining and enforcing patents and other rights for the Inventions shall continue beyond the termination of my engagement as a member of the SAB, and the Company agrees to compensate me at customary rates for comparable services rendered.

9.   I agree that, prior to the oral public disclosure and/or submission to any outside person of a manuscript describing or relating to my work as a member of the SAB or otherwise involving the Company, I will disclose and send to the Company a copy of the manuscript to be submitted and shall allow the Company at least sixty (60) days to determine whether such disclosure or manuscript contains subject matter for which patent protection should be sought prior to publication. If the Company notifies me that the oral presentation or manuscript contains material that consists of patentable subject matter for which patent protection should be sought, then I agree that I will withhold the proposed public disclosure for a maximum of three (3) months from the date of receipt of such notice from the Company in order to permit the Company to file patent applications directed to the patentable subject matter contained in the proposed disclosure. After the filing of a patent application by the Company, I will be free to submit the manuscript and/or make public the disclosures.

10.   I represent and warrant that my performance of all of the terms of this Agreement and my engagement as a member of the SAB does not and will not breach any agreement that I may have entered into or understanding that I may have; and I have not entered into any agreement that requires me to disclose any Confidential Information. If any provision(s) of this Agreement shall be declared invalid, illegal or unenforceable, such provision(s) shall be severed and all remaining provisions shall continue in full force and effect.

11.   This Agreement shall be effective as of the date on which I become a member of the SAB (the "Effective Date"). The term "Company," as used herein, shall include XYZ Corporation, its successors, assigns, legal representatives, subsidiaries and affiliates.

12.   Any notice required or permitted hereunder shall be given in writing and shall be deemed effectively given upon personal delivery to the party to be notified or upon deposit in the United States Post Office certified or registered mail or with an air courier, postage and fees prepaid, addressed to the Company at ___ _____, with a copy to: _____ _____or to myself at the address set forth below my signature on this Agreement, or at such other address as a party may designate by ten (10) day's advance written notice to the other party. Notwithstanding the foregoing, notice may be given by telex or telecopy, provided that appropriate confirmation of receipt is received.

13.   This Agreement shall be binding upon me, my heirs, executors, successors and assigns and administrators and shall inure to the benefit of the Company, and its representatives, successors and assigns. I understand that this Agreement is personal to me and may not be assigned by me.

14.   This Agreement shall be governed by and construed in accordance with the

laws of the _____.

Dated: _____, 200   _____

                                            Name:
                                            Address:

ACCEPTED AND AGREED TO:

XYZ CORPORATION
By:_____
[Name]   [Title]
Hereunto Duly Authorized

APPENDIX A-6

_____

NAME OF INVESTOR (please print)

INVESTOR QUESTIONNAIRE (INDIVIDUAL)

(ALL INFORMATION WILL BE TREATED CONFIDENTIALLY)

XYZ Corporation

_____

_____

      The information contained herein is being furnished by the undersigned in order to enable you to determine whether an offer and sale of Common Capital Stock, without par value of XYZ Corporation, a _____ corporation (the "Company"), may be made without registration of the shares under the Securities Act of 1933, as amended, and under certain state securities laws. I agree that the Company may present this Questionnaire to such parties including, but not limited to, governmental and regulatory authorities as it deems appropriate in order to assure itself that the offering will not result in a violation of the registration provisions of Federal or State Securities laws. I understand that this Questionnaire is not an offer of the shares or any other securities of the Company to me. If the shares are being purchased by a partnership, corporation or other entity, then a Questionnaire shall be completed by each of the equity owners of such entity.

1.   Personal.

      Full name:_____

      Residence address:_____

                              _____

      Home telephone:(___)_____

      Soc. Sec. Number:_____

      Date of birth: _____

      U.S. Citizen: ___ Yes ___ No

College attended:_____

                                          Degree:____   Year:

Graduate School:
attended:

                                          Degree:____   Year:

Employer:_____

Business address:_____

Business telephone:_____

Position or title: _____

Brief job:_____

_____

Marital Status:_____

Names and ages of
dependents, if any:_____

_____

_____

State in which I
maintain principal
residence or claim
domicile:_____

Other states in
which I maintain
a house or
apartment:_____

2.   <u>Bank and other references
which may be contacted:</u>

    (a)   Bank:_____

               Address:_____

               Account repre-
               sentative:_____
               Telephone:(____)_____

    (b)   Attorney:_____
               Address:_____

Telephone:(   ) _____

(c)   Accountant:_____
Address:_____

_____

Telephone:(   ) _____

3.   <u>Employment history.</u>

The following is a description of my principal employment (other than my current employment) during the last ten years or since graduation from college. I have provided specific information concerning the extend of vocationally related experience in financial and business matters.

FROM	TO	EMPLOYER	POSITION	BRIEF DESCRIPTION OF POSITION

4.   <u>Investment experience</u>

(a)   The frequency of my investments in marketable securities has been
( ) often; ( ) occasional; ( ) seldom;   ( ) never.

(b)   The frequency of my investments in private offerings or securities has been: ( ) often; ( ) more than once; ( ) never.

(c)   My private offering investment experience during the past five years consists of the following:

Name of venture	Activity venture (e.g., equipment leasing, real estate, oil and gas)	Form of venture (e.g., trust, corporation limited partnership)	Amount of original investment

(d)   I have previously made investments in:

Stock exchange listed securities	Yes___ No
Over-the-counter securities	Yes___ No
Commodities	Yes___ No
Options	Yes___ No
New Issues	Yes___ No
Margin purchases	Yes___ No

(e)   I have reviewed offering materials relating to the following types of investments in the last five years.   (Check all appropriate boxes).

Start-up companies	[ ]
Equipment leasing	[ ]
Research and development limited partnerships	[ ]
Oil and gas drilling programs	[ ]
Real estate syndications	[ ]
Stocks, bonds, or debentures	[ ]

5.   I consider myself to have such knowledge and experience in financial and business matters to enable me to evaluate the merits and risks of an investment in the Company.

                    Yes ___ No

6.   The following is a list of my professional licenses or registrations (including bar admissions, accounting certificates, real estate brokerage licenses, SEC or state broker-dealer registration):

_____

_____

_____

7.   I make one of the following representations regarding my net worth and related matters <u>and have checked the applicable representation</u>:

        ( )   a.   I certify that I have an individual net worth or joint net worth* with my spouse in excess of $1,000,000.

        ( )   b.   I certify that I have had an individual annual adjusted gross income** in excess of $200,000 in each of the two most recent tax years and I reasonably expect an individual annual adjusted gross income in excess of $200,000 during my current tax year. NOTE: IF YOU ARE BUYING JOINTLY WITH YOUR SPOUSE, YOU MUST HAVE A JOINT

ANNUAL ADJUSTED GROSS INCOME IN EXCESS OF $300,000 IN EACH OF THESE YEARS IN ORDER TO CHECK THIS BOX.

* As used herein, net worth means total assets (including principal residence) less total liabilities (including mortgages).

** As used herein "individual annual adjusted gross income" means "adjusted gross income," as reported for Federal income tax purposes, less any income attributable to a spouse or property owned by a spouse (unless that spouse is a co-purchaser) and increased by the following amounts (but not including any amounts attributable to a spouse or to property owned by a spouse unless that spouse is a co-purchaser): (i) the amount of any tax-exempt interest income received, (ii) amount of losses claimed as a limited partner in a limited partnership, (iii) any deduction claimed for depletion, and (iv) deductible amounts contributed to an IRA or Keogh retirement plan.

8.   My net worth or joint net worth with my spouse (excluding home, home furnishings, and appliances, and automobiles) is at least $_____; last year I had an income of at least _____$_____ , and I estimate that I will have an income in the current year of at least $_____. Please exclude income of spouse unless you are buying jointly.

9.   I make one of the following representations regarding my net worth relative to this investment <u>and have checked the applicable representation</u>:

( )   a.   My investment in the Company does not exceed 25% of my net worth (excluding home, home furnishings, appliances and automobiles). (Net worth may include the net worth of your spouse.)

( )   b.   My investment in the Company exceeds 25% of my net worth (excluding home, home furnishings, appliances and automobiles). (Net worth may include the net worth of your spouse.)

10.   The undersigned represents that the information contained herein is complete and accurate and may be relied upon by the Company and that the undersigned will notify the Company of any material change in any of such information prior to the undersigned's investment in the Company.

11.   <u>Designation of Purchaser Representatives</u>

(a)   In connection with my proposed investment in the Note, I will be relying upon the advice of a Purchaser Representative to evaluate the risks and merits of the investment: Yes____ No____ If yes, set forth below is the name, profession or occupation and business address of such Purchaser Representative and, if more than one, a brief explanation of the division of responsibility between them:

_____

_____
_____

IF YOU HAVE DESIGNATED A PURCHASER REPRESENTATIVE, THE ATTACHED PURCHASER REPRESENTATIVE'S QUESTIONNAIRE MUST BE COMPLETED AND SIGNED BY EACH PURCHASER REPRESENTATIVE DESIGNED. THE QUESTIONNAIRE MUST ALSO BE SIGNED BY THE INVESTOR.

The information contained herein is complete and accurate and I will notify you promptly of any change in any of such information occurring prior to any investment by me.

Dated: _____   _____
                                                          [Name]

                                              _____
                                              Name of Investor (please print)

APPENDIX A-7

SUBSCRIPTION AGREEMENT

XYZ Corporation

_____

_____

Gentlemen:

     In connection with the purchase, by the undersigned, of Common Stock, without par value (the "Shares") of XYZ Corporation, a _____corporation (the "Company") the parties hereto agree as follows:

     1.   Subscription. Subject to the terms and conditions hereof, the undersigned hereby irrevocably subscribes for and agrees to purchase _____ Shares and tenders herewith a check in the amount of $_____ payable to the order of the Company.

     2.   Acceptance of Subscription. The undersigned understands and agrees that this subscription is made subject to the unconditional right of the Company to reject any subscription, in whole or in part, for any reason whatsoever.

     3.   Special Account. The undersigned understands that the total amount subscribed will be, upon receipt, delivered to the Company for use by the Company without restrictions or escrow.

     4.   Representation and Warranties of the Undersigned. The undersigned understands and acknowledges that the Shares are being offered and sold under one or more of the exemptions from registration provided for in Section 3(b), 4(2) and 4(6) of the Securities Act of 1933, as amended (the "Act") including, Regulation D promulgated thereunder, that the undersigned acknowledges that the Shares are being purchased without the undersigned being offered or furnished any offering literature, prospectus or other material, financial or otherwise, and that this transaction has not been scrutinized by the United States Securities and Exchange Commission or by any regulatory authority charged with the administration of the securities laws of any state. The undersigned hereby further represents and warrants as follows:

(a)   the undersigned confirms that he understands and has fully considered, for purposes of this investment, the risks of an investment in the Shares and understands that: (i) this investment is suitable only for an investor who is able to bear the economic consequences or losing his entire investment, (ii) the purchase of the Shares is a speculative investment which involves a high degree of risk of loss by the undersigned of his entire investment, and (iii) that there will be no public market for the Shares and accordingly, it may not be possible for him to liquidate his investment in the Shares in case of an emergency;

(b)   the undersigned acknowledges that any statements made or materials provided contain the views of the management of the Company, and that the Company has not conducted any marketing studies or analysis with regard to the Company's prospects;

(c)   the undersigned confirms that he is: (i) an "Accredited Investor" as the term is defined pursuant to Regulation D promulgated under the Act; (ii) able to bear the economic risk of this investment, (iii) able to hold the Shares for the period of time set forth herein, and (iv) presently able to afford a complete loss of his investment; and represents that he has sufficient liquid assets so that the illiquidity associated with this investment will not cause any undue financial difficulties or affect the undersigned's ability to provide for his current needs and possible financial contingencies, and that his commitment to all speculative investments (including this one if his subscription is accepted by the Company) is reasonable in relation to his net worth and annual income;

(d)   the undersigned has such knowledge and experience in financial and business matters and that he is capable of evaluating the merits and risks of an investment in the Shares and of making an informed investment decision;

(e)   the undersigned has had the opportunity to discuss with his representatives, including his attorney and/or his accountant, if any, the tax consequences of his investment in the Shares;

(f)   the Shares are being acquired by the undersigned solely for his own personal account, for investment purposes only, and not with a view to, or in connection with, any resale or distribution thereof; the undersigned has no contract, undertaking, understanding, agreement or arrangement, formal or informal, with any person to sell, transfer or pledge to any person the Shares for which he hereby subscribes, any part thereof, any interest therein or any rights thereto; the undersigned has no present plans to enter into any such contract, undertaking, agreement or arrangement; and he understands the legal consequences of the foregoing representations and warranties to mean that he must bear the economic risk of the investment for an indefinite period of time because the Shares have not been registered under the Act and, therefore, cannot be sold unless they are subsequently registered under the Act (which the Company is not obligated, and has no intention, to do) or unless an exemption from such registration is available; the Shares will be considered "Restricted Securities" for purposes of Rule 144 promulgated under the Act;

(g) the undersigned understands that no Federal or state agency has passed on or made any recommendation or endorsement of the Shares and that the Company is relying on the truth and accuracy of the representations, declarations and warranties herein made by undersigned in offering the Shares for sale to the undersigned without having first registered the Shares under the Act;

(h) the undersigned consents to the placement of a legend on the Shares as required by applicable securities laws, including legends in form substantially as follows:

THE SECURITIES REPRESENTED BY THIS CERTIFICATE HAVE BEEN ACQUIRED FOR INVESTMENT AND HAVE NOT BEEN REGISTERED UNDER THE SECURITIES ACT OF 1933, AS AMENDED (THE "ACT"), OR UNDER ANY STATE SECURITIES LAW, AND NO INTEREST THEREIN MAY BE SOLD, DISTRIBUTED, ASSIGNED, OFFERED, PLEDGED OR OTHERWISE TRANSFERRED, AND THE SECURITIES REPRESENTED BY THIS CERTIFICATE MAY NOT BE SOLD UNLESS: (1) A REGISTRATION STATEMENT WITH RESPECT THERETO IS EFFECTIVE UNDER THE ACT AND ANY APPLICABLE STATE SECURITIES LAW OR (2) THE COMPANY RECEIVES AN OPINION OF LEGAL COUNSEL TO THE COMPANY OR OTHER COUNSEL TO THE HOLDER OF THESE SECURITIES (CONCURRED IN BY LEGAL COUNSEL TO THE COMPANY), STATING THAT SUCH TRANSACTION IS EXEMPT FROM REGISTRATION UNDER THE ACT AND APPLICABLE STATE SECURITIES LAWS. BY ACQUIRING THIS CERTIFICATE, THE HOLDER REPRESENTS THAT THE HOLDER HAS ACQUIRED SUCH CERTIFICATE FOR INVESTMENT AND THAT THE HOLDER WILL NOT SELL OR OTHERWISE DISPOSE OF THIS CERTIFICATE OR THE SHARES REPRESENTED THEREBY, WITHOUT REGISTRATION OR OTHER COMPLIANCE WITH THE ACT AND THE RULES AND REGULATIONS THEREUNDER.

(i)   The undersigned has not engaged any broker, dealer; finder, commission agent or other similar person in connection with the offer, offer for sale, or sale of the Shares and is under no obligation to pay any broker's fee, or commission in connection with his investment.

The foregoing representations and warranties are made by the undersigned with the intent that they may be relied upon in determining his suitability as an investor in the Company and the undersigned hereby agrees that such representations and warranties shall survive the sale by the Company to the undersigned of the Shares.

5.   Transferability.   The undersigned agrees not to transfer or assign this Agreement, or any of his interest herein, and Shares acquired pursuant hereto shall be made only in accordance with all applicable laws.

6.   Revocation. The undersigned agrees that he may not cancel, terminate or revoke this Agreement or any agreement of the undersigned made hereunder and that this Agreement shall survive the death or disability of the undersigned and shall be binding upon the undersigned's heirs, executors, administrators, successors and assigns.

7.   No Waiver.   Notwithstanding any of the representations, warranties, acknowledgments or agreements made herein by the undersigned, the undersigned does not waive any rights granted to him under Federal or state securities laws.

8.   Acknowledgments of the Undersigned.   The undersigned acknowledges that there have been no representations, guarantees or warranties made to him by the Company, its agents or employees, or by other person, expressly or implication, of any nature or kind.

9.   Continuing Effect of Representations, Warranties and Acknowledgments. The representations and warranties of Paragraph 4 and the acknowledgments of Paragraph 8 are true and accurate as of the date of this Subscription Agreement and shall be true and accurate as of the date of delivery to and acceptance by the Company, and shall survive such delivery and acceptance.   If, in any respect such representations, warranties and acknowledgments shall not be true and accurate prior to such delivery and acceptance, the undersigned shall give immediate written notice of such fact to the Company specifying which representations and warranties and acknowledgments are not true and accurate and the reasons therefore.

10.   Indemnification.   The undersigned acknowledges that he understands the meaning and legal consequences of the representations and warranties contained in Paragraph 4 and the acknowledgments contained in Paragraph 8, and he hereby agrees to indemnify and hold harmless the Company, its officers or any of its affiliates, salesmen, associates, agents or employees from and against any and all loss, damage or liability (including costs and reasonable attorney's fees) due to or arising out of a breach of any representation, warranty or acknowledgment of the undersigned contained in this Agreement.

11.   Miscellaneous.

(a)   All notices or other communications given or made hereunder shall be in writing and shall be delivered or mailed by registered or certified mail, return receipt requested, postage prepaid, to the undersigned at the address set forth below or to the Company at the address set forth above.

(b)   This Agreement shall be governed by and construed in accordance with laws of _____.

(c)   This Agreement constitutes the entire agreement between the parties with respect to the subject matter hereof and may be amended only be a writing executed by the parties.

IN WITNESS WHEREOF, the undersigned has hereby executed this Agreement this _____ day of _____, 200__.

_____
[Name]

XYZ Corporation hereby accepts the foregoing subscription subject to the terms and conditions hereof as of the _____ day of _____, 200__.

XYZ CORPORATION

By: _____

[Name]   [Title]
Hereunto Duly Authorized

INFORMATION

1.   Full name of Subscriber: _____

2.   Address for all correspondence: _____

3.   Social Security or
      _____
      Tax I.D. Number:

APPENDIX A-8

[NAME OF COMPANY]

INCENTIVE STOCK OPTION AGREEMENT

1. <u>Grant of Option</u>. (<u>NAME OF COMPANY</u>), a _____ _____ corporation (the "Company"), hereby grants to _____ (the "Optionee"), an option, pursuant to the Company's 200_ Stock Option Plan (the "Plan"), to purchase an aggregate of _____ (_____) shares of Common Stock ("Common Stock") of the Company at a price of $ _____ per share, purchasable as set forth in and subject to the terms and conditions of this option and the Plan. Except where the context otherwise requires, the term "Company" shall include the parent and all present and future subsidiaries of the Company as defined in Sections 424(e) and 424(f) of the Internal Revenue Code of 1986, as amended or replaced from time to time (the "Code").

2. <u>Incentive Stock Option</u>. This option is intended to qualify as an incentive stock option ("Incentive Stock Option") within the meaning of Section 422 of the Code.

3. <u>Exercise of Option and Provisions for Termination</u>.

(a) <u>Vesting Schedule</u>. Except as otherwise provided in this Agreement, this option may be exercised prior to the tenth anniversary of the date of grant (hereinafter the "Expiration Date") as follows:

(i) Immediately upon the date of grant, the Optionee may purchase up to _____ (_____) of the total shares subject to this option;

(ii) At the end of one year from the date of grant, the Optionee may purchase up to an additional _____ (_____) of the total shares subject to this option.

(iii) At the end of two years from the date of grant, the Optionee may purchase up to an additional _____ (_____) of the total shares subject to this option.

The right of exercise shall be cumulative so that if the option is not exercised to the maximum extent permissible during any exercise period, it shall be exercisable, in whole or in part, with respect to all shares not so purchased at any time prior to the Expiration Date or the earlier termination of this option. This option may not be exercised at any time on or after the Expiration Date.

(b)   Exercise Procedure.   Subject to the conditions set forth in this Agreement, this option shall be exercised by the Optionee's delivery of written notice of exercise to the Treasurer of the Company, specifying the number of shares to be purchased and the purchase price to be paid therefor and accompanied by payment in full in accordance with Section 4. Such exercise shall be effective upon receipt by the Treasurer of the Company of such written notice together with the required payment. The Optionee may purchase less than the number of shares covered hereby, provided that no partial exercise of this option may be for any fractional share or for fewer than ten whole shares.

(c)   Continuous Employment Required. Except as otherwise provided in this Section 3, this option may not be exercised unless the Optionee, at the time he or she exercises this option, is, and has been at all times since the date of grant of this option, an employee of the Company.   For all purposes of this option, (i) "employment" shall be defined in accordance with the provisions of Section 1.421-7(h) of the Income Tax Regulations or any successor regulations, and (ii) if this option shall be assumed or a new option substituted therefor in a transaction to which Section 424(a) of the Code applies, employment by such assuming or substituting corporation (hereinafter called the "Successor Corporation") shall be considered for all purposes of this option to be employment by the Company.

(d)   Exercise Period Upon Termination of Employment. If the Optionee ceases to be employed by the Company for any reason, then, except as provided in paragraphs (e) and (f) below, the right to exercise this option shall terminate three (3) months after such cessation (but in no event after the Expiration Date), provided that this option shall be exercisable only to the extent that the Optionee was entitled to exercise this option on the date of such cessation. The Company's obligation to deliver shares upon the exercise of this option shall be subject to the satisfaction of all applicable federal, state and local income and employment tax withholding requirements, arising by reason of this option being treated as a non-statutory option or otherwise. Notwithstanding the foregoing, if the Optionee, prior to the Expiration Date, materially violates the non-competition or confidentiality provisions of any employment contract, confidentiality and nondisclosure agreement or other agreement between the Optionee and the Company, the right to exercise this option shall terminate immediately upon written notice to the Optionee from the Company describing such violation.

(e)   Exercise Period Upon Death or Disability. If the Optionee dies or becomes disabled (within the meaning of Section 22(e)(3) of the Code) prior to the Expiration Date while he or she is an employee of the Company, or if the Optionee dies within three months after the Optionee ceases to be an employee of the Company (other than as the result of a discharge for "cause" as specified in paragraph (f) below), this option shall be exercisable within the period of one year following the date of death or disability of the Optionee (but in no event after the Expiration Date), by the Optionee or by the person to whom this option is transferred by will or the laws of descent and distribution, provided that this option shall be exercisable only to the extent this option was exercisable by the Optionee on the date of his or her death or disability. Except as otherwise indicated by the context, the term "Optionee," as used in this option, shall be deemed to include the estate of the Optionee or any person who acquires the right to exercise this option by bequest or inheritance or otherwise by reason of the death of the Optionee.

(f)　　Discharge for Cause. If the Optionee, prior to the Expiration Date, is discharged by the Company for "cause" (as defined below), the right to exercise this option shall terminate immediately upon such cessation of employment. "Cause" shall mean willful misconduct in connection with the Optionee's employment or willful failure to perform his or her employment responsibilities in the best interests of the Company (including, without limitation, breach by the Optionee of any provision of any employment, nondisclosure, non-competition or other similar agreement between the Optionee and the Company), as determined by the Company, which determination shall be conclusive. The Optionee shall be considered to have been discharged "for cause" if the Company determines, within 30 days after the Optionee's resignation, that discharge for cause was warranted.

4.　　Payment of Purchase Price.

(a) Method of Payment. Payment of the purchase price for shares purchased upon exercise of this option shall be made (i) by delivery to the Company of cash or a check to the order of the Company in an amount equal to the purchase price of such shares, (ii) subject to the consent of the Company, by delivery to the Company of shares of Common Stock of the Company then owned by the Optionee having a fair market value equal in amount to the purchase price of such shares, (iii) by any other means which the Board of Directors determines are consistent with the purpose of the Plan and with applicable laws and regulations (including, without limitation, the provisions of Rule 16b-3 under the Securities Exchange Act of 1934 and Regulation T promulgated by the Federal Reserve Board), or (iv) by any combination of such methods of payment.

(b)　　Valuation of Shares or Other Non-Cash Consideration Tendered in Payment of Purchase Price. For the purposes hereof, the fair market value of any share of the Company's Common Stock or other non-cash consideration which may be delivered to the Company in exercise of this option shall be determined in good faith by the Board of Directors of the Company.

(c)　　Delivery of Shares Tendered in Payment of Purchase Price. If the Optionee exercises options by delivery of shares of Common Stock of the Company, the certificate or certificates representing the shares of Common Stock of the Company to be delivered shall be duly executed in blank by the Optionee or shall be accompanied by a stock power duly executed in blank suitable for purposes of transferring such shares to the Company. Fractional shares of Common Stock of the Company will not be accepted in payment of the purchase price of shares acquired upon exercise of this option.

(d)   <u>Restrictions on Use of Option Stock</u>. Notwithstanding the foregoing, no shares of Common Stock of the Company may be tendered in payment of the purchase price of shares purchased upon exercise of this option if the shares to be so tendered were acquired within twelve (12) months before the date of such tender through the exercise of an option granted under the Plan or any other stock option or restricted stock plan of the Company.

5.   <u>Delivery of Shares; Compliance With Securities Laws, Etc.</u>

(a)   <u>General</u>. The Company shall, upon payment of the option price for the number of shares purchased and paid for, make prompt delivery of such shares to the Optionee, <u>provided</u> that if any law or regulation requires the Company to take any action with respect to such shares before the issuance thereof, then the date of delivery of such shares shall be extended for the period necessary to complete such action.

(b)   <u>Listing, Qualification, Etc</u>. This option shall be subject to the requirement that if, at any time, counsel to the Company shall determine that the listing, registration or qualification of the shares subject hereto upon any securities exchange or under any state or federal law, or the consent or approval of any governmental or regulatory body, or that the disclosure of non-public information or the satisfaction of any other condition is necessary as a condition of, or in connection with, the issuance or purchase of shares hereunder, this option may not be exercised, in whole or in part, unless such listing, registration, qualification, consent or approval, disclosure or satisfaction of such other condition shall have been effected or obtained on terms acceptable to the Board of Directors. Nothing herein shall be deemed to require the Company to apply for, effect or obtain such listing, registration, qualification, or disclosure, or to satisfy such other condition.

6.   <u>Nontransferability of Option</u>. Except as provided in paragraph (e) of Section 3, this option is personal and no rights granted hereunder may be transferred, assigned, pledged or hypothecated in any way (whether by operation of law or otherwise), nor shall any such rights be subject to execution, attachment or similar process. Upon any attempt to transfer, assign, pledge, hypothecate or otherwise dispose of this option or of such rights contrary to the provisions hereof, or upon the levy of any attachment or similar process upon this option or such rights, this option and such rights shall, at the election of the Company, become null and void.

7.   <u>No Special Employment Rights</u>. Nothing contained in the Plan or this option shall be construed or deemed by any person under any circumstances to bind the Company to continue the employment of the Optionee for the period within which this option may be exercised.

8.   <u>Rights as a Shareholder</u>. The Optionee shall have no rights as a shareholder with respect to any shares which may be purchased by exercise of this option (including, without limitation, any rights to receive dividends or non-cash distributions with respect to such shares) unless and until a certificate representing

such shares is duly issued and delivered to the Optionee. No adjustment shall be made for dividends or other rights for which the record date is prior to the date such stock certificate is issued.

9. Adjustment Provisions.

(a) General. In the event of a transaction described in Section 15(a) of the Plan, the Optionee shall, with respect to this option or any unexercised portion hereof, be entitled to the rights and benefits, and be subject to the limitations, set forth in Section 15(a) of the Plan.

(b) Board Authority to Make Adjustments. Any adjustments under this Section 9 will be made by the Board of Directors, whose determination as to what adjustments, if any, will be made and the extent thereof will be final, binding and conclusive. No fractional shares will be issued pursuant to this option on account of any such adjustments.

(c) Limits on Adjustments. No adjustment shall be made under this Section 9 which would, within the meaning of any applicable provision of the Code, constitute a modification, extension or renewal of this option or a grant of additional benefits to the Optionee.

10. Mergers, Consolidation, Distributions, Liquidations Etc. In the event of a merger, consolidation, distribution, liquidation or other similar event described in Section 16(a) of the Plan, the Optionee shall, with respect to this option or any unexercised portion hereof, be entitled to the rights and benefits, and be subject to the limitations, set forth in Section 16(a) of the Plan.

11. Withholding Taxes. The Company's obligation to deliver shares upon the exercise of this option shall be subject to the Optionee's satisfaction of all applicable federal, state and local income and employment tax withholding requirements.

12. Limitations on Disposition of Incentive Stock Option Shares. It is understood and intended that this option shall qualify as an "incentive stock option" as defined in Section 422
of the Code. Accordingly, the Optionee understands that in order to obtain the benefits of an incentive stock option under Section 422 of the Code, no sale or other disposition may be made of any shares acquired upon exercise of the option within one year after the day of the transfer of such shares to him, nor within two years after the grant of the option. If the Optionee intends to dispose, or does dispose (whether by sale, exchange, gift, transfer or otherwise), of any such shares within said periods, he or she will notify the Company in writing within ten days after such disposition.

13. Investment Representations; Legends.

(a)   <u>Representations</u>. The Optionee represents, warrants and covenants
that:

(i)   Any shares purchased upon exercise of this option shall be
acquired for the Optionee's account for investment only and not with a view
to, or for sale in connection with, any distribution of the shares in violation
of the Securities Act of 1933, as amended (the "Securities Act") or any rule
or regulation under the Securities Act.

(ii)   The Optionee has had such opportunity as he or she has
deemed adequate to obtain from representatives of the Company such
information as is necessary to permit the Optionee to evaluate the merits and
risks of his or her investment in the Company.

(iii) The Optionee is able to bear the economic risk of holding
shares acquired pursuant to the exercise of this option for an indefinite
period.

(iv)   The Optionee understands that (A) the shares acquired
pursuant to the exercise of this option will not be registered under the
Securities Act and are "restricted securities" within the meaning of Rule 144
under the Securities Act; (B) such shares cannot be sold, transferred or
otherwise disposed of unless they are subsequently registered under the
Securities Act or an exemption from registration is then available; (C) in any
event, an exemption from registration under Rule 144 or otherwise under the
Securities Act may not be available for at least two years and even then will
not be available unless a public market then exists for the Common Stock,
adequate information concerning the Company is then available to the public
and other terms and conditions of Rule 144 are complied with; and (D) there
is now no registration statement on file with the Securities and Exchange
Commission with respect to any stock of the Company and the Company has
no obligation or current intention to register any shares acquired pursuant to
the exercise of this option under the Securities Act.

(v)   The Optionee agrees that, if the Company offers for the
first time any of its Common Stock for sale pursuant to a registration
statement under the Securities Act, the Optionee will not, without the prior
written consent of the Company, publicly offer, sell, contract to sell or
otherwise dispose of, directly or indirectly, any shares purchased upon
exercise of this option for a period of 90 days after the effective date of such
registration statement.

By making payment upon exercise of this option, the Optionee shall be
deemed to have reaffirmed, as of the date of such payment, the representations made
in this Section 13.

(b)   Legends on Stock Certificates. All stock certificates representing shares of Common Stock issued to the Optionee upon exercise of this option shall have affixed thereto legends substantially in the following forms, in addition to any other legends required by applicable state law:

> "The shares of stock represented by this certificate have not been registered under the Securities Act of 1933, as amended, (the "Act"), and may not be transferred, sold or otherwise disposed of in the absence of an effective registration statement with respect to the shares evidenced by this certificate, filed and made effective under the Act, or an opinion of counsel satisfactory to the Company to the effect that registration under such Act is not required.

> "The shares of stock represented by this certificate are subject to certain restrictions on transfer contained in an Option Agreement, a copy of which will be furnished upon request by the Company".

14.   Miscellaneous.

(a)   Except as provided herein, this option may not be amended or otherwise modified unless evidenced in writing and signed by the Company and the Optionee.

(b)   All notices under this option shall be mailed or delivered by hand to the parties at their respective addresses set forth beneath their names below or at such other address as may be designated in writing by either of the parties to one another.

(c)   This option shall be governed by and construed in accordance with the laws of _____.

Date of Grant: [Name of Company]

_____, 20

                                        By:_____
                                        Title:_____
                                        Address:_____
                                        _____

OPTIONEE'S ACCEPTANCE

     The undersigned hereby accepts the foregoing option and agrees to the terms and conditions thereof. The undersigned hereby acknowledges receipt of a copy of the Company's 200_ Stock Option Plan.

OPTIONEE

Date:_____, 200__   By:_____

                                       Address:_____

                                               _____

                                               _____

APPENDIX A-9

[NAME OF COMPANY]

[Year] STOCK OPTION PLAN

1.   Purpose.

The purpose of this plan (the "Plan") is to secure for [NAME OF COMPANY] (the "Company") and its shareholders the benefits arising from capital stock ownership by employees, officers and directors of, and consultants or advisors to, the Company and its Parent and subsidiary corporations who are expected to contribute to the Company's future growth and success. Except where the context otherwise requires, the term "Company" shall include the parent and all present and future subsidiaries of the Company as defined in Sections 424(e) and 424(f) of the Internal Revenue Code of 1986, as amended or replaced from time to time (the "Code"). Those provisions of the Plan which make express reference to Section 422 shall apply only to Incentive Stock Options (as that term is defined in the Plan).

2.   Type of options and Administration.

(a)   Types of Options. Options granted pursuant to the Plan shall be authorized by action of the Board of Directors of the Company (or a Committee designated by the Board of Directors) and may be either incentive stock options ("Incentive Stock Options") meeting the requirements of Section 422 of the Code or nonstatutory options which are not intended to meet the requirements of Section 422 of the Code.

(b)   Administration. The Plan will be administered by the Board of Directors of the Company, whose construction and interpretation of the terms and provisions of the Plan shall be final and conclusive. The Board of Directors may in its sole discretion grant options to purchase shares of the Company's Common Stock ("Common Stock") and issue shares upon exercise of such options as provided in the Plan. The Board shall have authority, subject to the express provisions of the Plan, to construe the respective option agreements and the Plan, to prescribe, amend and rescind rules and regulations relating to the Plan, to determine the terms and provisions of the respective option agreements, which need not be identical, and to make all other determinations in the judgment of the Board of Directors necessary or desirable for the administration of the Plan. The Board of Directors may correct any defect or supply any omission or reconcile any inconsistency in the Plan or in any option agreement in the manner and to the extent it shall deem expedient to carry the Plan into effect and it shall be the sole and final judge of such expediency. No director or person acting pursuant to authority delegated by the Board of Directors shall be liable for any action or determination under the Plan made in good faith. To the extent permitted by applicable law, the Board of Directors may delegate any or all of its powers under the Plan to one or more committees or subcommittees of the Board of Directors (a "Committee"). If and when the Common Stock is registered under the Securities Exchange Act of 1934 (the "Exchange Act") the Board of Directors shall appoint one such Committee of not less than two members, each member of which shall be an "outside director" within the meaning of Section 162(m) of the Code and a "non-employee director" as defined in Rule 16b-3 promulgated under the Exchange Act). All references in the Plan to the Board of Directors shall mean the Board of Directors or a Committee of the Board of Directors to the extent that the Board's powers or authority under the Plan have been delegated to such Committee.

3.   Eligibility.

Options may be granted to persons who are, at the time of grant, employees, officers or directors of, or consultants or advisors to, the Company; provided, that the class of employees to whom Incentive Stock Options may be granted shall be limited to all employees of the Company. A person who has been granted an option may, if he or she is otherwise eligible, be granted additional options if the Board of Directors shall so determine.

4.   Stock Subject to Plan.

Subject to adjustment as provided in Section 15 below, the maximum number of shares of Common Stock of the Company which may be issued and sold under the Plan is [insert number] shares. If an option granted under the Plan shall expire or terminate for any reason without having been exercised in full, the unpurchased shares subject to such option shall again be available for subsequent option grants under the Plan. If shares issued upon exercise of an option under the Plan are tendered to the Company in payment of the exercise price of an option granted under the Plan, such tendered shares shall again be available for subsequent option grants under the Plan; provided, that in no event shall such shares be made available pursuant to exercise of Incentive Stock Options.

5.   Forms of Option Agreements.

As a condition to the grant of an option under the Plan, each recipient of an option shall execute an option agreement in such form not inconsistent with the Plan as may be approved by the Board of Directors. Such option agreements may differ among recipients.

6.   Purchase Price.

(a)   General. The purchase price per share of stock deliverable upon the exercise of an option shall be determined by the Board of Directors, provided, however, that in the case of an Incentive Stock Option, the exercise price shall not be less than 100% of the fair market value of such stock, as determined by the Board of Directors, at the time of grant of such option, or less than 110% of such fair market value in the case of options described in Section 11(b).

(b)   Payment of Purchase Price. Options granted under the Plan may provide for the payment of the exercise price by delivery of cash or a check to the order of the Company in an amount equal to the exercise price of such options, or, to the extent provided in the applicable option agreement, (i) by delivery to the Company of shares of Common Stock of the Company already owned by the optionee having a fair market value equal in amount to the exercise price of the options being exercised, (ii) by any other means (including, without limitation, by delivery of a promissory note of the optionee payable on such terms as are specified by the Board of Directors) which the Board of Directors determines are consistent with the purpose of the Plan and with applicable laws and regulations (including, without limitation, the provisions of Rule 16b-3 and Regulation T promulgated by the Federal Reserve Board) or (iii) by any combination of such methods of payment. The fair market value of any shares of the Company's Common Stock or other non-cash consideration which may be delivered upon exercise of an option shall be determined by the Board of Directors.

7.   Option Period.

Each option and all rights thereunder shall expire on such date as shall be set forth in the applicable option agreement, except that, in the case of an Incentive Stock Option, such date shall not be later than ten years after the date on which the option is granted and, in all cases, options shall be subject to earlier termination as provided in the Plan.

8.   Exercise of Options.

Each option granted under the Plan shall be exercisable either in full or in installments at such time or times and during such period as shall be set forth in the agreement evidencing such option, subject to the provisions of the Plan.

9.   Nontransferability of Options.

Except as the Board of Directors may otherwise determine or provide in an option, options shall not be assignable or transferable by the person to whom they are granted, either voluntarily or by operation of law, except by will or the laws of descent and distribution, and, during the life of the optionee, shall be exercisable only by the optionee; provided, however, that non-statutory options may be transferred pursuant to a qualified domestic relations order (as defined in Code Section 414(p)).

10.   Effect of Termination of Employment or Other Relationship.

Subject to the provisions of the Plan, the Board of Directors shall determine the period of time during which an optionee may exercise an option following (i) the termination of the optionee's employment or other relationship with the Company or (ii) the death or disability of the optionee. Such periods shall be set forth in the agreement evidencing such option.

11.   Incentive Stock Options.

Options granted under the Plan which are intended to be Incentive Stock Options shall be subject to the following additional terms and conditions:

(a)   Express Designation. All Incentive Stock Options granted under the Plan shall, at the time of grant, be specifically designated as such in the option agreement covering such Incentive Stock Options.

(b)   10% Shareholder. If any employee to whom an Incentive Stock Option is to be granted under the Plan is, at the time of the grant of such option, the owner of stock possessing more than 10% of the total combined voting power of all classes of stock of the Company (after taking into account the attribution of stock ownership rules of Section 424(d) of the Code), then the following special provisions shall be applicable to the Incentive Stock Option granted to such individual:

(i)   the purchase price per share of the Common Stock subject to such Incentive Stock Option shall not be less than 110% of the fair market value of one share of Common Stock at the time of grant; and

(ii)   the option exercise period shall not exceed five years from the date of grant.

(c)   Dollar Limitation. For so long as the Code shall so provide, options granted to any employee under the Plan (and any other incentive stock option plans of the Company) which are intended to constitute Incentive Stock Options shall not constitute Incentive Stock Options to the extent that such options, in the aggregate, become exercisable for the first time in any one calendar year for shares of Common Stock with an aggregate fair market value (determined as of the respective date or dates of grant) of more than $100,000.

(d)   Termination of Employment, Death or Disability. No Incentive Stock Option may be exercised unless, at the time of such exercise, the optionee is, and has been continuously since the date of grant of his or her option, employed by the Company, except that:

(i)   an Incentive Stock Option may be exercised within the period of three months after the date the optionee ceases to be an employee of the Company (or within such lesser period as may be specified in the applicable option agreement); provided, that the agreement with respect to such option may designate a longer exercise period and that the exercise after such three-month period shall be treated as the exercise of a non-statutory option under the Plan;

(ii)   if the optionee dies while in the employ of the Company, or within three months after the optionee ceases to be such an employee, the Incentive Stock Option may be exercised by the person to whom it is transferred by will or the laws of descent and distribution within the period of one year after the date of death (or within such lesser period as may be specified in the applicable option agreement); and

(iii)   if the optionee becomes disabled (within the meaning of Section 22(e)(3) of the Code or any successor provision thereto) while in the employ of the Company, the Incentive Stock Option may be exercised within the period of one year after the date the optionee ceases to be such an employee because of such disability (or within such lesser period as may be specified in the applicable option agreement).

For all purposes of the Plan and any option granted hereunder, "employment" shall be defined in accordance with the provisions of Section 1.421-7(h) of the Income Tax Regulations (or any successor regulations). Notwithstanding the foregoing provisions, no Incentive Stock Option may be exercised after its expiration date.

12.   Additional Provisions.

(a)   Additional Option Provisions. The Board of Directors may, in its sole discretion, include additional provisions in option agreements covering options granted under the Plan, including without limitation restrictions on transfer, repurchase rights, commitments to pay cash bonuses, to make, arrange for or guaranty loans or to transfer other property to optionees upon exercise of options, or such other provisions as shall be determined by the Board of Directors; provided that such additional provisions shall not be inconsistent with any other term or condition of the Plan and such additional provisions shall not cause any Incentive Stock Option granted under the Plan to fail to qualify as an Incentive Stock Option within the meaning of Section 422 of the Code.

(b)   Acceleration, Extension, Etc. The Board of Directors may, in its sole discretion, (i) accelerate the date or dates on which all or any particular option or options granted under the Plan may be exercised or (ii) extend the dates during which all, or any particular, option or options granted under the Plan may be exercised; provided, however, that no such extension shall be permitted if it would cause the Plan to fail to comply with Section 422 of the Code.

13.   General Restrictions.

(a)   Investment Representations. The Company may require any person to whom an option is granted, as a condition of exercising such option, to give written assurances in substance and form satisfactory to the Company to the effect that such person is acquiring the Common Stock subject to the option for his or her own account for investment and not with any present intention of selling or otherwise distributing the same, and to such other effects as the Company deems necessary or appropriate in order to comply with federal and applicable state securities laws, or with covenants or representations made by the Company in connection with any public offering of its Common Stock.

(b)   Compliance With Securities Laws. Each option shall be subject to the requirement that if, at any time, counsel to the Company shall determine that the listing, registration or qualification of the shares subject to such option upon any securities exchange or under any state or federal law, or the consent or approval of any governmental or regulatory body, or that the disclosure of non-public information or the satisfaction of any other condition is necessary as a condition of, or in connection with, the issuance or purchase of shares thereunder, such option may not be exercised, in whole or in part, unless such listing, registration, qualification, consent or approval, or satisfaction of such condition shall have been effected or obtained on conditions acceptable to the Board of Directors. Nothing herein shall be deemed to require the Company to apply for or to obtain such listing, registration or qualification, or to satisfy such condition.

14.   Rights as a Shareholder.

The holder of an option shall have no rights as a shareholder with respect to any shares covered by the option (including, without limitation, any rights to receive dividends or non-cash distributions with respect to such shares) until the date of issue of a stock certificate to him or her for such shares. No adjustment shall be made for dividends or other rights for which the record date is prior to the date such stock certificate is issued.

15.   Adjustment Provisions for Recapitalizations and Related Transactions.

(a)   General. If, through or as a result of any merger, consolidation, sale of all or substantially all of the assets of the Company, reorganization, recapitalization, reclassification, stock dividend, stock split, reverse stock split or other similar transaction, (i) the outstanding shares of Common Stock are increased, decreased or exchanged for a different number or kind of shares or other securities of the Company, or (ii) additional shares or new or different shares or other securities of the Company or other non-cash assets are distributed with respect to such shares of Common Stock or other securities, an appropriate and proportionate adjustment shall be made in (x) the maximum number and kind of shares reserved for issuance under the Plan, (y) the number and kind of shares or other securities subject to any then outstanding options under the Plan, and (z) the price for each share subject to any then outstanding options under the Plan, without changing the aggregate purchase price as to which such options remain exercisable. Notwithstanding the foregoing, no adjustment shall be made pursuant to this Section 15 if such adjustment would cause the Plan to fail to comply with Section 422 of the Code. If this Section 15 applies and Section 16 also applies to any event, then Section 16 shall be applicable to such event and this Section 15 shall not be applicable.

(b)   Board Authority to Make Adjustments. Any adjustments under this Section 15 will be made by the Board of Directors, whose determination as to what adjustments, if any, will be made and the extent thereof will be final, binding and conclusive. No fractional shares will be issued under the Plan on account of any such adjustments.

16.   Merger, Consolidation, Asset Sale, Liquidation, etc.

(a)   General. Subject to Section 16(b), upon the occurrence of an Acquisition Event (as defined below), or the execution by the Company of any agreement with respect to an Acquisition Event, the Board of Directors shall take any one or more of the following actions with respect to then outstanding options: (i) provide that such options shall be assumed, or equivalent options shall be substituted, by the acquiring or succeeding corporation (or an affiliate thereof), provided that any such options substituted for Incentive Stock Options shall meet the requirements of Section 424(a) of the Code, (ii) upon written notice to the optionees, provide that all then unexercised options will become exercisable in full as of a specified time (the "Acceleration Time") prior to the Acquisition Event and will terminate immediately prior to the consummation of such Acquisition Event, except to the extent exercised by the optionees between the Acceleration Time and the consummation of such Acquisition Event, (iii) in the event of a merger under the terms of which holders of the Common Stock of the Company will receive upon consummation thereof a cash payment for each share surrendered in the merger (the "Merger Price"), make or provide for a cash payment to the optionees equal to the difference between (A) the Merger Price times the number of shares of Common Stock subject to such outstanding options (whether or not then exercisable at prices not in excess of the Merger Price) and (B) the aggregate exercise price of all such outstanding options in exchange for the termination of such options, and (iv) provide that all or any outstanding options shall become exercisable in full immediately prior to such event. An "Acquisition Event" shall mean: (a) any merger or consolidation which results in the voting securities of the Company outstanding immediately prior thereto representing immediately thereafter (either by remaining outstanding or by being converted into voting securities of the surviving or acquiring entity) less than 50% of the combined voting power of the voting securities of the Company or such surviving or acquiring entity outstanding immediately after such merger or consolidation, (b) any sale of all or substantially all of the assets of the Company, or (c) the complete liquidation of the Company.

(b)   Substitute Options. The Company may grant options under the Plan in substitution for options held by employees of another corporation who become employees of the Company, or a subsidiary of the Company, as the result of a merger or consolidation of the employing corporation with the Company or a subsidiary of the Company, or as a result of the acquisition by the Company, or one of its subsidiaries, of property or stock of the employing corporation. The Company may direct that substitute options be granted on such terms and conditions as the Board of Directors considers appropriate in the circumstances.

17.   No Special Employment Rights.

Nothing contained in the Plan or in any option shall confer upon any optionee any right with respect to the continuation of his or her employment by the Company or interfere in any way with the right of the Company at any time to terminate such employment or to increase or decrease the compensation of the optionee.

18.   Other Employee Benefits.

Except as to plans which by their terms include such amounts as compensation, the amount of any compensation deemed to be received by an employee as a result of the exercise of an option or the sale of shares received upon such exercise will not constitute compensation with respect to which any other employee benefits of such employee are determined, including, without limitation, benefits under any bonus, pension, profit-sharing, life insurance or salary continuation plan, except as otherwise specifically determined by the Board of Directors.

19.   Amendment of the Plan.

(a)   The Board of Directors may at any time, and from time to time, modify or amend the Plan in any respect, except that if at any time the approval of the shareholders of the Company is required under Section 422 of the Code or any successor provision with respect to Incentive Stock Options, the Board of Directors may not effect such modification or amendment without such approval.

(b)   The termination or any modification or amendment of the Plan shall not, without the consent of an optionee, affect his or her rights under an option previously granted to him or her. With the consent of the optionee affected, the Board of Directors may amend outstanding option agreements in a manner not inconsistent with the Plan. The Board of Directors shall have the right to amend or modify the terms and provisions of the Plan and of any outstanding Incentive Stock Options granted under the Plan to the extent necessary to qualify any or all such options for such favorable federal income tax treatment (including deferral of taxation upon exercise) as may be afforded incentive stock options under Section 422 of the Code.

20.   Withholding.

The Company shall have the right to deduct from payments of any kind otherwise due to the optionee any federal, state or local taxes of any kind required by law to be withheld with respect to any shares issued upon exercise of options under the Plan. Subject to the prior approval of the Company, which may be withheld by the Company in its sole discretion, the optionee may elect to satisfy such obligations, in whole or in part, (i) by causing the Company to withhold shares of Common Stock otherwise issuable pursuant to the exercise of an option or (ii) by delivering to the Company shares of Common Stock already owned by the optionee. The shares so delivered or withheld shall have a fair market value equal to such withholding obligation. The fair market value of the shares used to satisfy such withholding obligation shall be determined by the Company as of the date that the amount of tax to be withheld is to be determined. An optionee who has made an election pursuant to this Section 20(a) may only satisfy his or her withholding obligation with shares of Common Stock which are not subject to any repurchase, forfeiture, unfulfilled vesting or other similar requirements.

21.   Cancellation and New Grant of Options, Etc.

The Board of Directors shall have the authority to effect, at any time and from time to time, with the consent of the affected optionees, (i) the cancellation of any or all outstanding options under the Plan and the grant in substitution therefor of new options under the Plan covering the same or different numbers of shares of Common Stock and having an option exercise price per share which may be lower or higher than the exercise price per share of the cancelled options, or (ii) the amendment of the terms of any and all outstanding options under the Plan to provide an option exercise price per share which is higher or lower than the then current exercise price per share of such outstanding options.

22.   Effective Date and Duration of the Plan.

(a)   Effective Date. The Plan shall become effective as of _____, but no Incentive Stock Option granted under the Plan shall become exercisable unless and until the Plan shall have been approved by the Company's shareholders. If such shareholder approval is not obtained within twelve months after the effective date of the Plan, no options previously granted under the Plan shall be deemed to be Incentive Stock Options and no Incentive Stock Options shall be granted thereafter. Amendments to the Plan not requiring shareholder approval shall become effective when adopted by the Board of Directors; amendments requiring shareholder approval (as provided in Section 19) shall become effective when adopted by the Board of Directors, but no Incentive Stock Option granted after the date of such amendment shall become exercisable (to the extent that such amendment to the Plan was required to enable the Company to grant such Incentive Stock Option to a particular optionee) unless and until such amendment shall have been approved by the Company's shareholders. If such shareholder approval is not obtained within twelve months of the Board's adoption of such amendment, any Incentive Stock Options granted on or after the date of such amendment shall terminate to the extent that such amendment to the Plan was required to enable the Company to grant such option to a particular optionee. Subject to this limitation, options may be granted under the Plan at any time after the effective date and before the date fixed for termination of the Plan.

(b)   Termination. Unless sooner terminated in accordance with Section 16, the Plan shall terminate, with respect to Incentive Stock Options, upon the earlier of (i) the close of business on the day next preceding the tenth anniversary of the date of its adoption by the Board of Directors, or (ii) the date on which all shares available for issuance under the Plan shall have been issued pursuant to the exercise or cancellation of options granted under the Plan. Unless sooner terminated in accordance with Section 16, the Plan shall terminate with respect to options which are not Incentive Stock Options on the date specified in (ii) above. If the date of termination is determined under (i) above, then options outstanding on such date shall continue to have force and effect in accordance with the provisions of the instruments evidencing such options.

23.   Provision for Foreign Participants.

The Board of Directors may, without amending the Plan, modify awards or options granted to participants who are foreign nationals or employed outside the United States to recognize differences in laws, rules, regulations or customs of such foreign jurisdictions with respect to tax, securities, currency, employee benefit or other matters.

[NAME OF COMPANY]

Date: _____ By: _____
                                                   [Name]   [Title]
                                            Hereunto Duly Authorized

APPENDIX A-10

REPURCHASE OF COMMON STOCK.

The Employee is hereby granted the right and option to purchase _____ _____(__) shares (the "Shares") of the Common Stock of the Company at a price of _____($__) per share for an aggregate purchase price, to be paid in cash, of _____($_____) Dollars (the "Subscription Price").

To insure the orderly continuation of the Company's business for an appropriate period of time, the Company and the Employee hereby agree as follows:

(A)   First Withdrawal Period

In the event that the Employee withdraws from the Company on or before _____ (the "First Withdrawal Period"), the Employee agrees that he will give up and forfeit all of the shares purchased and the Company shall have the right, but not the obligations, to repurchase from the Employee, or the legal representative of the estate of the Employee (the "Legal Representative"), as the case may be, all of the Shares owned by the Employee for the aggregate purchase price paid by the Employer, to be paid in cash, on the Closing Date, as hereinafter defined.

For purposes of this Article, the Employee shall be deemed to have withdrawn ("Withdrawn") from the Company upon the occurrence of any of the following events: (a) a voluntary termination by the Employee pursuant to Section ____ hereof; (b) death; (c) permanent disability (as hereinafter defined); or (d) a termination by the Company of the Employee's employment For Cause as defined in Article ___ hereof. The "Permanent Disability" of the Employee shall be as defined as noted in Article ____ hereof.

(B)   Second Withdrawal Period

In the event that the Employee withdraws between _____ and _____ (the "Second Withdrawal Period"), the Employee agrees that he will give up and forfeit two-thirds $(2/3^{rd})$ of the shares purchased (the "Forfeited Shares"). The Company shall have the right, but not the obligation, to repurchase from the Employee, or the Legal Representative, as the case may be, the Forfeited Shares owned by the Employee for an amount equal to the Appraised Value thereof as defined in Subsection D (ii) hereof.

(C)   Third Withdrawal Period

In the event that the Employee withdraws between _____ and _____ (the "Third Withdrawal Period"), the Employee agrees that he will give up and forfeit one-third (1/3rd) of the shares purchased (the "Forfeited Shares"). The Company shall have the right, but not the obligation, to repurchase from the Employee, or the Legal Representative, as the case may be, the Forfeited Shares owned by the Employee for an amount equal to the Appraised Value thereof as defined in Subsection D (ii) hereof.

(D)   Exercise of Repurchase Option

The Company's right and option to repurchase the Forfeited Shares shall be exercised by written notice (the "Notice of Exercise") given by the Company to the Employee or his Legal Representatives within thirty (30) days after the date of Withdrawal. The Notice of Exercise shall state that the Company is electing to repurchase the Forfeited Shares, and shall identify the number of Forfeited Shares to be repurchased (as determined pursuant to paragraph (A), (B) or (C) of this Section), the Closing Date and the proposed purchase price to be paid to the Employee. If the Company does not timely give a Notice of Exercise, the Company shall be deemed to have forever waived its option to repurchase the Forfeited Shares. At the Closing Date, the Employee shall deliver a stock certificate or stock certificates representing the Forfeited Shares to be repurchased by the Company, duly endorsed for transfer on the books and records of the Company free and clear of all liens, encumbrances and restrictions.

Subject to the provisions hereof, the total purchase price shall be paid, in full, in cash, on the Closing Date. If the total purchase price is equal to or less than $100,000 then the entire purchase price shall be paid in cash. If the total purchase price is in excess of $100,000 then the Company shall pay, in cash, on the Closing Date the sum of $100,000 and the balance of the purchase price shall be paid by the execution and delivery of a Corporate Promissory Note in the original principal amount of the total purchase price minus the amount paid of $100,000 (the "Principal Balance"), together with interest on the unpaid Principal Balance; and the Principal Balance, together with accrued and unpaid interest, shall be paid quarterly in arrears until paid in full. Interest shall be at the Prime Rate of Interest as published by Fleet Bank and fixed as of the Closing Date. The Corporate Promissory Note shall mature three (3) years after the Closing Date.

(i)   Closing Date:

The repurchase of the Forfeited Shares shall be consummated at the closing to be held on a date that is mutually agreeable to the Company and the Employee, but in no event more than thirty (30) days after the Notice of Exercise. Such transaction shall be consummated at 10:00 a.m. on such date (the "Closing Date") at the principal office of the Company or at such other time and place as the Company and the Employee mutually agree.

(ii)   Determination of the Purchase Price:

The Appraised Value shall be initially determined by the Employee and the Company and, if the parties are able to agree, then the amount determined shall be the Appraised Value.

If the Company and the Employee are unable to agree then the Appraised Value shall be determined by reference to an arms length completed financing with investors that has closed or is currently being offered by the Company to outside investors (the "Outside Financing") made in or within six (6) months of the date of the Withdrawal. If there is no Outside Financing within such six (6) month period, then the Appraised Value shall be determined by arbitration conducted in accordance with the rules and regulations then pertaining of the American Arbitration Association and the decision of the arbitrator shall be final and binding upon the parties. The parties shall endeavor to select an arbitrator. If the parties are unable to agree upon an arbitrator within a reasonable period of time, then the arbitrator shall be selected in accordance with the rules and regulations, then pertaining, of the American Arbitration Association. The arbitrator selected, shall be experienced in valuating early stage, biotechnology companies and the arbitrator, in reaching a decision, shall take into account the methodology for determining the Appraised Value that was utilized by the Company in the most recent Outside Financing.

(iii)   Forfeited Shares to be Repurchased:

The Forfeited Shares, for purposes of this Article, shall include any shares that may have been transferred by permission by the Employee, and any shares resulting from a stock dividend, distribution, stock split pursuant to a reorganization or recapitalization of the Company's stock or in a subscription to shares made available ratably to all of the Stockholders.

(iv)   <u>Acceleration of the Repurchase Periods</u>:

Notwithstanding anything to the contrary herein contained, in the event of the sale, merger or other business consolidation of the Company or an initial public offering of the Company's Shares, or in the event of a termination of the Employee without cause, the Withdrawal Periods shall be accelerated, and the provisions of this Article ___ shall be deemed null and void and of no further force or effect as of the date of the closing of the sale, merger or other business consolidation of the Company or an initial public offering of the Company's Shares or in a termination of the Employee without cause, e.g. meaning and intending that all of the Shares owned by the Employee shall be deemed fully vested and the Company shall have no right of repurchase.

Mr. Finn is a Senior Partner with the Boston based law firm of Rubin and Rudman, LLP. His practice is devoted to representing biotechnology and medical device companies in all areas of corporate law.

APPENDIX B

Business Plan Guidelines

Business Plan Guidelines

Throughout this book we have examined many of the most critical tasks and for managing a growing startup and early stage company, with an emphasis on high-technology firms. The reader should therefore be able to construct much of its business plan based upon the guidelines presented throughout this book.

A business plan serves as a detailed description of a company, explaining its mission and business model, products and services, intended markets and customers, financial projections, funding sought, means of exit, and the methods it will use to achieve its goals. The purpose of a business plan is two-fold. As a selling tool, it serves to describe the business in sufficient detail to attract investment capital. And because the most important attribute of an early stage company is the management team, the business plan provides a way for investors to form an impression about the quality of these individuals. As a management tool, the business plan serves as a blueprint for understanding and executing the business strategy. It forces the management team to detail specific milestones and create intricate details of company strategy and operations, such as market entry strategy, marketing strategy, revenue models, distribution strategy, etc. And the details of these topics must be written down in a way that can be easily read and understood by investors, as well as for the future reference of the management. Invariably, when a company is having difficulties, the solutions are almost always within or absent from its business plan.

A properly constructed business plan is essential for financing but only to the extent it gets the company a "first look" by an investor. A business plan is meaningless if the management team is unable to execute the strategies and achieve many of the milestones within such a plan. Thus, the true value of a well-thought out and properly constructed business plan is only reflected by the management team's ability to execute this plan. Remember, the business plan does not get a company funded, but rather, it serves as a resume to attract the closer attention of an investor. The due diligence process will ultimately determine the merits of funding. And if the management team can support all numbers and assumptions given in its plan and can demonstrate the ability to lead the company to success, investors will invest (assuming ROI criteria are fulfilled).

In closing, the business plan needs to represent both a sales tool and a management guide and it must be succinct yet persuasive. Finally, an effective business plan needs to capture the interest of the reader within the first 30 seconds or else it may face an expedited route into the trash bin. An effective plan should answer the following questions satisfactorily:

- What is the mission of the company?
- What services and products does the company provide?
- Who are your customers and why will they buy your services and products?
- How will the customers differentiate your services and products?
- Who are your competitors and what are their strengths and weaknesses?
- What is the competitive advantage of your company?
- When is the breakeven time?
- How much money is the company needing, how will it spend it, and when can the investors expect to receive their ROI?
- What is the exit strategy of the company?

Rather than going into detail and addressing each section of the business plan, I will now highlight the most important sections of a business plan, followed by a generic outline at the end of this section.

Market and Competitive Analysis

These sections have been combined here only to demonstrate their mutual dependence. The market analysis section should demonstrate sufficient detail and understanding of the industry and intended market, noting its size, growth rate and capacity, as well as any industry trends and regulatory changes that might affect customer spending patterns and how such possibilities could affect the intended markets. As well, it should discuss the position and customer reach of each major competitor. Finally, this data should be referenced when possible to increase credibility with the VCs.

Furthermore, this section should detail the specific market segmentation approach selected that is responsible for determining its intended customers and the strategy for targeting these groups. In addition, this section should present customer profiles including demographics, sighting actual numbers, revenue per customer, key decision makers within the customer organization, and percentage of overall industry. Finally, the market analysis section should address the reasons why the intended customers will choose the company's products over competitors.

A complete understanding of all competitors in the industry should be listed, including operational history, products, other markets served, pricing information, and customer base. The competitive analysis section should also address the company's products and compare them to those of the competitors, convincing the investor that the intended customers will opt for its products for compelling reasons. In addition, investors will want to know what sustainable competitive advantage the company offers, such as first-to-market, proprietary nature of the technology, production methods, or operations, customer relationships, and distribution channels. Finally, this section should analyze the barriers to entry and list the biggest threats to the company in terms of competitive attack. The strengths and weaknesses of the company as well as the competition should be listed and the overall business strategy should be centered on this information.

Sales and Marketing Plan

Having a great product is not enough to produce tremendous sales. Companies also need specific strategies focused on getting their products into the hands of the customer. Therefore, a detailed description of customers within the intended market should be listed with explanations for what the customer wants, how they make purchasing decisions, and who makes these decisions.

Utilizing both market analysis and customer profiling data, the plan should address specific methods for selling the product, to achieve the revenue growth assumed by the financial forecasts, including pricing, distribution channels, branding strategies, and possible strategic partnering arrangements. For more mature companies already engaged in sales and revenue growth, investors will want a description of the working capital cycle detailing the management of receivables, payables, and inventory. They will also want to know about the production process, any outsourcing, and sources of alternative suppliers.

Guidelines for Writing the Business Plan

- **Focus on the basics!** When the prospective investor has read the plan, he should come away with a feeling for what your company does, how it is unique, what market segment you intend to serve, why customers will buy your products, your exit strategy, how much money you need and for how long. Companies that spend too much time describing the technology rather than explaining the overall business appeal of the venture will receive minimal interest by VCs.

- **Make it easy to understand and read.** Do not use colored print, fancy fonts, or colored paper. The plan should be professional looking and will reflect the professionalism of the management team.

- **Always detail the competition.** One of the biggest pet peeves of VCs is for companies to say they have no competition. Often, this is a result of insufficient market analysis. Remember this rule: **All companies, regardless of how new, have competitors.** If you cannot find any than you simply have not performed adequate research.   Demonstrating that your company has competitors is not a bad sign, contrary to what entrepreneurs think. Rather, VCs want to see that companies have performed sufficient research, know their industry and market, and understand each competitor.   They want to see how you intend to deal with the competition, so make certain you identify them and address effective competitive strategies!

- **Always write your business plan.** Never hire a professional to do it. You are the best one that understands the business and even a professional will not have adequate understanding to construct a complete plan. You can, however, hire a professional to revise the plan, tie up loose needs, and basically clean it up making it have more investment appeal.

- **Provide references on all data** used for assumptions, such as market size, growth trends, etc.

- **Keep track of each plan issued**, being careful to number each one so you can keep track of who gets a plan.

- **Make sure the cover sheet is professional** and complete, as this serves as the initial first impression of the company. The cover sheet should contain the name of the company, the type of company (LLC, C corp, etc.), and the state of incorporation, company mailing address, phone number, fax, email, the president with home phone, and the date.

- **Do not use software programs to construct the financials.**   Each company is different and will have different needs. Constructing the financials enables the entrepreneur to think out each expense and understand all assumptions behind the revenue estimates.

- **Know your audience.** The business plan will experience many stages of evolution and a plan that may have been adequate to help secure angel financing may be unsuitable for venture capitalists. In general, a company needs to have a more comprehensive plan as more sophisticated investors are solicited. Remember, if your company cannot understand its audience, than chances are it will also have a difficult time understanding its customers and competitors.

- **Always have two different business plans** made available for review by prospective investors. One should be a condensed version, the other the extended version. Most investors will wish to review the condensed plan only after being impressed from the executive summary. If they continue to have interest, they may ask to inspect the extended plan as the start of their due diligence process.

- **Provide all three financials**: pro-forma cash flow statement, income statement, and balance sheet. This should consist of 5-year pro forma statements with monthly financial data for the first two years, then quarterly data.

- **Provide all relevant assumptions used for the financials**, such as those for the revenue growth, cost of goods, operating expenses, cash flow cycling times (accounts payable and receivables, inventory sales)

- **Seek as much outside feedback as you can get.** Remember that creating a well-written complete business plan is extremely difficult for even venture capitalists but the most important aspect of the plan is how well it reads.

The Executive Summary

This is perhaps the single most important document of the early stage company and management often fails to recognize the full magnitude of its importance. But this short document will determine if a venture capitalist will look at your business plan so its careful construction is critical. The summary should be constructed as a condensed version of the key points of the plan and include the company mission, vision, current status, description of products and services, the value proposition and its economic benefit, current round and total financing thus far, use of proceeds, how long the proceeds will last, market size and market share expectations, brief competitive landscape, exit strategy, financial summary, management team bios. If this sounds like a lot of material to fit within 2-3 pages, that's because it is. Yet each piece of information is a critical determinant for further consideration by an angel or venture capital.

Some of the mistakes I have seen in the executive summary is that companies focus too much trying to explain their "revolutionary" technology and leave out the details of the business proposition. In addition, they simply do not understand the meaning of "summary". The executive summary essentially highlights the most important portions of a business plan and saves the detail for the full plan. A well-written executive summary should contain a succinct summary of the most important aspects of the business plan and should be 2-3 pages in length. Remember, it is a summary and should only be written after the full plan has been completed. The following are a list of essentials to include in the summary:

- Vision, Mission, and Business Model
- Company Description
- Proof of Concept (technology or business model) and what problems it solves (include all patents)
- Description of the Market: size, participants, dynamics (profit margins, customer make up)
- Competition
- How your company is different
- Summary of the 5-year pro-forma financial statements
- How Much Money the company is seeking, for what purpose and for how long
- Management Profile
- Exit strategy

Sample Cover Page Format

Title of Business Plan

Name of company
Type of company structure

Date

Copy # of total #

THIS DOCUMENT CONATINS CONFIDENTIAL INFORMATION INTENDED FOR THE USE BY:

Name of Recipient
Title
Company

CONTACT:

Key contact
Title
Telephone
Fax:
Email:
Address

Business Plan Outline

Most individuals experienced in analyzing business plans will agree that there is really no set way to write a plan beyond including the essential elements. Business plans can be constructed in many different ways but the only thing that will determine their appeal is a delicate balance of comprehensiveness, organization, overall flow and ease with which it is read. The most important parts of the plan in order of importance are the executive summary, market analysis, marketing plan, sales and distribution strategy, and financial forecasts. While the exit strategy is of prime importance for investors, it is a derivative of the overall feasibility of the venture and efficiency of execution by the management team. Anyone can state an IPO exit at year five. What is most important is the design and execution of an overall business strategy that enables such an exit to materialize. Below is an outline of a complete business plan.

Cover Page

Table of Contents

Executive Summary
- Company Intro
- Concept and Mission
- Company's Products and Services
- Market Analysis and Trends
- Competitive Analysis
- Value Add of the Company
- Financing Amount, Purpose, and Time Span
- Milestones
- Management Profile
- Financial Summary
- Exit Strategy

Company History and Current Status
- How company started
- Founders and personnel

Business Model
- Nature of the business
- Profit margins of industry

Technology, Products, Services
- Description of technology (include diagrams if needed)
- Value Add
- Competitive Advantages
- Proprietary nature
- Current Statue of development

Market Analysis
- The Overall Industry
- Market Segments Targeted and rationale
- Customer Profiles (needs met/unmet, buying patterns)
- Describe how the company's products will met the needs of intended markets
- Describe All industry forces (suppliers, buyers, threat of substitutes)
- Barriers to entry

Competitive analysis
- Competitor Profiles (history, segments served, market share,
- Provide solutions to breech entry barriers
- Competitive Advantages (IP, etc.)
- Anticipated reaction from competitors upon market entry

Sales and Marketing
Marketing Strategy
- Identify customer purchasing decisions and trends
- Identify currents needs served and unmet by competition
- Identify company's positioning: quality versus price. Innovator versus adaptor, follower versus leader, private sector versus government

Sales
- Material, labor, overhead costs
- Methods of promotion and distribution
- Revenue model
- Customer selling approach

Management Profile
- Background info
- Capabilities
- Management Gaps
- Organizational chart

Financial Strategy
Financial Operations
- List of all loans and terms
- Operating budget
- Milestones
- Pro-forma income, cash flow, and balance sheet (by month for first year then by quarter for the remaining four years)

Financing
- Breakeven analysis
- Amount Needed, Time Period, Total amount required
- Capitalization table showing the amount raised and the percentage of ownership
- Exit Strategy

APPENDIX C

Detailed Explanations

C-1. Accredited Investors

It is important to fully understand the definition of an accredited investor, as provided by Rule 501 of Regulation D. The following represents only a short version of this definition. Readers are highly encouraged to read the definition in its entirety, which is provided by the link below. According to this rule, "accredited investors" shall mean any person who comes within any of the following categories, or whom the issuer reasonably believes comes within any if the following categories, at the time of the sale of the securities to that person:

- Any bank, savings and loan association, broker or, dealer, insurance company, investment company, business development company, Small Business Investment Company, and some employee benefit plans.

- Any private business development company.

- Any organization, corporation, business trust or partnership not formed for the specific purpose of acquiring securities offered, with total assets in excess of $5 million.

- Any director, executive officer or general partner of the issuer or of a general partner of the issuer.

- Any person with an individual net worth, or joint net worth with that person's spouse, at time of purchase that exceeds $1,000,000.

- Any person who had an annual individual income in excess of $200,000 in each of the past two years or annual joint income with spouse in excess of $300,000 in each of those years and has a reasonable expectation of reaching the same income in the current year.

- Any trust, with total assets in excess of $5 million, not formed for the specific purpose of acquiring the securities offered, whose purchase is directed by a sophisticated person.

- Any entity in which all of the equity owners are accredited investors.

Source: United States Securities and Exchange Commission, Regulation D: Rules Governing the Limited Offer and Sale of Securities Without Registration Under the Securities Act of 1933. www.sec.gov/divisions/corpfin/forms/regd.htm

C-2. Effects of Portfolio Diversification on Total Risk Reduction

Out of an investment portfolio of twelve companies, venture capitalists would love to have twelve homeruns but they realize that this is unrealistic, so they hope for one or two, knowing that there will be three or four complete failures, a couple of breakevens, and a few marginal returns. Therefore, in order to minimize venture fund risk and investment volatility, venture capitalists invest their pool of funds in a portfolio of companies, each with differing financial and business characteristics, so they will be diversified with respect to a variety of business and economic changes. In this way, companies will demonstrate different financial returns due to differing business dynamics based upon factors such as the industry, the stage of development, relative risk of the project, and many other variables. This investment management approach is based on the modern portfolio theory, similar to that used in the asset management of public securities.

In order to minimize portfolio risk one must first identify and measure the risk of each security relative to the overall portfolio. The most common method of measuring individual and portfolio risk is to measure each *security's volatility (fluctuations in market price with time), known as its beta (β), which represents the non-diversifiable risk portion of the total portfolio risk.* You will recall that because this type of risk is a result of broad events, it affects the entire market and therefore cannot be not decreased by the process of asset diversification. Therefore, *β is a measure of market risk or the risk that events will affect the entire market without prejudice.*

For publicly traded companies, market risk or beta is calculated by measuring the returns of a security versus the market returns over the same time period. The S & P 500 index is used as a broad measure of market performance and is assigned a value of +1.0. If the price of a security moves in the same direction and by the same amount as the S & P 500 index over a given time period, it has a beta of +1.0. Thus, for a security with a β = +1.0, a 2% increase in the S&P 500 over a specific time period should also result in a +2% increase in the security. Meanwhile, a 10% decline in the S&P 500 will result in a 10% decline in this security. If the security moves twice as much and in the same direction as the S & P 500 then it is assigned a beta of +2.0. Likewise, if a security moves in the opposite direction as the S & P 500 by a magnitude of one half of the S & P then it is assigned a beta of –0.5 (figures C-2.1 and C-2.2).

Figure C-2.1. Price Performance of Securities with Different Betas

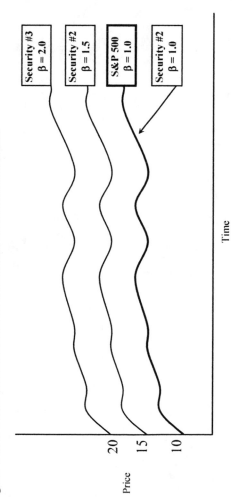

Figure C-2.2. Price Performance of Securities with Different Betas

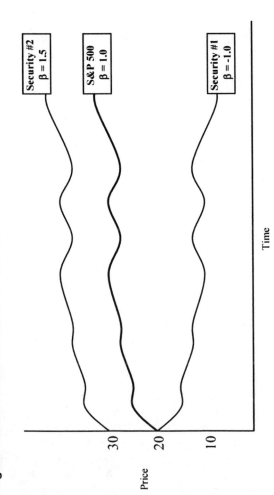

Regardless of the sign or direction, the higher betas are generally thought to be riskier then securities with lower betas because they are more volatile, or they experience larger price changes over a given time period. Because the market (as measured by the S&P 500 in this case) goes up and down one can develop a feel for the relative volatility of a security if its beta is known. Using betas, one can create a portfolio that is riskier than, as risky as, or less risky then the S & P 500 by assembling a portfolio with a composite beta of over +1, +1, and <+1 respectively. To calculate a composite beta of the entire portfolio, the percentage of each security relative to the entire investment amount of the portfolio is multiplied by its beta. This value will represent the weight of the beta in proportion to the portfolio. Finally, each of these proportionate beta vales are added and the total value is divided by the number of securities in the portfolio.

Constructing an investment portfolio and calculating the overall composite beta will allow the investor to select the level of risk (as defined by price volatility) they wish to assume. However, for private companies that have no active market, the use of betas in constructing a fund with a specific risk profile is not feasible since there is no standard with which to measure these betas (such as the S&P 500) and because company valuations do not change daily (since they are not traded on an active market). Therefore, venture capitalists consider a more crude method of determining what assets are different by looking at the *correlation coefficient* of each asset.

In the securities markets, correlation coefficients measure the degree of correlation between the price behaviors of selected securities and, similar to betas, can be either positive or negative, as the relative magnitude of this coefficient ranges from -1 to $+1$ to reflect the degree of negative or positive movement of each security. If a security has a positive correlation coefficient relative to another security, the price of both securities moves in the same direction. Likewise, if it has a negative correlation coefficient relative to the other security, it moves in the opposing direction. Similar to betas, if security A has a 0.90 correlation coefficient relative to security B, security A will demonstrate a 90% price movement relative to security B. Likewise, a -0.90 correlation coefficient will move 90% in the opposing direction. The main difference in using correlation coefficients rather than betas is that absolute price movements cannot be predicted relative to market movements since they are not associated with a an absolute standard value.

When two securities move in the same direction, they are said to be positively correlated. It does not matter if they both move downward in price (unlike with betas) as long as they move in the same direction (figure C-2.3). Similar to the calculation of composite betas, a composite correlation coefficient can be calculated for a portfolio by adding the proportionate contributions of each security, adding them, and dividing by the total.

However, we can get a rough measure of the additive effects of two positively correlated securities by adding them graphically. The cumulative effect of these two securities within a portfolio is that they will intensify the overall return over a given period. Thus, if two securities are positively correlated and their price declines, the declines will be additive and result in a large decline. Meanwhile for two securities with positive correlation coefficients that increase in price, the combined returns will be greater than each alone (figure C-2.4).

Figure C-2.3. Two Positively Correlated Securities (companies)

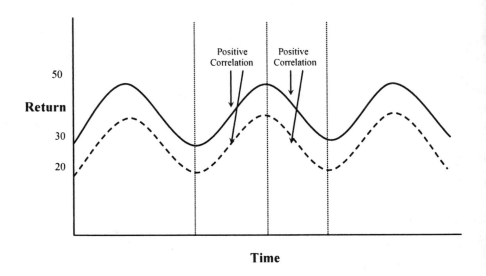

Figure C-2.5 shows two securities with equal but opposite correlation coefficients. Therefore, they are said to have negative correlations, such that when one security moves up during a given point in time, the other moves down an equal amount over the same time period. The cumulative affect this has it to cancel each other resulting in the straight line represented in Figure. These two examples were made simply to illustrate the concept by making them perfectly positive correlated in Figure C-2.5 and perfectly negatively correlated in Figure C-2.6.

Figure C-2.4. The Net Effect of Diversification on Volatility

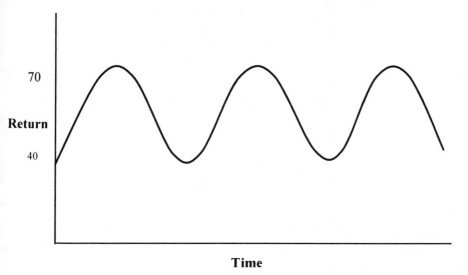

Figure C-2.5. Two Negatively Correlated Securities (companies)

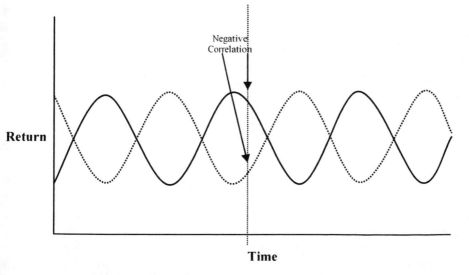

Although this graph represents two securities that are negatively correlated throughout the entire time period shown, a point has been selected on each security to illustrate that the relative correlation is determined at a specific point in time.

Figure C-2.6. The Net Effect of Diversification on Volatility

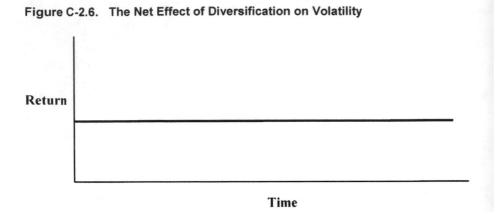

Return

Time

Now let us examine a plot of return versus time of two securities that are non-perfectly negatively correlated (figure C-2.7). After careful examination of both curves, you will notice that the top curve tends to go down as the bottom is going up and vice versa. Thus overall, they are negatively correlated and the correlation coefficient has a negative sign. However, because they do not move the same amount at a given time, they do not have a correlation coefficient of –1. Finally, notice that at some given points in time, both curves actually have brief periods of positive correlation interspersed within larger regions of negatively correlation, and this is what we would see in the real world, as no securities are ever perfectly correlated over a long period. However, these periods of positive correlation are minor relative to the overall movements and so the correlation coefficient is negative. We can liken these two investments with the performance of two portfolio companies in a venture fund. One of these companies could be computer networking while the other could be software.

Figure C-2.8 shows the resulting return of the two curves. Note that because the correlations were not perfect that we do not see a straight line, but rather a gradually increasing slope. Note that, unlike a public company traded on the stock market, the performance of venture-backed companies cannot be accurately assessed until the exit occurs, since is the only period when an accurate price will be known. Prior to this, only a rough estimation of ongoing performance can be approximated and will be based upon the financials, comparable companies, and market conditions. Therefore, if market conditions change, these performance estimations will change as well.

The goal of venture firms is to construct a portfolio of investments, each having a different correlation so that the performance characteristics of the entire portfolio (composite correlation coefficient) is less variable over a given time period due to diversification. This is done by selecting companies with different business dynamics, such as different sectors, different industries, different investment stages, and differing levels of committed capital. In the process of determining how much to invest in a particular industry, venture capitalists must examine and understand the various aspects specific for each industry so that they can establish an optimal balance of fund assets with regard to liquidation, leverage, and asset deployment. And because they only have one type of asset class with which to construct a diversified portfolio, the restrictions on the overall utility of the MPT are limited. However, it is thought *that increasing liquidity results from increasing levels of tangible assets and this may be used as a relative guide for determination of leverage constraints.* Because leverage increases portfolio risk and return, a sufficient level of liquidity must exist with each investment in order to justify a timely liquidation strategy. And over-deployment of capital to any one firm without a consideration of relative liquidity could result in diminished portfolio returns.

Figure C-2.7. Two Randomly Correlated Securities (companies)

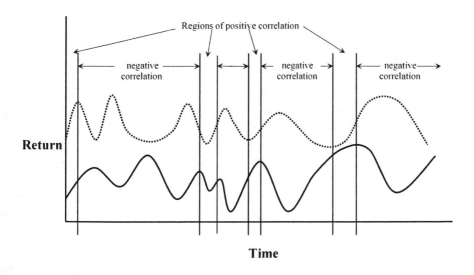

This figure illustrates the most common situation that occurs with two randomly selected securities, whereby there will be periods of positive and negative correlation over time. From the figure it can be assumed that the two securities are essentially negatively correlated overall, since the majority of time demonstrates opposing performance. Note that for each region of positive and negative correlation, the securities rarely demonstrate perfect correlation. Therefore, the numerical value will be either greater or less than 1.

Despite the rationale behind the MPT, it is much more difficult for venture capitalists to use MPT techniques because betas and correlation coefficient calculations are based upon historical data, namely previous market closing prices, and venture capitalists cannot accurately gauge a correlation coefficient for a company prior to investing in it.   Further difficulties arise due to the infrequency of valuation calculations made with private companies (usually quarterly) and due to the fact that they are very subjective (unlike the values used for calculating stock betas, i.e. closing prices).   Therefore, venture capitalists are left with industry gauges and data from companies that have already been funded for use in determining the best fit for the next investment.   Finally, one cannot loose sight of the fact that, while the MPT sounds like a nice way for venture funds to minimize risk, in fact it is not nearly as instrumental as in public securities but it does provide a basis for venture investment fund construction and management.

Figure C-2.8.   The Net Effect of Diversification on Volatility

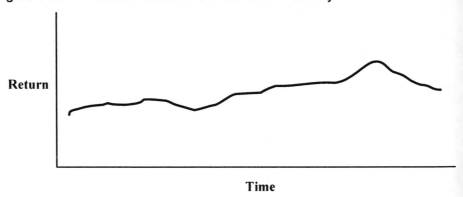

In order to appreciate the similarity between the private and public markets, keep in mind that much of the success of private companies is determined by the strength of the IPO market.   And a robust IPO market is a major indicator of strong stock market performance.   If a business or economic cycle experiences a prolonged recessionary environment, the private markets will suffer as well.   However, because there is a lag time that characterizes the reaction from public to private market performance, recessions lasting 3 or 4 quarters may escape adverse performance of private companies since the IPO window will only be closed for a short time period. During extreme periods whereby a recession is prolonged and the economic environment fails to show signs of near-term recovery, the leveraged buyout and merger/acquisition markets can be particularly lucrative due to decreased valuations of companies and distressed nature of corporate debt.   In such a scenario IPO opportunities are thereby diminished.

C-3. Venture Capital Due Diligence

Companies stand a much better chance of getting funded if they know what to expect from the due diligence process ahead of time. The process of venture capital due diligence can be thought of as consisting of two general processes. The first step is a request for documents, contact numbers, and product demonstrations. The second portion consists of interviews with management, board members, customers, and suppliers.

Initial Due Diligence Request List

A. Business
1. Business Plan/Powerpoint presentation
2. Term sheet of selected lead investor
3. Product literature/marketing material
4. Any market research/studies (internally produced or by professional research firms)
5. Competitive analysis (same as above) and summary of major competitors
6. Detail description of relationships with major suppliers, including contract manufacturers
7. List of current round participants and proposed allocation

B. Financial
1. Audited financial statements since inception
2. Projected financial statements with detailed assumptions (for the next 3-5 years, quarterly for current year)
3. Capitalization table/history of financing (dates, valuations, dollars in, type of security, etc.)
4. Pipeline report
5. Monthly shareholder letters going back 12 months
6. Summary of R&D expense since inception and projected R&D expenditure
7. All debt agreements including all proposed or completed for financing since inception
8. All correspondences with lenders

C. Legal

1. Significant employment agreements, compensation and benefit program contracts, and consulting agreements
2. Any information on pending, threatened or historical lawsuits or letters
3. Patents: (a) List of all patents (b) status, if applying (c) include patent numbers, descriptions and name of attorney and firm
4. Trademarks, service marks, copyrights
5. Name of lead attorney and firm
6. Documents relating to acquisitions or dispositions

D. Operating Agreements

1. Sales, agency, distribution, and advertising contracts
2. All joint venturing, licensing, and alliance agreements and contracts
3. All suppler contracts
4. Reference of outsource manufacturers
5. Lease contracts
6. Company warranties
7. Insurance policies
8. Customer service protocols

E. Corporate Records

1. Articles of Incorporation and By-Laws
2. Board of Directors and advisory committee meetings' minutes
3. Stock certificate form and stock record book
4. Shareholder meeting minutes
5. Annual and quarterly reports and other communications to stockholders since inception
6. Press clippings and news releases since inception

F. Other

1. List of alpha and beta customers (if applicable)
2. Alpha and potential beta customer references
3. Technical demonstration and performance specifications on alpha unit
4. All filings or material correspondence with state or federal regulatory agencies
5. Material government permits and licenses, if any
6. List of Board members and contact information
7. Organizational chart (with employee function)
8. Product: (a) brief description of the product(s), (b) stage of development, and (c) expected date(s) of commercialization

Interview Questions

A. Industry Assessment

1. What industry is the company involved in?
2. How would you categorize your company (service, manufacturing, distribution, etc.)?
3. How would you define the competitive structure of the industry (fragmented, oligopoly, monopoly, etc.)?
4. What is the regulatory environment of your industry (subject to government controls) and do you expect any changes to occur in the future?
5. What is the size of the industry?
6. What is the maturity of the industry?
7. What has been the five-year revenue growth rate of the industry and what is it expected to be over the next five years?
8. What has been the five-year earnings growth rate of the industry?
9. Explain the cyclical nature of the industry and how are sales and earnings affected? Can you provide a best and worst case scenario for the industry during business and economic cycles?
10. What are the major barriers to entry into the industry?
11. What is the success rate for new entrants into the industry?
12. What sources did you use to obtain the above information?

B. Products and Services

1. What is your company's current product line?
2. Which single product is most important for the success of the company?
3. Which product provides the least benefit for the company?
4. What makes your product unique?
5. Has all R&D been completed on all products?
6. How long did it take to develop each product?
7. What research has been conducted on competitive products?
8. What is the timetable for new product launches?
9. What are the revenue and market share estimates for all products over the next 12 months?
10. What will be the market share growth over the next 5 years and what is the company's market share target?
11. What are the margins for each product, and how are they expected to change as market share increases?

C. Sales and Marketing

1. Describe the marketing strategy
2. How does it compare with your competitors?
3. Does the company have purchase orders or letters of intent from potential customers to purchase products?
4. Does the company have a sales force?
5. Does the sales force have relevant industry experience?
6. Who are your largest customers, by percentage of sales?
7. How financially healthy are these customers?
8. How much repeat business do you anticipate?
9. What is the current credit policy for customers?

D. Competition

1. Who are you top four competitors in terms of sales?
2. How financially stable are they?
3. What is their strategic focus: Are they niche players, diversifying into other industries, or expanding into new markets?
4. How does your company differentiate itself from these competitors?
5. What are your competitors' greatest weaknesses?
6. Have the number of competitors increased of decreased since inception of your company and do you expect this to change?
7. What strategies do your competitors use in dealing with competition?
8. How do you plan to overcome the competition?

E. Production

1. Is the production automated or labor intensive?
2. Does the company self manufacture or subcontract?
3. Where is the production facility?
4. How long is the production cycle from raw materials to the customer?
5. To what extent does the company currently have the capacity to meet expected future demand and how long do you anticipate before capital expenditures will be required to meet excess demand?
6. What is the speed and flexibility of altering the production process to meet changes in demand?
7. What is the rate of production defects and what effects does this have on profit margins?
8. What are the most difficult challenges with the production process?
9. Are there any special environmental or government permits needed for production?
10. Are there any alternative production sites ready for use in case the current one has a problem?
11. What means of transportation does the company use to ship the product?

F. Suppliers
1. Who are the company's major suppliers?
2. Are they financially sound?
3. Do they work with your competitors and is there an exclusivity agreement in place?
4. Are they unionized?
5. Have they caused any bottlenecks?
6. What is there credit policy?
7. Who are your secondary suppliers?

G. Management
1. What is the management team's background?
2. Do they have previous experience with startups?
3. What is their experience with publicly traded companies?
4. What is their compensation package?
5. What is their percentage ownership in the company?
6. Have they invested any of their own capital in the company?
7. What is the vesting schedule?
8. Is the management team located within the same geographic area?
9. What was the process used in selecting the team?
10. Do any of the management team have experience with the competition?
11. How is the management team evaluated?
12. Are there any interim or part-time managers?
13. Do any of the managers have international experience or foreign language skills?
14. Has any member of the management team sued or been sued within the past five years?
15. Has any member of the management team been convicted of a felony?
16. Are there any civil or criminal charges pending against any member of the management?
17. Has any member of the management team ever been terminated from a management position?
18. Has any member of the management team filed for bankruptcy within the past five years?
19. Has any member of the management team ever been an officer of a company that has filed for bankruptcy?
20. Has any member of the management team been disciplined by a regulatory agency or professional association within the past five years?
21. Does any member of the management team have any health problems that should be mentioned?
22. Does the company have key-employee insurance?

23. Have all members of the management team signed the proper NDAs and non-compete agreements?
24. Have there been any problems with the management team and if so how were they resolved?
25. What are the biggest challenges of the management team?
26. Is there anything about the management team that you feel we should know?

H. Employees
1. What is the current number of nonmanagement employees and how many do you expect to have over the next 12 months and five years?
2. Does the company use independent contractors?
3. What is the selection process of employee hiring?
4. Have any of the employees worked for competitors?
5. What is the compensation package of employees?
6. How is employee performance evaluated?
7. What has been the rate of employee turnover since inception?
8. Are any employees or former employees involved with litigation with the company?
9. Are any employees exposed to any hazardous materials or areas during the manufacturing process?
10. How are the employees trained?

I. Corporate Finance
1. What are the revenue projections and growth rate over the next five years?
2. What are the earnings projections and growth rate over the next five yers?
3. When are sales reported (weekly, monthly, quarterly)?
4. How much cash does the company have?
5. How much access to working capital and lines of credit does the company have?
6. When is the company expected to be cashflow positive?
7. What are the key expense management areas of the company?
8. When does the company expect to be able to finance future growth from internal funds?
9. What percentage of stock is restricted and over what period?
10. Has the company used debt and does it plan to use debt?
11. Who is the accountant and primary bank?

J. Investment Parameters
1. Describe the company's fund-raising strategy.

2. What is the total amount of capital needed for this round of financing and what is the total amount of capital expected to be needed?
3. What will the current round of financing be used for?
4. How much money as been raised so far?
5. What are the terms and conditions of the current financing?
6. What will the total dilution be at the end of the funding?
7. Is all the equity diluted equally?
8. What types of securities has the company issued in the past and for what amounts?
9. What is the timetable for an IPO?
10. How much time has been devoted to fund raising activities?
11. What is the budget for fund raising activities?
12. What is the board composition?
13. What is the name of the securities attorney?

J. Business

1. What is the company's overall goal?
2. Who are the company's insurers?
3. Who are the company's accountants and auditors?
4. Who are the company's main attorneys?
5. Has the company completed all required corporate filings?
6. Does the company have all necessary licenses, building, and operating permits?
7. Has the company formed a general advisory board?
8. What is the history of the company?
9. Does the company have any tax problems?
10. Have there ever been any inquiries or reviews by taxing authorities?
11. List all real estate owned, leased or used by the company.
12. Are there any other lawsuits previously unmentioned which the company or its employees and directors are involved with or named in?

C-4. Bond Yields and Yield-to-Maturity

Bond Yields

While changes in short and long-term interest rates are frequently uncorrelated, occasionally there are brief periods where they have high correlation. When comparing bonds with equivalent credit quality, similar issuers, similar call features, and no sinking funds, those with longer maturity dates offer larger coupons (i.e. dividend rates) in exchange for the longer commitment of funds to entice investors to assume the larger risk of default that occurs with longer duration debt.

A bond's *current yield* reflects the percentage of dividends payable with respect to the current trading price of the bonds. For newly issued bonds, this yield is always equal to its *coupon or dividend rate* just after it enters the market since the price has not changed much. But as conditions change, so does the price of the bond, and because the dividend is fixed, the current yield will change. For instance, the credit quality of bond could increase, prompting an increase in the market price of the bond (since the risk of default has decreased). Other reasons for changes in the price of bonds include the bond market's expectations of future interest rate changes. Finally, when the Fed lowers the interest rates, previously issued bonds will show a drop in price since newly issued bonds will pay higher rates of interest.

When investors have expectations about the Fed's future decisions regarding interest rates changes, the market either discounts or attaches a premium price to bonds that were previously issued based upon whether future interest rates are expected to be higher or lower, respectively. If rates are expected to change prior to the maturity of the bond, its current yield will change to reflect this amount. In addition, the bonds' *yield-to-maturity* (YTM) is also changed based also on the time left until maturity. The YTM is similar to the current yield in that it is an expression of return percentage relative to the principal investment, except it also accounts for the maturation, or amount of time until the bond expires. In order to calculate the YTM, you must consider the price at which the bond can be purchased, its coupon rate, and the time left before it expires. Under a normal interest rate environment, a bond with a 15% coupon purchased at par value with a 5-year maturity will have a YTM of 15%. In contrast, that same bond, if purchased at a price below par will have a higher YTM since the dividend rate or coupon remains fixed. When comparing two bonds of equal time to maturity and call features, the price of each will fluctuate based upon many factors, such as interest rate expectations, the credit rating of the bond, business risk changes of the issuer, whether it has a sinking fund, whether it is callable or not, and its dividend rate.

Example.   An investor must choose between two investments. The first is the 10-year corporate bond from company A, selling for $500, paying a coupon of 10% that expires in 5 years. Meanwhile, company B has a bond that offers a 20% coupon and expires in 10 years. Both bonds were issued at an original price of $1000 each (par value). First determine the current yield of each bond, and then determine which bond provides the highest YTM. Assume the issuers are in the same industry, the bonds are not callable, they have the same credit rating, and there are no sinking funds.

Answer.   The bond of Company A has a coupon rate of 10% but a current yield of 20% since it is selling for half its original price. In contrast, the bond of Company B has a coupon rate of 20% which is identical to its current yield since it is selling at par. The bond of Company A has the highest YTM since both have the same current yield but Company A matures first.

C-5. Calculating the AMT*

   The AMT requires that taxpayers who may be eligible for the AMT to calculate their tax liability by two methods, the normal tax method and then the AMT method. The AMT method is calculated by adding back the deductions and exclusions from the normal method (such as personal exemptions, medical deductions and state and local taxes) so that a higher income is taxed. If the AMT is higher then the normal tax, the employee must pay both the normal tax rate plus the AMT amount. The AMT rate is 26% for taxable income up to $175,000 and 28% above this amount. Finally, if the amount of taxes paid using the AMT exceeds that amount which would have been paid using normal tax methods, the employee has generated AMT excess that may serve as a tax credit and can be applied in future years in those instances that the normal tax rate exceeds the AMT amount.

Regular taxable income

+ Medical/dental deductions

+ Specified miscellaneous itemized deductions subject to AMT

+ State/local/real estate tax deductions

+ Personal exemptions

+ Spread on ISO exercise

 = Preliminary AMT taxable income

   - $45,000 AMT standard exemption

= Actual AMT taxable income

   Multiply Actual AMT taxable income times 26% (up to $175,000) plus 28% times amounts over $175,000 to arrive at the tentative tax.

   AMT = Tentative tax - Regular tax

*Your CPA should always be consulted when calculating AMT and determining AMT eligibility

APPENDIX D

Competitive Analysis

D-1. Market Segmentation Analysis

Industry-Market Attractiveness Matrix

Industry/Market Evaluation Criteria	Weight of Criteria	Importance of Criteria	Weighted Score
Market Size (small/large,global/national/regional)			
Growth Rate (slowing/declining/accelerating)			
Profitability (current profitability, future expectations)			
Cyclicality (profit volatility)			
Seasonality (are profits seasonal?)			
Customers Average size Are needs changing? Is size increasing?			
Competitors Is competition high? Is it expected to increase?			
Supplier Reliability			
Extent of Industry Regulation			
Politics (Is the political climate stable?)			
Technology (What is the need for emerging technologies?)			
Entry and Exit Barriers (difficulty)			
Total			

Modified from: DePamphilis, D. 2001. *Mergers, Acquisitions and other Restructuring Activities* (chap 4).

D-2. Competitive Intelligence

Time Analysis per Task and per Question

Question	Research Request Tasks	Time (hrs)
1. What territories does the company sell in?	Locate and interview distributors	10
	Locate and interview OEMs	5
	Retrieve and review trade magazines	5
	Locate and interview store buyers	10
2. Whom does the company sell to?	Interview competitors	5
	Review annual report	2
	Review product literature	5
	Locate and retrieve press releases	3
	Locate and interview shipping companies	10
3. What are its distribution channels?	This question can be deduced from 1 and 2	
4. What markets does it hope to Penetrate?	Interview trade magazine editors	5
	Locate and interview Wall Street analysts	5
	Locate, retrieve and review latest analyses	5
	Locate and interview customers regarding approach sales force has taken with them	10
5. Is the company a low-cost producer?	Retrieve loan filings for equipment purchases	2
	Contact machinery suppliers for automation level of plant	10
	Examine union contracts	5
	Retrieve and review tax filings from tax assessors	5
	Locate and interview major suppliers	10
6. What products does it plan to release Next year?	Review patent filings	10
	Attend trade show and retrieve available product literature	10
7. Can the company afford to enter a Price war?	Can be deduced from question 5	
8. What is the company's advertising strategy? Where will it advertise this coming year?	Interview advertising staff for likely trade magazines	3
	Review three years of historical data from Leading National Advertisers, a source of advertising expenditures	5
	Interview advertising account reps from former agency	2

Taken from Fuld, L.M. 1995. *The New Competitor Intelligence.*

D-3. Self-Assessment

Business Attractiveness Matrix

Success Factor	Compared to Primary Competitor		
	Weight of Criteria	Importance of Criteria	Weighted Score
Market Share			
Product Line Breadth			
Sales Distribution (cost effectiveness)			
Price Competitiveness			
Facilities			
Production Capacity			
Product Quality			
R&D (Are you an innovator or follower?)			
Customer Service			
Profitability			
Total			

Modified from: DePamphilis, D. 2001. *Mergers, Acquisitions and other Restructuring Activities* (chap 4).

D-4. The State Department's Contact Numbers

▪ **The State Department's Asian, Pacific and European desks.**

Asia/Pacific Rim

China	202-647-6300/6796
Hong Kong	202-647-9141
Indonesia	202-647-3276
Japan	202-647-2912
Korea	202-647-7717
Malaysia	202-647-3276/9
Singapore	202-647-3276/8
Taiwan	202-647-7711
Thailand	202-647-7108

Europe

Belgium/Luxembourg	202-647-6071
Denmark	202-647-5669
France	202-647-2633
Germany	202-647-2005
Greece	202-647-6113
Ireland	202-647-6585
Italy	202-647-2453
Netherlands	202-647-6557
Portugal/Spain	202-647-1412
United Kingdom	202-647-6587

▪ **International Trade Administration's (ITA) Asian, Pacific & European desks.**

Asia/Pacific Rim

ASEAN Desk	202-482-3875
China	202-482-3583
Hong Kong	202-482-2462
Indonesia	202-482-3875
Japan	202-482-4527
Korea	202-482-4958
Malaysia	202-482-3875
Singapore	202-482-3875
Taiwan	202-482-4957
Thailand	202-482-3875

Europe

Europe-General	202-482-5638
Belgium/Luxembourg	202-482-5401
Denmark	202-482-3254
France	202-482-8008
Germany	202-482-2434/2435
Greece	202-482-3945
Ireland	202-482-4104
Italy	202-482-2177
Netherlands	202-482-5401
Portugal	202-482-3945
Spain	202-482-4508
United Kingdom	202-482-3748

D-5. Comparability of Two Licensing Agreements

Standards	Agreement #1	Agreement #2
Technology	Right to use worldwide patented technology to make. use, and sell FM stereo receivers and tuners and FM radios.	Right to use worldwide patented technology to make and sell compact disc players and certain other products.
Term	Effective January 1, 1988 Expires January 1, 1993	Effective January 1, 1988 Expires after 5 years---renews automatically for 5-year terms
Territory	Licensor is a U.S. corporation and Licensee is a Japanese company. No specific market area is given	Licensor is a French company and Japanese company—worldwide market
Exclusivity	Nonexclusive	Nonexclusive
Sublicensee	Nontransferable and nonassignable	Nontransferable. licensor cannot assign or sublease without consent
Termination Clauses	Licensor can terminate for default, bankruptcy, reorganization, takeover of licensee, or force majure	Licensee can terminate at the end of each 5-year term; either party can terminate for default, bankruptcy, or force majure
Trademarks of Trade Names	No	No
Technical Assistance	None	None
Payment Terms -Lump Sum	None	Equivalent of 1.1 billion yen in French Francs
-Royalty	0.2% of net sales in U.S. $-- credits given for apparatus sold in certain combination	1.3% of Net Selling Price in Francs or other currency acceptable to Licensor
-Minimum	None	None
Relationships	No other relevant agreements	Licensor waives all claims it may have against Licensee for prior use of the products

Ref: Parr, R.L., Sullivan, P.H. 1996. *Technology Licensing: Corporate Strategies for Maximizing Value.*

Notice that, while the technologies are not the same, they are somewhat similar in that they are both electronic components, and both have similar applications. That is, the right to make and sell these products, as opposed to components. Note however, that the two technologies differ in their relative age, FM stereo receivers being predated by several decades versus compact disc players. This will have an impact on the royalty since FM receivers cannot command a large price due to their maturity on the product life cycle curve. Hence the lump sum payment in addition to the royalty for the compact disc player license.

The term for the compact disc player renews every 5 years and is therefore a significant feature of this agreement since the ability of the licensor to renegotiate the terms is prohibited. The territory and exclusivity are obvious factors in determining the royalty rate since it affects the potential market that the licensee can reach. Exclusivity can refer to a geographic area, market area (such as to original manufactures versus direct consumers), or an industrial area.

Termination clauses should be considered carefully to determine the risk of license cessation. The use of the licensor's trademark or trade name in combination with the rights to its technology is very intrusive for the licensee and would obviously command a higher royalty rate due to the accessibility of the licensee's customer base as well as the risk of damage to the licensee's brand name and the loss of revenues resulting from any poorly manufactured products.

The amount of technical assistance provided by the licensor obviously adds value to the licensee, especially when the technology is new. The payment terms are the cumulative result of the aforementioned factors plus valuation considerations. The licensee must examine the costs of designing patents around the licensor's technology, the potential revenue and any added strategic benefits that may arise from the licensing arrangement to determine if the royalty is reasonable. Finally, the mutual relationship of the two parties can provide added benefit, such as supplier exclusivity, and the cancellation of all prior claims for the unauthorized use of the technology.

APPENDIX E

Investor Groups

E-1. State Incubation Associations

Alabama

Alabama Business Incubation Network
Devron A. Veasley, Chairman
1020 Ninth Avenue S.W.
Bessemer, AL 35022
Tel: (205) 481 2101
Fax: (205) 481-2100
E-mail: dveasley@mindspring.com

Alaska

PIN: Pacific Incubation Network
111 N. Market Street
Suite 604
San Jose, CA 95113
Tel: (408) 367-6134
Fax: (408) 938-3929
E-mail: info@pacincubation.org
Web Site: www.pacificincubation.org

Arkansas

Arkansas Business Incubator Management Association
c/o GENESIS Technology Incubator
1 U of Ark – Engineering Res. Center
Fayetteville, AR 72701
Tel: (501) 575-7227
Fax: (501) 575-7446

California

California Business Incubation Network
101 W Broadway
San Diego, CA 92101-8205
Sheila Washington
Tel: (619) 237-0559
Fax: (619) 237-0521

PIN: Pacific Incubation Network
111 N. Market Street
Suite 604
San Jose, CA 95113
Tel: (408) 367-6134
Fax: (408) 938-3929
E-mail: info@pacincubation.org

Web Site: www.pacificincubation.org
Colorado

Colorado Business Incubator Association
c/o Western Colorado Business Development Corp.
2591 B ¾ Rd
Grand Junction, CO 81503
Thea Chase
Tel: (970) 243-5242
Fax: (970) 241-0771
E-mail: tchase@gjincubator.org

Florida

Florida Business Incubation Association
1311 N. Highway US 1
Titusville, FL 32796
(321) 383-5200
Thomas G. Rainey, President
E-mail: trainey@trda.org

Indiana

Indiana Business Incubator Association
c/o A Business Center for Developing Enterprises
1100 W. Loyd Expressway Suite 113
Evansville, IN 47708
Tel: (888) 815-9758
Fax: (812) 426-6138

Louisiana

Louisiana Business Incubator Association
c/o LA Business & Technology Center
South Stadium Dr.
Baton Rouge, LA 70803
Charles D'Agostino
Tel: (225) 334-5555
Fax: (225) 388-3975

Maryland

Maryland Business Incubation Association
c/o Emerging Technology Center
2400 Boston St. Suite 300
Baltimore, MD 21224
President: Ann Lansinger
Tel: (310) 327-9150 ext. 1001
E-mail: annlansinger@etcbaltimore.com
Web: www.mdbusinessincubation.org

Michigan

Michigan Business Incubator Association
c/o Hastings Industrial Incubator
1035 E. State St.
Hastings, MI 49058
L. Joseph Rahn
Tel: (269) 948-2947
E-mail: lakelandboat@core.com

Mississippi

Mississippi Business Incubation Association
c/o Mississippi Development Authority
P.O. Box 849
Jackson, MS 39205-0849
Elizabeth Pittman
Tel: (601) 359-3595
Fax: (601) 359-2116
E-mail: epittman@mississippi.org

New Jersey

New Jersey Business Incubation Network
c/o NJIT Enterprise Development Center 1
240 Martin Luther King Blvd.
Newark, NJ 07102-2100
Stash Lisowski
Tel: (973) 643-5740
Fax: (973) 643-5839
E-mail: lisowski@admin.njit.edu

North Carolina

North Carolina Business Incubation Association
c/o Cape Fear Regional CDC
509 Cornelius Harnett Dr.
Wilmington, NC 28401
Rubin Sloan
Tel: (910) 815-0065
Fax: (910) 362-9697
E-mail: business@cfrcdc.org

Oklahoma

Oklahoma Business Incubator Association
c/o OK Dept. of Vocation & Technology Training
1500 W. 7th
Stillwater, OK 74074-4398

Jim Comer
Tel: (405) 743-5566
Fax: (405) 743-6821

Oregon

PIN: Pacific Incubation Network
111 N. Market Street
Suite 604
San Jose, CA 95113
Tel: (408) 367-6134
Fax: (408) 938-3929
E-mail: info@pacincubation.org
Web Site: www.pacificincubation.org

Pennsylvania

Pennsylvania Incubator Association
C/o Corry Redevelopment Authority
PO Box 38
Corry, PA 16407-9007
Richard Novotny
Tel: (814) 664-3884
Fax: (814) 664-3885
E-mail: movo@erie.net

Texas

Texas Business Incubator Association
9600 Long Point Road, Suite 150
Houston, TX 77055-4266
Chairman: Paul A. Barela
Tel: (713) 932-7495
Fax: (713) 932-7498
E-mail: info@tbionline.org
Web Site: www.tbiaonline.org

Virginia

Virginia Business Incubation Association
1354 8th St. SW
Roanoke, VA 24015
President: Lisa Ison
Tel: (540) 344-6402
Fax: (540) 345-0262
E-mail: lison@ncvc.net
Web Site: www.vbia.org

Washington

Washington Association of Small Business Incubators
5005center St
Suite D
Tacoma, WA 98409
Tel: (253) 284-0004
Fax: (253) 284-0007
E-mail: jbeletz@hotmail.com
Web site: www.williamfactory.com

Wisconsin

Wisconsin Business Incubator Assoc.
c/o Incubator WOW
1915 N. Martin Luther King Jr. Drive
Milwaukee, WI 53212-3641
Tel: (414) 263-5450
Fax: (414) 263-5456
E-mail: info@wwbic.com
Web Site: www.wwbic.com/

Regional Associations

PIN: Pacific Incubation Network
111 N. Market Street
Suite 604
San Jose, CA 95113
Tel: (408) 367-6134
Fax: (408) 938-3929
E-mail: info@pacincubation.org
Web Site: www.pacificincubation.org

E-2. Selected Incubators By State

California

- The San Jose Software Business Cluster http://www.sjsbc.org
  Started by Jim Robbins, this Silicon Valley incubator has been highly successful in helping companies growth through providing external resources, internal advice and access to capital. If you are in Northern California you have probably heard of it.

- NASA Commercialization Center Pomona Technology Center
  www.nasaincubator.csupomona.edu

- Panasonic Incubator www.vcpanasonic.com

Illinois

- Chicago Technology Park & Research Center (Chicago, IL)
  http://www.imdc.org/
  This biomedical incubator is located within the high powered Illinois medical district and has strong partnerships with many of the medical schools and biopharmaceutical companies within this district.

- EnterpriseWorks (Champaign, IL) http://www.tech.com/index.asp
  This incubator is located in research park at the University of Illinois and is supported by this university.

- Illinois Technology Enterprise Center (Chicago, IL)
  www.northwestern.edu/research/osi
  Sponsored by Northwestern University.

- Technology Innovation Center (Evanston, IL) www.theincubator.com
  The technology transfer and incubator facility of Northwestern University in Evanston.

Massachusetts

- Biosquare (Boston, MA) www.biosquare.org
  An incubator sponsored by Boston University, Boston Medical Center, and Boston University School of Medicine. This facility is enormous with over 700,000 square feet and state of the art lab facilities available for startup companies.

- PureTech Ventures (Boston, MA) www.puretech.com
  A biosciences incubator with real hands on experience and expertise in the biosciences.

New Jersey

- The Enterprise Development Center (Newark, NJ)
  http://www.njit-edc.org/
  An incubator sponsored by the New Jersey Institute of Technology.

New York

- Rensselaer Incubator Program (Troy, NY)
  http://www.rpi.edu/dept/incubator/homepage/
  Sponsored by Rensselaer Polytechnic Institute, one of the premier engineering and sciences colleges in the U.S., this incubator has been in existence for nearly 25 years and has assisted in graduating companies generating over $200 million in annual revenues.

- Broad Hollow Bioscience Park (Farmingdale, NY) http://www.bhbp.org/
  A new bioscience incubator sponsored by Farmingdale State University of New York with ties to Cold Spring Harbor Laboratory.

- Long Island High Tech Incubator (Stony Brook) http://www.lihti.org/
  Has five graduates that are public and has helped companies raise in excess of $100 million.

North Carolina

- BD & Co. Technologies (Research Triangle Park) www.bd.com/technologies/
  An incubator supported by Beckton, Dickinson, and Co. specializing in healthcare and biomedical ventures.

- The Ben Craig Center (Charlotte, NC)
  http://www.bencraigcenter.com/Default.htm
  Provides, incubation services and financing. Has a long history of success dating back to the early 1980s.

Ohio

- Omeris (Columbus, OH) www.omeris.org
  A biosciences incubator sponsored by local universities, hospitals and corporations.

Texas

- Austin Technology Incubator (Austin, TX) http://ati.ic2.org
  This incubator is sponsored by IC^2, a world-renowned high-tech commercialization center within University of Texas.

- Houston Technology Center (Houston, TX) http://www.houstontech.org
  This incubator is sponsored by the city of Houston, corporations, and venture firms and will no doubt put Texas on the map in biotechnology.

E-3. Angel Clubs & Networks

Arizona
Arizona Angels
Website: www.arizonaangels.com

California
Band of Angels
Website: www.bandofangels.com
Silicon Valley, CA

Sac of Angels
Website: www.etisacramento.org/angels.html
Sacramento, CA
Tel: (916) 498-1423

Tech Coast Angels
Website: www.techcoastangels.com
Los Angeles, CA

Golden Gate Angels
Website: www.ggangels.com
San Francisco, CA

Iron Horse Ventures
Website: www.ironhorseventures.com
Palo Alto, CA
Tel: (650) 857-0700

The Angels' Forum
Website: www.angelsforum.com
Palo Alto, CA

Sand Hill Angels
Website: www.sandhillangels.com
Silicon Valley, CA

The Sacramento Angels
Website: www.sacangels.com
Sacramento, CA

Georgia
Atlanta Technology Angels
Website: www.angelatlanta.com
Atlanta, GA

Illinois
Prairie Angels
Website: www.prairieangels.com
Chicago, IL
Tel: (773) 837-8250

Maryland
Baltimore-Washington Venture Group
Website: www.mbs.umd.edu/Dingman/docs/bwvg/index.htm
University of Maryland

Massachusetts
Investor's Circle
Website: www.investorscircle.net
Brookline, MA

Maryland Angels Council
Website: www.md-angels.com

North Carolina
Tri-State Investment Group
Chapel Hill, NC
Tel: (919) 968-3760

New Hampshire
The Breakfast Club
Milford, NH

New Mexico
Gathering of Angels
Website: www.gatheringofangels
Santa Fe, NM
Tel: 505-982-3050

New York
New York New Media Association
Website: www.nynma.org
Tel: (212) 785-7898

North Carolina
Charlotte Angel Partners
Website: www.capnc.com

truePilot
Website: www.truepilot.com
Research Triangle Park, NC

Tri-State Investment Group
Website: www.tignc.com

Chapel Hill, NC
Pennsylvania
Pennsylvania Private Investor Group
Website: www.ppig.com
Jenkintown, PA
Tel: (215) 884-9300 x 140

Virginia
The Dinner Club
Website: www.thedinnerclub.com
Vienna, VA
Tel: (703) 255-4930

Active Angel Investors
www.activeangelinvestors.com
Vienna, VA

GMU Century Cub Grubstake Breakfast
Website: www.centuryclub.org
George Mason University
Fairfax, VA

Washington
Alliance of Angels
www.allianceofangels.com

District of Columbia
Capital Investors
Website: www.capitalinvestors.com
Washington, D.C.

Washington Dinner Club
Website: www.washingtondinnerclub.com
Washington, D.C.

Womens' Angel Groups
Seraph Capital
Website: www.seraphcapital.com

WOMENAngels.net
Website: www.womenangels.net

E-4. Fund Raising & Venture Networks

a. Venture Forums & Conferences

Arizona Venture Forum
Florida Venture Capital Conference
Greater Midwest Venture Capital Coalition Forum
International Business Forum
Mid-Atlantic Venture Forum
New York Venture Capital Forum
North Carolina CEO Venture Forum
North Coast (Ohio) Growth Capital & Technology Showcase
North Jersey Venture Fair
Oklahoma Investment Forum
San Francisco Bay Area Venture Forum
Utah Venture Forum

b. Investment Meetings

Atlanta Venture Forum
Connecticut Venture Group
Dallas Venture Capital Group
Houston Venture Capital Association
Information Industry Association's Investor Conference
Long Island Venture Group
Missouri Venture Forum
New England Venture Capital Association
New York Venture Group
Northern California Venture Capital Association
Pennsylvania Private Investors Group
Toronto Venture Group
Western Association of Venture Capitalists
Western New York Venture Association

c. Investment Networks

The Capital Network
Environmental Capital Network
Georgia Capital Network
Investors Circle
Kentucky Investment Capital Network
LA Venture Network
Mid-Atlantic Investment Network
Northwest Capital Network
Pacific Venture Capital Network

Private Investor Network
Seed Capital Network
Technology Capital Network
Tennessee Venture Capital Network
Venture Capital Network of Minnesota
Washington Investment Network

References

Chapter 1: Entrepreneurship 101

Collins, J., Porras, J.I. *Building Your Company's Vision*. Harvard Business Review. September/October 1996, Volume 74 Issue 5, pp.65-77.

Chesbrough, H., Rosenbloom, R.S. "The Role of the Business Model in Capturing Value from Innovation: Evidence From Xerox Corporation's Technology Spin-Off Companies." *Industrial and Corporate Change*, Volume 11, Number 3, pp. 529-555.

Kolchinsky, Peter. *The Entrepreneur's Guide to a Biotech Startup*, third edition. © 2001.

Clarkson, K.W., Miller, R. L., Jentz, G.A., Cross, F.B. West's Business Law. seventh edition 1998 West Educational Publishing.

Pratt, J.W., Kulsrud, W.N. Federal Taxation. 2001. Houston: ARC Publishing.

Chapter 2: Venture Capital and Private Equity Basics

Belke, A., Fehn, R., Foster, N. *Does Venture Capital Spur Employment Growth?*

Yoder, J.A., Colvin, B.H., *Private Equity Gains Acceptance*, Pensions & Investments, September 20, 1999.

Prowse, S.D. "The Economics of the Private Equity Market." Federal Reserve Bank of Dallas. Economic Review. 1998 Third Quarter

Yoder, J.A. *Alternative Can Smooth Out Bumpy Returns*, Pensions & Investments, May 4, 1998.

Yoder, J.A. *A Primer on Alternative Investments*, Pensions & Investments, August, 1998.

Jagwani, S. *Supply and Demand of Venture Capital in the U.S.*, The Park Place Economist, vol.III.

Cohen, J.B, Zinbarg, E.D, Zeikel, A. 1987, Fifth Edition. Investment Analysis and Portfolio Management. Boston: Irwin.

Gitman, L.J., Joehnk, M.D. 1999, Seventh Edition. Fundamentals of Investing. New York: Addison-Wesley.

Zygmont, J. The VC Way. Cambridge: Perseus.

Bartlett, J.W. 1999. Fundamentals of Venture Capital. Lenham, MD: Madison Books.

Gompers, P., Lerner, J. 2000. The Venture Capital Cycle. Cambridge: MIT Press.

Camp, J.J.2002. <u>Venture Capital Due Diligence</u>. New York: John Wiley & Sons

"Three Keys to Obtaining Venture Capital". Pricewaterhouse Coopers, 9th ed.

"Mezzanine Debt—Another Level To Consider" An excerpt from Fitch Ratings Report. August 2003. Fleet Capital, CapitalEyes.
www.fleetcapita.com/resources/capeyes/a08-03-176.html

Levin, J.S., Ginsburg, M.D., Rocap, D.E. 2002 edition. <u>Structuring Venture Capital, Private Equity, and Entrepreneurial Transactions</u>. New York: Aspen Publishers.

Toll, D. *Private Equity Primer.* www.assetnews.com/ped/primer.htm

Chapter 3: Fundamentals of Raising Capital

Levin, J.S., Ginsburg, M.D., Rocap, D.E. 2002 edition. <u>Structuring Venture Capital, Private Equity, and Entrepreneurial Transactions</u>. New York: Aspen Publishers.

The Securities Act of 1933, The United States Securities and Exchange Commission.
http://www.sec.gov/divisions/corpfin/forms/securities.shtml

Chapter 4: Investor Profiles: Angels, VCs And Incubators

Benjamin, G.A., Margulis, J.B. 2000. <u>Angel Financing</u>. New York: John Wiley & Sons.

National Business Incubation Association. www.nbia.org
Richards, S. 2002. <u>Inside Business Incubators and Corporate Ventures</u>. New York: John Wiley & Sons.

Camp, J.J.2002. <u>Venture Capital Due Diligence</u>. New York: John Wiley & Sons.

Gompers, P., Lerner, J. 2000. <u>The Venture Capital Cycle</u>. Cambridge: MIT Press.

"Business Incubators in New York State". Empire State Development. Sept 2003.
http://www.nylovesbiz.com/pdf/NYSIncubators.pdf

Chapter 5: Intangible Assets: Intellectual Capital & Property

Pressman, D. 2003. <u>Patent It Yourself</u>. USA: Nolo.

Parr, R.L., Sullivan, P.H. 1996. <u>Technology Licensing: Corporate Strategies for Maximizing Value</u>. New York: John Wiley & Sons.

Craig, L., Moore, L. "Intangible Assets, Intellectual Capital or Property? It Does Make a Difference." <u>Front Range TechBiz</u>, Feb. 3, 2002.

Craig, L., Moore, L. "Towards a Strategy of Valuing Patents as Intellectual Capital." © 2003.

DePamphilis, D. 2001. Mergers, Acquisitions and other Restructuring Activities. San Diego: Academic Press.

Fuld, L.M. 1995. The New Competitor Intelligence. New York: John Wiley & Sons.

Pitkethly, R.H. "The Valuation of Patents : A review of patent valuation methods with consideration of option based methods and the potential for further research", WP 05/99, OIPRC Electronic Journal of Intellectual Property Rights, 2003. http://www.oiprc.ox.ac.uk/EJWP0599.html

Islam, S., Kremen, S.H. "Valuation of Computer Software Assets". Computer Forensics Online. http://www.shkdplc.com/cfo/articles/value.htm

Hicks, D., Buchanan, L. "Serial Innovators in the Markets for Technology", paper prepared for the ASEAT/Institute of Innovation Research Conference on: Knowledge and Economic and Social Change: New Challenges to Innovation Studies, April 7-9, 2003, Manchester, UK.

Copeland, M.V. February 20, 2003. "Public Issuance." Red Herring.

CHI Research, Inc. "Serial Innovators: Long-lived Small Innovative Firms". Vol. XI, No.1, March 2003.

Narin, F. "Tech-line Background Paper". August 19, 1999. To be published in "Measuring Stratgeic Competetnce", Imperial College Press Technology Management Series. http://www.chiresearch.com/docs/tlbp.pdf

Uniform Trade Secrets Act, National Conference of Commissioners on Uniform State Laws, as amended 1985. http://www.law.upenn.edu/bll/ulc/fnact99/1980s/utsa85.pdf http://nsi.org/Library/Espionage/usta.htm.

Halligan, M. R. "The Trade Secret Audit". www.rmarkhalligan2.com/trade/print.asp?id=10

The Economic Espionage Act of 1996: Computer Crime and Intellectual Property Section (CCIPS). October 1996. http://www.usdoj.gov/criminal/cybercrime/ipmanual/08ipma.htm

Raymond, D. June, 24 2002. "How to Find True Value in Companies". Forbes. http://www.forbes.com/asap/2002/0624/064_print.html.

The Trade Secret Office, www.thetso.com

Sorid, D. "U.S. trade-secret law to be tested in China case", Reuters. http://biz.yahoo.com/rc/031125/bizfeature_espionage_1.html

Davidson, S.A., Stack, A., Cole, S. "Reasonable Royalty Rates" CAmagazine.com

Chapter 6: Forming Competitive Strategies

Porter, M.E. 1996. "What is Strategy?" *Harvard Business Review.*

Porter, M.E. 1998. Competitive Strategy. New York: The Free Press.

Porter, M.E. 1985. Competitive Advantage. New York: The Free Press.

Day, D.S., Reibstein, D.J. 2002. Dynamic Competitive Strategy. New York: John-Wiley & Sons, Inc.

Sapienza, A.M. 1997. Creating Technology Strategies: How to Build Competitive Biomedical R&D. New York: Wiley-Liss.
Dixit, A.K., Nalebuff, B.J. Thinking Strategically. New York: W.W. Norton.
Financial Times. 2001. Mastering Strategy. Great Britain: Prentice-Hall.

O'Sullivan, K. October 2002. "Six Ways to Outrun the Competition". Inc.com http://pf.inc.com/magazine/20021015/24776.html.

Parr, R.L., Sullivan, P.H. 1996. Technology Licensing: Corporate Strategies for Maximizing Value. New York: John Wiley & Sons.

Fuld, L.M. 1995. The New Competitor Intelligence. New York: John Wiley & Sons.

Chapter 7: Alternative Growth Strategies: Licensing Agreements, Strategic Alliances and Joint Ventures

Parr, R.L., Sullivan, P.H. 1996. Technology Licensing: Corporate Strategies for Maximizing Value. New York: John Wiley & Sons.

DePamphilis, D. 2001. Mergers, Acquisitions and other Restructuring Activities. San Diego: Academic Press.

"Antitrust Guidelines for the Licensing of Intellectual Property," U.S. Department of Justice and the Federal Trade Commission, April 6, 1995.
http://www.usdoj.gov/atr/public/guidelines/ipguide.htm

Bartlett, J.W. 1999. Fundamentals of Venture Capital. Lenham, MD: Madison Books.

Reuer, J.J. and Leiblein, M.J, "Downside risk implications of multinationality and international joint ventures," *Academy of Management Journal.*

Chapter 8: Managing Growth

Damodaran, A. 2002, second edition. Investment Valuation. New York: John Wiley & Sons.

Dauber, N.A., Siegel, J.G., Shim, J.K. 1996. The Vest-Pocket CPA. Paramus, New Jersey: Prentice Hall.

Harris, R.S., Pringle, J.J. 1989. Introductory Corporate Finance. London: Scott, Foresman and Company.

Grouppelli, A.A., Nikbakht, E. 2000. Finance. New York: Barron's.

McEachern, W.A. 1994. Economics: A Contemporary Introduction. Third Edition. Cincinnati: South-Western Publishing Company.

Cohen, J.B, Zinbarg, E.D, Zeikel, A. 1987, Fifth Edition. Investment Analysis and Portfolio Management. Boston: Irwin.

Mills, A.R. "The Power of Cash Flows Ratios." Journal of Accountancy. Oct. 1998. www.findarticles.com/cf_0/m6280/n4_186/21224654/print.jhtml

Sapienza, A.M. 1997. Creating Technology Strategies: How to Build Competitive Biomedical R&D. Chapter 3. New York: Wiley-Liss.

Parr, R.L., Sullivan, P.H. 1996. Technology Licensing: Corporate Strategies for Maximizing Value. New York: John Wiley & Sons.

Chapter 9: Exit Strategies

DePamphilis, D. 2001. Mergers, Acquisitions and other Restructuring Activities. San Diego: Academic Press.

Galphin, T.J., Herndon, M. The Complete Guide to Mergers and Acquisitions. 2000 First Edition. San Francisco: Jossey-Bass.

Lajoux, A.R. The Art of M&A Integration. 1998. New York: McGraw-Hill.

Taulli, T. The Complete M&A Handbook. 2002. First Edition. New York: Random House.

Craig, V.V. 2000. Merchant Banking Past and Present. Division of Research and Statistics, FDIC Banking Review.

Gompers, P., Lerner, J. 2000. The Venture Capital Cycle. Cambridge: MIT Press.

Nasdaq. Going Public and Listing on the U.S. Securities Markets.

Chapter 10: Terms of Endearment: Term Sheets and Tactics

Wilmerding, A. 2000. <u>Term Sheets and Valuations</u>. Aspatore.

Wilmerding, A. 2003. <u>Deal Terms</u>. Aspatore.

Camp, J.J.2002. <u>Venture Capital Due Diligence</u>. New York: John Wiley & Sons

Chapter 11: Setting Valuation: Supply & Demand, Risk & Reward, Leverage & Control

Damodaran, A. 2002, second edition. <u>Investment Valuation</u>. New York: John Wiley & Sons.

Pratt, S.P. 2001. <u>The Market Approach to Valuing Businesses</u>. New York: John-Wiley & Sons.

DePamphilis, D. 2001. <u>Mergers, Acquisitions and other Restructuring Activities</u>. San: Academic Press.

Camp, J.J.2002. <u>Venture Capital Due Diligence</u>. New York: John Wiley & Sons

Chapter 12: Compensation & Employment

Leimberg, S.R., McFadden, J.J. 1999, sixth edition. <u>The Tools and Techniques of Employee and Retirement Planning</u>. Cincinnati: National Underwriter.

National Center for Employee Ownership (NCEO). <u>www.nceo.org</u>

Camp, J.J.2002. <u>Venture Capital Due Diligence</u>. New York: John Wiley & Sons

About the Author

Michael Stathis is the founder and Managing Director of Apex Venture Advisors, a venture capital consulting firm specializing in business strategy, fund raising, and technology consulting for early stage companies. Prior to forming Apex, Michael worked for two of the most respected investment banks on Wall Street, where he served in the capacity of asset management, securities analysis, and merchant banking. He obtained his Masters of Science from the University of Pennsylvania in physical biological chemistry and biophysics and has studied finance extensively.

Printed in the United States
56045LVS00004BA/8

9 780975 577615